HTML 3
INTERACTIVE
COURSE

KENT CEARLEY

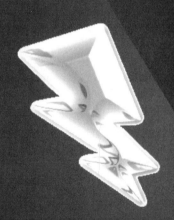

WAITE GROUP PRESS™

A Division of
Sams Publishing

Corte Madera, CA

PUBLISHER • Mitchell Waite
ASSOCIATE PUBLISHER • Charles Drucker

ACQUISITIONS MANAGER • Jill Pisoni

EDITORIAL DIRECTOR • John Crudo
MANAGING EDITOR • Dan Scherf
CONTENT EDITOR • Heidi Brumbaugh
COPY EDITOR • Merilee Eggleston
TECHNICAL REVIEWER • Robin Dumas

PRODUCTION DIRECTOR • Julianne Ososke
PRODUCTION MANAGER • Cecile Kaufman
DESIGN • Sestina Quarequio
PRODUCTION • Jude Levinson
ILLUSTRATION • Larry Wilson
CHAPTER OPENER ILLUSTRATION • ©Steven Hunt/Image Bank
COVER ILLUSTRATION • Robert Dougherty

© 1996 by The Waite Group, Inc.
Published by Waite Group Press™, 200 Tamal Plaza, Corte Madera, CA 94925.

Printed in the United States of America
96 97 98 99 • 10 9 8 7 6 5 4 3 2

Library of Congress Cataloging-in-Publication Data
Cearley, Kent.
      HTML 3 Interactive Course / Kent Cearley.
        p.   cm.
      Includes index.
      ISBN 1-57169-066-2
        1. Hypertext systems.   2. HTML (Document markup language)
  I. Title.
  IN PROCESS
  005.75—dc20

95-45826
CIP

Dedication

For my three favorite aliens: Rumiko, Kyle, and Ryan.

Message from the
Publisher

WELCOME TO OUR NERVOUS SYSTEM

Some people say that the World Wide Web is a graphical extension of the information superhighway, just a network of humans and machines sending each other long lists of the equivalent of digital junk mail.

I think it is much more than that. To me, the Web is nothing less than the nervous system of the entire planet—not just a collection of computer brains connected together, but more like a billion silicon neurons entangled and recirculating electro-chemical signals of information and data, each contributing to the birth of another CPU and another Web site.

Think of each person's hard disk connected at once to every other hard disk on earth, driven by human navigators searching like Columbus for the New World. Seen this way the Web is more of a super entity, a growing, living thing, controlled by the universal human will to expand, to be more. Yet, unlike a purposeful business plan with rigid rules, the Web expands in a nonlinear, unpredictable, creative way that echoes natural evolution.

We created our Web site not just to extend the reach of our computer book products but to be part of this synaptic neural network, to experience, like a nerve in the body, the flow of ideas and then to pass those ideas up the food chain of the mind. Your mind. Even more, we wanted to pump some of our own creative juices into this rich wine of technology.

TASTE OUR DIGITAL WINE

And so we ask you to taste our wine by visiting the body of our business. Begin by understanding the metaphor we have created for our Web site—a universal learning center, situated in outer space in the form of a space station. A place where you can journey to study any topic from the convenience of your own screen. Right now we are focusing on computer topics, but the stars are the limit on the Web.

If you are interested in discussing this Web site or finding out more about the Waite Group, please send me e-mail with your comments, and I will be happy to respond. Being a programmer myself, I love to talk about technology and find out what our readers are looking for.

Sincerely,

Mitchell Waite

Mitchell Waite, C.E.O. and Publisher

200 Tamal Plaza
Corte Madera CA 94925
415-924-2575
415-924-2576 fax

Internet email:
support@waite.com

Website:
http://www.waite.com/waite

CREATING THE HIGHEST QUALITY COMPUTER BOOKS IN THE INDUSTRY

Waite Group Press
Waite Group New Media

Come Visit
WAITE.COM
Waite Group Press
World Wide Web Site

Now find all the latest information on Waite Group books at our new Web site, **http://www.waite.com/waite.** You'll find an online catalog where you can examine and order any title, review upcoming books, and send e-mail to our authors and editors. Our FTP site has all you need to update your book: the latest program listings, errata sheets, most recent versions of Fractint, POV Ray, Polyray, DMorph, and all the programs featured in our books. So download, talk to us, ask questions, on **http://www.waite.com/waite.**

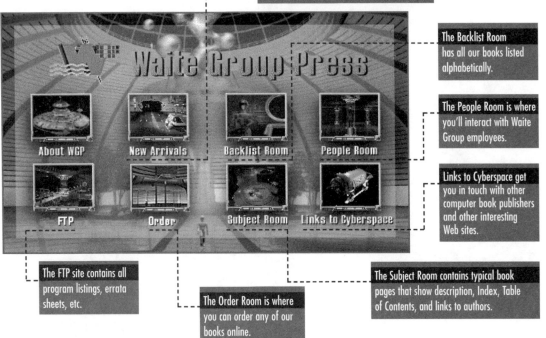

ABOUT THE AUTHOR

After an extended childhood as a Forest Service brat, growing up with backyards in most of the national forests, the author began his computer career in the urban sprawl of Tokyo, Japan. With a major in Clinical Psychology from the University of Maryland, and brief tangents into alternative careers in martial arts, bodyguard for women pro-wrestlers, and teaching English, he finally opted for the less hazardous pursuits of computer networks, Internet consulting, and writing. Currently a Network Analyst at the University of Colorado in Boulder, he has returned to the forests with plans of someday opening a small holographic coffee shop in the Rocky Mountains of New Mexico.

TABLE OF CONTENTS

CONTENTS

Chapter 5   The Nuts and Bolts of Web Servers .. 271

Chapter 7   Oracle Databases, VRML, OLE, and the Outer Limits 395

Acknowledgments

I would like to acknowledge Heidi Brumbaugh for her insight and guidance and Dan Scherf for his laid-back style of subtle persistence. Thanks also to Mitch Waite and Jill Pisoni for their capability and ease in virtual negotiations and counsel.

INTRODUCTION

This book is a hands-on course in HTML, the stuff Web pages are made of. But once you start writing HTML, you start to realize how much more you could do to your Web page with a little understanding of Web servers. And once you begin to understand a little more about Web servers, you notice some of the really nifty stuff you can do with CGI scripts. If you've ever read that book about giving a mouse a cookie to your preschooler, you'll know what I mean. (If you haven't, trust me, you don't want to give a mouse a cookie unless you have some scotch tape.)

The lessons ahead unfold along a path of growing sophistication in the use of the Web to deliver your message. The first two chapters explore the ins and outs of HTML from the basics, tables, and graphical bullets, to multimedia, glow-in-the-dark rulers, and imagemaps. The chapter that follows deals with squeezing content from the Internet itself using URLs. These small but powerful HTML tags can link your pages to non-Web resources and content. They can even be used to build Webs without Web servers. The chapter finishes with sessions on style and performance, rules of thumb and tricks of the trade for polishing your Web page's appearance and making its presentation snappy.

With the first three chapters under your belt, you can whip up a Web page from scratch. Chapter 4 begins your introduction to forms: pages that interact with their users. You'll cover all the form gadgets and gizmos, er, components, with time left to spare for writing some scripts behind the forms in both Perl and Visual Basic.

They say you can't really appreciate something unless you know how it's built. Well, some things anyway, and Web servers for sure. Chapter 5 covers Web servers, both the UNIX and Microsoft Windows varieties. You'll install a Web server on your Windows platform and learn how to tweak everything from files and directory access to username and password authorization to an individual Web page. You'll learn what logs to check, how to find who's looking at your pages, and an assortment of other procedures to get an inside view of how your Web server is being used. The last session shows you how to archive and cross-reference traffic from a listserver, allowing e-mail dialogs on any given topic to be stored in an online repository of hyperlinked content.

You're just getting warmed up. Chapter 6 introduces two different techniques for indexing the content of your Web pages. Using two public domain (free) products, you'll find out how to provide search capabilities that make finding a needle of text in a haystack of HTML as easy as entering a keyword on a form. You'll learn techniques that make writing scripts easier and more powerful, and develop this ability by creating games, animation, guest books, and access counters. By the end of Chapter 6 you'll be as familiar with the intricacies of scripts and interactive forms as you were with "plain" old HTML at the end of Chapter 2.

But you don't get off that easy! Chapter 7 covers practical topics at the cutting edge—or as close to the edge as printed media can get. You'll learn how to interface to an Oracle database using two different methods, both of which sidestep the costly and complex middle ware requirements of a traditional client/server. You'll learn how to create simple 3D objects using the Virtual Reality Modeling Language (VRML), and learn Java's role on a Web page. You'll discover how to drive Netscape's Navigator using OLE calls from Visual Basic, submitting forms to Web servers across the network from local Windows applications. Then onto security and how to use Pretty Good Privacy (PGP) to sign authenticated messages and transactions from a server, and beyond this, what the competing Web security models mean to a Web developer. Last but not least you'll learn how Digicash can be used to provide goods and services with virtual green.

I guess that's about it. As I watch this go to production with all the neat stuff happening out on the Web, I wish I could keep adding chapters on the fly. But I think my editors are tired of my begging for one last tweak, one last feature, and perhaps there's enough here to keep you busy having fun on the Web, the latest Internet frontier.

INSTALLATION

The companion CD-ROM contains all of the code for the sessions in the book, as well as various programs and utilities for your Web page development.

Since all of the code for the sessions in this book are on the companion CD-ROM, there is no need to type the code if you want to use it for your own projects. We will illustrate how to copy the files from the companion CD-ROM to your hard drive.

There are a few operating systems that are compatible with this CD. This section will walk you through the steps necessary for the most popular ones: Windows 3.x, Windows 95, and various flavors of UNIX. Each operating system will be discussed in turn.

For the following PC examples, we are going to assume that the CD-ROM drive you want to copy files *from* is the D: drive and the hard drive you want to copy files *to* is the C: drive. If your system is set up differently, please substitute the appropriate drive letters for your system. For UNIX users, these UNIX examples assume you will be using the mount point */cdrom*. If that is not the mount point you will be using, please substitute your mount point with the one in the example. In all cases, the mount point must exist or an error will occur. If the mount point directory does not exist, create the directory using the *mkdir* command and try remounting the CD-ROM.

WINDOWS 3.X

The following steps are for installing the programs onto your hard drive.

1. Open the File Manager.

2. In File Manager, locate the drive you want to copy to and click on it.

3. If you have a directory to copy the files to, skip to Step 4. Otherwise, create a new directory by selecting File, Create Directory. Type

   `HTML3IC`

   or a directory name of your choice and press ENTER or click on the OK button.

4. Click on HTML3IC or the directory you created.

5. Double-click on the D: drive icon. You should see three directories: ARCHIVES, PROGRAMS, and SOURCE. Double-click on the SOURCE directory. Drag the contents to the destination drive. If you only want to copy a few directories, control-click on the directories and drag the

selection to the destination drive. Depending on how fast your computer is and also depending on the options set for your computer, the copying process may take a few moments to a few minutes.

Installation of the programs on the CD-ROM can be accomplished the same way, with the exception that you will be double-clicking on the PROGRAMS directory instead of the SOURCE directory. After you copy the files from the CD-ROM to your hard drive, you can create a Program Group to launch them from (select File, New, Program Group from the Program Manager). Add the individual icons to this group (Select File, New, Program Item). When you are done, you may double-click on the icons to launch the programs.

When Windows copies a CD-ROM, it does not change the Read-only attribute for the files it copies. You can view the files, but you cannot edit them until you remove this attribute. To change it on all of the files, select the top-most directory with the files in it. In File Manager, select File, Properties and click on the Read-only checkbox to deselect it and click on OK.

The Icon Library Builder (found in \PROGRAMS\ICLBLD) has an installer called INSTALL.EXE. From the Program Manager, select File, Run and type in d:\programs\iclbld\install.exe and click on OK. Follow the on-screen prompts to successfully install this program. The NetManage Sampler can be installed by following the installation instructions in the section The Chameleon Sampler.

WINDOWS 95

The easiest way to copy files using Windows 95 is by using the Desktop.

1. Double-click on the My Computer icon. Your drives will appear in a window on the desktop.

2. Double-click on your hard drive and create a new folder, such as *HTML 3 Interactive Course*, by selecting File, New, Folder from the window menu. A folder called *New Folder* will be created on your hard drive with the name highlighted. Type in the name you want and press the ENTER key.

3. Go back to your drive window and double-click on the icon that represents your CD-ROM. You will see a window that has three folders in it: ARCHIVES, PROGRAMS, and SOURCE.

4. Double-click on the SOURCE folder. You will see a window with chapter folders in it. Select the directories you want to copy (control-click on the folders if you're not copying all of them) and drag your selection to the directory you created on your hard drive. You might need to reposition your windows to make the window for your hard drive visible. Depending on your system's performance, this may take a few moments to a few minutes.

Installation of the programs on the CD-ROM can be accomplished the same way, with the exception that you will be double-clicking on the PROGRAMS directory instead of the SOURCE directory. After you copy the files from the CD-ROM to your hard drive, you can create a Program Folder in your Start Menu to launch them from (select Open by right-clicking on the Start icon; select File, New Folder). Add the individual icons to this folder (Select File, New, Shortcut). When you are done, you may use the Start menu to launch the programs.

When Windows copies a CD-ROM, it does not change the Read-only attribute for the files it copies. You can view the files, but you cannot edit them until you remove this attribute. To change it on all of the files, select the top-most directory with the files in it. In the folder, right-click on the file or folder and select Properties; click on the Read-only checkbox to deselect it and click on OK.

The Icon Library Builder (found in \PROGRAMS\ICLBLD) has an installer called INSTALL.EXE. Select Start, Run and type in d:\programs\iclbld\install.exe and click on OK. Follow the on-screen prompts to successfully install this program. The NetManage Sampler can be installed by following the installation instructions in the section The Chameleon Sampler.

UNIX

Since there are many flavors of UNIX, there are many ways that a CD-ROM can be mounted. This section will illustrate how to mount a CD-ROM on a typical UNIX installation. In some versions of UNIX, having the CD-ROM in the drive when UNIX is started up will typically mount the CD-ROM. If your UNIX platform automatically mounts CD-ROMs, skip to Step 2; otherwise continue with Step 1.

1. While it is not necessary to be logged in as root, it may help in the mounting process. A few typical commands to mount a CD-ROM at the UNIX prompt are

```
mount /dev/cdrom /cdrom
mount -tiso9660 /dev/cdrom /cdrom
mount -f hsfs /dev/cdrom /cdrom
```

   If none of these commands work, you may be working with a non-standard implementation of UNIX. Please contact your systems administrator for further assistance.

2. Create and move into a directory that you would like to copy the files into, such as html_3_interactive_course, by typing

```
mkdir html_3_interactive_course
cd html_3_interactive_course
```

3. Copy all of the source code to your local drive by typing

```
cp /cdrom/source/* .
```

   or copy individual directories of source code by typing

```
cp /cdrom/source/chapter?/* .
```

   where chapter? is the name of the directory that corresponds to the chapter that you want to copy.

THE CHAMELEON SAMPLER

The NetManage Internet Chameleon is one of the most versatile and easy-to-use set of Internet tools in the world. Chameleon helps you sign up with an Internet provider, connect cleanly to the Internet, and access a variety of resources—including a pretty cool Web browser. The Chameleon package includes

- *Custom,* for connecting to the Internet
- *WebSurfer,* a full-featured World Wide Web browser
- *Gopher,* which lets you access any gopher menu worldwide
- *NEWTNews,* a Usenet newsreader
- *Mail,* a convenient way to send and receive e-mail
- *Archie,* which lets you search for a file over the Internet
- *Telnet,* for connecting to a remote computer
- *FTP,* for transferring files over the Internet
- *FTP Server,* which lets you allow others to download or upload files to your PC
- *Mail Utilities,* programs that help you compact or organize your mailbox files to save space
- *Ping,* to test if you're connected to a remote computer
- *Finger,* to check if a friend is connected to the Internet
- *Whois,* to get information about people registered in the NIC (Network Information Center) database

You can sample the Chameleon tools for 30 days at no charge. If you like what you see, you can register everything for 50 bucks.

Installing the Chameleon

In the installation directions here, we assume that your hard disk is the C: drive and your CD-ROM is the D: drive. If this doesn't match your computer, substitute C: or D: with the correct drive designation.

To copy the sampler software onto your hard disk, run the Setup program. While under Windows, select File, Run in the Program Manager. In the Run dialog box, type

```
d:\programs\ntmanage\disk_1\setup.exe
```

and then press the OK button.

The Setup program will ask you where to install the NetManage program. The default suggested is fine for most people. If you want it installed elsewhere, type in the drive and directory of your choosing and select Continue.

After a few moments, the Setup program will ask you to type in the path of the second batch of files. Select the 1 in *DISK_1* and change it to 2, and select Continue.

After another few moments, the Setup program will ask you to type in the path of the third batch of files. Select the 2 in *DISK_2* and change it to 3, and select Continue.

Click OK when Setup tells you that installation is complete. You are now ready to setup your Internet account!

Signing Up for an Internet Provider Account

If you don't already have one, the Chameleon package makes it easy to sign up with one of several popular Internet providers. If you'd like to sign up using the Chameleon software, run the Automatic Internet-Click to Start icon.

To learn about a particular Internet provider, click one of the tabs (other than NetManage) in the Select Internet Provider window. Most providers give you several hours (or even a month) of free trial time. To read about the locations an Internet provider can cover, the monthly price, and other important information, click the More Info button at the bottom of the screen. If you have specific questions, contact the provider directly.

When you're ready to begin the sign-up procedure, click the Signup button. You'll see a registration screen similar to the one in Figure I-1. Fill in your name (as it appears on your credit card), address, phone number, and credit card information.

You will not actually be charged any provider fees until you officially register with the service. You can cancel the registration transaction at any time during the sign-on process. If you do decide to register, your credit card number will be sent over a secure phone line.

As you work through the sign-up process, there may be other tabs asking for additional information. If so, click these tabs and fill in the forms.

Select the Phone List button at the bottom of the screen. The Phone List dialog appears, listing possible phone numbers you can use to register. If one of the numbers is in your area code, select it. Otherwise, select the toll-free 800 number.

If necessary, you can edit the registration phone number. Some systems, for example, require you to dial a 9 to reach an outside line. Just type in this 9.

Figure I-1 The easiest way to sign up for an Internet provider

When you've typed in all your vital stats, return to the first registration tab. Click Send to dial the toll-free number and begin the registration process. The icons to the right will light up as each stage of the dialing process is completed. The set of traffic lights tell you if each stage—initializing the modem, dialing, connecting, and communicating—has worked.

Note   You may need to click the Advanced button to specify special modem ports or commands.

Follow the instructions that appear as the registration proceeds. You will be given the option to select from various service and pricing plans. Your account information (username, e-mail address, password, dial-up number, and IP address) will automatically be configured into the Chameleon package. An interface will be created for the Custom program, which quickly and flawlessly connects you to the Internet.

That's it! You can now reboot your system to kick-start everything.

Registering the Chameleon Software

If you already have an Internet account, you can set up the Internet Chameleon software (shown in Figure I-2) and start using it within minutes. Run the Automatic Internet-Click to Start program.

Make sure the NetManage tab is selected, and then click the Signup button. You can now activate the software for a free 30-day demonstration period. After this period, the

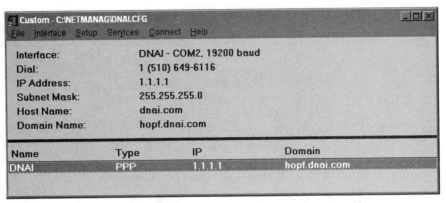

Figure I-2 The full Chameleon package in the Internet Chameleon program group

Chameleon software will no longer work. If you decide to register the Chameleon package (for $50), your credit card will be charged and your software will be activated permanently.

Fill in all the information on both forms, as shown in Figure I-1, including your credit card number (it won't be charged unless you complete the registration). You may need to contact your Internet provider for the Internet information on the second form.

Select the Phone button, and choose a local or toll-free phone number. Then click the Send button to dial in to NetManage and get your software activated.

Once you connect, you are given the following choices:

- Activate your software for a free 30-day demonstration.

- Purchase your software to activate it permanently.

- Configure your connection (if your Chameleon software has already been activated).

Connecting to the Internet

Now that you have selected a provider and registered your software, you can actually get hooked in to the Internet. To do this, you need to run the Custom program (Figure I-3) from Windows File Manager.

If you used the Chameleon package to sign up with your Internet provider, an automatic configuration file should have already been written for you. Otherwise, Chameleon comes with the configurations for most popular Internet providers. Select File, Open and look for the configuration file for your provider. If your provider is not

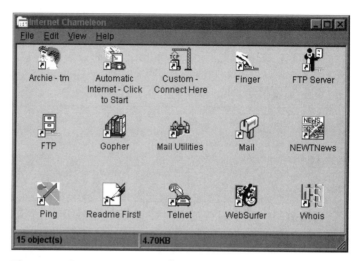

Figure I-3 Your customized on-ramp onto the Information Superhighway

listed, you'll need to contact them and ask what the proper settings are. They may even be able to send you a prewritten Chameleon configuration file.

If you do need to enter the connection settings yourself, use the appropriate values you have obtained from your Internet provider. You can verify or edit the following information under the Setup menu:

- IP Address
- Subnet Mask
- Host Name
- Domain Name
- Port
- Modem
- Dial
- Login
- Interface Name
- BOOTP

You may also need to fill in the following under the Services menu:

 Default Gateway

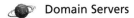 Domain Servers

Read Chapter 1 for more information about these terms.

Logging In

Once your configuration settings are in place, simply click the Connect menu to dial up your Internet provider and get connected. If all goes well, you should hear a small beep, and a program known as Newt will run. This program lets Windows communicate with the Internet. You can then minimize the Custom program and run the Internet application of your choice.

Logging Out

When you're done using the Internet, call up the Custom program and click the Disconnect menu.

Web Browsing with WebSurfer

WebSurfer is a full-featured World Wide Web browser similar to Mosaic. You can read all about browsers in Chapter 2 and about Mosaic in Chapter 5. To start exploring the Web, first use the Chameleon Custom program to connect to the Internet. Then run the WebSurfer program.

Like Mosaic, WebSurfer has a toolbar (see the top of Figure I-4) that acts as a short-cut for most commands. The toolbar contains

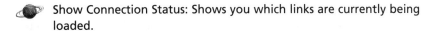 Show Connection Status: Shows you which links are currently being loaded.

Go to URL: Opens a specific Web URL (defined in Chapter 1).

Get URL: Reloads the current document.

Hotlist: Shows the list of your favorite Web pages for you to choose from. To go to a page, just double-click on it. You can also delete pages from the list by selecting the page and clicking Remove.

Make Hot: Adds the current Web page to your hotlist.

Back: Revisits the Web page you just came from.

Forward: Goes to the next Web page in the series, if applicable.

Home: Returns to the Web page you started from.

Cancel All: Stops the loading of the current Web page.

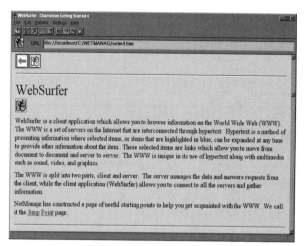

Figure I-4 The WebSurfer browser in all its glory

Loading a Web Page from the Internet

Like Mosaic, WebSurfer combines text and graphics on the same page. Any text in blue or graphics with a blue border are hypertext links to other Web pages, multimedia files, or Internet areas. To load a link, just click on it.

You can also load up a document directly. Just select Retrieve, Go To URL and type in the document's exact URL. Alternatively, you can type a document's URL in the Dialog bar's URL box and press ENTER to load it.

If the document is a Web page, it will be displayed. If the document is a graphic, sound, or movie, the WebSurfer program will attempt to call up a viewer program to display/play it. If the document is any other type of multimedia file, WebSurfer allows you to save the document directly to your hard disk.

To find out more about the current Web document, select Retrieve, Properties.

Loading a Web Page from Your Hard Disk

If you have any Web pages on your hard disk (perhaps ones that you've created yourself), you can easily use WebSurfer to view them. Select Retrieve, Open Local File. Choose the file you want to view and click OK.

You can even edit the current Web document—a very handy capability for Web developers. Select Retrieve, Edit HTML. Then access the Retrieve, Refresh From Disk menu item to reload the page in a flash and see what your edits look like.

THE eZONE

By buying this book, you have free access to the *HTML 3 Interactive Course* on Waite Group Press's eZone. As the back cover flap shows, there is an entire online support component that complements this book by providing dedicated support including personalized assistance from a HTML 3 expert; challenging online exams with immediate grading; access to additional resources and information; an area to interact with other readers of this book; a certificate of achievement demonstrating your successful completion of the course; and much more. There's no charge for these dedicated services; they're all part of the Interactive Course.

A sneak preview demo of the eZone is included on the CD in the \EZONE directory so that you can check out some of the kinds of available services; you'll need either Netscape Navigator 2 or later, or Miscrosoft Internet Explorer 3 or later to run it. A README file in the \EZONE directory explains how to run the demo.

To use the unprecedented eZone services (or just to check it out), visit us at: www.waite.com/ezone

Log on and learn HTML 3!

INTRODUCING HTML

INTRODUCING HTML

n this chapter you'll get an overview of the Internet and the World Wide Web, the pros and cons of various options for Internet connectivity, and how to set up your PC to start writing Web pages. Then, with the groundwork laid, you'll jump into *HTML*, or HyperText Markup Language, the lingua franca of Web publishing. By the end of the chapter you will have learned enough elements of *HTML* to create Web pages with headers, paragraphs, a variety of text formats, lists, and most importantly, hyperlinks to other pages. By then you'll be ready for Chapter 2, where you'll step through the doors to multimedia. There is much to cover. But to understand where you are heading, you should look briefly to where it all began.

THE INTERNET AND THE WEB

These first two sessions start from ground zero. If you already understand the differences between the Internet and the Web, know that a URL is not a female Yak, and have a (working) connection to the Internet, feel free to skip to Session 3. If you're still here, get ready for a nutshell tour of how all this madness known as the Internet and the World Wide Web got started, and whose fault it really is.

The Internet Phenomenon

This story has been told so often it's becoming folklore. Way back in the murky '60s, the Department of Defense funded a research project on internetworking. The goal was to reliably link computers across a network, and the first computer, or *node,* was hooked up at UCLA in 1969. Only two years later the number of nodes had grown to 15. Something was afoot. Well, okay, it did start off kind of slow, with just 62 nodes in the mid '70s, climbing steadily to 1,000 by the mid '80s. But then toward the late '80s things started to click. The National Science Foundation was funded to create a high-speed backbone to five supercomputer centers across the U.S., and to provide an infrastructure for regional networks. After this, connections exploded. More than 100,000 nodes were online at the end of the '80s, and most of the activity on the Internet centered around academic research and universities. By the mid '90s, the scope of the Internet was far wider, and in April of 1995 the government extricated itself entirely from the network, leaving by this time an estimated 4,000,000 nodes and an exponential growth rate. Figure 1-1 shows a graph of online traffic from December of 1992 up to the point that NFS-NET pulled out of the Internet provider business.

The '90s were also roughly the time the Internet went commercial. At one time the NSF restricted commercial traffic across its high-speed backbone. Since this backbone was heavily utilized, the restriction carried some legislative weight. It was considered bad form to advertise, vendors were tolerated only if they didn't mention their products, and violators were slapped with nasty messages and ostracized as uncool. But the NSF had been shifting its funding for the backbone to the commercial sector since 1993, and for a couple of years the situation was gray. Vendors were confused by the nature and culture of the Internet, and Internet veterans were confused by the changing commercialism of their home turf.

Of course, the new rules of the Next Generation Internet became abundantly clear to both parties as newbies from the online services such as Prodigy, America Online, and CompuServe found the onramps built by their providers and began an unprecedented influx of users that were affiliated with neither a company nor a university. The shifting user base, and the change of the Internet from a research to a commercial medium

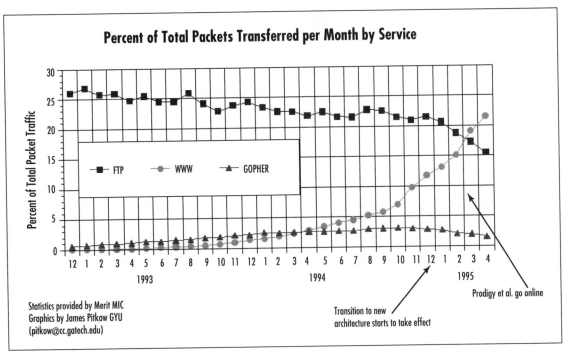

Figure 1-1
NSFNET traffic statistics

still has old-timers, newcomers, and legislatures alike guessing about its future and the rules of the game.

So Who Runs the Show?

No one. Even when the government was indirectly subsidizing the Internet through the Department of Defense, and later the NSF, it discovered to its alarm that the show was basically running itself. The Internet is not like a big bulletin board system where everyone has to log in to some major site. The Internet is a collection of independent computers, linked across a variety of local, regional, national, and international networks. Some players own some parts of some of these networks, but nobody owns them all. The Internet has been called the largest functioning anarchy in the world. It is a model of a system working without central authority. And this may explain some of the "attitude" you encounter on its various forums. Using the tired info-highway analogy, the parts of the Internet are like the city-owned roads, country-owned roads, etc. They all interconnect, they each have different ways of obtaining funds, and if they start putting in tollbooths, you can usually find another way around.

Enter the Web

The Internet is more than 20 years old, but the Web is just a baby. It first appeared in 1991, written by Tim Berners-Lee to help high energy physicists keep track of cross-references. He wrote the software in about two months and gave it away for free.

What the Web does is allow authors to put hypertext links in text, which readers can view with special browsers. A research paper by Dr. X mentioned in a piece of text can be retrieved by simply activating the link on the screen rather than tracking down the paper publication. The link brings up the paper referenced, it can be read or printed, and then the user can return to reading the original document, or follow new links in the paper by Dr. X.

The Web consists, in part, of *servers,* typically computer systems on the Internet, whose job it is to store documents. The Web's other vital part consists of *browsers* running on PCs, terminals, workstations, or RayBans that retrieve documents from the servers and display them onscreen. Pretty handy, but nobody really noticed the Web until some students at the National Center for Supercomputing Applications (NCSA) at the University of Illinois, Urbana-Champaign (UIUC) wrote a spiffy little product called Mosaic.

Mosaic was the first graphical browser of the World Wide Web. It made hypertext links accessible with a simple mouse click. It gave the Internet a pretty face. And since the NCSA Mosaic project was funded by the NSF, it was public domain software, and it spread like wildfire. For the first time Web users could see text and images on the same page, and could "surf" through hyperlinks with the flick of a wrist.

The first month after Mosaic's release for Microsoft Windows in November 1993, Web traffic for the first time exceeded 1 percent of the NSFNET's backbone traffic. This put it in eighth place behind protocols like e-mail, file transfer, Telnet, and Usenet News. One year later, Web traffic had moved from eighth place to second, weighing in at about 14 percent of the total traffic. As of 1995 it was the number one protocol moving across the Internet.

What's the Difference?

It's easy to get the Internet and the Web confused. Think of the Internet as the phone company and the Web as 1-800 numbers. The 1-800 numbers were a new way of using an existing technology. The Web is just another service on the Internet, like e-mail or file transfers. They are all services that use the Internet as a way to communicate, the way phones, answering machines, and faxes all use the "phone" lines. In fact, computer networks use phone lines as well, and the major phone services like MCI, Sprint, and AT&T are all active in providing the physical wiring that computer networks like the Internet run across.

Advantages of the Web

While the Internet had a number of services before the World Wide Web, they were not particularly easy to use. You generally had to have some understanding of UNIX (the most common server, or node, on the Internet), and most of the commands were textual, requiring you to memorize options and special commands that varied for each separate service. The Web browser provides a nice, friendly interface, not only to the World Wide Web, but to the other "legacy" services on the Internet as well. The Web uses special links called URLs, or uniform resource locators, to point to various Internet resources like FTP, Gopher, e-mail, Telnet, and others, as well as to find its own Web pages. To get to a resource, you just click the link with your mouse. No mess, no fuss. Here's a synopsis of what the Web browser has brought to the Internet users:

- **Everything under one hood.** The browser hides the complexity of having to know FTP in order to download a file, or of having to know Telnet in order to connect to an online service. The interface to a broad range of Internet services is provided via point and click, often making the other services indistinquishable from the Web's native hypertext.

- **Text and pictures on a page.** The Web browser can display text and graphics on the screen simultaneously. Parts of the text can be hyperlinks to other sources of information, and even pictures and images can be hyperlinks. Never underestimate the allure of graphics. Picture and image archives are some of the most heavily utilized repositories on the Internet.

- **Ease of use.** The same interface is used to access different forms of information, and everything is point and click. A beginner can begin accessing Internet services almost immediately after sitting down with the browser.

- **Easy to write.** It's easy to write hypertext. (Then why this big book? Well, it's powerful too!)

- **Free.** The Web provides incredible amounts of free and easily accessed information for research, exploration, and fun.

In fairness though, the Web wasn't the first service to integrate Internet resources under one hood; this distinction goes to Gopher. Gopher was developed at the University of Minnesota and provides a hierarchical menu structure for accessing Internet services. Gopher was growing in popularity—it did simplify the Internet—until it was overtaken by Mosaic.

Hypertext: The Way We Think

Hypertext has an interesting lineage that we won't get into, but it's basically been proposed as a model that more closely reflects the way we think than the hierarchical structures of Gopher. One thought tends to lead to another and another. If this model is implemented as links on the computer, information can be presented such that you can delve into particular areas that hold your interest, and theoretically dive as deep into these as you want to go. You could be reading a treatise by Freud, link to a definition of the superego, and from there to modern theories of morality and the meaning of anomie.

Of course, hypertext, if not architected or used well, can also be a bane. It can be argued that it encourages the attention deficient; it's not unusual to start researching the fjords of Greenland and end up pondering the social implications of Sigma's *Guide to Cows In Pinball*. The Web's equivalent of TV's channel surfing. Uh, where were we?

Home Pages

What a Web browser typically retrieves from a Web server is a *Web page*. These pages can contain text and images and hyperlinks to other pages. The *home page* is the page people load when they want to know about you or your company. It's the Web equivalent of an e-mail address. By entering the address (URL, remember?) of your page into their Web browser, users can browse a page that you have written in HTML.

Pages on the Web are written in HTML, and you'll learn to write in HTML from A to Z in the following sessions and chapters of this course. It takes about five minutes to learn to write a simple page, but the more you learn, the more polished your pages become, and the more sophisticated the options you will have at your disposal. The home page is the business card of the '90s. It's an online, multimedia, hypertext expression of your creative, personal, and professional presence on a medium accessible by millions.

To get started, you'll need to get connected to the Internet. If you're already connected, you can skip to Session 3; if not, Session 2 should help you get going. Before you move on, however, let's try a quiz.

1. The government pulled funding for the Internet in
    a. 1994
    b. 1995
    c. 1996
    d. 1993

2. Web browsers pull a variety of Internet services under one "hood." One popular way of doing this before the Web was
    a. using URLs
    b. with FTP
    c. with Gopher
    d. through hypertext

3. Why has hypertext been proposed as a model of information retrieval more similar to the way we think?
    a. because we typically think hierarchically
    b. because it is extremely fast

c. because it sounds better than saying we think like a gopher

d. because it can link any concept with any other concept

4. Who owns the Internet?
   a. the military
   b. the government
   c. an international coop
   d. no one

SESSION 2

GETTING CONNECTED

Technically, you do not need to be connected to the Internet to learn how to write Web pages. Most of the sessions and exercises writing HTML can be done on a PC without a network connection. In fact, you can install a Web server on your PC (covered in Chapter 4) and even go through the advanced sections on your own Web server/Web browser island without a modem in sight. But if you're serious about getting onto the Web, you will need an Internet connection. Fortunately, these are getting easier and easier to come by. In fact, by the time you read this, your local cable provider may even offer Internet connectivity.

What follows is a brief rundown on the many ways of connecting to the Internet. Included are the kinds of questions to ask potential providers, the kinds of services that are offered, and the hardware and software you will need. At the end of the session you'll learn what the minimal requirements are for a bare-bones connection—which is probably cheaper than you think.

Types of Connections

There are three basic ways individuals commonly access the Internet: SLIP (Serial Line Internet Protocol) or PPP (Point to Point Protocol) accounts, shell accounts, and accounts on online services. SLIP or PPP accounts are the most flexible. When you connect with one of these accounts you are a first-class citizen on the Internet. Your PC becomes another host, directly connected. You can usually offer and access the same Internet services as any other host, be it a UNIX system, mainframe, or Cray supercomputer.

Shell accounts offer you access to a computer that has access to the Internet. Sort of one step removed from the SLIP/PPP option. Typically these accounts are on computers running UNIX, and you can use Internet services on these systems, but not directly from your PC. The shell accounts are generally text-only interfaces to the Internet, but often a provider that offers PPP or SLIP will include a shell account on one of their systems, too. This could be useful to you in the later part of this course, when you will actually be creating scripts and files directly on the Web server. You don't need a shell account to run a Web browser, though.

The third way is arguably the easiest, but also the least flexible. You let America Online, CompuServe, or some other online network provide Internet services in addition to their regular fare. They have their own point and click menus to Internet services and try to make access easy and consistent with their other services.

Providers

Providers is the generic term given to the vendors of Internet services. They come in two major flavors: online services and Internet service providers (ISPs).

Online Services

These services typically started on their own turf, providing e-mail, online conferencing, and software downloads for their own members. Then they started providing links to selected Internet services as they began seeing the writing on the wall. These providers include America Online (AOL), Prodigy, CompuServe, and others. Most of these can provide you with space on their systems to create your own Web pages, and access through their Web browser to Web sites on the Internet. One drawback to these services is that you will probably have to use the Web browser they've picked out for you. At the time of this writing, the most popular Web browser is Netscape Navigator from Netscape Communications and is supported by neither AOL nor Prodigy. It can be supported through CompuServe at an extra price for PPP/SLIP access. Online services may serve a niche, but typically they are more expensive than direct Internet providers.

Internet Service Providers

Once ISPs were prolific mom and pop operations, but more and more they are becoming consolidated under large national providers. Often the providers in a local or regional area will still offer better rates, but depending on where you live, sometimes the national providers are the only ones available (besides the online services discussed above).

Finding Internet providers is something of a Catch-22. Most of them are listed on the Internet, but this kind of assumes you already have access to the Internet to find them, no? If you have a friend with an AOL, Prodigy, CompuServe, or other account who can send e-mail to the Internet (or you sign up for a free trial—hint, hint), you can get a list of these providers by sending a four-line message to ftpmail@decwrl.dec.com with the following content (no subject required):

```
connect nic.merit.edu
chdir /Internet/providers
get Internet-access-providers-us.txt
quit
```

This will get you a very large listing of the providers and the area codes they service. Another e-mail directory is PDIAL (Public Dial-up Internet Access List), which can be obtained by sending e-mail to info-deli-server@netcom.com with *send pdial* in the subject line and no message content. In both cases the e-mail response will be returned to whoever sent the message, so you don't have to include any return address.

Probably the easiest way of finding local providers, though, is to get a commercial Internet product like Spry's Internet in a Box, Internet Chameleon for Windows from Netmanage, or Onnet Explorer from FTP Inc. When these products are installed, they come up with a list of providers for your area code and will handle the connection and registration automatically.

Cable TV?

Major cable TV providers like TCI are really trying to crack into the online market. You might want to check with them about their immediate plans for Internet service. These companies have the capability of offering very high speed connections to the Internet by shaving one or two channels off their video bandwidth to your house. They're the ones to really watch for developments.

Questions to Ask

With any Internet provider, you'll need a basic checklist of information that will tell you if you're getting a competitive, or even adequate, deal. Here's what you'll need to ask about, and the answers you should be looking for:

- Speed. Very important. Make sure they offer at least 14.4Kbps (kilobits per second) connections. 28.8Kbps would be better. Any connection slower than 14.4 will take a painfully long time to load Web pages that are rich in graphics.

- Type of service. The answers you want to hear are PPP and/or SLIP to provide you with a direct connection to the Internet.

- Their Internet connection. What is the speed of their network's connection to the Internet? Good answers are T1 (1.5Mbps) or T3 (45Mbps), less than adequate answers are 56Kbps and ISDN, and anything less than 56Kbps is a bad, bad answer.

- Number of dialups. How many modems do they have, and typically how busy are they? If they give you the number, you can try calling it several times before you join to see how many busy signals you get. Test this during the hours you expect to be connected.

- Pricing. You will probably want a set number of hours at a fixed rate; usually this ranges from 25 to 100 hours a month, with everything over this billed at an hourly rate.

- Accounts. How many account names can you have? What if you want e-mail addresses for yourself and members of your family? Typically, providers will give you five or more at no extra charge.

Web space. Make sure they provide Web service, allowing you to create your own pages under your account. How much space do they give you for your own Web pages? Five MB is typical. A Web page usually doesn't take much space unless you're heavily into graphics.

Web scripts. Ask if they allow you to write your own Web scripts. Some providers control who can or can't write scripts, and offer this service only to their commercial accounts.

Domain names. And speaking of commercial accounts, ask how much they charge to register a domain name for your company, so you can have an address at www.yourcompany.com instead of using their generic domain name. A fee of $50 is about right.

Software. Do they provide you with SLIP or PPP software? A Web browser? An FTP client?

The Hardware

The hardware you will need depends on what you want to do with your Web browser. If you want to access pages with color graphics, sounds, and animation, you'll need at least

486/33 or faster processor (Pentium 75 or faster preferred)

4MB or more of memory (8–16MB preferred)

SVGA graphics, noninterlaced, .28 or .25 dot pitch, at least a 15" (17" preferred) monitor

420MB hard disk (more is better, especially if you're running other applications)

14.4Kb or faster modem (28.8Kb preferred)

The Software

For software you'll need SLIP or PPP if you are using an Internet provider. Typically the provider will supply this for you. Trumpet is a good Windows shareware package that provides both PPP and SLIP capabilities. Windows 95 has built-in PPP and SLIP support.

Next, you will need a Web browser. Netscape Navigator is probably the best choice; it currently has 70 to 80 percent of the Web browser market and provides advanced features that other browsers don't. Yet.

Last, you will need an FTP package. This will let you transfer Web pages that you write to your server. You can do your authoring on the PC, but when you get ready to have your page accessible to the world, you'll need to put it up on the server. While

Web browsers can download files to your PC using a built-in FTP, they cannot use it to transfer them up to the server. A good freeware FTP package is WS_FTP, and most Internet service providers will also provide you an FTP client free of charge.

On a Budget

You don't need whiz-bang multimedia capabilities to get onto the Web. Most of the Web pages on the Internet can be accessed in text mode. You still get all the hyperlinks and all the information content, you'll just miss out on the fancy graphics and menus. Some pages have all their links in the graphics, so if you go with a very cheap modem, these will take a loooonnng time to download, but they're generally the exception.

As forced obsolescence continues to push software into higher and higher end PCs, you can often find the best deals in the classifieds and secondhand computer stores for antique but usable discards. Antique refers to 386/33 or above at the time of this writing, but it could be a 486/33 by the time you read this. A minimal system that runs Microsoft Windows (the older 3.1 version), would be

- 386/33 processor or faster
- monochrome monitor w/graphics adapter
- 4MB memory
- 80MB disk
- 2400 baud modem

You can probably find this combination for $200 to $400. New versions of Web browsers expect 32-bit mode Windows, which requires either Windows 95 or Windows NT. Look for the versions that run strictly with Windows 3.1 (the Win32s libraries that allow Windows 3.1 to run 32-bit applications require too much overhead on this size machine, but on a 486/33 it would be no problem).

This combination won't give you color, and won't let you run much more than your Web browser at the same time, but it will connect you to the Web and allow you to access pages in text mode. It won't have blistering speed, but it should be acceptable as a "research" station.

QUIZ 2

1. What's the difference between a shell account and a SLIP/PPP account?
   a. You cannot access the Internet from shell accounts.
   b. Shell accounts are much slower.
   c. Shell accounts offer mainly text-based Internet services.
   d. Shell accounts cost more.

2. Why is the speed of the provider's connection to the Internet important?
    a. It determines the prestige of the site.
    b. High-speed connections will cost you more money.
    c. It has to handle the aggregate of all the provider's users going onto the Internet.
    d. It's not important; all Internet connections are relatively the same.

3. If a potential provider didn't offer space for individual Web pages, it would mean
    a. that you couldn't access the Internet
    b. that you couldn't use your Web browser through this provider
    c. that they were not running a UNIX server
    d. that you couldn't create home pages with your account

4. Online service providers typically offer
    a. direct connection to the Internet
    b. connection to the Internet through their applications
    c. PPP or SLIP accounts
    d. shell accounts

SETTING UP

Let's look at a simple model of how the Web works. Figure 1-2 illustrates the process. A Web browser on some PC or Mac, connected to the Internet via an Internet provider, retrieves Web pages from a Web server on the Internet. The Web page (written in HTML) can have links to other pages on other Web servers throughout the Internet, or to different pages on the same Web server and never branch off to anywhere else.

These links are typically called hyperlinks and are very flexible. A Web page can link not only to pages across the Internet, it can also link to pages on your own hard drive. In fact, in Netscape you can open a location, which is an address out on the Internet, or you can open a file, which is a page stored on your own PC. Figure 1-3 shows Netscape opening a local file. Note that you get the same Finder box that appears in other Windows applications for locating the Web page on your disk(s).

Pseudo Network

By opening local files, you avoid connect time charges while you learn to write HTML. But since a Web browser generally expects a network connection, you may need to fake it out. Make it think it has a connection so it won't display pesky messages like "Cannot Locate Network" when all you want to do is work by yourself on your own PC. This can be accomplished a couple of ways.

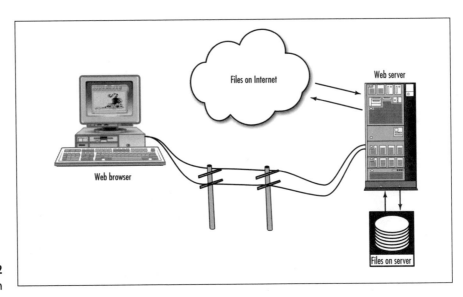

Figure 1-2
The Web in action

The Trumpet Fake

If you are using the Trumpet shareware product for your SLIP or PPP connection, use the following technique. When you first bring Trumpet up, it allows you to choose between various scripts for dialing into an Internet provider. It also has a Manual Login option, which lets you enter the phone number and control the modem directly instead of choosing an automated script. By selecting Manual Login and then pressing the <ESC> key, you will have turned on SLIP without connecting anywhere. Applications that look for a network when they come up, like Netscape, will see Trumpet and assume everything is okay. Now you can work with Netscape using local files and linking to other local files

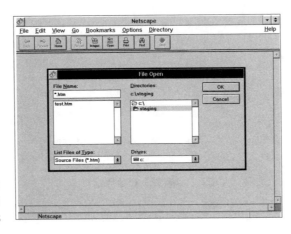

Figure 1-3
Netscape and local
Web pages

to your heart's content. Of course, if you try to open a URL, it will go nowhere, because you aren't really connected.

This technique is useful if you toggle back and forth between Internet connections to check your e-mail and browse the Web, and then hang up and work locally. To toggle from manual to an online connection, you merely go back into Trumpet and select the login script. You don't need to close Trumpet and restart it. Other SLIP and PPP products may work the same way. Try bringing them up without actually connecting to the network, and see if Netscape complains.

The Mozock Illusion

The second technique is to use a dummy network by putting the file mozock.dll in your c:\netscape directory and renaming it to winsock.dll. Now when you start Netscape, it will use this dummy Winsock library. If you have no Internet connection, or are connected via online services, this technique should work with no caveats.

If you also have the ability to dial in via SLIP/PPP, you'll need to make sure you close Netscape before making your Internet connection. If you don't, the dummy winsock.dll loaded by Netscape will conflict with the real winsock.dll loaded by your Internet software. After your connection is established, Netscape can be started and will ignore the dummy winsock.dll in its own directory, because your Internet software will have already loaded its own into memory.

Working Offline

Now that the details of how to work without an Internet connection have been ironed out, let's assemble the pieces needed to start writing Web pages. Assuming you've configured your system according to the guidelines in Session 2, and have a Web browser with either the SLIP/PPP stack like Trumpet or the mozock.dll setup in your Netscape directory, all you need now is an ASCII editor.

Editors

Web pages are written in plain ASCII. This means that if you use a word processor like WordPerfect or Microsoft Word, you'll need to export your text as DOS text before it can be read by a Web browser. This can be a hassle, and it's probably easier to use an ASCII editor that creates and saves files in this format by default. One such editor is a freeware product for Windows called PFE (Programmer's File Editor), written by Alan Phillips.

The following are step-by-step instructions for creating a Web page and viewing it with your browser. Don't worry about the HTML used in the page yet, just focus on the steps used to create and display the page. Perform each step on your own PC.

Creating a Local Web Page

1. Start the PFE editor and select File and click on New from the menu. (See the Installation section at the beginning of this book if you don't have

PFE installed yet.) This will create a new document window with a document named Untitled1.

2. Enter the following text in the document window:

```
<HTML>
<HEAD>
<TITLE>Local Web Page</TITLE>
</HEAD>
<BODY>
This is a local Web page
</BODY>
</HTML>
```

3. Save the document as c:\test.htm using the File and click on Save As menu option. Your screen should look like Figure 1-4 just before the save.

4. Now start up your Web browser, and open the local file c:\test.htm. You should see results like Figure 1-5 in your Web browser.

Now you can keep PFE running in one window and Netscape running in another, and toggle back and forth using the Windows command <ALT><TAB> (or the task bar in Windows 95), making changes and saving them from PFE, then clicking on the Netscape Reload button to refresh the page, picking up your latest changes.

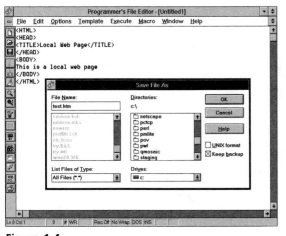

Figure 1-4
PFE saving a Web page

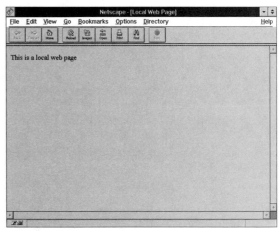

Figure 1-5
Browsing the local page

Filetypes

Web pages on your PC should end with an .htm filetype. On UNIX systems and Web servers on the Internet, the filetype is .html. When you transfer the pages you've developed on your local PC to your site on the Internet, you'll usually need to rename the files from the .htm to an .html extension. The exact procedure is covered next.

Working on the Web

To share your pages with the world, you'll need to transfer them to your Web site on the Internet. This can be done easily using FTP. After you've created and refined your pages, connect to the Internet and start up FTP. FTP allows you to move files from one system to another; Figure 1-6 demonstrates the use of WS_FTP to move from the PC (the "local" system on the left) to the UNIX system (the "remote" system on the right). The step-by-step procedure for doing these transfers is described below:

1. Run WS_FTP (see the Installation section at the beginning of this book if it is not already installed).

2. When the Session Profile dialog box pops up (Figure 1-7) click on New and fill out the information about the system you are connecting to. Your Internet provider should provide you with a host name, username, and password for logging on to the system. You'll also need to check on which subdirectory your Web pages go under; typically it is public_html. Figure 1-7 shows the profile filled out for a hypothetical site with

```
Host: www.surfers.com
Username: Barney
Password: Rubble (note that it is not displayed on the profile)
```

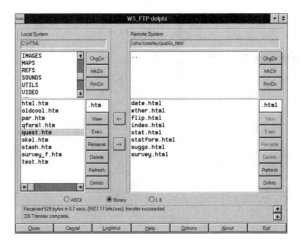

Figure 1-6
Transferring a Web page to a system on the Internet

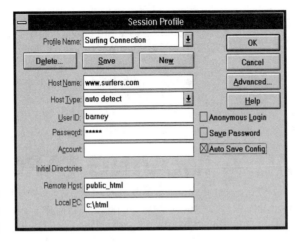

Figure 1-7
Session Profile
dialog box

```
Initial Directories: For Remote: public_html
For local c:\html
```

The profile name can be any handle nickname you want to call this system.

3. Now click on Save and OK and it will log you in to www.surfers.com. It will display the files in the local and remote directories.

4. Click on the local file you want to transfer, click on the ASCII option, and then click the arrow pointing from left to right to move this file into the remote directory.

5. It should now prompt for what the file should be called in the remote directory; it defaults to the same filename that is used on the PC. You'll want to override this default and call it test.html instead of test.htm.

6. WS_FTP will now show you a status bar of the transfer, and when it's complete, you can close and exit. The next time you come in, you don't have to go through steps 2 and 3; you can just click Connect and select the profile name followed by OK, and pick up from step 4.

You should now have a file called test.html on your Internet server. Open the file from Netscape, this time using Open and clicking on Location instead of Open and File. For location, enter the convention used by your provider to refer to their members' Web pages. Typically this is http://www.surfer.com/~barney/test.html, where *www.surfer.com* will be your provider's host name, *barney* will be your username, and *test.html* is the Web page you uploaded.

You've got all the ingredients needed to start whipping up Web pages, but just before you start to cook, Session 4 will cover a few conventions used in subsequent sessions.

It will also give you a little background. HTML is evolving like just about everything else on the Internet, and understanding why and how it was designed will give you a good foundation to begin mastering the Web. You can also come back to this section later if you want to jump right into HTML now and skip to Session 5. Later, as you develop more skills, you will probably be interested in learning a context for what you are doing.

HTML, A MOVING TARGET

When a Web browser displays a Web page, it reads in a text file and looks for special *tags*. These tags describe the text on the page and suggest how it should be displayed. The descriptive tags are what make up HTML.

When Tim Berners-Lee of CERN designed the first implementation of the Web, he designed a minimal set of tags that became retroactively known as HTML 1.0. Retroactive, because by the time an Internet task force got around to actually standardizing the language in 1994, it had already been extended, primarily to support the use of fill-in forms. The standards committee began work finalizing these extensions to the 1.0 base, calling the combination of 1.0 plus the ability to do forms HTML 2.0.

Of course, HTML wouldn't hold still, and before 2.0 became ratified, extensions were already popping up in the guise of HTML+ (or HTML 2.1, as some saw it). These "tweaks" to HTML 2.0 did not meet consensus agreement until the standards body defined a new target: HTML 3.0, which would include HTML 2.0 plus agreed upon features from the early HTML+ extensions.

And just when it looked as if the standards committees were catching up, a new browser entered the picture with an enthusiastic development team that wanted to give the Web community some nifty new features that the committee had promised but had yet to deliver. Netscape began introducing a number of enhancements to HTML, gaining both support and notoriety for their efforts.

HTML for Now

At the time of this writing, many of the features of HTML 3.0 have already been implemented in several browsers. In addition, some browsers have begun supporting some of Netscape's HTML extensions. And while figures vary, Netscape appears to have 70 to 80 percent of the Web browser market, giving it some influence in shaping de facto if not de jure standards.

HTML 3.0 is backwardly compatible with HTML 2.0. Which means, in theory, that using HTML 3.0 tags in a Web page that is viewed by an HTML 2.0 browser shouldn't break anything. At worst, the browser will ignore the 3.0 tags. The same goes with Netscape extensions. By definition a browser should ignore attributes and elements it does not understand in a tag. But some way of identifying these different standards will be useful in the sessions that follow.

HTML Conventions

This book covers HTML 2.0, most of the HTML 3.0 features that have been widely incorporated, and the Netscape 1.x HTML extensions. To differentiate between these, a special convention will be used. Tags that apply to HTML 2.0 or parts of HTML 3.0 in common use will be introduced without comment; all browsers should support these tags. Netscape extensions will be marked with NHTML to the side of the paragraph or text that introduces them, and HTML 3.0 enhancements that are not widely supported or that have not yet stabilized are flagged with an asterisk. The implications of using non-standard and evolving-standard tags (i.e., parts of HTML 3.1?) are discussed in the later sessions.

Here is an example of a tag, with options that are Netscape specific flagged. Attributes surrounded by square brackets are optional.

THE HORIZONTAL RULE TAG	
<HR	
[SRC=URL]	*
[SIZE=n]	NHTML
[WIDTH=n]	NHTML
[CLEAR=margin]	
>	

These syntax boxes may not contain all the attributes available for a tag. Some attributes will be listed in more advanced lessons that specifically utilize them. What you can expect in the syntax box is the syntax of the tag that will be used in the examples that follow it.

HTML is not the only component of the Web that's evolving. Web browsers continue extending functionality beyond the reaches of HTML. Most of these extensions try to make the browser more intelligent. Not only are browsers capable of loading text and links, some can simultaneously load and display multimedia content. When this is done successfully, the methods used are proposed back to the standards committees. It's definitely not the typical problem analysis, design, specification, and implementation model of conventional software development. It's the freewheeling Internet model of throw something out there, see how it works, fix it, compete to standardize, and repeat.

That's the history of and the forces behind HTML in a nickel tour. Now let's consider something more tangible: what HTML looks like.

The Anatomy of HTML

HTML elements consist of start and end tags. Start tags are delimited by < and > and end tags by </ and >. For example:

```
<TITLE>This is a title</TITLE>
```

<TITLE> is a start tag for the HTML title element. The elements are not case sensitive, so <TITLE>, <Title>, and <title> would all work equally well. Most authors make elements uppercase to separate them from the rest of the document. (We'll talk about what the <TITLE> tag actually does in Session 5.)

Start and end tags usually surround the text they are defining. In the example above, the text *This is a title* has been marked as the title.

Some elements have start tags but do not require end tags. An example of this is the line break element <BR>. It can be used as follows:

```
This is the first line.<BR>This is the second.
```

Attributes

Tags can optionally have text between the element name and the closing delimiter. For example:

```
<BR CLEAR>
```

This text is called an attribute. It's separated from the element name by at least one space. An attribute can also be of the format

```
<P ALIGN=clear>
```

with an attribute name, an equal sign, and a value. The value may also be enclosed in quotes:

```
<A HREF="http://www.surf.com/+barney/test.html">
```

While element and attribute names are not case sensitive, attribute values are. If, in the last example, the following was used instead:

```
<A HREF="http://www.surf.com/+barney/TEST.HTML">
```

the browser would not be able to find the file TEST.HTML if it was called test.html on the UNIX Web server. (In UNIX, filenames are case sensitive.)

Why Not WYSIWYG?

WYSIWYG, or What You See Is What You Get, editors are available for writing HTML on Microsoft Windows. So why aren't they used in this book? Two reasons.

The first is that HTML is really very easy. By knowing only four tags you can create an HTML document, and three of those are optional. By starting with minimal HTML and building as you go, you'll find that mastering HTML is probably much easier than you may first think. And as you move into the more advanced sections, you will be working on projects that go beyond the scope of what a WYSIWYG editor can provide. At times you will need to write scripts that generate HTML on the fly. If an editor has been doing this for you, mastering these techniques will be very difficult.

After you have mastered HTML, you can still use WYSIWYG packages or conversion utilities from existing word processors to build your HTML, but you will also be able to tweak the appearance of the page when the utilities don't do exactly what you want, or when What You See in the editor is not quite What You Get with the browser.

Another and probably the most important reason to learn HTML is that the standards are changing constantly. This is not chaos; it's perpetual reorganization. The difference? What is usually evolving is new and more exciting capabilities in HTML. This evolution usually starts in the browsers, then migrates relatively slowly to the standards, and then to the many converters, editors, etc., that generate HTML. By understanding HTML, you'll be able to explore new developments as soon as they become available, instead of waiting eight months until the next release of your WYSIWYG tool.

Now it's time to verify these assertions. In Session 5 you'll jump right into writing HTML, and by the end of this chapter, you'll be able to format text in a variety of sophisticated ways and turn an ordinary flat document into a hypertext landscape. But first, a few questions.

1. An HTML tag is?
   a. an HTML element name delimited by < and > for the start tag, and </ and > for the end tag
   b. an HTML attribute name delimited by < and > for the start tag, and </ and > for the end tag
   c. the element name within the delimiters < and > or </ and >
   d. the delimiters < and >

2. HTML attribute values are
   a. always included in double quotes
   b. always included in single quotes
   c. case sensitive
   d. not case sensitive

3. Netscape enhancements are
   a. HTML 3.0
   b. HTML+
   c. HTML 2.1
   d. Netscape-specific extensions to the HTML standards

4. What advantage does a text editor provide over a WYSIWYG editor for HTML?
   a. You can see what the HTML will look like on the browser as you are developing it.
   b. It will catch more mistakes.
   c. It allows you to take advantage of all existing and developing HTML options.
   d. It provides immediate feedback on the validity of your HTML.

WRITING HTML

So now you know that HTML stands for HyperText Markup Language, the language used to write hypertext documents on the World Wide Web.

A markup language might sound pretty exotic, but in principle it's no different from the red squiggles you used to get back on your essays in school. The squiggles, of course, told you what you needed to correct, change, or omit in the final edition (uhmm, assuming that wasn't your final edition!). The squiggles weren't part of the text, but described what should be done with it. This is the general characteristic of a "markup language." It is a set of instructions that tell what to do with the text. In the case of your teacher's squiggles, the markup language told some person (you) what to rewrite. In the case of HTML, the markup language tells some program (your Web browser) what to display.

You knew the markup language of your teachers, because it was usually

- In a different handwriting

- In bright red

- Signed "See me after class"

Well okay, probably just the first two for most of you, I mean us. The point is, a markup language needs to distinguish itself from the rest of the text. HTML does this through the use of special "tags." An example of an HTML tag, in this case telling a Web browser to bold the word "run" is

```
I told him not to <B>run</B>
```

Notice there is some "regular" text, *I told him not to,* and there are a couple of tags: <B></B>. There is also some apparently regular text surrounded by these tag things. This is typical HTML syntax. A tag is usually of the form *<tag> ... </tag>*. The value inside the < > is the name of the markup element or its abbreviation, like B (for bold), I (for italic), TITLE, HEAD, etc. The </ > is the closing tag, with the same element name, prefaced with a "/". Everything surrounded, or more properly, "enclosed," in these tags is affected by the markup element. So, if you wanted to bold the entire sentence, you would enclose it so:

```
<B>I told him not to run</B>
```

In place of red ink, you use this funny way of bracketing text to tell the browser when you're talking HTML and when you're just using regular text.

Of course, you couldn't have a markup language without something to mark up. A percentage of your World Wide Web pages could be just regular text, with smatterings of HTML markup thrown in to spiff them up. They can be much, much, more as well, but let's start with the minimal.

The minimal HTML document starts with a tag that tells the Web browser that everything between these tags is an HTML document; that tag is <HTML>. Its syntax is simply

---

THE <HTML> TAG

<HTML>
the html document
</HTML>

Didn't I tell you this was going to be easy?

Your document could be nothing more than a block of text:

```
<HTML>
The McIntroth Preserve, since its inception in the colonies in the early 1800s, has been
committed to the preservation of native strains of eastern seaboard boysenberry.
</HTML>
```

This is a perfectly legal Web page, written in HTML, viewable by Web browsers everywhere. Not all that exciting, but that's not your assignment…yet.

All other HTML tags will fall between <HTML> and its closing tag, </HTML>. Two other tags are recommended for every HTML document; these are <HEAD> and <BODY>. Their syntax in the HTML document is

---

THE <HEAD> AND <BODY> TAGS

<HTML>
    <HEAD>
    header tags (if any)
    </HEAD>
    <BODY>
    the html document
    </BODY>
</HTML>

So to make the document above truly proper, the tags would look like this:

```
<HTML>
<HEAD>
</HEAD>
<BODY>
The McIntroth Preserve, since its inception in the colonies in the early 1800s, has been
committed to the preservation of native strains of eastern seaboard boysenberry.
</BODY>
</HTML>
```

In proper HTML, the text of your document will go between the <BODY> tags. The only thing that usually goes between the <HEAD> tags is the <TITLE> tag, and that brings you officially into the lesson. Before you really start, though, a word on how things will unfold.

The rest of this chapter and Chapter 2 will introduce HTML elements one by one. You'll learn what the elements do, how the tags work in HTML, and how they are combined with other elements you've learned already. If elements and tags are already a little jumbled, just remember, the element is the name of a particular HTML markup "word" (or its abbreviation). Elements are used inside angle brackets; a tag is just a bracketed element name that shows in the text where the markup starts, and where it finishes (Figure 1-8).

You will be creating examples using a text editor and Web browser on your PC. Review Session 3 on setting up your browser if you don't have this working, because you'll need it from this point forward.

The Title

Now, on to the title. A <TITLE> tag has the following syntax:

THE <TITLE> TAG
<TITLE>*title text*</TITLE>

It's used this way:

```
<TITLE>The McIntroth Preserve</TITLE>
```

In HTML, the title can only go between the <HEAD> tags. In fact, <TITLE> is one of only a handful of HTML tags that are used in the heading section, that is, between <HEAD> and </HEAD>. A basic HTML document with a title looks like this:

```
<HTML>
```

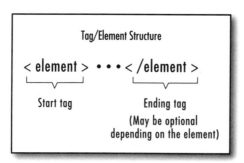

Figure 1-8
Tag/element
structure

```
<HEAD>
<TITLE> The McIntroth Preserve</TITLE>
</HEAD>
<BODY>
</BODY>
</HTML>
```

Try this as your first experiment. Open a new file with your editor and enter the HTML above. Save the file with a filetype of .htm; call it something like test.htm. Now open this file with your Web browser by selecting File and clicking on Open File from the Netscape menu. The page will be blank, but the title on the top border of your browser should read "The McIntroth Preserve," as shown in Figure 1-9. The title is rather subtle, and is usually not the first item of a Web page that catches the viewer's eye. It is important, however, in some less than obvious places. Bookmarks, for example.

When you "save a bookmark" to a Web page, your browser will save it by the title. If users add your page to their bookmarks and want to return to it in the future, they will have to identify it from their other bookmarks. Choose a title that gives enough information for them to recall the general content of your page.

The title is also used by search utilities on the Web. These are covered in Chapter 6, but essentially a variety of creatures, from spiders to robots to crawlers, exist on the Web to try to index and categorize the growing stores of information. These colorfully named programs "trawl" the Web, collecting titles, sometimes a little bit of content, and provide all these to Web surfers in search menus. If someone was looking for "Preserves," he or she would most likely hit the title and home page of The McIntroth Preserve. This is another way your choice of title plays a key role in the visibility of your page. Remember that a page is only allowed one title, so choose its content carefully. The title, in general, should be less than 65 characters.

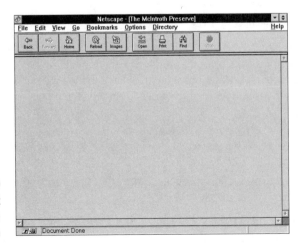

Figure 1-9
A title (and not much else!) in action

For now, let's leave the subtlety of titles for the "in your face" nature of the next HTML element.

The Header

Headers are a type of text element that tip the viewers to the subjects of the paragraphs that follow them. You've seen these for years in print; they let you know what information is unfolded in detail beneath them (just as this section's header does). They can help viewers orient themselves on the page, and orientation has become an important requirement in designing effective Web pages. The syntax for the header tag is

---

THE HEADER TAG

<Hn

        [ALIGN="*alignment*"]

>

header text

</Hn>

---

n is the level of the header.

ALIGN positions the header according to the alignment values "left" (the default), "right", "center", or "justify".

Headers come in six sizes: from the very large to the slightly larger than normal text. The header element is followed by a number, to tell the browser whether it's the jumbo size (1), the puny size (6), or some size in between (2–5). Unlike the title, you can have multiple headers of the same size in a document. The optional (remember the "[ ]" syntax) ALIGN attribute will specify how the header should be positioned on the page. A header with the following syntax:

```
<H1 ALIGN=center>The Beginning</H1>
```

would be centered. By default, the headers are left-justified. You'll use this default for the examples, which means you don't need to include the ALIGN attribute.

Let's add a header and breathe some life into the Preserve site. Open the file you created previously in your editor and add the following:

```
<H1>The History of McIntroth</H1>
The McIntroth family began its preserve to preserve the rare indigo
dye in the boysenberry, used to paint pachinko balls, which they exported
to the Orient.
```

Ah...let's go ahead and throw in all the other headers (in the name of science)!

```
<H1>The History of McIntroth</H1>
The McIntroth family began its preserve to preserve the rare indigo
```

```
dye in the boysenberry, used to paint pachinko balls, which they exported to the Orient.
<H2>The Great Boysenberry Shortage of 1812</H2>
<H3>The Great Boysenberry Shortage of 1812</H3>
<H4>The Great Boysenberry Shortage of 1812</H4>
<H5>The Great Boysenberry Shortage of 1812</H5>
<H6>The Great Boysenberry Shortage of 1812</H6>
```

This is all part of the body of an HTML document, or page, so you need to put it in the body section of the template you developed earlier, using the same title you used before:

```
<HTML>
<HEAD>
<TITLE> The McIntroth Preserve</TITLE>
</HEAD>
<BODY>
<H1>The History of McIntroth</H1>
The McIntroth family began its preserve to protect the rare indigo
dye in the boysenberry, used to paint pachinko balls, which they exported
to the Orient.
<H2>The Great Boysenberry Shortage of 1812</H2>
<H3>The Great Boysenberry Shortage of 1812</H3>
<H4>The Great Boysenberry Shortage of 1812</H4>
<H5>The Great Boysenberry Shortage of 1812</H5>
<H6>The Great Boysenberry Shortage of 1812</H6>
</BODY>
</HTML>
```

Now save the file and open it up in the browser. Figure 1-10 shows what you might encounter.

Now, with a few elements under your belt, you could find yourself in real trouble if you make an innocent assumption. You may have noticed that some elements, like <HTML>, actually enclose other elements like <HEAD> and <BODY>. You may be thinking, Hmmm, I think "The Great Boysenberry Shortage" would look really cool if it actually *spiraled into the void*; wonder what would happen if I put smaller and smaller headers inside one another like

```
<H1><H2><H3><H4><H5><H6>The Great Boysenberry Shortage of 1812</H6></H5></H4></H3></H2></H1>
```

Don't do this! Instead of gracefully spiraling text, you'll be looking at the clumsy antics of a majorly confused Web browser. Some elements include others by design, and this is called "nesting," but titles and headers cannot include each other, or themselves. You'll get to some examples of elements that can be nested when you cover lists in Session 7.

The actual size of a header on the screen depends on which font a given browser uses. You can't assume that it will be presented the same way it appears on your screen. The most you can assume is that <H1> will be larger than <H2>, etc., and that any header will usually be larger than normal text. Figure 1-11 shows Mosaic displaying the same HTML displayed by Netscape in Figure 1-10. Figure 1-12 shows the same headers as interpreted by yet another browser, called Quarterdeck Mosaic.

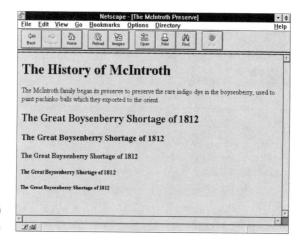

Figure 1-10
Headers galore

The examples have shown all HTML elements in uppercase. Remember, HTML is not case sensitive. HTML elements can be uppercase, lowercase, or mixed case; <TITLE>, <Title>, and <title> are all valid. Uppercase will be used for clarity for all HTML tags in these sessions.

Now, you have a header (some of you more than one), you have a title (hopefully, none of you more than one), and you have text. Great! Let's add some more text and then get to the fancy stuff already!

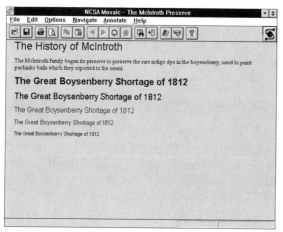

Figure 1-11
Headers by Mosaic

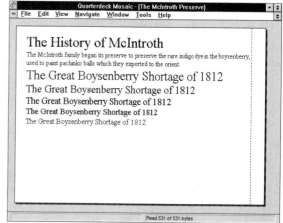

Figure 1-12
Headers by QMosaic

```
<HTML>
<HEAD>
<TITLE> The McIntroth Preserve</TITLE>
</HEAD>
<BODY>
<H1>The History of McIntroth</H1>
The McIntroth family began its preserve to protect the rare indigo
dye in the boysenberry, used to paint pachinko balls, which they exported
to the Orient.

Another family, the McKintrops, were bitter rivals of the McIntroths. And
for years they sent emissaries to China, trying to convince the royal court
that the Pennsylvania huckleberry in fact had better color gradients and
finish than the incumbent boysenberry.
</BODY>
</HTML>
```

But if you open this page with your browser, you'll discover something strange (Figure 1-13).

The two family histories are all mushed together. HTML will ignore whitespace, line breaks, and any other formatting you put in your text (except the spaces between words). It replaces multiple spaces with a single space, and gleefully strips out all of your indention, text alignment, tabs, and anything else that gives the appearance of formatting. HTML wants to control the whole show. Any formatting that is to be done must be done with its markup elements. To get things that look like paragraphs (i.e., line breaks between blocks of text or sentences), you have to use the HTML paragraph element.

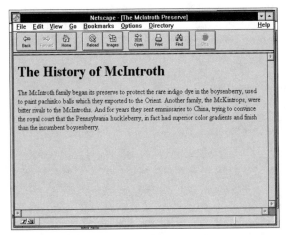

Figure 1-13
Something happened to the whitespace

The Paragraph

The paragraph element is used to separate blocks of text with blank lines. The syntax of a paragraph element is

---

THE PARAGRAPH TAG

<P
   [ALIGN="alignment"]
>
paragraph text
</P>

ALIGN positions the paragraph according to the alignment values "left" (the default), "right", "center", or "justify".

When the browser finds a <P> tag, it inserts a blank line before continuing, so this tag is usually used to indicate the start of a paragraph. The end tag, </P>, marks the end of the paragraph, as do other markup end tags:

```
<H1>The History of McIntroth</H1>
<P>The McIntroth family began its preserve to protect the rare indigo
dye in the boysenberry, used to paint pachinko balls, which they exported
to the Orient.</P>
<P>Another family, the McKintrops, were bitter rivals of the McIntroths. And
for years they sent emissaries to China, trying to convince the royal court
that the Pennsylvania huckleberry in fact had better color gradients and
finish than the incumbent boysenberry.</P>
```

It's a little early in the course to start bending rules, but the paragraph element doesn't actually require an ending </P>. Most Web authors just put a solitary <P> at the beginning of each paragraph. So the following is also legitimate HTML syntax:

```
<HTML>
<HEAD>
<TITLE> The McIntroth Preserve</TITLE>
</HEAD>
<BODY>
<H1>The History of McIntroth</H1>

<P>The McIntroth family began its preserve to protect the rare indigo
dye in the boysenberry, used to paint pachinko balls, which they exported
to the Orient.

<P>Another family, the McKintrops, were bitter rivals of the McIntroths. And
for years they sent emissaries to China, trying to convince the royal court
that the Pennsylvania huckleberry in fact had better color gradients and
finish than the incumbent boysenberry.
```

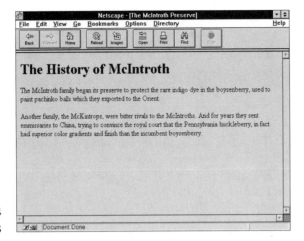

Figure 1-14
Paragraph tags

```
</BODY>
</HTML>
```

It's also common to separate paragraphs with a blank line when you're writing HTML. Even though it will be ignored by the browser, it gives a sense of how the markup tags will present the text. Open a new file with your editor and enter the HTML above. Save the file and open it with your Web browser. You should see results similar to those in Figure 1-14.

Yep! It worked. Note that you didn't need a paragraph element in the first paragraph, because the header automatically creates space between it and the next line. A header also contains an implicit line break, unlike normal text.

Now this is more like it. After finding that HTML strips out all semblance of your own formatting, you've regained a modicum of control. At least enough to do what basic documents do—make titles, subtitles, and paragraphs of text. In Sessions 6 and 7 you'll learn about formatting blocks of text and lists: bulleted lists, numbered lists, even lists within lists (nested lists). But first, a few questions...

Quiz 5

1. Which of the following is true?
   a. HTML tags are normally visible on the browser.
   b. A page should have only one title.

     c. You cannot have more than one header of the same size in a page.
     d. You cannot include headers within other headers.

2. Documents written in HTML, and put on the Web are called Web
     a. forms
     b. text
     c. browsers
     d. pages

3. One HTML element that can include all other HTML elements is
     a. <TITLE>
     b. <HEADER>
     c. <HTML>
     d. <H1>

4. The ending tag of an HTML element usually contains the element name preceded by what symbol?
     a. #
     b.)
     c. ?
     d. /

5. One important use of the title, other than a window title, is
     a. for bookmarks
     b. for linking to other pages
     c. for controlling the size of the text
     d. for starting a new paragraph

SESSION 6

BLOCK TEXT

In addition to the paragraph element, HTML has a few more tags that control the format of a block of text. This section will cover these, as well as explore word wrapping, line breaks, and ASCII art.

Quotes

The <BLOCKQUOTE> tag is like the paragraph tag in that it adds a line before the text, but it also adds a line after the text, indents the text from both the right and left margins, and generally displays it in a different font. The syntax for <BLOCKQUOTE> is

THE <BLOCKQUOTE> TAG

<BLOCKQUOTE>*text*</BLOCKQUOTE>

or

<BQ>*text*</BQ>   *

The <BQ> element can be used in browsers fully HTML 3.0 compliant in place
of <BLOCKQUOTE>.

It's used as follows:

```
<BLOCKQUOTE>
Since the American focuses on their future rather than their present or their past, the iso-
lation of the critical cause becomes paramount. If events in the world are conceived in
terms of a multiplicity of cause or even, more radically, in terms of multiple contigencies,
as with the Chinese, planning and the control of events and actions become more difficult.
The action orientation of the American, therefore, is conducive to a concept of simple cause
for events conceived as a linear chain of cause and effect.
</BLOCKQUOTE>
```

The separate font the browser uses when it sees <BLOCKQUOTE> causes the tagged
text to stand out from the surrounding text, as if you were quoting sections of text from
another source.

Addresses

Another useful format tag for blocks of text is the <ADDRESS> tag. Its syntax is

THE <ADDRESS> TAG

<ADDRESS>*address or signature text*</ADDRESS>

and it's used as follows:

```
<ADDRESS>
Edward Stewart /stewart@icn.research.org / University of Pittsburgh
</ADDRESS>
```

The <ADDRESS> tag is typically used for including either names and e-mail addresses or signatures at the bottom of an HTML document.

Let's combine the two new block formatting commands into the previous document
and see what they actually look like. Open a new file with your editor and enter the
following HTML:

```
<HTML>
<HEAD>
<TITLE>Cultural Patterns</TITLE>
</HEAD>
<BODY>
```

continued on next page

continued from previous page

```
<H1>Cultural Patterns</H1>

<P>In American Assumption and Values, Edward Stewart notes:
<BLOCKQUOTE>
Since the American focuses on their future rather than their present or their past, the iso-
lation of the critical cause becomes paramount. If events in the world are conceived in
terms of a multiplicity of cause or even, more radically, in terms of multiple contigencies,
as with the Chinese, planning and the control of events and actions become more difficult.
The action orientation of the American, therefore, is conducive to a concept of simple cause
for events conceived as a linear chain of cause and effect.
</BLOCKQUOTE>

<ADDRESS>
Edward Steward /stewart@icn.research.org / University of Pittsburgh
</ADDRESS>

</BODY>
</HTML>
```

Figure 1-15 shows the results.

Note that the blockquote text is offset nicely, indicating that the material is being quoted from some other source, and that the address block too is set off from the regular text, but also note that in both instances the line breaks put in the HTML are ignored. To explicitly direct the browser to start a new line, the <BR>, or line break, tag is needed. The syntax for <BR> is simply

---

**THE
 TAG**

```
<BR>
```

The <BR> tag is especially useful in cases like the <ADDRESS> block, where it would look better if each element of the address was displayed on a separate line. You can produce this effect with the <BR> tag as follows:

```
<ADDRESS>
Edward Stewart<BR>
stewart@icn.research.org<BR>
University of Pittsburgh
</ADDRESS>
```

The <BR> tag can be used in regular text as well. It can create a break in a line without inserting a blank line the way <P> would.

Another way of controlling how lines break is to use a special HTML tag indicating that the text is formatted just the way you want it to be, and the browser shouldn't muck with it. This is the preformat <PRE> tag. Its syntax is

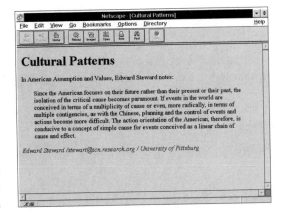

Figure 1-15
Blockquotes and
addresses

THE <PRE> TAG

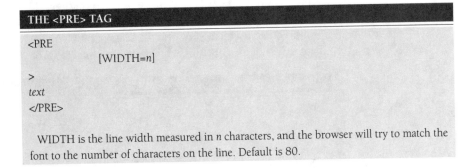

```
<PRE
            [WIDTH=n]
>
text
</PRE>
```

WIDTH is the line width measured in *n* characters, and the browser will try to match the font to the number of characters on the line. Default is 80.

<PRE> is used as follows:

```
<PRE>
This text should be displayed
in lines just the way they appear
here on my editor
</PRE>
```

The lines will be displayed as they are entered. For the <PRE> tag, the browser will usually use a fixed-width font. This means you can also slip in some ASCII art, which relies on characters being lined up correctly vertically. For example, the following (from Eric Raymond) can be displayed by protecting it with the <PRE> tag:

```
        (__)                    (__)                    (__)
        (\/)                    ($$)                    (**)
 /-------\/              /-------\/              /-------\/
/ | 666 ||              / |=====||              / |    ||
*  ||----||             *  ||----||             *  ||----||
    ~~    ~~                ~~    ~~                 ~~    ~~
Satanic cow             This cow is a Yuppie    Cow in love
```

It will work best if you are aligning text to use spaces rather than tabs in <PRE> blocks. Tabs may be expanded differently by different browsers.

<PRE> has an optional attribute to specify the width of the line. This could be useful if you are including a listing or report in a section of your HTML and wish the users to have the opportunity to scroll the screen to the right to pick up all the data in the right columns. The WIDTH attribute is used as follows:

```
<PRE WIDTH=132>
Col1            Col2          Col3         Col4        Col5       Col6
... spreadsheet data
</PRE>
```

Horizontal Tabs

Part of the reason to use <PRE> tags in HTML 2.0 was to align columnar data. While <PRE> works, you don't get a very polished look. The font looks like it was made by a mono-space typewriter and stands out awkwardly from the rest of the page. HTML 3.0 introduced two useful tags to solve this class of problem. One is <TABLE>, discussed in Chapter 3, and one is <TAB>, which is a horizontal tab. The syntax of the <TAB> tag is

THE <TAB> TAG *

<TAB
 	
      [ID=*identifier*]
      [TO=*identifier*]
      [IDENT=*en units*]
>
 	
ID is a name of the tab stop for the current position.
TO tabs to the position of a previously named tab stop.
INDENT is used in place of ID/TO and indents a number of "en" spaces, each one equivalent to half the point size of the current text.

The <TAB> tag in HTML 3.0 sets tab stops on your page, and allows other sections of text to begin at these stops. For example, the following HTML

```
Frog le<TAB ID=t1>gs<BR>
<TAB TO=t1>are hyperlinked to lily pads
```

would tab the second line so that the word *are* starts directly under the letter *g* in legs. You can set multiple tab stops, you just need to make the id of each unique. The id needs to start with an initial letter, but it can be followed by letters, numbers, or hyphens. <TAB ID=a-1>, <TAB ID=aaaaaa>, and <TAB ID=a1233rasdfas> are all equally valid.

Using the INDENT attribute specifies how far you want the text indented, instead of placing it relative to another marker by using the ID and TO attributes. Each unit of INDENT represents one-half the point size of the current font. A leading indent could be specified as follows:

```
<TAB INDENT=6>This is the start of something big.
```

Centering

Blocks of text can be centered using the <DIV> tag. Its syntax is:

> **THE <DIV> TAG**
>
> <DIV
>
>   [ALIGN="*alignment*"]
>
> >
>
> *text or blocks of text*
>
> </DIV>
>
> ALIGN positions the text according to the alignment values "left" (the default), "right", "center", or "justify".

The <DIV> tag can be used as follows:

```
<DIV ALIGN=center>
The<BR>
Beginning<BR>
Of<BR>
The<BR>
Story<BR>
</DIV>
```

Word Wrapping

In most blocks of HTML text, except for those defined by <PRE>, browsers wrap lines at spaces so they can squeeze all the text into the window on the browser. If you want to control where a line breaks, you can use the <BR> tag, and if you want to control where it doesn't break, you can use the   entity.

Nonbreaking Space

Entities are covered in greater depth in Chapter 2, but for now you can use   literally in place of a space to keep a line from being broken between two words. For example:

```
This may be a long paragraph, but please don't break between long sentences.
```

* * entered exactly as shown, in place of a space between *long* and *sentence* will cause the browser to see this as one long word. Since the browser won't break up a word, it will look for a space before or after these two on which to break the line. When the text is displayed,   looks the same as a space.

Nonbreaking Blocks

Netscape's HTML extensions provide another tag, <NOBR>, to protect a whole section of text from line breaks. Its syntax is

THE <NOBR> TAG	NHTML
3<NOBR>	

To make sure the entire sentence above ends up on a single line, you could use

```
<NOBR>This may be a long paragraph, but please don't break between long sentences.
</NOBR>
```

In HTML 3.0, the same effect can be achieved via

```
<DIV NOWRAP>
This may be a long paragraph, but please don't break between long sentences.
</DIV>
```

1. Why wasn't <BR> used after the final line in

```
<ADDRESS>
John McIntroth<BR>
McIntroth@mp.com<BR>
888-000-1212
</ADDRESS>
```

    a. The <ADDRESS> tag has an implied line break before and after its text.
    b. Only two <BR> tags are allowed in an <ADDRESS> tag.
    c. A maximum of two <BR> tags are allowed within an <ADDRESS> tag.
    d. The phone number line was supposed to display as part of the text following <ADDRESS>.

2. When will HTML break a line?
    a. when it reaches the right margin of a browser screen if <NOWRAP> or   are not specified
    b. whenever it sees a   element
    c. whenever it finds a new line in the text
    d. at the end of a paragraph or after a <BR> tag

3. Why shouldn't tabs be used to align columns in <PRE> blocks?
    a. They waste too much space.
    b. They are interpreted differently on different browsers.
    c. They are not permitted within <PRE> tags.
    d. It is difficult to align monotype fonts with tabs.

4. What is nonbreaking space?
   a. a space that continues indefinitely
   b. one or more spaces used to break a line
   c. a space that is not considered a space for breaking a line
   d. a space that will not damage a Web browser

SESSION 7

THE THREE TYPES OF LISTS

Word processors and presentation packages frequently use lists to organize a set of related points. Lists are an elegant means to emphasize key aspects of a topic and are usually set apart visually with graphical, character, or numeric *bullets*. Bullets are usually simple icons that flag the beginning of an item in a list of items. (Back in the "old" days, bullets were typically the lowercase "o" followed by a tab; today they can be check marks, smiley faces, or even bitmaps!) Here's an example of a list:

Things That Once Fell from the Sky

- Toads

- A 3,902-lb. stone

- Beans

- Space junk

Now, it may seem to the fledgling HTML author that it would be possible to create such a list using the <P> tag and the lowercase "o", with something like this:

```
<P>Things That Once Fell From The Sky
<P>o          Toads
<P>o          A 3,902-lb. Stone
<P>o          Beans
<P>o          Space Junk
```

and, running it through the browser, end up with Figure 1-16.

Yuck! Fortunately, there are some HTML tags just for lists that do a much nicer job. In fact, there are three types of tags, one for each of the following list types:

- <UL>   for unordered list (unnumbered)

- <OL>   for ordered list (numbered)

- <DL>   for a definition list (of terms)

Let's look at each one of these in turn.

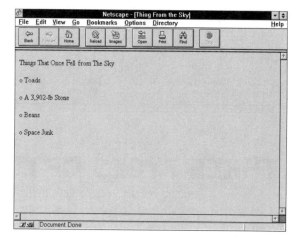

Figure 1-16
The poor man's list

Unordered Lists

The syntax for an unordered list is

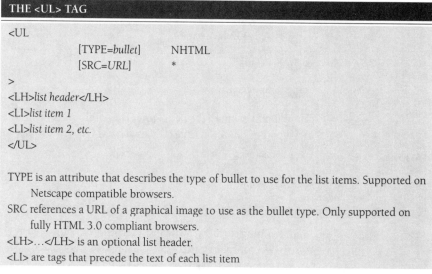

THE <UL> TAG

<UL

        [TYPE=*bullet*]   NHTML
        [SRC=*URL*]   *

>
<LH>*list header*</LH>
<LI>*list item 1*
<LI>*list item 2, etc.*
</UL>

TYPE is an attribute that describes the type of bullet to use for the list items. Supported on
    Netscape compatible browsers.
SRC references a URL of a graphical image to use as the bullet type. Only supported on
    fully HTML 3.0 compliant browsers.
<LH>...</LH> is an optional list header.
<LI> are tags that precede the text of each list item

Let's use <UL> first, and try to improve on the last example. Unordered lists preface each
list item with a bullet. An unordered list begins with the <UL> tag and ends with the
</UL> tag. In between are an optional list header enclosed with a beginning <LH> and
a closing </LH> tag, followed by the elements that make up the list. Each list element
is preceded by the special markup tag <LI> that identifies it as a list element. For example, the list above would appear as follows:

```
<UL>
<LI>Toads
<LI>A 3,902-lb. Stone
<LI>Beans
<LI>Space Junk
</UL>
```

If you put this in the complete body of an HTML page:

```
<HTML>
<HEAD>
<TITLE>Things That Once Fell from the Sky</TITLE>
</HEAD>
<BODY>
<P>Things That Once Fell from the Sky
<UL>
<LI> Toads
<LI> A 3,902-lb. Stone
<LI> Beans
<LI> Space Junk
</UL>
</BODY>
</HTML>
```

you get Figure 1-17.

In the HTML, one item was indented farther to the right than the rest. You'll notice that in lists, as in other areas of HTML documents, this formatting is ignored. All elements were aligned by the browser according to the HTML tags. Tabs and indentations can be helpful when authoring HTML in a text editor, but don't expect them to carry forward when the HTML is actually displayed in a browser.

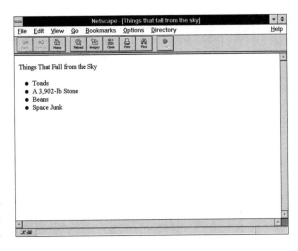

Figure 1-17
Example of the unordered list tag
<UL>

Ordered Lists

Ordered lists are much the same as unordered lists, but instead of a bullet, a number is used that automatically increments with each element. The syntax for the ordered list element is

THE <OL> TAG		
<OL		
	[TYPE=*counter type*]	NHTML
	[SEQNUM=*n*]	*
	[CONTINUE]	*
>		
<LH>*list header*</LH>		
<LI>*list item 1*		
<LI>*list item 2, etc.*		
</OL>		

TYPE is an attribute that describes the type of bullet to use for the list items. Supported on Netscape compatible browsers.

SEQNUM sets the starting sequence number for the list (default is 1).

CONTINUE picks up with the next sequence number from the last ordered list, instead of starting at 1.

<LH>...</LH> is an optional list header.

<LI> are tags that precede the text of each list item

List elements are identified the same way in ordered lists as they are in unordered lists, i.e., with the <LI> tag. Let's put the same items used above in a numbered list, but also extend the length of the elements to see what happens when they "wrap," or exceed the length of a single line on the browser. Let's also copy the list and use the <LH> tag on one to compare the effect of using a list header attribute with that of using a simple paragraph tag.

```
<OL>
<LH>Things That Fall from the Sky</LH>
<LI>Toads
<LI>A 3,902-lb. stone
<LI>Beans. Reported by a rancher in Brazil, apparently the beans were from
a storm in West Africa. The rancher tried to cook them, but they were too
tough to eat.
<LI>Space junk
</OL>

<P>Things That Fall from the Sky
<OL>
<LI>Toads
```

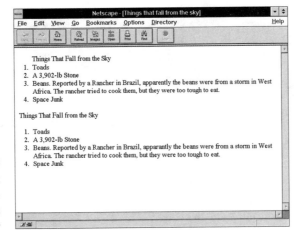

Figure 1-18
Numbered list
<OL> with
wrapping lines
and a list header

```
<LI>A 3,902-lb. stone
<LI>Beans. Reported by a rancher in Brazil, apparently the beans were from
a storm in West Africa. The rancher tried to cook them, but they were too
tough to eat.
<LI>Space junk
</OL>
```

When displayed, the text that wraps is displayed aligned under the beginning of the text above it, and aligned with the other list items. This acts like the block indent function in word processing. Some browsers will display the list header in a bold font, but in this example it is merely aligned with the list elements (Figure 1-18).

Definition Lists

Definition lists usually contain terms and their definitions. A definition list starts with a <DL> tag and ends with a </DL> tag. Its syntax is as follows:

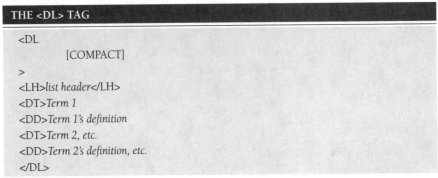

THE <DL> TAG

<DL
      [COMPACT]
>
<LH>*list header*</LH>
<DT>*Term 1*
<DD>*Term 1's definition*
<DT>*Term 2, etc.*
<DD>*Term 2's definition, etc.*
</DL>

continued on next page

THE <DL> TAG

COMPACT optionally requests the browser to reduce interitem spacing.
<LH>…</LH> is an optional list header.
<DT> are tags that introduce terms.
<DD> are the terms' definitions

The items of a definition list don't begin with the <LI> tag. Instead, the definition list items use two tags: <DT> to introduce the terms, and <DD> to define them.

An example should make this clear:

```
<P>Coffee Growing Countries and Characteristics of Their Exports
<DL>
<DT>Angola
<DD>Robusta. Strong flavor, but not much depth.
<DT>Columbia
<DD>Full body, balanced acidity, rich flavor.
<DT>Costa Rica
<DD>Spicy, aromatic, rich full body. Acidic.
<DT>Ethiopia
<DD>Sharp, pungent. Rich flavor.
<DT>India
<DD>Light body, mild.
</DL>
```

From this, the browser displays Figure 1-19.

Notice that the browser separated the terms from the definitions with a blank line; this is a unique characteristic of the definition list. If you want a little tighter spacing

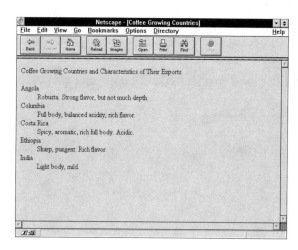

Figure 1-19
A definition list

between the term and its definition, you can use the COMPACT option in the <DL> tag as follows:

```
<P>Coffee Growing Countries and Characteristics of Their Exports
<DL COMPACT>
<DT>Angola
<DD>Robusta. Strong flavor, but not much depth.
<DT>Columbia
<DD>Full body, balanced acidity, rich flavor.
<DT>Costa Rica
<DD>Spicy, aromatic, rich full body. Acidic.
<DT>Ethiopia
<DD>Sharp, pungent. Rich flavor.
<DT>India
<DD>Light body, mild.
</DL>
```

Nesting Lists

While they are not part of HTML per se, nested lists are easily handled by most browsers. To nest lists, just include a complete list, with the opening tag, list items, and closing tag, inside of another. This will create indented lists of items. Most browsers will use different bullets for the nested list. Here is an example:

```
<H2>What you've learned so far</H2>
<UL>
<LI>      Titles
<LI>      Headers
<LI>      Paragraphs
<LI>      Basic Lists
          <OL>
          <LI>Unnumbered Lists
          <LI>Numbered Lists
          <LI>Definition Lists
          </OL>
<LI>      Line wraps in Lists
<LI>      Nested Lists
</UL>
```

And the browser displays Figure 1-20.

The indentations of the HTML in text form are strictly for clarity; they do not affect in any way how the nest lists are indented. The same results would have been achieved with all the tags beginning flush left.

A general rule of thumb is to nest lists no more than three levels, otherwise you may push past the right margins of some browsers, leading to unpredictable results.

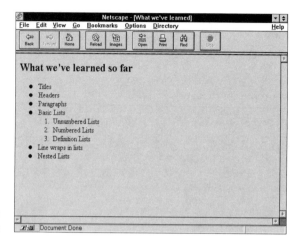

Figure 1-20
Nested lists

List Enhancements

Controlling the bullets used for list items was a popular request for HTML 3.0. Before the 3.0 specification included the SRC attribute in lists, Netscape had developed its own enhancements that allowed a greater variety of list bullets. If your browser does not support the new HTML 3.0 or the Netscape extensions, the option is simply ignored, and default bullets are used. You'll learn ways of creating your own bullets in Chapter 2, but if you are using Netscape, you can use the TYPE attribute with the tags <UL> and <OL>. <UL> can have a TYPE of "disc", "circle", or "square". <OL> can have a TYPE of "A" for ascending capital letters, "a" for lowercase letters, "I" for ascending, capital roman numerals, and "i" for lowercase of the same. Netscape has also added the TYPE option to the list element <LI> itself, so you can change the bullet of individual list items (as long as the bullet you choose is one of the allowable types for the list as a whole). For example, this is legal in Netscape:

```
<UL TYPE=square>
<LI>I'm a square but
<LI TYPE=circle>This item has a circle bullet!
<LI>default is to use the last bullet type...
<LI TYPE=square>switch back to square
<LI>and the last item...
</UL>
```

and it looks like Figure 1-21 in a Netscape browser.

You'll learn how to use the SRC option in Chapter 2, when you work with images. This option may or may not be supported on a given browser; it depends on how closely and aggressively the browser has chosen to implement the draft HTML 3.0 specifications.

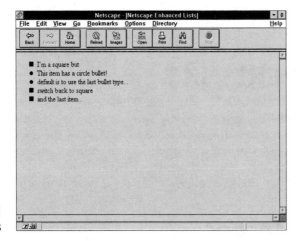

Figure 1-21
Enhanced lists

1. Which of the following is false?
   a. List items require special tags to identify them as items of a list.
   b. The type of list is specified in the opening and closing tags of the list.
   c. A list can have any number of items.
   d. Items for all types of lists are preceded with an <LI> tag.

2. An unordered list has what opening tag?
   a. <LI>
   b. <DT>
   c. <UL>
   d. <OL>

3. One thing that makes a definition list unique is
   a. You can have paragraph tags within the text of the items in the list.
   b. It can consist of multiple list items.
   c. It has two tags that identify a list item.
   d. It uses a different type size than other list types.

4. If an HTML extension is used, what generally happens in a browser that doesn't recognize the extension?
   a. The browser will display an "unauthorized extension" message.
   b. The browser will not work.
   c. The entire list will be ignored.
   d. The extension option will be ignored.

HYPERLINKS

Before finishing the first chapter of HTML, you should learn about the actual hypertext part of the hypertext markup language. All hypertext is done in HTML with a single markup tag: <A>. This tag is called an "anchor," and it defines the start and/or destination of a hypertext link. Anchors can link one place in your document to some other place. The other place could be in the same document, in another file, or across the Internet in a page on the other side of the world. Links are the key to HTML's power.

The Anchor

The syntax of an anchor tag is

THE <A> TAG

<A

       [HREF="*URL*"]

       [NAME="*id*"]

>

text that is linked or anchored

</A>

HREF points to a URL that is the destination of the hyperlink.
NAME defines a name that will be the destination of other hyperlinks

---

An anchor looks like this:

```
<A HREF="location">highlighted text</A>
```

The location is where the browser takes you when you click on the highlighted text. Only the highlighted text in this markup is visible to the viewer of your page, and it is usually displayed underlined, or in a different color, so viewers know they can click on the word or phrase to link to something (hopefully) related.

To assign a link to another file in the same directory that contains the file the viewer is reading, you could create a link such as the following:

```
<A HREF="biography.htm">My biography</A>
```

When viewers of this Web page click anywhere on the phrase *My biography,* the HTML document biography.htm is displayed in their browser.

When the mouse cursor passes over a link, it will typically change shape. Netscape's cursor, for example, changes from an arrow to a little hand (Figure 1-22).

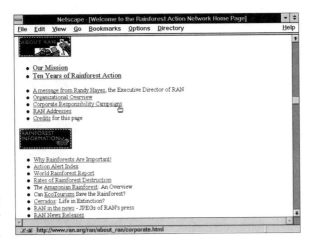

Figure 1-22
Netscape's cursor
on a link

Let's make a sample document that contains links to other documents in the same directory. You can practice on a hypothetical resume, and the links can contain information that elaborates on areas of experience that users might want to pursue in greater depth. In fact, you could send a resume like this on a disk, and a prospective employer (who is Internet literate) would be able to open and read it with a Web browser. First, you need to create the dates worked at various places, and the job titles. Links will be provided for more detail on each job. Open a new file called resume.htm with your editor and enter the following HTML:

```
<HTML>
<HEAD>
<TITLE>My Resume</TITLE>
</HEAD>
<BODY>
<P><A HREF="1992.htm">1991-1995</A> CEO, Vaporware Inc.
<P><A HREF="1991.htm">1990-1991</A> Mohave Tour Guide.
<P><A HREF="1987.htm">1987-1990</A> President and Chief Bottlewasher at Home Robotics.
</BODY>
</HTML>
```

Save this file, and create one of the files it links to in order to test the link. Open a new file called 1992.htm that describes experience at Vaporware, Inc.

```
<HTML>
<HEAD>
<TITLE>Vaporware Inc.</TITLE>
</HEAD>
<BODY>
From Jan. 1991 to Aug. 1995 I served as CEO for an innovative young software company which
marketed a variety of leading-edge products. These products included: x, y, and <A
HREF="z.htm">z</A>.
</BODY>
</HTML>
```

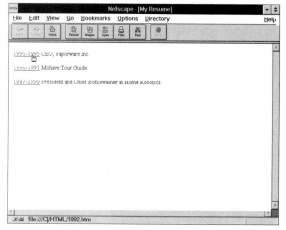

Figure 1-23
Resume links

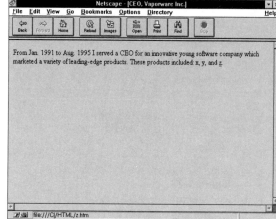

Figure 1-24
Linked!

Note that in the linked 1992.htm file, there is yet another link, for more information about product "z"! Now, give this sample a test drive.

Save 1992.htm and open resume.htm with your browser. You should see something like Figure 1-23.

Note that the cursor is over the link text, so it has changed to a hand. If you click the right mouse button now, you should see Figure 1-24.

If you click the large Back icon on the Netscape toolbar, the browser automatically takes you back to the resume document. This ability to backtrack is built into most Web browsers, and is indispensable at times in returning you to someplace you recognize.

This resume probably won't net any major job offers. But you can spiff it up a bit, and see how anchors work in conjunction with other markup tags.

Taking your initial resume, add headers, titles, paragraphs, and lists.

```
<HTML>
<HEAD>
<TITLE>My Resume</TITLE>
</HEAD>
<BODY>
<H2>John Serene</H2>
<H4>144 Metro Blvd. San Pedro, CA. 90018</H4>
Experienced in all phases of logistics, software, and automated home appliances. I am
resourceful, obstinate, and well liked by a few of my peers.
<UL>
<LI><A HREF="1992.htm">1991-1995</A> CEO, Vaporware Inc.
<LI><A HREF="1991.htm">1990-1991</A> Mohave Tour guide.
<LI><A HREF="1987.htm">1987-1990</A> President and Chief bottlewasher at Home Robotics.
```

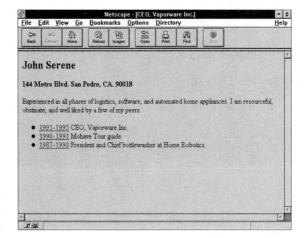

Figure 1-25
Resume with more
markup tags

```
</UL>
</BODY>
</HTML>
```

This results in Figure 1-25.

Linking Near

You can also link to locations within the same HTML document. This is similar to the Bookmark capability of word processors, which saves a place in your document that you can jump back (or forward) to from any other place in the document. To create one of these links, you first have to name the spot in the document that you will be jumping to. You do this with a "name anchor":

```
<A NAME="next">The Next Topic</A>
```

The piece of text *The Next Topic* is named "next". To link to this spot from anywhere else in the document, reference it with the following link:

```
<A HREF="#next">Go to the next topic</A>
```

Using links within a single page, you can fold the entire resume above into a single HTML document:

```
<HTML>
<HEAD>
<TITLE>My Resume</TITLE>
</HEAD>
<BODY>
```

continued on next page

continued from previous page

```
<H2>John Serene</H2>
<H4>144 Metro Blvd. San Pedro, CA. 90018</H4>
Experienced in all phases of logistics, software, and automated home appliances. I am
resourceful, obstinate, and well liked by a few of my peers.
<UL>
<LI><A HREF="#1992">1991-1995</A>CEO, Vaporware Inc.
<LI><A HREF="1991.htm">1990-1991</A>Mohave Tour Guide.
<LI><A HREF="1987.htm">1987-1990</A>President and Chief Bottlewasher at Home Robotics.
</UL>
<A NAME="1992">1991-1995 CEO, Vaporware Inc.</A>
<P>From Jan. 1991 to Aug. 1995 I served as CEO for an innovative young software company
which marketed a variety of leading-edge products. These products included: x, y, and <A
HREF="z.htm">z</A>.
</BODY>
</HEAD>
```

Linking Far

Okay, so you can distribute resumes on disk, but if this were all there was to hyperlinks, they wouldn't have achieved their current popularity. The secret door to links is in the location field of the anchor. These locations can be URLs, or uniform resource locators.

URLs are sort of the street address of a Web page on the Internet; you might have seen them in magazines or ads. Some examples are http://tvnet.com/WhatsOnTonite/index.html, http://www.sgi.com/fun/fun.html, and http://www.microsoft.com/pages/misc/whatsnew.htm. These point to HTML documents on the Internet. Chapter 3 covers what makes up a URL in great detail, but for now, just notice how these addresses can be incorporated in an anchor. If you wanted to include a link to Microsoft in your own Web page, you could build the link with the following:

```
<A HREF="http://www.microsoft.com/pages/misc/whatsnew.htm">My link to What's New at
Microsoft</A>
```

Now clicking on the text of the anchor will bring up Microsoft's page from across the Internet.

The anchor tag can link to much more that just other HTML. It is the technique used to access multimedia and other Internet services. But this is the domain of Chapter 2, where you'll explore the lights, sounds, and glitter of HTML and change hypertext to hypermedia right before your eyes.

1. Hyperlinks cannot link to the following:
   a. places within the same HTML document
   b. other HTML documents on disk

    c. HTML documents on the Internet

    d. computers you have no communication links to

2. The markup element for hyperlinks is the

    a. link

    b. URL

    c. anchor

    d. hyperlink

3. Which of the following is true?

    a. All hyperlinks in HTML use the same markup element.

    b. Different hyperlinks use different markup elements.

    c. All hyperlinks use the same URL.

    d. All hyperlinks end in </H>.

4. To go back to a page you previously visited

    a. requires a hyperlink pointing back to that page

    b. requires a bookmark

    c. can be done automatically by most browsers

    d. requires an anchor

MULTIMEDIA

CHAPTER 2

MULTIMEDIA

Welcome to Chapter 2, and some of the really fun stuff you can do with HTML! Now that you know some of the basics of HTML, hypertext, and the Web, you can push on to more advanced topics.

Starting with simple images, you'll pull graphics into your pages. You'll warp and woof text around the graphics' positions, and evolve the simple hyperlinks of Chapter 1 into hypermedia jubilees of music, voice, video, and animation.

After your conversion from hypertext to hypermedia, you'll learn techniques for adding impact to your Web pages. You'll dress up lists, make your own bullets, explore graphical rules and special characters, and make icons and graphical hotspots that link to other media at the click of a mouse. Finally, you'll learn how to include a link that a user can click to send you e-mail. Maybe they'll want to know how you did all that stuff they saw on your page!

 **PUTTING IMAGES ON A PAGE**

The <IMG> tag introduces pictures into HTML. The tag points to a graphics file, and wherever <IMG> appears in your HTML, a graphical image is displayed. The syntax for <IMG> is

THE <IMG> TAG:		
<IMG	SRC="*filename*"	
	ALT="*alt_filename*"	
	ALIGN="*alignment_type*"	
	ISMAP	
	WIDTH="*pixel_width*"	
	HEIGHT="*pixel_height*"	
	BORDER="*in_pixels*"	NHTML
	HSPACE=" *in_pixels*"	NHTML
	VSPACE=" *in_pixels*"	NHTML
	LOWSRC="*filename*"	NHTML
>		
<IMG> displays an image on a page.		

This chapter will cover almost every option for this tag, but let's start with its minimal syntax:

```
<IMG SRC="work.gif">
```

The <IMG> tag tells the browser to display an image file, and *SRC="work.gif"* tells it what image file to display. The example above points to a GIF image file. Don't worry if you don't know what a GIF image is right now; you'll get into details soon. Note that the image file needs to be in the same directory as the Web page for this syntax to work. Try out the <IMG> tag using the HTML that capped off the last session of Chapter 1. Be sure to copy work.gif into the same directory if it is not already there.

Open the Practice HTML Page created in Chapter 1 and add the <IMG> right after the <BODY> tag. Point SRC to a GIF file called work.gif and see what happens:

```
<HTML>
<HEAD>
<TITLE>Practice HTML Page</TITLE>
</HEAD>
<BODY>
<IMG SRC="work.gif">
<H2>Building an HTML Page</H2>
This is a sample page to explore the basic elements of HTML.
```

```
Included below are hypertext links within this document that provide
samples for each technique you've learned so far.<P>
<UL>
<LI><A HREF="para.htm">Paragraphs</A>
<LI><A HREF="unnumb.htm">Unnumbered Lists</A>
<LI><A HREF="numb.htm">Numbered Lists</A>
<LI><A HREF="nested.htm">Nested Lists</A>
<LI><A HREF="anchor.htm">Anchors ... like this!</A>
</UL>
</BODY>
</HTML>
```

Note <IMG> doesn't need an end tag.

Open your modified Web page in your browser. You should see something like Figure 2-1, displaying the graphical image work.gif on your practice page.

The work.gif image is 116 by 102 pixels, and it fits comfortably with the text already on the page. Notice that the image appears on the left of the page, and the text is aligned below it. This is the default behavior of <IMG> with no options specified. But <IMG> has several options. One even displays text instead of pictures.

The ALT Alternative

Before really starting to work with images, though, you need to consider how to handle a couple of situations you will run into writing pages on the Web:

 Browsers that don't support graphic images

 Users who intentionally choose not to display them

These two cases are significant, and it's important you learn how to accommodate them using the ALT attribute of the <IMG> tag.

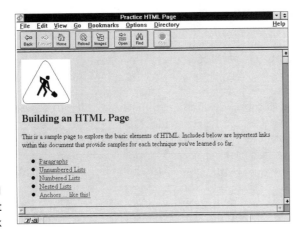

Figure 2-1
The <IMG> Tag at work

Lynx: The Legacy of Text

Historically, the majority of machines connected to the Internet have been UNIX systems, usually supporting a number of users. A common method of accessing these systems early on was via text-only terminals, or "dumb terminals," as they are called. Through clever use of ASCII characters, or using extended character sets, dumb terminals are capable of displaying crude graphic facsimiles. Some of these are quite ingenious, and are still found on e-mail signatures. But these terminals can't handle anything close to the complexity of the image formats in the GIF file you used in the last exercise.

Text-mode browsers like Lynx, ancestors of the graphical Web browser, developed so these terminals could still access the Web, Gopher, and other Internet services. But text-mode browsers can cause confusion if important information is only included in the graphic itself, and thus not displayed on the Web page. Information like a company e-mail address or a phone number in a GIF image with 3D fonts and rainbow colors may be impressive to Netscape and Mosaic users, but will leave the Lynx user clueless.

Using ALT

The ALT option tells the browser what text to display if it cannot display the image. So if your whiz-bang corporate logo with the gold sheen font is not displayed, the user can still get the essential information if you use the following syntax:

```
<IMG SRC="company.gif" ALT="Email us at: kites@kite.com">
```

Graphical browsers will not see the ALT text; instead they will see the image…unless. The second important consideration in using <IMG> may be more puzzling: why would a user with a browser capable of graphics turn them off?

A Picture Is Worth How Many Words?!

Speed. A growing (some say exploding) segment of the Web-using public is dialing in from home on relatively low speed serial lines. On these computers, a picture, in the form of a graphic, is worth considerably more than 1,000 words. In fact, let's do a rough calculation. A smallish GIF file that would take about a quarter of a browser screen is typically around 80K (approximately 80,000 characters). Say the average word is five characters, and adding a couple of spaces for good measure, you get 80,000 divided by 7, making the GIF equivalent to approximately 11,400 words! In Chapter 3 you'll learn tricks to trim this down, but an 80K file, transmitted to a browser across a 14.4 bps link, takes about 80 seconds. A good rule of thumb (until Internet comes over cable TV!) is to estimate about 1K (1,024 characters) a second transfer speeds for the average home user.

A typical user strategy for browsing the Web is to turn off the automatic image load feature for each page, navigate to the desired information, and then request image loads for specific pages. Without the ALT option, these users might lose their way, especially if the image has important information that is not included elsewhere on the page. Note that the text used in ALT cannot include HTML markup. Tags like <STRONG>, header tags, etc., are out; ALT wants regular text or special characters defined later. No tags!

So now you've seen how ALT is used to handle these cases. Let's look at more detail about the images themselves.

What Kind of Image?

The <IMG> examples so far have used SRC to point to a GIF image file. GIF is a popular format that you've probably run across if you've downloaded images from any online service. But GIF is only one of a number of graphics standards; what about JPEG, PCX, TIFF, and others? Can you use any graphics format in an <IMG> tag? The short answer is no. Among all the various formats, only a handful can be managed by the browser itself, and this handful boils down to three: GIF, JPEG, and XBM. Other formats can still be displayed on the Web, but not on the Web page along with your text, and not by using the <IMG> tag.

Each of the three formats that can be displayed by <IMG> have different characteristics. Examining these might make deciding which to use easier.

XBM

XBM is an X Windows bitmap, and only supports two colors. Most PC and Mac browsers can display these, but if you don't have UNIX, you might have a problem finding utilities that create them. GIF and JPEG, on the other hand, are standard formats for both the PC and the Mac.

GIF

GIF (Graphics Interchange Format) supports a maximum of 256 colors, and is generally preferred when you want crisp lines (e.g., you have text with the image, as in some icons), or have images with large blocks of single colors.

JPEG

JPEG (Joint Photographic Experts Group) supports up to 16.7 million colors and is very good at compressing photographic and photorealistic images. You can control the amount of compression, trading off size for quality. JPEG is a "lossy" compression scheme. This means it drops some bits here and there. Usually this is not important, or even noticeable, unless you have text or edges that are critical to your composition, in which case they could end up looking fuzzy.

A summary of image formats is outlined in Table 2-1, and more details and hints about GIF and JPEG and ways of using them optimally on the Web will be covered in Chapter 3.

Image Format	Description
GIF	CompuServe's Graphics Interchange Format. 256 colors, has special capabilities such as transparency and interlacing. Uses LZW compression. Widely available.
JPG, JPEG	Joint Photographic Experts Group. 16 million colors. Very efficient compression for photographic images.

continued on next page

continued from previous page

Image Format	Description
	User controllable trade-offs in image quality verses space on disk.
XBM	Bitmap image for X Windows. 2 colors.
BMP	Windows bitmap. Native to Window 3.x, and Windows 95 also supported by a variety of OS/2 applications. 16 million colors. RLE compression. Generally larger than other compressed image formats.
PICT	Macintosh Picture format. A native format on the Mac, analogous to BMP on Windows. Supports 16 million colors, is based on a QuickDraw display language.
TIFF	Tag image file format. A popular cross-platform image format for migrating between Mac and PC. 16 million colors. There are several "flavors" of TIFF, which sometimes leads to compatibility problems across platforms if options are not carefully matched.
PCX	PC Paintbrush format. 16 million colors.
TGA	TrueVision's Targa format. 16 million colors. Used in ray-tracing applications on PC and UNIX platforms (like POV).

Table 2-1 *Popular image formats*

Aligning Text with Images

So you've learned about two <IMG> options: SRC for pointing to GIF, JPEG, or XBM images you want to bring onto the page, and ALT for describing what to display if the browser cannot, or currently will not, display graphics. In Figure 2-1, the image kind of landed on the page and the text followed beneath it. Now it's time to take a look at a little finer control. The ALIGN option of the <IMG> tag controls where text is placed in relation to the image. The following HTML demonstrates three alignment options:

```
<HTML>
<HEAD>
<TITLE>Images and Text Alignment</TITLE>
</HEAD>
<BODY>
<IMG SRC="tower.gif" ALIGN="top"> On top!
<IMG SRC="tower.gif" ALIGN="middle"> Going down...at the middle!
<IMG SRC="tower.gif" ALIGN="bottom"> Where'd I put that bungee cord?!
</BODY>
</HTML>
```

Figure 2-2 illustrates the effect of each of these options.

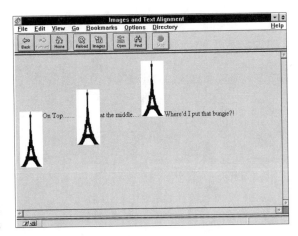

Figure 2-2
ALIGN options

Wrapping

What happens if you continue to pour text in, past the right margin of the browser? Let's start at the top and find out. Open an HTML file with your editor and, using the tower.gif image, specify ALIGN="top" followed by a long sentence or paragraph of text. What do you think will happen? Here's an example:

```
<HTML>
<HEAD>
<TITLE>The Tao of Text</TITLE>
</HEAD>
<BODY>
<IMG SRC="tower.gif" ALIGN="top">On top, but where do I go from here?
Maybe if the line is long enough I can tell where I'll end up.
</BODY>
</HTML>
```

Flowing Text Around Images

In Figure 2-3 you see the results of wrapping. When the line wraps, the rest of the text goes to the bottom of the image! This could be a surprise, especially to those experienced in other media where the image is part of a column, and text flows smoothly down the side. This capability was added in HTML 3.0 with two more ALIGN options: "right" and "left".

If you use the ALIGN="right" or ALIGN="left" options in the <IMG> tag, they will be ignored by browsers not fully HTML 3.0 compliant, defaulting to ALIGN="top". Edit the file you just created for the wrap experiment and change the ALIGN="top" to ALIGN="left". Bring the new version up in your browser and see if you get results similar to those in Figure 2-4.

The "left" option positions the image to the left of the text. The text flows down the right side, and when it clears the image at the bottom it wraps back to the left margin. The "right" option positions the image to the right of the text.

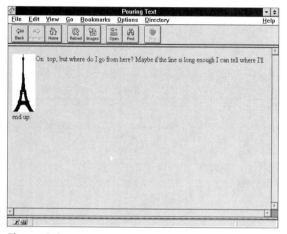

Figure 2-3
Wrapping with ALIGN

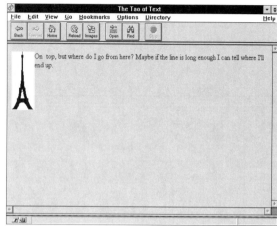

Figure 2-4
Text Flows

CLEAR

You don't have to completely fill the side of the image with text; you can use the <BR> line break tag with a CLEAR=ALL option to break off the text flow at any point. The text following the <BR> tag will be positioned below the image. The following change to the HTML illustrates this technique:

```
<HTML>
<HEAD>
<TITLE>The Tao of Text</TITLE>
</HEAD>
<BODY>
<IMG SRC="tower.gif" ALIGN="left">On top, but where do I go from here?
Maybe if the line is long enough I can tell
where I'll end up. <BR CLEAR=ALL>The story continues.
</BODY>
</HTML>
```

And the results are shown in Figure 2-5.

Height and Width for Speed

When using ALIGN="left" or ALIGN="right", you will also want to use the HEIGHT and WIDTH attributes. These options tell the browser, in pixels, how large the image will be. If you leave this out, the browser has to download the image before displaying any text, causing the page to appear sluggish. When HEIGHT and WIDTH are provided, the browser can block out a box to hold the image, display the text around it, and then fill in the box with the image. If the tower.gif image is 105 by 96 pixels, the HEIGHT and WIDTH options would be used as follows:

```
<HTML>
<HEAD>
<TITLE>The Tao of Text</TITLE>
```

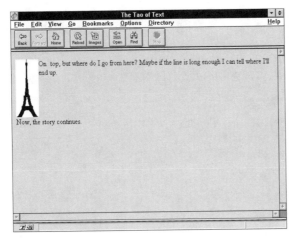

Figure 2-5
Using CLEAR=ALL
to reposition text

```
</HEAD>
<BODY>
<IMG SRC="tower.gif" ALIGN="left" WIDTH=|105■ HEIGHT=|96■>
On top, but where do I go from here?
Maybe if the line is long enough I can tell
where I'll end up.
<BR CLEAR=ALL>The story continues.
</BODY>
</HTML>
```

Borders and Spaces

The BORDER option is a Netscape enhancement that outlines the image with a pixel border. BORDER=0 turns off the border, BORDER=5 puts a five-pixel border around the image, creating a picture frame effect. Other Netscape options, VSPACE and HSPACE, create a similar effect, placing a pixel boundary above and below the image (VSPACE) or to the left and right of it (HSPACE). HSPACE and VSPACE can be used together to surround the entire image. Instead of a visible border, you get an invisible space to separate it from other images or from text.

While You Wait

Another Netscapism is the LOWSRC option. This option points to an image file that is supposed to be a low resolution copy of the one pointed to by SRC. This allows a Netscape browser to load the small, low resolution image first, and while the user is looking at it and the rest of the page, it is replaced by the larger, high resolution file.

The <FIG> Tag

The next graphics command to look at is the <FIG> tag, which is kind of <IMG>'s big brother. It offers greater flexibility in handling images, and while <IMG> is still the work-horse of the Web, especially for small graphics and simple formats, <FIG> offers some options that are hard to ignore. The syntax for <FIG> is

THE <FIG> TAG

```
<FIG              SRC="filename">
      <OVERLAY  SRC="filename">
      <CAPTION> ... </CAPTION>
      <CREDIT> ... </CREDIT>
      CLEAR="position"
      WIDTH="pixel_width"
      HEIGHT="pixel_height"
      NOFLOW
      IMAGEMAP
      MD="..."
</FIG>
```

<FIG> displays a figure with an optional overlay on the page.

You already know most of the <FIG> options from the <IMG> examples. Let's look at a few of the interesting differences and enhancements that <FIG> provides.

Where's the ALT?

One immediate difference is that the <FIG> tag requires an end tag, </FIG>. Another is that some options appear to be missing, such as ALT. How does <FIG> handle the case of the nongraphical or graphics option disabled browser?

The <FIG> tag permits HTML markup in between the beginning <FIG> and ending </FIG>. This markup will only be displayed if graphics disabled. This is much better than the simple character format of the <IMG> ALT option and is particularly useful if the image will be used as a menu, since the same menu could be depicted with hyperlinks for the nongraphical user.

HTML markup can also be used in the optional <CAPTION> and <CREDIT> tags with the <FIG> tag, and is displayed to both graphical and non-graphical browsers. Let's look at a sample <FIG> tag:

```
<FIG SRC="frog.gif">
      <CAPTION>This giant frog has been spotted in the
            prairies of the
            <STRONG>Midwestern US</STRONG>
      </CAPTION>
      <P>A giant frog terrorizes the Midwest
      <CREDIT>Photo by professional UFO photographer: Peter Caroll</CREDIT>
</FIG>
```

Figure 2-6 shows this displayed using the Arena browser.

Overlays

Another important difference between <FIG> and <IMG> is that the <FIG> element lets you specify two images. One, in <FIG SRC="filename"> is displayed first, and an optional second image can be overlaid on top of this image using the <OVERLAY SRC="filename"> tag, as in the following example:

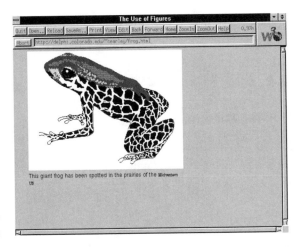

Figure 2-6
The frog

```
<FIG SRC="town.gif">
        <OVERLAY SRC="frog.gif">
        <CAPTION>Giant frog spotted near unsuspecting town</CAPTION>
        <P>A giant frog terrorizes the Midwest
        <CREDIT>Photo by professional UFO photographer: Peter
        Caroll</CREDIT>
</FIG>
```

Other Options

The IMAGEMAP option in <FIG> is like the ISMAP option in <IMG> and will be covered in Session 7, Imagemaps, at the end of this chapter. Imagemaps make various areas, or *hotspots,* of an image into hyperlinks.

The ALIGN option in <FIG> has a few more values than it does in <IMG>. The new values are:

 "bleedleft"   Aligns image with the right window border (Instead of just the text margin as with "left".)

 "bleedright" Aligns image with the left window border (Instead of just the text margin as with "right".)

 "justify"   Magnifies or reduces the image to fill the width of the screen between the two text margins

The other options, "left", "right", and "center", work as they do in <IMG>. When you use "left" and "right", text flows around the image just as it does with "bleedleft" and "bleedright". In "center" and "justify", text flow is disabled.

The CLEAR attribute is used if an image is already present in a margin. Its values have the following effects:

 "left"   Moves down until left margin is clear and displays the image "right"   Moves down until the right margin is clear and displays the image

<IMG> or <FIG>?

<IMG> has been part of the HTML language from the beginning, and is preferred for simplicity when dealing with small images or icons, as well as for accommodating non-HTML 3.0 compliant browsers.

<FIG> was introduced in HTML 3.0. It has quite a bit more flexibility than <IMG>, particularly in providing for nongraphical views of image material, and <FIG> provides powerful capabilities for building imagemaps on the client. You don't need to know what this means now, but you might prefer <FIG> for even your routine image requirements when you finish with Session 7.

Where to Get Graphics

Graphics for Web pages can be obtained from a number of sources. One of the best is the Web itself. Check the following URLs:

 http://www.yahoo.com/   Look under Computers and click on Multimedia and click on Pictures. They have links to several hundred archives of GIFs and JPEGs in every imaginable category.

 http://www.kodak.com/   Look under Digital Images.

Products such as CorelDRAW offer thousands of clip-art images on CDs, and provide the capability of transforming other image and clip-art formats to GIF or JPEG. Corel also sells a large inventory of stock photos on Kodak CD format. Each CD usually contains about 100 images, in varying resolutions. The images available cover the gamut from textures and landscapes to museum artifacts and faraway places. Similar photo CDs can also be economically produced from your own 35mm slides at photo processing shops or sometimes even your local supermarket!

Another option, especially for company pages, is the use of a scanner to capture company logos, graphics, and trademarks. And, of course, graphics for these purposes can also be created from scratch.

Before you leave the world of inline images for the broader expanse and multiple formats of external graphics, let's see what you've accomplished.

1. The ALT attribute of the <IMG> tag
   a. specifies the colors of the graphics image
   b. specifies the way text is aligned that follows the tag
   c. controls the position of the image on the page

    d. determines text that is displayed if the browser cannot, or will not, display graphics

2. Lynx is a
   a. graphical Web browser
   b. way to get from one place to another in hypertext
   c. graphics format
   d. text-based Web browser

3. When using the ALIGN="top" option, if the text after the <IMG> tag wraps on the browser screen, the text that wraps ends up
   a. on the next page
   b. immediately underneath the text preceding it
   c. at the top of the screen
   d. at the bottom of the image

4. A graphics format that you can*not* use with the <IMG> tag is
   a. GIF
   b. JPEG
   c. XBM
   d. PCX

EXERCISE 1

With the HTML elements learned so far, you can construct a fictional company brochure. You'll use image, title, header, and paragraph tags, along with URLs to link to related topics. With just these elements, you can created a fairly sophisticated presentation.

Open a new file with your editor and enter the following HTML

```
<HTML>
<HEAD>
<TITLE>Martian Expeditions</TITLE>
</HEAD>
<BODY>
</BODY>
</HTML>
```

This is the skeleton file. Now add a header and a company logo.

```
<HTML>
<HEAD>
<TITLE>Martian Expeditions</TITLE>
</HEAD>
<H2>Authentic Martian Expeditions</H2>
<IMG SRC="mars.gif" ALT="[MARS!]" ALIGN="middle">We're only a planet away!
<BODY>
</BODY>
</HTML>
```

Now add some filler, an unnumbered list of trip features, and wrap it up with a special offer:

```
<HTML>
<HEAD>
<TITLE>Martian Expeditions</TITLE>
</HEAD>
<BODY>
<H2>Authentic Martian Expeditions</H2>
<IMG SRC="mars.gif" ALT="[MARS!]" ALIGN="left">We're only a planet
away!
<UL>
<LI>Round trip from Miami
<LI>Immunizations for the Martian ZeeJee toad
<LI>10 Crew members, 2 onboard chefs
<LI>Tips and Free Travel Guides
</UL>
<P>Trade in Martian villages, sample local cuisine. See the 8 wonders of Mars,
and visit the forgotten tribe. Our native guides have decades of experience
with human tourists. You'll feel right at home with our posh accommodations,
and temperature controlled hoverships.
<p>Send us email for our free brochure, and automatic entry in our expedition
drawing. You may win a free trip for you and a friend!
Our email address is: expedite@mars.intergate.com
</BODY>
</HTML>
```

Note that the <P> tag keeps the text below from being concatenated with the text adjacent to the image. Also, ALIGN="left" was used to let text flow around the image. Let's see how the finished brochure looks (Figure 2-7).

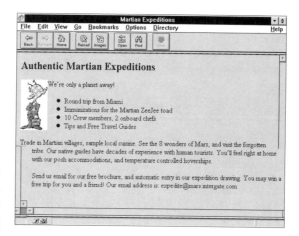

Figure 2-7
The Martian
expedition in
Netscape

HYPERMEDIA: IMAGES AND SOUND

Session 1 covered images displayed inline (i.e., on the Web page) by the browser . The <IMG> and <FIG> tags bring GIF, JPEG, or XBM images right onto your page. This session begins expanding these three options into a variety of other multimedia formats.

Hyperlinks to Images

Hyperlinks are not restricted just to other HTML documents. They can also point to other types of files or documents. Your hyperlinks to date have been of the form

```
<A HREF="somefile.html">Link To Page</A>
```

Clicking on the anchor text *Link to Page* brings somefile.html onto the browser screen. To link to another type of file, say a PCX graphics image, you would use the following:

```
<A HREF="somefile.pcx">Link To Image</A>
```

The browser knows this is not an HTML file by the filetype. HTML files end in .html or .htm; this file ends in .pcx. The browser also knows that it cannot display this file, since it is not HTML. What happens then when you click on the *Link to Image* anchor text? This is where the browser needs a *helper application*.

Helper Applications

Helper applications are other Windows or Mac programs that know how to handle these *external* formats. For example, the Microsoft Paintbrush program that comes with Windows understands the PCX graphics format. The browser can use this application to display the PCX file.

Configuring Helper Applications

In Netscape, the helper applications are configured under the Options and click on Preferences menu, in the Helper Applications options tab. Figure 2-8 displays this configuration box. Note the configuration specifies a filetype, an action, and extensions.

The filetype is a MIME (Multipurpose Internet Mail Extension) type and subtype. Don't worry about these now; they are generally sent in a preamble from the Web server to your browser, informing the browser about the type of document that is being sent. If a MIME type and subtype don't already exist for the type of format you wish to display, you can invent your own using the template suggested in Table 2-2.

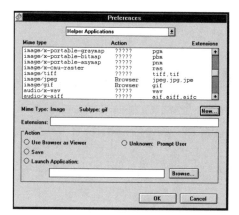

Figure 2-8
Helper application
configuration in
Netscape

The extension is, in DOS terminology, the actual filetype of the file. In the example above, somefile.pcx, the filetype is PCX.

The action column tells the browser what to do when this file is requested via a hyperlink. There are four options:

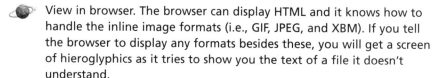 View in browser. The browser can display HTML and it knows how to handle the inline image formats (i.e., GIF, JPEG, and XBM). If you tell the browser to display any formats besides these, you will get a screen of hieroglyphics as it tries to show you the text of a file it doesn't understand.

 Save to disk. This option saves the hyperlinked file to disk, without even attempting to display it.

 Unknown: prompt user. This is the default for filetypes the browser doesn't understand. It will ask whether the user wants the file saved to disk, or which helper application it should launch to display it.

 Launch the application. This option correlates the filetype and extension with a local program that understands this filetype and that can be executed to display its contents.

To configure Netscape to use Paintbrush as a helper application to display PCX files, you can choose Create New Type from the Helper Applications options tab, specifying:

 Mime Type: image/pcx

 Extension: pcx

 Launch Application: c:\windows\pbrush.exe

Or you can do it the easier way. Open a local file with a PCX filetype, allowing Netscape to prompt you for what application to launch to display it.

In either case, be sure to select Options and click on Save Options to hang onto your changes.

MIME Subtypes	MIME Type	Content
gif,jpg,jpeg,bmp,tif,tiff,pcx,xbm,tga	image	graphic images
wav,au,snd,voc,aif,aiff,mid	audio	sound files
mpg,mpeg,avi,fli,mov,dvi	video	motion-video, animation
xls,dbf,wls,wpc,doc	application	application format (word processing, spreadsheets, etc.)

Table 2-2 *MIME template*

Extending the Principle

The same technique used with PCX graphics can be used for a variety of other formats, ranging from word processors, using filetypes like WPC, WPD, and DOC, to spreadsheets and database applications. Any application you have that displays or manipulates particular types of files can be configured as a helper application to Netscape for processing hyperlinks to those filetypes. For example, if you've configured WordPerfect as a helper application with the following:

```
Mime Type: application/wordperfect
Extensions: wpd,wpc
Launch Application: c:\wpc\wpc.exe
```

Then the following hyperlink:

```
<A HREF="review.wpd">Project Review</A>
```

when activated within the Web browser with a click on *Project Review*, will bring up WordPerfect with review.wpd.

Since these formats are not integral to the browser, they do not appear as seamless as the <IMG> formats. Users will see a second window open up, another application take over, and when it's finished displaying an image or document, the user will close the window and go back to the browser. But what these external formats lose in integration, they make up for in flexibility. Almost any type of external file can be handled by associating its filetype with a helper application in your browser.

Putting It to Use

Let's put a helper application to work. Configure your browser to use pbrush.exe to handle PCX filetypes using the instructions above, and then open a new file in your editor and enter the following HTML:

```
<HTML>
<HEAD>
<TITLE>The Face on Mars</TITLE>
</HEAD>
<A HREF="face1.pcx">Test link to a PCX file</A>
<BODY>
</BODY>
</HTML>
```

Clicking on the link should produce the results in Figure 2-9. The browser passes the PCX file to Paintbrush, and Paintbrush displays it in its own window.

A Better Helper

Since Paintbrush only handles a few image formats, namely PCX, DIB, and BMP, you'll probably want to use a more versatile helper application for graphics, like LVIEW1B (see the Installation chapter). This shareware application displays a wide range of formats, including PCX, GIF, JPG, TGA, and TIFF, and will be useful later when you begin actually manipulating images rather than just viewing them. To change from Paintbrush to LVIEW1B simply return to the Helper Applications configuration menu and edit the entry for PCX, replacing pbrush.exe with LVIEW1B as the Launch Application.

Thumbnails

Let's return to the face on Mars example again, and explore a versatile technique for handling an external image using a *thumbnail*. A thumbnail, displayed inline using <IMG>, is a small image that acts as a hyperlink to a larger or full representation of the same image. Thumbnails are popular in catalogs to show several products on a page and allow you to click on any single image to see it in greater detail.

By combining the <IMG> and anchor tags, you can link a small image to a larger one like so:

```
<HTML>
<HEAD>
<TITLE>The Face on Mars</TITLE>
</HEAD>
<H2>The Beginnings of a Gallery</H2>
<A HREF="face2.jpg"><IMG SRC="face1.jpg"></A>
To download the full 53K image of the face on Mars,
click the picture.
<BODY>
</BODY>
</HTML>
```

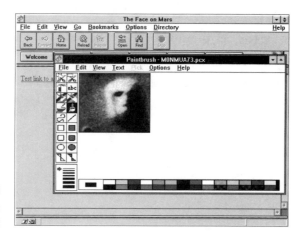

Figure 2-9
Helper application
at work

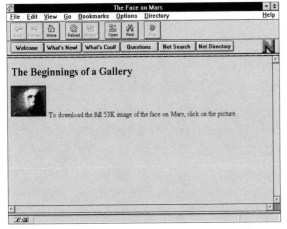

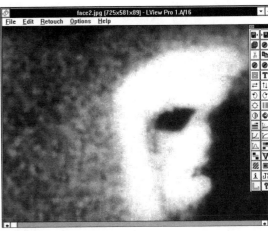

Figure 2-10
Example of a thumbnail

Figure 2-11
Loading the larger image by clicking the thumbnail

By inserting the <IMG> tag into the section of the <A HREF> anchor normally used for a link, a graphics link is created as displayed in Figure 2-10.

The small image in the <IMG> tag is linked with the anchor to the larger face2.jpg. Clicking on the thumbnail of the Mars picture brings up the large image in a helper application as shown in Figure 2-11 (in this case using LVIEW as the helper application for the filetype JPG).

Note the difference in resolution. The thumbnail (face1.jpg) is about 1K; the external image (face2.jpg) is about 50 times larger. Thumbnails offer a way to preview images you might be interested in before committing to a lengthy transfer. This general technique can be useful in many presentational contexts.

Hyperlinks to Sounds

Now that you know how to construct a hyperlink for an external image file like PCX, you also know how to link to a sound file. The only difference is in the filetype. Table 2-3 lists some of the more common audio formats found on the Web.

Filetype	Format
AIF,AIFF	Apple's Audio Interchange File Format
AU	Common UNIX sound format (NeXT, SUN)
WAV	Microsoft Waveform
IFF,MOD	Amiga sound formats
RA,RAM	RealAudio Format
VOC	Soundblaster Voice file
MID	MIDI format
SND	Can be NeXT, Mac, or Amiga format

Table 2-3 *Audio formats*

Audio Helpers

If you have a sound card installed in your system, you can use the Microsoft Windows multimedia interface through the MPLAYER.EXE program to play sounds supported by the soundcard. At a minimum, this should be the WAV and MIDI formats. Even without a sound card, though, you're not necessarily out of luck. You can use the SPEAKER.EXE program (see the Installation chapter) to set up a generic driver allowing you to play a number of sound formats through your PC speaker. Of course, the quality is not going to approach that of a sound card, but it may pass for voice grade audio. For MIDI (discussed shortly) or high-quality output, though, you'll need a real sound card.

Whether you are using the SPEAKER driver or have a sound card, you can associate most other sound formats with a shareware application called WHAM. WHAM, or Waveframe Hold And Modify, is a shareware utility (see the Installation chapter). It is the audio counterpart of the LVIEW utility above. It supports a wide variety of sound formats (AIF, AU, IFF, VOC, and WAV), and lets you modify, convert formats, and record sound files.

Let's build a practice page with a couple of sound files. Open a new file with your editor and enter the following HTML:

```
<HTML>
<HEAD>
<TITLE>A Web Page Recital, In Two Parts</TITLE>
</HEAD>
<BODY>
<H2>Sample Sound Files</H2>
<IMG SRC="sounds/note.gif">
<P>The following samples compare and contrast two different sound formats: WAV and MIDI.
<UL>
<LI><A HREF="spacemus.wav">This is a WAV file</A>
<LI><A HREF="moonlite.mid">This is a MIDI file</A>
</UL>
<P>Play each sound, and note how long (in seconds) each plays.
</BODY>
</HTML>
```

Note the syntax of the anchor tag. It's very similar to the PCX exercise you did above. The only real variation is in the filetypes; they're now MID and WAV instead of PCX. Remember that the filetype cues the browser to use a helper application to handle these formats when the anchor text is clicked.

Okay, if your helper application is configured, click each sound link in Figure 2-12. You'll discover that they are both approximately the same duration, about six seconds. But notice below the difference in their file sizes:

```
spacemus.wav    48K
moonlite.mid    11K
```

Music and MIDI

MIDI is a much more compact format than WAV. Rather than recording the actual sound waves, MIDI only records information about tracks, timing, notes, and instruments. The notes are regenerated with synthesizers or actual instrument samples on the

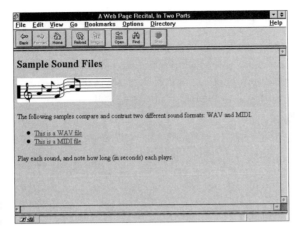

Figure 2-12
Sound format
comparisons

sound card. This results in complex, textured music that can be stored in a compact file. The only drawback (besides requiring a sound card for playback) is that MIDI doesn't handle voice, while most of the other formats can.

RealAudio

Formats handled by helper applications typically load the entire file referenced in the hyperlink before they actually display, play, or otherwise make the data available to the user. For sound files this can be annoying. It might take five minutes of transferring a file before you hear the first peep of what it is about. Wouldn't it make more sense to be able to listen to it as it was being transferred to your browser?

This feature is provided by a special audio helper application called RAPLAYER.EXE. This is a freeware player, but to play back their audio from a Web server requires purchasing Progressive Networks, Inc.'s server product, RealAudio.

RealAudio downloads a small file that points to the actual audio file. The player then starts on your PC as a helper application and starts playing the audio file during the downloads. This clever technique is sometimes called a *sidecar*. You'll see it again in the last chapter when you look at digital cash schemes, but in essence the sidecar is an application that connects and transfers data using your network independent of your browser.

When you install RealAudio (see the Installation chapter) you'll discover another intelligent feature: it automatically adds itself to your Netscape configuration file as a helper application.

Where to Find Sounds

Most sound cards also allow input via microphones or CDs. This means you can generate your own sound files for your Web page with whatever you can (legally) plug into the input lines of your sound card. Recording from audio input actually captures raw sound waves, so watch out! Unlike using MIDI, you can create extremely large files, extremely quickly!

You can also get sounds from CDs. Some multimedia companies advertise CDs full of royalty-free special effects and sound-bytes. And you can get them on the Web; check at http://www.yahoo.com/ under Computers and click on Multimedia, Sound.

For MIDI, products such as SuperJAM from Blue Ribbon Soundwork make it easy to create your own sound tracks, even if your humming sparks howls of protest from the neighborhood dogs.

So, you know how to whip pictures up in another application and provide sound-bytes or even symphonies at the click of a hyperlink. Try answering the questions below before you dive into the brave new worlds of video and animation.

QUIZ 2

1. External images are identified as such by their
   a. contents
   b. size
   c. filename
   d. filetype

2. "Thumbnail" images are
   a. pictures of the upper surfaces of thumbs
   b. large JPEG files
   c. small images that usually represent larger counterparts
   d. images that appear in the toolbar of a browser

3. Which of the following is *not* a sound format?
   a. SND
   b. AU
   c. WAV
   d. XBM

4. Which generally creates the smallest sound file?
   a. WAV
   b. SND
   c. XBM
   d. MIDI

5. The difference between inline images and those handled by helper applications is
   a. inline images are always smaller
   b. helper applications show images in their own window
   c. only external images can have 16.7 million colors
   d. inline images are always GIF files

EXERCISE 2

Create an HTML page that links images to sounds. Try to create an effect similar to the thumbnail, except instead of a small picture linked to a larger one, link a small picture to a sound file. Align the images on the left of the screen, and provide a short description of what users might expect to experience if they click the image.

Bonus question: How does the user know the images are "clickable"?

MOVIES ON THE WEB

Images and sounds add exciting dimensions to hypertext, but when you weave the two together into full-motion video, things get really interesting. A variety of video file formats is available on the World Wide Web; the most common being AVI, MOV, and MPEG (MPG). Like other hyperlinks to external files, the filetypes indicate both the format and the application your browser will use to handle it. Each of these formats can combine video, animation, sound, and music. But as you might suspect, this capability doesn't come cheap.

Video's Price

The format for full-motion video used for TV in North America is called NTSC and is defined as 704 by 480 pixels at 30 frames per second. A typical full-screen, color image on your computer is about 640 by 480, with 24-bit color, which requires about 900K. At 30 of these images per second, if they were uncompressed, you would need about 27MB for one minute of full-motion video! Trying to duplicate the capabilities of broadcast TV is probably the worst case scenario. More commonly, video on the Web is stored in quarter-screen frames (352 by 240). This, combined with compression techniques, can shrink storage requirements more than 3,000 percent.

But even compressed video can eat up large chunks of storage space and take several minutes to transfer. Nonetheless, many Web sites have found viable applications for video clips. Depending on your product and clientele, you may find this type of media is invaluable in promoting your page or product. Used with economy and discretion, a short, compressed video clip can make an impressive and lasting impact.

Video Guidelines

Here are some guidelines for using video. First, decide on the format. Like images, video comes in a variety of formats. As mentioned above, the most prevalent on the Web are AVI, MOV, and MPEG (or MPG). Since your primary concern is authoring for the Web, and there is such a variety of platforms, you should focus on interoperability rather than feature sets and bells and whistles. (These feature sets and bells and whistles are really interesting, but you'll want to invest in a good multimedia book to do them justice.) Let's look at the three most common formats and where they are typically used.

AVI

AVI is used extensively on Windows platforms. AVI files can be found on the Web and on several CD-ROM multimedia titles, but will probably not be your first choice for Web publishing. AVI hasn't really caught on with other platforms, and unless you have a captive Windows-based audience, you will need something more universal.

MOV

MOV is a little better. MOV is the Apple Macintosh QuickTime format. A player for QuickTime is available on Windows and you can, through special formatting, create QuickTime movies that can be displayed in both Mac and Windows environments. Your UNIX users, on the other hand, will have fairly limited options.

MPEG

That leaves MPEG, or MPG. This is becoming a very popular cross-platform video format, even more so with the advent of cheap decoder chips that are being bundled with graphics adapters. MPEG comes in two formats: MPEG 1 and MPEG 2. MPEG 1 is the most widely deployed, and it's the one covered below. MPEG 2 is designed for high-end video production applications.

MPEG 1 works with images at one-quarter broadcast quality (i.e., 352 by 240) at full-motion (30 fps) speeds. It's being used on CD-I (the Phillips Interactive CD format) and has been widely deployed with RCA's DSS home satellite dish systems. Not that people getting these services have quarter-size screens. MPEG decoders also work in conjunction with hardware that interpolates the images to the larger broadcast, or video-screen, format, and produces image quality roughly comparable to that of VHS.

Creating MPEG

One hitch with MPEG, though, is that while MPEG decoder/decompression is migrating to cheap, widely available chips, the encoding/compression part of the equation is still relatively expensive. Most of the video capture boards that you can buy to create your video segments for the Web store video in AVI, QuickTime, or M-JPEG (not the same as MPEG) formats. Getting the video from these formats into MPEG requires the use of a service bureau unless you have specialized hardware or software.

At the time of this writing, a real-time hardware encoder board for MPEG is around $3,000. A software-only MPEG encoder such as XingCD sells for $995. The latter can use a Pentium to convert previously captured AVI segments, and takes about one hour to produce one minute worth of MPEG. The entire process, from video capture to MPEG file on the Web, is illustrated in Figure 2-13.

Hyperlinks to Video

Adding a video clip to a Web page is very similar to adding the image and audio hyperlinks you built earlier. Let's add a link to an AVI file from the Martian Expedition page. (I couldn't talk Xing Technology into a complementary XingCD for MPEG conversion!)

```
<HTML>
<HEAD>
<TITLE>Martian Expeditions</TITLE>
</HEAD>
<A HREF="tie.avi">Exciting footage from our last expedition!</A>
<BODY>
</BODY>
</HTML>
```

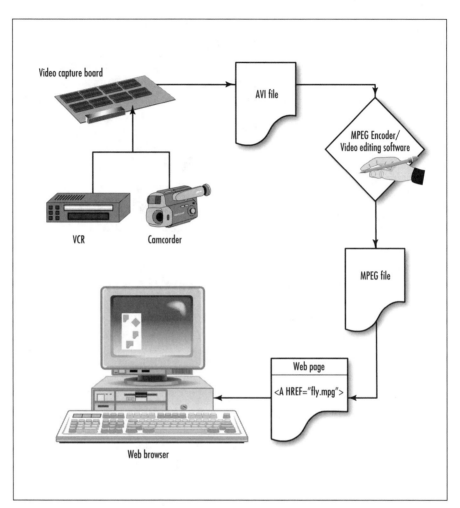

Figure 2-13
Capture to video
for the Web

Figure 2-14 shows Windows MPLAYER.EXE application displaying the AVI file when the hyperlink was activated.

Both the Apple and Microsoft video formats continue to evolve. The most interesting evolution is taking place in the way they are folding in interactive concepts like 3D surround views and the ability to virtually interact with objects. Taking advantage of these techniques usually requires development kits and, in the case of Apple, runtime licensing. Simpler techniques of capturing segments for small video sequences to be played on a generic Web browser is still more economical through the use of video capture boards to pull footage in from your camcorder, and MPEG conversion to put it in a format universally accessible to Web browsers. While it's well beyond the scope of this book to cover these techniques in detail, the next section will cover a few tips to keep in mind if you are considering creating your own video content.

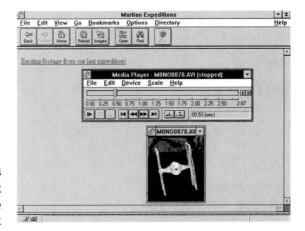

Figure 2-14
MPLAYER
displaying the
AVI hyperlink

Some Tips on Making Your Own Movies

If you use a quality video capture boards, you can expect to create video segments in the 320 by 240 resolution, 30 fps range. You'll need a fast disk (10ms or faster) and a fast processor (486/66 at least), lots of free disk space and memory (16MB RAM minimum), and a video editing package such as Adobe's Premier. If you have a hobbyist bent, this combination will provide you with hours of entertainment. Premier (for both the PC and the Mac) packages have all sorts of nifty effects, allowing you a variety of ways to superimpose one subject on another. In release 4.0, Premier provided features like 75 prefab transition effects (like wipes, dissolves, etc.), plus the ability to create your own. You'll want to check the multimedia magazines for comparisons if you're shopping for a video capture board. Quality in this arena does not necessarily correlate with price. As of this writing, Intel's Smart Video Recorder Pro is an excellent value at a reasonable price.

If you are a Mac user and you create a file with QuickTime, be sure to "flatten" it to create a format compatible for Windows QuickTime viewers. The flattening process creates a file with just the QuickTime data, rather than including the Macs native "resource fork," which is only interpretable with Macs. QuickTime has options for generating this format, and a variety of third party tools exist for this purpose as well.

Digital video can also be created from animation. Packages like Corel's Animator and various ray-tracing products can create surreal, photorealistic scenes for inclusion into AVI, QuickTime, or MPEG formats. Of course, you can also find video clips on the Web. Some popular MPEG video archives can be found at

> http://www.cs.tu-berlin.de/~phade/mpeg.html
> http://www.eeb.ele.tue.nl/mpeg/
> http://www.acm.uiuc.edu/rml/Mpeg

Scientific animations and visualization pages at

http://www.csc.fi/math_topics/Movies/
http://www.crs4it/Animate/Animations.html
http://www.tc.cornell.edu/Visualization
http://www.ncsa.uiuc.edu/General/NCSAExhibits.html

And the most up to date pointers to these individual archives at

http://www.yahoo.com/
under Computers click on Multimedia then click on Video

A sample page from the University of Illinois is shown in Figure 2-15.
For an MPEG helper application for Windows, see the Installation chapter.

What Else?!

Images, sounds, video, animation, music, that about covers all the sense modalities except
touch and…smell?!

In an April 1 edition of an Internet magazine, a company called Idaho Computing
introduced a product called ScentMaster. It was an add-on board for a PC that controlled
three external vials of "primary scents" and an aerosol adapter. It was advertised to interpret files with a filetype of OLF, and included a "scentor" that mixed scents based on
the OLF to synthesize up to 36 unique smells, including "roses," "new car," "roasted
coffee," and, gak, "dead animal in the wall"!

After taking several individuals, companies, and one Army consulting report in, it
was revealed as an April Fools' joke. It wasn't apparent even after the fact whether the
article fooled people because of their gullibility, or because of the imminent viability
of such an offering.

Well, this is about everything short of virtual reality that you can do with multimedia
and the Web. (And speaking of VR, check out VRML, or Virtual Reality Markup
Language, in Chapter 7!)

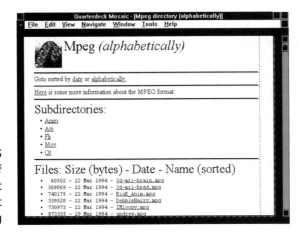

Figure 2-15
Sample sources of
MPEG movies at
http://www.acm.uiuc
.edu/rml/Mpeg

QUIZ 3

1. To play a one-minute, uncompressed TV commercial on the Web would require about how much space?
   a. 30K
   b. 300K
   c. 3MB
   d. 30MB

2. The QuickTime video format is primarily used by
   a. Windows
   b. UNIX
   c. the Web
   d. Apple

3. Probably the most widely used cross-platform video format is
   a. AVI
   b. QuickTime
   c. JPEG
   d. MPEG

4. Video segments are linked to on a Web page with which tag?
   a. <IMG...>
   b. <ALT...>
   c. <A HREF...>
   d. <P...>

SESSION 4

GRAPHICAL LIST BULLETS AND BUTTONS

After working with graphics and sound, it might seem like taking a step back to revisit the lowly list tag. But lists are versatile elements, and with them you can seamlessly integrate text and graphics. Recall that back in Chapter 1 when you were nesting lists, you produced a variety of bullets based on how deep the list items were nested, as in Figure 2-16.

Bullets and Lists

Using Netscape HTML enhancements, you were even able to specify the bullet to be used on an individual list item as a circle, square, number, or letter, but you were pretty much stuck with the bullet styles provided. Figure 2-17 introduces a new way of doing

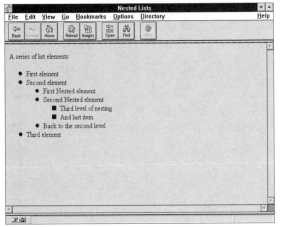

Figure 2-16
A list with all the HTML nesting levels

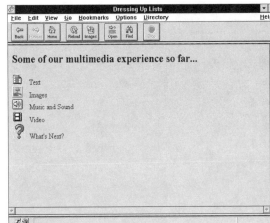

Figure 2-17
An image list

bullets, one that uses a variation of the definition list tag <DL> covered in Session 7 of Chapter 1.

Using the <IMG> Tag with Definition Lists

The <DL> element has two associated tags: <DT>, which introduces a term, and <DD>, which defines the term. These lists are handy for introducing glossaries, but Figure 2-17 was created by using the <DT> tag to specify an image as follows:

```
<DL COMPACT>
<DT><IMG SRC="bullet1.gif">
<DD>This is item 1
<DT><IMG SRC="bullet2.gif">
<DD>This is item 2
</DL>
```

The <DT> tag specifies an image using the <IMG> tag. This technique creates the appearance of user defined bullets that precede each of the text elements in the <DD> definition tags.

The COMPACT Option

The COMPACT option in the <DL> tag tells the browser to format the list elements with a minimal amount of free space between the elements. Without using COMPACT, your page might end up looking like Figure 2-18. Of course, if this is the effect you are looking for, that wouldn't be so bad. But note that in HTML, COMPACT does not control the format, it merely suggests to the browser that it should minimize the space. The same list might look different displayed in different browsers; as is illustrated in Figure 2-19. This is the QMosaic browser's version of the same HTML used in Figure 2-17. Even though the COMPACT option of <DL> is specified, QMosaic still arranges the item definitions below the item icons.

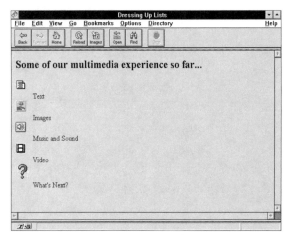

Figure 2-18
Netscape's interpretation without the <DL>
COMPACT option

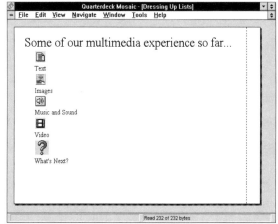

Figure 2-19
QMosaic's interpretation of <DL COMPACT>

Building Your Own

To start experimenting with this technique, the first thing you'll need is some graphical bullets. Several locations on the Web offer bullets and icons to use with your pages. Let's use Chris Stephens' Button, Cubes, & Bars link off of the Yahoo server. His page is shown in Figure 2-20.

Bullets on the Web

Chris has made it easy. Remember the thumbnails in Session 2? To retrieve a bullet, just click on the thumbnail. It loads the image to your helper application, and from there

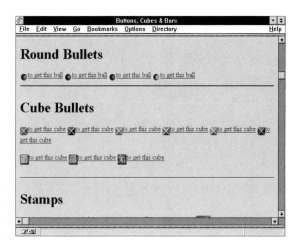

Figure 2-20
Bullets and icons
from Chris
Stephens

you can save it to disk and use it in your own HTML. In Netscape, bullets and icons can be retrieved off of Web pages, even if they aren't displayed as thumbnails (assuming they are public domain), by positioning your cursor on the image and clicking your right mouse button. It will bring up a menu with options on where to save the image you clicked on.

When you download these small icons from the Web, you'll notice that they are typically 32 by 32 bits, and usually only 16 colors. Most are also in GIF format, which makes any lines and text crisp in the relatively small image size. These characteristics combine to make the list bullets very quick to download. In fact, if you use the same image for all the bullets on your list, a browser will download the image just once. (Most browsers are smart enough to recognize that they already have this picture in their cache, so they will use it to format the rest of the list.) Conversely, if you use different images for each bullet, each image requires the browser to download it individually.

The Web is not the only source of prefab bullets. The 32 by 32 dimensions are suspiciously similar to those used by icons in Windows. In fact, with a couple of utilities, you can enlist Windows icons as serviceable bullets for HTML pages.

Converting Icons into Bullets

To change icons into bullets:

1. Select an icon, either individually, or from an icon library.

2. Use a graphics utility to export the ICO graphics format used by the icon to BMP format.

3. Convert the BMP to GIF for use in the <IMG> tag.

It's a shame you can't go from step 1 directly to step 3, but it's hard to find utilities that convert from ICO to GIF formats in one fell swoop. Let's walk through these steps with a live example.

Using the Icon Builder Library (see the Installation chapter), open all icons from the CD's \images directory using the Open All... button. Figure 2-21 shows the selection screen. Icon Builder lets you select the icons visually. Click on the barn.ico file in the From: window and move it into the To: window using the >>>Add>>> button. Repeat for as many other icons as you want to convert.

Once you've added all the icons you want, click on each one in the To: window, then click on Export Icon. Choose Bitmap File under Save File as Type as in Figure 2-22. Repeat until you've exported all the icons you moved into the To: window, saving each of them to disk as BMP files.

Start up LVIEW, the graphics utility (see the Installation chapter). This utility is needed to change the graphics format from BMP to GIF or JPG for use in the <IMG> tag. Open the BMP file you just created. From LVIEW's Retouch then click on Color Depth option menu, select Palette Image, Windows Palette, and deselect Dithering. Now save the file as a GIF87a format GIF file and voilà! You've made a bullet from an icon. Repeat this for each icon you exported in BMP format.

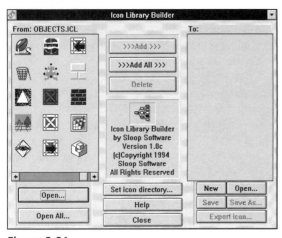

Figure 2-21
Selecting icons with ICL

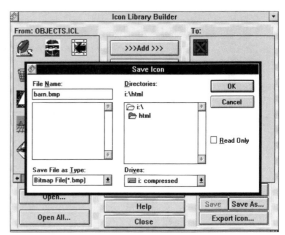

Figure 2-22
Saving the icon as a bitmap

Putting It to Use

Let's use the barn.gif bullet created above in a list. Open a new file in your editor and enter the following HTML. Feel free to substitute any other bullet you created above for barn.gif, and to replace the text with something related to your bullet.

```
<HTML>
<HEAD>
<TITLE>Custom List Bullets</TITLE>
</HEAD>
<BODY>
<H2>TOP 5 Reasons Build a Barn</H2>
<DL COMPACT>
<DT><IMG SRC="barn.gif">
<DD>You'd have a place for your goats so they wouldn't chew up your curtains all the time
<DT><IMG SRC="barn.gif">
<DD>Quarters for in-laws
<DT><IMG SRC="barn.gif">
<DD>A place for your son to practice his tuba
<DT><IMG SRC="barn.gif">
<DD>It's cheaper than buying a yacht
<DT><IMG SRC="barn.gif">
<DD>You can paint it really really really bright red and no one will
mind (more than the fact that you built it in the first place).
</DL>
</BODY>
</HTML>
```

Save the file, and open the HTML in your browser. Your results should be like those shown in Figure 2-23.

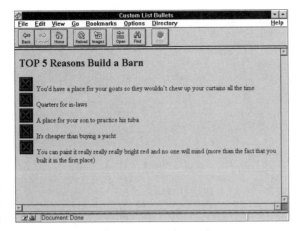

Figure 2-23
Browser with
barnyard icons

You may have noticed that bullets created from icons are kind of squarish, while those in Figure 2-21 have other shapes. This is because Windows icons use areas of color defined as *transparent,* which means they match the background so as to appear invisible. You'll learn how to do this in a few sessions.

Before we extend this technique to the next topic...do you remember Lynx? To accommodate text-mode browsers when you're making custom bullets, you can use the ALT attribute of the <IMG> tag, specifying ALT="o". This gives Lynx and its ilk at least the representation of a bullet rather than a jumbled list of text.

Buttons

You have all the basic ingredients necessary to expand this technique to create what's known as a *button.* A button is basically an icon that, when clicked, acts as a link. The principle is the same as that used in the thumbnail technique, except instead of linking to images, icons typically link to other pages.

Buttons to Navigate

To illustrate how buttons might be used, let's say you are developing a tutorial. The tutorial presents a sequence of slides, and includes hypertext to explain various terms in the presentation. When not following hyperlinks, the user will be following the presentation sequentially. You could manage this by putting a hyperlink called "Next" at the bottom of each screen, and "Next" is a good candidate for an icon. So is "Contents", "Help", and other navigational constructs that should ideally appear on each screen.

You probably don't need "Back", as this function is built into most browsers. Browsers know where you've been, but they don't know where you are going.

Let's build a template for a navigation page. The buttons used for Up (Contents), Next, and Help were converted from icons found in Microsoft's Visual Basic directory to GIF images on this book's CD. You'll find these in the \images directory of the CD; use them as the basis for your navigation page. Open a new file with your editor and enter the following HTML:

```
<HTML>
<HEAD>
<TITLE>Strategy Tutorials</TITLE>
</HEAD>
<BODY>
<H2>Strategy Tutorials</H2>
<H3>Samurai Inc.</H3>
<P>Our third lesson in strategy covers the Japanese concept of
"Shikkotai", which means to stick on your opponent like mud (or
lacquer, depending on the translator). The strategy is based on
all processes requiring optimal space to potentiate. By retreating,
you sometimes allow space for things to happen that could be prevented
by advancing. While counter-intuitive, the strategy is often effective
for just this reason. Your opponent does not expect it.<P>

<A HREF="help.html"><IMG SRC="help.gif"></A>
<A HREF="content.html"><IMG SRC="up.gif"></A>
<A HREF="lesson4.html"><IMG SRC="next.gif"></A>

</BODY>
</HTML>
```

Save and display the page in your browser. The results are shown in Figure 2-24.

Lists and Buttons Combined

You can, of course, combine graphical lists and buttons to make an even more sophisticated page. Let's use a hypothetical internal company page (as opposed to the "real" examples we've been using until now!) to demonstrate how this could work.

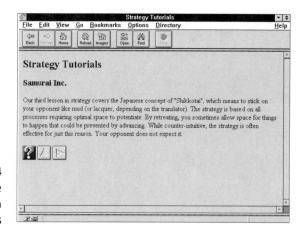

Figure 2-24
Netscape example of navigation buttons

Developing the page incrementally, first just sketch out the general categories. Open a new file with your editor and enter the following HTML:

```
<HTML>
<HEAD>
<TITLE>Samurai Company Page</TITLE>
</HEAD>
<BODY>
<DL COMPACT>
<DT>
<DD>Staff
<DT>
<DD>Phone Directory
<DT>
<DD>E-mail Directory
<DT>
<DD>General Policies
</BODY>
</HTML>
```

Now, in the <DT> slots, add some graphical bullets:

```
<DT><A HREF="staff.htm"><IMG SRC="staff.gif"></A>
```

Continue adding button links for each aspect of company information:

```
<HEAD>
<TITLE>Samurai Company Page</TITLE>
</HEAD>
<H2>The Samurai Company</H2>
<H3>Internal Home Page</H3>
<P>The Samurai Company is pleased to announce the availability
the following services for internal employees.<P>
<BODY>
<DL COMPACT>
<DT><DT><A HREF="staff.htm"><IMG SRC="staff.gif" HSIZE=32 VSIZE=32 BORDER=0></A>
<DD>Staff
<DT><A HREF="phone.htm"><IMG SRC="phone.gif" HSIZE=32 VSIZE=32 BORDER=0></A>
<DD>Phone Directory
<DT><A HREF="email.htm"><IMG SRC="email.gif" HSIZE=32 VSIZE=32 BORDER=0></A>
<DD>E-mail Directory
<DT><A HREF="policy.htm"><IMG SRC="policy.gif" HSIZE=32 VSIZE=32 BORDER=0></A>
<DD>General Policies
</BODY>
</HTML>
```

Save the file and display the results on your browser (Figure 2-25).

So you've learned two new uses for the <IMG> tag: adding impact to list items, and creating buttons as visual links to related information. You've explored how to find bullets on the Web, and how to put icons you may have lying around in Windows to use in HTML. I guess that just leaves you with a few questions…

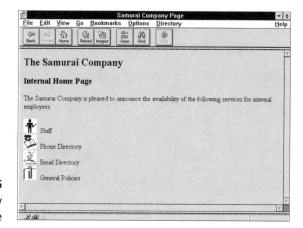

Figure 2-25
Internal company
page

1 The COMPACT option of the <DL> tag is useful for graphical lists because
   a. It reduces the size of the bullets.
   b. It changes the text font.
   c. It instructs the browser to minimize the space used to present the list.
   d. It instructs the browser to reuse bullets for better efficiency.

2. Bullets are generally
   a. BMP images
   b. PCX images
   c. ICO images
   d. GIF images

3. In order to use a Windows icon as a graphical bullet, you must
   a. make them smaller
   b. make them larger
   c. convert them to ICO images
   d. convert them to GIF images

4. A good way to provide list bullets for a text-mode browser is to
   a. use the COMPACT option
   b. use ALT="bullet"
   c. use ALT="o"
   d. use 32 by 32 images

5. An example of a button tag is
   a. <A HREF="page2.htm"><IMG SRC="next.gif" ALT="Next Page"></A>
   b. <IMG SRC="next.gif">
   c. <A HREF="page2.htm">Next.gif</A>
   d. <A HREF="next.gif"></A>

CHARACTERS, COMMENTS, AND TABLES

This session covers how to display special characters in Web pages, how to add comments to your HTML, and how to use tables to format text. Let's start with characters and learn how to put copyright and trademark symbols in your HTML, as well as use some seemingly innocuous characters that require special handling.

Special Characters in HTML

Some characters in HTML have special meanings.

HTML SPECIAL CHARACTERS	
<	is used to begin a markup tag.
>	is used to end it.
"	is used to include name values.
&	is the HTML escape character.

These characters are "reserved" for use in HTML tags. If you want to use them for other reasons on your page, you'll need to use an entity name or a special escaped character reference.

Character Entities

Character entity names are made up of three parts:

     &   A leading ampersand character

     name   symbolic entity name

     ;   A terminating semicolon

The following entity names are used for the characters above:

Character	Entity Name
<	&lt;
>	&gt;
"	&quot;
&	&amp;

So to enter the following in a Web page:

you would need the following HTML:

```
2 &gt; 3
```

Since > is a reserved character, it needs to be represented with an entity name: >. Applying the same rule, how would you display the following on a Web page?

```
He drew on the board, "3 > 2"
```

If you're thinking

```
He drew on the board, &quot; 3 &gt; 2 &quot;
```

you're absolutely correct. Be sure when you're using character entities to include the trailing semicolon (;). Forgetting this is a common mistake when you first begin to use entity references. Unlike most HTML statements, the entities are case sensitive. < is not the same at <. Forgetting this is another common mistake.

Using the & character as an escape character introduces the need for one more entity if you want to use & itself in the document. The & can be included in HTML by using the & entity.

Escaped Characters

Character entities name only a subset of all the characters available to you in HTML. The entire character set is shown in Table 2-4. Note that many of these characters do not have entity references. To display them on your Web page, you can use another technique: escaped character references.

Escaped characters consist of three elements, similar to the character entities. These elements are

      &   A leading ampersand character

      #*nnn*   A decimal number preceded by a # symbol

     ;   A terminating semicolon

The number *nnn* in the escaped character corresponds to the decimal number across from the character in Table 2-4. So an alternate way of specifying

```
>
```

which has a numeric value of 62, is

```
&#62;
```

This has the same effect as

```
&gt;
```

To spell Piñata, you could use the entity name in Table 2-4:

```
Pi&ntilde;ata
```

or you could use the decimal value:

```
Pi&#241;ata
```

This list show the Decimal and Hex codes for all the ISO Latin-1 characters. Note, in HTML, that any ISO Latin-1 character can be written as <code>&#xxx</code>, where <code>xxx</code> is the decimal code of the character.

TABLE 2-4

Char	Decimal	Hex	Entity Reference	Char	Decimal	Hex	Entity Reference
	160	a0		¡	161	a1	
¢	162	a2		£	163	a3	
¤	164	a4		¥	165	a5	
¦	166	a6		§	167	a7	
"	168	a8		©	169	a9	
ª	170	aa		«	171	ab	
¬	172	ac		-	173	ad	
®	174	ae		¯	175	af	
°	176	b0		±	177	b1	
²	178	b2		³	179	b3	
´	180	b4		µ	181	b5	
¶	182	b6		·	183	b7	
,	184	b8		¹	185	b9	
º	186	ba		»	187	bb	
¼	188	bc		½	189	bd	
¾	190	be		¿	191	bf	
À	192	c0	&Agrave;	Á	193	c1	&Aacute;
Â	194	c2	&Acirc;	Ã	195	c3	&Atilde;
Ä	196	c4	&Auml;	Å	197	c5	&Aring;
Æ	198	c6	&AElig;	Ç	199	c7	&Ccedil;
È	200	c8	&Egrave;	É	201	c9	&Eacute;
Ê	202	ca	&Ecirc;	Ë	203	cb	&Euml;
Ì	204	cc	&Igrave;	Í	205	cd	&Iacute;
Î	206	ce	&Icirc;	Ï	207	cf	&Iuml;
	208	d0	—	Ñ	209	d1	&Ntilde;
Ò	210	d2	&Ograve;	Ó	211	d3	&Oacute;
Ô	212	d4	&Ocirc;	Õ	213	d5	&Otilde;
Ö	214	d6	&Ouml;	x	215	d7	

continued on next page

continued from previous page

Char	Decimal	Hex	Entity Reference	Char	Decimal	Hex	Entity Reference
Ø	216	d8	&Oslash;	Ù	217	d9	&Ugrave;
Ú	218	da	&Uacute;	Û	219	db	&Ucirc;
Ü	220	dc	&Uuml;	Ý	221	dd	&Yacute;
‡	222	de	&THORN;	ß	223	df	&szlig;
à	224	e0	&agrave;	á	225	e1	&aacute;
â	226	e2	&acirc;	ã	227	e3	&atilde;
ä	228	e4	&auml;	å	229	e5	&aring;
æ	230	e6	&aelig;	ç	231	e7	&ccedil;
è	232	e8	&egrave;	é	233	e9	&eacute;
ê	234	ea	&ecirc;	ë	235	eb	&euml;
ì	236	ec	&igrave;	í	237	ed	&iacute;
î	238	ee	&icirc;	ï	239	ef	&iuml;
ò	240	f0	&eth;	ñ	241	f1	&ntilde;
ò	242	f2	&ograve;	ó	243	f3	&oacute;
ô	244	f4	&ocirc;	õ	245	f5	&otilde;
ö	246	f6	&ouml;	÷	247	f7	
ø	248	f8	&oslash;	ù	249	f9	&ugrave;
ú	250	fa	&uacute;	û	251	fb	&ucirc;
ü	252	fc	&uuml;	ý	253	fd	&yacute;
	254	fe	&thorn;	ÿ	255	ff	&yuml;

Table 2-4   *ISO Latin-1 Character Set*

Escaped characters are also handy when your keyboard doesn't have a particular character that is listed in the table. It can still be entered using the escape sequence.

Copyright and Registered Trademark Symbols

Netscape provides entity names for the following:

®	&reg;	for registered trademark
©	&copy;	for copyright

In browsers that do not handle the entity names for these symbols, the escaped character references can serve just as well:

®	&#174;	for registered trademark
©	&#169;	for copyright

Open a new file with your editor and enter several of these special characters. Mix escaped characters and entity names on your page and test the results in your browser. For example, enter the following HTML:

```
<HTML>
<HEAD>
<TITLE>Special Characters</TITLE>
</HEAD>
<BODY>
<H2>You ca&agrave;n use spe&#231;ial characters in headers</H2>
<UL>
<LI>Or in lists
<LI>you can use them to display literal tags like: &lt;IMG&gt; &amp;
&lt;P&gt;
</UL>
This corrupted text Copyright &copy; 2001 by Samurai, Inc.
</BODY>
</HTML>
```

The results are shown in Figure 2-26.

Comments

Just as you can in other languages, you can include comments in HTML. The syntax for a comment is

HTML COMMENTS

<!— *comment* —>
   comment is the text of your comment
Comments are internal notes in your HTML; they are not displayed by a browser.

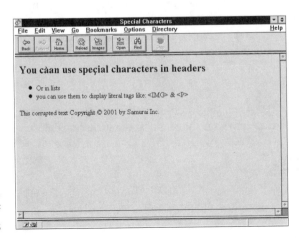

Figure 2-26
Smorgasbord of special characters

Comments are useful to you, the HTML author, for documenting your page. They are not viewable by the typical user (unless he or she looks at the HTML source). In HTML, an example of a comment is

```
<!-- Created 09/24/2001 by Jack McPhetridge -->
```

The text of your comment is preceded by <!— and the closing tag is —>. Comments are one of the few tags that break the normal format of HTML opening and closing conventions (*<tag>…</tag>*). A sample block of comments in HTML would be as follows:

```
<HTML>
<!-- This document was created 12/1/2004 to illustrate the concept -->
<!-- of headers for documenting HTML                               -->
<HEAD>
<TITLE>Sample Comments</TITLE>
</HEAD>
<BODY>
</BODY>
</HTML>
```

Comments can be added anywhere in your HTML, except within another tag (excluding, of course, <HTML>, <HEADER>, and <BODY>). Comments should not be nested, i.e., included within themselves.

Comment Gotchas

When rendered by browsers, comments have a few outstanding idiosyncrasies that you should be aware of.

In the past, some Web browsers have tripped up on the following syntax:

```
<!-- Come back and finish this list later....
<UL>
<LI>List item...
-->
```

You would expect the browser to assume that everything between the opening <!— and the closing —> is a comment. Some browsers, like Netscape, handle this as expected. Others will find the ending > in <UL> and end the comment there, leaving the following HTML fragment:

```
<LI>List item...
-->
```

They will then complain loudly about this incomplete segment. If you find yourself running into these browsers, be careful about including the > character in your comments.

Tables

Tables were one of the long-awaited features included in HTML 3.0. They replaced the primitive mechanism of <PRE> and </PRE>, which forced columnar information into rigid, left justified-rows of monospace text, and added greater controls to the placement of text and images on the screen. The syntax of the <TABLE> tag is

THE <TABLE> TAG

<TABLE		
	BORDER	
	BORDER=*"pixels"*	NHTML
	CELLSPACING=*"n"*	NHTML
	CELLPADDING=*"n"*	NHTML
	WIDTH=*"pixel-width"*	
<CAPTION>...</CAPTION>	ALIGN=*"position"*	
<TH>	ALIGN=*"position"*	
	VALIGN=*"vertical-position"*	
	NOWRAP	
	COLSPAN=*"rows"*	
	ROWSPAN=*"rows"*	
	WIDTH=*"pixel-width"*	
NHTML		
<TR>	ALIGN=*"position"*	
	VALIGN=*"position"*	
<TD>	ALIGN=*"position"*	
	VALIGN=*"position"*	
	NOWRAP	
	COLSPAN=*"rows"*	
	ROWSPAN=*"rows"*	
	WIDTH=*"pixel-width"*	
NHTML		
>		
<TABLE>		

Tables format text and images in columnar rows.

The <TABLE> tag holds the record for the tag with the most options you've covered so far, but tables aren't really that difficult to grasp.

Data in a table is organized like data in a spreadsheet. The table consists of rows that run from left to right across the screen, and the rows are made up of *cells*, which create vertical columns of data. The familiar tic-tac-toe diagram is a table of three rows across and three columns down. Each cell in tic-tac-toe holds a single character. Cells are the building blocks of tables. To build a table of the following tic-tac-toe board:

```
x|o|
‾‾‾‾
x|o|
‾‾‾‾
 |x|
```

you would enter the following HTML:

```
<TABLE>
<TD>x<TD>o<TD><BR>
```

continued on next page

continued from previous page

```
<TR>
<TD>x<TD>o<TD><BR>
<TR>
<TD><BR><TD>x<TD><BR>
</TABLE>
```

<TD> precedes the data for each cell. It doesn't require an end tag. <TR> tells the browser that this is the end of the cell data for this row; start the next cell on another row. Note that some cells have no data. This is fine; it indicates an empty cell, and in these cells you should put a blank line (<BR>) or a nonbreaking space entity ( ). Otherwise the table will not create a border between this cell and the next.

That's all there is to creating a simple table. Just remember that the table is built around the data in the cells. It will automatically figure out how many cells need to be on a row and how to format the text in the table as a whole.

Let's work with a slightly more complex example. Open a new file with your editor and enter the following HTML:

```
<HTML>
<HEAD>
<TITLE>Tables</TITLE>
</HEAD>
<BODY>
<H2>A Simple Table</H2>
<TABLE BORDER>
<CAPTION>Sample Table Layout</CAPTION>
<TH>Heading for Column 1
<TH>Heading for Column 2
<TR>
<TD>Data for Row 1, Col 1
<TD ALIGN="right">data for row 2, Col 2
<TR>
</TABLE>
</BODY>
</HTML>
```

When you display the results in your browser, it should look similar to Figure 2-27.

The BORDER option causes the table, rows, and cells to be framed with a visible border. The <CAPTION> tag within the table specifies the caption or label for the table. A caption can be aligned at the top or bottom of the table. Since the ALIGN option wasn't specified, it defaults to the top. The remaining tags format the data in the table.

ALIGN Options

The ALIGN option can be: "left", "center", or "right" (or "top" and "bottom" for the CAPTION tag). By default the data cells are aligned to the left, but ALIGN can also be used with the table row <TR> tag. This tag generally just begins a new row, but when it includes an ALIGN option, it sets the default alignment for all the cells in the row.

```
<TR ALIGN="center">
<TD>test
<TD>this
<TD>format
```

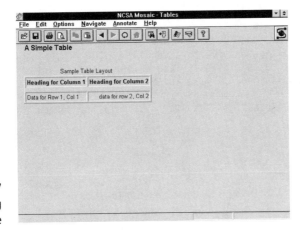

Figure 2-27
Mosaic displaying
a minimal table

produces the same effect as

```
<TR>
<TD ALIGN="center">test
<TD ALIGN="center">this
<TD ALIGN="center">format
```

Another option available to <TR>, <TH>, and <TD> tags is VALIGN. VALIGN aligns text vertically in the cell and can have a value of "top", "middle", "bottom", or "baseline".

<TH> Table Header Tag

Table header data is just like a data cell, except the text in the cells is displayed in a bold font. These cells are typically used for row or column headers, as in the case of Figure 2-27. Their default ALIGN option is "center".

Spanning Columns and Rows

The width of the columns is calculated from the cell data. If the data in a cell will be atypical of what is usually in that column or row, you may want to use ROWSPAN or COLSPAN to indicate how many rows this cell will span. Without using this, a cell with a long data value will be averaged with all the rest, and perhaps throw off formatting in the table. Relatively sophisticated overlapping headers can also be built using the ROWSPAN and COLSPAN options, as illustrated in the HTML below and the resultant table in Figure 2-28.

```
<HEAD>
<TITLE>Tables</TITLE>
</HEAD>
<BODY>
<H2>A More Sophisticated Table</H2>
<TABLE BORDER>
<CAPTION>Income Level and distribution</CAPTION>
<TR><TH COLSPAN=2><TH ROWSPAN=3>Number of<BR>Families<BR>1000
        <TH ROWSPAN=3>Percent of<BR>Families<BR>at income level
<TR>
```

continued on next page

continued from previous page

```
<TR><TH ALIGN=LEFT>Income Level
<TR><TH ALIGN=LEFT COLSPAN=2>Under $1,000<TD ALIGN=RIGHT>779<TD ALIGN=RIGHT>1.5
<TR><TH ALIGN=LEFT COLSPAN=2>$1,000-1,999<TD ALIGN=RIGHT>1,351<TD ALIGN=RIGHT>2.6
<TR><TH ALIGN=LEFT COLSPAN=2>$2,000-2,999<TD ALIGN=RIGHT>2,182<TD ALIGN=RIGHT>4.2
<TR><TH ALIGN=LEFT COLSPAN=2>$3,000-3,999<TD ALIGN=RIGHT>2,493<TD ALIGN=RIGHT>4.8
<TR><TH ALIGN=LEFT COLSPAN=2>$4,000-4,999<TD ALIGN=RIGHT>2,805<TD ALIGN=RIGHT>5.4
<TR>
<TR><TH ALIGN=LEFT COLSPAN=2>TOTAL<TD ALIGN=RIGHT>9,610<TD ALIGN=RIGHT>18.5
</TABLE>
</BODY>
</HTML>
```

NOWRAP

The NOWRAP option in a cell prevents the data in the cell from being wrapped onto another line when the table is formatted. Use this with caution, as it can produce long cell widths that cause users to have to scroll the screen to the right to see all of your table. By default, the browser will usually try to format a table to be displayed on a single screen without scrolling.

Netscapisms

Netscape has added several table enhancements to give you finer control over the presentation. They are

 BORDER=*n*. Given a value of 0, it compresses space reserved for borders between cells, allowing for compact tables. Given a numeric value, it enhances the table by creating a 3D appearance (try a value of 5 and see what it looks like).

 CELLSPACING=*n*. In the <TABLE> tag, this option controls the amount of space between individual cells; by default this value is 2.

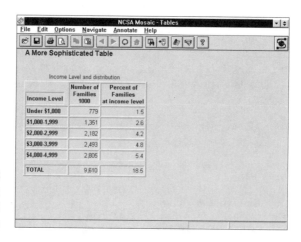

Figure 2-28
Mosaic with a more sophisticated table

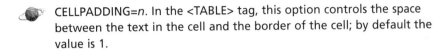
- CELLPADDING=*n*. In the <TABLE> tag, this option controls the space between the text in the cell and the border of the cell; by default the value is 1.

- WIDTH=*value* or *percent*. In the <TABLE> tag this attribute refers to the width of the table as a whole. The value is in pixels, the percent is the percentage of the page width. WIDTH used in the <TH> or <TD> tag specifies the width of the cell in absolute pixels or as a percentage of the table as a whole.

The <TABLE> tag also has advanced uses in input forms, which you'll cover in Chapter 4.

1. Which character cannot be used in normal text without a special escape sequence?
    a. !
    b. '
    c. lt;
    d. "

2. How would you write the following in HTML? large & small
    a. "large & small"
    b. large && small
    c. large &amp small
    d. large & small

3. What is the HTML 3.0 special character for copyright?
    a. cc
    b. &cc;
    c. &copyright;
    d. ©

4. Comments are ended with
    a. </comment>
    b. </!>
    c. </—>
    d. —>

5. The column widths of a table are determined by
    a. the WIDTH option
    b. the column data
    c. the column header
    d. the COLSPAN option

Using the <TABLE> tag, create a calendar depicting a month. It should have the name of the month and year at the top of the page, the columns should be labeled S, M, T, W, T, F, S for each day of the week, and it should have the correct numeric day of the month in the right cells. Make hyperlinks on a couple of the days to text describing an event that occurs on that day.

HINT: Remember to keep the borders on empty cells by using <TD>
.

SESSION 6

RULES, TRANSPARENT IMAGES, AND BACKGROUNDS

This is another multi-topic session. First we'll cover *rules*, the horizontal lines that section text on a page. You'll also learn to make a fancier variant of this technique called graphical rules. Then you'll dive deeper into image tricks in the section on *transparency*. Transparent images allow you to make sections of a graphic blend into the background of the page, creating images that seem to be more naturally part of your content. Finally, you'll learn techniques for using images as backgrounds, allowing you to superimpose other images and text on the same page.

Horizontal Rules

Making horizontal rules in HTML is easy. Just use the <HR> tag anywhere in your text, and you'll find a nice, horizontal rule cutting across the screen separating the images and text above the <HR> from the text that follows. The syntax of the <HR> tag is simply

THE <HR> TAG
<HR   WIDTH=*n*   NHTML   >   <HR> creates a horizontal rule across the page.

<HR> automatically creates a line break, so you won't need a <P> tag to separate two blocks of text if you use it. Open a new file with your editor and enter the following HTML:

```
<HTML>
<HEAD>
<TITLE>Drawing the Line</TITLE>
</HEAD>
<BODY>
<H2>Example of a Horizontal Line Tag</H2>
<HR>
```

```
Horizontal lines are a snap to make. Just throw the &lt;HR&gt; tag in
anywhere you would like to create an additional break between elements of
your page.
</BODY>
</HTML>
```

Save the file and open the HTML in your browser. Your results should look like Figure 2-29.

For a basic line, the kind provided by HTML, that's all there is to it. However, Netscape extensions to the <HR> tag allow for an option specifying the width of the line. Replacing

```
<HR>
```

in the last HTML example with the following:

```
<HR WIDTH=5>
```

results in a rule five pixels wide.

Graphical Rules

Lines add useful visual breaks in the presentation of material on the screen, but they are intrinsically pretty boring. It would be more interesting if the lines could be specified in various colors and textures. A special use of the <IMG> tag makes this possible.

Figure 2-30 shows a selection of graphical rules. This page is a contact sheet of rules created by Daniel McCoy, found by searching the Web (Netscape's DirectoryÍInternet Search option) for "rulers". Displaying a graphical rule is just another use of <IMG>. It's really just a long, skinny image! If you had a rule called rule1.gif, you could put it on the page in place of the rule above with the following HTML:

```
<HTML>
<HEAD>
<TITLE>Drawing the Line</TITLE>
</HEAD>
<BODY>
```

continued on next page

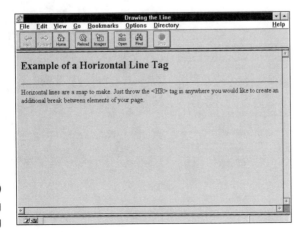

Figure 2-29
Netscape displaying
an <HR> tag

continued from previous page

```
<H2>Example of a Horizontal Line Tag</H2>
<BR><IMG SRC="ruler1.gif"><BR>
Horizontal lines are a snap to make. Just throw the &lt;HR&gt; tag in
anywhere you would like to create an additional break between elements of
your page.
</BODY>
</HTML>
```

The <BR> before and after the <IMG SRC="ruler1.gif"> tag should be used as a general precaution. It ensures that no text squeezes in to the right of the image. With <HR> you don't have to be as conscious of spacing; it automatically forces a line break. Figure 2-31 shows the page from Figure 2-29 with a graphical rule in place of the <HR> rule.

Next you'll examine one of these rules in detail with a helper application such as LVIEW, and learn how to make your own (Figure 2-32).

Making Your Own Graphical Rules

On LVIEW's title bar the rule's dimensions are displayed as 559 by 10 and it uses 64 colors. You could make a similar image easily with Paintbrush by opening a new file with these dimensions and filling it with a color or gradient. In fact, you might want try it as an experiment. In the following exercise, though, you'll be using Adobe's Photoshop and Kai's Filters to explore some more sophisticated options of the rule creation.

To make your own rule, open a GIF file of 559 by 10 pixels with a screen resolution of 72 dpi, just as you would if you were using Paintbrush, and then apply Kai's Mandelbrot filter. An example of this procedure in operation is shown in Figure 2-33.

The rule was saved to a GIF file called homemade.gif. Figure 2-34 shows the results when homemade.gif is used in the previous HTML in place of ruler1.gif.

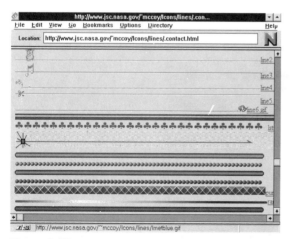

Figure 2-30
Graphical rules

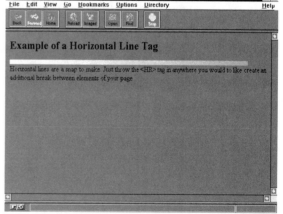

Figure 2-31
Graphical rule

Figure 2-32
A rule in LVIEW

Don't worry if you don't have Photoshop or Kai's Filters; they were used just to get a feel for the possibilities. You can produce similar results in Paintbrush, or CorelDRAW, or what have you by following the same steps:

1. Create a new image file of approximately 559 pixels wide by 10 pixels high. If you have an option for resolution, pick 72 dpi (dots per inch).

2. Fill the image with color, blends, fills, or whatever special effects are at your disposal.

3. Save the image as a GIF file. That's it. You've made a custom rule.

These rules all fit nice and neatly on the screen. If a rule exceeds the length of the screen (for example, on a laptop), most browsers just truncate the rule when it hits the right margin. The width of 559 pixels also assumes the common screen resolution of 640 by 480. If a higher resolution is being used by your user's browser, the rule may come up a bit short.

To accommodate text-mode browsers with your rule designs, you can use ALT="————" to create an old-fashioned hyphen rule to break up the text. You'll need enough hyphens to cover the whole width of your text rule, though; the tag won't automatically extend it to fit the screen.

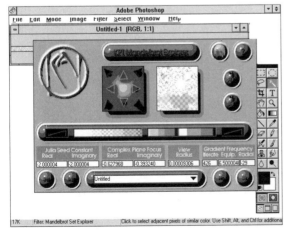

Figure 2-33
Photoshop and Kai ganging up to produce a rule

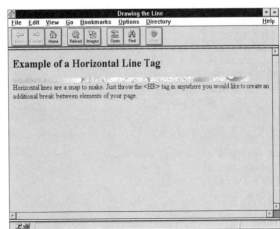

Figure 2-34
The homemade rule

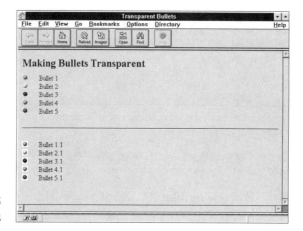

Figure 2-35
Transparent bullets

Transparent Images

Another handy technique using <IMG> is to display transparent images. Transparency is how a rectangular image is made to look like a shape. The rectangular background that is not part of the shape is made invisible (bitmap graphics are usually restricted to rectangular shapes). For example, Figure 2-35 shows several bullets with transparent backgrounds. Other bullets are displayed beneath them without transparency. Although these are separate images, the syntax appears identical in the HTML. Unfortunately, no options or attributes of the <IMG> tag tell the browser that an image is transparent; instead the trick lies in the way the image is created.

```
<HTML>
<HEAD>
<TITLE>Transparent Bullets</TITLE>
</HEAD>
<BODY>
<H2>Making Bullets Transparent</H2>
<DL COMPACT>
<DT><IMG SRC="green.gif">
<DD>Bullet 1
<DT><IMG SRC="yellow.gif">
<DD>Bullet 2
<DT><IMG SRC="blue.gif">
<DD>Bullet 3
<DT><IMG SRC="orange.gif">
<DD>Bullet 4
<DT><IMG SRC="purple.gif">
<DD>Bullet 5
</DL>
<HR>
<DL COMPACT>
<DT><IMG SRC="green2.gif">
<DD>Bullet 1.1
<DT><IMG SRC="yellow2.gif">
```

```
<DD>Bullet 2.1
<DT><IMG SRC="blue2.gif">
<DD>Bullet 3.1
<DT><IMG SRC="orange2.gif">
<DD>Bullet 4.1
<DT><IMG SRC="purple2.gif">
<DD>Bullet 5.1
</DL>
</BODY>
</HTML>
```

How Did the Bullets Get Transparent?

The key is in the image itself. Images that appear transparent are a special type of GIF format: GIF89a. The GIF format comes in two flavors, GIF87a, and GIF89a. The latter has the ability to display transparent images by assigning a color as a background color. You can use LVIEW to open any graphics image, specify a transparent color, and save the image in a GIF89a format. The basic steps are as follows:

1. Open the graphics image in LVIEW.

2. Select Options and click on Background Colors then click the Dropper button. The cursor will change into an eyedropper.

3. Move the eyedropper over the image to the color in the image you want to be transparent and click.

4. Return to Options and click on Background Colors. Everything that is not part of the background color you selected should be masked out in black. (This is the part of the image that will be displayed. The background will be invisible.)

5. Save the file as a GIF89a format GIF file.

Let's use a combination of graphics tools and techniques to enhance the bullets you used previously for lists. The graphical image in Figure 2-36 was created in Adobe Photoshop. It can be found on this book's CD in the \images directory, and is called tball.gif. Using LVIEW, open this image. Note that the background color on this image provides a high contrast to the other colors. This makes selecting the background easier from within LVIEW.

Follow these steps in LVIEW to make tball.gif's background transparent:

1. Select Options and click on Quantizing to turn off dithering, so you're working with solid colors. Next select Options and click on Background Color, and click the Dropper button. The cursor will change to an eyedropper. Move this eyedropper over to the upper left corner of the tball.gif image, away from the ball, and click.

2. Now select Options and click on Background Color again. The ball should be black. The black areas show you all the parts of the graphic that are not part of the background color.

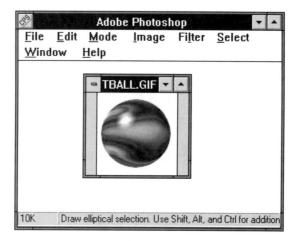

Figure 2-36
tball.gif

3. The last step is to save the image as a GIF89a file. Call it tball2.gif to distinguish it from the unmodified tball.gif.

Open a new file in your editor and enter the following HTML:

```
<HTML>
<HEAD>
<TITLE>Transparency Litmus</TITLE>
</HEAD>
<BODY>
<H2>The Litmus test of transparency</H2>
<IMG SRC="tball.gif" ALIGN="left">
First we'll display our original graphic.
<IMG SRC="tball2.gif" ALIGN="left">
And now the image after it has been processed by LVIEW, selecting the color
white to be transparent.
</BODY>
</HTML>
```

Your results should match Figure 2-37. The square border around the second image, tball2.gif, has disappeared! You can select any color to serve as the background color, and everywhere the background color wends through the image will "drop out," leaving transparent holes in the image.

Interlaced Images

LVIEW has another trick with images to explore before leaving the topic. GIF89a can save images as *interlaced*. Interlacing images creates a shudder effect, with the image being painted on the screen in multiple passes. The resolution gradually gets sharper and sharper until the whole image is resolved. When saving a GIF89a file in LVIEW under Options, there is an entry called Save GIFS Interlaced. To interlace a GIF image, simply check this option before saving the file. Browsers that don't support interlacing will simply display it as usual, ignoring the option.

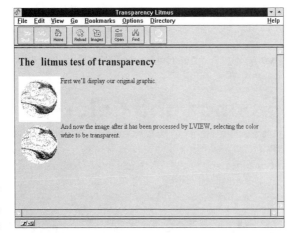

Figure 2-37
Transparent image
on a page

Adding Text to Images

LVIEW, as well as a number of other image editors, can also overlay text onto a graphic. The text can supplement a navigational button; for example you could insert the word "NEXT" under an arrow pointing to the right. Text can be used on toolbars. This function of text-as-graphics can let you use Windows fonts for constructing graphical titles and headers for your page.

Using LVIEW alone, you can construct the following title, displayed in Figure 2-38. When making the background for text transparent, be sure to set Options and click on Quantizing dithering off in LVIEW, or you may end up with a dithered background which, instead of being transparent, will appear like snowy TV reception.

Tips for Creating Rules and Transparent Images

- Rules should be about 560 by 10 pixels.

- Bullets should be 32 by 32 or 24 by 24 pixels.

- Icons are typically 32 by 32 pixels.

- When creating transparent images, be sure dithering is off.

- Be sure to save an image as GIF89a in order to use transparency and/or interlace.

Figure 2-38
A title created in
LVIEW

Select the 16-color Windows palette if you can for speed and size economies.

 Don't assume a particular background color will be used by browsers viewing your page.

Backgrounds and Color

HTML 3.0 added the ability to specify background images, or backdrops, for your Web pages, similar to the function that wallpaper serves on your Windows desktop. Netscape has added additional enhancements to control the color of a page background as well as the color of text and hyperlinks. The attributes controlling these options are specified in the <BODY> tag:

BACKGROUND/COLOR OPTIONS	
<BODY	
BACKGROUND=*"value"*	
BGCOLOR=*"#hex-value"*	NHTML
TEXT=*"#hex-value"*	NHTML
LINK=*"#hex-file"*	NHTML
VLINK=*"#hex-file"*	NHTML
ALINK=*"#hex-file"*	NHTML
>	
BACKGROUND allows an image to be used as a page background.	

The BACKGROUND option is assigned a URL pointing to a JPG or GIF image. For example, the following HTML uses one of the textured backgrounds from Netscape's home page:

```
<BODY BACKGROUND="http://home.netscape.com/home/bg/fabric/gray_fabric.gif">
```

Backgrounds are an easy addition to your Web page, and can produce some polished effects. To experiment with backgrounds, open a new file with your editor and enter the following HTML:

```
<HTML>
<HEAD>
<TITLE>Backgrounds</TITLE>
</HEAD>
<BODY BACKGROUND="http://home.netscape.com/home/bg/fabric/teal_pap.gif">
<H2>Testing Backgrounds</H2>
<HR>
<UL>
<LI>See how a few things look
<LI>With a little texture in another Background
</UL>
<P>This background came from Netscape's Background Page
</BODY>
</HTML>
```

Save your HTML and open it with your browser. You should see something like Figure 2-39, but in full color!

The image teal_pap.gif is 160 by 160 pixels. When an image is used as a background in HTML, it is *tiled* across the page. Tiling copies the image from left to right and top to bottom, filling the page with the pattern. In general you should keep images used for backgrounds small, 64 by 64 up to 180 by 180, in order to speed the download. You also do *not* want to use interlaced GIF files; they slow this tiling down considerably.

Text Colors

Sometimes a texture used for a background can make the text on your Web page difficult to read. Netscape has added several attributes to the <BODY> tag that control the color of text. For example, to change text from its default black to white in the previous example, the following HTML could be used:

```
<HTML>
<HEAD>
<TITLE>Backgrounds</TITLE>
</HEAD>
<BODY BACKGROUND="http://home.netscape.com/home/bg/fabric/teal_pap.gif" TEXT="#ffffff">
<H2>Testing Backgrounds</H2>
<HR>
<UL>
<LI>See how a few things look
<LI>With a little texture in another Background
</UL>
<P>This background came from Netscape's Background Page
</BODY>
</HTML>
```

The results are shown in Figure 2-40.

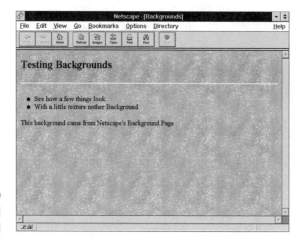

Figure 2-39
Textured
background

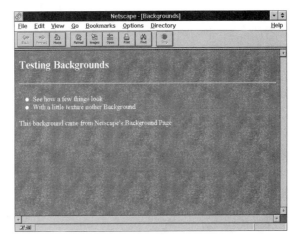

Figure 2-40
Textured
background with
colored text

In the Netscape options, colors are specified with numeric intensities of red, green, and blue. The numeric values for these intensities are in hexadecimal, and range from 0 (0) to 255 (ff in hexadecimal). To specify red, you would use

`#ff0000`

Don't worry, though; you don't need to learn a new number system to use Netscape options. Table 2-5 provides a quick reference for a few common, and some not so common, colors.

Color	Value	Color	Value
White	#ffffff	Aquamarine	#70db93
Green	#00ff00	Blue violet	#9F5F9F
Blue	#0000ff	Bright gold	#d9d919
Magenta	#ff00ff	Dark green	#2f4f2f
Cyan	#00ffff	Dark slate blue	#6b238e
Yellow	#ffff00	Dark turquoise	#7093db
Black	#000000	Dusty rose	#856363

Table 2-4   *Netscape's color options*

Figure 2-41
Selecting color
attributes

Another way to adjust colors is to use the RBG_BAR color utility by Daniel Dewey (see the Installation chapter). Figure 2-41 shows this utility at work. You can select any HTML text option and adjust the colors interactively.

Link Colors

Using Netscape enhancements, you can control the color of the following link text elements in HTML:

 LINK="#hex-value" Controls the colors of the text anchored in hyperlinks.

 VLINK="#hex-value" is the color of a visited hyperlink.

 ALINK="#hex-value" is the color of the active link.

Background Colors

The BGCOLOR="#hex-value" color attribute controls the color of the background screen when a background image is not used, or if images are turned off. If the background image is not loaded, and BGCOLOR is not specified, then the other color attributes (e.g., LINK, VLINK, ALINK) will be ignored.

QUIZ 6

1. Graphical rules are created using which HTML tag?
   a. <HR>
   b. <A>
   c. <IMG>
   d. <DL>

2. What are transparent images?
   a. images the browser cannot display
   b. images with the background color set to gray
   c. images without any color
   d. images with a background color selected as transparent

3. How large is a typical bullet?
   a. 560 by 50 pixels
   b. 640 by 480 pixels
   c. 128 by 128 pixels
   d. 32 by 32 pixels

4. Why would you want to make a background color in a rule transparent?
   a. to make it compatible with Lynx
   b. to make it display faster
   c. in order to use it with <IMG>
   d. if you wanted to use a nonrectangular shape as part of the rule

SESSION 7

IMAGEMAPS

This session covers a more sophisticated way of using images as hyperlinks. Up to now you've used two techniques for linking with images:

 Buttons, with the following syntax:

```
<A HREF="page2.html"><IMG SRC="next.gif"></A>
```

where clicking the inline next.gif image links to page2.html.

 Thumbnails, with the following syntax:

```
<A HREF="jumbo.jpg"><IMG SRC="tiny.jpg"></A>
```

where clicking the inline image tiny.jpg links to the larger jumbo.jpg.

In both cases a user can click anywhere on the picture to activate the link. The next technique you will learn allows you to be more selective; different links will be activated based on where in the image the user clicks. To do this you'll need to define *hotspots*.

Hotspots

Hotspots are regions on an image that activate a link. You can think of buttons and thumbnails as having one large hotspot that covers the entire image. Using imagemaps you can define as hotspots small sections of a larger image.

An image is two dimensional. It has an x axis that goes from left to right, and a y axis that runs from top to bottom. When an image is described as 100 pixels wide by 120 pixels high, that means the x axis runs from 0 to 99 starting from the top left corner, and the y axis, which also starts at the top left corner but runs *down*, goes from 0 to 119. The point at x,y coordinates 50,60 would be a point approximately in the middle of the image. Figure 2-42 illustrates the point.

Don't worry if you've forgotten everything you once knew about geometry; you've just covered about everything you need to know for imagemaps. In fact, you might have already intuited the general idea of imagemaps, which is to describe one or more hotspots, using x,y coordinates, and link these to Web pages. While you can define hotspots as individual x,y points, it would be pretty tedious work. Instead, you can use *shapes* that cover large regions of an image.

Shapes

The following shapes are used in defining hotspots:

 rect   Given x1,x2,y1,y2 coordinates, this shape defines a rectangular region of the image.

Figure 2-42
2D image with x
and y axis displayed

circle   Given x,y,radius coordinates, this defines a circular region.

polygon   Given x1,y1,x2,y2,x3,y3.....x(n),y(n), this defines an irregular region.

Shapes are used in an imagemap file, and not only do they need to coordinate information that defines their regions on the image, they need a URL that is associated with this region as a hyperlink. The syntax for the imagemap file is

IMAGEMAP FILE SYNTAX

shape   *URL*   *coordinates*

    shape is rect, circle, or polygon.
    URL is a valid URL.
    coordinates are the x,y coordinates required by the particular shape.

Building Imagemaps

Let's pull all this together now, and look at what is required to make an image into an imagemap.

1. Create an image file and reference it in your Web page using <IMG> and the ISMAP attribute.

2. Create an imagemap file that describes the hotspots on the image by associating shapes with URLs.

3. Make the <IMG> tag with the ISMAP attribute a link to the imagemap using <A HREF>, similar to the syntax for a button described in Session 4.

To summarize these steps, the imagemap requires an anchor that points to two elements: an image a user can click, and a file linking URLs to different regions of the image. An example of these two elements in a tag is

```
<A HREF="shapes.map"><IMG SRC="atlas.gif" ISMAP></A>
```

The file atlas.gif is the image, and shapes.map is the imagemap file, containing the shapes, coordinates, and URLs.

Examining the Image

Let's go through the procedure above one step at a time, building an imagemap for a tutorial. For the image, copy junk.gif (junk as in ship, not landfill) from the \images directory on this book's CD into a local directory. Open junk.gif with the LVIEW utility and check its dimensions. You should see something like the image in Figure 2-43.

Creating Hotspots

LVIEW displays the dimensions of the image (244 by 147) on its title bar. All of your hotspots will be within these coordinates. You could build these by hand, but the Installation chapter directs you to a nifty utility called Mapedit that will do all the work for you. Close LVIEW and start up Mapedit. Open junk.gif in Mapedit, and specify junk.map for the map file as shown in Figure 2-44.

The Create Type: choice you see in Figure 2-44 controls the format of the map file. In the past these map files were required to reside on the Web server, and the format for the map file varied slightly between NCSA and CERN type servers. NCSA is probably the most widely used, and the one you should choose for this exercise. It is the format of the server you'll be installing on your own PC in Chapter 5.

Now, this brings us to an interesting dilemma. To actually use the imagemaps you are creating in this exercise, you must either have access to a Web server, install your own Web server on your PC, or use an HTML 3.0 feature called client side imagemaps. This session is tailored toward the server option, but you'll learn how to make it a client side imagemap near the end of this session. What you learn for the server will still apply to the client.

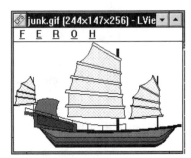

Figure 2-43
Image of a ship

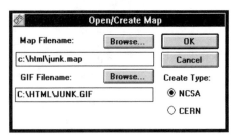

Figure 2-44
Creating hotspots with Mapedit

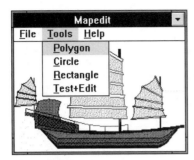

Figure 2-45
Mapedit tools

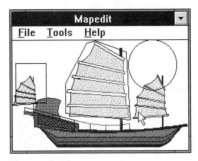

Figure 2-46
Creating a hotspot

Now, back to building the hotspots. Select a shape type from Mapedit's menu (Figure 2-45). Click somewhere on the image as a starting point and drag with the left mouse button to create the shape (Figure 2-46). After you have created the shape, click the right mouse button and you'll be prompted for the URL you want to associate with this region (Figure 2-47). Repeat this procedure for each hotspot you want to create. When you are finished, select the File and click on Default URL option shown in Figure 2-48 to specify what to link to if the user's mouse misses *all* of your hotspots! Now select FileÍSave to save your hotspots in the map file.

Create the following hotspots on the junk image:

- Use a rectangle to define the rudder, and for the URL, enter rudder.htm.

- Use a circle shape to define the crow's nest, and the URL will be crownest.htm.

- Use the polygon shape to define the sail, click on points all around the sail, and then use the right mouse button to close off the shape. Associate this region with sail.htm.

- Set the default to help.htm and save the map.

When you're finished, compare your results with those in the map file below. Don't worry about matching the x,y coordinates, just see if you're in the ballpark.

Figure 2-47
Associating a shape just
created with a URL

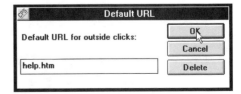

Figure 2-48
Specifying a default link

```
default help.htm
rect rudder.htm 4,30 46,83
circle crownest.htm 195,33 216,60
poly sail.htm 103,3 73,57 73,97 163,106 158,15 115,0
```

Linking the Map and Image

You've defined three hotspots and a default. Much easier than doing it by hand! Now that you've created junk.map, open a new file with your editor and enter the following HTML:

```
<HTML>
<HEAD>
<TITLE>Junker Tutorial</TITLE>
</HEAD>
<BODY>
<H2>A Visual Reference Page</H2>
<HR>
Click on any part of the ship below for a detailed
explanation.<P>
<A HREF="http://nautical.com/cgi-bin/imagemap/~jones/junk.map>
      <IMG SRC="junk.gif" ISMAP></A>
</BODY>
</HTML>
```

The results are displayed in Figure 2-49.
The anchor

```
<A HREF="http://nautical.com/cgi-bin/imagemap/~jones/junk.map>
```

points to the imagemap on the server. The imagemap is in Jones' directory. To get the syntax for this URL you'll need to touch base with whoever is managing your Web server. Just ask him or her what syntax you need to use to point to your imagemap. The rest of the tag,

```
<IMG SRC="junk.gif" ISMAP></A>
```

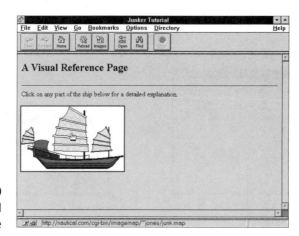

Figure 2-49
The visual
reference page

tells the browser that this is an imagemap, and whenever a user clicks anywhere on this image, to send the x,y coordinates of the click to the server specified in the <A HREF> portion. The server runs a program called imagemap, which matches the click on the image to a shape in the imagemap file in your directory on the server. Whatever URL is associated with the shape the coordinates fall inside of is the link taken by the user. You've completed your imagemap!

If you're using imagemaps on the server, you will also need to copy any HTML files you are linking to to the server as well. You'll also probably need to rename them from the DOS convention of .htm to the Web server's .html filetypes.

Client Side Imagemaps

In Session 1 of this chapter you learned about the <FIG> tag. Its IMAGEMAP option works exactly like that of the <IMG> tag. It sends coordinates to a Web server that matches them to a map file. But the <FIG> tag also allows you to map these hotspots locally, without involving the server. Here's an example of the syntax to do this with the tutorial you created above:

```
<FIG SRC="junk.gif">
<CAPTION>Junker Tutorial</CAPTION>
<P>Select an area of the image that you would like to learn about:
<UL>
<LI><A HREF="help.htm" SHAPE="default">Help</A>
<LI><A HREF="rudder.htm" SHAPE="rect 4,30 46,83">Rudder</A>
<LI><A HREF="crownest.htm" SHAPE="circle 195,33 216,60 ">Crow's
          Nest</A>
<LI><A HREF="sail.htm" SHAPE="poly 103,3 73,57 73,97
          163,106 158,15 115,0">Sail</A>
</UL>
</FIG>
```

And the complete HTML is

```
<HTML>
<HEAD>
<TITLE>Junker Tutorial</TITLE>
</HEAD>
<BODY>
<H2>A Visual Reference Page</H2>
<HR>
Click on any part of the ship below for a detailed
explanation.<P>
<FIG SRC=|junk.gif''>
<CAPTION>Junker Tutorial</CAPTION>
<P>Select an area of the image that you would like to learn about:
<UL>
<LI><A HREF=|help.htm'' SHAPE=|default''>Help</A>
<LI><A HREF=|rudder.htm'' SHAPE=|rect 4,30 46,83''>Rudder</A>
<LI><A HREF=|crownest.htm'' SHAPE=|circle 195,33 216,60 ''>Crow s
```

continued on next page

continued from previous page

```
                Nest</A>
<LI><A HREF=|sail.htm'' SHAPE=|poly 103,3 73,57 73,97
             163,106 158,15 115,0'>Sail</A>
</UL>
</FIG>
</BODY>
</HTML>
```

<FIG> has the added benefit of presenting a text menu of what can be selected from the hotspots if the graphic is not displayed.

Summary

Imagemaps are important tools, not just for visual dictionaries, but also for navigation. They can combine the function of several button bars, offering a graphical navigation "space." An example of this technique is employed on Waite Group's Lobby page, seen in Figure 2-50.

Note too, that this site has a way for text-based browsers to navigate to the same locations with the links below the imagemap.

1. A region that cannot be defined in an image type is a
   a. rectangle
   b. circle
   c. polygon
   d. cube

2. Regions of the image are defined in the
   a. URL
   b. imagemap

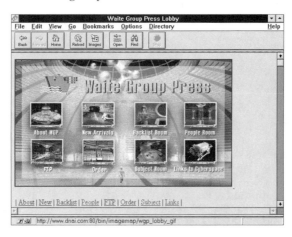

Figure 2-50
Waite Group's
Web site lobby

c. HTML

d. map file

3. The map file is

a. a graphical image of hotspots

b. a program run by the server

c. an option in the <IMG> tag

d. a text file defining regions and associated URLs

4. Which tag below is a valid sample of an imagemap?

a. <A HREF="http://nautical.com/cgi-bin/imagemap/~jones/ship.map"></A>

b. <A HREF="http://nautical.com/cgi-bin/imagemap/~jones/ship.map"><IMG SRC="ship.gif"></A>

c. <A HREF="http://nautical.com/cgi-bin/imagemap/~jones/ship.map"><IMG SRC="ship.gif" ISMAP</A>

d. <A HREF="http://nautical.com/cgibin/imagemap/~jones/ship.map">ship.gif</A>

TEXT TAGS

Tucked away in HTML are several tags whose sole purpose is changing the appearance of text. These tags provide effects such as highlighting, underlining, italics, and others, and they are organized into two broad categories:

 Physical markups

 Logical markups

Physical Markups

Physical markups describe fairly specifically how the text should look. They include the following tags:

PHYSICAL TAG	DESCRIPTION	
<B>...</B>	Bold	
<BIG>...</BIG>	Larger text than normal	NHTML
<SMALL>...</SMALL>	Smaller text than normal	NHTML
_{...}	Subscript	NHTML
^{...}	Superscript	NHTML
<I>...</I>	Italics	
<U>...</U>	Underline	
<TT>...</TT>	Fixed width	

Let's look at how these tags affect text in the sample HTML below. The result is shown in Figure 2-51.

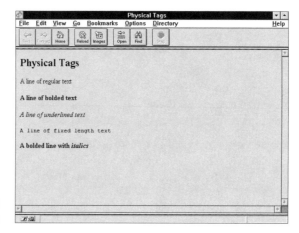

Figure 2-51
Physical tags

```
<HTML>
<HEAD>
<TITLE>Physical Tags</TITLE>
</HEAD>
<BODY>
A line of regular text<P>
<B>A line of bolded text</B>
<I>A line of underlined text</I>
<TT>two lines of fixed length text        tab to here</TT>
<TT>second line of fixed text             tab to here</TT>
<B>A bolded line with <I>italics</I></B>
</BODY>
</HTML>
```

The physical tags in the HTML tell the browser exactly what should be done to the text's appearance. Bold, italics–underline, each of these has a concrete representation on the screen. And while you'll find physical markups are commonly used on Web pages, it's generally preferable to use the next class of tags: logical markups.

Logical Markups

Logical markups are more in keeping with HTML philosophy, which is to be flexible in letting the browser decide the best presentation. To see what this means, note that while the physical tags are fairly explicit, the logical tags below are comparatively abstract:

LOGICAL TAG	DESCRIPTION
<CITE>…</CITE>	Citations
<CODE>…</CODE>	Source code listings
<EM>…</EM>	Emphasized text
<KBD>…</KBD>	Example of keyboard input
<SAMP>…</SAMP>	Literal characters
<STRONG>…</STRONG>	Strong emphasis
<VAR>…</VAR>	Variable name

The logical tags are more concerned with describing the text than with telling the browser how it should be displayed. Let's look at logical tags in various browsers that are all working with the following HTML

```
</HEAD>
<BODY>
<H2>Logical Tags</H2>
A line of regular text<P>
<CITE>Citation Style</CITE><P>
<CODE>Code, e.g. source code style</CODE><P>
<EM>Emphasized Text</EM><P>
<KBD>Text meant to represent keyboard input</KBD><P>
<SAMP>Sample style, e.g. for literal characters</SAMP><P>
<STRONG>Strong Emphasis</STRONG><P>
<VAR>Text to illustrate a variable name</VAR><P>
</BODY>
</HTML>
```

The results are shown on three different browsers in Figures 2-52, 2-53, and 2-54.

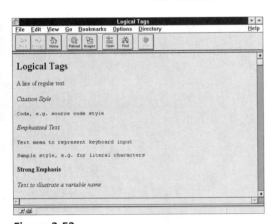

Figure 2-52
Logical styles in Netscape

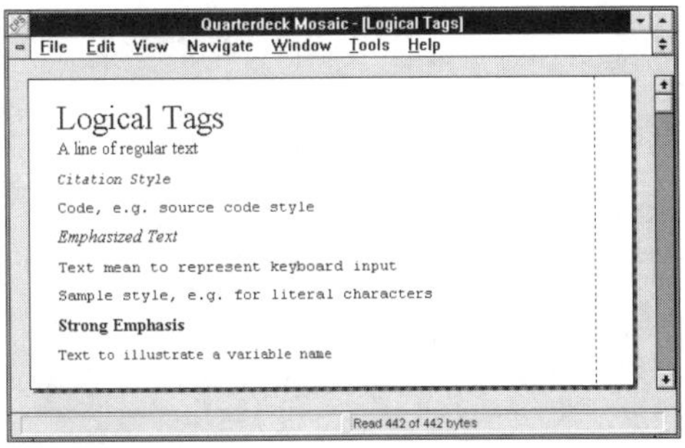

Figure 2-53
Logical styles in QMosiac

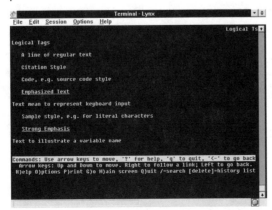

Figure 2-54
Logical styles in
Lynx

Using Text Tags

Most of the logical tags in these examples appear similar to some physical tag, but they can be rendered in other ways as well. The use of logical styles lets meaning be expressed with other forms of output than a display screen. For instance, a Web browser that reads text to the blind might be able to render <STRONG> or emphasized text, but the physical tags for bold or italics would have no meaning. Is italics a whisper, an exclamation, or a gong in the background?

Both physical and logical markups require a beginning and an ending tag. They are designed to be used in most places text is used in HTML: in headers, paragraphs, tables, list items, link anchors, and elsewhere.

Signing Your HTML

Authors sign their work in HTML in various ways. Your personal style or organizational guidelines will determine how you do it, but HTML provides you with several techniques.

Comments

One of the most common ways to sign a page is by using comment tags, the syntax of which was covered in Session 5:

```
<HTML>
<!-- This page was produced 03/01/2043 by -->
<!-- Matthew Lee                          -->
<HEAD>
<TITLE></TITLE>
</HEAD>
<BODY>
</BODY>
</HTML>
```

Using comments, your signature is not visibly on the page (unless users view the HTML source).

<ADDRESS>

A more visible option is to use the <ADDRESS> tag at the bottom of the document. The <ADDRESS> tag has a simple syntax:

THE <ADDRESS> TAG
<ADDRESS>...</ADDRESS>

It can be used as follows:

```
<HTML>
<!-- This page was produced 03/01/2043 by -->
<!-- Matthew Lee                          -->
<HEAD>
<TITLE>Junker Tutorial</TITLE>
</HEAD>
```

```
<BODY>
<H2>A Visual Reference Page</H2>
<HR>
Click on any part of the ship below for a detailed
explanation.<P>
<A HREF="http://nautical.com/cgi-bin/imagemap/~jones/junk.map>
        <IMG SRC="junk.gif" ISMAP></A>
<ADDRESS>Nautical Net Services Manager - info@nautical.net</ADDRESS>
</BODY>
</HTML>
```

This now appears on the page as in Figure 2-55.

mailto

The majority of browsers also support a special URL that a viewer can click to send you e-mail. A URL specifies both a location and a way of getting there. Up to now you've been working with just one type of URL: HTTP. The HTTP URL tells the browser that the method of getting to the resource is via the Web. The *mailto* URL, on the other hand, tells the browser that the method of getting to the location in the address part is to use e-mail. The syntax for this URL is

---

THE MAILTO URL

mailto:*name@e-mail.address*
name@e-mail.address is your Internet e-mail address.

mailto can be used to provide an e-mail hyperlink.

Most browsers have Internet e-mail capabilities built in. When they are configured correctly, this allows them to send e-mail directly to the recipient specified in the mailto when its URL is clicked. For example, you can use mailto with the following type of link:

```
<A HREF="mailto:name@email.address">e-mail me</A> if you want.
```

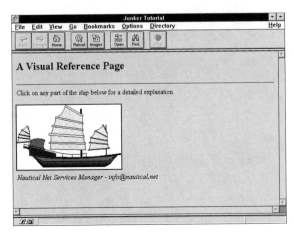

Figure 2-55
Author's signature
on the page

Clicking on the *e-mail me* text will cause the browser to bring up its e-mail interface (Figure 2-56), allowing users to type in a message to you, and in some cases, attach a document. Assuming your e-mail address was lee@nautical.net, you could add the following to your address block:

```
<HTML>
<!-- This page was produced 03/01/2043 by -->
<!-- Matthew Lee                           -->
<HEAD>
<TITLE>Junker Tutorial</TITLE>
</HEAD>
<BODY>
<H2>A Visual Reference Page</H2>
<HR>
Click on any part of the ship below for a detailed
explanation.<P>
<A HREF="http://nautical.com/cgi-bin/imagemap/~jones/junk.map>
        <IMG SRC="junk.gif" ISMAP></A>
<ADDRESS>Nautical Net Services Manager - send email to
        <A HREF="mailto:lee@nautical.net">this address</A></ADDRESS>
</BODY>
</HTML>
```

Let's put all this together in an exercise.

Exercise 8

Your client is Sarah Mangrave, who runs a successful flower company. She's heard about the Web, and when your Aunt Emma told her you were taking this course, she knew you could help her. Sarah wants a page that shows four or five of her flower arrange-

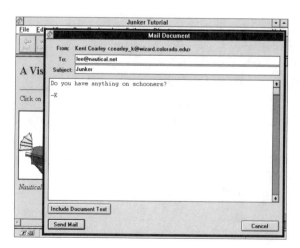

Figure 2-56
E-mail screen in Netscape

ments, along with descriptions. She wants her logo, her mailing address, and fax number on the page, and also she heard you could get e-mail from the Web, so she wants her AOL address on it as well. Use the images in the \images directory on the CD to build her online brochure. Make sure you include the following elements:

- A company page with a flowershop logo (pick any likely logo in the \images directory)

- The company title

- A graphical rule separating the logo and title from the rest of the page

- Four or five flower arrangements, images on the left, text descriptions on the right

- A contact area at the end with her e-mail address: Mangrave@aol.com using a mailto link

Use any backgrounds, colors, etc., that you like from the sessions you've covered so far. Have fun!

 **QUIZ 8**

1. The difference between physical and logical markups is
   a. Physical tags are more versatile.
   b. Logical tags specify exactly what the browser should do.
   c. Physical tags have more options.
   d. Logical tags describe the meaning of the text but not its presentation.

2. A tag generally used to specify the author of a document is
   a. <A>
   b. <CITE>
   c. <ADDRESS>
   d. <HEAD>

3. What would be the effect of the following HTML? <B>This is <I>it</I></B>
   a. The sentence would be bolded.
   b. The sentence would be in italics.
   c. "This is" would be in bold, and "it" would be italics.
   d. "This is" would be in bold, and "it" would be in bold and italics.

4. mailto is used in a
   a. comment block
   b. character tag
   c. logical tag
   d. URL

POWER HTML

POWER HTML

I n this chapter you'll work on two important sections of HTML that separate beginners from the adept: URLs and style. URLs open a host of Internet services to the HTML author. With the proper URL, your pages can access FTP, Gopher, Usenet newsgroups and articles, WAIS servers, LAN documents, and interactive Telnet and TN3270 sessions. And with techniques covered in the style sections, you'll learn a list of do's and don'ts for Web authors, gleaned from the hard-won experience of others. You'll avoid pitfalls and polish design skills on your way to HTML mastery. Get ready though; your first topic, URLs, will unleash your hyperlinks, giving them free rein to much more than HTML pages and files. With URLs you enter the native territories of the Internet itself.

URLS: ADDRESSES ON THE INTERNET

If you've been on the Web more than a week or two, you've run across *URLs*, or Uniform Resource Locators. You've been using URLs in your anchor tags (<A HREF="*url*"...>) to point to other Web pages in the exercises, and you've probably noticed them pop up in the Location field of your browser as you navigate from page to page. Every Web page on the Internet has an address in the form of a URL. In fact, it is becoming common for magazines and TV to drop references to company or individual home pages with URL references like http://www.microsoft.com/welcome.html (which is the actual URL to Microsoft's home page).URLs are like street addresses on the Internet (see Figure 3-1). They tell browsers how to get to a location, and what information to pick up when they get there. Like UPS, Federal Express, and the U.S. Postal Service, different services can get to the same address.

The URL above tells the client to make a World Wide Web connection and pick up an HTML page, but this is only one of several types of URLs.

URL Syntax

URL syntax is as follows:

> **URL SYNTAX**
>
> *method://location/method-specific-information*
> > *method* is the type of Internet service or protocol required to access a resource.
> > *location* is where to find this resource, or where to connect to this service.
> > *method-specific-information* is what you are requesting from the service once you get there. This information often includes local directory paths, filenames, etc.
>
> URLs describe where a resource is on the Internet, and how to retrieve it.

In the URL mentioned above, http://www.microsoft.com/welcome.html,

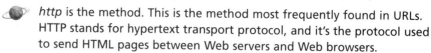

http is the method. This is the method most frequently found in URLs. HTTP stands for hypertext transport protocol, and it's the protocol used to send HTML pages between Web servers and Web browsers.

www.microsoft.com is the location. In this case, it's the Internet domain name of the Web server. As you recall from Chapter 1, Web servers on the Internet are referred to by their domain names or by their TCP/IP (Transmission Control Protocol/Internet Protocol) address (domain names are used to look up the TCP/IP address before connecting).

Figure 3-1
URLs are like street addresses

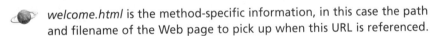 *welcome.html* is the method-specific information, in this case the path and filename of the Web page to pick up when this URL is referenced.

Methods

HTTP is the most popular method, but others include

FTP   File transfer protocol, e.g., access to anonymous FTP sites

File   Local files on your workstation or LAN

News   Usenet News groups and articles

Gopher   Client access to Gopher servers

WAIS   Index searches of WAIS server/databases

Telnet and TN3270   Interactive terminal sessions to hosts

You'll cover these in detail during this chapter. When you finish, your mastery of URLs will give your Web pages enormous power. You will be able to build hyperlinks that download files, connect to interactive services, perform lookups, reference newsgroups and specific articles, and even integrate information on your LAN. Understanding and being able to use the variations of the seven URLs listed above (including HTTP) provides your hyperlinks access to most of the services on the Internet. You'll see how the World Wide Web won a reputation as the great integrator of different technologies. With a knowledge of URLs, and the ability to write HTML, you will be able to exploit a Web browser's capacity to bring all this diversity together on one page.

A natural starting point is to look at the URL you've been using without much fanfare in your authoring to date. By understanding its structure, you'll pick up even more techniques, extending your expertise with this basic link.

HTTP

The syntax for the HTTP URL is

THE HTTP URL

http://*host*[:*port*]/*path*[*?search*]

HTTP URLs reference Web pages on the Internet.

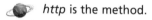 *http* is the method.

 *host* is the domain name of the HTTP server, or the TCP/IP address.

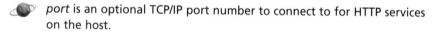 *port* is an optional TCP/IP port number to connect to for HTTP services on the host.

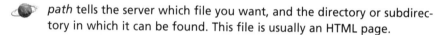 *path* tells the server which file you want, and the directory or subdirectory in which it can be found. This file is usually an HTML page.

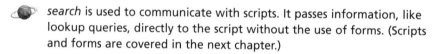 *search* is used to communicate with scripts. It passes information, like lookup queries, directly to the script without the use of forms. (Scripts and forms are covered in the next chapter.)

Paths

The path needs some explanation. Usually a path is just like a filename path on UNIX or DOS, with the subdirectories separated with a "/" (instead of the DOS "\" backslash). If the document on the server was in the accounting/payroll directory, and called tax.html, the path would be

```
accounting/payroll/tax.html
```

If the URL path ends in a trailing "/", the Web server will try to open a "default" document. This default varies with the type of Web server accessed, but it's usually one of the following filenames:

```
index.html, default.html, home.html, homepage.html
```

On some Web servers, if one of these default documents is not found, it will return a listing of all the files in the directory of the path used in the URL.

Path statements can go even further than referencing a page; they can also reference named anchors within the page. For example:

```
http://www.microsoft.com/test/docs/beta.html#Win98
```

refers to the page beta.html in directory test/docs/, and positions the browser at the anchor

```
<A NAME="Win98">Win 98 Beta Test Agreement</A>
```

that appears in the HTML. This can be a useful shortcut. With it, your link dives right into a specific segment of a large HTML document, so users see the relevant text immediately. The alternative, just linking to the document, leaves it up to the user to find the needle of relevance in a potential haystack of text.

Search

Another shortcut with the HTTP URL is to use the optional search syntax. For example, in Figure 3-2, the page written by David Koblas tracks foreign currency rates and displays various countries' currencies relative to the country you select.

Notice that in the Location field of the Netscape browser, this page's URL contains the search selector and a keyword requesting currencies relative to the American dollar. If you wanted to use a URL to this page, but one that shows currencies relative to the Japanese yen, you could change the search key and build a link as follows:

```
<A HREF="http://gnn.com/cgi-bin/gnn/currency?Japan">Currency Rates...Based on
Japanese Yen</A>
```

Results from using this URL with the new search syntax are shown in Figure 3-3. Whenever you see the search syntax in a URL, your browser is interacting with a *script*. It is the script that generates the HTML for the Web page you see displayed. A URL's ability to reference scripts enables more dynamic information to be returned, information that requires up-to-the-minute updates, such as currency exchange rates, weather reports, stock market prices, and so on. Using scripts, even static information can be tailored to user preferences or reading patterns. In Chapter 4 you'll see how to build these dynamic documents, but for now, just the syntax of the URL is key.

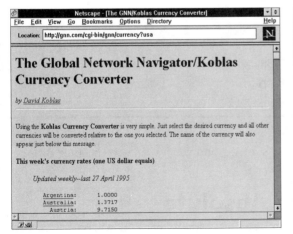

Figure 3-2
The Koblas Currency Converter

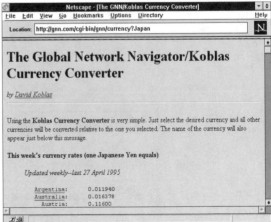

Figure 3-3
The Koblas Currency Converter, based on Japanese yen

Protected Characters

Search arguments bring up another issue. Sometimes you'll need to use search text with embedded spaces, like the one that appears in "South America." In a URL, there are sets of characters that are deemed "safe," and others that are "unsafe." This is because gateways and servers that the URL is filtered through might trip over spaces and funny characters that aren't part of their typical fare of vanilla text. And a space is unfortunately one of these "unsafe" characters. This doesn't mean you can't use it; it just means you have to represent it in another way. Unsafe characters can be used in URLs by encoding them with the escape sequence "%-*hexadecimal-value*". Table 3-1 shows a list of unsafe characters and their coding equivalents. So "South America", properly constructed in a search option, would look like this:

```
?South%20America
```

Character	Encoding
SPACE	%20
<	%3C
>	%3E
#	%23
%	%25
{	%7B
}	%7D
		%7C
\	%74
^	%5E
~	%7E
[	%5B
]	%5D
`	%60

Table 3-1 *URL protected character encoding*

Gopher URLs frequently use searches, and you'll use these encoding methods later this chapter in Gopher retrievals.

Relative Versus Absolute

You will often see HTTP URLs in Web pages with the following syntax:

```
<A HREF="test.html">Link to Test</A>
```

This lacks elements such as method and path, covered above. Why does it still work?

It works because the browser recognizes it as a "relative" URL, and fills in several defaults based on the page it just opened containing this hyperlink. Let's explore how this works with an example. The relative URL above has been included in the following HTML

```
<HTML>
<HEAD>
<TITLE>When Does Relative Become Absolute?</TITLE>
</HEAD>
<BODY>
This is a <A HREF="test.html">Link to Test</A>.
</BODY>
</HTML>
```

If this page was accessed by opening your browser to

`http://www.einstein.org/~albert/main.html`

when you clicked the *Link to Test* anchor, your browser would use http://www.einstein.org/~albert/ as the method, location, and path, and tack on the only clue you provided it: *test.html*, to produce an "absolute" link to

`http://www.einstein.org/~albert/test.html`

This all happens automatically. You can also tell the browser explicitly what to use for these defaults with the <BASE> tag.

<BASE>

The syntax for the <BASE> tag is

THE <BASE> TAG

<BASE HREF="*url*">
The BASE tag provides explicit defaults for relative URLs.

The <BASE> tag is found in the header section of your HTML document. For example:

```
<HTML>
<HEAD>
<TITLE>Home Base</TITLE>
<BASE HREF="http://www.einstein.org/~albert">
</HEAD>
```

In this HTML, all relative URLs are resolved using the value in the <BASE HREF> option. This could be useful if, for some reason, you didn't want to let the relative URLs default—say, for instance, if you copied this page from another server, and all its links were still in the other location.

Relative URLs are useful in your HTML to make your pages portable. If you hard-code the location and pathnames with absolute URLs, you will have to change all of your HTML if you move the pages from one directory, or from one platform, to another. With relative URLs you can just copy all the related files into the new hosts and/or directories.

Quiz 1

1. Which of the following is not a correct URL for HTTP?
   a. http://www.test.com/
   b. http://www.test.com/find?rates
   c. http://test.html
   d. http://www.test.com/test.html

2. Which URL below is an example of a "relative" URL?
   a. http://www.test.com/
   b. http://test.html
   c. test.html
   d. http://www.test.com/test.html

3. Relative URLs are used to
   a. provide the exact address of a Web page
   b. make Web pages more portable
   c. provide links to non-HTTP URLs
   d. provide links to documents related to the original

4. If you wanted to pass the search string "dogs and cats" with a URL referencing a search form, an example of correct syntax would be
   a. http://www.quiz.com/search?dogs and cats
   b. http://www.quiz.com/search?"dogs and cats"
   c. http://www.quiz.com/search?dogs_and_cats
   d. http://www.quiz.com/search?dogs%20and%20cats

Session 2

URLS FOR FTP, FILES, AND NEWS

The next three URLs are used to retrieve files from FTP servers, access local documents and directories off your PC drives or LAN, and retrieve groups and articles from Usenet News servers.

Accessing FTP Resources

FTP stands for file transfer protocol. It is commonly used on the Internet to copy files from one computer to another. FTP, like many Internet services, requires two parties: a client and a server. Before the Web wove its magical integration on the Internet, it was necessary to have a separate program on your PC just to do FTP. This FTP client would connect to FTP servers on the network to download or upload files. The files could be binary, as in the case of spreadsheets, word processing documents, etc., or they could be ASCII (plain text). Starting with Mosaic, Web browsers began to build in the FTP client's functionality. A Web browser, acting as an FTP client, can copy files directly from FTP servers. Often these servers have large repositories of data: shareware and freeware programs, documentation, games, and graphics. All the Web browser needs to access these files on an FTP server is a special URL. Once you understand the URL, you can tap into FTP servers as huge storage banks for your own purposes.

The syntax for the FTP URL is

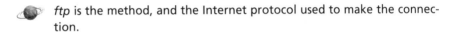

THE FTP URL

ftp://[user:password@]host[:port]/cwd1/cwd2/.../cwd3/filename[;type=option]

FTP URLs reference files and directories in FTP servers on the Internet.

- *ftp* is the method, and the Internet protocol used to make the connection.

- *user:password@* is an optional username and password used to log in via FTP. If blank, user defaults to "anonymous" and password defaults to your e-mail address. These defaults get you into most anonymous FTP sites on the Internet.

- *host* is the domain name of the FTP server, or the TCP/IP address.

- *port* is an optional TCP/IP port number to connect to for FTP services on the host.

- *cwd* is a series of 0 or more change directory commands. Superficially this may resemble the actual pathname of the file, but keep in mind that it is a sequence of directory commands that climbs down directory levels until it gets to the place the file is located.

- *filename* is the file to be retrieved using FTP.

- *type=option* specifies the type of transfer, and *option* can be "binary" or "ASCII". This option may not work, depending on your browser. When it is not specified, the filetype of the file is used to determine whether to retrieve the file in binary or ASCII mode.

An example of an FTP URL used in a hyperlink is

```
<A HREF="ftp://ftp.wuarchives.com/windows/bitmaps/x.bmp">To download the x bitmap,
click here.</A>
```

What your Web browser does when this link is activated depends on its filetype in the URL. If the filetype were .html" instead of .bmp in the example above, your browser would actually load it as a Web page! It may seem kind of strange to use FTP to link to Web pages, but some sites still use this technique. If they don't have a Web server, they can still provide Web pages using the older FTP protocol. In the case above, however, the filetype is recognized by the browser as a graphics file, and if a helper application is configured for BMP filetypes, the file will be displayed. Otherwise your browser will prompt you for a location to save x.bmp to disk.

A popular way of designating a host computer as an FTP server is to name it something starting with "ftp", much as "www" is commonly used to designate Web servers. The example URL above directs the browser to open an FTP session to ftp.wuarchives.com, then change directories from the default to /windows and then to /bitmaps. The URL then specifies a file, x.bmp, which your Web browser downloads as a binary file.

Note that no username and password were specified. ftp.wuarchives.com is one of those large shareware repositories mentioned above. It contains thousands of files, and offers these to Internet users logging in as "anonymous" and providing an e-mail address as a password. Other FTP servers, especially those internal to a company, will probably not allow anonymous logins (or will allow them only to users on its own local network.)

FTP Transfers

One reason for FTP's popularity is its guaranteed, 100 percent reliable file delivery. If you retrieve a file from an FTP server, and the transfer completes successfully, you typically don't have to worry about data being scrambled or "bits" being lost. FTP is built on network layers that ensure that you get what you asked for.

This is not to say that you will never end up with a file that is garbage. The culprit in this case is usually a file being transferred as ASCII when it is not really "plain text." This is a sure way to make a spreadsheet or word processing file unreadable. Most browsers do adequate jobs of matching the filetype with either ASCII or binary mode transfers. The type= option of the URL goes a step further, and lets you specify the correct mode even if the browser can't figure it out. Unfortunately, some browsers get confused when "type" is specified.

FTP or HTTP?

You can also use HTTP to transfer files. Here's the last example using HTTP instead of FTP:

```
<A HREF="http://www.wuarchives.com/windows/bitmaps/x.bmp">To Download the x bitmap,
click here..</A>
```

This assumes a Web server is running on www.wuarchives.com. If so, the file x.bmp is transferred using the HTTP protocol instead of FTP. The current version of the HTTP protocol is not as efficient as FTP for large file transfers, but it is just as reliable.

And on the flip side, you can use FTP URLs in places you may be accustomed to only using HTTP. In the <IMG> tag, this example:

```
<IMG SRC="ftp://ftp.graphics.com/image.gif" ALT="Logo">
```

picks up the inline image for a Web page using anonymous FTP from the FTP server at ftp.graphics.com.

Another example of FTP in place of HTTP was mentioned earlier, but not really elaborated on –the case of a service provider that offers FTP, but not personal home pages. You can work around this by placing Web pages in a directory accessible to the FTP server and using hyperlinks like:

```
<A HREF="ftp://ftp.wonk.com/user/joes.html">Link to Webless Job</A>
```

You can even use relative URLs in this page to reference other pages in the same FTP directory:

```
<IMG SRC="my.gif" ALT="Welcome to Joe's Webless Page!">
```

When a Web browser opens the page at ftp://ftp.wonk.com, it will resolve any relative URLs in the page using FTP as the default method, ftp.wonk.com as the address, and /user as the directory. This allows the Web browser to pick up the image my.gif in the example above using FTP. All this may or may not be practical—the point is to demonstrate some of the flexibility of URLs in seamlessly weaving together various Internet protocols.

While the FTP URL allows for username and password, this option should be avoided. If you put an FTP URL in your Web page with username and password, it doesn't even require a hacker to view the source and glean a valid login to your system.

EXERCISE 2

The FTP URL can be used to turn your Web browser into a friendly interface for browsing through anonymous FTP sites. Here are a few popular FTP sites on the Internet:

- ftp.wustl.edu
- dftnic.gsfc.nasa.gov
- ftp.sunet.se
- ftp.netcom.com

Construct FTP URLs to browse each of these sites and open them in your Web browser to see what happens. You don't need to build a page with a hyperlink, just open the URL with your browser's Open Location option. Using some of the sites above, find a directory of GIF images and note the location. Place one of the images in a Web page as an inline image.

For example, open ftp://dftnic.gsfc.nasa.gov and point and click your way to the following file:

```
/images/gifs/astronomy/andromeda.gif
```

Now put the complete FTP URL into an <IMG> tag:

```
<IMG SRC="ftp://dftnic.gsfc.nasa.gov/images
/gifs/astronomy/andromeda.gif">
```

The two URLs you've covered up to now are designed to access resources on the Internet. What if all you have, or need, is a local PC or a LAN that is not connected to any network? The next URL might just fit the bill.

Local Files

The File URL allows you to reference pages on your PC's disk. You've been doing this implicitly for the exercises. When you use the Open File command in your browser menu, rather than the Open Location command, you are actually opening a File URL. In fact, you could plug the File URL syntax into Open Location and it would produce the same effect as Open File. File URLs have the following syntax:

THE FILE URL
file:/*path*/*filename*

File URLs reference files and directories on local PCs or LANs.

 file is the method.

 path is the directory path. Unlike FTP, this is not a series of change directory commands (although it might have the same effect), this is an actual file path.

 filename is the name of the file.

For example, to specify a file on your local PC's C: drive in a hyperlink, enter

```
<A HREF="file:/c:\html\test.htm">Test link to local disk</A>
```

Relative links will also work from this page. If a link in test.htm above, refers to

```
<A HREF="next.htm">Next Page</A>
```

The browser will look for next.htm under the c:\html directory. Note that this URL is different from the last URLs in a couple of ways. Only one "/" follows the method. The path is specified with the local file conventions; in DOS these are backslashes "\" instead of the UNIX forward slash "/" convention (although most browsers will accept either variant for DOS files).

LAN Pages

Using the same syntax, you can also refer to paths on your *LAN*. LANs, or Local Area Networks, typically map network drives to regular drive letters on your PC like M: and N:. A file on the LAN can be accessed on your PC by using this drive letter, a directory, and the filename. For example, a departmental schedule called work.gif might be on the M: drive under \schedule and be referenced with

```
M:\SCHEDULE\WORK.PRJ
```

This file could be accessed by anyone in your department, but probably not by anyone from the Internet. The "local" in LAN implies a limited clientele.

Web pages on your LAN are referenced using the File URL. A Web page called billing.htm in the same directory could be referenced as

```
file:/m:\schedule\billing.htm
```

The File URL can contain relative links to pages in the same directory just as HTTP and FTP URLs can.

Tactical Uses for LAN-Based Web Pages

LANs can be used to host Web pages for companies without Internet connections. But even companies with Internet links can benefit from LAN-based Web pages. A local home page on a network drive will load extremely quickly compared to even high-speed links to pages on the Internet. This access speed can be leveraged by using File URLs to point to other types of PC documents, bringing them all into a Web page menu. If you have a lot of word processing documents, spreadsheets, or even "canned" queries to a database used by some common application, you can link to all these files from your LAN page. With the proper helper applications configured, users can rapidly find documentation, and browsers can automatically activate the appropriate application to read it. The Web browser in this case serves as a type of shell to pull together a number of separate formats, much as it does on the Internet, but this time closer to home.

Another useful technique is to point all departmental users of a LAN to an internal page on the LAN with the File URL. This page, in turn, can have hyperlinks out onto the Internet. Users outside of the local LAN do not have access to the internal home page, which results in a simple but effective security mechanism.

But now let's turn attention back to the Internet at large, to a dynamic, voluminous info-expanse called Usenet News.

News URL

Usenet News, like FTP, consists of clients and servers. News clients read *articles* from the server, and articles are organized under topics called *newsgroups*. The articles in Usenet News are not the type of articles you find in conventional newspapers, despite the similarity of their names. Usenet News articles are *posted* by users with News client software, often in response to what other users have posted. It's like an extended dialog organized under topic areas called newsgroups. Usenet News *servers* collect all the articles posted by the News clients and forward them to other Usenet servers across the Internet so everyone reading a newsgroup sees more or less the same set of articles. Each newsgroup, of which there are thousands, has an average reader base of about ten thousand users.

As they do for FTP, most Web browsers have integrated News clients that can read articles from News servers. As they don't for FTP, some browsers also allow you to post to, or update, these servers. Now that you know the two fundamental entities of Usenet News, newsgroups and articles, it's time to introduce the News URL syntax:

THE USENET NEWS URL

news:*newsgroup*
news:*article-id*

News URLs refers to newsgroups or specific articles on Usenet News servers.

For these URLs to work, you will need to have a new server configured in your browser. In Netscape this is part of the Options and click on Preferences and click on Mail and News menu. Typically this must be configured to point to a News server offered by your Internet provider or organization.

The News URL comes in two varieties. The first, news:*newsgroup*, connects your browser to the entire newsgroup, which may be useful to advertise a source of information about a broad topic. For example:

```
<A HREF="news:comp.infosystems.www.announce">Web Announcements</A>
```

links you to discussions about the latest announcements on the Web.

The News client on the Web browser doesn't work as seamlessly as the FTP client. Try opening the URL above in your Web browser and see what happens. You don't need to use the anchor, just open the following location:

```
news:comp.infosystems.www.announce
```

Make sure your News server is configured before you try this. Compare your results with Figure 3-4.

Note the status line at the bottom of the screen. The cursor in the window is over an article announcing "PERSONAL: Bevelizer - 3D GIF Button Maker" and the article-id is shown in the status bar in Netscape as news:420bri$35a@holly.aa.net. This is an example of the second type of the News URL, news:*article-id*. If you open this URL, your browser will load this specific article rather than listing the article in the newsgroup. An example is shown in Figure 3-5. Try opening one of the articles listed in the newsgroup experiment you did above. Remember, you'll have to position the cursor over the article anchor to see the actual id. You can, of course, just click on the article, but that would be cheating.

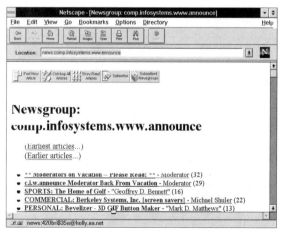

Figure 3-4

Netscape showing newsgroup
comp.infosystems.www.announce

Figure 3-5

Netscape opening a news:*article-id* URL

You'll want to exercise some caution linking directly to articles in your Web pages. Old articles "roll off" of the News server very quickly, and pointers to articles that are more than a week old will probably link off into the ozone.

Local News?

News servers can also be set up locally, and don't necessarily have to participate with other Internet News servers. Local News servers can be used to create your own internal News groups. Since many Web browsers have fully functional News clients, allowing users to read and post messages, this is an easy way to make a "collaborative" application. You can create your own newsgroups centered around projects or special interests. For an example of this, check out what Netscape has done with private newsgroups from their home page.

Setting up a News server is beyond the scope of this section (and book!), but News servers can be obtained free over the Internet, and many of the books on setting up Internet services have sections on installing and configuring Usenet News. Food for thought.

Well, FTP, File, and News haven't yet exhausted the possibilities of the URL tag. In Session 3 you'll cover Gopher, Telnet/TN3270, and WAIS. After that, you will have pulled about everything the Internet has to offer into your hyperlinks.

1. FTP URLs used in HTML on the Web typically do not use the optional user-name password because
   a. It is not supported by some clients.
   b. It is server specific.
   c. It exposes the username and password access to a server.
   d. It is invalid.

2. Unlike HTTP, FTP URLs
   a. can download files
   b. can be used in <IMG> tags
   c. can be used as graphical rules
   d. can be used to access non-Web servers

3. In a File URL
   a. You cannot use relative links.
   b. You can access network drives.
   c. You cannot use images.
   d. You require a host name.

4. A client knows where the News server is when it links via a News URL because
   a. It is specified in the URL.
   b. It is relative to where the URL was accessed.
   c. It is configured in the browser.
   d. There is only one News server on the Internet.

GOPHER, WAIS, AND TELNET

Gopher was the predecessor of the Web in many ways, and Gopher servers still contain large quantities of useful data. Gopher archives are usually indexed for text retrieval, and you will learn how to access and search Gopher servers with a new URL.

WAIS (pronounced "ways"), or Wide Area Information Servers, is another indexed database of information spread across the Internet. These servers can be a little trickier to access, and you'll learn techniques for using Web gateways and helper applications to get what you need.

Telnet will bring up the rear as arguably one of the oldest interactive protocols on the Internet, and you'll use its URL to connect to hosts on the Internet as a terminal.

Gopher

About two to three years BW (before the Web), Gopher was one of the hottest services on the Internet. Structurally, Gopher is much like the Web, with Gopher clients that browse Gopher servers for information. Organizationally, however, Gopher is quite different. Gopher servers make plain-text documents available through hierarchical menus. This provides a way to control complexity and make navigation easy, especially for classes of information that fall naturally into hierarchies, like corporate policies and procedures, manuals, organizational guidelines, etc. Items in a directory could be files or links to other Gopher servers. It sounds kind of like hypertext, but the links are not embedded in the text of the documents. In Gopher the links are outside the text, in the menu hierarchies.

Gopher evolved into Gopher+, which provides a rudimentary capability for handling forms and accessing different versions of the same document, based on what the client platform can support.

Gopher and Gopher+ servers were (and are) used to store large text repositories, primarily because text indexing was built into Gopher. Using its indexes, Gopher allows keyword and Boolean searches to be done on any part of the Gopher directory tree. Gopher clients bring up the documents with the keyword or phrase of the search highlighted.

It's important to understand Gopher's development in order to understand how you can use its services from the Web. Large amounts of data are stashed in Gopher sites, and you can pull this information into Web pages, leveraging the utility of Gopher's text-search capabilities with the Gopher URL. The URL has the following syntax:

THE GOPHER URL

gopher://host[:port]/resource-type/[gopher-selector-string]

Gopher URLs access documents, menus, and search forms on Gopher servers.

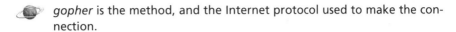 *gopher* is the method, and the Internet protocol used to make the connection.

host is the domain name of the Gopher server, or the TCP/IP address.

port is an optional TCP/IP port number to connect to for HTTP services on the host.

resource-type is a single character field specifying the type of Gopher resource being accessed. Some of the more useful Gopher resources include

Type code	Description
0	Text file
1	Directory
7	Indexed query
h	HTML file(!)

Gopher-selector-string is the document name or query string, depending on the resource type specified. This field is blank if the resource type is a directory(1).

Let's put the URL to use. For this exercise you'll need to be connected to the Internet. Once you're connected, open the following URL from your browser's Open Location menu:

```
gopher://gopher.senate.gov/1
```

This is the most basic link to the top directory of the Gopher server at gopher.senate.gov. Your Web browser screen should look similar to what's shown in Figure 3-6.

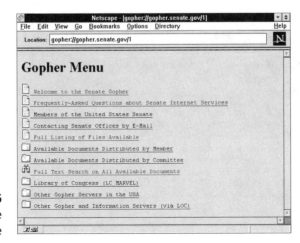

Figure 3-6
Gopher link to the
top of the tree

Note that your Web browser is acting as if it were a Gopher client. If you click on any of the menu levels, you "walk" down the hierarchy of the directory, just as if you were a bona fide Gopher client.

This Gopher site appears to have been set up to publish results of various senatorial committees. Click on the Full Text Search link and enter "web" when prompted for the search phrase. Your results will vary, but your browser screen should look similar to Figure 3-7. You've just done an indexed search using Gopher.

Look closely at the Location box on the Netscape browser screen and you'll discover the URL used to perform this search. Also note a common artifact in Gopher URLs: the selector string frequently duplicates the resource type. You don't have to duplicate this when you are constructing the URL for your Web page. For example, to hardcode a search for "UFO" in the senatorial reports, so you could just click on this in your Web page for an up-to-the-minute report on recent activity, you could use the URL used for the "web" search above, substituting "ufo" as the search string. Try this by opening the following URL:

```
gopher://ftp.senate.gov:/7g/search?ufo
```

The optional port (70) was removed from the URL above, and the extra "7" in the resource type was dropped. Other than that, it is the same URL that appeared in Figure 3-7. To make this search into a hypertext link on a Web page, you could use the following syntax:

```
<A HREF="gopher://ftp.senate.gov:/7g/search?ufo">Recent Senate UFO info</A>
```

If you wanted to make the search a little more sophisticated, say, instead of tracking the illusive UFOs, you wanted to track the equally evanescent Social Security, you would need to be a little trickier. Since you have a space between the keywords, and a space is one of those "unsafe" characters in a URL, you need to use its encoded equivalent shown back in Table 3-1. To practice safe queries, open the following URL in your browser:

```
gopher://ftp.senate.gov/7g/search?social%20security
```

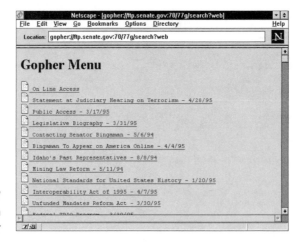

Figure 3-7
Searching with
Gopher

The space is encoded as %20. The search returns links to all the documents containing the phrase "social security". Click on any one of them to read the document. You'll note that most Web browsers will not highlight the search keywords in the text as the Gopher browsers do. As a workaround, in Netscape you can use the Edit and click on Find (or simply Ctrl-F) to search within the document for the keywords used in the query.

One document turned up in both queries:

```
Independence For Social Security
```

Here is the paragraph that Netscape's Find located:

```
Social Security system has declined to the point where a recent
survey of 18- to 34-year-olds revealed that 46 percent of
respondents believed in UFO's, while only 28 percent believed their
Social Security will be there when they retire.
```

There it is: the hidden link between Social Security and UFOs.

WAIS

WAIS offers search and retrieval of text data, but it is very different from Gopher and the URLs covered so far. Up to now, the URLs you've encountered have been supported by the Web browser itself. To use WAIS URLs, however, requires most Web browsers to use special gateways.

WAIS stands for Wide Area Information Servers, and it is trademarked by WAIS, Inc. WAIS evolved on the Internet as a powerful index and search application. With WAIS it is possible to do full word indexes on a variety of data types, including multimedia and HTML, and query this data with powerful combinations of "natural" language and Boolean terms. Results from WAIS searches come back ranked by relevancy to your query from 1 (low) to 1,000 (high). Whether a document is relevant to your query is assessed by criteria like the number of times your keyword was found in the document, whether it was found in an important place (like a paragraph heading or a title), etc. You can also tell WAIS, "this document is kind of like what I'm looking for," and it goes back to work using that document and your criteria to hone the results further.

All this power does not come cheap. WAIS is relatively complex to install and maintain, and it is more integrated with Gopher than the World Wide Web. Still, large databases exist on the Net indexed with WAIS, and they can be accessed with a little finesse with browsers such as Netscape.

The WAIS URL has the following syntax:

THE WAIS URL

wais://host[:port]/database[?search]

WAIS URLs search WAIS databases, typically through Web gateways.

---

 wais is the method, and the Internet protocol used to make the connection. Be forewarned, most Web browsers will squawk if you try to connect directly with this URL. More on this below.

- *host* is the domain name of the WAIS server, or the TCP/IP address.

- *port* is an optional TCP/IP port number to connect to for HTTP services on the host.

- *database* is the WAIS database to be searched.

- *?search* is the literal "?" followed by the WAIS search string.

Most Web browsers will need to access WAIS databases through special gateways that translate Web to WAIS and back again when the results are obtained. One of these gateways is run by WAIS, Inc., at http://www.wais.com/. Open this URL in your Web browser, and select their Directory of Servers. You should see something similar to Figure 3-8. From here you can search the list of WAIS servers that might handle a given topic.

Let's try a search on databases that maintain information on Aborigines. Scroll down the page to the search prompt and enter "aborigines". This searches for WAIS servers that have information on this topic. Figure 3-9 shows the search screen, and Figure 3-10 the results of your query. Note the small check boxes beside the search results. Checking one of these tells WAIS to use this document, along with the keyword(s), to narrow your search further. Play around with these searches for a while until you get the hang of it.

WAIS provides a gateway to search a set of WAIS servers, eliminating the need to use the WAIS URL. It is possible that future browsers may incorporate WAIS client capabilities; then you could use the URL directly. But, it's hard to predict whether the Web will support WAIS' early popularity the way Gopher did. Several Web indexing solutions stand in direct competition to this venerable workhorse. Some will be covered in greater detail in Chapter 6, when you look into building your own indexing solutions. In the interim, let's wrap up the URL tour with the next topic.

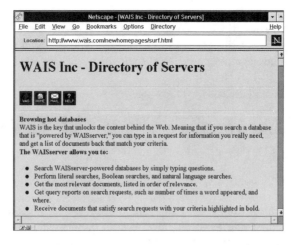

Figure 3-8
The WAIS gateway

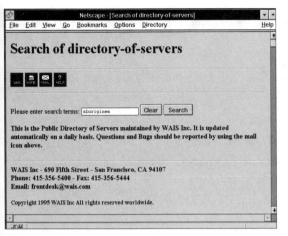

Figure 3-9
WAIS search for servers

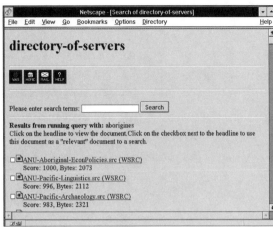

Figure 3-10
WAIS servers with information about Aborigines

Telnet and TN3270

Telnet is a protocol used to connect terminals to servers. It provides access to a host of character-based, interactive services. In the old days it was popular and economical to use dumb terminals to connect via Telnet to smart servers shared by multiple users. TN3270 is a variant of Telnet generally used to connect to IBM mainframes (3270 is a common class of terminals used by these mainframes), and the same strategy applied.

Telnet and TN3270 are supported by most browsers in a sort of hybrid way. Netscape provides a good example. Look in Netscape's Options and click on Preferences menu, under Applications and Directories. You'll note a field for a Telnet application and one for a TN3270 application. Entering the name of your Telnet and TN3270 client executable will allow Netscape to use these URLs. Once these fields are configured, activating Telnet or TN3270 URLs launches the application with a destination, and optionally a username and password.

Many organizations find themselves straddling several islands of information. Depending on when in the company's life cycle a project is initiated seems to dictate what type of server it ends up on. A surprising amount of useful information is still locked in the recesses of the mainframe, and is still accessed daily with interactive terminal sessions. HTML may be useful in folding these into one port of entry, allowing at least a common menu to a company's disparate services. Telnet and TN3270 URLs can also be used by help desks and other places in an organization where a single menu to separate resources can be helpful.

The Telnet and TN3270 URLs have the following syntax:

TELNET AND TN3270 URLS

telnet://[user][:password]@host[:port]
tn3270://[user][:password]@host[:port]

Telnet and TN3270 URLs connect interactively to host computers.

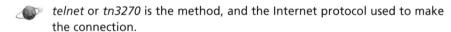 *telnet* or *tn3270* is the method, and the Internet protocol used to make the connection.

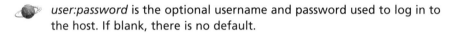 *user:password* is the optional username and password used to log in to the host. If blank, there is no default.

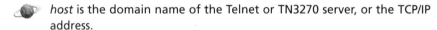 *host* is the domain name of the Telnet or TN3270 server, or the TCP/IP address.

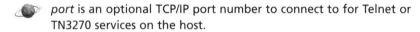 *port* is an optional TCP/IP port number to connect to for Telnet or TN3270 services on the host.

There are still surprisingly numerous Telnet resources on the Internet. One hypertext archive of Telnet resources can be found by opening the following URL:

```
http://www.einet.net/hytelnet/START.TXT.html
```

Figure 3-11 shows what should be displayed in your browser. These links have been organized by a program called HYTELNET, which maintains pointers to the vast majority of Telnet-accessible resources. If you follow the links down a few levels, you will bottom out on a Telnet or TN3270 URL. Clicking this will activate your Telnet or TN3270 client application and connect you with a server. The HYTELNET screens do a good job of telling you what username to use to log in when prompted, and what the general menus will look like on the service you are connecting to. Figure 3-12 shows a Telnet session to a campus information system at Columbia University. You probably won't end up at Figure 3-12, but follow the links from the page in Figure 3-11 down to the point you actually connect to a server before continuing.

When you connect to an interactive server using either of these URLs, you will no longer be looking at this information with your Web browser. Instead, a Telnet application will take over the screen to connect to the service. When you disconnect, and close the Telnet application, you return to the Web browser.

Businesses with corporate information on mainframe computers can usually "script" these Telnet connections, forcing them to go to a particular screen in an application (and nowhere else!). This could be very useful for an organization's Web page, offering news and bulletins, perhaps about availability and downtimes, all folded into the same page with other corporate info.

Sometimes services like WAIS and Gopher are offered via Telnet. This provides another technique for accessing WAIS through Telnet using a Web browser. Of course, the more of these "translations" you go through, the less likely you will be to emerge unscathed. It's usually better to keep it simple and direct; nevertheless, you'll seldom find that an Internet service cannot be accessed through some means, however twisted, via the Web.

Figure 3-11
Telnet services on the Internet

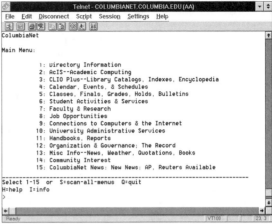

Figure 3-12
A campuswide information system via Telnet

What's in a Name?

URLs might seem innocuous enough, but beneath their surface brews an irksome issue. The URL syntax is a type of addressing scheme. Part of its syntax defines where to go to connect to a service, or to pick up a Web page, and what the architects of the Web really wanted was a way to uniquely identify the page independent of location. Why?

So that when a popular page moves from one spot on the Internet to another, it doesn't leave a trail of broken links in its wake. IP addresses and host names are pretty much fixed to a physical location on the Internet. What's being explored by Internet task forces are methods to make the names more abstract, less tied to *where* they are and more related to *what* they are, ultimately trying to end up with a *URN,* or uniform resource name, that is not dependent on a physical location. The tradeoff is that pages may then be easy to nail down, but translating a page's virtual name to its current physical location (it still needs to exist somewhere) may require searching through an exponentially growing space. Can it be done? Stay tuned! In particular, watch http://www.ics.uci.edu/pub/ietf/uri/ for information from the group working on this problem. Unless, of course, their page moves!

1. Gopher is
   a. a site in Indiana
   b. a search and retrieval protocol
   c. a document type
   d. hierarchically organized directories and documents

2. One problem with using WAIS is that
   a. There are extensive amounts of data available.
   b. There are relatively few WAIS databases.
   c. It is not directly supported by most Web browsers.
   d. It is a commercial product.

3. Which of the following is the correct Gopher URL to search for "Foxes" and "Geese"?
   a. gopher://mother.goose.edu/7search?Foxes and Geese
   b. gopher://mother.goose.edu/7search?"Foxes and Geese"
   c. gopher://mother.goose.edu/7?search?Foxes%20and%20Geese
   d. gopher://mother.goose.edu/7?search?"Foxes%20and%20Geese"

4. Telnet URLs can be used to
   a. transfer files
   b. jump to non-HTML pages
   c. log in to interactive services
   d. send mail

URL GOTCHAS

You've now covered all the major URLs used in writing HTML. You have used URLs to pull together a variety of Internet services under the control of a single Web browser, and this is their forte. But URLs also have their quirks. Most beginning Web authors have been stung by one or more of the following "gotchas."

Trailing "/"

Some HTTP URLs appear to be pointers to host names or addresses without an HTML page specified. They may appear as

```
http://www.mistletoe.com/
```

Yet when you open this URL in the browser, it displays either a Web page or a directory of files.

This syntax was discussed briefly in the section on HTTP URLs in Session 1. The URL above tells the Web server that you want the default Web page at this location. On some servers, for example, the default Web page is index.html. Since no page was specified in the URL above, the Web server will look in the default directory on www.mistletoe.com and look for a file index.html in that directory. If this default file does not exist, the server may, based on options set in its configuration, return a list of the files in the directory.

URLs to default pages and directories are commonplace on the Web. What can be confusing, though, is that sometimes you will discover URLs like this:

`http://www.mistletoe.com`

and they work. Sometimes. Some browsers append the trailing "/" for you before requesting this URL from the Web server. In these cases, you may never realize that the syntax is technically invalid and will choke some percentage of browsers that interpret it strictly according to correct HTML syntax. This can be avoided by remembering to always include a trailing slash if you are not referencing a specific file or script in an HTTP URL.

Your Domain Is Not My Domain

Another common mistake is using partial domain names in the host section of the URL. Someone at Mistletoe, Inc., might get by with the following URL:

`http://www/~fred/home.html`

Fred and everyone else at Mistletoe Inc., may be able to open this page without a hitch. Their local network assumes that if they don't use a domain name, the server should plug in their default domain name, mistletoe.com, filling out the URL to

`http://www.mistletoe.com/~fred/home.html`

But when Sally tries to follow one of these links on Fred's page, from her company at volksmitten.com, the URL is interpreted as

`http://www.volksmitten.com/~fred/home.html`

and she gets the infamous message, Unable to locate this server, blah blah blah.

The motto: If your URLs contain a host name on your network, be sure to use the entire host name *and* the complete domain name.

Files in the Hood

The File URL suffers the same susceptibility as the domain name. File URLs point to specific locations on the local disk or local area network. These local and LAN disks are not typically accessible by the outside world, so URLs referencing file pages should have limited visibility. (Don't send a memo out to everyone on comp.infosystem.www.announce saying, "Check out my cool home page at file:/c:/html/cool.htm." unless you're insulated for some major flameage!)

Even people on the same office or departmental network as you may not be able to access these URLs unless they have the same drive mappings. What may be the M: drive on your machine may be the P: drive on someone else's, causing the File URL link to break. So use the File URL with caution, remembering that these are not generally accessible from the Internet.

Relative URLs

Back in Session 1 you were introduced to relative (partial) and absolute (full) URLs. Relative URLs are URLs with some parts missing, and the browser and/or Web server fills in the missing parts. This makes the URL shorter and more portable. But parts are not all equal in a URL. Some parts, if missing, can cause a URL to break. Generally, it is safe to use relative URLs in the following ways:

Pathnames

You can omit the pathname on URLs that refer to files in the same directory as the document just retrieved. For example, if your home page is

```
http://www.risingstar.com/users/ishtar/home.html
```

and in home.html you reference another file in the same directory with a URL:

```
<A HREF="http://www.risingstar.com/users/ishtar/music.html">My Favorite Music</A>
```

you can instead leave out the method and path info:

```
<A HREF="music.html">My Favorite Music</A>
```

This is safe.

Server Names

You can also omit the server and specify another path:

```
<A HREF="/users/sirius/home.html">The Dog Star</A>
```

This works because the browser uses the current document to fill in the missing information. Since the document with this link came from

```
http://www.risingstar.com/
```

this will be the default method and server for other pages linked to from this one. This is safe.

Unsafe

So what's unsafe? Most other types of relative URLs. Especially those that assume certain operations will be performed relative to directories such as

```
http://../../test.html
```

Some servers may also have "aliases" set up for various directories. In some Web servers this can cause the relative references to files in the same directory to break. While both of the examples above are generally safe, be sure to test relative URLs on your particular server.

Missing Quotes

This can be a slippery one. If you have a block of HTML, and one of your anchors is missing a closing quote:

```
<P>The Order of PI Web Server is a resource site for all those mathematical
explorers, hobbyists, and tourists, interested in
exploring the esoteric nature
of thinking by numbers. Or as <A HREF="leibniz.html>Leibniz</A>
once said:
```

```
<blockquote>
     Music is the pleasure the human soul experiences from counting
     without being aware that it is counting
</blockquote>
```

the missing quote (in this case after *leibniz.html,*) can cause unpredictable results. On some browsers the HTML may appear to work normally, and if you have used one of these faulty anchors to test your HTML, you may not catch the problem. That's why it is always a good idea to view your HTML with at least three different browsers (see Session 6 for information on some automated syntax checkers on the Web that also assist with this problem).

Some browsers will try to include the rest of the text as a URL. This creates the strange phenomenon of "black holes" of HTML. Since the browser assumes it's a URL, it won't display it. Other browsers may actually lock up the user's PC. This won't leave the lasting impression of your Web page that you're looking for!

Spaces Before the Link

This problem is not catastrophic, but it can be annoying. When you create the text representing your link, i.e., the anchor text for the link, be sure not to insert a leading or trailing space. Here's an example of the wrong way to do it:

```
<A HREF="music.html"> My Favorite Music</A>
```

Sometimes, as it may for missing quotes, the browser will compensate; other times it will leave a jutting underscore to the left of the anchor text. The anchor will still work as a hyperlink, but the space is a telltale sign of sloppy Webmanship.

That brings you to the end of a laundry list of things that can go wrong with URLs. Given time and experience, you will come up with your own pet problems, but these pointers should help you avoid those that hit budding authors right out of the gates.

Used appropriately, URLs add a powerful capability to your Web authoring arsenal. You can use URLs to weave in services that are not intrinsically part of the World Wide Web; this is the primary reason the Web has gained its incredible popularity. To pull everything under one "hood," or client interface, is both elegant and powerful. But before you take a break, let's make sure none of the subtleties of URLs will come back to bite you.

1. Which of the following is an example of a relative URL?
   a. <A HREF="http://www.quiz.edu/user/home.html">A</A>
   b. <A HREF="http://www.quiz.edu/home.html">B</A>
   c. <A HREF="http://www.quiz.edu/~user/home.html">C</A>
   d. <A HREF="home.html">D</A>

2. Which of the following is not a valid URL?
   a. <A HREF="http://www.quiz.edu/">A</A>

b. <A HREF="http://www.quiz.edu">A</A>
c. <A HREF="home.html">C</A>
d. <A HREF="http://www.quiz.edu/~fred/>D</A>

3. In which instance is the File URL inappropriate?
   a. to test HTML pages on your own PC
   b. to serve pages on your LAN if the LAN drive is mapped consistently for all
      of your LAN users
   c. to serve as your personal bookmark file
   d. to allow Internet users access to local LAN information

4. Which of the following is a valid URL?
   a. <A HREF="http://www/home.html">A</A>
   b. <A HREF="http://www.quiz.com>B</A>
   c. <A HREF="http://www.quiz.com/>C<A>
   d. <A HREF="/user/fred/home.html">D</A>

SESSION 5

STYLE 101

In the remaining sessions you'll look at some characteristics of well-designed Web pages. Up to now, you've focused on the mechanics of HTML and, along the way, assembled most of the building blocks for constructing HTML documents. With what you've learned, you can do or approximate nearly everything that can be done in HTML (barring forms, which you'll cover in Chapter 4). But as with any art, there is technique, and there is expression.

While HTML is still a relatively new form of expression, many basic principles of graphic design still apply. This session will touch on some of these basics, as well as totally new principles specific to the unique requirements of the Web. This session and the next two present information on style, consistency, and performance. These guidelines have been formed through trial and error on the Web. But you will also discover that the guidelines leave much up to the Web author. After weighing the pros and cons of various approaches, you will be the final judge as to which aspects of style you adopt, and how they will work into your own unique creations of content on the Web.

Presentation Versus Content

In Session 1 you learned about the philosophical distinction between presentation and content. In discussions of style, this issue returns to center stage. Emphasizing content means that you focus on describing what type of information is in the page, rather than how it is to be visually presented.

While this is the philosophical ideal and intent of HTML, most practicing Web authors have their feet in both courts. They are concerned with the content, but they also want some control over the appearance, or presentation, of the page. This conflict forces authors to constantly test their pages with a multitude of browsers, always measuring the effect of any change through the lens of Mosaic, Netscape, Lynx, Arena, etc.

The goal of style with an emphasis on content is not to look your best, but rather to look good on most browsers and not look bad on any. There are some ways to get around this "common denominator" approach; you'll learn about those, and some trade-offs, a little later. First, let's jump right into one of the hotspots in the dichotomy between presentation and content.

Highlights

In Chapter 2 you were introduced to highlighting tags. To recap briefly, bold <B>, italic <I>, underline <U>, are part of the handful of elements that tell exactly how you want the text presented. These tags are referred to as "physical styles." Another class of tags, more in keeping with the idea of defining content rather than presentation, are the "logical styles," among them the emphasis <EM>, strong emphasis <STRONG>, citations <CITE>, code <CODE>, and sample <SAMP> tags. Presentation (physical) styles can often be translated to content (logical) styles. Here are some examples:

<B>**Bold**</B>	<STRONG>**Strong**</STRONG>
<I>*Italic*</I>	<EM>*Emphasized*</EM> or
	<CITE>*Citation*</CITE>
<U><u>Underline</u></U>	any of the above, based on content

While logical styles are generally recommended over physical styles, the jury is still hung on which is ultimately "better." Logical styles, for example, have the bad habit of proliferating indefinitely. There are arguably as many ways to define content as the content itself, and while there are a handful of physical style tags, the number of logical styles continues to expand in each new HTML specification.

Don't Click Here

A common habit of those new to HTML and hypertext is to include links with anchors like "Click me for more information." Some of the same content arguments are applicable here: not everyone reading your page is going to have anything that even remotely "clicks," and if they do, it might not be connected to their computer, and they might not like hearing about it. A much more sophisticated approach is to weave your links into your text as naturally as possible. So instead of

`For more information about this topic `<u>`click here`</u>`.`

slightly reword to make your link part of the flow:

<u>`More information`</u>` on this topic is available.`

Figure 3-13 shows an example of pages weaving links into normal text, with a Web page on James Joyce by R. L. Callahan. Several links are peppered throughout the page, but not a single "Click me".

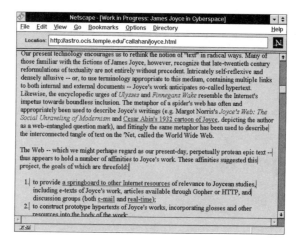

Figure 3-13
Don't "click here"

Another, more subtle, point about hyperlinks is that intentionally or not, they emphasize sections of your text. Most browsers underline or color anchored text, and this may inappropriately stress parts of your sentences. It also causes users to pause to decide whether they want to take the link or not, possibly interrupting the flow of your presentation. Often this can be avoided by moving links to the perimeter of your text, either before or after blocks of material.

Rule Sparingly

Horizontal rules <HR> are a useful way to segment areas of your page, but they are often misused. A general guideline is to use no more than one rule per screen (a screen is a typical display screen of 640 by 480 pixels.) Rules can often be eliminated completely by the liberal use of vertical space in your page.

Page Lengths

A good length for a Web page is no more than two (640 by 480 pixel) screens. This allows for quick navigation to and through your page. But while this size may be optimal for the interactive browsers, you can exceed this limit if you have information someone might want to print. It is frustrating and wasteful to chase down and print multiple links to collect an entire document. If chances are that someone will need to print your information, and it consists of several pages, you could do a few things:

 Add a link for the entire HTML document, while still providing links to individual pages for interactive browsers.

 Add a link for the document in postscript or PDF, or some other printable format so it can be downloaded and printed.

Graphics

Graphics are an important part of the Web's appeal, but beginners have a common tendency to misuse them. Graphics in a document should be relatively small, between 20 and 30K. Larger than this, and they make your Web page load sluggishly.

Graphics should also not be too wide. A typical PC monitor displays a 640 pixel wide by 480 pixel high resolution. Of this, the Web browser can usually fit an image less than 350 pixels wide onto the screen. Larger than 350 pixels, and the user will need to use the scroll bars to see the entire image.

It's also a good idea to center the image if you are not using "left" or "right" alignments. This creates a more uniform appearance across a wide variety of screen sizes. Images can be centered as follows:

```
<P ALIGN="center"><IMG SRC="image.gif"></P>
```

Backgrounds

In HTML 3.0, and even before with NHTML, it became possible to specify a background image in the <BODY> tag. This image is layered behind your text and can introduce a problem known as *flooding*. A flooded page is one that is unreadable because the colors in the background image obscure the default or user customized colors for text on the Web browser. Even if you are using the same default text colors to design the page, the background image can be rendered darker or lighter on another monitor, making it hard to test for potential problems. Use this option sparingly, and with backgrounds that offer high contrast to your text colors.

Advertise Size

If you have links to external files, in particular to large images or multimedia formats, be sure to indicate on the link how large the file is. This common courtesy allows your users to make intelligent decisions on whether to download a document. It can be very annoying to click on a file of unknown size that will take an unknown duration to transfer. File sizes are typically advertised in kilobytes (K) or megabytes (MB).

Common Mistakes

In Session 4 you covered classes of mistakes common when using URLs. Now you'll cover some more general HTML errors. These mistakes are so well known (and remembered!) that it's best you learn about them here so they will never happen to you (or so you'll have a place to look for help when they do!).

 Entity references with missing ";". When using the special entity references, & < > " these are easy to omit. No great calamity, but they may be hard to catch in dense thickets of text.

 Missed end tags. A popular mistake is forgetting to close blocks of formatted text. The results can be very puzzling. Sometimes HTML with missing end tags works fine on one browser, and given Murphy's law, usually on the browser you use to check the page. Other browsers might display a variety of pathological behaviors. Everything from strange artifacts on the screen (you should not take advantage of this, no matter how cool it looks) to documents that partially load, or links that don't work, even though the URL is correct.

One way to avoid missing tags when writing "straight" HTML, is to put the end tag in as soon as you put in the start tag. So if you are building a list, first create the skeleton:

```
<OL>
<LI>
</OL>
```

then go back and fill it in. The same applies to blocks of text surrounded by <BLOCK-QUOTE></BLOCKQUOTE>, <PRE></PRE>, etc.

 Mixed head and body. This too leads to unpredictable results. Only put elements in the header section that belong there, and be sure to put in the end tag for the heading, </HEAD>, followed by the start tag for the body, <BODY>.

 Omitting <HEAD>, <BODY>, and <HTML>. Most browsers will handle this by default, assuming it's an HTML document. But there are some cases, such as backing up to a previous link, in which the browser will not reload the page correctly. Adding the appropriate <HTML>, <HEAD>, and <BODY> tags will fix the problem immediately.

Writing Neat HTML

When writing HTML, use space and formatting liberally in your source document. Even though this formatting is ignored by the browser, it makes the document much more readable as you, or others, maintain and enhance the page. Compare the following two HTML documents. Both display exactly the same results on the browser, but which would you rather work with as an author?

Version 1:
```
<HTML>
<HEAD>
<TITLE>Marshal McLuhan And Hypermedia</TITLE>
</HEAD>
<BODY>
<H1>Marshal McLuhan And Hypermedia</H1>
Some thoughts and extracts on McLuhan's contribution to the field. McLuhan once said:
<blockquote> Today we're beginning to realize that the new media aren't just mechanical gim-
micks for creating worlds of illusion, but new languages with new and unique powers of
expression.</blockquote> McLuhan was particularly interested in how mediums of communication
appropriate one another. Some questions he had about Television are interesting to rehash in
the context of Hypermedia. Examples of which are: <UL><LI>Consider the power of a medium to
impose its own spatial assumptions and structures. What kind of space is evoked by film -vs-
```

```
television -vs- Hypermedia?<LI>Sound waves become visible on the fuselage of jets before
they break the sound barrier. Are human sense modality translatable to one another at vari-
ous intensities?</UL> We will continue to explore connections between McLuhan and Hypermedia
in the issues of this digest that follows.
</BODY>
</HTML>
```

Version 2:
```
<HTML>
<HEAD>
<TITLE>Marshal McLuhan And Hypermedia</TITLE>
</HEAD>
<BODY>
<H1>Marshal McLuhan And Hypermedia</H1>

Some thoughts and extracts on McLuhan's contribution to the field. McLuhan once said:

<blockquote>    Today we're beginning to realize that the new media aren't just mechanical
                gimmicks for creating worlds of illusion, but new languages with new and
                unique powers of expression.
</blockquote>

McLuhan was particularly interested in how mediums of communication appropriate one another.
Some questions he had about Television are interesting to rehash in the context of
Hypermedia. Examples of which are

<UL>
<LI>    Consider the power of a medium to impose its own spatial assumptions and structures.
What kind of space is evoked by film -vs- television -vs- Hypermedia?
<LI>    Sound waves become visible on the fuselage of jets before they break the sound bar-
rier. Are human sense modality translatable to one another at various intensities?
</UL>

We will continue to explore connections between McLuhan and Hypermedia in the issues of this
digest that follows.

</BODY>
</HTML>
```

The versions are identical in the browser, as shown in Figure 3-14.

Still, most of us would rather work with the second version, so use formatting liberally when building HTML. Insert spaces between paragraphs, indent blockquotes and
citations, and use levels of indentation for nested lists:

```
<OL>
        <LI>
        <LI>
        <UL>
                <LI>
                <LI>
        </UL>
        <LI>
        <LI>
</OL>
```

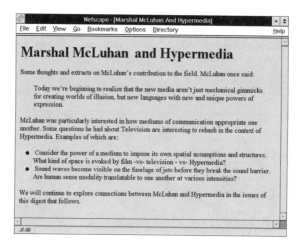

Figure 3-14
Marshall McLuhan

Be sure to keep everything in ASCII text, though. If your editor lets you bold, underline, or use italics, don't put these in your HTML. They are generally special characters that only make sense to the editor and can majorly confuse your browser. Tabs and carriage returns are okay.

In Session 6 you'll dig more into style by creating a common look and feel for all your Web pages.

1   Content is stressed over presentation in HTML because
    a. Content gives the author more power over how the page appears.
    b. The browser has more control over presentation than the author does.
    c. Content is superior to presentation.
    d. You cannot design for presentation using HTML.

2. A logical style element
    a. defines how the text will be presented on the browser
    b. describes the content of the text but not how it will be presented
    c. defines both the content and the presentation
    d. is not content based

3. The best text to use for a link anchor is
    a. something explicit like "Click here"
    b. something unrelated to the text so the user knows it is going somewhere else
    c. bolded text
    d. text that is part of the meaning of the link

4. A well-designed Web page
    a. contains all of the text related to the information being presented
    b. contains no more than one screen of information
    c. generally contains between one and two screens of information
    d. contains all the text necessary to print all related information

Session 6

CONSISTENCY

Web pages shouldn't stand alone. In well-designed Web sites, pages cooperate, creating a whole that makes the parts more intelligible. Consistency is vital in making such a scheme work.

Disorientation is a common experience for both new and veteran hypertext users. With three or four clicks of the mouse, users can circle the world and back, so it's important to have some useful landmarks to help them know where they are, how to get back to where they've been, and even hints on where to go next.

The first consistency requirements you'll learn are five elements that should be included in every Web page you publish. Building a template with the following elements provides sort of a "prefab" structure that you can rapidly assemble into a well-designed page. When you layer in the navigational aids that follow the five essentials, you will have developed a personalized template into which you can just drop information and content to flesh out a page.

The Five Basic Ingredients

The five basic ingredients of every HTML document are listed below.

Author and/or Contact

If the contact is a company, you will probably want to use a generic e-mail address, like "publications@rdoe.inc.com" rather than "jjones@rdoe.inc.com". If J. Jones gets snagged by an HTML headhunter, important messages to the company may bounce against his or her defunct address. If this is your personal page, on the other hand, you'll want to make sure the headhunter and fans know who you are.

Link to Local Home Page

This goes on every page. Given the nature of the Web, you can't assume that everyone is beginning at the same starting point and following the links down. The user could be bailing in from some other link to somewhere deep in the dusty corners of the sprawl. The user may be completely lost, or may assume your page is part of the company he or she just branched from. This can also happen with users using bookmarks to specific pages. Always show them a way home.

Company Name

When applicable.

Date Created and Last Revised

This gives users an idea of the recency, and sometimes, therefore, the validity of the information. Be sure to use unambiguous date formats such as February 10, 2001, or 10-Feb-2001. After all, this is the World Wide Web, not the U.S. of A. Web; users in other countries could misinterpret 2-10-01.

Copyright Notice

The copyright notice is optional, but you might use it if you want to try to scare away those who would use your content without approval or credit. Nobody on the Internet actually knows the full implications of copyrights. In the print world, anything you write is owned by you, with or without a copyright notice. On the Internet, your content can be incorporated into links, and it becomes ambiguous as to whether your content is being used or merely referenced. If the content of your page is copied or printed, however, instead of merely linked, it becomes a more tangible violation of copyright.

A sample copyright notice is included in the templates below.

Templates

Now let's build a sample template with these essential ingredients for you to tuck away. A good template saves a lot of repetitive busywork, and helps ensure a consistent look to all your pages. With your editor, open a new file and enter the following HTML:

```
<HTML>
<TITLE>Essential Ingredients</TITLE>
</HEAD>
<BODY>
<A HREF="home.html">Back to LaRouche Home Page</A>
<HR>
J Jones at <A HREF="mailto:sales@lbi.com">sales@lbi.com</A>
<ADDRESS>
LaRouche Business Consultants<BR>
LBC, Inc.<BR>
<EM>Created: 07-Feb-2001</EM>
<EM>Updated: 28-Feb-2001</EM>
</ADDRESS>
Copyright &copy; 2001 LBI
</BODY>
</HTML>
```

When you're finished, open the newly created page in your Web browser. Your results should look like Figure 3-15.

There are various ways to format this basic information, and you should tailor it to your own style. For example, the <TABLE> element in HTML 3.0 can be used to provide the same basic information but with a radically different appearance. Create a new file with the following HTML and compare its appearance to the previous template:

```
<HTML>
<HEAD>
<TITLE>Essential Ingredients II</TITLE>
</HEAD>
<BODY>
<TABLE BORDER=5>
<TR>
</TR>
<TD ALIGN-RIGHT>Author</TD>
<TD COLSPAN=2><B>J Jones</B></TD>
```

```
</TR>
<TR>
<TD ALIGN-RIGHT>Comments to</TD>
<TD COLSPAN=2><B><A HREF="mailto:sales@lbi.com">sales@lbi.com</A></B></TD>
</TR>
<TR>
<TD ALIGN-RIGHT>Home Page</TD>
<TD COLSPAN=2><B><HREF="home.html">Home</A></B></TD>
</TR>
<TR>
<TD ALIGN-RIGHT>Company</TD>
<TD COLSPAN=2><B>LaRouche Business Consultants<BR>
        LBC, Inc.</B></TD>
</TR>
<TR>
<TD ALIGN-RIGHT>Created</TD>
<TD COLSPAN=2><B>07-Feb-2001</B></TD>
</TR>
<TR>
<TD ALIGN-RIGHT>Updated</TD>
<TD COLSPAN=2><B>28-Feb-2001</B></TD>
</TR>
<TR>
<TD COLSPAN=3><B>Copyright &copy; 2001. All Rights Reserved.</B></TD>
</TR>
<TR>
</TABLE>
</BODY>
</HTML>
```

Your results should be similar to those shown in Figure 3-16.

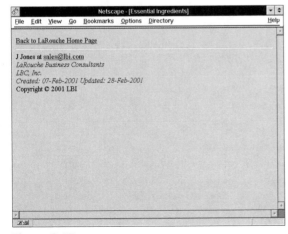

Figure 3-15
Building a template

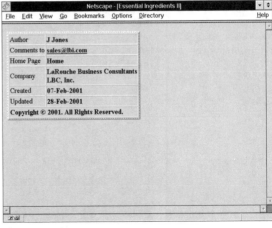

Figure 3-16
Using the <TABLE> element for basic information

Navigation Templates

In addition to the five basic elements, most Web pages need an additional layer of consistency in the form of navigational aids. One of these aids, the Home Page link, was covered above. Others you will want to include are Next, Prev, Up, or Contents, and perhaps, for symmetry, fold the Home Page link with these instead of putting it in the contact information.

There is a variety of navigational styles. These include the graphical menu, icon menus, buttons, and text links. You'll look at each approach, and find the one most suited to your page content.

Graphical Menus

Graphical menus take control of the page. They are usually large and embed all navigational controls into one imagemap. They often appear as the home page of a company, and provide a visual directory of services. Figure 3-17 shows an example of this kind of menu at the Waite Group Press's home page.

The URLs for each option are located in the imagemap related to this graphics file, so the HTML menu page itself is fairly sparse. In fact, the entire menu is actually in the <IMG SRC="lobby.gif" ALT="Waite Group Press" ISMAP> tag. The other images in the HTML are button links, which are described below.

```
<HTML>
<HEAD>
<TITLE>Waite Group Press Lobby</TITLE>
</HEAD>
<BODY>
<a href = "/bin/imagemap/wgp_lobby_gif">
<IMG SRC="lobby.gif" ALT="Waite Group Press" ISMAP></a>
<P>
<A HREF="../about.html">About</a>|
<A HREF="new_gif.html">New</a>|
<A HREF="backlist_gif.html">Backlist</a>|
<A HREF="people1_gif.html">People</a>|
<A HREF="data_gif.html">ftp</a>|
<A HREF="order_gif.html">Order</a>|
<A HREF="subject_gif.html">Subject</a>|
<A HREF="links_gif.html">Links</a>|
</BODY>
</HTML>
```

You can use techniques to compensate for the size of the graphics files needed with this type of menu. They will be discussed in Session 7.

You won't want to use the graphical menu for every page, but as an entry point to your company, or your home page, it gives you complete control over appearances. You can even emulate other GUI interfaces, making the page Windows or Mac-like, or you can go for the totally surreal and imaginative.

Icon Menus

Icon menus are illustrated in Figure 3-18. This technique uses a handful of smaller graphical images that serve the same purpose as the composite image in the last example.

The HTML for the icon menu in Figure 3-18 uses the <IMG> tag in the anchors. It also uses a special twist: the block is surrounded with the preformatting tags <PRE>:

```
<pre>
<A HREF="Hot.html"><IMG ALIGN=middle SRC="/GIFS/ReadMe.gif" WIDTH=50 HEIGHT=44></A> <A
HREF="Hot.html">Important! Read Me First!</A>    <A HREF="WhatsNew.html"><IMG ALIGN=middle
SRC="/GIFS/New.gif" WIDTH=50 HEIGHT=44></A> <A HREF="WhatsNew.html">What's New</A>

<A HREF="Corp/AboutAdobe.html"><IMG ALIGN=middle SRC="/GIFS/Adobe.gif" WIDTH=50
HEIGHT=44></A> <A HREF="Corp/AboutAdobe.html">About Adobe</A>                    <A
HREF="Acrobat/Acrobat0.html"><IMG ALIGN=middle SRC="/GIFS/Acrobat.gif" WIDTH=50
HEIGHT=44></A> <A HREF="Acrobat/Acrobat0.html">Adobe(TM) Acrobat(TM)</A>

<A HREF="Products.html"><IMG ALIGN=middle SRC="/GIFS/Products.gif" WIDTH=50 HEIGHT=44></A> <A
HREF="Products.html">Adobe Products</A>                <A HREF="Tips/TT.html"><IMG
ALIGN=middle SRC="/GIFS/Lightbulb.gif" WIDTH=50 HEIGHT=44></A> <A HREF="Tips/TT.html">Tips
&amp; Techniques</A>
```

Note that two images and hyperlinks are specified on each line within the <PRE> block; this creates the two-column menu. Another way to do this would be to use a table.

Buttons

The third navigational technique, using buttons, continues the trend toward faster and faster page transfers. The large graphical menu generally takes the longest to transfer

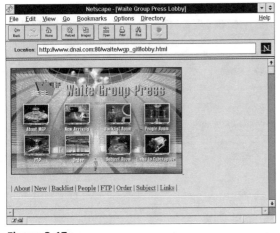

Figure 3-17
Waite Group Press's graphical menu

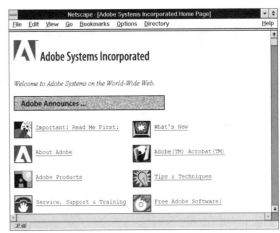

Figure 3-18
An icon menu

completely to your browser, icons are the second slowest, and buttons turn out to be pretty speedy. You can think of buttons as just smaller icons that you either assemble as a group of individual images or present as a single image. As a single image, the buttons become a "button bar," using the imagemap technique of their larger cousin, the graphical menu. Figure 3-19 shows an example of a button bar.

You can provide the same navigational options with a plain old text links approach, and this will transfer blindingly fast. Of course, it looks a little spartan, but it accomplishes the same end. Often text links are provided in addition to the navigation styles listed above. This accommodates the text-mode browsers, as well as those zipping through links with inline images turned off.

Combinations

Back in Session 5, the optimal page size was roughly calculated as a maximum of two screens. If a page has more than one screen, a user must scroll down to read the entire page. If the user then has to scroll back up to click on a navigation link, it will become very tiresome. Especially if the designer has taken consistency to heart and made all of his or her pages like this!

A better convention is to provide navigational tools at the bottom of the page, or at both the bottom and the top. This technique is demonstrated on the Waite Group's home page. Figure 3-17 shows the first screen and the graphical menu, Figure 3-20 shows the button bar at the bottom of the page.

Pick a style of navigation that you like, and that suits your material and audience. Once your templates are built, you can concentrate on the content of your pages, knowing that it will snap into place in a quality framework that will orient your audience.

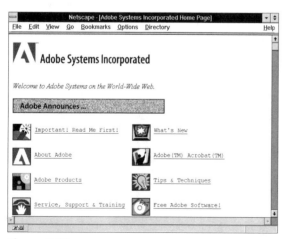

Figure 3-19
A button bar

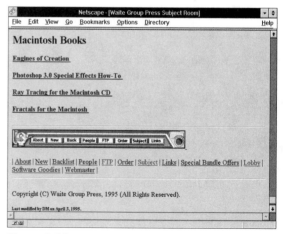

Figure 3-20
Combination with button bar

Consistency and Content

Some consistency rules also apply to page content. Not that you want to structure all information in the same way, but certain routine checks should be made in the text of your pages.

For example, it's important to use consistent filenames in URLs. If you are writing pages on a UNIX system, you probably already know that UNIX filenames are case sensitive. "This.html" is not the same page as "this.html". Establishing conventions keeps errors from creeping into your HTML. Some authors put the first letter of an individual word in caps, so they would reference the file BasicDocumentation.html with initial caps, while others would reference it all in lowercase.

Another potential problem on UNIX Web servers is that some implementations support blanks in the filenames, making "Basic Documentation.html" a valid filename. In order to make your URLs portable, you will want to replace the blanks with the hyphen "-" or underscore "_", and this, too, you will want to do consistently.

Annoying problems with formatting can arise when the paragraph tag <P> is not used correctly. <P> is used to insert a paragraph break between text before and after it. Tags that already create a break, like <HEAD>, <ADDRESS>, <BLOCKQUOTE>, and <PRE> should not have <P> tags before or after them.

You shouldn't put paragraph tags before a list, either, or between list elements. These rules will help eliminate odd differences in your layout when viewed by different browsers.

Testing

Testing the usability of your pages should become part of your authoring process. Here are some elements of testing for style and content that you may want to consider:

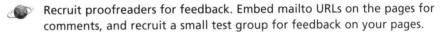 Recruit proofreaders for feedback. Embed mailto URLs on the pages for comments, and recruit a small test group for feedback on your pages.

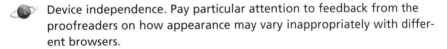 Device independence. Pay particular attention to feedback from the proofreaders on how appearance may vary inappropriately with different browsers.

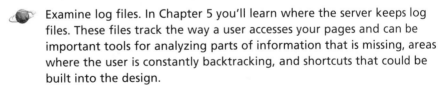 Examine log files. In Chapter 5 you'll learn where the server keeps log files. These files track the way a user accesses your pages and can be important tools for analyzing parts of information that is missing, areas where the user is constantly backtracking, and shortcuts that could be built into the design.

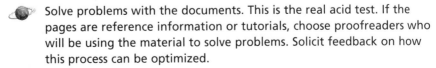 Solve problems with the documents. This is the real acid test. If the pages are reference information or tutorials, choose proofreaders who will be using the material to solve problems. Solicit feedback on how this process can be optimized.

Even with well-designed, concise stylistic content, you can still leave bad impressions if users have to suffer through long delays to read your pages. Session 7 deals with ways of tuning the time it takes to transfer a page from the server to a browser, controlling another important variable in a user's perception of your pages.

1. A link to the home page is important because
   a. Users can then find the author of the page.
   b. Users may have linked to your pages from other sites.
   c. It contains the copyright information on your site.
   d. The home page contains all the navigational aids.

2. The graphical menu should be used
   a. on every page for orientation
   b. on the home page to provide a map of your site
   c. instead of text links, because it is faster to load
   d. in place of icons, because it contains more information

3. Consistency on Web pages is
   a. important for orienting users new to your Web site
   b. only useful in the navigational aids of a page
   c. automatically provided by HTML
   d. achieved by closely mimicking paper documentation

4. Why should file naming conventions for Web pages be standardized?
   a. to prevent user confusion
   b. to make the pages more portable to other servers
   c. to reduce mistakes by the Web author
   d. UNIX requires file naming standards

Build a complete template with the essential information for your Web page, including the basic navigational aids.

SESSION 7

PERFORMANCE

Performance on the Web refers to how long it takes to load a page, and this depends on two primary factors: the speed of the link(s) and the amount of data that needs to be transferred. Between the Web server that stores the page and the Web browser that reads it lies a mesh of communications links. The slowest of these links are usually connections from home, which are typically through low-speed modems. The fastest links are through parts of the Internet "backbones," where traffic merges from the small network subsidiaries into large pipes of high-speed communication bandwidth using the latest networking technologies.

A page that might take a few seconds to load from work might take some poor soul dialing in from Prodigy or AOL five minutes to view. Just as the author of pages must take into account the variety of browsers and differences in presentation, he or she must also keep in mind the variety of speeds at which pages will be transferred. Millions of people using the major online services are dialing in at speeds between 9,600 and 28,800 bits per second; a good rule of thumb is that if a Web page takes more than 30 seconds to load over these connections, you will hinder the utility of your presentation.

If you keep to two screens worth of information, HTML markup and text should load in much less than 30 seconds in the circumstances above, but the inline images on your page could take longer. Tuning these images can significantly impact the transfer speed of your page.

Tuning Inline Images

The size of an inline image determines how quickly it can be loaded. In the lessons in Chapter 2 on the <IMG> tag, you discovered that in terms of file size, a simple image is equivalent to a surprising amount of plain text. Two screens of HTML, even very dense text, will weigh in at about 4,000 bytes (or characters). A small GIF occupying one-quarter of one screen, however, is equivalent to about 6,000 bytes, or approximately three screens of HTML all by itself!

You manipulate four characteristics of an image to improve your page's performance:

 Dimensions

Number of colors

Type of compression

Reusability

Each of these characteristics is discussed below.

Dimensions

The dimensions of an image simply describe how big the image is in pixels. One way to speed up performance is to specify these dimensions in the markup. Doing this lets the browser block out a space for the image and begin displaying text immediately. Since the browser knows what part of the screen will be used by the image, it doesn't have to wait until the entire image is downloaded to begin formatting text on the page. While the overall transfer time may not be significantly different (since the browser still has to transfer the same amount of information), it appears faster to the user because the frames for the images pop up in the document right away. In both the Netscape extensions and HTML 3.0, the <IMG> tag has options for WIDTH and HEIGHT that correspond to the pixel size of the image.

For example, a quarter-screen image (1/4 of 640 by 480) would be 320 by 240 pixels, and in your HTML the <IMG> tag would look like this:

```
<IMG WIDTH=320 HEIGHT=240 SRC=test.gif>
```

Number of Colors

GIF images can contain 256 colors, JPEG images can contain 16 million. On most browsers that run under Windows, you typically only get about 50 colors. Windows uses 16 colors from its 256-color palette (for Super VGA systems), and the browser typically takes the rest for its menus, buttons, etc., leaving about 50 entries in the palette free. The way palettes are combined in Windows is pretty complex, and beyond the scope of what you need to know as a Web author, but realizing that your inline images will in most cases not be displayed in 256 colors, much less true color, may let you optimize by dropping information that can't be used. This situation will change as Windows evolves to more readily handle true color, but even so you'll want to analyze your image to see how many colors you really need. The answer might be surprising.

To prove this for yourself, you can adjust the number of colors using LVIEW. Start LVIEW and open the file fractal1.gif from the \images directory of this book's CD. This is a GIF image of 320 by 240 pixels, and a size of 55,696 bytes. Load it into LVIEW and select RetouchÍColor Depth. Click the Palette image button and the Custom number of colors button and set the number of colors to 50. An example of this option screen is displayed in Figure 3-21.

After you enter 50 in Custom colors and click OK, LVIEW calculates the best mix of 50 colors to accurately represent your image. You'll notice the results appear fine at 50 colors, and saving the file results in a new size of 33,743 bytes, shaving off about 20K. Since 1K equates to about one second of transfer time, this cosmetic change eliminates 20 seconds, or almost half of the download time required for this image!

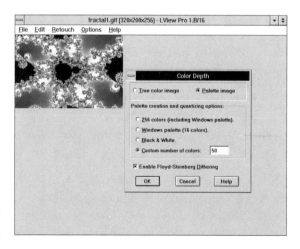

Figure 3-21
LVIEW tuning color
depth

Type of Compression

Most browsers support both GIF and JPEG as inline images. When is one preferable to the other? The rules of thumb are

 JPEG is better at storing full-color photographic or gray-scale images, especially if you want your scenes to have realism.

 GIF is used for black-and-white images with only a few, distinct colors (as opposed to color blends), line drawings, and graphics with text.

If you are scanning pictures to use as images on the Web, you'll need to consider the implications of these compression styles. GIF starts out throwing away most of the color information right off the bat, but even so you will typically get compression ratios from 5:1 to as low as 2:1.

JPEG achieves 10:1 to 20:1 compression ratios without breaking a sweat on full-color images, and can go as low as 100:1 in some cases.

Once you have an image in GIF, converting it to JPEG can produce some very strange results. If at all possible, decide on the format you need when you originally create the digitized image and stick to it.

Reusability

This is where consistency on your pages pays off in terms of performance. If you use the same navigational bar or buttons on all your pages, users of them will only pay the penalty for downloading these images once. As browsers go from page to page on the Web, they keep images they've already downloaded *cached*, that is, tucked away on the local disk or in memory, so they don't have to pester the server to download them again. This provides a graphical template for moving around your documents while actually only downloading the new HTML markup and text.

Besides navigational bars and buttons, reusability works with graphical bullets and rules as well. Avoid the compulsion to decorate list items with bullets of all colors of the rainbow. Each of these bullets will need to be retrieved separately, multiplying the time it takes to render your page. If you use a single bullet style, the bullet will be downloaded once and reused for each list item, achieving much faster load times.

Tuning Sounds

Sounds are analogous to images in many ways. More bits and bytes give you more depth and realism, but you need to look at how much is needed to really make a difference.

Sounds can be sampled at different rates, and these frequency rates correspond to the number of colors captured in their visual counterparts. Eight bits per sample is used for mono sound, and 16 bits per sample for stereo. How frequently the sound is sampled varies from phone quality at 8 kHz to CD-quality stereo at 44.1 kHz. A 60-second audio clip of phone-quality mono sound would take up about 512K, while the same 60-second sample at CD quality mushrooms to about 10MB!

For simple voice annotations to your Web page, CD-quality sound would be overkill. Even for recorded music, you can approximate FM radio quality with a sample rate of 22.050 kHz and 16 bits per sample. You will usually find the sample rate and number of bits per sample as options on your recorder application. As you did in the exercise adjusting color depths with LVIEW, you should experiment during recording with samples rates and bits per sample to see if you can reduce the size of the sound file without noticeable differences in the quality.

For purely instrumental music, MIDI is probably the best sound option of all. Since MIDI records information about the music, but leaves the actual reconstruction of the song to the player, it has very compact disk requirements, often a fraction of those of the same music recorded digitally.

Sound, except in the case of RealAudio (covered in Chapter 2), is not played simultaneously with the display of the page. Since it doesn't have this "inline" capability, the way images do with the <IMG> tag, it is not as critical to the performance of the page as a whole. Sound files are usually individually and discretely linked to with the anchor tag, and if it is a large sample, you can always warn the unaware user. In fact, as discussed in Session 5, this courtesy of advertising the size of files attached to a link is an important technique to incorporate.

Label Large Files

If you offer thumbnails of large graphical images, or links to any type of multimedia, it is good form to label the size of the files if they are larger than about 100K. This allows the user to decide whether he or she wants to download them at that time, come back later, or skip them. You can use something like the following:

```
<A HREF="mondo.wav">WAV file of Moose Calls  [512K]</A>
```

Alternate Paths

When designing for a large number of different browsers, connection speeds, and user preferences, sometimes the lowest common denominator strategy is not effective. While it's more work, in some cases you may need to create different paths through your document. One path can serve the material as minimal text, with text navigational links. A second path can be a "low-resolution" option, offering economically sized buttons, conservative use of standard bullets, and reduced color graphics. The third path, for those with high-speed corporate connections or direct Internet implants in the forebrain, can go all out with sophisticated graphical menus and navigation bars, virtual rooms, spaces, and corridors, and whatever else you may devise. This combination of techniques provides access to your pages for the most viewers while satisfying your creative urge to push a medium to its max.

The multiple path approach can also be used if you want to maximize appearance for specific browsers, offering options like Select your viewer preference: Netscape, Mosaic, Hot Java, etc. An example of this technique is shown in Figure 3-22.

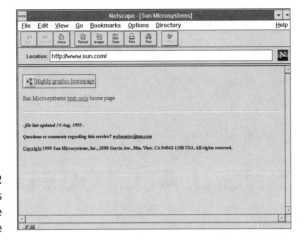

Figure 3-22
Alternate paths
from Sun's home
page

The Sun Microsystems page begins with a graphical menu. If you have images turned off, as in Figure 3-22, you see only the anchor text "Highly graphic homepage" and another hyperlink option, "text-only homepage". This technique provides a *welcome page* as the point of entry for users, allowing them to select the type of home page they want to see based on the capabilities of their links and browsers.

QUIZ 7

1. Why should you label links to large files?
   a. to allow the user to choose whether to download or not
   b. because all links should be labeled with complete information about external files
   c. so the user will know if the file has changed
   d. so you can sort your links by file size

2. What are two ways to reduce the transfer time of an image?
   a. Reduce the number of colors and always use JPEG compression.
   b. Reuse the image on multiple pages, and only use scanned images.
   c. Don't use scanned images and choose the appropriate compression.
   d. Reduce the number of colors and explicitly specify the dimensions of the image in the markup.

3. As a rule of thumb, how many characters per second can be transmitted across a typical modem link?
   a. 10,000
   b. 100
   c. 1,000
   d. 1,000,000

4. What other variables may affect transfer time besides the speed of the user's modem?
   a. external links in the file
   b. large sound files
   c. traffic on any link between the browser and the server of the Web page
   d. amount of disk space on the user's PC

PUTTING IT ALL TOGETHER

For this session, let's meet out on the Web. You'll look at some examples of good style, and pick apart how they're done. You'll study them with the principles and rules of thumb covered in this chapter in mind, and perhaps pick up some ideas that will contribute to the real-life pages you want to design.

The Online Brochure

The first page you'll examine is an example of the large graphical menu. Connect to the following URL with your browser:

```
http://www.rezn8.com/
```

This is the home page of ReZ.n8 Productions, a creator of special effects for studios. Their page is shown in Figure 3-23. The graphic is a relatively large GIF file (507 by 380), and it is an imagemap, so various hotspots take you to different parts of their menu. It took about 25 seconds to load with a 14.4 bps modem connection. The hotspots are not visually presented as buttons, but as icons. This page is clean and visually appealing, a good model for an online brochure. Its weak points might be that it is not readily

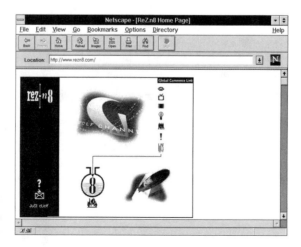

Figure 3-23
ReZ.n8 Productions
home page

apparent where the icons take you, and the image uses 256 colors when it would probably look almost identical, and load much faster, with a smaller palette. It could also use interlacing to good effect.

An advantage to this type of home page is the simplicity of the HTML. Here is the source for the ReZ.n8 home page:

```
<html>
<head>
<title>ReZ.n8 Home Page</title>
</head>
<body>
<a href="/cgi-bin/mapper/lowrez/maps/lowreztop.map"><img
src="/lowrez/pics/lowreztop.gif" ismap></a>
<p>
568472 accesses, 10/26/94 to 09/04/95<p>
<hr>
The material shown on our pages is provided for demonstration and testing purposes only.
<hr>
<b>Copyright&#169 ReZ.n8 Productions, Inc.; 1994</b>
</body>
</html>
```

Note the use of the escape encoding and the numeric value of the copyright symbol. Note also that a GIF image was used for the menu; this makes the small text on the menu crisper, and the boundaries of the lines clearer.

Combination Page

The next page (Figure 3-24) is from vivid studios, an online design firm specializing in multimedia. It uses a combination of a graphical menu and a navigational button bar. The beginning of their source HTML is

```
<html> <head> <title>vivid studios</title> </head>
<body>
<A HREF="/img/vividBanner.map"><img src="vividBanner.gif" ISMAP border=0
ALT="[vivid studios]"></A>

<A HREF="/img/miniBanner.map"><img src="miniBanner.gif" ISMAP border=0
ALT="[navigational banner]"></A> <p>


<H2>Welcome to vivid studios' website</H2>

Wouldn't want to be the last on your block to know what's going on in the
ever-trendy world of multimedia, now would you? Entangle yourself in our website
and find out more: <p>
```

Note that the graphical menu also serves as the corporate logo. Small icons delineated with an imagemap link to some of the same locations that appear on the navigational bar beneath it, but in a much more visual representation. The navigation bar is the same width as the graphical menu, and both are, as the last example was, relatively large. The

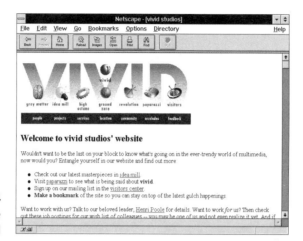

Figure 3-24
Combination page
at vivid

graphical menu is 500 by 140 pixels and is 21,358 bytes. The navigational bar is 500 by 30 pixels, and only 1,256 bytes. Part of the major size difference between the two is due to the navigational bar's using only 16 colors, while the graphical menu uses the full GIF complement of 256.

The 500-pixel width of the images fills the width of a typical 14" monitor running at 640 by 480 resolution. Figure 3-24 shows it displayed on an 800 by 600 resolution, where it takes up a little more than half of the screen width. The next image, for the navigational bar, starts beneath the first because it doesn't have room to be displayed to the side. A potential gotcha, if the resolution is higher, is that the navigational bar will slide up to the right of the graphical menu, probably not the effect its creators had in mind. To prevent this from happening, no matter what the user's resolution, add a line break tag to the end of the first image:

```
<A HREF="/img/vividBanner.map"><img src="vividBanner.gif" ISMAP border=0
ALT="[vivid studios]"></A><BR>

<A HREF="/img/miniBanner.map"><img src="miniBanner.gif" ISMAP border=0
ALT="[navigational banner]"></A> <p>
```

Icon Menus

The next example is at http://www.cdrom.ibm.com/. This is IBM's online catalog of interactive CDs. As you can see in Figure 3-25, it's organized as an icon menu. Each icon is 160 by 100 pixels and linked to a topic page graphically represented by the icon. Beneath the icons are text hyperlinks to the same content. A snippet of the source HTML is shown below:

```
<HTML>
<HEAD>
<TITLE>Multimedia Studio</TITLE>
</HEAD>
<BODY>
```

```
<IMG SRC="graphics/masthead.gif" ALIGN=MIDDLE ALT="IBM Multimedia Studio">
<p>
Welcome to the IBM Multimedia Studio,
an electronic catalog of
interactive CDROM software!
<pre>
<A HREF="informat/infmenu.htm"><IMG SRC="graphics/information.gif" ALT="Information"></A>
<A HREF="entertai/entmenu.htm"><IMG SRC="graphics/entertainment.gif" ALT="Entertainment"></A>

<A HREF="educatio/edumenu.htm"><IMG SRC="graphics/educ2.gif" ALT="Education"></A>   <A
HREF="promotio/promenu.htm"><IMG SRC="graphics/promo2.gif" ALT="Special Promotions"></A>
</pre>
<ul>
<li><A HREF="informat/infmenu.htm"> Information</A>
<li><A HREF="entertai/entmenu.htm"> Entertainment</A>
<li><A HREF="educatio/edumenu.htm"> Education</A>
<li><A HREF="promotio/promenu.htm"> Promotions</A>
</ul>
<hr>
```

The designer of this page wanted to be sure the icons for the menu lined up in rows with two icons in each. To do this, he or she used the preformat <PRE> tag and put two images on the same line, followed by a line break in the source HTML and the next two images on the same line.

Mutability

Now let's look at one of the most dynamically changing pages on the Web and look for clues on maintaining such mutable content. The site is Yahoo, at http://www.yahoo.com/.

Yahoo provides a directory of pages on the Web organized by category. Many browsers are distributed with links directly to Yahoo as a directory of services, and it is probably one of the most frequently accessed pages on the Web. As such, you might

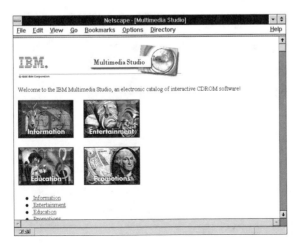

Figure 3-25
An icon menu

expect it to have evolved some performance optimizations. Let's see what they might be. Figure 3-26 shows the Yahoo home page.

Yahoo has an imagemap performing double duty as the company logo and the menu of services. While the graphical menu approach usually results in slower load times, Yahoo's page loads in about six seconds. The secret is in the image. The graphical menu is 450 by 70 pixels, but contains only four colors! This produces a file size of only 2,800 bytes; no wonder it loads so quickly! From the source HTML, you can see they have also optimized for the browser by explicitly specifying the dimensions of the image:

```
<HTML>
<HEAD>
<TITLE>Yahoo
</TITLE>
<base href="http://www.yahoo.com/">
</HEAD>
<body>
<CENTER>
<a href="/bin/top1"><IMG width=450 height=70 border=0 hspace=0 ismap
src="/images/main.gif"></a><br>
</CENTER>
<BR>
```

Yahoo also provides optimizations in areas, like the search field, that are especially important to the types of service it is providing. The text on the page is uncluttered. Subject categories are shown with links, but all of the company and miscellaneous information is tucked behind the Info link on the graphical menu. The Write Us link prominently displays a feedback mechanism to e-mail comments on the page. The New link offers a view of what has recently changed on the site, a better approach than placing a Last Changed date on the page with no pointers to what has actually been updated.

Figure 3-27 shows a few levels deeper in the Yahoo pages. The Info and Write Us links are tagging along as part of the menu, and each category is labeled with a

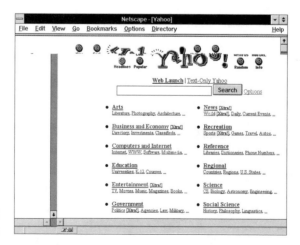

Figure 3-26
Yahoo

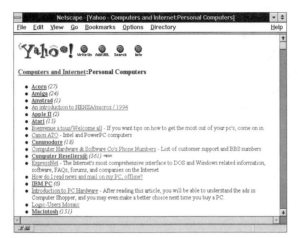

Figure 3-27
Yahoo
subcategories

number indicating the number of topics under this topic. Topics that are new at this level have a small New icon appended to the text link using the following HTML:

```
<LI><a href="/Business_and_Economy/Companies/Computers/Resellers/"><b>Computer
Resellers@</b></a> <i>(361)</i> <img alt=" [new]" src="/images/new.gif">
```

Note the ALT=" [new] " that flags the category for text-only viewers.

Well, that wraps up the lesson on style. You've been through the gamut this chapter. You've studied URLs in depth, you've learned how to avoid common mistakes, you've studied design heuristics and building templates, and you've taken "flat" HTML about as far as it can go. In Chapter 4 you'll move into an area of HTML that will let you interact with your viewers, and find out what they're thinking.

1. The main disadvantage of the graphical menu for navigation is
   a. You can't link to multiple places from a single graphic.
   b. It has to be loaded with an external link.
   c. It can take a long time to download if not created with care.
   d. It's not consistent across different browsers.

2. What was a potential problem with vivid's home page?
   a. A character entity tag was not followed by a semicolon.
   b. None.
   c. A link was not closed.
   d. The navigation menu might not have ended up under the graphical menu on a large screen.

3. Even if you didn't provide an ALT option in your image, you could still accommodate a text browser by
   a. describing the image with text

b. putting in an external link to the image

c. adding a link to a page specifically for text-mode browsers

d. making the image transparent

4. Why is a link to a home page sometimes seen on the home page itself?

a. because you may be coming in from somewhere else

b. to provide a consistent format

c. in case you forget you were at the home page

d. to advertise that this is the home page

INTERACTIVE FORMS AND SCRIPTS

INTERACTIVE FORMS AND SCRIPTS

U p to now you've been folding a variety of content into your Web pages. You've presented images and text, you've formatted and emphasized, you've added video and music and hyperlinks to the outer limits of the Web. But all of this is still like telvision before Nintendo.

In this chapter you'll look at ways of making Web pages interactive. The way you'll do this is with forms. A form is a special type of Web page. In addition to all the standard elements you've learned to date, forms add additional elements for creating fields a user can fill in with information. What you do with this information is up to your imagination. Typical uses are questionnaires, guest books, and order forms. More unusual uses are digital grafitti boards, games, remote control of robotic arms, and tours through virtual landscapes. In the following sessions you will

191

cover all the elements used to construct forms, and you will build a few complete applications. But a journey of a thousand miles starts with…

WHAT ARE FORMS?

To get a firm handle on forms, let's dip into how HTML has been working behind the scenes. Specifically, let's look at how the Web browser and the Web server interact, and at the difference between how a form and a regular Web page behave. Figure 4-1 illustrates how a regular Web page interacts with the browser and the Web server.

The browser asks the server for a Web page, passing the server the URL that describes how to locate the page. The Web server locates the page, usually on its local

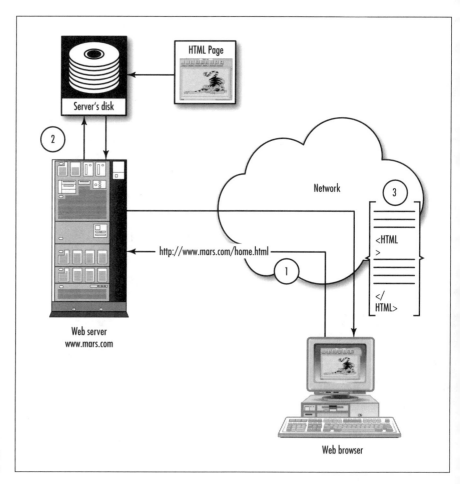

Figure 4-1
Browser retrieving
a Web page

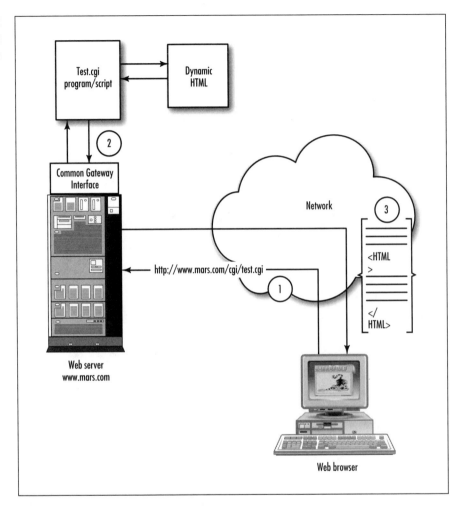

Figure 4-2
Browser submitting a form

disks, and sends the requested Web page back to the browser, then waits for another request. The Web page is usually a page of HTML, and, of course, this page may have other URLs to other servers, where the process repeats.

In this simplified scenario, the server's job is to transfer pages stored in its directories that are requested by Web browsers. Since pages must be transferred from the server's directory to your Web browser via a network, the URLs have explicit directions about which server to pester and what file to pester it for.

Forms work basically the same way. But instead of asking the Web server for a file, a form requests the server to run a program. Instead of returning some precomposed Web page, the server returns a new page, built on the fly by the program. Programs add a whole new layer of flexibility to the Web. Figure 4-2 demonstrates what happens when a URL points to a program rather than an ordinary Web page.

Let's hold detailed discussion of what programs can do for a little later. Right now let's concentrate on the HTML tags that are used to create a form.

A classic form consists of three elements: the <FORM> tag, input fields, and a submit button.

The <FORM> Tag

The <FORM> tag, like the <BODY> tag, is a container. <FORM>...</FORM> contains a section of HTML that makes up the form. Tags placed between <FORM> and </FORM> can be regular HTML in addition to some special elements defined just for forms. The syntax of the <FORM> tag is

---

THE <FORM> TAG

```
<FORM
         [ACTION="url"]
         [METHOD="method"]
         [ENCTYPE="type"]

    >
</FORM>
```

ACTION is the name of the program to be run when this form is submitted.
METHOD is how the data filled in on the form is passed to the program.
ENCTYPE is how the data is encoded.

ACTION is the only required attribute in the <FORM> tag. It is a URL to the program to be executed when the form is submitted. The URL looks the same as the URLs you have been using up to now to reference Web pages; the only difference is that a URL in the <FORM> tag points to a program that is run, rather than to a page that is retrieved.

METHOD can be either "POST" or "GET". These options determine how data from your form is passed to the program. The default is "GET", which tacks all the data onto the URL when it calls the program. While this is the default, this method is not generally used, because it can sometimes result in your form data being truncated before the program ever receives it. "POST" is a more reliable delivery method, and should be your preferred method. Reasons why will become clearer soon.

ENCTYPE is included for completeness. It only has one value: "x-www-form-encoded". This is the default, so you can ignore this field until it sprouts more options in future versions of HTML.

The <FORM> tag in an HTML document looks like this:

```
<HTML>
<HEAD>
<TITLE>Sample Form with No Input Fields</TITLE>
</HEAD>
<BODY>
<FORM ACTION="http://myhost.com/test.exe" METHOD="POST">
Form elements and other HTML go here...
</FORM>
```

```
</BODY>
</HTML>
```

This is how a form is defined in an HTML document, but it's still lacking two other ingredients to make it a fully functional: input fields and a submit button.

Input Fields

Input fields are special elements that are found only between <FORM> tags. They allow users of your Web page to enter information that is sent to you (or rather, to your program). Input fields are created on forms with three different tags: <INPUT>, <SELECT>, and <TEXTAREA>. You'll cover all of these before the end of the chapter, but right now let's focus on <INPUT>, and use it to create a simple input field. The syntax of the <INPUT> tag is

---

THE <INPUT> TAG

```
<INPUT
        [TYPE="field-type"]
        [NAME="field-name"]
        [SIZE=width]
        [VALUE="default-value"]
        [MAXLENGTH=maxchars]
>
```

TYPE controls what type of input the field is for.
NAME is a variable name used to reference this field from a program.
SIZE is the default width of the field in number of characters.
VALUE is the default data for the field.
MAXLENGTH is the maximum number of characters permitted in the field.

The <INPUT> tag has eight different values for the TYPE attribute, listed in Table 4-1.

TYPE Value	Description
text	Regular text input field (the default).
password	A text field that masks input as it is entered.
hidden	An invisible text input field. Unlike "password", this field doesn't appear on the Web page.
checkbox	A set of boxes that can be clicked on or off.
radio	A set of buttons, usually mutually exclusive, the user can click on or off.
image	An image that the user can click on to submit the form.
submit	A button that the user can click on to submit the form.
reset	A button that resets all the input fields on the form to their default values.

Table 4-1 *Input types*

The NAME attribute will be used later, when you start to write scripts and programs. It is used to refer to the data of a specific input field. NAME is a required attribute for all types of input except "submit" and "reset".

The SIZE attribute works as you would expect it to, defining the length of the input fields. Its primary use is with the text input types ("text", "password", and "hidden").

The SIZE attribute controls how big the input field appears on the screen, but unless MAXLENGTH is specified, the amount of text that can be entered in this field is unlimited. MAXLENGTH provides a way to limit the amount of data to fixed number of characters.

VALUE is the default value for the fields when the form first comes up. If no VALUE is specified, the fields will be blank.

One of the most common ways to use the <INPUT> tag is as follows:

```
<INPUT TYPE="text" NAME="username" SIZE=40>
```

Let's experiment with this to see how it appears on a Web page. Open a new file with your editor and enter the following HTML:

```
<HTML>
<HEAD>
<TITLE>HyperFiction Contest</TITLE>
</HEAD>
<BODY>
<H2>The HyperFiction Contest</H2>
Enter the information below for more details. Qualify for thousands of dollars in prizes, in
our first annual Hypertext Fiction awards!
<HR>
<FORM ACTION="http://myhost.com/test.exe" METHOD="POST">
<P>Please enter your name: <INPUT TYPE="text" NAME="name" SIZE=40>
</FORM>
The HFC Annual awards are sponsored by the James Joyce association for disassociated text.
</BODY>
</HTML>
```

Save the file, then open it with your Web browser. Your screen should look like Figure 4-3.

Notice on Figure 4-3 that you can have HTML before and after the <FORM> tag. You can insert any HTML tags between the <FORM> tag you like. The only restriction is that you cannot have <FORM> tags nested within <FORM> tags. Note also that the NAME attribute of the <INPUT> tag does not show up on the form itself. Values of the NAME attribute are used by the program on the server as variable names for the fields that contain values.

Now all you need is a way to submit the form once it's filled out.

Submitting Forms

Submitting forms is how data in the input fields of a form is actually sent to the program back on the server. A special button was designed just for this purpose. The following creates a button on a form for submitting data:

```
<INPUT TYPE="submit" VALUE="Send Info">
```

The VALUE attribute in a submit button is used to put a label on the face of the button.

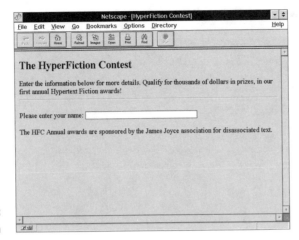

Figure 4-3
Start of a form

To finish the design of the HyperFiction form, let's add a submit button and a few more input fields. Open the file you used for the previous exercise, and enter the new HTML below:

```
<HTML>
<HEAD>
<TITLE>HyperFiction Contest</TITLE>
</HEAD>
<BODY>
<H2>The HyperFiction Contest</H2>
Enter the information below for more details. Qualify for thousands of dollars in prizes, in
our first annual Hypertext Fiction awards!
<HR>
<FORM ACTION="http://myhost.com/test.exe" METHOD="POST">
<P>Please enter your name: <INPUT TYPE="text" NAME="name" SIZE=40>
<P>E-mail address: <INPUT TYPE=''text'' NAME=''address'' SIZE=60>''<P><INPUT TYPE=|submit''
VALUE=''Send Info''>
</FORM>
The HFC Annual awards are sponsored by the James Joyce association for disassociated text.
</BODY>
</HTML>
```

Save your file and open it in your browser. Compare your results with those in Figure 4-4.

Sometimes browsers will submit a form that has only one input field after the user presses the <ENTER> key in this field.

Congratulations! You've completed your first form. You used the <FORM> tag to carve out a piece of your Web page to use as a form. You added <INPUT> tags to accept data entry from users of your form, and you put a simple button on the form for submitting the data.

In these early stages of design, you don't need to be too concerned with writing the application program that will eventually deal with your input fields. In fact, in devel-

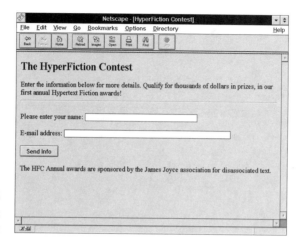

Figure 4-4
HyperFiction
Contest form

oping forms, you will often find yourself concentrating on the design and testing of the form first, and then developing the application later.

In some cases, you won't even need to write an application. Your Web server may provide you with several canned applications, some of which you can use to echo the results of your form back, showing you what NAME="*value*" pairs from your input fields were passed to the server. This is useful in testing. To see if your server has this echo application, try the following URLs in your ACTION attribute. Substitute your server's Internet name for *www.test.com*:

```
<FORM ACTION="http://www.test.com/cgi-bin/test-cgi" METHOD="POST">
<FORM ACTION="http://www.test.com/cgi-bin/echo" METHOD="POST">
```

Other canned applications can e-mail you the results of your forms. This might be quite sufficient to allow users to request information, or even to submit orders. A server script will provide you with nicely formatted output from your forms, but a quick and dirty way to get your form data e-mailed without relying on a server is to use the following URL:

```
<FORM ACTION="mailto:user@address" METHOD=POST>
```

When Netscape, Mosaic, and a high percentage of other browsers process this type of form ACTION statement, the input data from the form will be "mailed" to you. It's going to look pretty strange, because the data in the NAME="*value*" pairs is encoded, but at least it will be recognizable feedback during construction of your practice forms.

An application called MFORM will take an encoded form that was e-mailed using ACTION="mailto...", and format the message into comma-delimited data for import into spreadsheets and databases. MFORM runs in Windows, and allows you to use and process forms for data entry without having to write application scripts on the server. MFORM will play a part in an example in an upcoming lesson.

You can use one of the echo scripts or the e-mail option to start getting a feel for how the data in fields on your form is sent to the server.

After all this scaffolding, you're probably anxious to start whipping out order forms, travel vouchers, and payroll checks, etc. But first let's do a quick check to make sure you're ready for the road.

QUIZ 1

1. A form is usually associated with what on the server?
   a. an HTML file
   b. a URL
   c. a program
   d. a user

2. What happens if you don't include a METHOD statement in a <FORM> tag?
   a. The form will not work.
   b. The browser will assume you wanted to use "POST", since that's the safest.
   c. METHOD is an <INPUT> tag option, not a <FORM> tag option.
   d. The browser will default to METHOD="GET".

3. What happens when you use one of the "echo" programs as the ACTION URL in your forms?
   a. It echoes back your form.
   b. It doesn't return anything, but lets you test your form.
   c. It returns a status letting you know you reached the server okay.
   d. It returns the field names and values filled out in your form.

4. The purpose of the submit button is
   a. to define a form
   b. to define fields on the form that are sent to the server
   c. to specify the server
   d. to send the form data when the user clicks on it

SESSION 2

TEXT FIELDS

This is a busy lesson. In it, you will learn all of the text input elements, including a few more variations of the <INPUT> tag, and be introduced to two more tags: <SELECT> and <TEXTAREA>. You'll also learn about a button that zaps all the input fields on a form, either clearing them or returning them to their default values.

In Session 1 you used an <INPUT> tag with the TYPE="text" attribute. In this type of field, text appears in the field as the user enters it. For most types of data this is appropriate, but when entering passwords, secret keys, and birthdays, users might not want the text to appear on the screen. To preserve their secrets from onlookers, use the TYPE="password" attribute of the <INPUT> tag.

Passwords and Secret Decoder Messages

<INPUT TYPE="password"> protects the contents of a field from prying eyes. Anyone looking over the user's shoulder will see the text entered as a series of ******. The real text is, of course, passed to the application program along with the rest of the form data. If you are using the mailto URL to experiment with forms, be aware that these fields are e-mailed in plain text. The only place they are protected is on the screen itself when the user is filling out the form. Like all the other <INPUT TYPE=> values (except "submit" and "reset"), "password" requires a NAME attribute. Let's see how this works. Open a new file in your editor and enter the following HTML:

```
<HTML>
<HEAD>
<TITLE>The Bleating Edge MediaZine</TITLE>
</HEAD>
<BODY>
<H2>The Bleating Edge MediaZine</H2>
<P>This month's issue deals with the recent legislation mandating Slipper Chips to be part
of the manufacture of tennis shoes. This would allow approved agencies, through the proper
warrants, to track the anonymous whereabouts of highly paid athletes, insuring compliance
with contractual terms and agreements.
<P>To retrieve this month's issue, you must be a paid subscriber.
<HR>
<FORM ACTION="http://myhost.com/test.exe" METHOD="POST">
<P>Please enter your name: <INPUT TYPE="text" NAME="name" SIZE=40>
<P>And your Subscription # <INPUT TYPE="password" NAME="password" SIZE=40>
<P><INPUT TYPE="submit" VALUE="Browse Issue">
</FORM>
To subscribe to the B.E.M. use our
<A HREF="http://myhost.com/subscribe.exe>convenient subscription Form.</A>
</BODY>
</HTML>
```

Save the file and open it in your browser. When the form comes up, enter a name and password in the input fields. Your screen should now look like Figure 4-5. The name appears as entered, and the password is a series of asterisks, just as advertised.

Just Forget It!

Before leaving the <INPUT> tag, one other TYPE value deserves special mention. That is TYPE="reset". This option creates a button on the form that clears all the input fields. If the fields are given default values with the VALUE="xxx" attribute, it returns the fields to these values. Fields without default values become blank.

This option saves the user from having to use the <BACKSPACE> or <DELETE> keys to clear fields. It can also help when the user wants the field to revert to a default value.

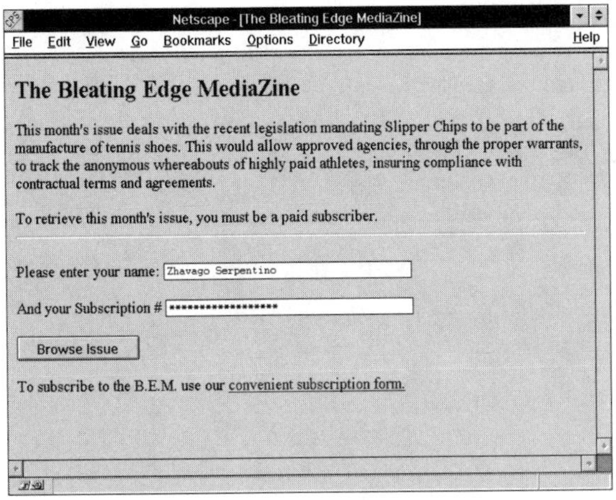

Figure 4-5
Password field for
subscription
number

The reset button is usually provided along with the submit button as standard fare on a typical form.

Its complete syntax, as it would appear on the form, would be

```
<INPUT TYPE="reset" VALUE="Clear">
```

The VALUE attribute, as in the case of "submit", defines the label that appears on the button. Open the same file you used in your last example and let's add a reset button:

```
<HTML>
<HEAD>
<TITLE>The Bleating Edge MediaZine</TITLE>
</HEAD>
<BODY>
<H2>The Bleating Edge MediaZine</H2>
<P>This month's issue deals with the recent legislation mandating Slipper Chips to be part
of the manufacture of tennis shoes. This would allow approved agencies, through the proper
warrants, to track the anonymous whereabouts of highly paid athletes, insuring compliance
with contractual terms and agreements.
<P>To retrieve this month's issue, you must be a paid subscriber.
<HR>
<FORM ACTION="http://myhost.com/test.exe" METHOD="POST">
<P>Please enter your name: <INPUT TYPE="text" NAME="name" SIZE=40>
<P>And your Subscription # <INPUT TYPE="password" NAME="password" SIZE=40>
<P><INPUT TYPE="submit" VALUE="Browse Issue">
<INPUT TYPE=''reset'' VALUE=''Clear''>
</FORM>
To subscribe to the B.E.M. use our
<A HREF="http://myhost.com/subscribe.exe>convenient subscription Form.</A>
</BODY>
</HTML>
```

Save the file and open it in your browser. Figure 4-6 shows what you should see. Play with the form a bit, enter text in the name and subscription fields, and then click reset and note what happens.

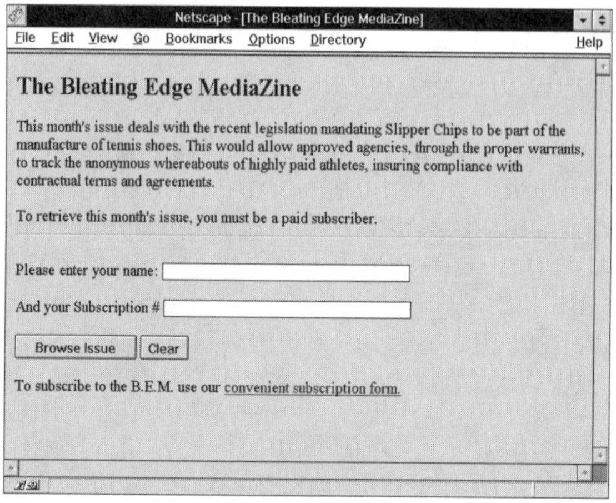

Figure 4-6
Completed form:
submit and reset
buttons

The next type of text input field is not an attribute of the <INPUT> tag at all. It's a field with a tag of its own called <TEXTAREA>.

For Spacious Fields

The <TEXTAREA> tag creates a multiline text entry field. Its syntax is

THE <TEXTAREA> TAG

```
<TEXTAREA
        [NAME=""]
        [ROWS=nn]
        [COLS=nn]
>
</TEXTAREA>
```

NAME is the symbolic name of the field, not displayed on the form.
ROWS are the number of vertical rows.
COLS are the number of horizontal columns.

<TEXTAREA> fields automatically have scroll bars. They are free-form fields and contain unlimited amounts of text. The ROWS attribute is the number of characters wide the text box is, and the COLS attribute is the number of characters high. Note also that <TEXTAREA> requires a closing </TEXTAREA> tag.

You can use <TEXTAREA> in a form for memos and open-ended free-form text input. For example, let's create a form for reporting PC problems. <TEXTAREA> will be the problem description field. Open a new file in your editor and enter the following HTML:

```
<HTML>
<HEAD>
<TITLE>PC Problem Reporting</TITLE>
</HEAD>
```

```
<BODY>
<H1>PC Problem Reporting</H1>
This automated help desk will diagnose and repair your PC given a clear and comprehensive
description of the problem. After entering your problem description below, please step back
away from your desk as the electromagnetic fields produced by the cellular automata used for
repairs can molecularly alter caffeine patches and nanic implants.
<HR>
<FORM ACTION="http://www.ainova.com/cellbyte.exe" METHOD="POST">
<P><STRONG>Problem Description:</STRONG>
<P><TEXTAREA NAME="problem" ROWS=5 COLS=55>
</TEXTAREA>
<P><INPUT TYPE="submit" VALUE="Submit">
<INPUT TYPE="reset" VALUE="Clear">
</FORM>
</BODY>
</HTML>
```

Save the file and open it in your browser. Figure 4-7 illustrates the appearance of the <TEXTAREA> tag in your HTML.

You may have noticed that the VALUE attribute is missing in the <TEXTAREA> tag. This doesn't mean you can't assign <TEXTAREA> a default value, it just means that you have to do it a little differently. Default values for the <TEXTAREA> tag are entered between the tags. They must be in regular text, though—straight ASCII—no HTML or fancy stuff. New lines are honored, however, so line breaks you put in your editor show up in the default text. Here is a sample of using default text:

```
<P><TEXTAREA NAME="problem" ROWS=5 COLS=55>
If your problem is with the monitor, just press SUBMIT,
otherwise, replace this with your problem description.
</TEXTAREA>
```

If you include this snippet in your HTML from the previous example, you get the result displayed in Figure 4-8.

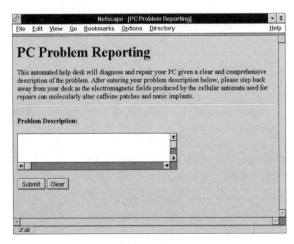

Figure 4-7
The <TEXTAREA>
tag in action

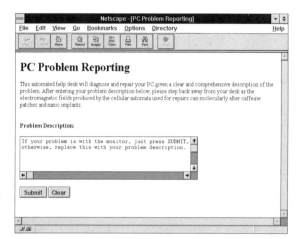

Figure 4-8
<TEXTAREA> with
default values

The next tag still deals with text but introduces elements used for building menus.

Making Choices

The <SELECT> tag lets the user pull down menus of items, and then select an item by clicking on it. You're probably familiar with these in Web browsers and other GUI applications. They provide a convenient way for users to pick from one or more alternatives. The syntax for the <SELECT> tag is

THE <SELECT> TAG
<SELECT
[NAME=""]
[SIZE=*nn*]
[MULTIPLE]
>
<OPTION [SELECTED]> *first option*
<OPTION [SELECTED]> *second option*
</SELECT>
NAME is the symbolic name of the field, not displayed on the form.
SIZE is the number of option lines displayed. Default is 1.
MULTIPLE, if present, means multiple options can be selected.
<OPTION> indicates one or more options after the start <SELECT> tag.
[SELECTED], if present, means the option is selected by default.

The actual appearance of options in the <SELECT> tag may vary based on the browser. On most browsers, specifying a size of 1 will display only the first option, and provide a drop-down selection menu for the remaining ones. For example, the following syntax:

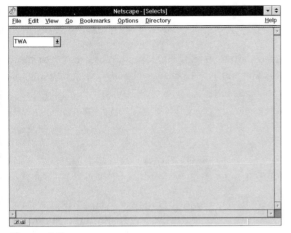

Figure 4-9
<SELECT> rolled up

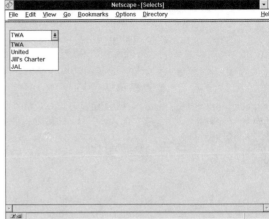

Figure 4-10
<SELECT> rolled down

```
<SELECT NAME="firstchoice" SIZE=1>
<OPTION> TWA
<OPTION> United
<OPTION> Jill's Charter
<OPTION> JAL
</SELECT>
```

created Figures 4-9 and 4-10 in Netscape. Figure 4-9 shows this menu's default state, and Figure 4-10 shows what the screen looks like when a user has clicked to pull down a menu.

If a SIZE option greater than 1 is used, the browser creates a scrollable list. Changing SIZE=1 to SIZE=3 in the example above creates the effect shown in Figure 4-11.

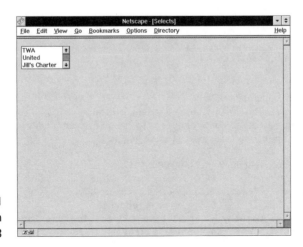

Figure 4-11
<SELECT> with
SIZE=3

If the MULTIPLE option is specified, the user can select more than one option. With MULTIPLE, the options are always represented as a scrollable list, regardless of what is specified in SIZE.

The SELECTED attribute is used within an <OPTION> tag to create one or more default selections. To default to Jill's Charter in the example above, you can use the following HTML:

```
<SELECT NAME="firstchoice" SIZE=1>
<OPTION> TWA
<OPTION> United
<OPTION SELECTED> Jill's Charter
<OPTION> JAL
</SELECT>
```

You're now ready to design a more functional form. First you'll construct the basic form template and solicit some of the usual information, like name and customer id. Open a new file in your editor and enter the following HTML:

```
<TITLE>Consumer Vengeance, Inc.</TITLE>
</HEAD>
<BODY>
<H2>Consumer Vengeance Clearinghouse</H2>
<P>Please fill out the information below to order any of our
convenient form letters. Please use your customer id to place an order. To receive a
customer id, call our toll free operators at 1-800-MAKEME.
<HR>
<FORM ACTION="http://www.cvc.com/order" METHOD="POST">
<BR>Please Enter your name: <INPUT TYPE="text" NAME="name" SIZE=40>
<BR>Your Customer number  : <INPUT TYPE="password" NAME="custno" SIZE=40>
<BR><INPUT TYPE="text" NAME="email" SIZE=40> E-mail address
<BR><INPUT TYPE="submit" VALUE="Order">
<INPUT TYPE="reset" VALUE="Clear">
</FORM>
</BODY>
</HTML>
```

Now add a free-form text field for an address, and a selection menu for the type of form letter the user is ordering:

```
<TITLE>Consumer Vengeance, Inc.</TITLE>
</HEAD>
<BODY>
<H2>Consumer Vengeance Clearinghouse</H2>
<P>Please fill out the information below to order any of our
convenient form letters. Please use your customer id to place an order. To receive a
customer id, call our toll free operators at 1-800-MAKEME.
<HR>
<FORM ACTION="http://www.cvc.com/order" METHOD="POST">
<BR><INPUT TYPE="text" NAME="name" SIZE=40> Name
<BR><INPUT TYPE="password" NAME="custno" SIZE=40> Customer Number
<BR><INPUT TYPE="text" NAME="email" SIZE=40> E-mail address
<P>Enter The Recipient's Name, Company, and Mailing Address for the Form Letter:
<BR><TEXTAREA NAME="recipient" ROWS=4 COLS=55></TEXTAREA>
```

```
<P>Enter Type of Form Letter:
<BR><SELECT NAME=|formlet■>
<OPTION> Tenant Deposit Complaint
<OPTION> Contesting Charge for Defective Mechandise
<OPTION> New Car Lemon Letter to Dealer
<OPTION> Freedom of Information Act Request
<OPTION> Social Security Refund
<OPTION> Media Damage
</SELECT>
<P><INPUT TYPE="submit" VALUE="Order">
<INPUT TYPE="reset" VALUE="Clear">
</FORM>
</BODY>
</HTML>
```

Save the file and bring it up in your browser. Figure 4-12 shows your final product.

This form provides a hypothetical order form for a company that delivers a product (in this case, complaint letters) via e-mail. Note that the input fields were defined before their corresponding text to enable the form elements to line up. Other ways of lining elements of a form up will be covered in Session 4. Now it's time to review what you've learned.

1. The SIZE option in the <SELECT> tag controls
   a. how wide the <SELECT> field is
   b. how many <OPTION> tags are allowed
   c. how many <OPTION> tags are displayed
   d. how long the text of an option can be

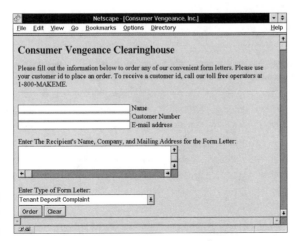

Figure 4-12
The consumer
order form

2. The TYPE="reset" option of the <INPUT> tag is used to
   a. resubmit the form
   b. clear all the values on the form
   c. reset all the values on the form to their default values
   d. delete the form

3. To assign default values to a <TEXTAREA> field
   a. Use the VALUE= option.
   b. Put the text between <TEXTAREA> and </TEXTAREA>.
   c. Put the text in the NAME= option.
   d. <TEXTAREA> is an input only field; you cannot assign it values.

4. To set a default OPTION in the <SELECT> tag
   a. Use the VALUE= option.
   b. Put the text after the <OPTION>.
   c. Put the text inside of the tag.
   d. Use the SELECTED option in the <OPTION> tag.

RADIO BUTTONS, CHECK BOXES, AND CUSTOM BUTTONS

In this lesson you'll put the finishing touches on form design. Radio buttons, check boxes, and custom buttons are the remaining three elements that can be used on forms. When you master these, you will have mastered all of the design elements that can appear on a form (except for one, but it doesn't really "appear" on the form). Not a bad three session's work!

Radio Buttons

Radio buttons are a TYPE attribute of the INPUT tag. To briefly review, the generic syntax of the INPUT tag is

THE ABBREVIATED <INPUT> TAG
<INPUT
[TYPE="*field-type*"]
[NAME="*field-name*"]
[SIZE=*width*]
[VALUE="*default-value*"]
[MAXLENGTH=*maxchars*]
>

Using TYPE="radio", that is, <INPUT TYPE="radio">, creates a radio button on a form. Radio buttons present mutually exclusive options; when one is selected, the others are automatically deselected. (They're like the dial on a radio, which you can only have tuned to one channel at a time, even though many channels are available. Hence the name.) A typical use for radio buttons is for something like payment options:

```
<INPUT TYPE="radio" NAME="cr" VALUE="M">Master Card
<INPUT TYPE="radio" NAME="cr" VALUE="V">Visa
<INPUT TYPE="radio" NAME="cr" VALUE="A">American Express
```

Figure 4-13 illustrates how this HTML segment appears on a form.

Notice that in this figure, none of the circles is selected. You can choose a default entry, which shows up selected on the initial form, by adding a CHECKED option to one of the <INPUT> tags:

```
<INPUT TYPE="radio" NAME="cr" VALUE="M">Master Card
<INPUT TYPE="radio" NAME="cr" VALUE="V">Visa
<INPUT TYPE="radio" NAME="cr" VALUE="A" CHECKED>American Express
```

Now American Express will come up selected, as in Figure 4-14. If the user clicks Visa or MasterCard, American Express is automatically deselected.

The syntax for the radio button follows the same syntax as described in the <INPUT> tag, but a few of the attributes are used in special ways. The NAME attribute must be the same for each selection that belongs in the group. In the example above, the symbolic name "cr" holds the value of the type of credit the user selects.

Notice in Figure 4-14 that what is actually displayed as the options on screen is the text after the tag. The VALUE attribute is not used for display; rather, it tells the browser what to pass back to the server. For example, if MasterCard is selected, the value "M" is passed back. This makes it easier for the program on the server to process the return value. The VALUE attribute is required on radio buttons, and each button's VALUE should be unique.

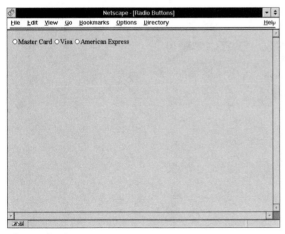

Figure 4-13
Radio buttons

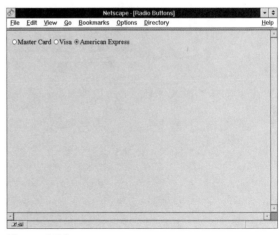

Figure 4-14
Radio button selected

Check Boxes

Check boxes are like radio buttons, but you can select more than one at a time, using the CHECKED option to indicate as many items as desired. For check boxes, TYPE="checkbox" is used in the <INPUT> tag instead of TYPE="radio". An example of check box code follows:

```
<INPUT TYPE="checkbox" NAME="toppings" VALUE="P">Pepperoni
<INPUT TYPE="checkbox" NAME="toppings" VALUE="X" CHECKED>Extra Cheese
<INPUT TYPE="checkbox" NAME="toppings" VALUE="G">Green Peppers
<INPUT TYPE="checkbox" NAME="toppings" VALUE="A" CHECKED>Anchovies
<INPUT TYPE="checkbox" NAME="toppings" VALUE="O">Onions
```

NAME="toppings" identifies all these as belonging to the same check box group. The VALUE attribute is required, and should be unique, just as it is for radio buttons. Check boxes look a little different from radio buttons on the screen. Figure 4-15 illustrates the check box group defined above.

Radio buttons and check boxes are very useful for online surveys and questionnaires, as you'll see in Session 4.

Custom Buttons

There is another type of button that has a flashier use in forms than submit and reset do. It's called the image button. Image buttons combine the functions of an inline image and a submit button. In future version of HTML, this will probably be an option of TYPE="submit", but currently it has its own type: TYPE="image". Here is an example of an image used as a submit button:

```
<INPUT TYPE="image" NAME="sub" SRC="go.gif" ALIGN="top">
```

The inline image go.gif will be placed on the form as a button. When it is clicked, all the data filled in on the form so far will be sent to the server, just as if a regular sub-

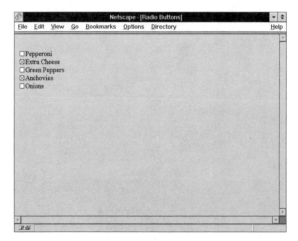

Figure 4-15
Check boxes

mit button had been clicked. Figure 4-16 illustrates the use of an image button on the order form used in Session 2. You can have multiple image buttons in the form, as well as a mixture of image and submit buttons.

ALIGN works as it does with an inline image, specifying where text will be aligned in relationship to the image. The default is ALIGN="bottom".

Revisiting the Order Form

Before moving on, let's put together what has been covered so far. Your project will be to build a comprehensive order form. The form should have the following ingredients:

- Customer name, address, phone, and e-mail
- Method of payment
- Ship To address
- Items ordered
- Totals

Don't worry too much about style right now; you'll refine that in the next lesson. Just make sure you have a clear idea of how all the items in the ingredients list will map to form elements. Let's take them step by step.

Building an Order Form

Building the first part of this form will be easy. You'll gather a handful of elements for the customer name, address, phone, and e-mail, and write a short thank you on the order. Order forms are usually accessed by users after they've seen other parts of your online catalog, so the structure focuses on allowing them to order something they've seen, rather than describing company products.

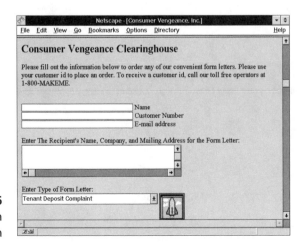

Figure 4-16
Order form with
an image button

With that in mind, let's construct the first section of the order form for a hypothetical company that deals in holograms. Open a new file with your editor and enter the following HTML:

```
<HTML>
<HEAD>
<TITLE>Jane's Holographic Outlet</TITLE>
</HEAD>
<H2>Thanks For Ordering From Jane's Holographic!</H2>
<HR>
<FORM ACTION="mailto:orders@jh.com" METHOD="POST">
<p>Your Name:
<BR>
<INPUT TYPE="TEXT" NAME="oname" SIZE=30  MAXLENGTH=30>
<P>Your Address:
<BR>
<TEXTAREA NAME="oaddress" ROWS=4 COLS=30>
</TEXTAREA>
<P>Daytime Phone:
<BR>
<INPUT TYPE="TEXT" NAME="ophone" SIZE=20  MAXLENGTH=20>
<P>Your E-mail Address:
<BR>
<INPUT TYPE="TEXT" NAME="oemail" SIZE=50 MAXLENGTH=50>
</FORM>
<BODY>
</BODY>
</HTML>
```

Everything should be familiar. The ACTION attribute of the form is a mailto URL, which will mail the user's order to you. Later, when you're familiar with scripts, you can actually record the order directly into a database. The <TEXTAREA> element was used for the address instead of creating multiple input fields for street address 1, street address 2, city, etc.

Now let's work on the next section: method of payment. Add the following just before the </FORM> tag:

```
<HR>
<H3>METHOD OF PAYMENT:</H3>
<P>
Entering your credit card number is optional. If you are concerned with
Internet security, just fill out the Form, leaving the credit card info
blank. Jane's will call you at your daytime phone number to get your credit information.
<P>
<SELECT NAME="ctype" SIZE=1>
<OPTION SELECTED>VISA
<OPTION VALUE>MASTERCARD
<OPTION>Call Me For Credit Info
</SELECT>
CARD #:
<INPUT TYPE="text" NAME="crno" SIZE=20  MAXLENGTH=30>
EXP.DATE:
<INPUT TYPE="TEXT" NAME="expdate" SIZE=8  MAXLENGTH=10>
<HR>
```

The <SELECT> element was used for the credit card info instead of a radio button. This allows the other credit information to fit on the same line, and makes the form a little more compact. Note the MAXLENGTH attributes associated with date and credit card number. This gives a little buffer in case this form is still in use in the year 2000, and/or credit card numbers expand in length.

You've also given the users an out if they're a little nervous about sending their credit card number across the Internet.

The Ship To section is similar to the first section. The NAME attributes have to be changed, to keep the variables separate from the customer's name and address. You can also add an area for personalized text to put on a gift card. Add the following to your HTML, just before the </FORM> tag:

```
<HR>
<H3>PLEASE SHIP TO:</H3>
SHIP TO (RECEIVER'S NAME):
<BR>Leave blank if same as address above
<BR>
<INPUT TYPE="text" NAME="sname" SIZE=30  MAXLENGTH=30>
<P> Receiver's Address:
<BR>
<TEXTAREA NAME="saddress" ROWS=4  COLS=30>
</TEXTAREA>
<P> Ship Via:<br>
<INPUT TYPE="RADIO" NAME="svia"  VALUE="FedEx">FedEx Overnight
<INPUT TYPE="RADIO" NAME="svia"  VALUE="TwoDay Priority">Two-Day
Priority
<INPUT TYPE="RADIO" NAME="svia" VALUE="FirstClass">First Class
<P> Gift Card to Read:
<TEXTAREA NAME="gcard" ROWS=4 COLS=30>
</TEXTAREA>
```

Radio buttons have been added to let users select a shipping method. Now you can move into the actual line items ordered. Add the following, again just before the </FORM> tag:

```
<HR>
<H3>Holographic Items Ordered:</H3>
BUTTONS:
<BR>
<SELECT NAME="btns" SIZE=1>
<OPTION SELECTED>
<OPTION>$15 Humphrey Bogart
<OPTION>$15 Mars Landing
<OPTION>$15 Time Particle
<OPTION> No Button
</SELECT>
QUANTITY:
<INPUT TYPE="text" NAME="btnqty" VALUE="" SIZE=3  MAXLENGTH=5>
COST (PRICE x QUANTITY): $
<INPUT TYPE="text" NAME="btncost" VALUE="" SIZE=5  MAXLENGTH=10>
<BR>
<SELECT NAME="btns" SIZE=1>
<OPTION SELECTED>
```

continued on next page

continued from previous page

```
<OPTION>$15 Humphrey Bogart
<OPTION>$15 Mars Landing
<OPTION>$15 Time Particle
<OPTION> No Button
</SELECT>
QUANTITY:
<INPUT TYPE="text" NAME="btnqty" VALUE="" SIZE=3  MAXLENGTH=5>
COST (PRICE x QUANTITY): $
<INPUT TYPE="text" NAME="btncost" VALUE="" SIZE=5  MAXLENGTH=10>
<BR>
<SELECT NAME="btns" SIZE=1>
<OPTION SELECTED>
<OPTION>$15 Humphrey Bogart
<OPTION>$15 Mars Landing
<OPTION>$15 Time Particle
<OPTION> No Button
</SELECT>
QUANTITY:
<INPUT TYPE="text" NAME="btnqty" VALUE="" SIZE=3  MAXLENGTH=5>
COST (PRICE x QUANTITY): $
<INPUT TYPE="text" NAME="btncost" VALUE="" SIZE=5  MAXLENGTH=10>
```

Jane's Holographic only carries a limited stock of buttons. If the company had a larger inventory, you could make the item fields blank, rather than using the <SELECT> tag, and you would probably want to add an item#. For Jane's three products, though, this should be sufficient.

Now for the totals. Add the following to your HTML to wrap up the form. Insert it just before the </FORM> tag:

```
<HR>
<H3>Order Total:</H3>
<HR>
SUBTOTAL:
<INPUT TYPE="text"  NAME="subtotal" VALUE="" SIZE=8 MAXLENGTH=10>
<P>Please add $1.50 for shipping and handling (no item limit). For
orders outside of the continental U.S. <A HREF="mailto:rates@jh.com">
send email</A> for rates, include your destination!
<P>TOTAL Including Shipping:
<INPUT TYPE="text"  NAME="total" VALUE="" SIZE=8 MAXLENGTH=10>
<P>Would you like to send a comment to Jane's?:
<BR>
<TEXTAREA NAME="comments" ROWS=4 COLS=30>
</TEXTAREA>
<P>
<INPUT TYPE="submit" VALUE="E-mail Order">
<INPUT TYPE="reset" VALUE="Clear Form">
<P>
```

One of the current limitations of HTML forms is that you cannot have the form calculate totals for users until they submit the information. When the form above is e-mailed, you'll have to check carefully for errors in arithmetic, complete shipping addresses, etc.

In this respect it's not much different from a paper form, but what it lacks in validation it makes up for in speed and accessibility.

That completes the order form! When it's all put together, you have a scrollable order form with sections separated by horizontal lines as seen in Figure 4-17. When the form is submitted, all the information will be e-mailed to the address mailto:orders@jh.com. Since this is a mailto URL, it doesn't require any interaction with the Web server, or any application scripts. The data from the form is encoded (more on encoding in Session 4) and e-mailed from the user's browser to Jane's e-mail address.

QUIZ 3

1. A custom submit button is created by
   a. specifying an image type on a regular submit button
   b. using an <INPUT TYPE="submit" SRC="go.gif"> syntax
   c. using the TYPE="image" option of the <INPUT> tag
   d. pasting an image onto the submit button

2. Radio buttons
   a. can be used to receive multiple options simultaneously
   b. should each have a different NAME
   c. are used for selecting mutually exclusive options
   d. provide dials for selecting numeric quantities

3. A form
   a. cannot span more than one screen
   b. can have scroll bars by using the SIZE option in the <FORM> tag
   c. Can only be scrolled horizontally
   d. must have the submit button on the first screen if it is scrollable

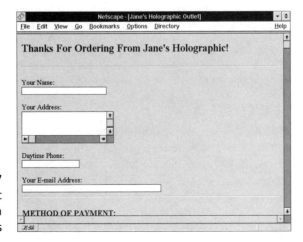

Figure 4-17
The Holographic order form with scroll bars

4. A check box is used for
   a. mutually exclusive options
   b. a single option that can be on or off
   c. a single character input field
   d. multiple options that can be chosen simultaneously

A SCRIPTLESS FORM

In this session you'll build a questionnaire with the skills you've developed. You'll learn some advanced techniques for formatting your form using tables, and you'll find out what forms that are e-mailed actually look like. Taking the e-mailed form, you'll extract the data from the questionnaire and append it to an Access database or an Excel spreadsheet.

The Questionnaire

A questionnaire can be a useful way to collect information on the Web. It can be filled out in seconds, and it provides a way to get feedback from customers, browsers, and other sundry travelers through your pages. The questionnaire will have to provide some benefit to the user, though. Not too many people are thrilled with voluntarily providing detailed information about themselves, especially in this day and age.

Try asking about potential services of interest to the users, or provide a way for users to influence what's on your pages. These types of surveys make it in your users' interest to respond. Questionnaires can also have much more limited scope, of course.

One useful application for a questionnaire is within your organization. Departments can put up anonymous questionnaires asking for ratings on various services, and offer Web suggestion boxes for improving their business processes. Questionnaires can also provide entertainment. For example, Figure 4-18 illustrates an online confessional.

Before tackling a confession booth, you'll need to cover the building blocks of an online survey. You have a lot of HTML elements at your disposal, but it may not be intuitive to you yet how these can be used to solicit a range of information. Let's construct a questionnaire that employs a wide variety of response formats. You can then extrapolate parts of this example to whip out a vanilla questionnaire for any occasion.

The Scenario

Joe Windbag decides that what the Web needs is an online dating service. But ever since he lost $10,000 in a yak dairy substitute, he has become leery of new markets. Especially those he doesn't quite understand, like yaks and Webs. What Joe really wants is to do a survey and find out what type of things people might like in an online dating service, and how better to find this out than by putting up a Web "storefront" and asking for opinions? Joe turns to you. You set him up with a Web page on a commercial provider and then begin working on designing his questionnaire.

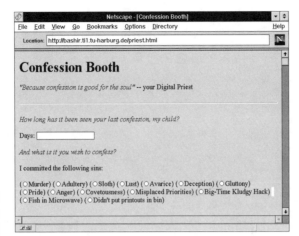

Figure 4-18
The infamous
online confessional

The Rough

First, build a simple form template. You want this questionnaire e-mailed to Joe, since it's not clear that the idea is going to fly, and Joe doesn't want to pay extra for a commercial account that allows scripts on the server. Open a file with your editor and enter the following HTML to start the questionnaire with a framework:

```
<HTML>
<HEAD>
<TITLE>The Date Web</TITLE>
</HEAD>
<BODY>
<H1 ALIGN="center">The Date Web</H1>
<H3 ALIGN="center"><I>Snag the Guy or Gal of Your Dreams!</I></H3>
<HR>
<STRONG>The Date Web</STRONG> by Spinsters Inc. is introducing a new service for
the busy professional. Our Web binds time and space, allowing you unprecedented contacts
with complete anonymity.
<P>In order to best suit your needs, we would like to customize
the service to your requirements. Before fully deploying The Date Web
we would like to hear how it would best fit your expectations.
<P>Please take a moment to fill out the following questionairre. Your
responses will determine the nature of the service and directly affect
its benefits and utility to you. Your responses are strictly anonymous.
<HR>
<FORM ACTION="mailto:survey@yakproducts.com" METHOD="POST">
<INPUT TYPE="submit" VALUE="Submit">
<INPUT TYPE="reset" VALUE="Clear Form">
</FORM>
</BODY>
</HTML>
```

The form is set. You've got the company introduction, the rationale for the questionnaire, and the form is ready to fire out responses to your e-mail address. Now you can get down to the nitty-gritty of finding out just what the lovelorn of cyberspace are look-ing for in a service. First it will be useful to get some idea about their age and gender to help identify your market. Add the following HTML to your work in progress:

```
<H3>About You...</H3>
<STRONG>Sex:</STRONG>
<SELECT NAME="sex">
<OPTION>Male
<OPTION>Female
</SELECT>
<BR>
<STRONG>Age:</STRONG>
<INPUT TYPE="radio" NAME="age" VALUE="lt20">Under 20
<INPUT TYPE="radio" NAME="age" VALUE="20some">20 - 29
<INPUT TYPE="radio" NAME="age" VALUE="30some">30 - 39
<INPUT TYPE="radio" NAME="age" VALUE="40some">40 - 49
<INPUT TYPE="radio" NAME="age" VALUE="40some">50 - 59
<INPUT TYPE="radio" NAME="age" VALUE="60plus">60 and over
```

Now add another section, using some HTML formatting, to identify what users are look-ing for:

```
<H3>About the Service...</H3>
<STRONG>What services do you feel are requirements:</STRONG>
<PRE>
Scanned Pictures                        <INPUT TYPE="checkbox" NAME="Q1a">
        Voice Samples                   <INPUT TYPE="checkbox" NAME="Q1b">
        Private Response Boxes          <INPUT TYPE="checkbox" NAME="Q1c">
        Anonymous Chat Rooms            <INPUT TYPE="checkbox" NAME="Q1d">
        Anonymous e-mail boxes          <INPUT TYPE="checkbox" NAME="Q1e">
        Match on both partners criteria <INPUT TYPE="checkbox" NAME="Q1f">
        Selectively ignore              <INPUT TYPE="checkbox" NAME="Q1g">
        Other:                          <INPUT TYPE="TEXT" NAME="Q1other" VALUE="">
</PRE><P>


<strong>
Please rank the following statements in order of importance,
by selecting the phrase you feel corresponds with each rank...
</strong>
<br>
where <strong>1.</strong> is the most important rank, <strong>2.</strong>
the second most important rank, <strong>3.</strong><br> etc. Please use
a given number only once per statement.

<P><STRONG>Things I would most like to know about a potential partner are...
</STRONG>

<P><select name="physical">
<option selected>1
<option>2
<option>3
<option>4
</select>
```

```
Physical Description

<P><select name="interests">
<option>1
<option selected>2
<option>3
<option>4
</select>
Interests, Hobbies, Sports

<P><select name="skills">
<option>1
<option>2
<option selected>3
<option>4
</select>
IQ, Education, Occupation

<P><select name="mood">
<option>1
<option>2
<option>3
<option selected>4
</select>
Personality, State of Mind
```

Figures 4-19 and 4-20 show some of what you have so far.

When a user fills out the form and submits it, you will receive something similar in content to the following as your e-mail message:

```
sex=Female&age=20some&Q1a=on&Q1b=on&Q1c=on&Q1e=on&Q1f=on&Q1g=on
&Q1other=Rorschack+tests&physical=1&interests=3&skills=4&mood=2
```

Figure 4-19
The Date Web questionnaire—screen 1

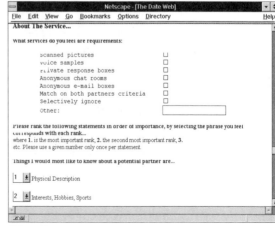

Figure 4-20
The Date Web questionnaire—screen 2

Yeck! This is the encoding that a Web browser does to its data before sending it to the server, or in this case, the e-mail recipient. Let's look at what the browser is actually doing when it encodes the data.

First, it separates each variable=value pair with an ampersand (&). Then, if it finds any spaces in the data the user entered, it converts them to pluses (+). Note that for the radio box variable (age), only one value is assigned (age=20some). For the check boxes, each check box has a value assigned (e.g., Q1a=on, Q1b=on, etc.) Since you didn't specify a value in the check boxes, they default to "on" if they were checked (if they aren't checked, they simply aren't included in the encoded data string). If a user enters any special characters like tabs or quotes in any of the fields, they will be encoded as a hexadecimal string in form of %nn, where *nn* is the hexadecimal number corresponding to the character's ASCII value.

It would be a real pain to decode this message manually and enter it in your questionnaire database. Luckily, the MFORM utility can be used to streamline the process. To process this encoded data, you need to go through these four steps:

1. Save the mail message as a text file. If you use Eudora, you can do this using Save As from the file menu. It's best to use the file extension .mfm, since that is what MFORM looks for first. In this example, the encoded mail message was saved as q.mfm.

2. Start the MFORM application. (Installation instructions are at the beginning of the book.) From within MFORM, open the q.mfm file you saved in step 1 above. You'll see the encoded message in the Encoded Text window.

3. Click Convert. This converts the encoded text to a comma delimited format for importing into Access (or other databases). The result is shown in Figure 4-21. Note that the field names are in the first row of comma delimited data, and the data elements are in the second. This allows you to create a new table from scratch when you import into Access.

4. Now save the file as q.txt. This saves the decoded text in comma delimited format.

5. Import this file into Access. On Access import options, choose Text (Delimited), Create New Table, and check the box that says First Row Contains Field Names.

Figure 4-22 shows the results of the steps with the data stored in an Access table. To append more results to the table, just follow the same steps, but in Access import options, select Append to Existing Table instead of Create New Table.

When using a database table to store form results, you'll want to predefine the table with all the fields that can be used in the forms. Check boxes, for example, may or may not send a field of data, depending on whether the box was checked. If you import using

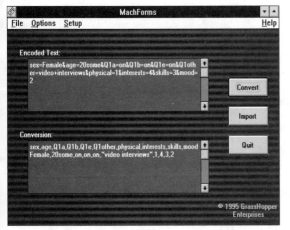

Figure 4-21
MFORM conversion of questionnaire results

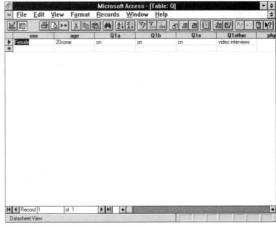

Figure 4-22
Access table with successful import

MFORM with the first row as field names, it will be able to find and update the proper fields, even if some fields are not present.

Tables and Forms

Now that you've stepped through the entire questionnaire building process, from form design to database update, let's return to the form itself, and explore some methods of refining its appearance.

With the introduction of tables in HTML 3.0, fields can be presented in a more versatile way. You'll remember from Chapter 2 that the basic syntax for the <TABLE> tag is (considerably simplified):

THE ABBREVIATED <TABLE> TAG	
<TABLE [BORDER]>	Begins the table. Optional border.
<TD>	Table cell1.
<TD>	Table cell2, etc.
<TR>	Starts a new row.
</TABLE>	Ends the table.

Using tables, input fields can be aligned, justified within cells, and the whole presentation can be structured much more aesthetically. Let's look at what tables can do with simple form constructs first.

When you first started building forms, you built input fields like the following:

```
<P>Name
<BR><INPUT TYPE="text" NAME="name" SIZE=35 MAXLENGTH=35>
<BR>Company
```

continued on next page

continued from previous page

```
<BR><INPUT TYPE="text" NAME="company" SIZE=35 MAXLENGTH=35>
<BR>Address
<BR><TEXTAREA NAME="Address" ROWS=4 COLS=35>
</TEXTAREA>
<BR>Phone
<BR><INPUT TYPE="text" NAME="phone" SIZE=12 MAXLENGTH=20>
<BR>Fax
<BR><INPUT TYPE="text" NAME="fax" SIZE=12 MAXLENGTH=20>
<BR>Email
<BR><INPUT TYPE="text" NAME="e-mail" SIZE=50 MAXLENGTH=60>
<P><INPUT TYPE="submit" VALUE="Submit">
<INPUT TYPE="reset" VALUE="Clear">
```

Figure 4-23 shows how such a form would look.

Using <BR> for line breaks instead of <P> tags makes the fields more compact on most browsers, but it still looks a little sprawled. Let's see what you can do with tables. Open a new file and enter the following HTML:

```
<TABLE BORDER>
<Caption>Application Form</Caption>
<TD>Name
<TD><INPUT TYPE="text" NAME="name" SIZE=35 MAXLENGTH=35>
<TD>Phone
<TD><INPUT TYPE="text" NAME="phone" SIZE=12 MAXLENGTH=20>
<TR>
<TD>Company
<TD><INPUT TYPE="text" NAME="company" SIZE=35 MAXLENGTH=35>
<TD>Fax
<TD><INPUT TYPE="text" NAME="fax" SIZE=12 MAXLENGTH=20>
<TR>
<TD>Address
<TD rowspan=4><TEXTAREA NAME="Address" ROWS=4 COLS=35>
</TEXTAREA>
<TR>
```

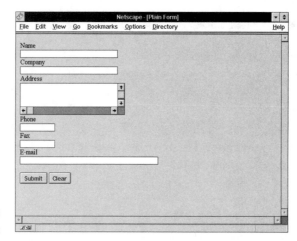

Figure 4-23
Plain input form

```
<TD>
<TD><INPUT TYPE="submit" VALUE="Submit">
<TD><INPUT TYPE="reset" VALUE="Clear">
<TR>
<TR>
<TR>
<TD>Email
<TD colspan=2><INPUT TYPE="text" NAME="e-mail" SIZE=50 MAXLENGTH=60>
<TR>
</table>
```

Save the file and open it in your browser. You should see a much-improved form design illustrated in Figure 4-24. Remember that table cells can also hold images, so you can replace the generic submit button with image buttons to improve the appearance even further.

1. When importing data from e-mail forms into Access, why predefine the fields? MFORM puts them on the first row for you.
   a. You cannot use the first row of data to create fields in a new Access database.
   b. Predefined fields offer better validation.
   c. If you don't predefine fields, MFORM will not be able to load more data.
   d. Some fields, like check boxes, would be missing if they had no data.

2. Why is it a good idea to use MAXLENGTH on all fields that will be imported to a database?
   a. It's easier to report.
   b. It works better in e-mail.
   c. It prevents data from being truncated.
   d. Data must be exactly the same length as the database fields.

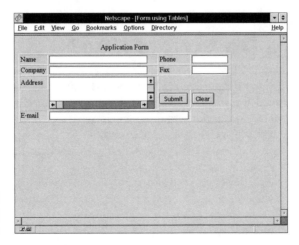

Figure 4-24
Input form using tables

3. The purpose of a default value on a check box is
   a. to put the value in the box
   b. to check the box, if a value is present
   c. to return the value if the box is checked
   d. VALUE is not a valid option on a <CHECKBOX> element

4. Why would you use an e-mail form instead of one with regular scripts?
   a. for faster response
   b. because e-mail forms are handled automatically by the Web server
   c. because e-mail forms allow more flexible form design
   d. because e-mail forms don't need to be processed by a Web server

Back in Session 3 you created an order form for Jane's Holographic. Redesign this form using one or more tables between <FORM> and </FORM>. What do tables do to the data when it is e-mailed with the mailto URL?

WRITING SCRIPTS

Now it's time to take the plunge! In this session you'll go to the heart of script writing with *CGI* scripts. CGI (Common Gateway Interface) scripts are basically programs that the Web server runs for a form. They can be written in whatever language is available on the Web server. Scripts can be written in industrial strength languages like C or C++, or they can be in interpreted languages like the UNIX C, Bourne, and Korn shells, Perl, etc. Some platforms have languages that are uniquely theirs, so if you run a Windows Web server, for example, you can use Visual Basic for your CGI scripts.

Where Do Scripts Live?

Scripts, like HTML, must reside on the Web server. Unlike HTML, though, scripts usually live in a specific directory called *cgi-bin*. This directory is protected so that not just anyone can plop scripts into it. You need to be a friend (or a paying customer!) to have the Webmaster move your scripts into cgi-bin so they can be run by forms. As always, however, there are a couple of workarounds.

An option in a Web server's configuration files, for example, can allow you to run scripts out of your own directory. This option, known as a *ScriptAlias* or the *Exec* directive, can allow any directory on the server to store and execute scripts referenced by forms. In Chapter 5 you'll learn how to set this option yourself as you go through the steps of setting up your own Web server. For now, you will need to arrange with the Webmaster to run scripts out of your own directory, or access to the cgi-bin directory.

Just before diving into scripts, let's revisit the <FORM> tag and review how it works. The <FORM> tag ties the Web form to the CGI script, and the <FORM> tag's options control how data transfers from browser to server. Let's follow the <FORM> tag and its attributes upstream, and see what it delivers to the script.

Review of <FORM>

The <FORM> tag uses the ACTION attribute to request a script by name and location. In scripts that reside in cgi-bin directories, it's common to see a <FORM> tag like this:

```
<FORM ACTION="/cgi-bin/test.cgi" ...>
```

When the Web server options allow scripts in other directories, cgi-bin could be conspicuously absent, and the ACTION option would look more like a URL:

```
<FORM ACTION="~jane/bin/test.cgi" ...>
```

Besides ACTION, another key attribute in the <FORM> tag is METHOD. Remember the "POST" and "GET" options? These options determine how data passes to your script. You'll learn about these in a minute, when you get a little closer to the actual scripts.

All this chapter you've worked with input tags that collect data on a form and ship it off somewhere with the click of a submit button. Now it's time to follow the data all the way through.

How Forms Send Data

In your scriptless mailto form in Session 4, you learned that data from the form was encoded before it was sent out over e-mail. This is not just a property of mailto; the same encoding is used before the data is passed to a script.

Once the data is encoded, it is not simply handed over to the script, even though it appears so from the ACTION URL. Before it gets to the script, it has to go through a middleman, and that's where the CGI comes into play.

The Middleman

CGI, the Common Gateway Interface, is a key player in any scripts that you write, and it's important to understand where it fits into the process. In fact, the scripts and programs you write to process form data are commonly called CGI scripts. In Figure 4-25 you can see that the CGI not only passes data from the form to the script, but it is also responsible for returning any output from the script back to the Web browser. With the CGI taking care of these two responsibilities, the script's job becomes pretty easy. Scripts don't have to negotiate the intricacies of communication that is taking place between the browser and the server; they are handed input on a silver platter, and whatever output they send is faithfully transcribed by CGI and returned to the user who submitted the form. Let's look at what scripts get on their "silver platter."

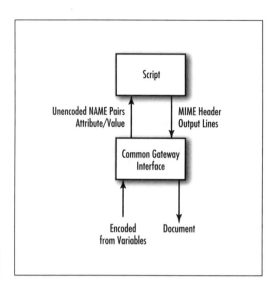

Figure 4-25
The CGI middleman

How the CGI Passes Data to Scripts

When the user clicks the submit button, the input data is encoded, sent to the server, and turned over to the CGI. Depending on the METHOD in the <FORM> tag, the CGI puts the data in *environmental variables* and *command-line arguments*, and in the case of METHOD="POST", data is also passed through the *standard input* of the program. These three sources of input data are well known in programming, and most languages have simple methods for retrieving input from them.

Environmental Variables

Environmental variables are variables a program can retrieve from the system in which it is running. In MS-DOS for example, you often see these variables set in the autoexec.bat file with statements like:

```
SET CONFIG=c:\windows\whizbang.ini
```

The variable CONFIG has been set to a value of "c:\windows\whizbang.ini". A program running in the DOS environment can "query" the environment for the value of these variables. In a DOS batch program, for example, the value of CONFIG can be displayed with a statement like:

```
ECHO %CONFIG%
```

Command-Line Arguments

Command-line arguments are data that is passed to the program by including it on the same line that you use to execute the program. If you executed a DOS batch file at the C:\> prompt with the following syntax:

```
C:\>test and here is some data
```

the DOS test.bat file would run, and *and here is some data* would be passed as command-line arguments. The operating system, in this case DOS, usually breaks up the data, putting one word, or token, in each argument. The example above generates five arguments, with the following values:

```
Argv[1]="and"
Argv[2]="here"
Argv[3]="is"
Argv[4]="some"
Argv[5]="data"
```

Argv[1] refers to the first argument, Argv[2] the second, etc. Most systems also put the program name itself into argument zero, so

```
Argv[0]="test"
```

To print the arguments to the screen in DOS the same way you printed the environmental variable, you would use the syntax

```
ECHO %1 %2 %3 %4 %5
```

Standard Input

When a typical program is run, it usually has several files automatically opened for its use. In the examples above, the standard output for a DOS batch file is the monitor. Whatever is sent to output with commands like echo are seen on the screen. Standard input, on the other hand, is usually the keyboard. In both cases, though, input and output can be redirected. In DOS, instead of standard input coming from the keyboard, it can be piped from another batch file:

```
dir | more
```

In this syntax, the vertical bar represents a "pipe." The pipe sends the standard output of the dir command to the standard input of the more command. Pipes are used frequently in UNIX. One program does a particular part of a task and sends its output to the next program in the pipe, which transforms it further, and when output finally comes out the end of the pipes, you have the data just the way you intended (hopefully!). This flexibility means you don't have to rewrite programs if your input is coming from dir in one instance and TYPE in another.

When the CGI sends data to your script via standard input, in essence it is just another program that is piping data to your script. Standard input streams are designed to handle virtually unlimited amounts of data. This capability can be important in choosing "GET" or "POST" as your METHOD on the <FORM> tag.

"GET" and "POST"

And now let's revisit "GET" and "POST", seeing how each passes data using one of the techniques described above. This simple form can provide an example (you don't need to enter it):

```
<FORM ACTION="http://myhost.com/test" METHOD="GET">
<P>Please enter your name: <INPUT TYPE="text" NAME="name" SIZE=40>
```

continued on next page

continued from previous page

```
<P>E-mail address: <INPUT TYPE="text" NAME="address" SIZE=60>
<P><INPUT TYPE="submit" VALUE="Send Info">
</FORM>
```

Assume the user entered "Sarah Zinfandel" for the NAME variable, and "zinfandel@instanbul.com" for the e-mail address. The data is encoded as

```
name=Sarah+Zinfandel&address=zinfandel@instanbul.com
```

and sent to the server.

Now, based on the METHOD, the CGI will hand this to the script in one of two ways:

```
METHOD="GET"
```

puts the entire encoded data into the environmental variable QUERY_STRING.

```
METHOD="POST"
```

passes the encoded data via standard input and puts the total number of characters passed to standard input in the environmental variable CONTENT_LENGTH.

What about the command line? Command-line arguments are created when a tag like the following is used:

```
<FORM ACTION="~mydir/test?quick check">
```

Since no METHOD was specified, METHOD defaults to METHOD="GET". The data after the question mark is placed in both the command-line arguments for the script as

```
Argv[1]="quick"
Argv[2]="check"
```

and since it is a METHOD="GET", the same data is also encoded in the QUERY_STRING variable as

```
QUERY_STRING="quick+check"
```

These are the ways the script gets data from the form, or in the case of the last example, from data in the ACTION statement itself. For most conventional languages, environmental variables, command-line arguments, and standard input are the easiest way to retrieve data. And the CGI wants to make things as easy as possible.

Sending Data back to the User

Sending data back is even easier than retrieving it. You just have to send it to one place: standard output. Standard output is where most output statements like print, echo, putc(), etc., go by default. If the CGI wasn't there to catch this, it would normally just go to the screen.

But you can't just send anything back. The Web server is expecting you to send back a valid document so it can return the document to the browser. This document is usually HTML, but it can also be an image, a sound file, plain text, etc. These document types are the MIME types you learned in Chapter 2. The first line of output from the script needs to tell the server what type of document it will be sending back to the browser.

To do this, the first line you need to send is a line describing the content type. If your script is sending back HTML, the line will look like this:

```
Content-Type: text/html
```

followed by a blank line. Then just send the regular HTML that you would write in your pages. Most of your scripts will be using the text/html content type, but if you're curious, you can see a larger list of content types by looking in your browser's helper applications menu under Options and click on Preferences (in Netscape).

Here's an example of sending back a simple HTML document from a script. This script is written in a UNIX shell language called the Bourne shell. It's very similar to the DOS batch commands used in the previous examples:

```
#!/bin/sh
echo "Content-Type: text/html"
echo
echo "<HTML><HEAD>"
echo "<TITLE>Just Returned From My Script!</TITLE></HEAD>"
echo "<BODY>"
echo "<H1>This is all it takes!</H1></BODY></HTML>"
```

This creates an HTML document on the fly that is passed back to the browser. (The *#!/bin/sh* just tells the operating system what type of shell language you are using).

Besides returning MIME documents, you can also return a URL referencing another document. In this case the browser will automatically link to the URL and display this other document without missing a beat. This is called redirection. If instead of building the HTML in your script, you wanted to refer a browser to an HTML document that already exists, you would use a Location command:

```
Location: <URL>
<blank line>
```

For example, to refer the user to a file on your own server (i.e., a relative URL) you would use

```
Location: ~jane/result.html
```

And in a script like the last example, you would use

```
#!/bin/sh
echo "Location: ~jane/result.html"
echo
```

You can use any valid URL, so the redirection can be to an FTP file, a Gopher site, etc.

That's all there is to output! The CGI takes care of delivering whatever you send back to the browser. The scripts communicate only with the CGI through these very simple and direct mechanisms.

So enough with the theory, let's write some scripts!

Script Flavors

Oops. I guess a little conceptual stuff still remains. You'll need to pick a scripting language. Which one depends on the platform your Web server is running on. If it runs on a UNIX system, your choices are the various flavors of UNIX shells: C shell, Bourne shell, or Korn shell; languages like C or C++; and utility languages like Perl. On Windows you can use Visual Basic, Visual C++, DOS batch commands, and Perl. On OS/2 you can use Rexx, C—and Perl. Hmmm, seems to be a recurrent theme here.

Perl is probably the most popular language for writing CGI scripts. In part this is due to the large number of platforms it has been ported to. But it's also due to properties of the language itself. Perl has powerful functions for manipulating text, and it has several add-on libraries developed cooperatively on the Internet for working with HTML and the CGI environment. Perl is also pretty easy to read and understand. We'll use it for the script exercises. See what you think.

A Dash of Perl

Let's cover a handful of commands in Perl that you'll use to create a script below. This is a minitutorial in the span of a paragraph or two, but it should give you the necessary ingredients to write your first script. It doesn't take that much.

The first statement of every Perl program needs to point to where Perl is on the system it is running. In most cases, where Perl is in the /usr/local/bin directory, it will look like this:

```
#!/usr/local/bin/perl
```

This line tells the system that this is a Perl program, and tells it where to find the Perl interpreter.

The first actual Perl command you will need is the *print* command. It can be used as follows:

```
print "Hello World!\n";
print "This is my first Perl Program!!!";
```

Note that the semicolon at the end of a line is very important. Without it, Perl will complain about syntax errors and your program will not run. The \n causes a line break. To print a blank line, you would use

```
print "\n";
```

With just the first line and the print statement you can create a CGI script that returns an HTML document:

```
#!/usr/local/bin/perl
print "Content-Type: text/html";
print "\n";
print "<HTML><HEAD><TITLE>";
print "A Perl CGI Script";
print "</TITLE></HEAD><BODY>";
print "<H1>This will work</H1>";
print "</BODY></HTML>";
```

This will return the results through the CGI to the browser, and seems to take care of the output. But how do you access input variables from a form using Perl? For this, you'll use a Perl library designed to make this easy. You will first have to include the library in your Perl script, right after the first line:

```
#!/usr/local/bin/perl
require("cgi-lib.pl");
```

The *require* statement in Perl pulls the library cgi-lib.pl into your program. It assumes this library can be found in the Perl system library, and if there is any scripting going on in your Web server, cgi-lib.pl will probably be there. If not, you can pull it off the CD that comes with this book, put it in your own directory, and add a special line before the require statement that tells Perl where to look for cgi-lib.pl. Let's assume you've had to put cgi-lib.pl in a subdirectory under your home account called cgi-lib.pl. Your first three lines of Perl script will look like the following:

```
#!/usr/local/bin/perl
@INC("$HOME/cgilib");
require("cgi-lib.pl");
```

Now to get the input from the form, add the following line (which calls a routine in cgi-lib.pl):

```
&ReadParse;
```

This puts all the input variables on the form into a Perl array. It doesn't matter if the data was sent via "GET" or "POST"; it handles either automatically. The Perl array name that stores the form data is *$in*. To reference elements in this array, you would use the following syntax:

```
$in{'keyname'}
```

This is what's called an associative array. Each element is indexed by a value. The value is the name of the input variable on the form. For example, if you had the field <INPUT TYPE="text" NAME="address" SIZE=20> on your form, and the user entered "38 Birch Street", you would retrieve this value in your Perl script by referencing the array element *address*:

```
$in{'address'}
```

This statement references the form variable called *address*. To print out what the user entered in the address field, enter

```
print $in{'Address'};
```

In this example, it would print

```
38 Birch Street
```

If you want to surround this with other text, just separate it with commas:

```
print "You live at: ",$in{'Address'}," is that correct?";
```

and get the following:

```
You live at: 38 Birch Street is that correct?
```

Any input variable name assigned in your form will be stored in this array when you enter the &ReadParse; command.

One last bit of esoterica and you're licensed for Perl. When you create a Perl script on a UNIX system, after you save it, you need to make sure it is flagged as *executable*. If it's not executable, UNIX doesn't know that it's a program. To set the executable flag, use the following command in your script (let's say the script is named "query-results"):

```
chmod a+x query-results
```

That's the nickel tour. Many fine tutorials exist on Perl; some of them are even on the Web. Don't worry if it hasn't quite jelled at this point. You'll come back to Perl in a real example very soon. In fact, right after you look at the steps for creating a script from A to Z (er, 1 to 3).

Three Steps to Creating a Script

Writing a script requires the following:

1. **Designing the input form.** You need to know what variables are being passed, what meaning they have on the form, and how they should be used in the script. Are you collecting data to be stored in a file or a database? Are you asking for information to be used for an online search?

2. Writing the script, the part of the process that actually interprets and acts on the data from the form.

3. Sending back the output. What do you want to send back? Are you building an HTML page for results, are you merely trying to find which URL to direct viewers to, or are you sending back graphics or other multimedia content based on the data provided in the form?

Your First Script

Let's put the three-step formula into practice. First, create a form using the following HTML:

```
<FORM ACTION="http://yourhost.com/~your-username/echotest" METHOD="POST">
<P>Please enter your name: <INPUT TYPE="text" NAME="name" SIZE=40>
<P>E-mail address: <INPUT TYPE="text" NAME="email" SIZE=60>
<P>Mailing address: <TEXTAREA NAME="address" ROWS=5 COLS=45></TEXTAREA>
<P>Do you make homebrew?</B>
<INPUT TYPE="radio" Name="hb" VALUE="Yes" CHECKED>Yes</B>
<INPUT TYPE="radio" Name="hb" VALUE="No">No</B>
<P><INPUT TYPE="submit" VALUE="Send Info">
</FORM>
```

This HTML can reside either on your PC or under your account on the Web server. For the ACTION part of the <FORM> tag, specify a location where your script will reside.

The script needs to be on the Web server, and its location can be arranged with your local Webmaster.

Log in to the system that will run your scripts and use an editor on the system to create the following script:

```perl
#!/usr/local/bin/perl
require("cgi-lib.pl");
print "Content-Type: text/html\n\n";
print "<HTML><HEAD><TITLE>";
print "Results for: ",$in{'name'};
print "</TITLE></HEAD><BODY>";
print "<H1>Just For You</H1>";
print "<P>Hi ",$in{'name'}," !\n";
print "<HR>";
print "<P>You live at ",$in{'address'};
print "<P><STRONG>Is this Correct?</STRONG>";
print "<P>Homebrewer? Lessee...",$in{'hb'};
print "<P>You like homebrew!" if $in{'hb'}='Yes'
print "</BODY></HTML>";
```

Call this script "echotest". Make sure it is executable, and make sure you have the right locations in the script for both Perl and cgi-lib.pl. Your Webmaster should be able to help you set this up initially. At this point, don't tell him or her that you're after their job, wait until Chapter 7.

Now open the HTML form in your browser, fill in some input data, and submit the form. If your script executes successfully, it should echo back the values you entered on the form to your browser. If you run into problems, Session 6 looks at troubleshooting in detail.

QUIZ 5

1 If you use METHOD="GET" on a form, where will the script find the input data from the form?
   a. standard input
   b. command line
   c. in an environmental variable
   d. in a special file

2. For a script to send output back to a Web browser
   a. It needs to find the Web browser's address and open a channel.
   b. It sends output to the standard output.
   c. It sends output to a special HTML pipe.
   d. It has to initiate contact with the Web browser directly.

3. The first line a script needs to send back is
   a. <HTML>
   b. a blank line
   c. a MIME header
   d. a line break

4. Scripts are typically found where?
   a. on the Web client
   b. as part of a form
   c. on the Web server in a /script directory
   d. on the Web server in a /cgi-bin directory

SESSION 6

SCRIPTS AS FRONT-ENDS

In this session you will continue to develop and refine your script writing technique. As you start writing more sophisticated scripts, a checklist of common mistakes and a solid test plan will prevent you from getting struck with the bane of tyro scripters: the infamous screen of death. With a map of pitfalls and a plan of attack, you'll learn how to save a user's form input on disk, and how to search and view the disk file from a form once it's there. Besides returning the contents of a file, you will also return a graphical image dynamically, allowing you the sleight of hand of changing images each time a page is accessed. Without wasting another moment, let's pick up your checklist and file a flight plan into the heart of script writing…the adventure continues.

Testing and Troubleshooting Scripts

If not approached with some modicum of discipline, script writing can be extremely frustrating. After initial success with some small scripts, many aspiring Web authors jump straight into a large opus. Understanding the CGI, the simplicity of the interface, and having mastered most elements of HTML, the Web author may think that scripts are only an incremental step. That by adding a knowledge of a language like Perl on a catch as catch can basis, a full and glorious forms application will unfold before his or her very eyes.

This first blush of enthusiasm is usually frustrated by some extremely nitpicky requirements that snag the project at every turn, until a certain number of flight hours are logged, and a systematic method begins to emerge from experience that helps avoid these pitfalls. To help you sidestep as much annoyance as possible, some of the common snags are bulleted below, and these are followed by a time-tested recipe for staying tightly on track during the development of a project.

Things That Can Go Wrong

 Your script is not executable. To run a script on a UNIX platform, the file must be flagged as executable. When you create a file, it doesn't, by default, set this flag. You have to set it later with the chmod a+x prog-name command. This is easy to forget. If you create a subdirectory for your script files, make sure that files from the directory can be read and executed by the world. The chmod command also works for directories:

chmod o+rx dirname. A symptom that this is the problem is a message from the server, stating, "Your client does not have permission to get URL ...".

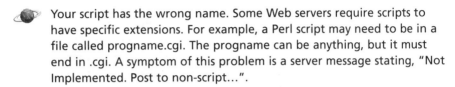 Your script has the wrong name. Some Web servers require scripts to have specific extensions. For example, a Perl script may need to be in a file called progname.cgi. The progname can be anything, but it must end in .cgi. A symptom of this problem is a server message stating, "Not Implemented. Post to non-script...".

Your script is not where it can be executed. You don't have permission to run scripts out of your HTML directory. A symptom of this can be a number of obscure messages; sometimes the server may complain about difficulties finding the script, rather than lack of authorization: "The Requested URL was not found...".

Your script is not being executed. Browsers operate differently. Most keep a cache of forms. If you are revising your form, either the input data or the scripts you are calling, you need to make sure to reload it before testing. This can be frustrating but obvious once you realize what's happening, as your script continually seems to ignore new data on your form, or your form seems to still be calling an old script. Sometimes it may be useful to flush the memory and disk cache if results are particularly squirrelly.

Your script has internal errors. Probably the most common message received by beginners is the infamous "Server Error 500", and it usually means something is syntactically wrong with your script. One way to find the errors is to print the system error log, which should have some information about the problem. You'll need to ask your system administrator where this log is, and then print out the tailend of it, where it keeps the most recent errors. In UNIX running NCSA flavors of Web servers, the error log is typically in /usr/httpd/logs/error_log, and you can use the UNIX tail command to print the last screen of entries: tail /usr/httpd/logs/error_log. The best way to eliminate this class of errors, however, is to follow the procedures discussed later.

Development and Testing

The following approach will help you catch errors while they are still small, and ensure that you are building your application on a stable foundation. This plan will quickly become second nature, enabling you to develop sophisticated scripts component by component, plugging well-tested and reliable prefabs together into large, error-free architectures. And imagine, you thought you were just writing scripts!

Session 5 introduced a high-level, three-step procedure for writing scripts. You developed the form, wrote the script that processed input from the form, and designed what went back to the browser. This time you'll zero in on the way events flow between these high level steps to make a solid application. It doesn't just go one, two, three. It's more like one, two, two, one, two, three. The stutter step is key. Here's the expanded outline of a test/development procedure:

 Design the form. This is the fun part, plus it gives you a nice illusion that the project is further along than it really is. With all the oohs and ahhs you collect on the interface, you'll want to avoid embarrassment should anyone actually click that submit button. More pragmatically, designing the form helps you think about the functions you'll need behind the scenes based on what options you are allowing the user. The interface is the easiest piece to change, and you can refine it at this stage until it looks as if it has all the pieces the user requires. Changing the interface is cheap; after all, you're not changing the script behind it, just its appearance. But the main reason, again, is that this part's the most fun.

 Write a minimal script. The function of this script is just to echo what was input to the form. This achieves a couple of very important goals. It makes sure your protections are okay (e.g., file and directory permissions), and it ensures that the data you think is being passed from the form is actually there, especially in the variable names you are expecting. You can use a subroutine that comes with the cgi-lib.pl library to print all the variables passed to your script. Here is a short example:

```perl
#!/usr/local/bin/perl
require ("cgi-lib.pl");
&ReadParse;     # Brings all the Form variables into the %in array
print "Content-Type=text/html\n\n";
print "<HTML><HEAD><TITLE>";
print "Variable Listing";
print "</TITLE></HEAD><BODY>";
print "<H1>Variables Passed From Form</H1>";
print &PrintVariables(%in);
print "</BODY></HTML>";
```

 Test the script by itself, i.e., stand-alone. In this stage, you go ahead and write the script, but when you're finished, hardcode the variables that will be passed from the form and test the script from your UNIX account, not from the form. For example, if the variables *name* and *address* were being passed from the form to your script, called register.cgi, here's what it would look like accepting input from the form:

```perl
#!/usr/local/bin/perl
require ("cgi-lib.pl");
&ReadParse;     # Brings all the Form variables into the %in array
print "Content-Type=text/html\n\n";
print "<HTML><HEAD><TITLE>";
print "Variable Listing";
```

```
print "</TITLE></HEAD><BODY>";

... do something with %in{'name'}...
... do something with %in{'address'} ...

print "</BODY></HTML>";
```

If you just ran this from UNIX (instead of running it via the Web form), the %in array would have no values. These are normally obtained from standard input passed by the CGI and loaded with the &ReadParse subroutine in cgi-lib.pl. To fake all of this out so you can run the script interactively, make the following changes:

Comment out &ReadParse by putting a # in front of it. This causes Perl to skip this line:

```
# &ReadParse;   # Brings all the Form variables into the %in array
```

Assign the values to the %in array yourself:

```
$in{'Name'} = "John Doe";
$in{'Address'} = "5596 Pennsylvania";
```

Now test the program by running it from the command line:

```
register.cgi
(or ./register.cgi or perl register.cgi)
```

You should see the results that would typically be passed back to the CGI interface appear on your screen. You'll also see any errors the script has that are normally written to standard output and only appear in the system error logs. You can do even more debugging by running this script with Perl flags that give you more information. For instance,

```
perl -w register.cgi
```

will print out warning messages about your syntax or the operations of your script. The following,

```
perl -d register.cgi
```

will run Perl with the debugger.

After your stand-alone script is running as you would expect it to, take out the comment on &ReadParse, and comment out your explicit assignments to the %in array. Now you're ready for the live test, and you should've bypassed all the Things That Can Go Wrong by following this simple procedure.

Now that you've got the secret map, you're ready to hit the territory. Let's get started on a little more useful and educational project than just parroting what was entered on a form. Ready?

Your Second Script ... Any Suggestions?

For your second script project you'll write an anonymous suggestion box. This application allows members of your department, organization, or simply visitors to your page to make anonymous suggestions. With slight variations, the suggestion box can also become a guest book, comment box, or other type of feedback form. You could even modify the suggestion box for brainstorming, focusing it on a specific idea or policy. Before doing this, however, let's outline what you need to accomplish.

A suggestion box presents a form that allows free-form text input into a suggestions field. When the form is submitted, a script will save the suggestions to a file. The script will need to keep appending to the file as new suggestions come in. It will also need to be able to view the file, in order to review the suggestions. Since you might not want just anyone to review suggestions, you'll need to protect this part of the application with a secret password. Now that you've got the general gist of things, use the development procedure discussed above to build the suggestion box.

The first step is to design the form. (The whole procedure, of course, assumes you first have a fairly clear idea of what your objectives are for the application.) Designing the form will help mold the overall idea into something concrete. This may lead to refinements in the original idea, and that's a natural part of the process.

So let's design the form. You'll need an input box for the suggestions. The <TEXTAREA> tag should work nicely. You'll also need a button for submitting the suggestion, and a button for clearing the form. Add to this a View button, and a password field to make sure the user is authorized to view the suggestions file. Lay out the HTML in your mind for this initial form, and compare what you come up with to the sample below:

```
<HTML>
<HEAD>
<TITLE>The Suggestion Box</TITLE>
</HEAD>
<BODY>
<H1 ALIGN="center">The Suggestion Box</H1>
<FORM ACTION="http://test.home.com/~smith/suggs.cgi" METHOD="POST">
<BLOCKQUOTE>Please enter your suggestions below. This is an anonymous service, no
records or information is kept about the source of the suggestion. All
suggestions are reviewed by the VP of Finance.</BLOCKQUOTE>
<HR>
<TABLE>
<TD><TEXTAREA NAME="Suggestions" ROWS=8 COLS=65>
</TEXTAREA>
<TR>
<TD ALIGN="right"><INPUT TYPE="image" NAME="buttons" SRC="buttons.gif">
<TR>
<TD ALIGN="right">Password: <INPUT TYPE="password" Name="secret" SIZE=20>
<TR>
</TABLE>
</FORM>
</BODY>
</HTML>
```

Open a new file with your editor and enter the HTML above, or enter the form with your own interface design. Just make sure you stick to the same input variables so you can track with the script. Figure 4-26 shows what you should have come up with if you used the HTML above.

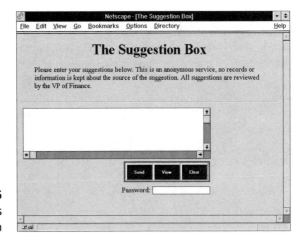

Figure 4-26
The suggestions
form

Note that in Figure 4-26 the submit button wasn't used. An <INPUT TYPE="image"...> with three options, Send, View, and Clear, was used in its place. You'll recall that the TYPE="image" option provides an alternative to the generic submit button, replacing it with a graphical image the user can click to submit any data entered on the form. But along with the data, the browser will also send the x and y coordinates of where the mouse pointer clicked on this image. It does this by sending two variables:

```
name.x
name.y
```

where *name* is the value assigned to the NAME attribute.

When the input image in Figure 4-26 named "buttons" is clicked by the user, the browser sends back the x and y coordinates of the mouse pointer in variables *buttons.x* and *buttons.y*. Since it's a horizontal bar, you're only concerned with the x-axis. If *buttons.x* is less than 85, the user clicked the Send option; if *buttons.x* is greater than or equal to 167, then the Clear option was clicked. If the value of x falls in neither of these ranges, the user must have selected the middle option, View. These x values are in pixels, and you can find out how long each button is in pixels by opening the image buttons.gif in LVIEW. So the input image replaced the need for a submit button, but what about reset?

Usually reset does not communicate with the Web server. The browser just clears all the values and resets them to the defaults on the local form. When you try to use a button bar for this function, the server will receive *buttons.x* > 167 and do nothing specifically to the form. To simulate the function of a local reset, you can use a redirection, causing the browser to reload the form. For example, if you named the form above "suggs.html", when the user clicked the Clear button, the script could send back:

```
Location: suggs.html
<blank line>
```

to the CGI. The CGI would then cause the Web browser to reload the form, along with its default values. Perhaps not as elegant as <INPUT TYPE="reset">, but a tradeoff for putting all the submit functions in a graphical button bar.

Now, when you're finished tweaking the form, and this might go on for a while, you're ready to write the suggs.cgi script. Remember that the first function of this script is just to echo back the input variables on the form. You can accomplish this with the script you wrote back in the Development and Testing section. Call this script suggs.cgi (and make sure it's working before moving on). Note in particular what happens when you click various spots on the button bar. This is another way of finding out what the *buttons.x* thresholds are for each button. Once you've got the script working and you've discovered where the beginning and end of each button is (it will be echoed back to your screen every time you click the button bar), move on to the next step in the procedure: writing the actual code for the script.

For this next step, you'll need to learn a few more Perl constructs. First, since you are testing the value of *buttons.x* to see whether Send, View, or Clear was clicked, you'll need to know how conditionals in Perl work:

```
if ($in{'button.x'} < 85) {      # The Send Button
      do this ...
      }
elseif ($in{'button.x'} > 167) {      # The Clear Button
      do this ...
      }
else {                                # The View Button
      do this ...
      }
```

Using these Perl statements, you can test for all three conditions of the button bar. The *do this...* part is a place for Perl statements that you haven't filled in yet. Note that you don't need a semicolon after the curly braces "}". This is one of the few places where semicolons aren't used at the end of a Perl statement. All the statements between the braces will still need to end in a semicolon. You can also use the if statement to test for data that is missing from a form:

```
if (!$in{'Suggestions'}) {
      # complain about no suggestions...
      }
```

The ! means "not". The statement above is read: "If there is not a value for *$in{'Suggestions'}*, then do the following." To check the password field, enter

```
if ($in{'secret'} ne "Swordfish") {
      # bzzzzt ... bad password
      }
```

This is read: "If what was entered in the form text variable *secret* is not equal to 'Swordfish', the user didn't know the password."

The second Perl construct you need is some way to add information to a file. The information you want to add is contained in the $in array. Remember, this array has all the variables that were entered on the form. To write to a file from Perl, you need to open it with a statement like:

```
open(SUGGESTIONS,">>/users/home/smith/suggestions.dat");
```

The first argument to open, *SUGGESTIONS*, is a "filehandle" Perl associates with the actual filename, which is provided in the second argument: /~*smith/suggestions.dat*. The filename includes the complete directory path to the file, and the funny >> sign in front of it means that you want to append data to this file. You'll want to do a couple of things in UNIX to make this file ready for your script. First, you can create an empty file with the touch command:

```
touch /users/home/smith/suggestions.dat
```

then change the protections so the Web server has access to it:

```
chmod o+rwx /user/home/smith/suggestions.dat
```

To actually put data into this file now, you can use the Perl print statement that you already know. For example, to put "Hello World" in this file, you would enter

```
print(SUGGESTIONS "Hello World\n");
```

Note that there is no comma, just a space, between the filehandle and the "Hello World" string sent to the file. To put what was entered in the suggestion box in the form above into the file, use

```
print(SUGGESTIONS $in{'Suggestions'});
```

When you're finished writing to a file, be sure to close it:

```
close(SUGGESTIONS);
```

Let's start with these building blocks and develop the first part of the script. First write out in (almost) ordinary English what you want to do:

```
If send was entered then
        if suggestions are empty send back a comment
        else
                add their suggestions to the suggestions file
                send them back a thank you
Elseif View was entered
        if the password is ok
                send the file back to their browser
        else
                send back invalid password message
Else it must be clear
        send a redirect to the initial Form
```

This is known as *pseudocode*. It's not really a scripting language, but it's close enough that it helps organize how the script will be written. Fleshing out a program in pseudocode is usually an integral part of writing a script, so it wasn't mentioned as a separate procedure. Once you have the gist of the script in pseudocode, you need to turn it into Perl. Try writing the part for the Send and Clear buttons in Perl, and check your results with the code below. (Leave the View part empty for now; you need to learn one last trick to get that working.)

```perl
#!/usr/local/bin/perl
require ("cgi-lib.pl");

# Set some variables used later...they are easier to change
# here, than hunting for them later in the script
$suggfile = "/users/home/smith/suggestions.dat";
$password = "swordfish";

&ReadParse;     # Brings all the form variables into the %in array
if ($in{'buttons.x'} < 85) {     # Send Button was clicked
        if (!$in{'Suggestions'}) {
                print "Content-Type: text/html\n\n";
                print "<HTML><HEAD><TITLE>";
                print "No Suggestions";
                print "</TITLE></HEAD><BODY>";
                print "<H2>Suggestion Box was Empty!</H2>";
                print "</BODY></HTML>";
                }
        else {
                open(SUGGESTIONS,">>$suggfile");
                print(SUGGESTIONS $in{'Suggestions'});
                print(SUGGESTIONS "\n-----------------\n\n");
                close(SUGGESTIONS);
                print "Content-Type: text/html\n\n";
                print "<HTML><HEAD><TITLE>";
                print "Thank You";
                print "</TITLE></HEAD><BODY>";
                print "<H2>Thanks for your Suggestions!</H2>";
                print "</BODY></HTML>";
                }
        }
elsif ($in{'buttons.x'} > 167) { # Clear Button was clicked
        print "Location: suggs.html\n\n";
        }
else {          # Must have been the View Button Then
        }
```

Now test this procedure by commenting out the *&ReadParse* line, and assigning the value of *Suggestions* yourself:

```perl
#!/usr/local/bin/perl
require ("cgi-lib.pl");
# &ReadParse;   # Brings all the Form variables into the %in array
$in{'Suggestions'} = "This is a sample suggestion";
.
.

.
[the rest of the script]
```

Run the script, *not* the suggestion form, from UNIX. Check the suggestions file, to make sure it entered the suggestion, by typing it out. In UNIX the equivalent of the type command is the cat command:

```
cat /users/home/smith/suggestions.dat
```

You should see your sample suggestion, followed by a separator line of hyphens.

Now test it without a suggestions variable, by commenting out

```
# $in{'Suggestions'} = "This is a sample suggestion";
```

The script should display the HTML that complains about no suggestions to your screen. If everything checks out, you only need one more piece to complete the project.

To view a file, you need to get Perl to print the file to the screen. Remember that since the script is called from the CGI, everything that is output to standard output, in this case the screen, is sent back to the Web browser. Of course, you'll need to send the HTML headers and preamble stuff first, then send the file, then send the ending </BODY> and </HTML> tags. To display a file to standard output from within Perl, you can open the file and print it as follows:

```
open(SUGGS,"/users/home/smith/suggestions.dat");
print <SUGGS>;
close(SUGGS);
```

Fit this snippet into the View section after testing for a correct password. When you're done, check it against the following, completed script:

```
#!/usr/local/bin/perl
require ("cgi-lib.pl");
$suggfile = "/users/home/smith/suggestions.dat";
$password = "swordfish";
&ReadParse;     # Brings all the Form variables into the %in array
if ($in{'buttons.x'} < 85) {     # Send Button
        if (!$in{'Suggestions'}) {
                print "Content-Type: text/html\n\n";
                print "<HTML><HEAD><TITLE>";
                print "No Suggestions";
                print "</TITLE></HEAD><BODY>";
                print "<H2>Suggestion Box was Empty!</H2>";
                print "</BODY></HTML>";
                }
        else {
                open(SUGGESTIONS,">>$suggfile");
                print(SUGGESTIONS $in{'Suggestions'});
                print(SUGGESTIONS "\n----------------\n\n");
                close(SUGGESTIONS);
                print "Content-Type: text/html\n\n";
                print "<HTML><HEAD><TITLE>";
                print "Thank You";
                print "</TITLE></HEAD><BODY>";
                print "<H2>Thanks for your Suggestions!</H2>";
                print "</BODY></HTML>";
                }
```

continued on next page

continued from previous page

```
        }
elsif ($in{'buttons.x'} > 167) { # Clear Button
        print "Location: suggs.html\n\n";
        }
else {          # View Button
        if ($in{'secret'} ne $password) {
                print "Content-Type: text/html\n\n";
                print "<HTML><HEAD><TITLE>";
                print "Not Authorized";
                print "</TITLE></HEAD><BODY>";
                print "<H2>Not Authorized For View</H2>";
                print "</BODY></HTML>";
                }
        else {  # Password was OK!
                print "Content-Type: text/html\n\n";
                print "<HTML><HEAD><TITLE>";
                print "Suggestions File";
                print "</TITLE></HEAD><BODY>";
                print "<H2>Suggestions File</H2><HR>";
                print "<FORM ACTION=\"sug-edit\" METHOD=POST>";
                print "<TEXTAREA COLS=65 ROWS=16>";
                open(SUGGS,$suggfile);
                print <SUGGS>;
                close(SUGGS);
                print "</TEXTAREA>";
                print "<P><INPUT TYPE=\"reset\">";
                print "</FORM>";
                print "</BODY></HTML>";
                }
        }
```

You can now test the new View section using the same techniques used to test Send and Clear. After all the checks work out at the terminal, uncomment the *&ReadParse*, comment out all your explicit variable assignments, and you're ready to test it with the form!

The script used in the example was very verbose. There are several ways to make it more compact and efficient. For example, you could have written the HTML for the canned conditions like No Suggestions, Invalid Password, and Thank You in an actual HTML file, and used the redirection technique you used for Clear to automatically load these pages. You could also put the standard HTML headers and ending document tags into subroutines. You'll discover many other shortcuts if you delve deeper into Perl.

1. To append data to a file in Perl you need to
   a. use a special print statement
   b. open the file in a way that means you are appending data
   c. never close the file
   d. write to different files and combine them later

2. After including cgi-bin.pl in your Perl script, what do you need to do to print a text variable called *name* from a form?
   a. *print $name;*
   b. *print $in{'name'};*
   c. *&ReadParse;* and then print *$in{'name'};*
   d. *print {'name'};*

3. You receive an error back from the server, saying, "Server Error 500". What does this mean?
   a. The server is down.
   b. The server could not access your script.
   c. Your script had some internal error.
   d. Nothing, this is a normal status message.

4. What is the error log used for?
   a. keeping track of server accesses
   b. security
   c. it's part of the CGI
   d. recording errors, usually problems with scripts

EXERCISE 6

Add a delete function to the View screen. In Perl you can delete a file by opening it with one ">" instead of two ">>":

```
open(RESET,">/user/home/smith/suggestions.dat");
close(RESET);
```

You do not need to check the password before the delete; the user had to enter a valid password to be in the View screen in the first place.

Replace the section testing for the View button with the following code:

```
else {           # View Button
        if ($in{'secret'} ne $password) {
                print "Content-Type: text/html\n\n";
                print "<HTML><HEAD><TITLE>";
                print "Not Authorized";
                print "</TITLE></HEAD><BODY>";
                print "<H2>Not Authorized For View</H2>";
                print "</BODY></HTML>";
                }
        else {   # Password was OK!
                print "Content-Type: text/html\n\n";
                print "<HTML><HEAD><TITLE>";
                print "Suggestions File";
                print "</TITLE></HEAD><BODY>";
                print "<H2>Suggestions File</H2><HR>";
                print "<FORM ACTION=\"sug-edit\" METHOD=POST>";
                print "<TEXTAREA COLS=65 ROWS=16>";
```

continued on next page

continued from previous page

```
open(SUGGS,$suggfile);
print <SUGGS>;
close(SUGGS);
print "</TEXTAREA>";
print "<P><INPUT TYPE=\"reset\">";
print "<INPUT TYPE=\"submit\" VALUE=\"Delete\">";
print "</FORM>";
print "</BODY></HTML>";
}
}
```

Create a sug-edit.cgi similar to the following:

```
#!/usr/local/bin/perl
require ("cgi-lib.pl");
$suggfile = "/users/home/smith/suggestions.dat";
&ReadParse;    # Brings all the Form variables into the %in array
open(RESET,">$suggfile");
close(RESET);
print "Content-Type: text/html\n\n";
print "<HTML><HEAD><TITLE>";
print "Action Complete";
print "</TITLE></HEAD><BODY>";
print "<H2>Suggestion Box Was Cleared!</H2>";
print "</BODY></HTML>";
```

PERL AND VISUAL BASIC

With a modest project under your belt and some functional Perl syntax at your disposal, you're ready for the next frontier. Here you will explore some of the little-known fringes: sending output that isn't HTML back to the Web browser, finding other ways that scripts can be activated outside the confines of forms, and learning a few more Perl tricks for making your CGI scripts easier.

After that you say good-bye to Perl scripts, until the last project in the chapter, and learn another scripting language: Visual Basic. Visual Basic offers some unique advantages for integrating CGI scripts with the application interfaces available on Windows. A busy session! Let's get started.

Delivering More Than HTML

In the last script project, all of the output you sent back to the user (with the exception of the Location: redirect) was HTML. If you experimented a little, you might have noticed a side effect of this. When users entered data in the suggestion box, they could actually enter HTML. For example, a suggestion could contain something like:

```
I <STRONG>REALLY</STRONG> want Charmin tissue in the bathrooms!
```

This could be useful, and it's exploited in some chat applications with scripts similar to the one you developed for suggestions. An advantage is that users can add markup and even hyperlinks to their comments, and see them displayed when they view the file. A disadvantage is that you have to be on the lookout for tags that might cause problems. An opening <STRONG> tag without an ending tag would emphasize the rest of the suggestions, including those appended after the one with the dangling tag. Session 6's script protected itself against this by putting the text in a <TEXTAREA> box when viewing the suggestions. If it didn't "wrap" the text with this tag, it would have displayed and interpreted any HTML included with the text.

But you don't have to use HTML as the content type. In fact, you've got all of the MIME types to choose from. You could have sent the suggestions (or any other text file) back as follows:

```
print "Content-Type: text/plain\n\n";
open(SUGGS,$suggfile);
print <SUGGS>;
close(SUGGS);
```

No fuss, no mess. No need for pesky <HTML> tags and headers and closing tags. Of course, not very exciting output either, just monospace text, but maybe this is all you need for some applications. You can use the same technique to send other types of files. A more interesting one is the graphics file.

A GIF file, for example, can be sent back to the client from a CGI script with the following:

```
print "Content-Type: image/gif\n\n";
open(GIF,"frogleg.gif");
print <GIF>;
close(GIF);
```

This would cause the Web browser to display the image as if an <HREF> to a GIF file were clicked. This has some small utility. Perhaps you can determine from the form what picture to show someone and return precisely the picture they would like to see. If you have an extensive catalog, this is more refined than building a gazillion links to every picture in your inventory. But you can also use this to create a neat effect, and that brings us to a different topic.

Other Ways Scripts Can Be Activated

All of the examples so far have illustrated scripts being activated through the ACTION attribute of a form. They can also be called from an <IMG> tag. The usefulness of this might not be apparent at first. In fact, it may not be apparent at the end of this example either, but it's kind of fun getting there. <IMG> is expecting an instream image back, of course, so your script should return a GIF or JPEG file. Who's to say, though, that it has to return the same image each time it's called? Let's add a little variety to your home page, by making it use a randomly selected image each time it is accessed. Kind of like switching wallpaper in Windows every time you start up.

First, set up an array of images to choose from in Perl:

```
$image[1] = "icecream.gif";
$image[2] = "pickles.gif";
$image[3] = "relish.gif";
$image[4] = "mustard.gif";
```

These are the images on a hypothetical hot dog kiosk (it could happen). The Perl array is indexed by numbers instead of by values as the *$in* array was.

Now you need to generate a random number between 1 and 4. Since Perl can do anything, this is not a problem:

```
$roll = int(rand(4)) + 1;
```

Rather than get into the details of this function, if you use it as above, it will return a number between 1 and 4. Just change 4 to whatever the highest number is, and it will work.

So *$roll* now equals a number between 1 and 4. That's all you need. Create a script like the following:

```
#!/usr/local/bin/perl
$image[1] = "icecream.gif";
$image[2] = "pickles.gif";
$image[3] = "relish.gif";
$image[4] = "mustard.gif";
$roll = int(rand(4)) + 1;
print "Content-Type: image/gif\n\n";
open(GIF,"frogleg.gif");
print <GIF>;
close(GIF);
```

Call it random-image.cgi or something equally clever, and reference it in your HTML as

```
<IMG SRC="http://test.home.com/~smith/random-image.cgi">
```

You'll have people lined up at your hot dog kiosk in minutes.

Closing Perl Tricks

Before dragging you from Perl and into the wild and GUI world of Visual Basic, here are a few miscellaneous tricks to make your script writing easier.

Earlier you entered

```
print "Content-Type: text/html\n\n";
print "<HTML><HEAD><TITLE>";
print "Suggestion Box Was Cleared!";
print "</TITLE></HEAD><BODY>";
print "<H2>Suggestion Box Was Cleared!</H2>";
print "</BODY></HTML>";
```

You can also enter

```
print "Content-Type: text/html\n\n";
print <<"ENDHTML";
<HTML>
```

```
<HEAD>
<TITLE>Suggestion Box Was Cleared!</TITLE>
</HEAD>
<H2>Suggestion Box Was Cleared!</H2>
</BODY>
</HTML>
ENDHTML
```

This instructs Perl to print everything up until it finds a piece of text in the script with the characters ENDHTML, and then stop. Using this technique you can include HTML pages in your CGI. It makes it a little easier to prototype.

If you really get lazy, er, I mean efficient, you can write subroutines to automatically generate headers and trailers:

```
sub html_trailer {
        print "</BODY>";
        print "</HTML>";
        }
sub html_header {
        $title = $_[0];
        print "Content-type: text/html\n\n";
        print "<HTML><HEAD><TITLE>$title</TITLE>";
        print "</HEAD><BODY><H1>$title</H1>";
        }
```

Include them in the bottom of your script, and then you can use them as follows:

```
&html_header("Suggestion Box Was Cleared!");
&html_trailer;
```

You'll learn more Perl tricks as you go along. In fact, writing CGI scripts is one of the most enjoyable ways to play with Perl.

Other Types of Scripts

While Perl is probably the most common CGI scripting language, you can also use other languages. The Windows HTTPd software, based on NCSA's UNIX Web server, provides a CGI interface for Visual Basic. Its operation is quite a bit different from the CGI on UNIX platforms, but the experience you've gained with Perl and the UNIX CGI will make assimilating the differences much easier.

If you haven't already installed the Windows HTTPd software, you'll need to for developing the scripts in the rest of this session. The instructions are in the Installation section of this book.

Windows and Visual Basic are a potent combination. Visual Basic is one of the easiest languages for programming on the Windows platform. As a native Windows language, it can also harness the power of other Windows applications using software components in the form of custom controls (VBXs) and Object Linking and Embedding (OLE). With these components, it is surprisingly easy to write sophisticated applications using very minimal Visual Basic code. The power of Visual Basic in CGI scripts is this ability to leverage not only its own intrinsic functionality, but that of the entire suite of Windows applications. Before deciding how to glue all this functionality together for access via the Web, let's begin with a more limited scope; comparing and contrasting the Windows CGI with the UNIX CGI.

The first major difference is that the Windows CGI doesn't pass the variables entered on a form through environmental variables, standard input, or command-line arguments. Instead the CGI puts most everything into a temporary .ini file. An .ini file is a text file with name=value pairs clustered in sections. For example, here are the contents of the clock.ini file, which stores preferences about the display of the Windows Clock application:

```
[Clock]
Maximized=0
Options=0,0,0,0,0,0
Position=44,44,252,270
```

A Windows application can use Windows system calls to retrieve the variable name *Maximized* in the section *[Clock]*, for example. The system call will return the value "0". Many applications have their own .ini files where they store configuration information. The Windows CGI uses a temporary .ini, which it passes to your Visual Basic CGI script.

The CGI's .ini has seven sections, but only a few are of immediate interest. Here is a sample of the first section that is of use:

```
[Form Literal]
name=Fred Flintstone
address=23 Rubble Lane
zipcode=5
```

This is how the [Form Literal] section might look when name, address, and zip code fields were filled in on the forms page. If, however, the string on the value size of the equation is greater than 254 characters, say for a comments field, the CGI puts it in another file and references it in another section:

```
[Form External]
comments=c:\temp\hs125sdgs.00 500
```

This line means the CGI has put the decoded string in a temporary file called c:\temp\hs125sdgs.00 and that the file has 500 characters of data.

If the string value has more than 65,536 characters, the reference goes into yet another section, which points to an offset in another file that we won't talk about here (for more information check the following file that came with the installation: \\info\wincgi.htm). You can find all the variables you need for the next two lessons in either [Form Literal] or [Form External].

The Windows Web server also provides you with a utility similar to cgi-lib.pl in Perl. This is the cgi.bas file. It needs to be included in your Visual Basic project, and it has the Main entry point to your script. You need to use the Visual Basic Project Options menu to select Sub Main as the entry point. This is analogous to including cgi-lib.pl with *require cgi-lib.pl* in Perl.

cgi.bas

The file cgi.bas is a set of routines you can use to retrieve data from the sections of the .ini, and to send output back through the CGI to the Web browser.

This will make more sense if you just do it, so double-click on the Visual Basic icon, and follow these steps:

1. When VB first comes up, you have a new project and a form. You don't need the form, so select the File menu and choose Remove File. It will remove the default form1.frm from the PROJECT1 menu.

2. Select the File menu again, choose Add File, and add c:\httpd\cgi-src\cgi.bas. This is like including cgi-lib.pl in Perl.

3. Select the Project option under the Options menu. Your Start Up Formshould say Sub Main. This means the first function called in the application will be one named Main. This is found in the cgi.bas file. Click OK.

4. Now select the File menu, and choose New Module. This will be where you put your script code. Create a subroutine in this module called CGI_Main that takes no arguments. This is the routine that cgi.bas will call after it has initialized all the CGI variables.

Now all that's left is for you to enter code in the CGI_Main subroutine, which you'll get to below. You can add other subroutines and functions called from within CGI_Main, and you can add other modules if you like. These two, though, cgi.bas and a module with a CGI_Main subroutine, are the bare essentials needed for every Visual Basic CGI script. Let's use a call to the cgi.bas module to write a script that just sends HTML back to the browser. We can deal with processing form variables next.

Unlike the UNIX CGI, you can't just send output through the pipe and assume it will go back to the browser through the CGI. With Visual Basic you need to use the Send function provided in cgi.bas. To send back a sample HTML document, enter the following in the CGI_Main subroutine you created above:

```
Sub CGI_Main()
        Send ("Content-Type: text/html")
        Send("")
        Send("<HTML><HEAD><TITLE>Wow!</TITLE></HEAD>")
        Send("<BODY><H1>I'm in Visual Basic Now!!!</H1></BODY></HTML>")
End Sub
```

After you enter this, return to the File menu and choose Make Executable File in the c:\httpd\cgi-win directory and call it test1.exe. Start your Windows Web server, if it's not started already, by double-clicking the Httpd icon. Now open your browser and connect to the following URL:

```
http://127.0.0.1/cgi-win/test1.exe
```

The host address, 127.0.0.1, is a special IP address used to connect to yourself. Since your Web server and browser are running on the same machine, this address tells the browser it doesn't need to go out on the network. This type of address can only be used on your own PC. If you want to allow someone else to connect to your Web server, you'll need to give them a real IP address that you have configured in your network software.

If you connected successfully, the Web server will execute the test1.exe module, and you should see the HTML you coded in your CGI_Main() subroutine returned on your browser's screen. Once this basic mechanism is working, it will be easy to incrementally extend the functionality to process input fields on a form.

Let's whip up a small data entry form to add a little more challenge. Open a new file in your editor and add the following HTML:

```
<HTML>
<HEAD>
<TITLE>Corporate Phone Directory</TITLE>
</HEAD>
<BODY>
<H2>Corporate Phone Directory</H2>
<HR>
<FORM ACTION="http://127.0.0.1/cgi-win/test2.exe" METHOD=POST>
Name: <INPUT TYPE="text" NAME="name" SIZE=25>
<BR>Phone: <INPUT TYPE="text" NAME="phone" SIZE=12>
<BR>Ext: <INPUT TYPE="text" NAME="ext" SIZE=6>
<BR>Department: <INPUT TYPE="text" NAME="dept" SIZE=20>
<P><INPUT TYPE="submit" VALUE="Add"><INPUT TYPE="reset" VALUE="Clear">
</FORM>
</BODY>
</HTML>
```

Since all the values are fewer than 254 characters, you can retrieve them from the [Form Literal] section of the temporary .ini file using a function provided in cgi.bas called GetSmallField. For example, to retrieve the name, enter

```
Dim cName as String
cName = GetSmallField("name")
```

In Visual Basic, you can then concatenate a variable with a string as follows:

```
"The name is: " & cName
```

So on the send command, you can have

```
send ("Name: " & cName)
```

Let's write a simple Visual Basic CGI script to echo the results of this form using what you've covered so far. Call the module test2.exe, and when you're finished, compare your results with the code below.

```
Sub CGI_Main()
        Dim cName as String
        Dim cPhone as String
        Dim cExt as String
        Dim cDept as String
        cName = GetSmallField("name")
        cPhone = GetSmallField("phone")
```

```
cExt = GetSmallField("ext")
cDept = GetSmallField("dept")
Send ("Content-Type: text/html")
Send("")
Send("<HTML><HEAD><TITLE>Your Input</TITLE></HEAD>")
Send("<BODY><H1>Is This What You Entered</H1>")
Send ("Name: " & cName)
Send  ("<BR>Phone: " & cPhone)
Send ("<BR>Ext: " & cExt)
Send ("<BR>Department:" & cDept)
Send("</BODY></HTML>")
End Sub
```

1 How can you send back an instream GIF file from a script?
   a. just like HTML; just print the GIF file instead of HTML
   b. using redirection
   c. by including it in an <HTML> document
   d. by using a MIME header for image/gif

2. Other than in the ACTION keyword of a <FORM> tag, what is another way scripts can be called?
   a. in a <SELECT> option tag
   b. through mailto:
   c. through a URL in an <IMG> tag
   d. through an ACTION option in the <BODY> tag

3. How does the Windows CGI pass form variables to a Visual Basic application?
   a. through standard input
   b. through an .ini file
   c. through environmental variables
   d. through DDE links

4. What two essential ingredients does a VB application need to run as a CGI script?
   a. cgi-lib.bas and vgi.bas
   b. cgi-lib.bas and a Main entry point
   c. cgi.bas and a module with CGI_Main subroutine
   d. cgi.bas and a cgi_main.bas

INTERMEDIATE SCRIPTING

In Session 7 you just scratched the surface of Visual Basic scripting. In this lesson you'll jump in a little further, developing a complete phone directory application using Microsoft Access as a database.

The Application

The phone directory is a simple application, but it exploits a variety of database access techniques. A user can add, view, change, list, and delete records in a corporate phone book. Users can also request data formatted for a report. Using the Windows Web server, an application can support up to 16 concurrent users running on a 486/66 class PC or higher. The shell of the application can be used as a framework for more sophisticated database applications, and with a few minor changes, it can use ODBC to access remote databases as a client/server implementation. Using the development steps covered previously, the first stop in the application design will be the appearance of the screens.

Note that this project assumes some familiarity with Visual Basic. Due to the material that will be covered, and the time required to complete it, we won't dwell on the details of Visual Basic syntax. Not that anything fancy is going on (in Visual Basic anyway); just a lot of code and a short amount of space.

The Screens

The Phone Page application consists of two general purpose screens shown in Figures 4-27 and 4-28.

Most of the application's functions springboard from the list screen and its toolbar. The names in the phone book will be listed in a <SELECT> tag, where they can be selected for deletions, edits, and viewing more detailed information. The HTML for the list screen is

```
<HTML>
<HEAD>
<TITLE>The Phone Page</TITLE>
```

Figure 4-27
List screen

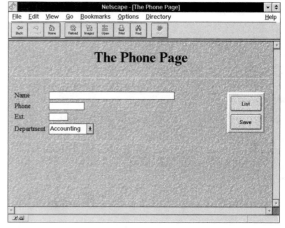

Figure 4-28
Detail screen

```
</HEAD>
<BODY BACKGROUND="gr.gif">
<H1 ALIGN="center">The Phone Page</H1>
<HR>
<FORM ACTION="http://127.0.0.1/cgi-win/phone.exe" METHOD="POST">
<TABLE>
<TD VALIGN="top" ALIGN="center"><STRONG>Names:</STRONG>
<TR>
<TD WIDTH=80% VALIGN="top" ALIGN="middle"><SELECT NAME="list" SIZE=13>
<OPTION>        
</SELECT>
<TD ROWSPAN=10><INPUT TYPE="image" BORDER=0 SRC="lbutton.jpg">
<TR>
</TABLE>
<INPUT TYPE="hidden" NAME="screen" VALUE="D">
</FORM>
</BODY>
</HTML>
```

A few embellishments are thrown in: background graphics for texture, beveled tool-bars, and some table optimizations. The &*nbsp*; is a nonbreaking space character entity. Generally this entity is used in places where you don't want the browser to break up words by wrapping them to the next line. For example:

```
this test should all stay together
```

By using   instead of regular spaces, you ensure that the browser will keep all the text above on a single line, rather than wrapping the text on a space boundary if the sentence runs into the right margin. The use of   in the example is a little nonstandard, and it circumvents a problem with some browsers. Without any data in the <OPTION> tag, <SELECT> becomes invisible on many Web browsers, so the   entities place data (spaces) in the <OPTION> tag. This lets the user know a field is there, even if no data is stored in the database yet.

The second screen, Figure 4-28, is a multipurpose detail screen. It provides a data entry form for adding new members to the directory, and it provides a form for view-ing detailed information about members selected in the list screen. Well, not a lot of detail, but it's easily extended. The HTML for this form is

```
<HTML>
<HEAD>
<TITLE>The Phone Page</TITLE>
</HEAD>
<BODY BACKGROUND="gr.gif">
<H1 ALIGN="center">The Phone Page</H1>
<HR>
<FORM ACTION="http://127.0.0.1/cgi-win/phone.exe" METHOD="POST">
<TABLE>
<TD>Name
<TD WIDTH=85%><INPUT TYPE="text" NAME="name" SIZE=45>
<TD>
<TD ROWSPAN=4 ALIGN="right"><INPUT TYPE="image" BORDER=0 SRC="dbutton.jpg">
<TR>
```

continued on next page

continued from previous page

```
<TD>Phone
<TD><INPUT TYPE="text" NAME="phone" SIZE=12>
<TR>
<TD>Ext.
<TD><INPUT TYPE="text" NAME="ext" SIZE=6>
<TR>
<TD>Department
<TD><SELECT NAME="dept">
<OPTION>Accounting
<OPTION>Purchasing
<OPTION>Budget
<OPTION>Sales
</SELECT>
<TR>
</TABLE>
<INPUT TYPE="hidden" NAME="screen" VALUE="D">
</FORM>
</BODY>
</HTML>
```

In both of these listings lurks a tag you haven't encountered yet, the <INPUT TYPE="hidden">. It uses the same syntax as the <INPUT> tag introduced in Session 3, and the example used above was

```
<INPUT TYPE="hidden" NAME="screen" VALUE="D">
```

Let's examine how this works.

Hidden Variables

Hidden variables do not appear on the Web browser, but they are still sent with the form to the CGI script. It's as if a user entered something in VALUE="", but he or she never got a chance to see it! Hidden variables are useful for keeping track of interactions between the Web server and browser.

For example, a user may retrieve one piece of information in a query that is used in another query to zero in on something related. Rather than having to re-enter the information, you could save it in a hidden variable on a subquery form. This is a technique used to preserve *state* information. State just means a type of memory, where the server using hidden variables in the CGI script remembers what a particular user did last. Normally the server doesn't keep any state information, and it treats each request from a Web browser as if it had never heard from the client before. Hidden variables can be used to build short-term memory into interactions. You'll get a better feel for these variables as we build the Phone Page application.

Echo

And speaking of which, you're ready for the next step. Having finished the fun part, uhm, part of the fun part, you can now write the minimal script that returns what was entered on the forms. This will be a snap. It's basically just a clone of what you wrote in Visual Basic in Session 7, except you're echoing different variables. Once you have created pages with the HTML above for the forms, open a new project in Visual Basic following the steps in the last session. Enter the following Visual Basic code into a new module in the project (call it phone.bas):

In the Declarations section of the phone.bas module, enter

```
Global cName As String
Global cPhone As String
Global cExt As String
Global cDept As String
Global cList As String
Global cMode As String
Global cScreen As String
Global cMode As String
```

And in the CGI_Main subroutine in phone.bas, enter

```
Sub CGI_Main ()
    cName = GetField("name")
    cPhone = GetField("phone")
    cExt = GetField("ext")
    cDept = GetField("dept")
    cScreen = GetField("screen")

    Send ("Content-Type: text/html")
    Send ("")
    Send ("<HTML><HEAD><TITLE>Echo</TITLE></HEAD>")
    Send ("<BODY><H1>Variables...</H1>")
    Send ("<HR>")

    Send ("Name: " & cName)
    Send ("<BR>Phone: " & cPhone)
    Send ("<BR>Ext: " & cExt)
    Send ("<BR>Dept: " & cDept)
    Send ("<BR>Screen (Hidden): " & cScreen)

    Send ("</BODY></HTML>")
End Sub
```

A new function, GetField, was used above instead of the GetSmallField function provided by the CGI. GetField is just a clone of the GetSmallField function, except that when a variable is not found, the function returns an empty string rather than an error. You can extend this function later to transparently handle fields that are larger than 254 characters, although you won't need to do that for this example. Here is the GetField function; you can include it in your phone.bas module:

```
Function GetField (key As String) As String
    Dim i As Integer

    For i = 0 To (CGI_NumFormTuples - 1)
        If cgi_FormTuples(i).key = key Then
            GetField = Trim$(cgi_FormTuples(i).VALUE)
            Exit Function          ' ** DONE **
```

continued on next page

continued from previous page

```
        End If
    Next i
    '
    ' Field does not exist
    '
    GetField = ""
End Function
```

One important caveat: the variable names are treated as case sensitive in this CGI. This means that a variable called NAME="name" on your form will not be picked up with a call like

```
$x = GetSmallField("Name")
```

This is one of the things you will have discovered right away by using the echo procedure in your skeleton script.

Now save the project and create an executable following the steps in the last session. Call your executable phone.exe and put it in the c:\httpd\cgi-win directory. Now you can bring up the list and detail Web forms in your browser and test them against the phone.exe script, which should just echo what you enter back to the browser. Make sure the Windows Web server is running by double-clicking on Httpd before testing your script.

Running Stand-Alone

In Perl you tested your scripts by assigning dummy values to the $in variables and commenting out the *require "cgi-lib.pl";* line. Visual Basic requires a few more steps. First you'll need to add a global variable to phone.bas that tells the application whether you're running in test mode or from the CGI:

```
Global Standalone As Integer
```

Then you'll need to add a new form to the project, so you can enter variables interactively and test the results without going through the Web forms and Web server. An example of this type of stand-alone, Visual Basic form is shown in Figure 4-29.

Note that this is a Visual Basic form, not a Web form. It has input fields for the same variables that would ordinarily be passed by the Web forms, including the hidden variables. In fact, it's the hidden variable *screen* that tells whether you're being called from the list form or the detail form, and you can manually set it on the stand-alone form. Also note the input boxes for List Command and Detail Command; these will simulate clicking somewhere on the toolbar.

Next you'll need to add the following at the very beginning of the CGI_Main subroutine:

```
If Not Standalone Then
  cName = GetField("name")
  cPhone = GetField("phone")
  cExt = GetField("ext")
  cDept = GetField("dept")
  cScreen = GetField("screen")
```

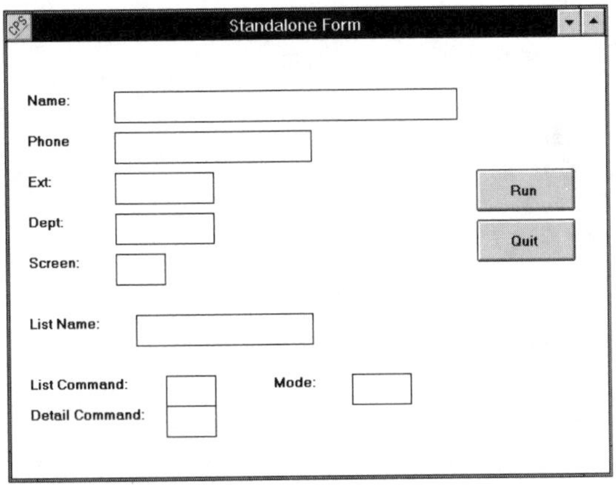

Figure 4-29
The stand-alone
form

```
cList = GetField("list")
cMode = GetField("mode")
End If
```

This prevents CGI_Main from trying to acquire the variables from the CGI if it's running in stand-alone mode. The Click Procedure of the Run button activates the following code:

```
Standalone = True
cName = text1
cPhone = text2
cExt = text3
cDept = text4
cScreen = UCase$(text5)
cLbutton = UCase$(text6)
cDbutton = UCase$(text7)
cMode = UCase$(text8)
cList = text9
CGI_Main
```

The form variables are assigned from the input fields on the Visual Basic form, and the stand-alone switch is set to True before calling CGI_Main. This simulates CGI_Main being called from the cgi.bas routine. But you also need to change the Project Options so the Startup Form is FORM1 rather than Sub Main. This gives control to your interactive Visual Basic form, instead of the Main CGI entry point in cgi.bas.

Now you can drive the application interactively from Visual Basic. Not quite as simple as commenting out a line in a Perl script, but Windows' claim to fame has not historically been simplicity!

The good news is you're almost done. The only other tweak you need to make for stand-alone testing is to do something with the Send function in cgi.bas.

Send returns your output to the CGI to deliver to the client. Instead of modifying the Send function, you can write another function in phone.bas that calls Send if Standalone is False, but directs the output somewhere else if Standalone is True. Here is a function called CGI_Send that is smart enough to recognize what mode you are running in:

```
Sub CGI_Send (s As String)
      if Standalone then
             debug.print s
      else
             Send(s)
      endif
End Sub
```

When running in stand-alone mode, this routine will send the output to Visual Basic's Debug window, letting you check exactly what would be sent back to the Web browser during testing.

You're now officially prepared for testing. Fortunately, you don't need to build this testing framework twice. You can reuse the same general structure for future Visual Basic projects. To turn off stand-alone, and run as a CGI script, you merely need to change the Project Options back to Startup Form: Sub Main, and you're set.

Pseudocode

Now sketch out in pseudocode what the application will do. Pseudocode will help identify the functions you need to write, and help conceptualize the entire process. You can expand it like an accordion, starting with the outermost functions and developing detail to handle each case. For example, you could start like this:

```
load cgi variables from Form
if screen = list then...
else ... ' screen is detail
```

Screen was the hidden variable that tells you whether the script is being called from the list form or the detail form. Each has different options. First, let's expand the list form options, since this is the first form a user will access:

```
load cgi variable from web form
if screen = list then...
      command = get the command (can be View, Edit, Delete, Report, or Null)
      if View
             find the record they selected
             set view mode
             send the detail web form with info
      if Edit
             find the record they selected
             set edit mode
             send the detail web form with info
      if Add
             set variables to blanks
             set add mode
             send the empty detail web form
      if Delete
```

```
        find the record they selected
        delete it
        send the list web form with a status message
    if Report
        send a report web form
    if None of the above
        send the list web form again (default)
if screen = detail then ...
    command = get the command (can be Save or List)
    if Save
        if mode is add
            make sure name isn't blank
            add record
            send the detail web page again saying we added
        if mode is edit
            make sure name isn't blank
            find the record using the name selected in List web form
            update it with changes
        otherwise we must be in View mode
            say they can't modify the record
    if List
        send the list web form
```

From the pseudocode it looks as if the list and detail forms will have to be sent back to the user from various places, sometimes with an optional message. This makes them good candidates for a general purpose function. Let's then design two subroutines in pseudocode that take care of this:

```
Sub list_html (msg as string)
    take snapshot of database
    fill out the OPTION attributes in <SELECT> with names
    display any messages
    send hidden variables
End Sub

Sub detail_html (msg as string)
    populate fields in forms with global variables
    display any messages
    send hidden variables
End Sub
```

These subroutines go in the phone.bas module. They each take an optional message string, and if the string is present, it is displayed on the bottom of the form. The hidden variables are *screen*, since both screens use the same script; *mode* to tell if Edit, View, or Add has been selected; and *list*, which remembers the name selected from the list form.

You also need a subroutine that processes the buttons. This routine tests the x and y coordinates and finds out which button was clicked. It returns a simple value you can test in the main code. This insulates the code from the toolbar, allowing you to switch toolbars and submit formats. The button subroutine can also do some validity checks so the main routine stays as simple as possible.

Real Code

Now let's turn the pseudocode into Visual Basic code with calls to functions and sub-routines (that you'll write later):

```
Sub CGI_Main ()
    If Not Standalone Then
        cName = GetField("name")
        cPhone = GetField("phone")
        cExt = GetField("ext")
        cDept = GetField("dept")
        cScreen = GetField("screen")
        cList = GetField("list")
        cMode = GetField("mode")
    End If
    If cScreen = "L" Then
        bCommand = List_command()
        Select Case bCommand
            Case "V"            ' View
                get_record (cList)
                cMode = "V"
                Detail_html ("")
            Case "E"            ' Edit
                get_record (cList)
                cMode = "E"
                Detail_html ("")
            Case "A"            ' Add
                cName = ""
                cPhone = ""
                cExt = ""
                cDept = ""
                cMode = "A"
                Detail_html ("")
            Case "D"            ' Delete
                delete_record (cList)
                List_html ("Record Deleted!")
            Case "R"            ' Report
                Report_html
            Case Else           ' Null
                List_html ("Invalid Command")
        End Select
    ElseIf cScreen = "D" Then
        bCommand = Detail_command()
        Select Case bCommand
            Case "S"            ' Save
                If cMode = "A" Then
                    If cName = "" Then
                        Detail_html ("Name Cannot Be Blank")
                    Else
                        Add_record
                        Detail_html ("Record Added")
                    End If
                ElseIf cMode = "E" Then
```

```
            If cName = "" Then
                Detail_html ("Name Cannot Be Blank")
            Else
                Update_record (cList)
                Detail_html ("Record Changed")
            End If
        Else
            Detail_html ("Cannot Change Record")
        End If
    Case Else        ' List or other
        List_html ("")
    End Select
Else
    List_html ("")
End If
End Sub
```

This pretty much follows the pseudocode. Initially you will write the main routine, inventing functions and subroutines as you go to keep focused on the higher level of what you are doing. Eventually though, you'll have to break down and write the lower level routines. Since this application is included on the accompanying CD, try to use this framework and develop the underlying routines as an exercise.

Notice that get_record is looking up a record selected in the <SELECT> field by a name value. How else could you allow a user to choose from a set of names, and then look up the detailed record? The technique you decide on will be the backbone of the application. This technique of using the name has some implications that must be dealt with in the design.

First, since this is the key for lookups, you can't allow a blank field to be entered. Second, if a user was modifying the record, he or she might modify the name field. Since the record is not actually changed until the Save button is clicked, it needs to be looked up again. Remember the stateless nature of the Web server: once a user is sitting on a form, like the detail screen, the Web server has no connection with what is happening. It doesn't know that the user is editing a record in a database, and even though the user is presented with that illusion, he or she is in fact editing local form variables. When the user saves the record, the script gets control once again and needs to figure out what the user is trying to change. The hidden variable *list* contains the key the script uses to find the right record. Then the script can implement the changes.

Here are the database routines that are referenced in the main routine. First is a function that looks up a record, given the name of an employee:

```
Sub get_record (nm As String)
Set db = OpenDatabase(dbname, True, False)     ' Open the Access Database
Set ss = db.CreateSnapshot("select * from phone where name='" & Trim(nm) & "'")
                            ' Lookup the record
If ss.EOF Then                              ' If not found
    cName = ""                              ' set fields to blank
    cPhone = ""                             ' for Web form
    cExt = ""
    cDept = ""
```

continued on next page

continued from previous page

```
Else                                        ' If found
    cName = ss("Name")             ' put the records values
    cPhone = ss("Phone")           ' into the web form
    cExt = ss("Ext")               ' input variables
    cDept = ss("Dept")
End If
ss.Close                                    ' Cleanup
db.Close
End Sub
```

This routine, as you can tell from the CGI_Main subroutine, looks up a record in the database by the name selected in the list screen, and fills in global variables with the records contents. A slight variation in the OpenDatabase command, and it could be retrieving records using ODBC, going against remote SQL databases as well. All the other syntax in this and the following routines could stay the same. The next routine adds records to the database:

```
Sub Add_record ()
Set db = OpenDatabase(dbname, True, False)   ' Open the Access Database
Set tb = db.OpenTable("phone")               ' Open the specific table
tb.AddNew                                        ' Add a new record
tb("Name") = cName                               ' fill in the fields
tb("Phone") = cPhone                         ' with fields from the
tb("Ext") = cExt                             ' Web form
tb("Dept") = cDept
tb.Update                                        ' Apply the changes
tb.Close                                         ' Cleanup
db.Close
End Sub
```

The Add_record() routine takes the values filled out on the Web form and appends them to the Microsoft Access database. The next function removes records that are no longer needed:

```
Sub delete_record (nm As String)
Set db = OpenDatabase(dbname, True, False)     ' Open Access Database
Set ds = db.CreateDynaset("select * from phone where name='" & nm & "'")
If Not ds.EOF Then                                 ' Lookup record to delete
    ds.Delete                                  ' if found, delete it
End If
ds.Close                                           ' Cleanup
db.Close
End Sub
```

The Delete_record routine looks up the name selected, and if it finds it, it deletes it. The next function changes data in an existing record:

```
Sub Update_record (nm As String)
Dim cq As String
Set db = OpenDatabase(dbname, True, False)
Set ds = db.CreateDynaset("phone")
cq = "Name = '" & Trim(nm) & "'"
ds.FindFirst cq
```

```
If Not ds.NoMatch Then
    ds.Edit
    ds("Name") = cName
    ds("Phone") = cPhone
    ds("Ext") = cExt
    ds("Dept") = cDept
    ds.Update
End If
ds.Close
db.Close
End Sub
```

The Update_record routine looks up the record, like delete, but this time if it finds it, it changes its contents to reflect what is in the Web form's variables.

The only other actual database call needed, is in the List_html and Report_html routines that build HTML with the entire contents of the database:

```
Sub List_html (msg As String)
CGI_SEND ("Content-Type: text/html")
CGI_SEND ("")
CGI_SEND ("<HTML>")
CGI_SEND ("<HEAD>")
CGI_SEND ("<TITLE>The Phone Page</TITLE>")
CGI_SEND ("</HEAD>")
CGI_SEND ("<BODY BACKGROUND=""/images/gr.gif"">")
CGI_SEND ("<H1 ALIGN=""center"">The Phone Page</H1>")
CGI_SEND ("<HR>")
CGI_SEND ("<FORM ACTION=""/cgi-win/phone.exe"" METHOD=""POST"">")
CGI_SEND ("<TABLE>")
CGI_SEND ("<TD VALIGN=""top"" ALIGN=""center""><STRONG>Names:</STRONG>")
CGI_SEND ("<TR>")
CGI_SEND ("<TD WIDTH=80% VALIGN=""top"" ALIGN=""middle""><SELECT NAME=""list"" SIZE=13>")
Set db = OpenDatabase(dbname, True, False)
Set ss = db.CreateSnapshot("select * from phone order by name")
If ss.EOF Then
    CGI_SEND ("<OPTION>        ")
Else
    Do Until ss.EOF
        CGI_SEND ("<OPTION>" & ss("Name"))
        ss.MoveNext
    Loop
End If
ss.Close
db.Close
CGI_SEND ("</SELECT>")
CGI_SEND ("<TD ROWSPAN=10><INPUT TYPE=""image"" BORDER=0 SRC=""/images/lbutton.jpg"">")
CGI_SEND ("<TR>")
CGI_SEND ("</TABLE>")
CGI_SEND ("<INPUT TYPE=""hidden"" NAME=""screen"" VALUE=""L"">")
CGI_SEND ("<INPUT TYPE=""hidden"" NAME=""mode"" VALUE=""" & cMode & """>")
CGI_SEND ("</FORM>")
If msg <> "" Then
    CGI_SEND ("<P ALIGN=""center""><STRONG>" & msg & "</STRONG>")
```

continued on next page

continued from previous page

```
End If
CGI_SEND ("</BODY>")
CGI_SEND ("</HTML>")
End Sub
```

The Report_html routine is basically a clone, with slightly different HTML. It includes all of the database elements, so a printed listing can be obtained:

```
Sub Report_html ()
CGI_SEND ("Content-Type: text/html")
CGI_SEND ("")
CGI_SEND ("<HTML>")
CGI_SEND ("<HEAD>")
CGI_SEND ("<TITLE>Phone Listing</TITLE>")
CGI_SEND ("</HEAD>")
CGI_SEND ("<BODY BACKGROUND=""/images/gr.gif"">")
CGI_SEND ("<H1 ALIGN=""center"">Phone Listing</H1>")
CGI_SEND ("<P>")
CGI_SEND ("<TABLE BORDER>")
CGI_SEND ("<TH>Name")
CGI_SEND ("<TH>Phone")
CGI_SEND ("<TH>Extension")
CGI_SEND ("<TH>Department")
CGI_SEND ("<TR>")
Set db = OpenDatabase(dbname, True, False)
Set ss = db.CreateSnapshot("select * from phone order by name")
Do Until ss.EOF
    CGI_SEND ("<TD>" & ss("Name"))
    CGI_SEND ("<TD>" & ss("Phone"))
    CGI_SEND ("<TD>" & ss("Ext"))
    CGI_SEND ("<TD>" & ss("Dept"))
    CGI_SEND ("<TR>")
    ss.MoveNext
Loop
ss.Close
db.Close
CGI_SEND ("</TABLE>")
CGI_SEND ("</BODY>")
CGI_SEND ("</HTML>")
End Sub
```

The routine that creates the Detail_html screen doesn't have any database access. It merely fills in what has been set in global variables by calls to the other routines. It will take the value assigned to the department in the database and map it to one of the options in <SELECT>. It also keeps the value of the hidden variable *list*, which contains the unmodified name for lookups during the Save process:

```
Sub Detail_html (msg As String)
Dim depts() As String, i As Integer

Dim maxdepts As Integer
maxdepts = 4
ReDim depts(maxdepts)
```

```
depts(0) = ">Accounting"
depts(1) = ">Purchasing"
depts(2) = ">Budget"
depts(3) = ">Sales"
For i = 0 To maxdepts - 1
If depts(i) = (">" & cDept) Then
    depts(i) = "SELECTED" & depts(i)
End If
Next i

CGI_SEND ("Content-Type: text/html")
CGI_SEND ("")
CGI_SEND ("<HTML>")
CGI_SEND ("<HEAD>")
CGI_SEND ("<TITLE>The Phone Page</TITLE>")
CGI_SEND ("</HEAD>")
CGI_SEND ("<BODY BACKGROUND=""/images/gr.gif"">")
CGI_SEND ("<H1 ALIGN=""center"">The Phone Page</H1>")
CGI_SEND ("<HR>")
CGI_SEND ("<FORM ACTION=""/cgi-win/phone.exe"" METHOD=""POST"">")
CGI_SEND ("<TABLE>")
CGI_SEND ("<TD>Name")
CGI_SEND ("<TD WIDTH=85%><INPUT TYPE=""text"" NAME=""name"" MAXLENGTH=45 VALUE=""" & cName &
""" SIZE=45>")
CGI_SEND ("<TD>")
CGI_SEND ("<TD ROWSPAN=4 ALIGN=""right""><INPUT TYPE=""image"" BORDER=0 SRC=""/images/dbut-
ton.jpg"">")
CGI_SEND ("<TR>")
CGI_SEND ("<TD>Phone")
CGI_SEND ("<TD><INPUT TYPE=""text"" NAME=""phone"" VALUE=""" & cPhone & """ SIZE=12
MAXLENGTH=12>")
CGI_SEND ("<TR>")
CGI_SEND ("<TD>Ext.")
CGI_SEND ("<TD><INPUT TYPE=""text"" NAME=""ext"" VALUE=""" & cExt & """ SIZE=6 MAXLENGTH=6>")
CGI_SEND ("<TR>")
CGI_SEND ("<TD>Department")
CGI_SEND ("<TD><SELECT NAME=""dept"">")
For i = 0 To maxdepts - 1
    CGI_SEND ("<OPTION " & depts(i))
Next i
CGI_SEND ("</SELECT>")
CGI_SEND ("<TR>")
CGI_SEND ("</TABLE>")
CGI_SEND ("<INPUT TYPE=""hidden"" NAME=""screen"" VALUE=""D"">")
CGI_SEND ("<INPUT TYPE=""hidden"" NAME=""mode"" VALUE=""" & cMode & """>")
CGI_SEND ("<INPUT TYPE=""hidden"" NAME=""list"" VALUE=""" & cList & """>")
CGI_SEND ("</FORM>")
If msg <> "" Then
    CGI_SEND ("<P ALIGN=""center""><STRONG>" & msg & "</STRONG>")
End If
CGI_SEND ("</BODY>")
CGI_SEND ("</HTML>")
End Sub
```

That's it in a nutshell. Once everything checks out, you can kick it out of debug mode and see it in operation in the following figures.

Figure 4-30 shows the Phone Page directory, populated with a few initial entries in the Microsoft Access table. Note that Churchland is selected in Figure 4-30. Figure 4-31 shows what happens when the View button is clicked.

While viewing this entry, the user tried to make some changes, which the Web form apparently permits, and then clicked Save. Figure 4-32 shows the resulting screen.

Figure 4-33 illustrates the report, containing all of the fields for each entry in the database.

1. Why is the interaction between Web servers and Web browsers called stateless?
   a. Web browsers sometimes lose track of servers.
   b. Web servers keep information about clients but not vice versa.
   c. After sending output to a Web browser, a Web server retains no information about the connection.
   d. Web clients can be connected in multiple ways.

2. What general problems exist for Web applications that edit database records on the server?
   a. They can't look up by key.
   b. They have to have exclusive access.
   c. Record locking is difficult to implement.
   d. They can only access limited amounts of data.

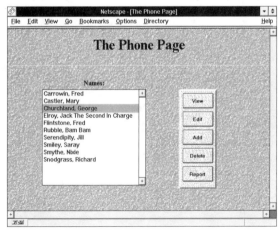

Figure 4-30
The Phone Page directory

Figure 4-31
Viewing an entry

Figure 4-32
Invalid change

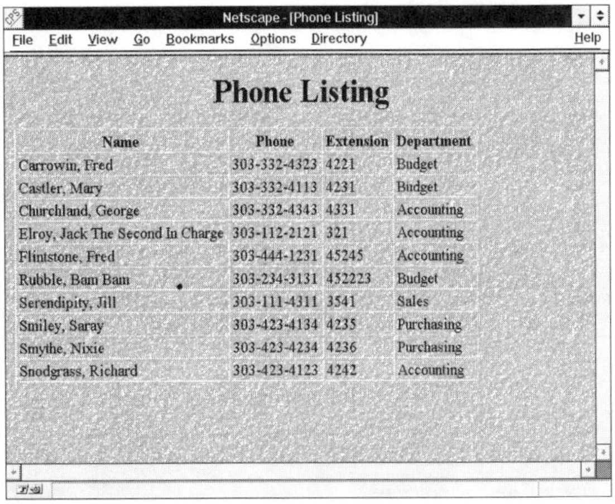

Figure 4-33
Phone Page report

3. A hidden variable is used for
   a. entering passwords
   b. controlling the Web server
   c. saving information between browser and script
   d. screen spacing

4. Why couldn't the script keep state information in its memory?
   a. The CGI doesn't give it any memory to spare.
   b. It's not permitted.
   c. A script generally ends after it returns results to the browser.
   d. It would require too much memory.

THE NUTS AND BOLTS OF WEB SERVERS

THE NUTS AND BOLTS OF WEB SERVERS

n this chapter you'll learn the craft of the Webmaster.

Sooner or later most Web authors are pulled into managing a Web server. Some do it in pursuit of control—they find options available to them as a Webmaster that they would have to beg, bribe, or blackmail their server administrator into providing. Some do it out of curiosity, in order to find out what's going on behind the curtains of their Web pages and CGI scripts. Some do it for profit, and some do it for fun. But whatever the motivation, being a Webmaster, like writing pages in HTML, is really pretty easy.

After installing, configuring, protecting, and squeezing all the functionality you can out of your Web server, you will leave this chapter as a fully fledged and duly appointed Webmaster, king or queen of your own www.domain. The skills you develop will be required for advanced Web applications, in which

273

the boundaries between browser and server blur. In Chapter 6 you will use these skills to write interactive Web applications, page animations, and other goodies. But let's not get distracted too early.

JUMPING IN

In Chapter 4 you installed the WinHttpd Web server for use with your Visual Basic scripts. You set it up with instructions from the Installation chapter, but basically you just brought it up to experiment with the CGI and Visual Basic. Now it's time to learn more details about how to manage the server.

Connecting to Your Server

If you installed the Web server on a system at work, chances are you already have a TCP/IP network address. This same address will be the address for your Web server, and anyone with TCP/IP access to your machine can open a Web page on your server with the following URL:

```
http://your-ip-address/
```

If your IP address was 112.45.0.3, then the following would work:

```
http://112.45.0.3/
```

If your PC has a domain name, it can be used in place of the IP address. For example, if your domain name was smith.enterprise.com, your Web server could be accessed via

```
http://smith.enterprise.com/
```

TCP/IP addresses on the Internet need to be unique, and the process for registering and acquiring an address helps ensure that your IP address is not being used anywhere else in the world. If you are not connected to the Internet, and you don't plan to be connected, you can make up your own TCP/IP address for testing with your Windows Web server. In either case, connected or not, you'll need to have TCP/IP running on your system to use the Web server.

Another possible scenario is that you are using your PC at home, and connect to the Internet through a service provider. Generally with this type of connection, you are given an IP address dynamically when you dial in, and this address will most likely change from session to session. Your Web server address will only be good for that session, so you will probably be doing most of your testing and development offline, as if you had no Internet connection.

In each of the scenarios above, you can always use an IP address of 127.0.0.1. This address, as you'll recall from Chapter 4, is a special TCP/IP address that connects to yourself. Let's use 127.0.0.1 to test the server. Double-click on the Httpd icon to start your Web server, then open your browser to the following URL:

```
http://127.0.0.1/
```

Your Home Page

What you will see as your first page, after you make this connection, is displayed in Figure 5-1.

Remember from Session 1 in Chapter 3 that when a URL is opened with a path or filename, the HTTP server will return a default document, in a default path. For WinHttpd, this is index.htm, in c:\httpd\htdocs. If you replace index.htm, or edit it in place, it can serve as your new server's default home page. If you are connected to a network, other people can access your server using a URL with your host name or address. And if you are on the Internet, congratulations; your server can now be accessed by millions who have no idea you've only set it up five minutes ago.

Some Web servers are even easier to configure than this one. If you are using Netmanage's Chameleon product, and you have their full product suite, you will have an icon labeled Personal Web Server. One click of this icon, and you get the short configuration screen displayed in Figure 5-2.

Once the default document name, default directory, and default port (usually 80) is specified, Netmanage's Web server starts up and takes URL requests just like the WinHttpd server. That's about a 60-second installation. Don't be surprised to start seeing Web servers being bundled in Internet suites, the same way word processors are bundled in office suites.

What Did You Do?!

If you're saying, "It can't be this easy," well, you're kind of right. Several decisions were made for this installation that you will want to weigh more carefully before setting up

Figure 5-1
Windows HTTPD default page

Figure 5-2
Netmanage's Personal Web Server configuration

a "real" server. Using WinHttpd, you inherit 16-bit Windows 3.x as a platform, you inherit a CGI interface to Visual Basic and MS-DOS, and you inherit the limitations of WinHttpd itself, which is a max of approximately 16 simultaneous users of your server. This environment is perfectly adequate for development and testing, or even for a small departmental server. It can be dedicated to a particular function no other Web server is handling in your company, like pulling data from a Microsoft Access database. You did that in Chapter 4.

But a Windows server is not the first choice for a large application, or one that is going to get beat on by the masses as they churn through your server for compelling content. Luckily you have several other options.

Platforms and Servers

A Web server is a combination of a hardware platform, an operating system, and the Web server software that runs on them. Web server software runs on almost anything from an Amiga, Mac, or PC to Data Generals, Tandems, and IBM mainframes. Almost any platform that can be connected to a TCP/IP network has Web server software somewhere that you can download.

This doesn't mean, however, that servers on all platforms run equally well. A Web server needs to be able to handle multiple requests from the network as efficiently as possible. If, the operating system the server runs on has trouble handling more than a single task, as DOS does, the server's performance will be sluggish and perhaps unstable. If the platform doesn't have a good CGI interface, the utility of forms and scripts on the platform will be limited. And if a platform doesn't have good tools for managing the Web server's configuration, logs, and security, the server will be cumbersome to manage and hard to maintain. Just because a platform *can* run a Web server, doesn't mean it *should* run a Web server.

Decisions, Decisions: UNIX Versus NT

In the early '90s, most Web servers ran on UNIX. The hardware could vary—Suns, DECs, HPs—but the operating system was UNIX. UNIX was the platform of choice for most TCP/IP related services: FTP, Telnet, e-mail, Gopher, etc. And because TCP/IP was an intrinsic part of UNIX and the de facto network protocol of the Internet, UNIX servers were the backbone of the Internet.

But while UNIX ruled the Internet, the desktop belonged to Microsoft. And Microsoft was making a bid for Windows NT to be the server of choice for its desktop clients. As of the time of this writing, NT had caught up to UNIX in the number of Web server implementations available, including commercial and freeware servers. NT has the potential of offering a simpler platform on which to install and maintain Web servers. The learning curve for maintaining a secure Windows NT server is much shorter than that for its UNIX counterpart. But the jury is still out on which you should choose for an industrial strength Web server.

UNIX has been evolving for more than 20 years, and networking, multitasking, and Internet services are part of its native heritage. Price performance, at the time of this writing, still seems to favor UNIX. UNIX runs on a large number of hardware platforms, allowing the savvy Webmaster to pick the platform with the fastest processor, the best-tuned UNIX, and the best software suites for the cheapest price. The UNIX operating system is still a competitive market for features and support.

Ideally, it shouldn't matter. UNIX or NT will probably both serve your purposes within similar margins. Focus your decision on the features of the Web server software—features that will vary widely with both operating system and hardware platforms.

Server Features

You'll learn more about the features as you get into the lessons on configuring your Web server. But a high-level overview of some of them might include how pages and directories (or paths) can be protected, how access information is logged, and what types of scripting languages are supported. An important aspect of Web server software that is tied to the platform is the availability of "external" tools and utilities such as log reporting and statistic tools, search engines and indexing utilities, gateways available on the platform to other sources of information like WAIS, and databases. These tools will often give your Web server the particular functionality you require, and in these cases, the platform becomes an important contributor to what is, or is not, available.

Server Topologies

People can get philosophical, and some even a bit religious, when they start thinking about the "right" Web server, and the "right" platform. But before you begin to make hard and fast decisions, you should delve more into the workings of typical Web servers. Since you already have one installed and functional, let's take a look at how it is laid out.

The WinHttpd server has a directory tree as follows:

```
c:\httpd cgi-bin
         cgi-dos
         cgi-src
         cgi-win
         conf------maps
         htdocs----demo
                   images
         icons
         logs
         support
         httpd.exe
         httpd.log
```

The server executable, httpd.exe, is at the main directory root. This can be pulled into your Windows desktop using File Manager, and will be the icon you use to start up the Web server. The file httpd.log, found in the main directory, tracks basic information about the server startup and will list any problems in initializing. The CGI directories back at the top of the listing store the two different types of CGI scripts that WinHttpd can run. The \cgi-dos directory stores DOS scripts, which can be .bat files or dos.exe and .com programs. DOS Perl can also be run from the CGI interface. The \cgi-win directory is for running Windows applications like Visual Basic or Visual C++. Sample Visual Basic applications that use the cgi-win interface are found in \cgi-src.

The \conf directory contains the server configuration files. You'll use these files to set up and customize server security, control access to directory trees, define how the server identifies various MIME types, and other sundry goodies.

The default location for holding your HTML pages is the \htdocs directory. If an HTML page is referenced with

```
http://112.45.0.3/test.htm
```

the server will look in c:\httpd\htdocs\ for the file test.htm. Note that the images directory is a subdirectory off of this directory, allowing you to specify images as

```
<IMG SRC="images/balloon.gif">
```

The \logs directory contains the error and access logs. The error log is useful when running CGI scripts. You can view the contents of the error log for clues on what happened in an unsuccessful script. The access log records every connection to your server, where the connection is from, which page was accessed, and how many characters were transferred.

The \support directory contains the utilities provided with WinHttpd to manage the server. Included are programs to schedule, automatically stop and restart the server, add users and passwords, etc.

To explore more of this server, you can access its online documentation through http://127.0.0.1/httpddoc/overview.htm. Understanding the layout and where to find its online documentation will help you when you come back to the WinHttpd configuration after this session—after you know more about what you want to configure and why. To get there though, you won't be studying WinHttpd; instead you will investigate another Web server, the grandfather of all Web servers.

The Grandaddy of Web Servers...Setting the Mold

CERN and NCSA Web servers are the original two servers from which most other implementations are derived. They are both still viable and robust servers in their own right; CERN runs on UNIX and VMS platforms, and NCSA runs on UNIX and Windows NT. The Web server used above (WinHttpd), evolved from NCSA's.

In Session 2 you will examine NCSA's Web server on a UNIX platform. You will note many similarities, particularly in directory structures, with the Windows implementation. You will also get a feel for how applications on the Internet are transferred, unpacked, and installed on UNIX platforms. This will be valuable for retrieving other nifty utilities on the Net designed to make the Webmaster's life more productive.

This first session you have explored a functional Web server, discovered what its various directories hold, and learned how to use both local and Internet connections. You've learned what logs to look in for information, and what the basic capabilities of a Windows platform are for providing Web services. In Session 2 you scale into the "real" world with a working UNIX Web server, but first a quick review of the material.

QUIZ 1

1. What file is loaded by default when you connect to the WinHttpd server?
   a. c:\httpd\index.htm
   b. c:\httpd\welcome.htm
   c. c:\httpd\htdocs\index.htm
   d. c:\httpd\htdocs\test.htm

2. What does connecting to a host at IP address 127.0.0.1 do?
   a. connects to the Internet
   b. connects you to a WinHttpd server
   c. connects to info.gov
   d. connects to yourself

3. Where would you look if your Windows HTTPD server did not stay up when you ran c:\httpd\httpd.exe?
   a. c:\httpd\logs\access.log
   b. c:\httpd\logs\error.log
   c. c:\httpd\httpd.log
   d. It should display errors on the screen.

4. What is in the c:\httpd\support directory?
   a. log files
   b. help files
   c. system documentation
   d. files and utilities for running the server

SESSION 2

THE UNIX WEB SERVER

In this session you'll install a UNIX server. It's not quite as turnkey as the Windows equivalent, but it will introduce you to a very large segment of Web server presence. At the time of this writing, UNIX still holds the trump card for Web server implementations. Because of the wide range of platforms that run UNIX, from the lowly micros to the liquid-cooled supercomputers, it provides a base that can grow as demand for service grows. This expandability, along with the UNIX's native utilities for working with the Internet, make it an attractive platform for the professional Webmaster.

The National Center for Supercomputing Applications at the University of Illinois, more commonly known as NCSA, distributes one of the most widely used and emulated of the Web servers. The Windows Web server you worked with in the last session was modeled after the NCSA version. The NCSA server targets UNIX platforms and is distributed as both executable, ready-to-run programs and as C source code. NCSA's home page is at http://hoohoo.ncsa.uiuc.edu/.

The easiest way to install the NCSA server is to use the executables, or binaries, as they are called in UNIX. As of the time of this writing, NCSA has binaries available for the following platforms:

- Silicon Graphics, Inc.–SGI Indigo, IRIX 4.0.5.

- Silicon Graphics, Inc.–SGI Indy, IRIX 5.2.

- Sun Microsystems–SPARCserver 690MP, SunOS 4.1.3.

- Sun Microsystems–Sparc 20, Solaris 2.3

- Sun Microsystems–Sparc 20, Solaris 2.4

- International Business Machines–IBM RS/6000 Model 550, AIX 3.2.5

- Hewlett-Packard–HP 9000 model 715, HP-UX 9.05

- DEC–Dec Alpha, OSF/1 3.0

- DEC–Dec Mips 3100, Ultrix 4.0

- Intel-based PC–Pentium 90, Linux 1.2.8

Software you download from NCSA for the UNIX server will be compressed and tarred. This isn't as painful as it sounds. It's the counterpart of ZIP in the PC world. Let's look at the procedure step by step for downloading and unpacking a binary Web server kit from NCSA. The sample platform in this case is an IBM RS/6000.

1. First you will want to change directories to /usr/local, or some similiar directory on your system. The Web server subdirectories will be created in this directory.

2. From this directory, get the binary file from NCSA using FTP. You could just click on the FTP URL from your Web browser client, and your browser would download the server software for you, but if you are running a PC, you would still need to upload it to your UNIX system. In this example, the file is transferred via FTP directly to the RS/6000:

```
cd /usr/local
$ ftp
ftp>open ftp.ncsa.uiuc.edu
ftp>binary
ftp>cd /Web/httpd/Unix/ncsa_httpd/current
ftp>get httpd_1.4.2.aix.tar.Z
ftp>quit
```

3. Now unpack the file with the following commands:

```
$ uncompress httpd_1.4.2.aix.tar.Z
$ tar -xvf httpd_1.4.2.aix.tar
```

These commands will create a directory called /usr/local/httpd_1.4.2 with the Web server executable, and a number of subdirectories for configuration files and documents.

4. Since these procedures just create the essential directories, you'll need to create an additional directory as a default location for Web documents:

```
$ mkdir /usr/local/httpd_1.4.2/htdocs
```

And one for the server logs:

```
$ mkdir /usr/local/httpd_1.4.2/logs
```

5. Now set your default directory to /usr/local/httpd_1.4.2/conf. This is the directory with the three configuration files that control the entire operation of your Web server. Copy the configuration files that came with the distribution to their operational names:

```
$ cp access.conf-dist access.conf
$ cp httpd.conf-dist httpd.conf
$ cp srm.conf-dist srm.conf
```

Now you have a backup with the original defaults in the "-dist" filenames.

These three files each have a surprising number of parameters, but you'll just need to set a few to get the server working. In Session 3 you'll be back into these files, using them to tune and configure the Web server. Here are the minimal configuration changes to these files needed to make your server operational:

 access.conf

Find and change the following lines (the # lines are comments, just as they are in Perl):

```
# /usr/local/etc/httpd/ should be changed to whatever you set ServerRoot to.
        <Directory /usr/local/etc/httpd/cgi-bin>

# This should be changed to whatever you set DocumentRoot to.
        <Directory /usr/local/etc/httpd/htdocs>
```

Change these directories to the ones you used for the installation:

```
# /usr/local/etc/httpd/ should be changed to whatever you set ServerRoot to.
        <Directory /usr/local/httpd_1.4.2/cgi-bin>

# This should be changed to whatever you set DocumentRoot to.
        <Directory /usr/local/httpd_1.4.2/htdocs>
```

 httpd.conf

Find and change the following lines:

```
# ServerAdmin: Your address, where problems with the server should be
```

continued on next page

continued from previous page
```
# e-mailed.
ServerAdmin you@your.address

# ServerRoot: The directory the server's config, error, and log files
# are kept in
ServerRoot /usr/local/etc/httpd
```

Change these to reflect your e-mail address and the location of the Web server files. If you are following the configuration example above, ServerRoot would be set as follows:

```
# ServerRoot: The directory the server's config, error, and log files
# are kept in
ServerRoot /usr/local/httpd_1.4.2
```

 srm.conf

Find and change the following lines:

```
# DocumentRoot: The directory out of which you will serve your
# documents. By default, all requests are taken from this directory, but
# symbolic links and aliases may be used to point to other locations.

DocumentRoot /usr/local/etc/httpd/htdocs

# Aliases: Add here as many aliases as you need, up to 20. The format is
# Alias fakename realname

Alias /icons/ /usr/local/etc/httpd/icons/

# ScriptAlias: This controls which directories contain server scripts.
# Format: ScriptAlias fakename realname

ScriptAlias /cgi-bin/ /usr/local/etc/httpd/cgi-bin/
```

To reflect the actual location of the Web documents, add the following:

```
# DocumentRoot: The directory out of which you will serve your
# documents. By default, all requests are taken from this directory, but
# symbolic links and aliases may be used to point to other locations.

DocumentRoot /usr/local/httpd_1.4.2/htdocs
# Aliases: Add here as many aliases as you need, up to 20. The format is
# Alias fakename realname

Alias /icons/ /usr/local/httpd_1.4.2/httpd/icons/

# ScriptAlias: This controls which directories contain server scripts.
# Format: ScriptAlias fakename realname

ScriptAlias /cgi-bin/ /usr/local/httpd_1.4.2/cgi-bin/
```

That's it! Not as straightforward as the Windows Web server; as you can see, UNIX has quite a few more twists.

At the Starting Line

On a UNIX system, a Web server can be started one of two ways. The first is called *stand-alone*. Stand-alone means that you manually start it, either from the shell or from a script that is run each time the UNIX system is restarted. The other way is through *inetd,* which only starts the server if there is an attempt to make a Web connection to your server. Stand-alone is usually preferred if your server is going to be heavily utilized, so let's start with that.

To start up your newly installed, modestly configured UNIX Web server, enter the following:

```
/usr/local/httpd_1.4.2/httpd -d /usr/local/httpd_1.4.2
```

You will need to do this from the *root* account, because Web servers use a reserved IP port (80), which is not accessible to processes without privileges. When the server starts up, it will change its identity from root to the user/group specified in the httpd.conf file. By default this is user "nobody" with a group of -1. If this combination doesn't exist on your UNIX system, use some other nonprivileged account that will be the process owner of your Web server.

If the server has a problem with any of the configuration files, it will display the error at your terminal and end abruptly. If it comes back with your shell prompt, it has successfully taken off and is running as a *daemon* in the background. (Daemons are UNIX processes that run semiautonomously, kind of like DOS TSRs).

Shutting Down

When the Web server starts up, it creates a special file in its /logs subdirectory. This file is called httpd.pid and contains the process id of the server daemon. This id is used by the system to identify the Web server, and is used by a special UNIX command to shut it down:

```
kill 'cat /usr/local/httpd_1.4.2/logs/httpd.pid'
```

This combination of commands feeds the process id stored in httpd.pid to the UNIX kill command, which stops the process.

After you make changes to the configuration files, you may want the server just to restart itself. Rather than using the shutdown command above, followed by a manual startup again, you can combine both functions with the following command:

```
kill -HUP 'cat /usr/local/httpd_1.4.2/logs/httpd.pid'
```

This kills the process and restarts it in one fell swoop.

Directories

Note that the UNIX directory structure is very similar to that of the Windows Web server:

```
/usr/local/httpd_1.4.2/
        httpd                    the server executable or binary
        /cgi-bin                 for the system cgi scripts and imagemap
        /conf                    server configuration files
        /logs                    server access, error logs
        /htdocs                  default Web page directory
```

Utilities

If you peek into cgi-bin, you'll see utilities that are different from the ones in Windows. Some of these you can play with later…or right away, to test the integrity of the server, of course:

fortune   Returns a random saying if /usr/games/fortune is on your system

calendar   Given a date, returns a monthly calendar using the UNIX cal command

finger   A simple interface to the finger command

mail   Web form to e-mail interface

jj   Order a submarine sandwich…?

uptime   Shows how long your Web server is up, and how many max users

UNIX for Free: The Linux Alternative

UNIX might not sound too exciting, unless you already happen to work in an environment with workstations just lying around underutilized. But UNIX doesn't have to run on a high-powered workstation with RISC processors. It's also becoming very popular on the lowly PC. Linux is probably one of the better known of several UNIX implementations that run comfortably on a 486 with 4MB of memory. Linux is freeware, obtainable over the Internet, though due to its size, it is usually preferable to pick it up on a CD.

With Linux you can use the same NCSA server installed above. NCSA even has a binary version for Linux. You can also get Perl, gnu C++ compilers, and other goodies as freeware. Linux does a good job multitasking processes and is much more robust than Windows in this regard. Many commercial Web servers run on Linux. If you get interested in UNIX, this might be your ticket.

Now that you've brought up a Web server on both Windows and UNIX, it's time to move on to configuring its operations. Once you've mastered the server environment, you will have a good handle on what can be done with the Web from start to finish.

Quiz 2

1. What does ServerRoot refer to in the configuration files?
   a. the address at NCSA where the server software was retrieved
   b. the main directory, which has the log, conf, and cgi-bin subdirectories
   c. the directory with the default Web page
   d. the home directory of the Webmaster

2. What is the difference between starting a Web server stand-alone and starting it inetd?
   a. Stand-alone starts automatically when someone connects to the server.
   b. inetd must be started from the command line.
   c. Stand-alone must be started from the command line or in a script.
   d. inetd is used for heavily utilized Web servers.

3. Why do you need to start the Web server from a privileged account?
   a. because it needs access to system files
   b. because all daemons are privileged
   c. because it uses a TCP/IP port that requires privileges to use
   d. because only accounts with privileges know how to start Web servers

4. What is Linux?
   a. a debugger for UNIX
   b. a type of tissue
   c. a version of UNIX that runs on a PC
   d. a Web server for a PC

Session 3

FILES AND DIRECTORIES

Now that the server is installed, let's start looking at ways the configuration files control its behavior. Changing various configuration keywords, or *directives,* as they are called, can drastically affect the server's response to simple URLs passed from a Web browser. The configuration files and directives discussed below apply to both the WinHttpd server and the UNIX NCSA server.

The first important use of configuration files is to control how URLs map onto the Web server's directories.

URLs and the Web Server

If a URL such as the following, with no directory or filename, is specified:

http://www.test.com/

the server looks for the following parameters:

SRM.CONF DEFAULT DOCUMENT DIRECTIVES

DocumentRoot   *directory*
    directory is the default directory for documents requested from
    the server and is used when no path is specified in the URL.
DocumentRoot specifies the default document directory.

DirectoryIndex   *filename*
       filename is the name of the HTML file opened if no filename is
       specified in the URL.
DirectoryIndex specifies a default Web page.

If, for example, the srm.conf file had the following lines:

```
DocumentRoot          /usr/local/http_1.4.2/htdocs
DirectoryIndex  index.html
```

the URL given above would be translated by the server into the following path and file-name:

```
/usr/local/http_1.4.2/htdocs/index.html
```

This process is shown in Figure 5-3.

Note that /usr/local/http_1.4.2/htdocs is the *absolute* pathname of the document on this server. An absolute path reflects the physical directory structure on the server. This structure is hidden from Web browsers, and URLs with path statements do not refer to actual, absolute paths on the server. Instead, the URL paths go through a translation process. The example above demonstrates what happens when no path is specified.

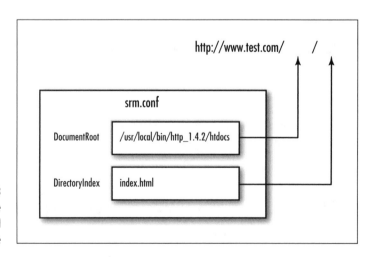

Figure 5-3
Building the
default path and
filename

If a URL contains some path information like the following:

```
http://www.test.com/vpsales/reports/annual.html
```

the server will take the path /vpsales/reports/ and pre-pend the DocumentRoot path, producing

```
/usr/local/http_1.4.2/htdocs/vpsales/reports/annual.html
```

If annual.html wasn't specified as the document, the server would append index.html as the document name.

Paths used in URLs don't have to actually exist on the Web server. Through the use of an Alias, a URL pathname can be invented that maps to an absolute pathname on the server. The Alias directive's syntax is

---

SRM.CONF ALIAS DIRECTIVE

Alias   *fake-name real-name*
          fake-name is a pathname you invent.
          real-name is the absolute path it maps to on the server.
The Alias directive maps a fake pathname to a real one in URLs on the Web server.

For example, you might use a completely different directory for your product's catalog information. It is not in a subdirectory under /usr/local/http_1.4.2/htdocs. Instead, the documents are in the /usr/docs/catalog/ directory. Short of redefining DocumentRoot, how would you direct URLs to these pages? Note that the following URL would *not* work:

```
http://www.test.com/usr/docs/catalog/
```

As you saw in the previous example, the URL would be translated to

```
/usr/local/http_1.4.2/htdocs/usr/docs/catalog
```

Adding the following Alias directive to srm.conf gets around this problem:

```
Alias    /catalog/              /usr/docs/catalog/
```

Now the URL http://www.test.com/catalog/brochure.html will be mapped to the following path and file:

```
/usr/docs/catalog/brochure.html
```

The last type of mapping is what happens when a /~username is found in the URL. The UserDir directive is used to control this mapping, and its syntax is

---

SRM.CONF USER DIRECTORY DIRECTIVE

UserDir   *directory*   (not applicable in WinHttpd)
           directory is the name of the subdirectory in the user's directory that contains
           all of his or her Web pages and Web subdirectories.
The UserDir directive specifies the name of the directory that is appended onto a user's
home directory if a ~user request is received.

If the UserDir directive in srm.conf is set as follows:

```
# UserDir: .
UserDir public_html
```

then the path for /~username URLs is the user's home directory with the UserDir appended. If a user's directory was

```
/users/home/raphael
```

and the srm.conf UserDir directive was set as above, the following URL:

```
http://www.test.com/~raphael/test.html
```

would map to the following path and file:

```
/users/home/raphael/test.html
```

These examples illustrate how URLs are translated by the Web server, and the way this mapping is controlled by directives in the srm.conf file. The actual stepwise procedure the Web server goes through to translate a URL is outlined below. When a Web server gets a URL from a browser, it

1. Checks the beginning of the path to see if it maps to any Alias defined in srm.conf. If so, it does the translation from fake path to real path and finds the document.

2. Checks for /~username in the path. If found, and if UserDir is set, it translates to the user's home directory and finds the document.

3. If none of the above pans out, it puts DocumentRoot at the beginning of the path and finds the document.

So srm.conf, and in particular the directives DocumentRoot, DirectoryIndex, Alias, and UserDir, are key players in defining how a Web server translates URL paths to find Web pages. They work toward the same end, that of hiding the absolute paths to the documents. This makes it easy to move directories and documents around on the server. In fact, using the following directive in srm.conf, you can move the documents to another server entirely:

SRM.CONF REDIRECT DIRECTIVE

Redirect   *fake-path replacement-url*
           fake-path is the pathname in the current URL.
           replace-url is the URL to redirect any requests for the fake path to.
The Redirect directive tells the browser where to look for documents that have moved.

To use this directive to redirect all requests for /catalog/ to another server, www.sales.com, you could have an entry like the following in srm.conf:

```
Redirect           /catalog/                http://www.sales.com/catalog/
```

The redirect happens transparently. The first thing the browser trying to connect to http://www.test.com/catalog/brochure.html will see is the page from http://www.sales.com/catalog/brochure.html!

Finding Scripts

How does a Web server tell the difference between a Web page and a Web script? The answer is not as easy as it seems. Scripts frequently have no filetypes on UNIX, just filenames. If the server picks up a file in a directory, and it cannot determine what type of file it is by its filetype, it will use the directive DefaultType in the httpd.conf file to decide what to do. The syntax for this directive is

HTTPD.CONF DEFAULT TYPE DIRECTIVE
DefaultType   *mime-type*
mime-type is the MIME header returned to the browser if the server can't figure out what type of document is being requested.
The DefaultType directive specifies the default MIME header for unknown documents.

The default entry in httpd.conf for this directive is

`DefaultType    text/plain`

Which means, if the server can't figure it out, it returns the file as a plain text document. Why then don't scripts just get returned to the browser as text?

The reason is the ScriptAlias directive in the srm.conf file. Its syntax is

SRM.CONF SCRIPT DIRECTIVE
ScriptAlias   *fake-directory real-directory*
fake-directory is the directory used by URLs to reference scripts.
real-directory is where the scripts are actually stored on the server.
The ScriptAlias directive identifies directories with scripts.

ScriptAlias defaults to the following:

`ScriptAlias    /cgi-bin/              /usr/local/etc/httpd/cgi-bin/`

Which means that any URL with /cgi-bin/ specified is asking for a script in the /usr/local/etc/httpd/cgi-bin/ directory. What follows the /cgi-bin/ pathname will be the name of the script. You can have multiple ScriptAlias directives in srm.conf.

Another technique for identifying scripts, which does not use ScriptAlias, will be discussed in Session 4, when you learn how to allow users on the server to run scripts out of their own directories. But besides just locating Web pages and scripts, srm.conf can be used to customize a feature for serving files without writing a single line of HTML.

Fancy Directories

A handful of srm.conf directives control a useful facility for automatically serving the contents of directories. If no file is specified on the URL, and the default index.html is not present, then a directory listing is returned. An example of this is shown in Figure 5-4.

Compare this simple default behavior to the same directory shown in Figure 5-5. This is the FancyIndexing option. FancyIndexing is one of several directives in srm.conf that control the display of directories Those directives are

SRM.CONF DIRECTORY INDEXING DIRECTIVES	
IndexOptions	FancyIndexing ScanHTMLTitles
	FancyIndexing turns on use of Icons, Header, Readme, and description text.
	ScanHTMLTitles displays HTML <TITLE> text instead of just file names.
AddIconByType	(*nongraphical-text, icon-image*) *mime-type*
	nongraphical-text displays an icon beside the filetype for nongraphical browsers.
	icon-image is the image displayed for the filetype for graphical browsers.
	mime-type is the type of file the *icon-image* and *nongraphical*-text apply to.
AddIcon	*icon* *file-type* or *directory*
	icon is the image displayed for the filetype.

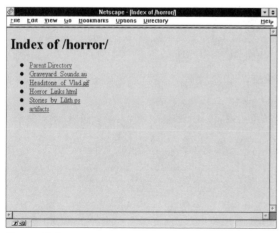

Figure 5-4
Simple directory listing

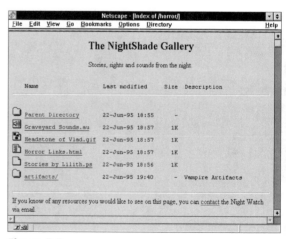

Figure 5-5
FancyIndexing

SRM.CONF DIRECTORY INDEXING DIRECTIVES

	file-type is the name or wildcard mask for the file.
	directory is the directory to map to the icon
DefaultIcon	*icon*
	icon is the icon displayed when filetype is not matched to either AddIconByType or AddIcon directives.
IndexIgnore	*filename(s)*
	filename(s) are filenames to mask in the directory listing.
HeaderName	*filename*
	filename is the name of the HTML file displayed at the head of the directory listing as *filename*.html.
ReadmeName	*filename*
	filename is the name of the HTML file displayed at the end of the directory listing as *filename*.html.
AddDescription	*descriptive-text*　　*directory*
	descriptive-text is descriptive text of subdirectories.
	directory is the subdirectory path.

Directory indexing directives control the presentation of directory indexes.

Each of these will be discussed in turn.

When FancyIndexing is activated, with the following line in srm.conf:

```
IndexOptions    FancyIndexing
```

the server scans a directory and maps filetypes to icons that it has defined in the AddIconByType directive. Several icons are already provided with the NCSA server in the /icons directory (which, incidentally, is an Alias). Here are a few:

```
# AddIcon tells the server which icon to show for different files or filename
# extensions

AddIconByType (TXT,/icons/text.xbm) text/*
AddIconByType (IMG,/icons/image.xbm) image/*
AddIconByType (SND,/icons/sound.xbm) audio/*
AddIcon /icons/movie.xbm .mpg .qt
AddIcon /icons/binary.xbm .bin

AddIcon /icons/back.xbm ..
AddIcon /icons/menu.xbm ^^DIRECTORY^^
AddIcon /icons/blank.xbm ^^BLANKICON^^

# DefaultIcon is which icon to show for files which do not have an icon
# explicitly set.

DefaultIcon /icons/unknown.xbm
```

The AddIcon directive also assigns icons to special elements like directories and parent directories. The DefaultIcon directive specifies what to use if the file doesn't fit in any of the previous mappings.

These icons appear to the left of the file in the directory listing. The filenames listed will be the actual names of the files in the directory. They don't have to be restricted to these names, though. If the files are HTML documents, you can make the server scan the files and display the <TITLE> tags instead of just the filenames by adding the following option to IndexOptions in srm.conf:

```
IndexOptions FancyIndexing ScanHTMLTitles
```

Be careful with this option, though; it makes the server do the extra work of collecting all the titles from within HTML documents in a directory. If your server gets heavily used, you probably don't want to use this.

Ignore Me

You can also tell the server to ignore certain files when building the automatic directory index. This is useful for skipping some of the files starting with a period. The IndexIgnore directive controls what is ignored, and its default is usually adequate:

```
IndexIgnore    */.??* */README* */HEADER*
```

This says ignore all files beginning with a period (.), and all files starting with README or HEADER. The reason you may want README and HEADER ignored is that these are special files that can be used with the IndexOptions directive.

README and HEADER

If a file called HEADER.html is present, the server will use display this at the top of the directory listings. The HEADER.html can have header tags, e.g., <H1>, and HTML describing the contents of the listing displayed beneath it. README.html serves a similar function at the end of the listing.

By default the server looks for a file called HEADER.html, then HEADER, and README.html, then README. The filenames used are controlled by the following directives:

HeaderName   HEADER
ReadmeName   README

An example of the HEADER and README files used in Figure 5-4 are

```
HEADER.html
<H2 ALIGN=center>The NightShade Gallery</H2>
<P ALIGN=center>Stories, sights and sounds from the night.</P>


README.html
If you know of any resources you would like to see on this page, you
can <A HREF="mailto:lilith@sumeria.su">contact</A> the Night
Watch via email.
```

Descriptions

The AddDescription directive controls what shows up in the description field for files displayed in the directory listing. It is used as follows:

```
AddDescription  "Vampire Artifacts"     /home/smith/horror/artifacts
```

This adds the description "Vampire Artifacts" to the subdirectory /home/smith/horror/artifacts. This directive can provide a description for a subdirectory, as shown in this example and Figure 5-5, or it can provide descriptions for individual files.

The Web server's ability to display directory structures and contents is similar in some ways to what Gopher provides. No HTML is required to make files of any type available to Web browsers.

Some useful features of directory listings are

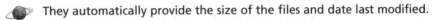 They automatically provide the size of the files and date last modified.

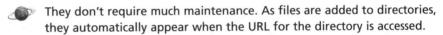 They don't require much maintenance. As files are added to directories, they automatically appear when the URL for the directory is accessed.

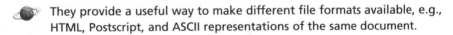 They provide a useful way to make different file formats available, e.g., HTML, Postscript, and ASCII representations of the same document.

 They provide an alternative to FTP URLs for serving files meant for downloading by clients.

1. If the DocumentRoot directive in srm.conf is set to /usr/local/docs, what would the Web server use for the path and filename when it received the following URL: http://server/test/my.html?
   a. /test/my.html
   b. /usr/local/docs/my.hmtl
   c. /usr/local/docs/test/index.html
   d. /usr/local/docs/test/my.html

2. With DocumentRoot the same as in the question above, why would the following URL fail: http://server/usr/local/docs/test/my.html?
   a. It would be mapped to /usr/local/docs/usr/local/docs/test/my.html.
   b. It wouldn't fail, it would return the same document as Question 1.
   c. It wouldn't be able to find index.html because my.html was specified.
   d. It would be mapped to /usr/local/docs/test/index.html.

3. With the UserDir directive in srm.conf set to public_html, what path and filename would the following URL map to: http://server/~fred/?
   a. /usr/local/docs/fred/index.html
   b. Fred's user directory followed by /public_html/index.html

    c. /usr/local/docs/~fred/index.html

    d. /usr/local/docs/~fred.html

4. What's the difference between fancy and simple indexing?

    a. Simple indexing does not display the file size.

    b. FancyIndexing is sorted by filename.

    c. Simple indexing does not display HTML documents.

    d. FancyIndexing shows icons for document types and can display HTML surrounding the directory listing.

PROTECTION

By default, the Web servers you installed in the first two sessions do not limit access to the server. Unless access is already being controlled in your environment via firewalls or gateways, anyone on the Internet can connect to your Web site and retrieve Web documents. This might be just what you want. If not, you have two options available for controlling who gets in.

You can control access by address. Based on the incoming TCP/IP address, or host name, you can deny or allow access to Web documents within directories. An address can refer to a specific host, like janet.BigWampum.com, or it can refer to a network domain, such as everyone from the Big Wampum company: .BigWampum.com.

You can also control access by user, checking a username and password before allowing any pages to be retrieved from a directory. The username and password file is one created by utilities that come with the Web server. Each of these methods will be covered in this session.

Protecting Trees

Access directives are found in the Web server's access.conf configuration file. The access directives control whole directories and all their subdirectories, rather than individual Web pages. This is a key point to remember for the rest of the session. Individual Web pages or forms are not protected; *directory trees* are protected.

Access directives are surrounded by an opening and a closing tag, just as HTML tags are. The syntax for this tag is

ACCESS.CONF ACCESS CONTROL DIRECTIVE	
<Directory *absolute-directory-name>*	
AuthUserFile	*absolute-path-and-filename*
AuthGroupFile	*absolute-path-and-filename*
AuthName	*authentication-realm*
AuthType	Basic

ACCESS.CONF ACCESS CONTROL DIRECTIVE	
AllowOverride	*directives*| None	All
<LIMIT *method*>	
order	[allow,deny]	[deny, allow]
deny from	*ip-address*	*domain-name*
allow from	*ip-address*	*domain-name*
require user	*username*
require group	*groupname*
</LIMIT>	
</Directory>	

absolute-directory-name is the pathname to the directory protected by these rules.
The <Directory> directive specifies rules for protecting documents within a directory.

Multiple pairs of these <Directory> tags can be included in the access.conf file. Each tag can specify a separate directory protected with separate rules. Let's examine how to protect the main document directory from outside networks.

Limiting Access to Local Domain

The <Limit> tag is used with the <Directory> directive to define exactly how the directory is being protected. The option method can be specified within the <Limit> tag:

```
<Limit method>
</Limit>
```

The method can be GET and/or POST.

Most documents, even forms, are initially retrieved using a GET. The POST will only be used in special cases discussed later. Only one <Limit> tag can be used within a given <Directory> tag.

The directives used within the <Limit> tag for controlling access by host are

 *order*   Defines whether deny or allow should be evaluated first.

 *deny*   Defines what to deny access.

 *allow*   Defines what to allow access.

For example, the following directive limits access to the main Web server's directory, and all its subdirectories, to users from the test.com domain:

```
<Directory /usr/local/httpdocs>
<Limit GET>
        order deny, allow
        deny from all
        allow from test.com
</Limit>
</Directory>
```

The detailed elements of this directive are

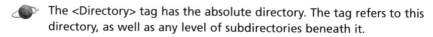

The <Directory> tag has the absolute directory. The tag refers to this directory, as well as any level of subdirectories beneath it.

order indicates the server should look at *deny* first, and then allow only the exceptions.

deny using the option *from all* rejects everybody, no matter where they are from.

allow using the option *from test.com* lets anyone from the test.com company to squeak in.

If allow had specified *jane.test.com*, instead of just *test.com*, then only the host jane.test.com could access the directory, instead of any host with test.com as the last part of its domain name. But what if you want to allow multiple networks in, or conversely, you want to allow everyone in except one or more networks?

Multiple Domains and IP Subnets

To permit not only test.com, but BigWampum.com and clarity.com access to the default directory, you would change the directive as follows:

```
<Directory /usr/local/httpdocs>
<Limit GET>
        order deny, allow
        deny from all
        allow from test.com BigWampum.com clarity.com
</Limit>
</Directory>
```

To switch this, and allow everyone in except these networks, just make a few swaps:

```
<Directory /usr/local/httpdocs>
<Limit GET>
        order allow, deny
        deny from test.com BigWampum.com clarity.com
        allow from all
</Limit>
</Directory>
```

Note that the order needed some tweaking. If the same order was used as in the previous example, the server would have denied the restricted domains first, then permitted them again, because allow permits everyone!

Besides network names, you can also use TCP/IP addresses in the deny and allow directives:

```
deny from 128.145.1.0
```

Or to restrict an entire network:

```
deny from 128.145
```

or a subnet:

```
deny from 128.138.1
```

Limiting Access to Users

Controlling access by host and network is mostly transparent to the users. They either get in without a hassle, or they receive a message in their browser similar to Figure 5-6. With the next level of protection, user authentication, users are challenged by the server when they try to access the protected directory tree. The challenge consists of a username/password prompt; without a correct response, the user is stopped in his or her tracks.

The username/password file is not the username and passwords that might already be on the server. It is a special file just for the Web server. Because of this, accounts can be set up for Web users that may or may not have valid accounts on the system the Web server is running on.

To protect a directory using username and password, a few more directives are required. Here is an example:

```
<Directory /usr/local/httpdocs>
AuthUserFile /usr/local/httpd_1.4.2/conf/.htpasswd
AuthGroupFile /dev/null
AuthName Admin Access
AuthType Basic
<Limit GET>
        require user smirnoff
        </Limit>
        </Directory>
```

The new directives are

 AuthUserFile This points to the username/password file. You'll learn to create this in a minute.

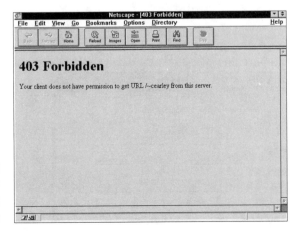

Figure 5-6
Denied access because of network address

AuthGroupFile   This points to /dev/null, which is the UNIX equivalent of saying nowhere. This file is used for group authorizations, which you aren't using just yet.

AuthName   This gives an arbitrary name for the domain being protected.

AuthType   This takes the only option currently available: Basic.

require user   In the <Limit> directive, this tells the server that only a given user can access this directory. But that user needs to know the password.

With this in place, note the result of attempting to open the default directory with http://www.test.com/ in Figure 5-7.

Once the successful password is entered, you can access any document in the directory. Note in Figure 5-7 that the AuthName is displayed in the prompt box.

How Authentication Works

But how does this work? Working with forms in Chapter 4, you learned that Web servers are stateless, which means they don't keep track of users from one interaction to another. Why doesn't the Web server keep asking for username/password with each new Web page you access under a protected directory?

The secret is in the browser. If a Web browser supports authentication (and most do), that means it will stash the username/password, as well as the authentication realm, and reuse these as it navigates from page to page. If it tries to access information in another authentication realm, the server will prompt for a new username/password.

Creating the Password File

The password file was referenced in the previous example as

```
AuthUserFile /usr/local/httpd_1.4.2/conf/.htpasswd
```

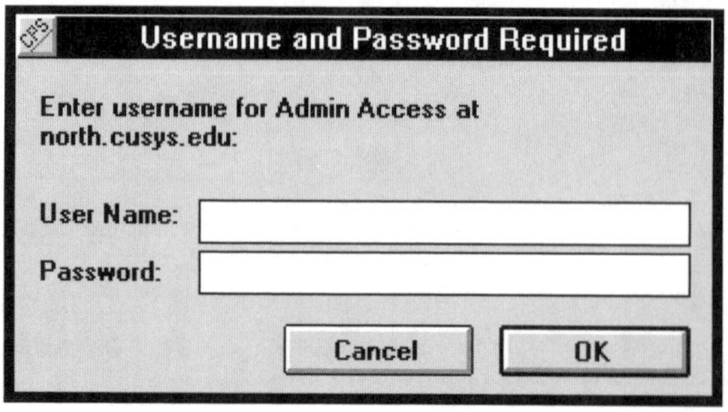

Figure 5-7
Username
and password
protection

Username and Password Required

Enter username for Admin Access at
north.cusys.edu:

User Name:

Password:

Cancel   OK

The server assumes this file already exists, so you'll need to create it before restarting the server with this new directive. To create the Web server password file, you'll need to use a utility found in the /support directory called htpasswd. The syntax for htpasswd is

THE HTPASSWD COMMAND
htpasswd [-c] .htpassword-file username

-c	is an optional argument, and if present will create the .htpassword file.
.htpasswrd-file	is the file to be created, or edited.
username	is the new or existing user in the .htpassword-file.

The htpasswd command creates and maintains the Web user password file.

To create the .htpasswd file referred to in the example with the username "smirnoff", you would use the following:

```
htpasswd -c /usr/local/httpd_1.4.2/conf/.htpasswd smirnoff
```

Don't use the -c flag again after the password file has been created; it will wipe out the file! To add more users, or to change smirnoff's password, just use

```
httpasswd /usr/loca/bin/httpd_1.4.2/conf/.htpasswd username
```

Passwords are stored encrypted in this file, but you still need to take precautions to protect it. Ideally it should be located outside of any directory tree accessible by Web browsers.

Access Groups

Groups are just an extension of the username/password authentication method. In addition to a password file, you can create a *group file* that has names of one or more users. The group file can be created with an ordinary text editor, and each line has the following format:

```
group-name: user1 user2 user3 etc.
```

So let's make a group file with smirnoff and a couple of more users, and create an arbitrary group called "vips". The file will be called .htgroups and contains the following line:

```
vips: smirnoff swartz lemon
```

Now you can use the following directory to deny everyone, except those belonging to the group "vips", access to the main document directory:

```
<Directory /usr/local/httpdocs>
AuthUserFile /usr/local/httpd_1.4.2/conf/.htpasswd
AuthGroupFile /usr/local/httpd_1.4.2/conf/.htgroups
AuthName Front Door
AuthType Basic
<Limit GET>
        require group vips
</Limit>
</Directory>
```

The users will still need to know their individual passwords to log in. It will not be apparent to them that they are also being identified with one or more groups, although it is this group membership that authorizes them to enter a particular directory.

Other Directories...

Username and group protections can be combined with host and network protections, as shown in the following example:

```
<Directory /usr/local/httpdocs>
AuthUserFile /usr/local/httpd_1.4.2/conf/.htpasswd
AuthGroupFile /usr/local/httpd_1.4.2/conf/.htgroups
AuthName Front Door
AuthType Basic
<Limit GET>
        order allow, deny
        deny from test.com BigWampum.com clarity.com
        allow from all
        require group vips
</Limit>
</Directory>
```

These directives combine both types of access control. The first directives applied are deny and allow. So only users *not* from the test.com, BigWampum.com, or clarity.com networks who are members of the group "vips" (and remember their passwords) can access the main directory.

These examples have all used the default directory specified back in the srm.conf file. Other directories can be protected as well, each with its own <Directory> tag:

```
<Directory /usr/local/httpdocs>
<Limit GET>
        order allow, deny
        deny from bother.com competitor.com
        allow from all
</Limit>
</Directory>

<Directory /home/jack/top-secret-ufo-stuff>
AuthUserFile /usr/local/httpd_1.4.2/conf/.htpasswd
AuthGroupFile /usr/local/httpd_1.4.2/conf/.htgroups
AuthName Secret Door
AuthType Basic
<Limit GET>
        order deny, allow
        deny from all
        allow from test.com
        require group vips
</Limit>
</Directory>
```

```
<Directory /home/robertson/funstuff>
AuthUserFile /usr/local/httpd_1.4.2/conf/.htpasswd
AuthGroupFile /usr/local/httpd_1.4.2/conf/.htgroups
AuthName Private Room
AuthType Basic
<Limit GET>
       require user robertson
</Limit>
</Directory>
```

The access.conf file can also control all the user directories on your Web. For example, if all the user directories were under the /home root directory, you could use the following to protect everyone against offsite access (assuming your site is test.com):

```
<Directory /home>
<Limit GET>
       order deny, allow
       deny from all
       allow from test.com
</Limit>
</Directory>
```

Since the <Directory> directive applies to everything in the /home directory and all the subdirectories beneath it, all users with home directories like:

```
/home/finance/smith
/home/budget/jones
/home/sales/fred
```

are protected by the directive above.

Delegating Control

Unless specifically restricted, users can also control their own directories by creating a file called *.htaccess* in the directory they want to protect. The directives in .htaccess look just like the directives under <Directory>, except they don't need the <Directory> tag. The directory is assumed to be the one in which the .htaccess file is found.

Users can maintain their own password and group files, and control which networks can access their directories. This is a way of delegating security controls instead of specifying them globally within access.conf.

For example, if a user whose Web directory is in /users/home/fred/public_html wants to limit access to only his friends at snaggle.net and himself at woof.com, he could create an .htaccess file in his public_html directory with the following entries:

```
<Limit GET>
       order deny, allow
       deny from all
       allow from snaggle.net fred.woof.com
</Limit>
```

Controlling Delegation

Delegating control can also get out of hand. Perhaps you want to delegate to some people, but want to explicitly control others. A directive called *AllowOveride* restricts which part of the family business you give away. The syntax of the AllowOveride directive is

```
AllowOverride   directives
```

If not specified, AllowOverride defaults to allow all directives in .htaccess files. To prevent users from controlling their own access permissions, assuming all the users were in under the /home directory, you would use the following:

```
<Directory /home>
AllowOverride None
</Directory>
```

Even if the users don't all fall neatly under the /home directory, they still need to use the subdirectory specified in UserDir directive in srm.conf for Web access via ~username. You can use wildcard syntax to protect all public_html directories no matter where they are located via

```
<Directory /*/public_html*>
AllowOverride None
</Directory>
```

Obscure Cases

If you are using scripts to call other scripts, you might run into a case where a user has access to one script, but not the one that script calls. Since the user did the equivalent of a GET to retrieve the initial script, the access rules in <Limit GET> were in effect. The second script, though, called by the first, might be called with a POST. With no <Limit> directives applying to it, it is a potential security hole. To patch it, merely include the following in the <Limit> directive:

```
<Limit GET POST>
```

This protects both the initial script and any scripts posted to under this directory.

1. How would you restrict access to /usr/local/docs from everyone except the people in your network? Assume your host address is joe.smurfs.edu.

```
a. <Directory /usr/local/docs>
   <Limit GET>
          order allow, deny
          deny from joes.smurfs.edu
          allow from all
   </Limit>
   </Directory>
```

```
b. <Directory /usr/local/docs>
   <Limit GET>
           order allow, deny
           deny from smurfs.edu
           allow from all
   </Limit>
   </Directory>
c. <Directory /usr/local/docs>
   <Limit GET>
           order deny, allow
           deny from all
           allow from smurfs.edu
   </Limit>
   </Directory>
d. <Directory /usr/local/docs>
   <Limit GET>
           order deny, allow
           deny from all
           allow from joes.smurfs.edu
   </Limit>
   </Directory>
```

2. How would you add a user, "joe", to an existing password file called upass?
   a. httpasswd -c joe upass
   b. httpasswd upass joe
   c. httpasswd -c upass joe
   d. httpasswd -a joe upass

3. How is the group file maintained?
   a. It's maintained with httgroup.
   b. It's created automatically when users are added with httpasswd.
   c. There is an option of the httpasswd utility to specify the group of a user.
   d. It's maintained with a regular text editor; it's just a normal file.

4. If you restrict access to a directory by both network addresses and username/password, which takes precedence?
   a. If network is specified, the username section is ignored.
   b. If username is specified, the network section is ignored.
   c. You can't specify both.
   d. Network is checked first, and if it passes, then username/password is checked.

SESSION 5

SERVER DIRECTIVES

A few important directives were omitted from Session 4.. They don't fall within the scope of access controls per se, but they are keys to important functionality on the Web server.

Options is one of these. Options controls directives that permit or restrict the ability to run scripts in a directory, whether an index listing of a directory's contents is generated if a default page doesn't exist, and whether Web browsers can follow links from a user's directory into other directories on the system. Options also contains a directive that allows information to be dynamically included in a page before it leaves the server. This somewhat controversial technique, known as *server side includes*, is available on NCSA Web servers. After covering the Options directive and learning how to use server side includes, you'll briefly cover how imagemaps are processed on the server.

The Options Directive

The Options directive is used inside inside the <Directory> tag in the access.conf file. Its syntax is

ACCESS.CONF OPTIONS DIRECTIVE

```
<Directory>
        Options      one or more of the below
```

None	None of the options listed below are enabled.
All	All of the options listed below are enabled.
Indexes	Allows indexes to this directory.
FollowSymLinks	Follows links to other directories.
SymLinksIfOwnerMatch	Follows links only if the same owner created them.
ExecCGI	Allows CGI scripts to execute in this directory.
Includes	Allows server side includes in this directory.
IncludesNoExec	Allows server side includes but no scripts.

```
</Directory>
```

The Options directive controls script, includes, and symbolic link permissions.

The following is a typical example of the use of the Options directive:

```
<Directory /usr/local/etc/catalog>
Options Indexes SymLinksIfOwnerMatch
AllowOverride None
<Limit GET>
        order deny, allow
        deny from all
        allow from test.com
</Limit>
</Directory>
```

The option Indexes you've seen at work with plain and fancy indexing. By default an index to a directory will be returned if the directory is referenced in a URL but does not have a default index.html page. For example:

```
http://testserver.edu/catalogs/
```

To turn off this behavior, configure an Options directive with None, or with the Index option omitted. This will cause the URL above to return the message

```
403 Forbidden
Your client does not have permission to get URL /catalogs/ from this server.
```

The FollowSymLinks option refers to the capability in UNIX to have a directory or file that is really a pointer to some other directory or file in a different location. If FollowSymLinks is enabled, the Web server will treat these links as if they were part of the directory specified in the <Directory> tag, inheriting the same access controls.

The SymLinksIfOwnerMatch option allows access through these links only to other directories or files that you own.

The ExecCGI option permits scripts to be run in a directory and the subdirectories under it. Usually the server knows whether a file is a script or not by whether it is in one of the ScriptAlias directories defined in the srm.conf file. Since the ExecCGI option can be used in a directory that has HTML as well as scripts, the server needs to know which file is a script file. To identify scripts, you'll need to add a directive to srm.conf, describing the filetype that your scripts use:

```
AddType application/x-httpd-cgi .cgi
```

This entry tells the Web server to treat files with a filetype of .cgi as CGI scripts. You could then create a Perl script in a directory with the ExecCGI option and call it

```
prespoll.cgi
```

If ExecCGI is enabled on the user "smirnoff"'s directory, then this script could be executed with the following HTML:

```
<FORM ACTION="http://www.yourserver/~smirnoff/prespoll.cgi">
```

Like Web pages, the script needs to be accessible for world read and execute. You can make sure that it is with the chmod command:

```
chmod o+rx prespoll.cgi
```

The Includes and IncludesNoExec options are going to require a short detour into server side includes. These allow NCSA type servers to both include other documents and to run scripts as part of a document before the results are returned to the Web browser. They're a controversial feature, but skip the politics for now and just concentrate on how they work.

Server Side Includes

Server side includes are simply statements within an HTML document that direct the server to include other HTML, or to run a script whenever the document is retrieved. Obviously this goes above and beyond any HTML tag's capabilities, and in fact users never see these includes as part of the HTML, even if they view the source back on the Web browser. Includes are used strictly between the document and the server. Here's how it's done.

First, the document has a special directive that the server recognizes as a request for a server side include. The directive's syntax is

THE SERVER SIDE INCLUDES DIRECTIVE

<!—#command options—>
Commands:

config	Controls some parameters that determine how the server parses the include document
include	Points to a file to include in the document
echo	Prints the value of a predefined variable
fsize	Prints the size of a specified file
flastmod	Prints the last modificaton date of a specified file
exec	Executes a shell command or CGI script and "folds in" the results

Server side includes contain commands that dynamically change the content of a page.

This lesson will not cover all of these commands and options; just a few of the more common ones will be demonstrated. For more detailed information, consult the server documentation at http://hoohoo.ncsa.uiuc.edu/.

Second, the srm.conf file must contain information that tells the server which files to parse for server side includes. This directive is

```
AddType text/x-server-parsed-html .shtml
```

This directs the server to only look for server side include commands in filetypes of .shtml. You could use also use .html; this makes the server search all HTML files for possible commands before sending the pages on to the Web browser, and it can really bog down your server. That's why when server side includes are enabled, they are usually directed to look only in specific files. When these two criteria are met—server side include directives are in an HTML file, and the server has been told which files to look for them in—you're ready to start using some of the commands.

One of the most popular of these commands is the include itself, not surprising, since this command performs the directive's basic function, which is to let you pull in another file on the fly. You can point to the file you want to include in two different ways: virtual or relative. Virtual specifies the same type of path you would use in a URL to the server. For example, the following uses a virtual path command:

```
<!--#include virtual="/~smirnoff/standard.html"-->
```

The relative option specifies a file to include relative to the current file, so to pick up another file in the same directory, you would enter

```
<!--#include file="standard.html"-->
```

The following HTML will pull in a middle section. This middle section could be a text file on the server that is being constantly updated with information; in this case it is the error_log file from the Web server:

```
<HTML>
<HEAD>
<TITLE>Testing Server Side Includes</TITLE>
</HEAD>
```

```
<BODY>
<H2>Display The Latest Web Server Error Log</H2>
<HR>
<PRE>
<!--#include virtual="/logs/error_log"-->
</PRE>
</BODY>
</HTML>
```

The file is called error.shtml, and an Alias for the log's directory has been specified in srm.conf so the virtual path could be used. This was a workaround. Absolute paths are not permitted in the include command.

What it brings down when accessed via URL http://www.test.com/~smirnoff/error.shtml is displayed in Figure 5-8.

It's generally not a good idea to do this in real life. By defining an Alias for the log's directory, you have opened up a part of the server's files that are usually restricted from Web browser access. To correct this problem, let's password protect this directory, making it available only to a single user: "smirnoff". The following in the access.conf should do the trick:

```
<Directory /usr/local/httpd_1.4.2/logs>
Options None
AllowOverride None
AuthUserFile /usr/local/httpd_1.4.2/conf/.htpasswd
AuthGroupFile /dev/null
AuthName Admin Access
AuthType Basic
<Limit GET>
        require user smirnoff
</Limit>
</Directory>
```

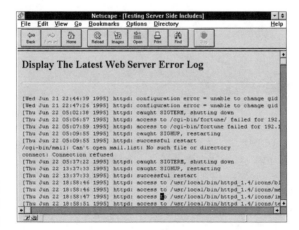

Figure 5-8
Including the
error log

And now when errors.shmtl is accessed, a username/password prompt pops up. This demonstrates that server side includes still work through the access control mechanisms of the server.

The other include commands can provide various specialized functions, and the exec option is usually avoided as a potential security risk (you'll learn why in Session 6). Before you go on, though, you should know about one other command of server side includes that is seen frequently.

The *echo* command sends information stored in variables back with the HTML page as it's retrieved. On small servers it's a popular feature. If you set the following in srm.conf:

```
AddType text/x-server-parsed-html .html
```

then in any directory that has the Option Includes directive set, you can add the following in your pages to automatically include the last time the document was modified:

```
<HTML>
regular html stuff...
<!--#config timefmt="%A, %d-%b-%y"-->
<B>This Page Last Updated: <!--#echo var="LAST_MODIFIED"--></B>
```

This displays the modification date of the page automatically. The config directive was used to change the default way the time is displayed, from day, date, time, and time zone, to simply day and date. Other useful variables that can be displayed with the echo command are

DATE_GMT	Current Greenwich Mean Time
DATE_LOCAL	Local date and time
DOCUMENT_NAME	Filename of this document
DOCUMENT_URI	Virtual pathname of the document
LAST_MODIFIED	Date/time of last change made to the document

The server is very picky about the syntax of commands for server side includes. For example, if you have a space between the "LAST_MODIFIED" string and the trailing —>, the example above will not work.

ImageMaps

The last server option to be covered is server imagemaps. Imagemaps are not controlled by directives, but they are somewhat similar to server side includes in that the server will take certain actions as directed in the page. Or in this case, in an image on the page.

First, a quick review. In HTML a hotspot can be defined on a GIF file by associating it with another file that describes the coordinates of the hotspot. For example, in the following HTML:

```
<A HREF="http://www.test.com/cgi-bin/imagemap/~jacob/ohio.map">
<IMG SRC=ohio.gif ISMAP></A>
```

when a mouse button is clicked on *ohio.gif* on the Web browser, the following process unfolds on the Web server. Figure 5-9 shows the ImageMap process.

1. A program called imagemap located in cgi-bin is executed. It is passed the x,y coordinates of the mouse click and the path/filename, /~jacob/ohio.map, as an argument.

2. imagemap reads ohio.map for the coordinates, and the x,y coordinates are compared with entries in the map file for a hit. When a match is found, the URL specified in ohio.map for these coordinates is linked to.

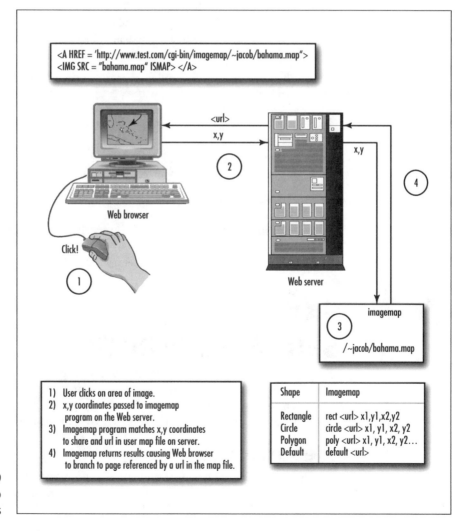

Figure 5-9
The imagemap process

1. What steps need to be completed before scripts can be executed out of user directories?
    a. The directories need to be given the ExecCGI option, and srm.conf needs to be configured with a script filetype.
    b. Nothing.
    c. The directories need to be given the ExecCGI option.
    d. The directories need to be given the Includes option.

2. What are symbolic links?
    a. HTML tags that link to other documents
    b. links to include other documents
    c. files or directories that are actually pointers to other files or directories
    d. links that have graphical tags

3. Why isn't configuring .html filetypes as server side includes generally recommended?
    a. The server confuses them with ordinary Web pages.
    b. The server has to look in each HTML file to see if any commands are present.
    c. Web browsers will not be able to process the files.
    d. The server will think Web pages are scripts and try to execute them.

4. Why won't the following work? <!—#include="/usr/local/docs/test.txt—>
    a. You can't include a text file.
    b. "/usr/local/docs/text.txt" probably specifies an absolute path.
    c. There is a syntax error.
    d. The .txt filetype needs to be set up in srm.conf to specify an include file.

SESSION 6

SERVER SECURITY

The access control directives you've mastered so far provide two ways of protecting document directories: protection by network or host address, and protection by username/passwords. While these are relatively secure, they aren't 100 percent. Before Webmasters develop a false sense of security, they need to look at some hard facts.

Weaknesses

Only permitting certain networks in, like acme.com, relies on another Internet service called the *Domain Name System,* or DNS, server, to provide your Web server with the correct network name. When a Web browser connects to a Web server, the server typically receives only the TCP/IP address, and must ask the DNS server for the domain name through a mechanism called reverse DNS lookups. If the DNS server has been hacked, it may report just what the Web server wants to hear, and allow access to a bogus address. And though the Web server directives also give the ability to screen based on IP addresses, it is in some ways easier to spoof an IP address than to trick a DNS server, so this method doesn't provide additional security.

What about usernames and passwords? After all, they are under direct control of the Web server; don't they offer secure protection? Not really. The main problem here is that the Web browser sends the username and password out across the network in what is called "cleartext." The passwords are not encrypted, and a variety of public domain tools allow Joe or Jane Hacker to watch all the packets going back and forth across popular network mediums like Ethernet. This is one reason the credit card companies are a bit paranoid about commerce on the Internet, and why encryption standards like SSL and S-HTTP (discussed in Chapter 7) are seen as important technology for a commercial Internet.

But don't hang it all up at this point and decide you need to plunk down big dollars for a commercial server. These potential security problems are worst-case scenarios. If you do have something that absolutely must be protected at all costs, then, naah, you probably want a commercial server with encrypted authentication, or firewalls and proxies to sequester behind. But if your server uses adequate safeguards, as discussed below, it will be no worse off than any of the other Telnet, FTP, and e-mail hosts that make up the dozens of nodes on the Internet today. In fact, technology is rapidly closing off many of these exposures, independent of encrypted sessions.

Bottom Line

The bottom line? Sensitive information, military secrets, and trusted family recipes probably require better security than is available on a noncommercial Web server that is not protected by firewalls. But information for the general public, or for limited sets of the public, like subscribers or special interest groups, can be adequately protected by the basic access control mechanisms of the servers you've studied—barring a personally directed and sustained attempt to hack into your systems (which would probably penetrate any other security techniques as well).

Tricky Protections

As mentioned above, many technologies are evolving to close security exposures. Routers that link sites to the Internet, for example, are often configured to prevent IP address "spoofing." Etherswitches and network segmentation are making it more and more difficult to find points where "eavesdropping" is viable. And the widescale use of LANs offers other techniques for protecting Web documents.

Let's say you have a Web server attached to the Internet, and you have a number of users in your department for whom you would like to provide information. It's not unusual for them to all be connected to the same departmental LAN. In this scenario, the limitations of the File URL can actually provide a measure of security for the LAN users. You could reference Web pages and documentation from the Web server with File URLs pointing to LAN-based documents. The Web browsers on the local LAN will know how to retrieve these documents, but if any users outside of your LAN, use a drive mapping like

`FILE:/M:\AUDITS\INDEX.HTM`

they will find their browsers trying to access their local M: drive!

Even if you feel your network backbone is secure against eavesdroppers, and the DNS server is secure and well managed, you'll still need to tighten up a few more areas on the Web server to avoid any internal holes. The first of these is user directories.

User Directories

Enabling user directories with the UserDir directive in srm.conf lets users write their own Web pages and reference them in ~username URLs. This makes the job of the Webmaster easier. He or she doesn't have to constantly be shuffling users' pages into some document directory under his or her control. Things can just evolve. But without changing some defaults that come packaged with the Web server software, this evolution could lead to future problems. One potential problem is with symbolic links.

Symbolic Links

Symbolic links are a feature of UNIX. You'll remember from Sesssion 5 that this feature allows directories or files to really be links to other directories or files. So while a directory listing might look like a neat hierarchy of files and subdirectories, some of these files might be in other directories, and some of the directories might be on other parts of the system. This can quickly defeat the directory-based protection of the Web server's access controls.

For example, you might have given permission for a user to run scripts in his subdirectories. He might in turn create a symbolic link to the anonymous FTP directory where people from anywhere can upload files. This now means you've let anyone from anywhere write scripts to run on your Web server! This can be circumvented with the following directive on the user's directories:

```
<Directory /home/users>
Options Indexes
AllowOverride None
</Directory>
```

This gives the server the ability to index the user directories (see simple and fancy indexes in Session 3) but nothing else. The server won't follow symbolic links, so it won't allow the user to run scripts. A less drastic alternative would be to follow symbolic links, but only to files and directories owned by the user:

```
<Directory /home/users>
Options Indexes SymLinksIfOwnerMatch
AllowOverride None
</Directory>
```

This type of exposure demonstrates the importance of the directory trees on a Web server. The server will not allow access to documents outside of directory trees that it has set up with Alias directives in srm.conf and with the UserDir directive. Symbolic links could compromise this control, allowing a Web browser to examine directories and files outside of the Web document directories.

The AllowOverride None directive is another important security control. It prevents these rules from being superseded by an .htaccess entry in a user's directory.

User Script Exposures

When user-written scripts are permitted on the server, via a directive like

```
<Directory /home/users>
Options Indexes SymLinksIfOwnerMatch ExecCGI
AllowOverride None
</Directory>
```

the Web server will run scripts using its own username rather than that of the script's owner. Scripts can access objects on the system as if they were the Web server. This could lead to trouble.

Such trouble is commonly not malicious, but instead a result of users learning to write scripts and leaving holes in them that can be exploited through their forms. For example, some scripts will at times use input or variables from a form to pass to a system command. It could be an innocuous string like a lookup value, passed to a system utility like grep to search through a certain file for it. Maybe a user is just coming up to speed on forms and writes a simple script that does something like this:

```
#!/usr/local/perl
print "You entered: @ARGV\n";
```

and the form is called with an argument of

```
`ls -l`
```

The actual UNIX command ls -l would be executed, producing a directory listing that would be returned as the argument. Other UNIX commands besides ls could have been entered, with less germane consequences.

Most interpreted script languages, including the UNIX shells, Perl, etc., have special characters that can be used to invoke commands. These commands can be ways of escaping from the script and performing a hacker's own agenda. One way to protect your users and server from accidental exposure is through the use of wrappers.

Wrappers

CGIWrap, available from http://wwwcgi.umr.edu/ at the University of Missouri-Rolla, provides a useful solution. By installing this program in one of your cgi-bin directories, user scripts can be invoked via the following:

```
http://myserver.net/cgi-bin/cgiwrap?user=username&script=scriptname
```

where *username* is the name of the user who wrote the script, and *scriptname* is the name of the script. The user scripts need to be moved into cgi-bin, so there is some administrative overhead, but the scripts don't need to be individually inspected. CGIWrap takes care of filtering the variables so no escape commands can be entered, and it runs the script as if it were being run by the owner of the script, rather than the Web server.

Includes

Server side includes suffer from some of the same exposures that user scripts do, particularly the exec command, which triggers a CGI script or actually executes a shell command. While legitimate cases have been made for the Includes and other commands, most Webmasters restrict the ability of users to invoke the exec command. To allow Includes without exec capabilities, you would use the following directives in access.conf:

```
<Directory /home/users>
Options IncludesNoExec
AllowOverride None
</Directory>
```

Excluding Robots

Robots and spiders are automatic programs that scan the Web for information. They aren't pernicious, but they might be a bother, adding additional load to your server, and perhaps advertising information that you would not like to see globally distributed. While no standards committee exists to define proper robot protocol, many of the larger robots will look for a robots.txt file in your main directory. If the contents of this file are

```
# beat it
User-agent: *
Disallow: /
```

the robot should slink off without attempting to scan through all of your directories. More information about robots and directives for the robots.txt file can be found at http://web.nexor.co.uk/mak/doc/robots.html.

1. How could network- or IP-based security on the server be compromised?
   a. It can't be; it's airtight.
   b. If the server is down, the controls won't be in effect.
   c. The server relies on other services to validate the network and IP addresses.
   d. By eavesdroppers.

2. Why can't outside users access local File URLs?
   a. because they can be password protected
   b. because they are not in the directory trees
   c. because LAN drives are like local drives and are unknown to the server
   d   because it's not an HTML standard

3. How can symbolic links create exposures?
   a. What's linked to is not covered under the access controls of the directory.
   b. Users could link to scripts even though their directory does not have the ExecCGI option.
   c. Security doesn't apply to links.
   d. Users might extend their rights outside of their directory tree.

4. What exposures are there with user-written CGIs?
   a. None, if they use a secure language like Perl.
   b. None, if the ExecCGI option is used.
   c. Input from forms may be interpreted as system commands.
   d. There is no way to control them.

SESSION 7

SERVER TOOLS

Web servers run for days or even weeks with very little attention. If your server is heavily utilized, however, you will want to monitor a few things frequently. One of these is the log files. The NCSA server creates four log files by default in the logs subdirectory:

error_log   Logs all errors encountered by the server, such as errors running scripts, problems with authentication, attemps to override directory protections with .htaccess files, etc.

access_log   Logs files transferred from the Web server, and the hosts requesting them

agent_log   Tracks the type of browsers accessing the Web server, e.g., Mosaic, Netscape, etc.

referer_log   Tracks documents referencing your server from other Web servers, and what documents they pointed to

Left to their own devices, these logs will continue to grow and can get surprisingly large, surprisingly fast. To clear a log, just rename it and restart the server (if you are using the stand-alone startup method; if you use inetd, skip the restart step). The steps needed to rename the access_log and restart the stand-alone server are

```
cd /usr/local/httpd/logs          change default to the log directory
mv access_log 1297-access_log     rename it to mmyy-access_log
kill -HUP `cat httpd.pid`         restart the server
```

Besides just accumulating information, you have to purge or archive periodically, and the logs can be used for reporting activity on your Web server. Several tools have been developed to make the Webmaster's life easier; getstats from ftp.eit.com is one of these. The getstats program is written in C and needs to be compiled on your system. It consists of one file: getstats.*nnn*.c, where *nnn* is the current version number. At the top of this file a few default directories are coded for your Web server. Edit these to reflect valid directories on your server, compile it, and it's ready to use.

Figure 5-10 shows an example of a small section of access_log displayed on the terminal.

Figure 5-11 shows a quick summary of the same log provided by running the following:

```
getstats -M -c
```

The -M option tells getstats to use the "common" log format, which more Web server providers have started to adopt, including the NCSA version. The -c asks for a concise, summary type report.

Other reporting options are

-m	Shows monthly report with total number of accesses for each month.
-w	Shows weekly report breaking down access counts by day.
-hs	Shows hourly summary.
-r	Shows number of requests by request name. Use this option to find your most popular documents.
-dn	Shows a domain name report. It details which domains accessed your server and how many requests were made from each.

These options just scratch the surface of the getstats suite. You can select log entries based on strings, look for or exclude certain hosts, you can specify date ranges, file size thresholds, and more.

To make this set of options a little more manageable, getstats also provides an HTML interface. To enable this feature, you'll need to complete the following steps:

1. Edit the getstats.c program and turn on the CGI option by uncommenting #*define CGI*.

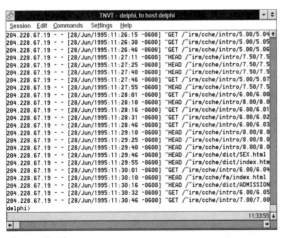

Figure 5-10
access_log in its native format

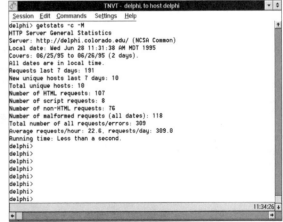

Figure 5-11
getstats concise report option

2. Edit statform.c that comes with the getstats package and put in the default log file to analyze, the root directory, etc., just as you did originally for getstats.

3. Compile getstats and statform and move both executables into one of your cgi-bin directories. Make sure both are executable by the Web server (*chmod a+rx <filename>*).

4. Edit statform.html and point it to the statform program in /cgi-bin/.

5. Put statform.html somewhere and open it in a URL.

These steps should result in the form appearing in Figure 5-11.
For log crunching sessions that will last a long time, you can use a statform option on the form requesting the results to be e-mailed to you.

RefStats

If you start managing your own Web server, you're probably going to be curious about whose Web pages are pointing to your own. The referer_log in the /logs directory contains detailed information about where people are coming from to see your Web pages; a handy utility called Refstats, written by Benjamin Franz, pops this information up into a page of HTML. The utility is a Perl CGI script, obtainable from http://www.netimages.com. Just change the *$HTTPDPATH* variable in the script to point to your root directory and then plop it into /cgi-bin/. Open a URL to the script, for example:

```
http://myserver.earth.orb/cgi-bin/refstats
```

and you'll be treated to a display similiar to that shown in Figure 5-13.

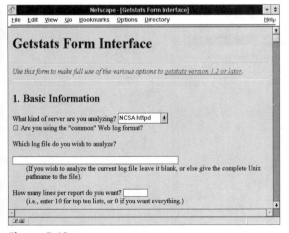

Figure 5-12
getstats with a Web interface

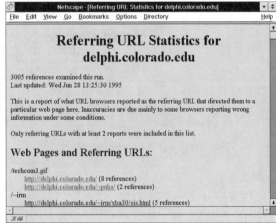

Figure 5-13
RefStats page–where they are all coming from

What about the error_log, you say? You could get fancy if you like, and someone is probably writing a utility even as you read this to format and prettify errors, but usually the basic

```
tail /usr/local/httpd/error_log
```

works to display the most recent errors, followed periodically by

```
cat /dev/null > /usr/local/httpd/error_log
```

to clear out the file.

HTML Validation

One of the perks of running a Web is the several services available to take a URL and parse it for valid HTML syntax. Some of these get quite fancy, validating strict and loose interpretations of the standards, validating HTML 2.0, 3.0, Mozilla extensions, etc. When you were writing HTML and displaying it in your own browser for practice, you couldn't really hand out a URL pointing to your local disk. But now that you've almost cleared the ranks as Webmaster, you can not only validate, but can use the nifty inline images that certify your page is HTML 2.x or 3.x approved. Figure 5-14 shows the form for a service at http://www.halsoft.com/html-val-svc/. These types of services also offer the scripts to run the validation at your own site.

Another validation tool that will come in handy is one used to verify links on your server. The Web changes daily, and the price of not keeping up to date is dead-end links. Fortunately, you can automate the process with a Web utility that checks your pages periodically, making sure all the links are valid and listing those that are not. This utility, verify_links, comes from the same source as the getstats utility. It has binary executables available for most platforms that NCSA runs on. Follow these steps to retrieve and install the file:

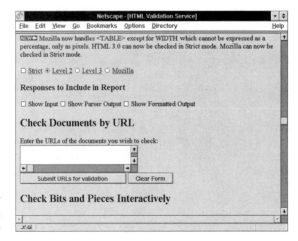

Figure 5-14
HTML validation
service

1. Change your default directory (*cd*) to your cgi-bin directory (as configured in httpd.conf).

2. FTP the verify_links.tar file from ftp.eit.com in the directory /pub/wsk/<OS TYPE>/webtest/. The <OS TYPE> here is your operating sytem type: AIX, Solaris, sunos, etc. This ensures you get the correct executable for your system.

3. Now untar the file, using *tar -xvf verify_links.tar.*

4. Step 3 will create new directories under cgi-bin. You should end up with the executable in /admin/webtest/verify_links.

That's it. Now open http://yourserver/cgi-bin/admin/webtest/verify_html and you should get the form shown in Figure 5-15.

This utility allows you to enter the name of a Web server document and check all of the links.

WebCopy

The last stop in your grab bag of Web administration goodies is a utility used to migrate pages from one Web server to another. This may prove more useful than you initially think. As you begin setting up Web servers, you will probably start on one system, hop to another, and another, until you have pages in various stages of development strewn across them all. When you finally reach that ultimate plateau where you want to consolidate all of your artistry under a unified front, you'll find this command very handy.

WebCopy is a Perl script (what else?) that retrieves a URL, copying it from the remote location to the current directory. It can also retrieve all the URLs this URL references (although it stays on the same host, otherwise you could inadvertently fill up your terabyte hard disk with the whole World Wide Web!).

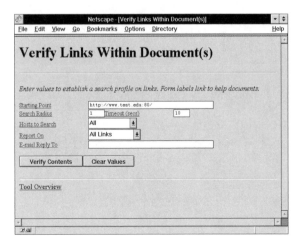

Figure 5-15
verify_links form

Let's go through some examples to demonstrate how this works. First, the easy case, retrieving a single Web page from another server:

```
webcopy http://myotherserver.mars.orb/cool.html
```

This copies cool.html into the current directory. If you want to get not only cool.html, but all the images it references, you can use the -i, or include inline images, option:

```
webcopy -i http://myotherserver.mars.orb/cool.html
```

And to get a page and all the files it refers to in the same directory (including image files), use the -r, or recurse HTML documents, option:

```
webcopy -ri http://myotherserver.mars.orb/cool.html
```

More options are available. You can get the complete list of options by entering

```
webcopy -h
```

You can spend a lot of your time playing with utilities to save time. You know it's becoming an obsession when you start spending days looking for just the right tool, when you could have done the job in a few minutes with tools at hand. Sorry to break it to you, but there's currently no known cure for this affliction.

Quiz 7

1. What Web server log keeps information on what Web documents are pointing to your server?
   a. access_log
   b. referrer_log
   c. httpd_log
   d. No specific log does this.

2. How would you archive a log running a stand-alone Web server?
   a. rename it
   b. copy it to tape
   c. rename it and restart the server
   d. restart the server

3. Why do you need a Web server to use the HTML validation service mentioned in this chapter?
   a. You have to be authorized.
   b. The URL needs to be somewhere accessible to the Internet.
   c. You don't; it can also validate from your local disk.
   d. The validation service uses Web server security.

4. What is not a valid use for WebCopy?
   a. to relocate HTML documents to another server
   b. to relocate inline GIF images to another server

c. to verify links
d. to relocate an HTML document and all documents it refers to on the same
server to another server

ADDING CONTENT

By the time you reach this session, you will already have learned most of the bare necessities (and maybe a tad more) for keeping a Web server up and running smoothly. You've approached it from both ends now, from designing the pages to serving HTML and tinkering with the inner workings reserved for Webmasters only. And now that you are ensconced on the server, you are about to discover another way to generate HTML—automatically!

A collection of tools falling under the umbrella of converters, generators, and widgets (yes, that is a technical term) enables a Webmaster to generate incredible amounts of content on their servers with very little manual effort. This makes the Webmaster look very productive. But if you've heard the term garbage in, garbage out, you know some of the dangers involved. Picking among all the sundry utilities that change postscript to HTML, text to HTML, rtf to HTML, probably even sawdust to HTML, a few gems are worth considering. This session focuses on one that provides a "value-added" service by migrating a listserver's native format to HTML. It's rolled into a product called Hypermail.

Hypermail

As part of your general initiation to the Internet, you've probably been exposed to *listservers*. Listservers, for the uninitiated, provide e-mail addresses that go to a group of people rather than a single recipient. They usually provide ways to sign up for a topic, like spelunking, and allow you to send and receive e-mail from the group as a whole. Sometimes they even let you sign off of the list when you are no longer interested (sorry, a joke for the initiated). Lists can be extremely helpful; questions get answered, interesting discussions wax and wane—but lists have frustrations as well.

Murphy's law of listservers dictates that the important piece of information you are looking for will have been discussed and resolved before you join the list. A subclause of this same law states that you will delete a message as having no practical relevance to anything you are doing, only to discover the next week that it could save you man-years of effort. This is where Hypermail leverages the capabilities of the Web to overcome these listserver limitations.

Hypermail takes a file of messages, in UNIX mailbox format, which coincidentally is also Eudora's mailbox format—more on this below–and builds a set of cross-referenced, hyperlinked, whiz-bang HTML documents that can be browsed by date, subject, sender, recipient, or threads (connected conversations). E-mail addresses are changed to mailto pointers, allowing you to zap out an e-mail for clarification on a point made months ago, even though you might receive a resounding "huh?" in response. In essence, Hypermail provides a knowledge base focused around a topic that has evolved naturally in the course of the life of the lists.

Lists and listservers can be set up internally by companies for questions and answers about policies, benefits, vacation spots, restaurants, whatever. And stored in Hypermail, the information serves as an extensible reference encyclopedia (without the drudgery of actually having to sit down and produce it all).

Hypermail can be obtained via anonymous FTP from ftp.eit.com in the /pub/web.software/hypermail directory. It runs on UNIX, and has binaries available for the following platforms at the time of this writing:

 SunOS 4.1.3

 Solaris 2.3

 IRIX 5.2

 OSF/1 2.0

And, of course, source code is available for the platforms that didn't hit the top four.

Installing Hypermail

Installing Hypermail requires you to move the Hypermail binary into some directory in your PATH statement, typically /usr/local or /usr/bin. If you need to obtain and compile the source, follow these steps:

1. Retrieve the hypermailxxx.tar file from ftp.eit.com in the /pub/web.software/hypermail directory; xxx is the most current release of Hypermail (and probably the only tar file out there anyway).

2. Untar the file with the UNIX tar command *tar -xvf hypermailxxx.tar.*

3. In the newly created (by tar) hypermail subdirectory, edit config.h and Makefile to reflect where your Web server is and other local variables.

4. Type in *make* to compile the files and create the hypermail executable.

5. Move the executable to a directory in one of the directories in your PATH statement, like /usr/local, /usr/bin, etc.

That's it. Hypermail has one of the better behaved installations. The latest instructions in the README file should be checked out, though, before you install. This file will be in the hypermail subdirectory.

Using Hypermail

Hypermail reads a mailbox, which is just a regular UNIX file with a bunch of mail messages appended to each other, and produces a set of indexes and HTML documents in a directory. If the directory already exists, Hypermail will append the new content of the mailbox to what already exists; otherwise, it will create a directory from scratch. To create a Hypermail directory using a mailbox called "good-wines", enter

```
hypermail -m WWW-literature -d  /archives/WWW-literature
```

This reads the mail messages in WWW-literature and generates the indexes and HTML in /archives/WWW-literature.

Now you can use the following URL to access the archives:

```
http://wwwtestserver.zu/~johnson/archives/WWW-literature/
```

Hypermail has created a default index.html document in this directory that will be picked up automatically. In the good-wines directory you'll find four files:

 author.html

 date.html

 index.html

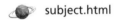 subject.html

plus a bunch of *nnnn*.html files, one for each mail message, where *nnnn* starts at 0001 and increments. These are the individual mail files cross-referenced and sorted by author, date, and subject. Figure 5-16 is an example of an archive created by Hypermail.

Importing Eudora

In the Eudora directory on the PC, you will find a set of files with filetypes .mbx and .toc. The .mbx filetypes are Eudora folders. By default Eudora has an In, Out, and Trash Folder, or Mailbox. These can be FTPed to a Web server and run through Hypermail to create an archive. The steps you would go through are

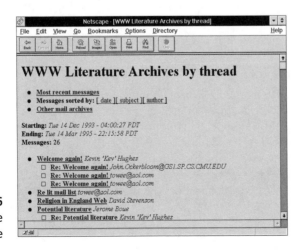

Figure 5-16
Hypermail archive
of WWW literature

1. FTP the filename.mbx file to your public_html directory on the Web server.

2. Enter the following command: hypermail -m "filename.mbx" -d archive.

3. Open a URL from your browser to http://yourserver/~username/archive/.

You should see an indexed list of your mailbox. With this feature you can turn the mailboxes you've stashed away in Eudora as a member of various listserver groups into extensively cross-referenced and globally accessible HTML archives on your server. You can update the information by repeating the process. Don't worry about accidentally having two copies of the same mail message; Hypermail is smart enough to figure out if it already has a message in the archive and will not duplicate it. It will just pick up the new ones.

Other Options

You can embed a reference to a page of information about this archive using the -b flag, and insert a title for the archive using the -l flag as follows:

```
hypermail -m "wines.mbx" -d "archive/wines"
        -l "Good Wines Archive" -b "http://myserver.com/aboutwine.html"
```

Another way of using Hypermail allows you to set up an e-mail alias on a UNIX system that can update archives automatically whenever the alias receives a message. This is done by adding an entry to the sendmail aliases file, usually in /etc/aliases or /var/adm/sendmail/aliases. After entering the following entry in aliases (without any line breaks):

```
list1: "|/usr/local/bin/hypermail -i -u -d /archive/list1 -l \"Mailing List Archive 1\""
```

run the command

```
newaliases
```

to apply the alias updates. Now any messages sent to the user "list1" on this this server will automatically be archived in /archive/list1 by Hypermail.

Summary

Well, you've installed a Web server or two, tinkered with most of the options in the three configuration files that control its operations, and practiced using some utilities to track who is using the server and from where. You took a serious look at the issues around security, and explored the various ways of protecting Web directories and the pages they contain. You were introduced to some utilities for validating HTML and making sure links were up to date in Web pages on the server, and finished up with utilities for moving Web directories from one place to another and turning listserver and Eudora messages into cross-referenced HTML archives. In Chapter 6 you'll move into indexing documents on a server, and a variety of advanced scripting techniques.

1. A limitation of listservers addressed by Hypermail is
   a. Listservers are typically restricted to only a few people.
   b. Hypermail adds hypertext capabilities to standard e-mail.
   c. Listservers don't usually retain archives of e-mail messages.
   d. Listservers don't allow questions and answers.

2. Hypermail can automatically general HTML pages from
   a. listservers
   b. Eudora
   c. mailboxes
   d. text files

3. To use Hypermail with Eudora mailboxes, you have to
   a. run Hypermail on your PC and then upload the HTML files
   b. upload your Eudora mailbox(es) to the Web server and run Hypermail on it
   c. forward your Eudora mail to Hypermail
   d. Hypermail only works with native UNIX mail.

4. Hypermail cross-references mail by
   a. author, date, title
   b. date, author, subject
   c. subject, e-mail address, author
   d. date, size, subject

INDEXING, WEB GAMES, AND ADVANCED SCRIPTS

## CHAPTER 6

INDEXING, WEB GAMES, AND ADVANCED SCRIPTS

This chapter takes your HTML and CGI scripting skills to the next level. A lot of advanced functionality on the Web owes a debt to building blocks and tools available in the public domain. These public domain products leverage ordinary CGI scripts, allowing them to bolt together powerful applications with a little CGI assembly and serve up the results in easy-to-use HTML pages and forms. These applications can let you search and retrieve large text archives using indexes, create and manipulate graphics dynamically, animate pages, provide glitzy access counters to user pages, and add guest books and online chat forums.

Many Web effects are made simple by packages that just need a CGI script as an intermediary; others rely on advanced features of certain browsers and more sophisticated uses of scripting languages.

329

Each application discussed in the following sessions should extend your understanding of what's possible on the Web, and take you far beyond the simple home pages of chapters past. So what are you waiting for?

INDEXING WEB DOCUMENTS

The Web is a growing maze of information, with new outposts and frontiers popping up daily. And as more and more information comes online, it becomes correspondingly more difficult to find any given piece of information. Directories like Yahoo (http://www.yahoo.com/) have popped up to help categorize broad topic areas, permitting drill-downs into deeper and deeper subcategories. These directory services usually rely on self-registration; Webmasters register their pages under the proper category and subclass. Other types of services, like Lycos (http://www.lycos.com/), search for keywords in a Web page's title or contents, relying on Web spiders or robots to comb the expanding hyperverse, crawling from site to site and indexing the content of all the pages they find.

On the scale of the Web as a whole, finding and classifying information appears daunting, but on the scale of local Web servers, a variety of tools provides efficient search and retrieval for growing text and HTML archives. These are critical components of the Webmaster's arsenal, and with a little CGI scripting, they are easy to add to your server.

Keep It Simple

Web indexing lets users search entire document trees or Web servers for keywords. No matter how dense and involuted the hyperlinks, the entire local fabric can be scanned for pieces of information relevant to spontaneous criteria. Figure 6-1 illustrates the type of services you may want to offer. Sun Tzu's *The Art of War* has been translated into Web pages on a local server. All the text that makes up the document has been indexed for lookup and retrieval. The Art of War can be searched for any keywords entered on the form, and the results, i.e., the pages with text containing the keywords, will be returned to the user's browser. Three components have gone into making this application:

- The search form (shown in Figure 6-1).

- The script that the form calls

- The indexes and index program that the script uses to look up the keywords

The application is built on an indexing product, so let's look at this first. The example above uses a keyword lookup, but most indexing products allow *Boolean searches* in addition to simple keywords. A Boolean search is a combination of keywords using and, or, and not. For example, the Boolean phrase

```
planets or stars
```

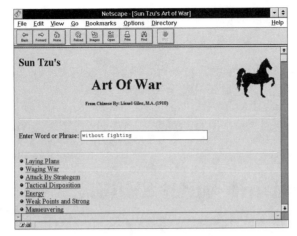

Figure 6-1
Query form for
Sun Tzu

would search all documents for mention of the word "planet" or the word "stars", return-ing documents that matched either criterion. Keywords don't have to be explicitly marked in the documents. In fact, the indexes you will use for the project in this session will be able to find any word in the document. In this sense every word becomes a keyword. Web indexing adds a powerful normalizer to the naturally dissipative function of hyper-links; and Web indexing software can, at an early stage, offer tremendous value to your Web server offerings.

Even if you are sold on the idea, you still must sort through an array of Web soft-ware from the complex to the simple. Let's start with the simple, with an indexing product called SWISH, designed for ease of use.

SWISH Knows HTML

It's helpful if a Web indexing product understands HTML. If it doesn't, it might do a number of annoying things, like index comments, index the word "Title" umpteen times, and return pointers to files rather than URLs. Web indexing is something of a special indexing problem, and you need to keep issues like these in mind when evaluating pos-sible solutions.

SWISH stands for Simple Web Indexing System for Humans, and it understands HTML. It was created in reaction to complex configuration and installation requirements of the first generation indexing tools like WAIS. Let's install SWISH and see if it lives up to its name.

Installing SWISH

To install SWISH, perform the following steps:

1. FTP the SWISH package from ftp.eit.com in /pub/web.software/swish/swish.11.tar.Z.

2. Uncompress and untar it: *uncompress swish.11.tar.Z | tar -xvf.*

3. Change default to the newly created swish.11 directory.

4. Read the README file for instructions on how to compile it.

5. After compiling, move the SWISH executable into a directory in your search path, like /usr/local/bin.

SWISH is written in very generic C and should compile on just about anything with a C compiler. You can delegate these steps to the system administrator; all you'll really need for the rest of this session is to have the compiled SWISH program somewhere in your executable path.

Searching with SWISH

To use SWISH you must first build an index of the files and/or directories you will be searching. The public domain version of the Sun Tzu archives was obtained from the Project Gutenberg home page (http://jg.cso.uiuc.edu/PG/welcome.html). It can be found on this book's CD under */text/suntsu*. You can upload the HTML files in this directory onto your Web server to complete the following exercises. Place the SunTzu HTML files in a directory called /suntzu. For example, the directory of Web pages for a user called "jones" is as follows:

```
/~jones/suntzu/scroll1.html
               /scroll2.html
               /scroll3.html
               etc.
```

Each "scroll" contains the text of one of the 13 chapters in *The Art of War*. To build an index of these files, change directory to /suntzu and enter the following:

```
swish -i .
```

The -i option instructs it to create an index, and the "." tells SWISH to index everything in the current directory and all the directories below it. You could give SWISH a specific directory tree, or even specific files instead of the ".". SWISH indexes every file that it finds in these directories and creates an index called index.swish in the current directory.

After an index has been created, you can use the swish command to search for keywords. By default SWISH will look in the current directory for the index.swish file. For example, in the index you just created, search for the Boolean phrase "without and fighting":

```
swish -w without and fighting
```

You should receive back something like the following:

```
# SWISH format 1.1
search words: without and fighting
# Name: (no name)
# Saved as: index.swish
# Counts: 6386 words, 16 files
# Indexed on: 09/09/95 15:38:48 MDT
# Description: (no description)
# Pointer: (no pointer)
```

```
# Maintained by: (no maintainer)
1000 ./sun2.html "sun2.html" 9553
714 ./sun3.html "sun3.html" 13474
714 ./sun5.html "sun5.html" 14342
714 ./sun8.html "sun8.html" 14296
571 ./sun10.html "sun10.html" 16771
571 ./sun6.html "sun6.html" 16135
428 ./sun7.html "sun7.html" 20673
285 ./sun9.html "sun9.html" 25255
142 ./intro.html "intro.html" 78116
142 ./sun11.html "sun11.html" 56713
.
```

Ten documents in the SunTzu archive have the words "without" and "fighting" in them. They are ordered by SWISH according to the ones it thinks are most relevant. The number on the left is a ranking; 1000 is the most relevant and 1 is the least. These ranks are based on weights given to the number of times the keywords are found in the document, and where they are found (e.g., the word in a title would be more significant than the word in the text), etc.

In SWISH, if two keywords are entered without a Boolean term between them, it is assumed that you want a Boolean "and". For example:

```
swish -w without fighting
```

is the same as

```
swish -w without and fighting
```

In and of itself this could be pretty useful, just to keep track of personal information. To keep track of Web information, however, to really use SWISH, you'll need to refine this procedure a little by making changes to its configuration. Create a configuration file called swish.conf and add the following entries:

```
IndexDir /home/jones/public_html/suntzu
IndexFile /home/jones/indexes/index.swish
IndexOnly .html .txt .gif .ps .jpg
FollowSymLinks yes
NoContents .ps .gif .jpg
ReplaceRules replace "/home/jones/public_html""http://www.test.com/~jones"
# Files matching the following criteria will NOT be indexed
FileRules filename is index.html
FileRules pathname contains admin demo trash testing
FileRules title contains construction examples
FileRules directory contains .htaccess
```

Let's go over these options individually.

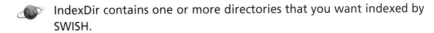 IndexDir contains one or more directories that you want indexed by SWISH.

IndexFile is the path and name of the file SWISH will create for the index.

- IndexOnly tells SWISH to only index files with these filetypes.

- FollowSymLinks is similar to its use in access.conf (see Chapter 5, Session 5), and controls whether symbolic links to files or directories will be followed when looking for documents to index.

- NoContents tells SWISH not to try to index the contents of these files, just to remember their filenames.

- ReplaceRules controls how the physical directory names map to the virtual names and aliases used in URLs on this server.

- FileRules excludes files from indexing based on their name, a name found in their path, or a word found in the <TITLE> tag or a directory.

These options give you fine-grain control over just what SWISH puts in the index file. The configuration file is only used by SWISH when it's building the indexes, and you'll need to point to it on the command line:

```
swish -c /usr/local/swish/swish.conf
```

The -c says that what follows is the path and filename of the SWISH configuration file. Try reindexing with this new configuration file.

Now let's use the same search criteria, this time with the -f option, which points to the location of the index, since you can't always assume it will be in the current directory:

```
swish -f /usr/local/swish/indexes/swish.index -w without and fighting
```

The same search criteria now return the following:

```
# SWISH format 1.1
search words: without and fighting
# Name: (no name)
# Saved as: index.swish
# Counts: 6386 words, 16 files
# Indexed on: 09/09/95 16:17:41 MDT
# Description: (no description)
# Pointer: (no pointer)
# Maintained by: (no maintainer)
1000 http:/www.test.com/~jones/suntzu/sun2.html "sun2.html" 9553
714 http:/www.test.com/~jones/suntzu/sun3.html "sun3.html" 13474
714 http:/www.test.com/~jones/suntzu/sun5.html "sun5.html" 14342
714 http:/www.test.com/~jones/suntzu/sun8.html "sun8.html" 14296
571 http:/www.test.com/~jones/suntzu/sun10.html "sun10.html" 16771
571 http:/www.test.com/~jones/suntzu/sun6.html "sun6.html" 16135
428 http:/www.test.com/~jones/suntzu/sun7.html "sun7.html" 20673
285 http:/www.test.com/~jones/suntzu/sun9.html "sun9.html" 25255
142 http:/www.test.com/~jones/suntzu/intro.html "intro.html" 78116
142 http:/www.test.com/~jones/suntzu/sun11.html "sun11.html" 56713
.
```

Much better; SWISH now returns a URL to the file with the requested text, but it's still not ready for prime time. To automate these searches and make them available to forms on a Web page, you'll need to write a script that formats SWISH output into something a little more HTMLish. Open a new script called find_swish.cgi on your server and enter the following Perl code:

```perl
#!/usr/local/bin/perl;
require "cgi-lib.pl";
require "shellwords.pl";
&ReadParse;
$query = $in{'query'};                      # Get Query Field
$swish_options = $in{'options'};        # Get Hidden field with index path
open(SEARCH,"swish $swish_options -w $query |") || die "Can't open pipe";
```

This Perl script opens a *pipe* to the swish program. A pipe is a connection between programs that allows one to read or write to the other. In this case, the Perl script is reading the SWISH output from the swish -w command. Now add the following to this script:

```perl
$hits = 0;
print &PrintHeader;
print "<HTML><HEAD><TITLE>Indexed Search</TITLE></HEAD><BODY>\n";
while ($_ = <SEARCH>) {
        @toks = &shellwords;            # Parse line into tokens
        if ($toks[0] =~ /\d+/) {         # If first token is a digit, it's a hit
                if ($hits == 0) {          # Build List Header
                        print "<H3>Search Results Sorted By Relevance</H3>\n";
                        print "<HR><UL>\n";
                        }
                print "<LI><A HREF=\"$toks[1]\">";
                print "$toks[2]</A>\n";
                print "<BR>Relevance: $toks[0]\n";
                print "<BR>Size: $toks[3]\n";
                $hits++;
                }
        elsif ($toks[0] =~ /err:/) {    # Error or not Found
                shift(@toks);
                $errstr = join(' ',@toks);
                }
        }
}
close(SEARCH);
if ($hits > 0) {
        print "</UL>\n";
        }
else {
        print "<P>Search String <STRONG>$query</STRONG> Not Found\n";
        print "<BR>$errstr\n";
}
print "</BODY></HTML>";
```

This remaining section of Perl code strips away the lines that are not URLs (i.e., not prefaced with a relevance number), and looks for a line with "err:" just in case the keywords were not found or some other error occurred. It wraps the results in HTML that it outputs to the CGI. The Perl script has made SWISH into an accomplice, using

SWISH's index search capabilities behind the scenes. Now you just need a form that passes the two variables used in the script:

$query   which contains the boolean query passed to swish -w
$options   which contains the -f path/filename of the index for SWISH to use

Interfacing with Forms

For the form, only a simple text input box is needed. You'll recall from Session 1 of Chapter 4 that with only one input field, the form is submitted when the user presses <ENTER>. Open a new HTML file with your editor and enter the following:

```
<HTML>
<HEAD>
<TITLE>Sun Tzu's Art of War</TITLE>
</HEAD>
<BODY>
<IMG width=114 height=108 vspace=10 ALIGN=right
        SRC="images/horse.gif">
<H2 ALIGN=left>Sun Tzu's</H2>
<H1 ALIGN=center>Art Of War</H1>
<H6 ALIGN=center>From Chinese By: Lionel Giles, M.A. (1910)</H6>
<HR>
<FORM ACTION="/cgi-bin/find_swish.cgi" METHOD="POST">
Enter Word or Phrase:
<INPUT TYPE="text" NAME="query" SIZE=40>
<INPUT TYPE="hidden" NAME="options"
        VALUE="-f /home/jones/indexes/index.swish">
</FORM>
<HR>
<IMG SRC="images/red.gif">
<A HREF="suntzu/scroll1.html">Laying Plans</A><BR>
.... links to individual Chapters in Sun Tzu
</BODY>
</HTML>
```

Note that the variable *options* is a hidden variable. Users don't really need to see where the SWISH indexes are kept for these archives. The ACTION option in <FORM> points to the Perl script you created to interface with SWISH. Save the form and open it in your browser. You should see results similar to those in Figure 6-1.

Figure 6-2 shows the results of entering "without fighting" in the query input field.

To Use with Other Indexes

To reuse this same script for other archives and other indexes, you merely change the hidden option variable on the search form. You can experiment with indexes in various directories for separate archives, and later, if you want to save space, you can combine indexes with SWISH by using the following command:

```
swish -M index1 index2 ... outputfile
```

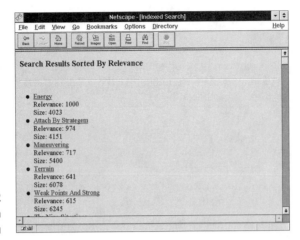

Figure 6-2
Query results from
Sun Tzu

The last file specified is the file that will be created by merging all the indexes together. This removes any redundant word data and usually reduces the disk space used.

Other Interfaces

A "canned" forms interface to SWISH is available at http://www.eit.com/software/wwwwais/. Whether prepackaged form interfaces like this one will work for you depends on your unique requirements. If they don't, at least you know how to roll your own.

Fast and Easy

All right, SWISH lives up to its name. It really is simple, especially once everything is set up. So what's missing? The release of SWISH available at the time of this writing didn't allow for incremental updates to your index. This means that if only a single file changes, the new information cannot be added to the existing index without recreating it. This gets time-consuming as your archive or document space grows. SWISH also can't be used for indexing large files containing individual records. It would simply return the pointer to the file itself. And what if you can't spell what you're looking for? Session 2 will introduce an industrial strength indexing program used by large servers with demanding requirements. It can do incremental updates, find keywords even if you misspell them in the query, return pointers to records in a large archived file, plus much more.

Despite any shortcomings, SWISH is a fast way to get up and running with a Web index. It cuts through much of the complexity associated with other indexing products like WAIS, and it provides a good foundation for understanding the way other indexing works and how to use a form's interface to offer query capability to your data.

EXERCISE 1

SWISH has a command-line option to specify context criteria. This lets you search only certain spots in an HTML document, like the <TITLE>, <HEAD>, or <BODY> tags. By using the -t option, followed by:

H	for <HEAD>
B	for <BODY>
T	for <TITLE>
H	for <H1> to <H6> tags
E	for emphasized tags, e.g., <B>,<I>,<EM> or <STRONG>
C	for comments

you can confine the search to these areas. For example, to search for text only in the <TITLE> or <H1>...<Hn> tags, enter

```
swish -t Th -w pickles
```

Expand your search form to provide check boxes on the form for these areas, defaulting them to all checked. Modify the script to pick these up and add them to the options passed to SWISH.

QUIZ 1

1. If you created a SWISH index using the command swish -i., what would be indexed?
   a. Everything in the current directory.
   b. Everything specified in a swish.conf file in the current directory.
   c. Everything in the current directory and all of its subdirectories.
   d. Nothing; the -i option means interactive query.

2. What is in the index.swish file?
   a. An index of keywords extracted from titles and headers.
   b. Configuration information.
   c. A keyword index to all the words in the files indexed.
   d. The results of the last query.

3. What will the following command search for? *swish -w oranges or apples*
   a. oranges or apples in the titles
   b. any document with both oranges and apples
   c. any document with oranges but without apples and vice versa
   d. any document with either oranges or apples

4. Why is the swish.conf file useful when writing scripts?
   a. It is required when the SWISH command is used in scripts.
   b. It allows you to refer to different SWISH indexes simultaneously.
   c. It is used to merge SWISH indexes before searching.
   d. It is used to translate pathnames into URLs.

PROFESSIONAL INDEXING

Glimpse is the next indexing application you will explore. Glimpse is SWISH on steroids. In addition to the SWISH's Boolean queries and selective file indexing, Glimpse brings the following to the table:

- Speed. Quoting from the documentation, "find 296 lines containing 'whitehouse' in 8750 files occupying 104MB took 6 seconds on a Sun Sparc 5". Your application will start out a little more modest, but you should have room to grow.

- Misspelled words. Glimpse can find keywords even if you're not sure how they are spelled.

- Multiple line records. Instead of just returning a line of text with the keyword, or a pointer to a file, Glimpse can return a paragraph, or an arbitrarily delimited block of text.

- File pattern matching. This is the ability to use search criteria not only for keywords within files, but for selecting files themselves, e.g., only files in a certain directory, or with certain filenames or filetypes.

- Compressed files. Glimpse can index and search compressed files, both in standard compression formats and using its own compression engine.

- Incremental updates. Indexes can be updated with new information on files that have changed since the last index was built. No need to rebuild the entire index.

- Glimpse server. An optional process that can be always running on your server ready to handle Glimpse queries.

Glimpse stands for Global Implicit Search, whatever that means. It was written at the University of Arizona and has found its way into some heavy-duty applications on the Internet. The Harvest package, which provides large-scale Web caching, uses Glimpse as its underlying search and retrieval caddy. Glimpse comes in three pieces:

- GlimpseIndex   The component that creates the indexes

- Glimpse   The piece that looks things up in the index

- GlimpseServer   An optional server than can help marshal Glimpse queries

Information can be obtained on how to download Glimpse from http://glimpse.cs.arizona.edu:1994/ Glimpse has binary executables for Suns and DEC Alphas that can save you a compile step if you have one of these platforms.

Installing Glimpse

Glimpse installation is a little more involved than installing SWISH, and it changes slightly from release to release. After downloading the compressed file from the URL above, read a file called README.install in the glimpse directory. It outlines a step-by-step procedure based on the system you are installing on.

Once Glimpse is compiled and linked (if you didn't get the binaries), you can move its executables into your execution path and use it from the command line much the same as SWISH.

Using Glimpse

Let's start with the same task you performed with SWISH: indexing the current directory and everything thereunder. Change the default to the directory with the Sun Tzu archives, and enter the following command:

```
glimpseindex .
```

The Sun Tzu archives are hardly your average 200MB files, but you probably won't notice the difference from where you're sitting.

Glimpse does a few things very differently from SWISH. First, it creates a whole population of files in your home directory:

.glimpse_index	This is the real index file.
.glimpse_include	Filenames you want explicitly included. Initially blank.
.glimpse_exclude	Filenames you don't want indexed. Initially blank.
.glimpse_filenames	A list of all the filenames it did index.
.glimpse_filters	Rules for what to do to certain files before Glimpse tries to index them.
.glimpse_messages	Status on how many words each file contributes to the index.
.glimpse_partitions	Internal file for Glimpse itself.
.glimpse_statistics	Miscellaneous statistics about the index.

So, one index and lots of auxiliary files. You don't need to be concerned with the aux files; just don't be shocked when you see them in your home directory.

To create these files in some location other than your home directory, use the -H option as follows:

```
glimpseindex -H /usr3/archive/indexes
```

Now all the index files will be built in the /usr3/archive/indexes directory. To look something up that you've indexed, use the glimpse command. Let's look up "fighting". If you let the indexes default to your home directory, you can simply enter

```
glimpse 'fighting'
```

You should get something back similar to the following:

```
/home/jones/public_html/suntzu/scroll2.txt:   2. When you engage in actual fighting, if victory
```

```
/home/jones/public_html/suntzu/scroll2.txt: 17.   Therefore in chariot fighting, when ten or
                                                   more chariots
/home/jones/public_html/suntzu/scroll3.html:       in breaking the enemy's resistance without
                                                   fighting.
/home/jones/public_html/suntzu/scroll3.html:       troops without any fighting; he captures
                                                   their cities
/home/jones/public_html/suntzu/scroll5.html:       is nowise different from fighting with a
                                                   small one:
/home/jones/public_html/suntzu/scroll5.html:  5.   In all fighting, the direct method may be
                                                   used
/home/jones/public_html/suntzu/scroll5.html: 22.   When he utilizes combined energy, his
                                                   fighting
/home/jones/public_html/suntzu/scroll5.html: 23.   Thus the energy developed by good
                                                   fighting men
/home/jones/public_html/suntzu/scroll6.html:       prevent him from fighting.  Scheme so as to
                                                   discover
/home/jones/public_html/suntzu/scroll7.html: 26.   In night-fighting, then, make much use of
                                                   signal-fires
/home/jones/public_html/suntzu/scroll7.html:       and drums, and in fighting by day, of flags
                                                   and banners,
```

Glimpse shows the record in which it found the keyword. By default a record is a line in a file. Note that Glimpse doesn't return the pesky header information that SWISH did.

Now let's play with some other options. Just entering a word like "ground" in a query will return "underground," "groundless," "foreground," etc. If you're really serious about finding just the word "ground," use

```
glimpse -w ground
```

The -w option means match only a whole word. To make the search case insensitive, add -i:

```
glimpse -i -w  ground
```

Booleans are specified differently in Glimpse than in SWISH. To search for "ground" and "water", you would enter

```
glimpse ground;water
```

To search for "ground" or "water", enter

```
glimpse ground,water
```

And to search for the phrase "ground water", enter

```
glimpse 'ground water'
```

Several powerful search patterns can be used with Glimpse, including searching for sequences at the beginning or end of a line, using wildcards and regular expressions that can be investigated in the Glimpse documentation.

If you put the indexes somewhere other than in your home directory, use the same option as in GlimpseIndex to point to the location of the directories:

```
glimpse -H /usr3/archives/indexes -i -w ground
```

Note that the search results from Glimpse return the filename and the line containing the keyword. If you want a little more of the context surrounding the keyword, you can have Glimpse return a paragraph by using the record delimiter option:

```
glimpse -d '$$' -w 'ground'
```

This returns (partial list):

```
/home/jones/public_html/suntzu/scroll11.html: 47. On contentious ground,I would hurry up my
rear.

/home/jones/public_html/suntzu/scroll11.html: 48. On open ground, I would keep a vigilant
eye on my defenses.  On ground of intersecting highways, I would consolidate my alliances.

/home/jones/public_html/suntzu/scroll11.html: 49. On serious ground, I would try to ensure a
continuous stream of supplies.  On difficult ground, I would keep pushing on along the road.

/home/jones/public_html/suntzu/scroll11.html: 50. On hemmed-in ground, I would block any way
of retreat.  On desperate ground, I would proclaim to my soldiers the hopelessness of saving
their lives.

/home/jones/public_html/suntzu/scroll11.html: 66. Forestall your opponent by seizing what he
holds dear, and subtly contrive to time his arrival on the ground.
```

The $$ is a special symbol meaning paragraph. This not only returns a paragraph, but also searches by paragraph as a unique record, rather than by each line, which is the default. Instead of accepting either the default line or the paragraph, you can also specify a string of up to eight characters that will be used to separate records in the file.

For example, if you are archiving a printed report, you could use a string like "Page No." to separate the individual pages into records. You could also use a field name on files generated by exporting text from a database in field=value pairs. Be careful, though; if the delimiter doesn't appear in the data, then the entire file will be returned on a successful match!

Glimpse and the CGI

A set of utilities has been written to accompany Glimpse called GlimpseHTTP. The utilities are a collection of CGI scripts, HTML pages, and C source code for building a user-managed archive of Glimpse indexes. You can look into this if you wish, but GlimpseHTTP implements a very structured way of indexing and retrieval through Web documents that kind of runs counter to the seat of the pants operation into which you've been so carefully indoctrinated. So let's skip it and modify the SWISH script to handle Glimpse.

One advantage to writing scripts with Glimpse is that it doesn't return all the extra comments that SWISH does. Glimpse gives you the name of the file and then the line or record that matches the query. The disadvantage is that Glimpse doesn't know HTML from a hole in the ground. You'll have to convert the directories to URLs yourself. But it will be good scripting experience. Let's make some strategic modifications to the SWISH script to start to accommodate Glimpse. Copy your find_swish.cgi to a file called find_glimpse.cgi and then open it and make the following changes:

```perl
#!/usr/local/bin/perl
require "cgi-lib.pl";
&ReadParse;
$query = $in{'query'};            # Get Query Field
$g_options = $in{'options'};      # Get Hidden field with index path
open(SEARCH,"glimpse $options $query |");
```

The last line uses the glimpse command in the SEARCH pipe instead of SWISH and expects options to be passed from the form.

```perl
while (<SEARCH>) {
        $url = "http:\/\/www.test.com\/\~jones";
        $path = "\/home\/jones\/public_html";
```

The variable *$url* replaces the variable *$path* in the filenames returned from Glimpse. You cannot just enter

```perl
        $url = "http://www.test.com/~jones";
        $path="/home/jones/public_html";
```

because forward slashes "/" are special characters in Perl scripts. Like the special characters in HTML, you need to represent them differently so Perl doesn't confuse them with its own syntactical elements. To specify a special character like this in Perl, you need to preface it with the Perl escape character, which is "\". "\" tells Perl not to interpret the next character as Perl, but to just accept it as it is. So your code ends up looking kind of funny; any time you want to say "/", you have to use "\/". The next section of the script will use these variables to examine the results from Glimpse:

```perl
chop;
if (/$path/) {            # If filename displayed by glimpse
    @fields = split(/:/); # separate path/filename: first line
    $link = $fields[0];
    $anchor = $fields[1];
```

If *$path* is found in the line returned by Glimpse, it must be a line with a filename. This line also contains the first line of text in the record, with the keyword separated as follows:

```
/home/jones/public_html/suntzu/scroll11/scroll11.html: 47. On contentious ground,I would
```

The split(/:/) function breaks this field in half. The half with the filename is stored in $fields[0], and the part with the line of text containing the keyword is stored in $fields[1]. These are assigned the variables *$link* and *$anchor,* respectively:

```perl
    $link =~ s/$path/$url/;
    $anchor =~ s/^\s+//g;
```

Now a little editing is done to each field. In *$link*, which is the filename, *$url* is substituted for *$path,* changing

```
/home/jones/public_html/suntzu/scroll1.html
```

to

```
http://www.test.com/~jones/suntzu/scroll1/html
```

and *$anchor* is stripped of any leading spaces. *$anchor* and *$link* can now be used to create a hyperlink, linking the line with the keyword back to the page it came from:

```
print "<P><A HREF=\"$link\">$anchor<\/A><BR>\n";
}
else {                              # If multiple lines per field,
        print "$_<BR>"; # print them after the hyperlink
        }


}
close(SEARCH);
print "</BODY></HTML>\n";
```

You need to use the Perl escape "\" character for some more forward slashes "/", and also in order to use the double quote character in the script. The whole script looks like this:

```
#!/usr/local/bin/perl
require "cgi-lib.pl";
&ReadParse;
$query = $in{'query'};          # Get Query Field
$g_options = $in{'options'};   # Get hidden options
print &PrintHeader;
print "<H2>Search Results...</H2><HR>";
open(SEARCH,"glimpse $g_options $query |");
while (<SEARCH>) {
        $url = "http:\/\/www.test.com\/\~jones";
        $path = "\/home\/jones\/public_html";
        chop;
        if (/$path/) {            # If filename displayed by Glimpse
        @fields = split(/:/); # separate path/filename: first line
        $link = $fields[0];
        $anchor = $fields[1];
        $link =~ s/$path/$url/; # convert path/file into URL
        $anchor =~ s/^\s+//g;    # strip out leading spaces
        print "<P><A HREF=\"$link\">$anchor<\/A><BR>\n";
        }
else {                              # If multiple lines per field,
        print "$_<BR>"; # print them after the hyperlink
        }

        }
        close(SEARCH);
        print "</BODY></HTML>\n";
```

The form that calls this script form can still look exactly like Figure 6-1; you've just replaced the underlying CGI script and indexing engine. The hidden options variable in the search form should be set to

```
<INPUT TYPE="hidden" NAME="options" VALUE="-H /home/jones -y -i -w"
```

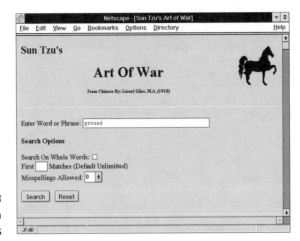

Figure 6-3
Query form with
Glimpse options

You can also implement a few more command-line options to take advantage of Glimpse's capabilities:

-y	Prevents Glimpse from issuing any interactive prompts
-w	Lets the user search on word boundaries
-#	Allows a given number of misspellings in a word, from 0 to 8
-L n	Specifies the maximum number of hits returned, n

Modify the form used in Figure 6-1 to ask for these options. Then modify the script to put the options in the hidden $option string before calling Glimpse. Figure 6-3 shows one example of what the form might look like.

Your script should now look something like the following:

```perl
#!/usr/local/bin/perl
require "cgi-lib.pl";
&ReadParse;
$query = $in{'query'};                # Get Query Field

$g_options = "-d'\$\$' -H /usr/doc/indexes -y ";      # Initial option defaults
$g_options = "$g_options -w " if $in{'word'} eq "X";
$g_options = "$g_options -$in{'misspells'}";
$hits = $in{'hits'};
$g_options = "$g_options -L $hits" if $hits =~ /\d+/;

print &PrintHeader;
print "<H2>Search Results...</H2><HR>";
open(SEARCH,"glimpse $g_options $query |");
while (<SEARCH>) {
        $url = "http:\/\/www.test.com\/~jones";
        $path = "\/home\/jones\/public_html";
        chop;
        if (/$path/) {                # If filename displayed by glimpse
        @fields = split(/:/); # separate path/filename: first line
```

continued on next page

continued from previous page

```
    $link = $fields[0];
    $anchor = $fields[1];
    $link =~ s/$path/$url/; # convert path/file into URL
    $anchor =~ s/^\s+//g;    # strip out leading spaces
    print "<P><A HREF=\"$link\">$anchor<\/A><BR>\n";
    }
else {                             # If multiple lines per field,
    print "$_<BR>"; # print them after the hyperlink
    }


    }
    close(SEARCH);
    print "</BODY></HTML>\n";
```

The result of a query is shown in Figure 6-4.

Glimpse can be very picky about the order of the options in your command line. Be sure to study the Glimpse documentation if you are adding additional options to your script. Another potential gotcha is that when Glimpse indexes are created, they are not given world read access. You'll need to change the access of the Glimpse indexes for the Web server to be able to read them. For example, in the directory with the indexes, issue: *chmod a+r .glimpse*.*

Revisiting the Indexing Options

The bare-bones "*glimpseindex /directory* is probably not what you will want for full-blown indexing. Several options can be tacked on to extend this minimalist beginning.

One important feature that is missing in the default settings is the indexing of numbers. Unless explicitly specified, glimpseindex will not index any numeric content of your data. To force it to index numbers, add the -n option:

```
glimpseindex -n .
```

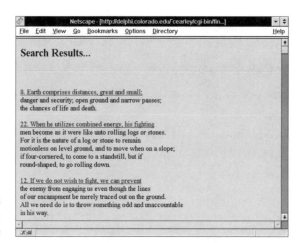

Figure 6-4
Search results of a
Glimpse query

To add incrementally to an already established index, causing it to revise the index based on changes or additions to files, use the -f option:

```
glimpseindex -f .
```

This adds files to the index that were created or modified since the index was created. If no index actually exists, GlimpseIndex will go ahead and create one. For small changes this works fine. If your data is being deleted and added in batches, though, you are often better off rebuilding the entire index for the sake of efficiency.

When you are building indexes, you have three options as to what type of indexes to create.

1. -o   Creates small indexes, e.g., 7 to 9 percent of the combined size of all the files indexed.

2. -b   Creates medium size indexes, e.g., 20 to 30 percent of the combined file sizes.

This produces a faster search, at the tradeoff of using more disk space.

3. If neither -o nor -b is specified, a tiny index is built. This index is typically 2 to 3 percent of the combined file sizes. Tiny index is the default if no option is specified.

To add directories to an existing index, use the -a option:

```
glimpse -a /anotherdir
```

The same procedure applies: Glimpse will traverse /anotherdir, and all its subdirectories, adding to the existing index.

GlimpseIndex automatically tries to determine if a file should be indexed or not. It will exclude any files with filetypes .o, .gz, .Z, .z, .hqx, .zip, or .tar, plus any filetypes entered in .glimpse_exclude.

More nifty features of Glimpse can be gleaned from the documentation that comes with the distribution, particularly if you want to get into the compressed file features, which veer a little south of what's strictly necessary for interfacing Glimpse with CGI scripts.

1. Why was an escape character necessary in the Perl CGI script for Glimpse?
   a. The glimpse index requires an escape code to initialize.
   b. Without an escape, the index would not return control.
   c. The script needed to use special reserved characters like "/", "$", and "\".
   d. To protect the HTML.

2. What feature does Glimpse have that SWISH doesn't?
   a. Boolean searching
   b. ability to index multiple files and subdirectories
   c. ability to search for partial words
   d. ability to incrementally add files to the index

3. If you don't specify where to put the index files, Glimpse will put them
   a. in the directory in which Glimpse is run
   b. in your home directory
   c. in the home directory of the Web server
   d. in a temporary file area

4. If you use the -d'$$' (paragraph) option in Glimpse, Glimpse will
   a. search each line but return the paragraph with the line the keyword was found in
   b. search each paragraph and return the line the keyword was found in
   c. return the entire file if the keyword was found
   d. search each paragraph and return the paragraph if the keyword was found

ADVANCED PERL CGI LIBRARY

Most of the CGI scripts you've been working with have been written in Perl. By including the cgi-lib.pl routines, you have been able to access form input variables easily. Before getting into some of the more advanced scripting applications, however, it's time to meet cgi-lib's big brother, CGI.pm. It's not CGI after hours, it's CGI *perl module* written by Lincoln Stein, and it works with the latest release of Perl: 5. Perl 5 is mostly backwards compatible with release 4 of Perl, which at the time of this writing was still the most widely used version. Perl 5 runs all of the Perl scripts developed so far in this book, plus it offers even more interesting features for CGI authors. If you're not sure which version of Perl is on your system, enter the following command:

```
perl -v
```

You'll either get something like

```
This is perl, version 5.001
```

or

```
This is perl, version 4.0
```

You'll need to upgrade to Perl 5 to use CGI.pm. (The upgrade is free, just like Perl 4.0.)

Installing CGI.pm

This is probably the easiest installation in the book. Use the following URL to download CGI.pm:

```
http://www-genome.wi.mit.edu/ftp/pub/software/WWW/CGI.pm
```

Now copy this to your Perl library, usually at /usr/local/lib/perl5:

```
cp CGI.pm /usr/local/lib/perl5
```

You're done!

Hello Fred

Let's look at a minimalist Perl5/CGI.pm script that simply returns the "Hello World" equivalent in CGI. This script returns Hello *x*, where *x* is the value you entered in a text field called Name that references this script in its <FORM ACTION=URL> tag.

```
use CGI;
$query = new CGI;
print $query->header;
print $query->start_html("Hello");
$name   = $query-param('name');
print "Hi there $name!";
print $query->end_html;
```

Here is the HTML that is generated when this script is called:

```
<HTML>
<HEAD>
<TITLE>Hello</TITLE>
</HEAD>
<BODY>Hi there Fred!
</BODY>
</HTML>
```

Let's dissect the important elements of the script, starting with

```
use CGI;
```

This is the equivalent of

```
require "cgi-lib.pl"
```

in previous Perl 4 scripts. It tells Perl to load the CGI handling routines. But now it gets different. This creates an *object* called *$query*:

```
$query = new CGI;
```

$query looks like an ordinary Perl variable, but it is really an object with all the input values from the form stored inside of it. It also has a bunch of functions, or methods as they are called in object programming, to generate HTML and retrieve specified variables from the form. To call the functions (i.e., use the methods) that are part of the *$query* object, you use the $query->method technique:

```
$query->header;
```

This CGI.pm method returns the following Perl string:

```
"Content-Type: text/html\n\n"
```

The following method assigns the argument "*Hello*" to the <TITLE> tag:

```
$query->start_html("Hello");
```

and returns the following stock HTML string:

```
"<HTML><HEAD><TITLE>Hello</TITLE></HEAD><BODY>"
```

The next method returns the value of the form variable called *name:*

```
$query->param('name');
```

It can be used to assign a string to the value of any parameter. In the example it returned the string

```
"Fred"
```

The final method is

```
$query->end_html;
```

and returns the following HTML:

```
</BODY></HTML>
```

Note that all of these $query->methods just return values; they still need to be printed before anything is actually displayed or returned through the CGI.

You might be thinking you could've done the same thing back in the lessons with cgi-lib, albeit with a smidgeon more code. So what's the big deal? You're just getting warmed up!

Contestants One, Two, and Three

In the case of multivalued fields, like those created by <SELECT> tags with MULTIPLE options or check boxes, a variable can have more than one value. The old cgi-lib tacked a suffix onto each one of these values, so a check box on a form like this:

```
Pick Your Favorite Color(s):
<INPUT TYPE="checkbox" NAME="color" VALUE=blue>blue
<INPUT TYPE="checkbox" NAME="color" VALUE=cherry>cherry
<INPUT TYPE="checkbox" NAME="color" VALUE=watermelon>watermelon
<INPUT TYPE="checkbox" NAME="color" VALUE=pipestone>pipestone
<INPUT TYPE="checkbox" NAME="color" VALUE=rust>rust
```

could return

```
color = blue
color_1 = pipestone
color_2 = rust
```

and you would have to figure out in your script whether one or more of these were entered. CGI.pm puts the values for *color* in a Perl array. The array may have one or more values, and you can employ the rich set of Perl functions to manipulate arrays (or lists, as they're called in Perl) to process them any way you like. To print one or more of the colors picked, you could use

```
print "You picked: join(",",$query->param('color'))";
```

which uses the Perl function join to build a string separating each element in the list with a comma.

You can process all the values in an array using a loop:

```perl
while($query->param('color')) {
        print "$_";
        }
```

The $_ variable contains one by one each of the values in *color*. You can add standard Perl pattern matching to the loop:

```perl
while($query->param('color')) {
        if (/rust/) {
                print "RUST??!!!!";
                }
        else {
                print "$_ is ok.";
                }
        }
```

Once you get a set of values in a list, Perl can do some pretty amazing things with it. You'll learn some by example, but a good book for serious CGI authors is *Programming Perl* by O'Reilly & Associates. It's for Perl 4, but hopefully a new version will be coming out soon (meanwhile, the Perl 4 stuff still applies in Perl 5).

All in One

Now, back to CGI.pm. Besides nifty ways to obtain form variables, CGI.pm has a suite of methods for creating them. You haven't really explored using scripts to create form variables, and this is where it gets interesting. Here's an example of a single script that both creates a form, and then processes the form once it's filled in. Open a new script file on your Web server and enter the following Perl code:

```perl
#!/usr/local/bin/perl
use CGI;
$query = new CGI;
print $query->header;
print $query->start_html("What's Your Name?");
print $query->startform;
print "Please Enter Your Name: ",$query->textfield('name');
print $query->endform;
print "<HR>";
if ($query->param('name') ne "") {
        print "<HR>";
        print "Your Name Is: ",$query->param('name');
        }
print $query->end_html;
```

Save this script as ftest.cgi and open it in your browser with a URL something like this:

```
http://myserver.com/~me/myscripts/ftest.cgi
```

Your results should be similar to Figure 6-5. The HTML the script created is below:

```html
<HTML>
<HEAD>
<TITLE>What's Your Name?</TITLE>
```

continued on next page

continued from previous page

```
</HEAD>
<BODY>
<FORM METHOD="POST" >
Please Enter Your Name: <INPUT TYPE="text" NAME="name" VALUE=""   >
</FORM>
<HR>
</BODY>
</HTML>
```

Note that the action URL of the form defaults to this script, since it wasn't specified. METHOD="POST" is the default set by $query->startform. If you now fill in the name "Ralph" and press <ENTER>, you get the results displayed in Figure 6-6.

Did you notice? A subtle thing is going on here. Lincoln refers to it as "sticky" variables. The values filled in when the form was first displayed are automatically retained by CGI.pm when it displays the form the second time. This comes in handy when you are checking input fields for valid values. If one of the fields has invalid or missing data, you don't want to force the user to fill out the entire form again. CGI.pm takes care of this automatically. You can send back a message on the form confident that all the user's input will still be there.

Other CGI Form Elements

As you might suspect, CGI.pm has a few more elements for creating forms. In fact, it supports most of the HTML form elements. In the following examples, *$query* is used as the CGI object. In real scripts this variable name will be whatever was created in the line specifying

```
$var = new CGI;
```

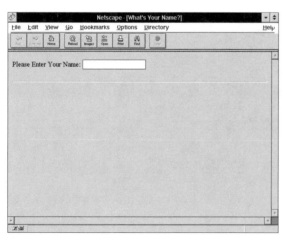

Figure 6-5
First form pass

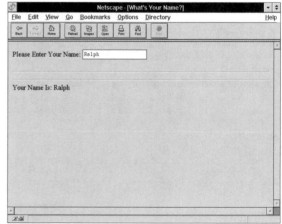

Figure 6-6
Second form pass

What follows below is a whirlwind tour through the CGI functions. Each function corresponds to an HTML form element, so it will be an exercise in mapping what you already know about forms to how the elements are created using CGI.pm. You won't spend a lot of time on any one of them; the goal is just to acquaint you in this session with the general syntax of the tools you will need to use in future exercises.

Input Text

In CGI.pm, <INPUT TYPE="text"> becomes

print $query->textfield('name', 'initial value', size, maxsize)

- *name* is required; this is the name of the text field in the form.

- *initial value* is optional; if not specified the field will be blank.

- *size* is optional; the size of the text field.

- *maxsize* is optional; the maximum size of the text field.

Example:

```
print $query->textfield('Address');    #defaults to size 20
```

Retrieved via

```
$Address = $query->param('Address');
```

This retrieval technique works the same on all the following elements, so it won't be repeated. Other retrieval techniques will be introduced with elements as needed.

A field's value can be set in the initial value parameter, but values can also be set elsewhere in the script. To assign a single value to the form variable *Address*, enter

```
$query->param('Address','56 Hollywood Blvd');
```

To assign multiple values to *Address*, enter

```
$query->param('Address','56 Hollywood Blvd','Hollywood, CA','90030');
```

These newly assigned values will "stick" as the new defaults, unless the Reset button is clicked.

Input Textarea

In CGI.pm, <TEXTAREA> becomes

print $query->textarea('name', 'initial value', rows, cols)

- *name* is required; this is the name of the text field in the form.

- *initial value* is optional; if not specified the field will be blank.

- *rows* is optional, the number of rows in the text field.

- *cols* is optional, the width of the lines in the text field.

Example:

```
print $query->textarea('memo','',12,60);
```

Input Password

In CGI.pm, <INPUT TYPE="password"> equates to

> print $query->password_field(*'name','initial value', size, maxsize*)

- *name* is required; this is the name of the text field in the form.

- *initial value* is optional; if not specified the field will be blank.

- *size* is optional, the size of the text field.

- *maxsize* is optional, the maximum size of the text field.

Example:

```
print $query->password_field('secret',,16);
```

Input Hidden

In CGI.pm, <INPUT TYPE="hidden"> becomes

> print $query->hidden(*name,'value1','value2'...*)

- *name* is required; this is the name of the text field in the form.

- *value1* through *valuen* are one or more values associated with this variable.

This form element can be used to pass a list back and forth on a form containing state information. You'll use this feature in the next section to build an interactive game. This field is unlike the other fields; it's not "sticky." That is, the field is reset to the value list you specify on this line each time the form is called.

Example:

```
print $query->hidden('vipcodes','Groucho','Harpo');
```

To assign a list of hidden values to a Perl array, use

```
@Secrets = $query->param('vipcodes');
```

Pop-Up Menus

The CGI.pm equivalent of <SELECT SIZE=1> is

> print $query->popup_menu(*'name',*
>   [*'item1','item2'...*],
>   *'selected item',*
>   {*'item1'=>'value1', 'item2'=>'value2'...*})

- *name* is required; this is the name of the <SELECT> field in the form.

🪐 *['item'...]* parameters are the list of menu items the user will see.

🪐 *'selected item'* is optionally one of the list of menu items that should be selected.

🪐 *{'item1'='value1'...}* is optionally the value that is really passed back to the script when an item is selected.

Examples:

```
print $query->popup_menu('Payment',['Visa','MC','First Virtual','DigiCash'])
print $query->popup_menu('Prize',
      ['Jaguar', 'Round-Trip to Hawaii', '$100,000','Candybar'],
      'CandyBar',
      {'Jaguar'=>'car', 'Round-Trip to Hawaii'=>'trip',
               '$100,000'=>'money','Candbar'=>'bummer'}
      );
```

If in the last example, the user picked $100,000 on the Web form, the value returned to

```
print $query->param('Prize')
```

would be

```
money
```

Scrollable List

The CGI.pm counterpart of <SELECT SIZE=>1> is

print $query->scrolling_list('name',
['item1','item2'...],
['selected item1','selected item2'...],
size,
multiple,
{'item1'=>'value1', 'item2'=>'value2'...})

🪐 *name* is required; this is the name of the <SELECT> field in the form.

🪐 *['item'...]* parameters are the list of menu items the user will see.

🪐 *['selected item',...]* is optionally one or more items in the list of menu items that should be selected.

🪐 *size* is optionally the number of lines of the list that should be visible when displayed (the rest are scrolled).

🪐 *multiple* is optionally a value of 'true' or 'false' set to allow multiple selections.

🪐 *{'item1'='value1'...}* is optionally the values really passed back to the script when an item is selected.

Examples:

```
print $query->scrolling_list('Toppings',
        ['Extra Cheese', 'Mushrooms', 'Olives', 'Green Peppers'],
        ['Extra Cheese', 'Mushrooms'],
        3,
        'true');
```

To load the results into a Perl list called @Pizza_Toppings, enter

```
@Pizza_Toppings = $query->scrolling_list('Toppings');
```

Check Box Groups

<INPUT TYPE="checkbox"> in HTML turns into the following in CGI.pm:

print $query->checkbox_group('*name*',
['*item1*','*item2*'...],
'*selected item*' or ['*item1*','*item2*'...],
line breaks,
{'*item1*'=>'*value1*', '*item2*'=>'*value2*'...})

- *name* is required; this is the name of the check box group in the form.

- *['item'...]* parameters are the list of menu items the user will see.

- *'selected item' or ['items'...]* optionally are one (in the first case) or multiple (in the second) boxes to be checked by default.

- *line breaks* is 'true' or 'false' depending on whether you want each check box separated on a new line ('true') or just displayed from left to right ('false').

- *{'item1'='value1'...}* is optionally the value that is really passed back to the script when an item is selected.

Examples:

```
print $query->checkbox_group('Send_Info',
        ['Products', 'Services', 'Memberships', 'Discounts'],
        'Products',
        'true');
```

Retrieve in a standard Perl list:

```
@info = $query->param('Send_Info');
```

Each box checked will return its value.

Creating a single check box rather than a group of related check boxes can be done with the following:

```
print $query->checkbox('InfoReq',1,'Y','Send Info?');
```

which creates a form variable called *InfoReq*; turns it on by default *1*; returns the value *Y* if it stays on; and prompts the user with *Send Info?*. You can test it in your script via

```perl
if ($query->param('InfoReq') eq "Y") {
    print "Here's the info you requested...";
}
```

Radio Button Groups

In CGI.pm, <INPUT TYPE="radio"> turns into the following:

print $query->radio_group(*'name'*,
['item1','item2'...],
'selected item',
line breaks,
{'item1'=>'value1', 'item2'=>'value2'...})

- **name** is required; this is the name of the radio button group in the form.

- **['item'...]** parameters are the values assigned to each button, and what the user will see by default.

- **'selected item'** is optionally the button to select by default. If not specified, the first radio button is selected.

- **line breaks** is 'true' or 'false' depending on whether you want each radio button separated on a new line ('true') or just displayed from left to right ('false').

- **{'item1'='value1'...}** is optionally the value that is displayed next to the radio button (not what is passed back to your script).

Examples:

```perl
print $query->radio_group('Payment',
    ['Cash', 'Visa', 'MasterCard', 'Discovery'],
    'true');
```

A single value is returned from

```perl
$query->param('Payment');
```

Submit and Reset

The submit button in CGI.pm (<INPUT TYPE="submit"> in HTML) is created with the following:

$query->submit(*'button-label','value'*);

- **'button-label'** is what appears on the button.

- **'value'** is optionally what is passed back to your script.

If you have multiple submit buttons on a form, you can find out which one was clicked via

```
if  ($query->params('button-label') eq value)...
```

In CGI.pm, <INPUT TYPE="reset"> has two slightly different relatives. One will undo recent changes to the form, but not set everything back to default value. It is

```
print $query->reset;
```

The other resets everything back to the default values:

```
print $query->defaults;
```

Image Button

A clickable image button of the kind created in HTML with <INPUT TYPE="image"> can be created in CGI.pm with the following syntax:
Example:

```
print $query->image_button('Nav','/images/navigate.gif','MIDDLE');
```

This example would load the image in /images/navigate.gif in a button called *Nav*, and set the optional alignment to MIDDLE (other choices are TOP and BOTTOM). When the button is clicked, it can be tested via

```
$x = $query->param('Nav.x');
$y = $query->param('Nav.y');
```

The above runs down all the functions you need to know to generate complete forms from Perl scripts using CGI.pm. As you can see, CGI.pm has almost every form element covered. Before you actually dive into using them, let's take a quick detour into debugging to see how it has been simplified with these new functions.

The Really Nice Stuff

Back when you were using the cgi-lib.pl functions, testing scripts was cumbersome. You were probably tempted to shortcut the process and just execute the script from a form rather than fuss around with the details of setting environmental variables and then changing everything back before testing from the form. You also probably tripped a few Server Error 500 messages and spent some time browsing the tailend of the error log to debug your scripts.

You can put all of this behind you now. CGI.pm makes debugging scripts simple. In fact, you don't need to change a thing to test the script from the command line instead of testing it from a form. Here's how it's done.

Let's pick on the simple script you created at the beginning of the session to ask for a name. If you called the script ask.cgi, just run it from the command line via

```
./ask.cgi
```

It will prompt you with the following:

```
(waiting for standard input)
```

Just enter one or more variables, each on its own line:

```
name='Rasputin of New Jersey'
address='Stateside'
^d
```

The *^d* is generated by holding the <CTRL> key and pressing "d". Use this when you run out of variables. Note that the sample script just uses the *name* variable, but it doesn't hurt anything to add more variables, like *address*. When you press <CTRL>+d, you'll get the following on your screen:

```
Content-type: text/html

<HTML><HEAD><TITLE>What's Your Name?</TITLE>
</HEAD><BODY><FORM METHOD="POST" >
Please Enter Your Name: <INPUT TYPE="text" NAME="name" VALUE="Rasputin
of New Jersey"  ></FORM>
<HR><HR>Your Name Is: Rasputin of New Jersey</BODY></HTML>
```

Pretty nifty, eh? If you want the script to dump all the variables passed to it, you can use the function

```
print $query->dump;
```

You'll receive a nicely formatted HTML list of all the name=value pairs assigned in the form.

Advanced Uses

CGI.pm comes with more advanced features, like saving and restoring values from a form to a file, and self-referencing URLs. These will be left for you to pursue in the CGI documentation; you won't need them for what's coming.

You should now have a core set of functions to help you whip out forms in nothing flat for the projects that follow. This will be useful, because you will be concentrating on other things, and expediency in generating values and retrieving them from the CGI will be assumed.

Just before this though, a couple of dangling functions should be mentioned. To send a redirect from CGI.pm simply enter

```
print $query->redirect('http://elsewhere.net');
```

then exit your script quickly without generating any further output. The user will immediately go to this redirect URL, just the way you would expect redirect to function.

If you want to print another content type besides HTML, pass its MIME type in

```
print $query->header('image/gif');
```

This can be followed with lines that output a GIF image. Okay, now you're finished! Almost.

QUIZ 3

1. CGI.pm's major difference from cgi-lib.pl is
   a. It allows you to retrieve values from a form.
   b. It lets you write output back to the CGI.
   c. It has functions for creating forms.
   d. It interfaces with Perl.

2. What is the smallest number of statements needed in CGI.pm to send back an HTML page?
   a. 1
   b. 2
   c. 3
   d. 4

3. What is meant by "sticky" variables?
   a. variables that clump together
   b. variables that keep their values each time the form is passed back
   c. variables that accept input
   d. variables that cannot be separated from a page

4. What is one use for sticky variables?
   a. to keep a user from having to re-enter all the data on a form if only one field is invalid
   b. for security
   c. for controlling the amount of information contained on a form
   d. to freeze a user's screen, disabling hyperlinks

SESSION 4

THE GAMESTER

Games feature prominently in the evolution of computing. From artificial intelligence to the genesis of operating systems, games often present the most subtle challenges and the most instructive solutions. UNIX is reputedly the result of Ken Thompson's needing a file system to program a game called Space Travel. And while you won't be developing the next generation operating system in this book, games are a way of developing more expertise in CGI scripting. And who knows what may spring from these humble beginnings?

Games are dynamically interactive. If what you had on your screen just kind of sat there in a nonfluid state, it wouldn't be called a game. It would be called work. Just kidding. Let's develop a Web game to learn how CGI scripts can be made interactive. In order for a script to be interactive, it has to surmount one basic design hurdle of the Web: statelessness.

Statelessness was touched on briefly in Chapters 4 and 5, but this time it's going to be a major concern. To review, Web interactions between the browser and the server are basically one shot deals. The browser asks for something, the server returns it. The browser fills out a form, the server does something with the data and sends something back. Each time the browser requests something from the server, it's as if the server never heard from the browser before. This makes interacting with a large number of anonymous clients easy. It's much better than each client having to log in, carry on the network counterpart of a conversation, and then log out when they are done. Instead, it's more like somebody yelling, "What's the price of watermelons?" and somebody else yelling back, "Five bucks." They don't yell back, "Hey, aren't you the guy that just asked about pinto beans? Are you going to buy something or what?"

Obviously this won't work too well with a game. It would be difficult to get a very sophisticated game going if the server didn't remember who was playing, and that the player had moved once already. Maybe paper, rock, scissors would work, because you win or lose with one interaction. But very few people in a Euclidean universe can win checkers in a single move. As a CGI author, you'll have to circumvent the statelessness of the Web server with your secret weapon: the hidden variable.

Hidden Variables and State

Hidden variables are never seen by the user of your CGI script. They are little pieces of information that can be sent back with a Web page to keep track of what that page just did with your script on the server. This makes these variables popular carriers of "state" information for CGI applications. During the rest of this session, you'll explore an interactive puzzle that uses hidden variables to track a user's progress and determine when (and if) the user solves it. The puzzle is illustrated in Figure 6-7. It's the kind of puzzle that has you sliding tiles around trying to create a certain pattern. Only one vacant spot on the board exists, so it takes some planning, or luck, to rearrange the tiles in the desired pattern.

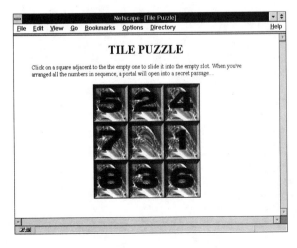

Figure 6-7
The slider puzzle

The Slider Puzzle

To do this on the Web you need GIF or JPEG images, one for each tile, plus one that is blank. These can be found on the CD accompanying this book (/images/slider), but you can just as easily generate your own. The tiles used in this project are simple numbers, and the goal will be to try to arrange them sequentially. They could just as easily be pieces of a picture. You could still use them as numbers in your script, then you would know when the picture was assembled correctly. This will be an exercise later, so you might want to think about how the script can be adapted. But first things first.

The pseudocode for the project looks something like this:

```
Present the initial tile puzzle
While not solved {
        Check player's move, if valid present new tile arrangement
        }
```

If pseudocode were a valid scripting language, you would be done. But until then, you'll need to translate it into Perl. Let's write a subroutine that will display the tiles, since it looks as if it needs to be used a couple of times in the script:

```
sub DisplayTiles {
        local ($i);
        $i = 0;
        print "<CENTER>";
        foreach $seq (@_) {
                print $query->image_button("button$seq",
                        "../images/$seq.gif");
                $i++;
                if ($i==3) {                # Display three to a row
                        print "<BR>\n";
                        $i = 0;
                        }
                }
        print "</CENTER>";
        }
```

Subroutines are a construct in Perl that you haven't covered yet. They are ways of breaking up a complex program into smaller pieces that can be called individually. To call the subroutine above, passing the sequence number of the tiles, you could use the following Perl syntax:

```
&DislayTiles(0,1,2,3,4,5,6,7,8);
```

The subroutine would print out the following:

```
<INPUT NAME="button0" TYPE="image" SRC="0.gif">
<INPUT NAME="button1" TYPE="image" SRC="1.gif">
<INPUT NAME="button2" TYPE="image" SRC="2.gif"><BR>
<INPUT NAME="button3" TYPE="image" SRC="3.gif">
<INPUT NAME="button4" TYPE="image" SRC="4.gif">
<INPUT NAME="button5" TYPE="image" SRC="5.gif"><BR>
<INPUT NAME="button6" TYPE="image" SRC="6.gif">
```

```
<INPUT NAME="button7" TYPE="image" SRC="7.gif">
<INPUT NAME="button8" TYPE="image" SRC="8.gif"><BR>
```

This subroutine takes care of displaying the tiles in the proper sequence; it just needs to be told what the sequence is. Perl puts the list of values passed to the subroutine in the special list: @_. Note that the variable $i is defined as a *local* variable. If you didn't do this, you might conflict with a variable $i defined somewhere else in the Perl script, and it might not like the fact that the DisplayTitles routine assigns it its own values. As a local variable, even if the $i variable exists elsewhere, it won't be the same $i as is used in the subroutine. The $i++ construct adds 1 to whatever value $i already has, so it acts as a counter. The rest of the syntax should be familiar.

This subroutine will display the tiles. Now you need a subroutine that will read the tile the user clicked and move it to the vacant slot. Since the tiles are displayed on a form as image buttons, the browser will have passed two variables for the tile that was clicked: *button.x* and *button.y*. Problem is, it could be any button, from button0 to button8. A simple loop should let you figure out which one it was:

```
sub CheckTile {
        local ($clicked, $i);
        $clicked = 0;
        # Find the tile that was clicked
        for ($i=0; $i<=8; $i++) {
                if ($query->param("button$i.x")) {
                        $button = $i;
                        last;
                        }
                }
```

The only thing new here is the *last* statement. This tells Perl to stop this loop (the *for* loop) immediately. You've found your tile.

Now that you know which tile was clicked, you need to see if the move was legal. Legally the user can only click titles that are next to the empty slot. If the empty slot is represented by 8.gif, this leads to an interesting puzzle for the CGI author: how do you tell if the tile clicked is next to 8? The figure is two dimensional, like this:

```
0 1 2
3 4 5
6 7 8
```

but your list was passed to the subroutine like this:

```
0,1,2,3,4,5,6,7,8
```

Let's try to translate. If the number clicked has an 8 to the right or left of it, it's a valid move, and you can just swap places. The other valid move is if the number is above or below it. Hmmm. Since this is an array of 3 by 3, above would mean -3, and below should be +3. And since 8 is a key tile, you need to keep track of where it is so you can do these calculations. Let's add the following to the subroutine:

```
sub CheckTile {
        local (*tiles) = @_;
        local ($button, $i, $empty, $clicked, $null_tile, $array);
```

continued on next page

continued from previous page

```perl
$clicked = 0;
$array = 3;
$null_tile = 8;
# Find the tile that was clicked
for ($i=0; $i<=8; $i++) {
        if ($query->param("button$i.x")) {
                $button = $i;
                last;
                }
        }

# Find where the empty tile is in the list:
for ($[..$#tiles) {
        $empty = $_ if ($tiles[$_]) == $null_tile;
        $clicked = $_ if ($tiles[$_]) == $button;
        }
```

And now to check if the move is legal:

```perl
# Clicking the empty tile is not permitted
if ($button == $null_tile) {
        return 0
        }

# Check to see if tile clicked is adjacent to empty tile
if    (($empty == $clicked-1) ||
        ($empty == $clicked+1) ||
        ($empty == $clicked-$array) ||
        ($empty == $clicked+$array) ) {
                $tiles[$empty] = $tiles[$clicked];
                $tiles[$clicked] = $null_tile;
        }
else {
        return 0;
        }
}
```

Okay, this is some pretty dense Perl code. What you've done is to check the button that was clicked to see what position it occupies in the list. Remember that the list is the sequence of tiles and how they are arranged on the screen, first three on the top row, second three on the second row, etc. Once the position of the clicked tile in the list is determined, it is compared to where the empty tile (8) is. If the empty tile is legally adjacent, above or below, their positions are switched on the spot. If not, the subroutine returns a value of 0, which means "false" in Perl. The main routine can check this value and print out a message if the result is "false"; otherwise the subroutine has determined the move was legal and has returned the revised list. All the main routine has to do is display the tiles using the DisplayTiles routine and return the current list sequence as a hidden variable, ready for the next move.

But wait, what if the puzzle is solved?! You need a routine to check to see if everything is in the proper order:

```
sub Solved {
        local(@tiles) = @_;
        local($j);
        for ($j=0; $j<=$#tiles; $j++) {
                return 0 if ($j != $tiles[$j]);
                }
        return 1;
        }
```

This routine looks through each element of the array and tests to see if the value is equal to its position in the array. If, in the puzzle, 0.gif is in position 0, 1.gif is in position 1, etc., all the way down, the puzzle is solved.

So subroutines have been written that do all the dirty work. This is called "bottom up" coding, and is usually a workable approach if you have an overall idea of the structure. With bottom up coding, you solve little interesting parts of the problem and then bring all the solutions together to solve the problem as a whole.

The overall solution now is as follows:

> Display initially random tiles
> Repeat until solved
> Rearrange tiles according to user clicks
> Congratulate user!

Oops, you need a routine to mix up the tiles to start with. Let's add one more subroutine:

```
sub Mixup {
        local(@temp);
        local(*tiles) = @_;
        push(@temp,splice(@tiles, rand(@tiles),1)) while @tiles;
        @tiles = @temp;
        }
```

The Perl push and splice operations on arrays go beyond the scope of this simple session on the Web tile game, but trust that this routine will completely and randomly resequence any array passed to it.

Now, putting everything together in a bare-bones script:

```
#!/usr/local/bin/perl
use CGI;
$query = new CGI;
print $query->header;
print $query->start_html("Tile Puzzle");
print "<H1 ALIGN=center>TILE PUZZLE</H1>";
print "<BLOCKQUOTE>";
print "Click on a square adjacent to the the empty one ";
print "to slide it into the empty slot. When you\'ve arranged ";
print "all the numbers in sequence, a portal will open into a ";
print "secret passage....<P>";
print "</BLOCKQUOTE>";
print $query->startform,"\n";
if (defined(@tiles = $query->param('tilelist'))) {
$query->delete('tilelist');
```

continued on next page

continued from previous page

```
            if (!&CheckTile(*tiles)) {
                    print "<H3>Sorry That Move Is Not Legal</H3>";
                    }
            elsif (&Solved(@tiles)) {
                    print "<H3>Congratulations!! You Solved It!<H3>";
                    print "You may <A HREF='portal.html'>proceed</A><P>";
                    }
            }
    else    {
            @tiles = (0..8);
            &Mixup(*tiles);
            }
    &DisplayTiles(@tiles);
    print $query->hidden('tilelist',@tiles);
    print $query->endform,"\n";
    print $query->end_html;
```

Let's look at what the script accomplishes. The script is checking to see if a tile list has already been created (which means this is not the first time the script was called). If it hasn't been, it creates one, mixes up the pattern randomly, and displays the results while tucking the sequence away in a hidden variable sent back to the browser.

If the hidden variable has already been assigned, the script picks up the tile sequence from the variable, checks to see if the move is valid, and if the puzzle is solved. The tile list is changed by the CheckTile routine and the hidden variable is updated with the new sequence. CGI.pm resets all hidden variables to their default; only the visible tags have "sticky" values. This is kind of a nuisance for maintaining state information, but the workaround is to delete and recreate the variable with a new set of defaults. Now just tack the subroutines written above onto the end of the script, and the Web Tile Puzzle script is complete.

Extending the Idea

With slight modifications you could use the same technique to implement other games, like Concentration, Master Mind, etc. You've learned how to keep track of a series of interactions with the server using a hidden variable. This is the basic mechanism behind a large percentage of interactive games you'll find on the Web.

1. What subroutines would need to be changed if the tile were 4 by 4 instead of 3 by 3?
   a. Mixup, Solved, CheckTile, DisplayTiles
   b. Mixup, Solved
   c. CheckTile
   d. Solved

2. What else could have been used for the image besides input fields?
   a. an inline image

b. a hyperlink

c. a table

d. an imagemap

3. Why didn't you just use a variable with a sticky value instead of the hidden variable you had to keep reinitializing?

a. All the sticky variables are displayed so the user can change them.

b. Hidden variables are the only variables that can maintain state information.

c. The information kept changing, so something had to be reinitialized .

d. Sticky variables can't hold arrays.

4. What is the simplest way to modify the game to display a visual puzzle instead of numeric puzzle?

a. Rewrite the main routine.

b. Rewrite the subroutines.

c. Make 1.gif … 8.gif contain a picture.

d. It is impossible.

CREATING GIFS ON THE FLY

Now for something fancy. With the tile game, you played with a kaleidoscope of tiles that shifted at the click of a mouse. This lesson, you'll play with some tools that let your script generate graphics on the fly. You'll still be using the CGI.pm library, but you will need to add a couple more ingredients to your server's repertoire.

First you will need gd, a graphics library for creating GIF images dynamically. It is available via anonymous FTP from isis.cshl.org in /pub/gd/gd1.1.1.tar.Z. After uncompressing and untarring via

```
uncompress gd1.1.1.tar.Z
tar -xf gd1.1.1.tar
```

follow the directions in the README to install.

The gd library is a set of modules callable from C programs to create and manipulate GIFs. To make this accessible to your Perl scripts, you need one more ingredient: GD.pm. This is a Perl 5 interface module to the gd libraries written by the same busy author who produced CGI.pm. It is available from http://www-genome.-wi.mit.edu/ftp/pub/software/WWW/GD.pm.tar.Z. Follow the same procedures you did when unpacking gd, except do the uncompress and tar from your /usr/local/source/perl5.001/ext library (or wherever your path is for the Perl 5 source code and its ext subdirectory). Then follow the installation notes.

Creating and Displaying Objects

Documentation for GD.pm can be found on its home page (http://www-genome.wi.mit.edu/ftp/distribution/software/WWW/GD.html) , so there's no need to spend time here detailing its functionality. Instead, let's just jump right in and build something.

To create a simple object, like a red circle in a blue background, open a new script file on your Web server and enter the following Perl code:

```perl
#!/usr/local/bin/perl
use CGI;
use GD;
$query = new CGI;
print $query->header("image/gif");

# Create a new image. Give it 100x100 pixels, default if not
#       specified is 64x64
$image = new GD::Image(100,100);

# The first color allocated will be the background color of the image
$black = $image->colorAllocate(0,0,0);

# Define some other colors
$red    = $image->colorAllocate(255,0,0);
$blue   = $image->colorAllocate(0,0,255);
$white  = $image->colorAllocate(255,255,255);


# Draw a red circle in the middle
$image->arc(50,50,50,50,0,360,$red);

# Draw a rectangle filled with blue
$image->filledRectangle(60,60,75,75,$blue);


# Convert it to GIF format and send it back to the Browser
print $image->gif;
```

Opening this script with a URL from your browser will give you the results shown in Figure 6-8.

Let's go through what happened step by step:

```perl
#!/usr/local/bin/perl
use CGI;
use GD;
$query = new CGI;
print $query->header("image/gif");
```

The script uses both the CGI library that you used in Session 4 and the new GD library. A new CGI element was created and used to print the MIME header indicating that this will not be HTML, but a GIF image.

```perl
# Create a new image. Give it 100x100 pixels, default if not
#       specified is 64x64
$image = new GD::Image(100,100);
```

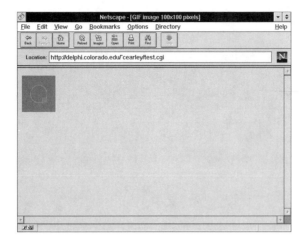

Figure 6-8
A simple
homemade GIF

Just as *$query* represents an object used to interact with the CGI, *$image* is a newly created image object. All the operations done on the image will be done through this object. It was initialized at 100 by 100 pixels.

```
# The first color allocated will be the background color of the image
$black = $image->colorAllocate(0,0,0);

# Define some other colors
$red    = $image->colorAllocate(255,0,0);
$blue   = $image->colorAllocate(0,0,255);
$white  = $image->colorAllocate(255,255,255);
```

A few colors are now created in the image's palette. In addition, a variable was created to refer to each color. These color variables are used as arguments in other image functions. The colors are combinations of RGB values; each value can range from 255 to 0 and control the amount of red, green, or blue that makes up the color. All red is 255,0,0, all blue is 0,0,255. To make magenta, which is a combination of red and blue, you would use 255,0,255. You've encountered this RGB scheme before in setting Netscape background colors.

The next part of the script draws a circle using the arc function. Arc takes the following arguments:

```
arc(cx,cy,width,height,start,end,color)
```

cx,cy are the coordinates to the center of the arc.

width, height are the dimensions of the arc.

start,end are degrees the arc will sweep around the circle. 0 to 360 is a complete circle.

color is the line color.

```
# Draw a red circle in the middle
$image->arc(50,50,50,50,0,360,$red);
```

The next line draws a rectangle filled with a solid color specified in the color argument. The syntax is

```
filledRectangle(x1,y1,x2,y2,color);
```

```
# Draw a rectangle filled with blue
$image->filledRectangle(60,60,75,75,$blue);
```

And finally, the image is converted from its internal format to a GIF image and printed, all with a single function:

```
# Convert it to GIF format and send it back to the Browser
print $image->gif;
```

Manipulating Graphics

The GD graphics library has other functions for creating polygons, turning on and off single pixels, tiling, etc. Let's focus on a few more that are of immediate use to Web images: transparency and interlacing.

To set a color of an image as transparent, enter

```
$image->transparent($black);
```

To make the image interlaced, enter

```
$image->interlaced('true');
```

Not only can you do this with images you are creating in GD's format, but you can open a GIF that is already created and manipulate it with GD functions. The following snippet loads a GIF file called target.gif, locates the color from its palette that is closest to white, and sets it as the transparent color. Then it makes the GIF interlaced:

```
open(GIF,"target.gif");
$image->newFromGif GD::Image(GIF);
$white = $image->colorClosest(255,255,255);
$image->transparent($white);
$image->interlaced('true');
print $image->gif;
```

The color $white is used as the transparent color in the GIF image. But $white was first allocated as the color closest to the RGB values 255,255,255, with the colorClosest function. This is because a GIF is loaded with its own palette, and if you don't know the exact RGB combination of what appears to be a color similar to white in the image, your odds are not very good of guessing it. The color 250,250,250 looks very similar to 255,255,255. If most of the background appears white or black, or some other easily discernible color, you can use colorClosest to let the function figure out what shade it is. The other alternative is to load the GIF into a utility like LVIEW and find out the exact RGB value of a pixel in the background.

You can *flood-fill* regions of an image with the following:

```
fill(x,y,color)
```

Given an x,y coordinate on the image, and a color that has been allocated, GD will fill the area with the color until it runs into a pixel of a color different from that of the pixel at x,y. You can use this function, along with the previous example of loading an already existing GIF file, to make an interesting project.

A Coloring Book

A Web coloring book displays an image that a user can color by clicking on different sections. The user can select from a palette of colors with radio buttons, and you can build the entire application in a few lines of Perl. Figure 6-9 shows what the project looks like to the user.

Behind the scenes you'll need to take care of the following:

- Keep a history of where the user clicks and what color was selected.

- Apply the history of changes to the image on the fly. You don't modify the original GIF.

- Distinquish between when the script is being called to present the image, and when it's being called to present the page.

The first two are similar to what you did with the tile puzzle. Hidden variables can be used to keep track of each color change. The last requirement is new. You encountered it when you pointed to a script to return a random GIF, but this time the requirements are a little trickier. Let's sketch out roughly what needs to be done in Perl:

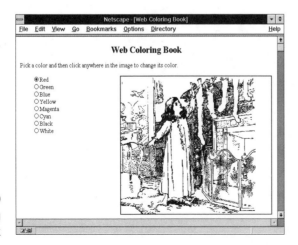

Figure 6-9
The Web coloring book

```
#!/usr/local/bin/perl
use GD;
use CGI;
$query = new CGI;                                  # create CGI object
if ($query->param('image')) {                      # see if variable image present
        open(GIF,"../images/target.gif");          # if so open a gif file
        $image = newFromGif GD::Image(GIF);        # translate it to a GD file
        close GIF;                                 # no longer need the GIF
        &apply_changes;                            # apply any image modifications
        print $query->header("image/gif");         # Send MIME image header
        print $image->gif;                         # Translate back to gif and
        exit 0;                                    # send the image
        }
```

If the script is called with the syntax

http://location/script?image=1

it will display the image and exit. You can use the above as the URL for the <IMG> SRC
option in the form. Without the *?image=1* tagged onto the end, the script will display the
initial form, and handle the coloring book functions. The rest of the script is as follows:

```
print $query->header;                                       # Regular form
print $query->start_html("Web Coloring Book");
print "<H2 ALIGN=center>Web Coloring Book</H2>";
print "Pick a color and then click anywhere in the image ";
print "to change its color.\n ";
print $query->startform,"\n";
$tag = "?image=1";                                          # Assume first time
if ($query->param('pict.x')) {                     # if picture already
        @x = $query->param('xclick');              # clicked then get
        @y = $query->param('yclick');              # the old x,y and
        @c = $query->param('clist');               # color values
        $nx = $query->param('pict.x');             # get the new ones
        $ny = $query->param('pict.y');             # (just clicked)
        $ncolor = $query->param('color');
        $query->param('xclick',@x,$nx);            # and add to the old
        $query->param('yclick',@y,$ny);            # updating the hidden
        $query->param('clist',@c,$ncolor);         # variables
        $tag = "&image=1";                                  # tag as not new
        }
$my_url = $query->self_url;                                 # get hidden variables

# Refer to this script for image... use the self_url retains passes all
#       the variables set up to now back to the script for processing the
#       image
print $query->image_button('pict',"$my_url$tag",'RIGHT'),"\n";

# Color choices
print $query->radio_group('color',['0','1','2','3','4','5','6','7']
        ,'0',
        'true',
        {'0'=>'Red','1'=>'Green','2'=>'Blue','3'=>'Yellow','4'=>'Magenta',
         '5'=>'Cyan','6'=>'Black','7'=>'White'});
```

```
# State information about previous x,y clicks and colors
print $query->hidden('xclick'),"\n";
print $query->hidden('yclick'),"\n";
print $query->hidden('clist'),"\n";
print $query->endform,"\n";
print $query->end_html;
```

Only a couple of new elements here. The *$my_url* variable is obtained from the *$query* object using the method $query->self_url. This variable is used to associate the image in the button with the script, so you can pass back a modified picture. It also makes sure all the form variables are passed. If you simply used

```
print $query->image_button('pict',"color.cgi?image=1",'RIGHT'),"\n";
```

the browser would connect to the script to display the image, but none of the hidden variables containing the x,y coordinates or color choices would be transmitted. Self_url creates a link that preserves state information.

Three different arrays are being kept: @x, @y, and @c. These hold each x, y coordinate and color selections made by the user. The current combination of x and y, obtained from the *pict.x* and *pict.y* values of the <INPUT TYPE="image"> object, and the color, obtained from the radio buttons, are appended to the x,y,c values already recorded. This array is used by the next subroutine:

```
sub apply_changes {
local(@x,@y,@c,$i);
$ctable[0] = $image->colorAllocate(255,0,0); #Red
$ctable[1] = $image->colorAllocate(0,255,0); #Green
$ctable[2] = $image->colorAllocate(0,0,255); #Blue
$ctable[3] = $image->colorAllocate(255,255,0); #Yellow
$ctable[4] = $image->colorAllocate(255,0,255); #Magenta
$ctable[5] = $image->colorAllocate(0,255,255); #Cyan
$ctable[6] = $image->colorAllocate(0,0,0); #Black
$ctable[7] = $image->colorAllocate(255,255,255); #White
@x = $query->param('xclick');   # Collect x,y and color
@y = $query->param('yclick');   # values from the hidden
@c = $query->param('clist');    # variables
for ($i=0; $i<=$#x; $i++) {     # apply each in sequence
        $image->fill($x[$i],$y[$i],$ctable[$c[$i]]);
        }
}
```

which consecutively applies each color to the x,y coordinate with GD's fill function. The values of the color radio selections are mapped into a color index array of preassigned colors. What results is an interactive coloring book, suitable for kids of all ages.

QUIZ 5

1. What does the GD fill function do?
   a. It fills an entire image with a color.
   b. It changes one color in an image to another.

c. It changes the color of a section until it hits pixels of a color different from the section.

d. It changes multiple colors in an image to a single color.

2. When setting a transparent color of a GIF in the example, why was the colorClosest function used?

a. It would be hard to guess the exact RGB numbers of a color in the GIF file.

b. Transparent colors only work by approximating regular colors.

c. Transparent colors cannot be exact RGB values.

d. The closest value to white will always be the transparent color in a GIF file.

3. To display an existing GIF file, which GD functions need to be used?

a. $image->newFromGIF, $image-gif

b. $image->gif

c. $image = new GD::Image, $image->newFromGIF,$image->gif

d. $image->DisplayGif

4. What color is assigned to the background when a GD image is created from scratch?

a. None, it is transparent.

b. The first color allocated with the colorAllocate function

c. The last color allocated with the colorAllocate function

d. The color assigned with backgroundColor function

EXERCISE 5

Black could be used for the outline of an image to color. Modify the script to prevent any blocks of black from being filled. The following function returns the color table index for the color under an x,y coordinate:

```
$index = $image->getPixel(x,y);
```

The next function returns the index of the color closest to the RGB values specified (black in this case). Its index can be compared to the above to see if black was selected.

```
$black = $image->colorClosest(0,0,0);
```

SESSION 6

POOR MAN'S WEB ANIMATION

The session deals with a couple of Netscape extensions for Web page animation. This goes a little beyond the concept of dynamic documents that change based on user inter-action. These extensions permit documents to change at automatic intervals. The extensions are recognized by the client, so the scripts can be written on any server, and they fall into two categories referred to as *server push* and *client pull*.

Client Pull

Client pulls are implemented with a <META> tag in the header of your HTML. The tag has the following format:

```
<META HTTP-EQUIV="Refresh" CONTENT=n>
```

where *n* is the number of seconds to delay before automatically refreshing the page. If you wrote an HTML page like the following:

```
<HTML>
<HEAD>
<META HTTP-EQUIV="Refresh" CONTENT=10>
</HEAD>
<BODY>
<H2>You Will See This Again </H2>
</BODY>
</HTML>
```

the browser would retrieve the page, wait ten seconds, and then reload the page. The refresh is a one-time directive; it means refresh once after ten seconds. But when the page loads again, if it has a new refresh directive, the process will repeat indefinitely. In and of itself this wouldn't be very useful. In fact, it would be downright annoying. But another option on the <META> tag gives you a little more flexibility:

```
<META HTTP-EQUIV="Refresh" CONTENT="n; URL=url">
```

 n is the number of seconds to delay before automatically refreshing the page.

 url is the URL to link to after the specified number of seconds has expired.

Using this syntax you can wait a few seconds, then link to a page that doesn't have a client pull. This is the basic technique of an application convention you're probably well acquainted with: the splash page.

Splash Pages with Client Pulls

Implementing a splash page with what you know now about client pulls is easy. You build your splash page like so:

```
<HTML>
<HEAD>
<META HTTP-EQUIV="Refresh" CONTENT="5;URL=home.html">
</HEAD>
<BODY>
<H2 Align=center>Welcome To Water Emporium</H2>
<HR>
<IMG SRC="banner.gif">
<A HREF="home.html">Home Page</A>
</BODY>
</HTML>
```

This flashes Water Emporium's expensive designer logo on the screen for five seconds and then replaces the screen with their home.html page. Note that a visible hyperlink was put into this page as well for those browsers not equipped for client pulls.

You can also use a time of 0 seconds. This causes the browser to load the new page as soon as the first one is completely displayed. A possible application for an interactive course in speed reading?

What if the user is really fast, or really impatient, and clicks the *home.html* link before the refresh interval is up? It will automatically cancel the refresh and activate the link. In fact, this is one way out of a client pull.

Escaping Client Pulls

Activating a link terminates the refresh. Other ways to stop a client pull are to close the window or click the Back button (unless this goes back to a document with a client pull!).

Other Strange Uses

The <META> tag for the client pull can be returned with other types of headers, like the redirection header. It would then mean: get this URL now, wait *n* seconds and then go get this other one. This could be used in a script to create an automatic tour through a set of pages, kind of like a slide show, with chances to bail out of the canned presentation by selecting a link that appears on a page before the refresh countdown expires. It can also make for some interesting poetry...

Automatic Agents

One handy use for client pull is to keep an eye on certain things happening on your server (or elsewhere). For example, if you would like to keep track of errors happening on the Web server, you could create a simple script as follows:

```perl
#!/usr/local/bin/perl
use CGI;
$q = new CGI;
print $q->header;
print "<HTML><HEAD><META HTTPD-EQUIV='Refresh' CONTENT=30>";
print "<TITLE>Display Error Log</TITLE>";
print "<BODY><H2>Server Error Log</H2><HR>";
print "<PRE>";
`tail /usr/local/etc/httpd/error_log`;
print "</PRE>";
print $q->end_html;
```

This script would print the tailend of the error log every 30 seconds until you left the page.

Server Push

Client pulls are controlled by the client. The Web browser sets the timer, and when it expires, the browser takes action, either reloading the current page or branching to a URL specified in the <META> tag. With server pushes, as you might expect, the control shifts to the server. The server keeps open a connection with the client, telling the browser that it has more to send. It does this with an experimental MIME header.

MIME headers encapsulate the content of data passing between the server and the client. Usually these headers represent distinct chunks of data, such as Content-Type: text/htm, or Content-Type: image/gif, but MIME also has formats that represent multipart documents. This means many pieces of information can be included in a single message. For example, many different GIF files could be transmitted, and the browser would display them one after another.

This multipart functionality was used to add an experimental MIME format called multipart/x-mixed-replace, which means, multiple files are coming, but each one replaces the previous one. The browser then will get rid of the previous object and replace it with the next one that is sent by the server, and continues to do this until the server has no more to send. Using this facility to swap images in place can produce a rudimentary type of animation. An example will make this clearer.

The format for the multipart MIME header is

```
Content-type: multipart/x-mixed-replace;boundary=SomeString
```

where *SomeString* is an arbitrary string used to delimit each image, or object.

To send down two GIF images, 1st.gif and 2nd.gif, the following script would implement a server push:

```perl
#!/usr/local/bin/perl
$| = 1;
print "Content-type: multipart/x-mixed-replace;boundary=thatsit\n\n";
print "--thatsit\n";
print "Content-type: image/gif\n\n";
open (GIF,"1st.gif");
print (<GIF>);
close (GIF);
print "--thatsit\n";
print "Content-type: image/gif\n\n";
open (GIF,"2nd.gif");
print (<GIF>);
close (GIF);
print "--thatsit--\n";
```

Note that "thatsit" is used to mark the beginning of a new MIME object; the string is preceded by two dashes "--" before every Content-type header, and at the very end it is also followed by two dashes indicating the end of the entire multipart message.

Another new element is at the begining of the Perl script. The funny looking line:

```
$! = 1;
```

is easy to miss, but it's very important. It tells Perl not to buffer the output but to send it out immediately. If this weren't present, the operating system might decide, for efficiency, to wait until you had a certain number of output lines pending before it would actually write them to the CGI. This would cause the user's page to lock up.

What happens when you run the script above is that one image appears on the page, and is immediately replaced with another. This script can be referenced as part of the URL for an inline image:

```
<IMG SRC="/cgi-bin/flipit">
```

It gets more fun when a series of images are replaced in succession. For the next example you'll write a simple to loop to display five GIF images successively. You can use this to cause a company banner to scroll on the screen from right to left, or to animate a graphical rule. Just remember that all the images need to be the same size. Here is the script to use:

```perl
#!/usr/local/bin/perl
$| = 1;
print "Content-type: multipart/x-mixed-replace;boundary=thatsit\n\n";
for ($i=1; $i <= 3; $i++) {
        print "--thatsit\n";
        print "Content-type: image/gif\n\n";
        open (GIF,"../images/$i.gif");
        print (<GIF>);
        close (GIF);
}
print "--thatsit--\n";
```

If this script were called dynarule.cgi, it could be used to animate a graphical rule in a larger form by referencing it with an inline image tag:

```
<BR><IMG SRC="dynarule.cgi"><BR>
```

Stopping Pushes

Pushes can be stopped by simply clicking the Stop button on the browser. They are also stopped when you leave the page, either following another link, or using the Back link built into the browser.

Gotchas

On some servers, notably NCSA's, you need to be careful when specifying the content-type header. NCSA seems to have problems, at least in the current release, if any spaces occur in the content type. For example:

```
Content-type multipart/x-mixed-replace; boundary=thatsit
```

would be problematic, because of the space between *replace;* and *boundary*.

Another common mistake is not to include the *$|=1;* statement in Perl, to force the output to be unbuffered.

Some servers, like CERN, have also reported problems if the script name is not prefaced with the characters "nph-". This tells the server that this is a nonparsed-header file, and the script will be generating its own content headers. It doesn't seem to be necessary with the more recent releases of the NCSA server, but if you run into problems, try renaming dynarule.cgi to nph-dynarule.cgi.

Pros and Cons

Server pushes are generally more efficient than client pulls, especially for animating images. Each new connection to the Web server requires a few seconds of overhead to set up and tear down the connection to the browser. Since server push keeps this connection open, it doesn't incur the latency of several discrete requests.

Of course, keeping a connection open uses up server resources. A connection is usually turned around quickly, and doesn't span too long an interval of time. This allows relatively small servers to handle a large number of requests. With server pushes holding a connection open, it is more likely that the server will have to handle more than one request at the same time. This requirement for concurrency puts additional load on server processing.

Client pulls are less efficient, for the reasons explained above. They have to reestablish connection with each interval. But no connection is maintained over time. So for applications that refresh in longer intervals, like 30 seconds and longer, client pulls might be the way to go.

QUIZ 6

1. Client pulls
   a. are when a server refreshes the client automatically
   b. are when a client requests animation from the server
   c. are when a client reloads itself or branches to a URL after an interval
   d. are when a client reloads itself when told to by the server

2. Client pulls and server pushes
   a. are only available in Netscape servers
   b. are available on any server and HTML 3.0 browser
   c. are available on any server and Netscape browser
   d. are available on HTML 3.0 servers and Netscape browsers

3. One potential disadvantage of a server push is
   a. It requires constant reconnection to the server.
   b. It cannot be interrupted.
   c. It keeps a connection open to the server.
   d. It cannot be used with Perl.

4. When writing Perl scripts that implement server pushes, it is important to
   a. make sure a delay is placed in between each image
   b. make sure output is unbuffered
   c. check for user interruption
   d. not have a timeout in the script

SESSION 7

THE GUEST BOOK

Guest books, found in vintage tourist stops and ritzy restaurants, also have a counterpart on the Web. Figure 6-10 shows a guest book page at

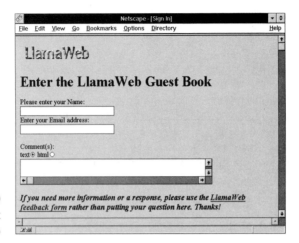

Figure 6-10
The guest book at
LlamaWeb

http://www.webcom.com/~degraham/. A guest book allows users of your site to sign their names, offer comments and suggestions, and leave behind a stamp of their presence without resorting to virtual graffiti (for ideas on a virtual graffiti board, check out http://www.ncb.gov.sg/BOG/—in Singapore no less!).

Let's start the design of the guest book with the form itself. Note on the guest book in Figure 6-10 that the potential signee can see the most recent signatures of visiting guests. This is part of the appeal. You'll need to make sure your guests have the instant satisfaction of seeing their signatures recorded online for worldwide perusal. So the form will have an area for their signature, followed by a scrollable section of the signatures to date. Try to get a firm idea of what you would do to create this page before reading further.

The Form

Obviously, this is not just a simple form. One section of the form lets users enter signatures, but on the same page are displayed scrollable entries in the guest book. Most likely this page will need to be a form generated by a script. The script would print the form part of the page and follow it with the text of a guest book file of some sort. Such a script might look like this:

```
use CGI;
$query = new CGI;
print $query->header;
print $query->start_html("BareBones Guestbook --- The Beginning");
print "<H2 ALIGN=center>Celestial Scents Guest Book</H2>";
print "Please sign your name and enter any comments you would";
print "like to share below. Celestial Scents is honored to ";
print "have you as a visitor. (Please note, some information ";
print "about you will be filled in automatically when you ";
print "sign. This information is obtained from your Web browser.<P>";
print $query->startform("POST","/cgi-bin/addcomments.cgi"),"\n";
print "Your Name: ",$query->textfield('name','',50),"<P>";
```

```
print "Comments: ",","<BR>",$query->textarea('comments','',5,60);
print "<P>",$query->submit('Submit');
print $query->defaults('Reset');
print $query->endform,"\n";


&display_guestbook("guests.dat");


print $query->end_html;
```

This script displays the part of the form the user can sign, then passes the buck to the &display_guestbook subroutine to display existing signatures. It is hoped that this subroutine will somehow magically display the guest book, folding it onto the current form. In the startform function of the CGI library, another script, addcomments.cgi, was specified, to add signatures to the guest book.

The Scripts

It now appears only one subroutine and a small script are needed for a functional guest book. If it were this easy, why doesn't every page have one? Hmmm. Let's proceed cautiously just in case. The &display_guestbook routine seems pretty straightforward. Assuming that addcomments.cgi puts data from the form into this file, all that should be necessary is to display the file. This can be done readily enough in Perl:

```
sub display_guestbook {
        local ($fn) = @_;
        open(GUEST,"<$fn");
        print   <GUEST>;
        close(GUEST);
        }
```

You open a filename passed to the subroutine and print it. The Perl syntax:

```
local($fn) = @_;
```

creates a local variable called *$fn*, and assigns it to the filename passed to &display_guestbook ("guests.dat" in the example above). The file is then opened, printed to standard output, and closed. That's done. What about the addguestbook.cgi script?

Updating the Guest Book

Input from the form is written to the guest book file. Each user's signature should be separated from those of other users, so addguestbook.cgi will need to throw in some HTML to separate blocks of signatures. It will also need to screen what is coming in to make sure no metacharacters are in the input that could compromise the security of the script. And finally, it will need to lock the file while it's doing the update so the file won't become corrupted if another user is trying to enter a signature at the same time. Let's look at these requirements individually.

First, before data ever hits the guest book file, you need to check the input for metacharacters. Rather than complaining with a nasty message, let's just zap metacharacters from the input fields and press on. Here's the first part of the addguests.cgi script:

```
#!/usr/local/bin/perl
```

continued on next page

continued from previous page

```
use CGI;
$query = new CGI;
$name = $query->param('name');
$comments = $query->param('comments');


$name    =" y/a-zA-z0-9_-+ \t<>\"\/\a\%\]//cd;
$comments =" y/a-zA-z0-9_-+ \t<>\"\/\a\%\]\n//cd;
$comments =" s/\n/<BR>/g;
```

The last two bizarre-looking lines of Perl delete everything in the $name and $comment strings that is not alphanumeric, or a few other permitted characters (numbers,_,+,-,tabs,",/,@,%,<,>). The $comments variable also allows the user to press return in the comment fields, then substitutes this for <BR>. Look up the *substitution* commands in Perl for more info on how to use these functions.

Next you need to lock the file you are about to update. Locking it allows the script to make changes safely. The following lines insure this:

```
#!/usr/local/bin/perl
$LOCK_EX = 2;
$LOCK_UN = 8;

use CGI;
$query = new CGI;
$name = $query->param('name');
$comments = $query->param('comments');

$name    =" y/a-zA-z0-9_-+ \t<>\"\/\a\%\]//cd;
$comments =" y/a-zA-z0-9_-+ \t<>\"\/\a\%\]\n//cd;

open(GUEST,">>guests.dat");
flock(GUEST, $LOCK_EX);
seek(GUEST, 0, 2);
.... add stuff
flock(GUEST,$LOCK_UN);
```

The GUEST file is opened with the ">>" syntax, which means append. (This will open the file for update and go to the bottom.) The function flock operates on the filehandle GUEST based on the flags passed. The flag $LOCK_EX requests an exclusive lock and waits until it happens. If it does have to wait, because of another process updating guests.dat for example, you'll need to ensure you're still at the bottom of the file once the lock is performed. The seek(GUEST, 0, 2) does this for you. Now name and comments are added to the file and flock is called again, this time to unlock the file.

The last step in the script is to fill in the part in the middle that "adds stuff" to the guests.dat file:

```
#!/usr/local/bin/perl
$LOCK_EX = 2;
$LOCK_UN = 8;

use CGI;
$query = new CGI;
$name = $query->param('name');
```

```
$comments = $query->param('comments');

$name    =" y/a-zA-z0-9_-+ \t<>\"\/\@\%\]//cd;
$comments =" y/a-zA-z0-9_-+ \t<>\"\/\@\%\]\n//cd;

open(GUEST,">>guests.dat');
flock(GUEST, $LOCK_EX);
seek(GUEST, 0, 2);

print GUEST "<HR>";
print GUEST "<STRONG>$name</STRONG><BR>";
print GUEST "$comments<P>";

flock(GUEST,$LOCK_UN);


print $query->header;
print $query->start_html;
print "<H2>Your Signature and Comments Have Been Added To Guestbook!</H2>";
print "<P>Thanks!";
print $query->end_html;
```

Figure 6-11 shows the fictional guest book in operation. It's already captured a celebrity signature.

It's Upside Down!

While the guest book is fully functional, it's not yet fully usable. For example, you might notice as you add entries for practice that the latest entries always come up last. This

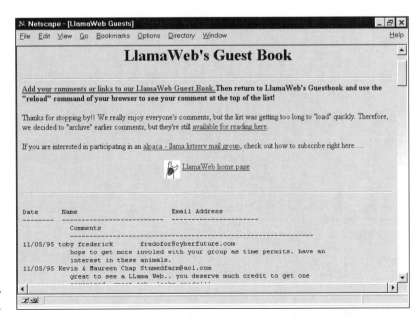

Figure 6-11
Celestial Scents
guestbook

is no way to treat a guest! Ideally the guest book should show the most recently entered entries at the top of the page and the older ones as you scroll down. This appears obvious to the user, but you may be scratching your head about how to get a file to print upside down from your script. Here's a thought on the subject: when displaying the form, print the file in reverse. Instead of

```perl
sub display_guestbook {
        local ($fn) = @_;
        open(GUEST,"<$fn");
        print   <GUEST>;
        close(GUEST);
        }
```

use

```perl
sub display_guestbook {
    local ($fn) = @_;
    open(GUEST,"<$fn");
    print reverse <GUEST>;
    close(GUEST);
    }
```

And while you're at it, you should also take this opportunity to add some more information about the user, including a date and time stamp for the record. A lot of information about the user is already stored in variables by the time your script is called. For example, from the CGI library, you can access the following that may be of use:

  remote_host()   Returns host name or IP address of the user

  remote_addr()   Returns the user's IP address specifically

🌑 referer()   Returns the URL that got the user here

These can be accessed like the other CGI functions. For example $query->remote_host() returns a string with the remote host (if *$query* was used for the CGI object).

You can also use a local Perl function to the local date and time:

```perl
($sec,$min,$hour,$mday,$mon,$year,$wday,$ydat,$isdat) = localtime(time);
```

Putting this all together, the completed addguest.cgi script contains

```perl
#!/usr/local/bin/perl
$LOCK_EX = 2;
$LOCK_UN = 8;

use CGI;
$query = new CGI;
$name = $query->param('name');
$comments = $query->param('comments');

$name =~ y/a-zA-z0-9_-+ \t<>\"\/\@\%\]//cd;
$comments  =~ y/a-zA-z0-9_-+ \t<>\"\/\@\%\]\n//cd;
$comments =~ s/\n/<BR>/g;
($sec,$min,$hour,$mday,$mon,$year,$wday,$ydat,$isdat) = localtime(time);
local(@day_of_week) = ("Sun","Mon","Tue","Wed","Thu","Fri","Sat","Sun");
```

```
local(@month) =
local(@month)=("Jan","Feb","Mar","Apr","May","Jun","Jul","Aug","Sep","Oct","Nov"
,"Dec");
$date = "$day_of_week[$wday], $month[$mon] $mday, $hour:$min";

open(GUEST,">>guests.dat");
flock(GUEST, $LOCK_EX);
seek(GUEST, 0, 2);

print GUEST "<HR>";
print GUEST "<STRONG>$name</STRONG><BR>";
print GUEST "$date<BR>";
print GUEST "$comments<P>\n";

flock(GUEST,$LOCK_UN);

print $query->header;
print $query->start_html;
print "<H2>Signature and Comments Added To Guestbook!</H2>";
print "<P>Thanks!";
print $query->end_html;
```

Look Ma! HTML!

While the addguests.cgi script screens out all metacharacters that could cause problems, it does allow in basic HTML tags. Users who know HTML can dress up their comments considerably, providing markup and links and even inline images. This can get out of hand. For example, if someone entered </HTML> as a tag, he or she might show up as the solitary guest amongst a host of invisible others. To restrict the ability to include HTML in the guest book, take out the <> characters from the permissible characters in the filters:

```
$name     =       $name =~ y/a-zA-z0-9_-+ \t\"\/\@\%\]//cd;
$comments =       $comments =~ y/a-zA-z0-9_-+ \t\"\/\@\%\]\n//cd;
```

That's it! A usable guest book ready for bells and whistles. You'll probably want to keep an eye on the file size, however. Trim it off or archive it if it grows too large. This will help keep response time to the guest book snappy.

Note The example didn't have a pathname for the guests.dat file. You'll need to put a fully qualified pathname for the location of the file on your system. You'll also need to make sure the file is world writable with the chmod o+w guests.dat command. Remember, you are not accessing this file with your account and login; rather, the Web server is accessing it, most likely with the default user "nobody".

QUIZ 7

1. Why was <BR> substituted for line feeds in the comment field?
   a to protect the script from metacharacters
   b. to separate the records for each line in the file
   c. because line feeds should not be used in files

    d. so the record could be displayed as HTML and preserve the line breaks the user entered

2. What happens if user A is trying to sign the guest book but user B has it locked?
   a. The script will return an error.
   b. User A's changes will write over user B's.
   c. The script for user A will wait until user B is finished, then add user A's signature.
   d. User A's changes will not be written to the guest book.

3. When the user signs the guest book, and then returns to it using the browser's Back arrow, why isn't the signature there?
   a. The file must have been locked.
   b. The user is looking at the guest book caches by the browser; he or she needs to use Reload to pick up the recent page.
   c. Some error occurred during the process.
   d. It's there, it's just at the bottom of the file, so the user should scroll down.

4. How could you address the problem in Question 3?
   a. Make sure the file was not locked when the script was run.
   b. Put a link on the Your Comments Added page that would link back to the guest book script forcing a refresh.
   c. It can't be addressed; it's just the nature of the browser.
   d. Reverse the file so the most recently added signature is displayed first.

Extra Credit:

    Why didn't the print reverse GUEST command print the name, date, and comments in reverse order, too?
   a. Because the file was opened in reverse.
   b. Because the guest book script was also revised to print name, date, and comments in reverse order.
   c. Because it prints out lines in reverse, and name,date, comments are one line.
   d. It does print name, date, and comments fields in reverse order.

EXERCISE 7

Describe how you could modify the guest book to support Interactive "chat" sessions.

ACCESS COUNTERS

Counters are the little numbers on a page that tell how many times it has been accessed. On fancy pages they are graphical numbers; on your pages they'll be graphical LEDs. To get this effect you'll need to put together what you've learned so far, along with just a little bit more. The little bit more part will be a short detour into special types of files call DBMs.

Perl and DBM Files

On UNIX systems, DBM, or database management files, are used to efficiently store, and more importantly, quickly retrieve records. Database management is a slight exaggeration. DBMs are not really designed to hold the stuff you would put in a relational database like Microsoft Access or Oracle. Typically, they hold only a pair of data elements: keys and values. Given a key, the DBM routines can zing back a value associated with this key.

Perl also has this key=value mechanism built into one of its own data types called an associative array. For example, the following:

```
%ideal_weekend=(
        'Sat', 'Saturday'
        'Sun', 'Sunday',
        'Mon', 'Monday',
        'Tue', 'Tuesday',
        'Wed','Wednesday');
```

creates the associative array %ideal_weekend, and assigns it a set of key=value pairs. Now to get the value of 'Mon', i.e., use the abbreviation to look up the value, you can use the following Perl syntax:

```
$today = $ideal_weekend{'Mon'};
```

and the value of $today will be "Monday". The curly braces are used on an associative array instead of the square brackets used on a normal array. Note also that when you are referring to an array element, the name is $ideal_weekend rather than %ideal_weekend, which refers to the associative array as a whole.

If these associative Perl arrays, which are stored in memory, could somehow be stored in key=value pairs on disk, you would have a natural way to store and retrieve data with Perl. Coincidentally, here's where the DBM routines come in. This function:

```
dbmopen( %myarray,'/usr/fred/mydata',0666);
```

will bind a DBM file called /usr/fred/mydata to an associative Perl array called %myarray. If the file does not exist, the 0666 option specifies a MODE in which the file will be created. These are regular UNIX file mode flags for creating the file. You can find more detail on mode options with the UNIX equivalent of help:

```
man chmod
```

For our purposes the 0666, which lets anyone read or write to the file, should work fine. The DBM routines will create two files:

```
/usr/fred/mydata.dir
/usr/fred/mydata.pag
```

These now hold any data put into the associative array %myarray, until the file is closed with

```
dbmclose(%myarray);
```

Let's open a DBM file, creating it if it doesn't exist, and load it with the values assigned before in %ideal_weekend:

```
dbmopen( %ideal_weekend,'/usr/fred/weekends',0666);
%ideal_weekend=(
        'Sat', 'Saturday'
        'Sun', 'Sunday',
        'Mon', 'Monday',
        'Tue', 'Tuesday',
        'Wed','Wednesday');
dbmclose(%ideal_weekend);
```

An important thing to note here is that any values assigned in the array before the dbmopen will be wiped out when dbmopen is used. That's why the assignments in the example came after dbmopen.

Not only are the values now in the %ideal_weekend array, they are also recorded on disk, in the files

```
/usr/fred/weekends.dir
/usr/fred/weekends.pag
```

Later, in some other program, you can open these files and the array will automatically be available to Perl. For example, this code from a Perl script written and run sometime after the one in the previous example:

```
dbmopen( %ideal_weekend,'/usr/fred/weekends',0666);
print $ideal_weekend{'Mon'};
dbmclose(%ideal_weekend);
```

would print

```
Monday
```

To update a value in the DBM file, simply assign it a new value in the Perl associative array that is bound to the DBM. The keys are unique, so if you assign a new value for 'Mon', it replaces what was there before. A couple of more operations that will come in handy:

```
$delete $ideal_weekend{'Mon'}  # To Delete A Key=Value
if defined($ideal_weekend{'Mon'} # To Test if A Value Exists
```

What Perl accomplishes with DBM is a way to retain data in a file that is simple to look up later. This comes in very handy for page counters.

What to Count

What the page counters represent is the number of times a page has been viewed on some browser. How do you get this information? If you said, "The access_log," you're right! And you've been doing your homework. In fact, some pages do use this approach. But let's look for something easier. Scanning the log file for hits on a particular page sounds like too much work. Anybody else?

A server side include? You're getting very warm. In fact, that technique is even more popular than scanning the log. The disadvantage to that approach is that you need to turn server side includes on for all your HTML files (or at least the files in directories where you want to maintain counters). This can lead to considerable overhead, and opens a potential security hole.

About the only thing left is the venerable <IMG SRC> trick, no? This allows you to call a script when the browser tries to download the image. Of course, it's expecting an image back, and would complain mightily if you sent back some dweeby numeric like a page count. But what if you sent back a GIF that just happened to have the graphical access counter? It just might work.

So much for the mechanism; what kinds of tricks does the script need to know? Well, first it needs to be able to update and retrieve information about the page and the number of times it has been accessed. DBM can handle this, and using the following variable from the CGI library, you can obtain the URL of the page calling you for an access count:

```
$myurl = $query->referer();
```

Putting these two concepts together, you can create a Perl snippet that will look up the URL in a DBM file (creating it if it doesn't exist). The URL will be the key; the value is the access count. If the URL key is not defined, create it, and set the access to 1. If it does exist, add one to the access count. Once you are done, check your code with the subroutine below. You should have something like the following:

```
dbmopen("%access,"/usr/local/etc/counts",0666);
$myurl = $query->referer;
if defined($count = $access{$myurl}) {
        $access{$myurl} = $count + 1;
        }
else    {
        $count = 1;
        $access{$myurl} = $count;
        }
dbmclose(%access);
```

Any time any page calls this script, that page's URL will be incremented or added to the DBM file. A variable called $count will contain the access counts for the page. Now you just need to turn this into a GIF file. For this you'll use the trusty GD library routines you used for Web games.

Copy Image

You actually could use the GD library directly to create a GIF with a number to send back. GD has a string function, and by creating an image block large enough to contain the numbers you wanted in it, and writing on the image with a function like

```
$myimage->string(gdSmallFont,5,5,"$count",$red);
```

you could actually pull it off. It won't quite give you the effect that you can produce with a little more effort. Try it, though, and see if you agree.

Another function of the GD library permits you to copy one image into another. This technique can be used to copy small panels of numbers, represented in their own GIF files, into an odometer of sorts. The copy function is

```
copy(source,dstX,dstY,srcX,srcY,width,height)
```

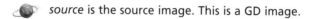 *source* is the source image. This is a GD image.

dstX, dstY are the x,y coordinates in the source to copy from.

srcX,srcY are the x,y coordinates in the image you're copying to.

width, height is the width and height of the region to copy.

For example, let's create an image file, load a GIF file, and copy the GIF into the GD image file, then print the GD out, converting it to GIF in the process. Whew! It's shorter in code than in English!

```
$destimage = new GD::Image(100,100);   # New GD image 100x100 pixels
open (GIF,"test.gif");
$srcimage = newFromGIF GD::Image(GIF); # Copy GIF into GD format
close(GIF);
$destimage = copy($srcimage,0,0,0,0,25,25,);   # copy a 25x25 pixel block
$print $destimage->gif;
```

Five lines of code. A GD object of 100 by 100 pixels was created, a GIF file that already existed was loaded into a separate, newly created, GD object. A square of 25 by 25 pixels from the GIF was copied into the the 100 by 100 pixel object, and the object was printed as a GIF file back through the CGI.

All you need now is a set of GIF images that represent LCD numbers. The images will each be 15 by 20 pixels, and they will be called 0.gif through 9.gif. You'll need to calculate how many you need based on how many digits are in *$count*. Perl makes this easy; *$count* can be used either as a number or as a character value. To find out how many characters wide it is, enter

```
$len = length($count);
```

The variable *$len* will be 2 if *$count* is a two-digit number, etc. To peel numbers off of *$count* one at a time, use

```
for ($i=0; $i<length($count); $i++) {
        print "Digit $i+1 is: $substr($count,$i,1);
        }
```

If *$count* were 1934, this routine would print

```
Digit 1 is: 1
Digit 2 is: 9
Digit 3 is: 3
Digit 4 is: 4
```

You have all the ingredients to construct a GD object, load the appropriate GIF(s) into the object, and present it back to the calling routine as a GIF counter. Go ahead and try to finish the Perl routine you started above, completing the access counter application. Compare your complete script with the script below. The steps needed in the completed script are

1. Look up a URL. If it exists, increment the count. If it doesn't, create an entry with a count of 1.

2. Create a GD image with a width of the number of digits in the count * 15. The height will be 20.

3. Copy the individual GIF files representing each digit in the count into the new GD object.

4. Send the GD object back to the CGI as a GIF file.

Your script should look something like the following:

```perl
#!/usr/local/bin/perl
use CGI;
use GD;
$query = new CGI;
dbmopen(%access,"/home/test/counts",0666);     # Open DBM with absolute path
$myurl = $query->referer();                     # What page accessed me?
if (defined($count = $access{$myurl})) {         # If in the database
        $access{$myurl} = $count + 1;            # increment the counter
        }
else    {                                       # otherwise create a new
        $count = 1;                              # entry and initialize
        $access{$myurl} = $count;
        }
dbmclose(%access);                              # All done and updated
$len = length($count);                          # Now process the count
$destimage = new GD::Image(15*$len,20);         # allocate for length of
$dstX = 0;                                       # digits
for ($i=0; $i<$len; $i++) {
        $gf = substr($count,$i,1);              # peel off number as character
        open (GIF,"../images/$gf.gif");         # tack it onto the GIF name
        $srcimage = newFromGif GD::Image(GIF);  # Copy GIF into GD format
        close(GIF);
        $destimage->copy($srcimage,$dstX,0,0,0,15,20);
        $dstX = $dstX + 15;                     # bump copy to next position
}
$|=1;
print $query->header("image/gif");              # MIME type of image
print $destimage->gif;                          # convert and send as GIF
```

Anywhere on your page that you want an access counter, you can use the following tag:

```
<IMG SRC="script-name">
```

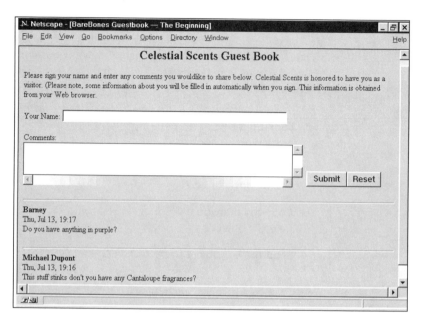

Figure 6-12
LED access counter

where *script-name* is the path and name of the script just created. Figure 6-12 shows the newly written access counter at work.

A couple of important notes: you will want to protect this script with the server protection mechanisms covered in Chapter 5, at least to the point of restricting it to local network access. Otherwise, you've given the Internet a free access counter that anyone can include in their pages with a simple <IMG SRC=> pointer.

Also, since the GIF images that make up the LCDs are provided on the CD under \images, you can change the colors, sizes, etc. In fact, with what you already know, you can make a simple addition to the script to make the background transparent, which allows the LCDs to look like they are part of the background of the page itself. Throw in a little animation, and your friends will really start to worry about you.

Limitations

Technically, this type of counter does not actually record all of the accesses to your page. It only records accesses with graphical browsers (when they load inline images). But this can also be an advantage; it tells you how many times your page was accessed in all its graphical glory. Those just passing through in search of commodity information are allowed to slide by without note or comment.

1. How would you make the counter's background transparent?
   a. use the GD function $image->transparent() on the GIF counters

    b. use the GD function $image->transparent() on the *$srcimage GD* object that holds the GIF objects

    c. use the GD function *$image->transparent()* on the *$destimage* the GIFs are moved into

    d. use the GD colorAllocate on the *$destimage* to set a default background color, then use $image->transparent passing this color as an argument

2. Why does the height of the counter image always remain the same no matter how many digits there are?

    a. The height field automatically adjusts with the copy command.

    b. The height field is ignored when using GIF files.

    c. Only the width field changes as more GIFs are added; they are all the same height.

    d. Only the width field changes; any number could be used for the height.

3. Why was $|=1 used in the counter script?

    a. to set the maximum number of GIF files

    b. to make sure the DBM file was closed

    c. to reset the counter

    d. to make sure the image was not buffered

4. What would be a potential obstacle to storing both a counter and a date in the DBM file, along with the URL?

    a. You would have to continually update the date.

    b. The date would overwrite the counter.

    c. The counter would overwrite the date.

    d. The value is a single value; you would have to concatenate the two and split them out again when accessing.

EXERCISE 8

Write a form and a script that will display all the URLs in the access file, and optional zero the file. To loop through an associative array in Perl, you can use the following syntax for the associative array %access:

```
while (($key,$value) = each %access) {
      print "URL = $key Access Count = $value\n";
      }
```

ORACLE DATABASES, VRML, OLE, AND THE OUTER LIMITS

ORACLE DATABASES, VRML, OLE, AND THE OUTER LIMITS

The topics in the following sessions skirt the fringes of what's evolving on the Web. They start with the Web's hooks into large relational databases. Using Oracle as representative, you'll discover ways to use SQL from Perl and write HTML with stored procedures. The topics then slide into other realms of the cyber landscape. Using Virtual Reality Modeling Language to construct three-dimensional spaces, home pages turn into home spaces, and you'll pop through one of these virtual corridors to touch upon Java, a powerful language that allows you to write scripts on the client. After Java, you'll explore client side scripting a little further, using OLE Automation to control Netscape from Visual Basic, learning how to retrieve URLs and post HTML forms from a Visual Basic application. The next topic explores the uses of PGP in your scripts, to send digitally signed messages from

397

a Web server, and to lay the foundation for understanding public and private key cryptography. Secure servers are next: what they buy you, how you can use them. The chapter ends with digital cash, and an experiment for setting up your own goods and services and charging cyberbucks to retrieve them. A lot to cover, so let's get started!

DATABASES AND THE WORLD WIDE WEB

While hypertext is a flexible way to organize free-form text, it is not the best choice for all applications. More conventional record formats, with data elements structured in repeating fields like name, address, and zip code, are often better suited to relational databases. Using forms and CGI scripts, the Web can effectively access relational data, usually far more efficiently than relational databases can extend to handle hypertext.

To maximize the Web's capabilities for dipping into relational data, a short excursion into the "cultural" differences between these two approaches is necessary.

Hypertext Versus the Relational Database

HTML is the language of the Web. You've seen how it is used to retrieve Web pages and initiate scripts through its use of URLs. In the world of the relational database, SQL (Structured Query Language) plays a similar role. SQL is the common language used to retrieve, update, delete, and otherwise manipulate data stored in a relational table. Figure 7-1 illustrates the difference between hypertext and relational databases.

Web pages are a polymorphous lot. You never know when you click a URL if you'll get a dense block of narrative text, a sparse outline of hyperlinks to other sources, a multimedia brochure, or a huge imagemap of a warthog with hotspots. Relational tables, on the other hand, are pretty boring.

They contain records, called rows, and each row contains exactly the same type of data as all the other rows in a table. Different tables can have different record structures. An employee table may contain names, addresses, hire-dates, etc., while an insurance table could contain providers, payment plans, and coverage; but within a single table every record has the same structure. Linking employees to their insurance policies is not done in the tables themselves; instead, it is done with SQL, and may look something like this:

```
select all employees.name where insurance.provider = "MegaHealth";
```

SQL can be executed in a variety of ways. It can be used in scripts, or within traditional application programming languages like COBOL and C. It can even be used

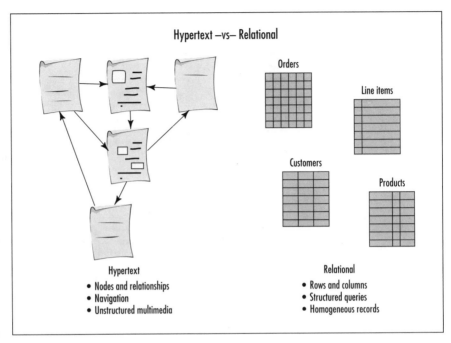

Figure 7-1
Hypertext versus
relational DBMs

internally in the database itself to create tables that are combinations and subsets of other tables. These are called views. For your purposes, you'll use SQL in scripts. After culling what is needed from the relational tables, the scripts will return results through the CGI to the Web.

Before diving in, though, another ingredient of relational databases needs to be explored: how they work on a network.

Relational Databases and Networks

SQL is not enough. Just as HTML would be pretty limited if it only worked on local files on your PC, SQL only begins to hit its stride when used across a network. And just as Web servers require a network protocol called HTTP to talk to browsers, SQL needs some way of communicating between client and server. For this it uses *middleware*.

Middleware

Middleware has been called the slash in client/server. It's big and ugly and it costs lots of money. All network browsers, whether they are Netscape, Mosaic, or Jill's Webrover (soon to be released?) use the same protocol (HTTP) to pass HTML. An SQL client on a PC, however, needs a different protocol depending on whether the database server is Oracle, Sybase, Informix, or one of eighteen other relational implementations. The

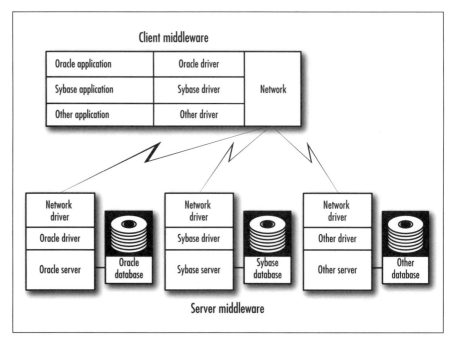

Figure 7-2
The middleware
stack

relational server needs a separate side of the middleware piece to talk to the client. This infamous middleware stack is depicted in Figure 7-2.

What if some of your data was in Oracle, some in Informix, and some in Sybase? Or what if you wanted to write an SQL "script" that worked with any of these databases? Even though SQL is universally understood by all relational databases, each client middleware piece has different conventions that govern how it receives the SQL from the client application. This means five different SQL scripts for five different servers. Or you could use ODBC.

ODBC

ODBC stands for Open Database Connectivity. It is a way of passing SQL across the network, through the proprietary middleware layers, that is transparent to an SQL script. The script doesn't need to know or care what flavor of relational database is on the server. As Figure 7-3 demonstrates, it doesn't really eliminate the individual stacks, it just adds another layer on top so the client application doesn't have to think about them. In Chapter 4 you used a Visual Basic interface to a Microsoft Access database. By changing the Open command from

```
Set db = OpenDatabase(dbname, True, False)
```

to

```
Set db = OpenDatabase("empdb",False,False,"UID=fred;PWD=frenchfry")
```

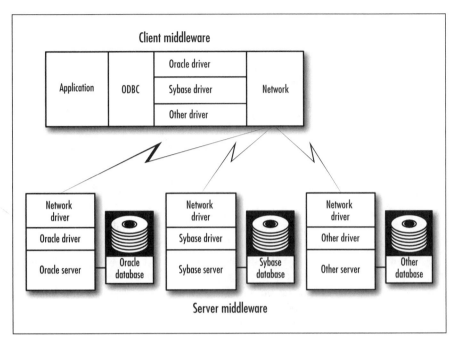

Figure 7-3
The ODBC stack

you could use an empdb database defined in the odbc.ini file. This entry could point to a corporate employee database running Sybase on a UNIX server, for example. The rest of the program would work pretty much as it was written. This is one strength of ODBC in the middleware equation.

ODBC on UNIX?

Initially ODBC was available only for Microsoft Windows, but today it is also available for UNIX platforms. This means you could use native scripting languages on UNIX with the universal ODBC widget to access any relational database. If you did this with Perl, for example, you could start using it in your CGI scripts. Feasible, but not necessary.

Now that you understand how a bread-and-butter client/server is implemented in the real world, let's look at how it can be deconstructed for the Web.

Just Say No to Middleware

Even with ODBC, the relational vendors get dollars for every middleware client. This part of the equation has sunk many client/server projects. With the vendors charging $100 per client for the middleware software, and then charging per client on the server side, the final totals for projects of even a modest scope can be alarming. Take into account the fact that the middleware client software comes out with new releases every year, and that installing the updates incurs maintenance costs, and you may be looking for alternatives…like the Web.

The Web has been a great integrator for the Internet, rolling up the various applications like FTP, Telnet, and Gopher into simple URLs navigated with the click of a mouse. The Web has also begun simplifying the middleware stacks of database vendors, eliminating the need for ODBC and proprietary client and server middleware, and rolling everything up into HTTP between the Web browser and the Web server. If servers, or more specifically, the CGI scripts, know how to access the database, the clients can be blissfully ignorant of the whole sticky middleware proposition. Figure 7-4 shows how this works.

Web forms pass query data to the CGI scripts on the Web server. CGI scripts query the database with SQL and return the results in HTML. The Web server can be on the same server as the relational database server, eliminating network overhead between the scripts running the SQL and the database. The effect is to sidestep the middleware layers of Figure 7-2.

All that remains is to figure out how the CGI scripts talk SQL to the relational databases. Luckily, a variety of mechanisms exist to do this, but let's pick one that uses Perl, building on what you have already learned. The following package runs against Oracle, one of the most popular and scalable of the relational technologies.

Oraperl

Oraperl is Perl 4 extended with 12 added functions for calling an Oracle database. (At the time of this writing, it was not yet ported to Perl 5.) The functions can connect to an Oracle database, log in with a username and password, send SQL queries, and retrieve results. Oraperl can be found at: http://dozer.us.oracle.com:8080/ in the Downloadables section (this is Oracle's home page of Web related resources).

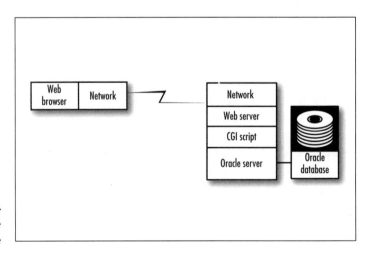

Figure 7-4
The middleware
alternative

SQL

It will be useful to know a bit of SQL before jumping into Oraperl. Table 7-1 is a quick rundown of some common SQL statements and what they do with a database.

Datatype	Description
CREATE TABLE	Creates a new relational table. When using this you'll need to define the fields (called columns) that make up the record, like name, address, zipcode.
	Example:
	CREATE TABLE sales (customerid INTEGER, orderdate DATE);
	Creates a table called sales with two fields: customerid and orderdate.
DROP TABLE	Deletes a table, and all of its data from a database.
	Example:
	DROP TABLE sales;
	Deletes the table named sales and all of its data (if any).
SELECT	The meat and potatoes of SQL, SELECT looks up values and returns them from one or more tables.
	Example:
	SELECT customerid,orderdate FROM sales WHERE customerid = 1;
	Retrieves the fields customerid and orderdate from the table called sales for all the rows with customerid equal to 1.
INSERT	Adds new records to a table.
	Example:
	INSERT INTO sales (customerid, orderdate) VALUES (1,'06-JUL-99');
	Adds a new row to the table named sales with a customer id of 1 and an order date of 06-JUL-99.
UPDATE	Changes the values of existing records (rows).
	Example:
	UPDATE sales SET orderdate='01-JAN-99' WHERE customerid = 1;
	Changes the value of orderdate to 01-JAN-99 in all the rows of the table that have a customer id of 1.

Table 7-1   *SQL flyby*

Oraperl Example

The following script in Oraperl prints all the rows of the employee table to your screen (stdout):

```
#!/usr/local/bin/oraperl
$lda = &ora_login('empdata', 'www_test', 'password') || die $ora_errstr;
$csr = &ora_open($lda, "select * from employees")     || die $ora_errstr;
while (@data = &ora_fetch($csr)) {
        print join('/',@data),"\n";
        }
warn "$ora_errstr" if $ora_errno;
&ora_close($csr)        || die $ora_errstr;
&ora_logoff($lda)       || die $ora_errstr;
```

Each individual function is discussed shortly, but the general flow is as follows:

1. Log in to the Oracle database with a database name, a user id, and password using &ora_login.

2. Take the identifier returned from &ora_login and use it as a parameter in &ora_open along with an SQL statement to be executed.

3. Use the cursor returned by &ora_open to retrieve the results of the SQL statement by passing the cursor to &ora_fetch. This returns the fields in a Perl list. Keep retrieving results until *&ora_fetch* is false.

4. Check for errors.

5. Free up the SQL statement with &ora_close.

6. Log out of the database with &ora_logoff.

The line:

```
die $ora_errstr;
```

prints out the Oracle error if the statement has a problem. Before writing a more substantial script, let's look at the Oraperl functions.

Essential Oraperl Functions

$lda = &ora_login(*database, username, password*)

This function is required before any other Oraperl functions are called. It logs into the database and establishes a link to send SQL and retrieve results.

 *database* is the Oracle database name.

 *username* is a username defined in Oracle.

password is the password for the Oracle username.

Returns:

A scalar variable representing a login identifier (*$lda*).

$csr = &ora_open($lda, *SQL statement* [, *rows*])

This function allocates and returns a cursor to receive the results of an SQL query.

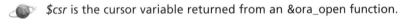 *$lda* is the value returned from &ora_login when successfully connected and logged in to the database.

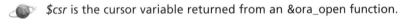 *SQL statement* is any valid SQL statement.

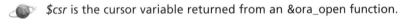 *rows* is an optional integer specifying how many rows should be cached in the return buffer for the cursor. Default is 5.

Returns:

A scalar variable identifying the cursor that holds the results of the SQL query ($csr).

&ora_fetch($csr [,trunc])

&ora_fetch is used to retrieve the results from an SQL SELECT statement used in &ora_open.

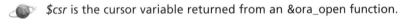 *$csr* is the cursor variable returned from an &ora_open function.

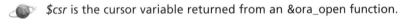 *trunc* is an optional value specifying whether to truncate LONG or LONGRAW datatypes if they are larger than the default 80-byte buffer. A nonzero value means truncation, a zero value means stop the program with an error.

Returns:

If you assign a scalar value to the &ora_fetch function, e.g.:

```
$nfields = &ora_fetch($csr,1)
```

it will return the number of fields in the row returned by an SQL SELECT statement. If you assign a list value, e.g.:

```
@row = &ora_fetch($csr,1)
```

then &ora_fetch will return the row of data, one field per list element. Any null values will be undefined in the Perl array.

Usage notes:

&ora_fetch returns rows until it runs out of data or encounters an error. Unfortunately, to differentiate between running out of data and encountering an error, you'll need to check the value of *$ora_errno* at the end of the loop. For example:

```
while (@data = &ora_fetch($csr, 1)) {
    # do something with the data
    }
warn $ora_errstr if $ora_errno;
```

&ora_bind($csr,*value1*,*value2*,*etc.*)

This substitutes variables into an SQL statement, if the SQL statement was used with placeholders in the &ora_open function.

🪐 *$csr* is the cursor identifier returned from the &ora_open function.

🪐 *value1...value(n)* are values substituted into a special type of &ora_open parameter that looks like this:

```
$csr = &ora_open($lda,'select * from emp where name=:1');
```

The *:1* is a placeholder for a variable that will be substituted later with the &ora_bind function. In this case &ora_open doesn't execute the SQL statement because it is not complete. It will be executed when &ora_bind uses the *$csr:*

```
&ora_bind($csr,'Fred');
```

Now you can use &ora_fetch to retrieve the results, exactly as if you had used

```
$csr = &ora_open($lda,'select * from emp where name=Fred');
```

Returns:
&ora_bind returns the number of rows affected by the command, or a value 'OK' if no rows were affected.

Usage notes:
You can use &ora_bind over and over again against the same $csr to look up different values, or in INSERT or UPDATE statements to make changes.

&ora_close($csr)

&ora_close is used to release the cursor identifier when the SQL statement is no longer needed. It's the cleanup for &ora_open.

🪐 *$csr* is the cursor identifier returned by the &ora_open function.

&ora_logoff($lda)

&ora_logoff logs you out of the database. It's the cleanup from &ora_login.

🪐 *$lda* is the database identifier.

These half-dozen functions are the essentials your scripts will need to manipulate an Oracle database. A few more, used in special circumstances, are covered next.

Commitment

Most relational databases allow you to back out of changes that you didn't really mean to make, and most will assume you don't really mean to make changes requested via

SQL until they see a *commit* statement. If you are writing a modest update script that adds data to tables, you can specify that Oraperl automatically assumes you are serious and commits each change to the database when the statement is executed. You can do this by calling the following function at the beginning of your script:

```
&ora_autocommit($lda,1);
```

This statement applies to operations at the database level (*$lda*), not the individual SQL statement level (*$csr*). A nonzero value means autocommit is enabled; a value of zero will disable autocommit and force committing changes manually with the following function:

```
&ora_commit($lda);
```

Autocommit is disabled by default, which can be a rude surprise. If you forget to use &ora_commit, or set &ora_autocommit, you'll find your Oraperl updates never seem to change any of the Oracle table data.

But you may also rely on this behavior. If autocommit is not enabled, and you want to back out of all of the changes made since the last commit, you can use this function:

```
&ora_rollback($lda);
```

Shortcuts

Some SQL commands, like DROP TABLE, don't return data that needs to be fetched. If you don't need to use placeholders and bind substitution values, you can use the

```
&ora_do($lda,$sql-statement)
```

function.

This statement doesn't require &ora_open and &ora_close to be called. It just zaps an SQL statement to the database and it's done. The whole script for dropping a table could be

```
#!/usr/local/bin/oraperl
$lda = &ora_login('empdata', 'www_test', 'password') || die $ora_errstr;
&ora_do('DROP TABLE sales'); || die $ora_errstr;
&ora_logoff($lda)          || die $ora_errstr;
```

Like &ora_bind, &ora_do returns the number of rows affected by the command, or 'OK' if no rows are affected.

The Long Story

While fetching data returned from a SELECT, Oraperl tries to allocate space to hold the value of each field. It has a slight problem with fields that are of type LONG or LONG-RAW. These fields can be up to two gigabytes in size, and Oraperl can't tell in advance how much space will actually be used. It makes a guess at 80 bytes, but if the values exceed this, it will flag the field as truncated. If you don't tell Oraperl to ignore the truncation, your script will bomb with an error. The default 80 assumption can be changed by setting the *$ora_long* variable to whatever you would like to preallocate for these fields.

Frills

The following functions are not essential to using SQL, but are useful for retrieving information from Oracle in your scripts:

```
@titles = &ora_titles($csr [, $truncate])
```

This returns the title of each field returned in the csr query. The fields are strings, and the strings are truncated to the length of the field unless the optional $truncate$ value is used and specified as zero.

```
@lengths = &ora_lengths($csr)
```

This returns the length of each field in the csr query in an array of integers.

```
@types = &ora_types($csr)
```

This returns the type of each field. Oracle datatypes are listing in Table 7-2.

Datatype	Description
CHAR(size)	Fixed-length character strings up to 32767 bytes.
DATE(DATE)	Dates and times.
LONG (LONG VARCHAR)	Stores large, variable length character strings up to 2GB!
NUMBER(precision,scale) (FLOAT,NUMERIC, DECIMAL,DEC,INTEGER, INT,SMALLINT,REAL, DOUBLE,PRECISION)	All types of numbers.
LONG RAW	Long binary strings.
RAW(size)	Binary strings of less than 2,000 bytes.
VARCHAR2(size)	Variable-length character strings of up to 32,767 bytes.

Table 7-2   *Oracle datatypes*

Oraperl Scripts

Here are a few scripts you can use to experiment with Oraperl. You'll look at sample scripts for creating tables, inserting and deleting data, and searching and listing records.

Creating Tables

Using the Oracle datatypes listed in Table 7-2, let's write an Oraperl script to create an Oracle table with the following fields:

Empid, FirstName, LastName, Department, Phone

Here's a sample:

```
#!/usr/local/bin/oraperl
print "Enter Password: ";
system 'stty' , '-echo';        # turn echo off
$pw=<STDIN>;
system 'stty' , 'echo';         # turn echo back on
chop($pw);

$lda = &ora_login('whse','www_script',$pw);
&ora_do($lda, 'DROP TABLE employees');
&ora_do($lda, <<END_OF_CREATE) || die $ora_errstr;
CREATE TABLE employees (
        empid integer primary key,
        firstname CHAR(15),
        lastname CHAR(25),
        dept CHAR(45),
        phone CHAR(80),
        notes VARCHAR2(2000),
        hired DATE)
END_OF_CREATE
&ora_commit($lda) || print $ora_errstr;
&ora_logoff($lda);
```

The DROP TABLE before it's run is useful in the early stages when you are revising the table design. It deletes the table before recreating it. The script prompts for a password that it uses to log in to Oracle as "www_script". This eliminates the need to hardcode the password in the script.

Sequence Numbers

Note that the empid field is created as a primary key. A primary key is used to uniquely identify a record. If you already have an employee ID that is unique for each individual, you can use it in this field, but Oracle also provides a means to automatically generate a unique key using a sequence number. This is useful for record types like purchase orders and invoice numbers. In Oracle you can create a sequence number for the table above by using the following SQL:

```
#!/usr/local/bin/oraperl
print "Enter Password: ";
system 'stty' , '-echo';        # turn echo off
$pw=<STDIN>;
system 'stty' , 'echo';         # turn echo back on
chop($pw);

$lda = &ora_login('whse','www_scripts',$pw);
$cmd = "create sequence empseq start with 1 increment by 1 nomaxvalue nocycle cache 20";
&ora_do($lda, $cmd) || die $ora_errstr;
&ora_commit($lda) || print $ora_errstr;
&ora_logoff($lda);
```

You'll need the DBA (database administrator) to grant you SEQUENCE privileges (CREATE, ALTER, and SELECT) to manipulate these in Oracle. The sequence object *empseq*, created above, can now be used to generate unique values. Whenever you need a new value for adding a new record to the employees' table, retrieve it via an SQL reference to

```
empseq.nextvalue
```

For example, to add a new employee, use the following SQL:

```
insert into checkout values empseq.nextval,'Fred','Flintstone', ...
```

This returns the next sequence number, and increments *empseq* for the next time it is used.

Insert and Delete

To insert records using Oraperl and the CGI, you can use the cgi-lib library for Perl 4 (CGI.pm only works with Perl 5). Here's an example of a script that retrieves form input values for employee data and adds them to the employees' table in Oracle:

```perl
#!/usr/local/bin/oraperl
require 'cgi-lib.pl';

&ReadParse(*in);
$lda = &ora_login('p:whse','www_scripts','sinatra') || print $ora_errstr;

$sql = "insert into employees values
            (chkoutseq.nextval,
            \'$in{'first'}\',
            \'$in{'last'}\',
            \'$in{'dept'}\',
            NULL,NULL,NULL)";

&ora_do($lda,$sql) || print "$ora_errstr\n";
&ora_commit($lda)  || print $ora_errstr;
&ora_logoff($lda);
```

To change the values of an existing record, just modify the SQL string above to

```perl
$sql = "update employees
        set lastname = \'$in{'last'}\',
            firstname = \'$in{'first'}\',
            dept = \'$in{'dept'}\'
        where empid = $in{'empid'}";
```

Here's the value of the unique key; without it, you would have trouble updating precisely the record you want, especially since there could be duplicates. This same unique id can be used to delete a record:

```perl
$sql = "delete from employees where empid = $in{'empid'}";
```

Searching and Listing

This next Oraperl script will look up an employee ID passed from a form, and print the last name and first name of the matching employee:

```perl
#!/usr/local/bin/oraperl
require 'cgi-lib.pl';
```

```
&ReadParse(*in);
$lda = &ora_login('p:whse','www_scripts','sinatra') || print $ora_errstr;

$csr = &ora_open($lda, 'select lastname,firstname from employees where empid = :1') || die
$ora_errstr;


&ora_bind($csr, $in{'empid'))  || die $ora_errstr;

if (($lastname,$firstname) = &ora_fetch($csr)) {
        print "$lastname,$firstname\n";
        }
else {
        die $ora_errstr if $ora_errno;
        print "unknown\n";
}

&ora_close($csr);
&ora_logoff($lda);
```

Since you used &ora_open in this script, you needed to use &ora_close before logging out to release any storage allocated for the cursor. The next example takes a username, password, and table name passed from a form, and prints the contents of the table (careful!):

```
#!/usr/local/bin/oraperl
require 'cgi-lib.pl';

&ReadParse(*in);
$lda = &ora_login('p:whse',$in{'username'},$in{'password') || print    $ora_errstr;

$csr = &ora_open($lda, "select * from $in{'table'}")  || die $ora_errstr;

while (@data = &ora_fetch($csr)){
        print join("', '", @data),"\n";
        }
warn "$ora_errstr" if $ora_errno;

&ora_close($csr)        || die $ora_errstr;
&ora_logoff($lda)       || die $ora_errstr;
```

Debugging Oraperl

If you include the following line at the beginning of your Oraperl scripts:

```
$ora_debug = shift if $ARGV[0] =~ /^-#/;
```

you can then invoke the script in debugging mode by entering -#d on the command line. For example, the script dump.cgi contains

```
#!/usr/local/bin/oraperl
require 'cgi-lib.pl';
$ora_debug = shift if $ARGV[0] =~ /^-#/;
```

continued on next page

continued from previous page

```
#
# Dump all records from the employee table
#
$lda = &ora_login('p:whse','www_scripts','sinatra') || die $ora_errstr;
$csr = &ora_open($lda,"select firstname from employees
                where firname='Arnold'") ||
                die $ora_errstr;
#
while (@data = &ora_fetch($csr)) {
        print join('/',@data),"\n";
        }
#
# Cleanup
#
warn "$ora_errstr" if $ora_errno;
&ora_close($csr);
&ora_logoff($lda);
```

Running

```
dump.cgi -#d
```

from the command line generated the following detailed information about the interaction between Oraperl and Oracle (partial listing!):

```
?func: info: ora_debug set to d
ora_login: entry: ora_login("p:whse", "www_scripts", "sinatra")
ora_getlda: entry: ora_getlda(void)
ora_getcursor: entry: ora_getcursor(void)
ora_getcursor: malloc: got a cursor at 0x1400f7b80
ora_getcursor: malloc: got a csr at 0x1400f7c00
ora_getcursor: exit: returning 0x1400f7b80
ora_getlda: malloc: got hda at 0x1400b5600
ora_getlda: exit: returning 0x1400f7b80
set_sid: entry: set_sid(p:whse)
set_sid: info: setting TWO_TASK to p:whse
set_sid: entry: set_sid(<NULL>)
set_sid: info: no value to reset ORACLE_SID/TWO_TASK
ora_login: conv: lda 0x1400f7b80 converted to string "0x1400f7b80"
ora_login: exit: returning lda 0x1400f7b80
ora_open: entry: ora_open(0x1400f7b80, "select firstname from employees
        where firstname='Arnold'", 5)
ora_open: conv: string "0x1400f7b80" converted to lda 0x1400f7b80
check_lda: entry: check_lda(0x1400f7b80)
ora_findcursor: entry: ora_findcursor(0x1400f7b80)
ora_findcursor: exit: is a cursor
check_lda: exit: is an lda
ora_getcursor: entry: ora_getcursor(void)
ora_getcursor: malloc: got a cursor at 0x1400f7f00
ora_getcursor: malloc: got a csr at 0x1400f7f80
ora_getcursor: exit: returning 0x1400f7f00
count_colons: entry: count_colons("select firstname from employees
        where firstname='Arnold'")
```

```
count_colons: exit: count_colons: returning 0
ora_open: info: statement contains 0 colons
ora_open: info: statement returns 1 fields
ora_open: malloc: got data array 1 items 8 bytes at 0x1400eefc0
ora_open: malloc: got len array 1 items 2 bytes at 0x1400eefe0
ora_open: malloc: got rcode array 1 items 8 bytes at 0x1400ef000
ora_open: malloc: got type array 1 items 2 bytes at 0x1400ef020
ora_open: malloc: got field 0, 80 bytes at 0x140100000
ora_open: malloc: got rcode 0, 10 bytes at 0x1400ef040
ora_open: info: Field 0, length 15, type 1 (character array)
ora_open: malloc: got ora_result 8 bytes at 0x1400ef060
ora_open: conv: csr 0x1400f7f00 converted to string "0x1400f7f00"
ora_open: exit: returning csr "0x1400f7f00"
ora_fetch: entry: ora_fetch(0x1400f7f00, 0)
ora_fetch: conv: string "0x1400f7f00" converted to csr 0x1400f7f00
check_csr: entry: check_csr(0x1400f7f00)
ora_findcursor: entry: ora_findcursor(0x1400f7f00)
ora_findcursor: exit: is a cursor
check_csr: exit: is a csr
ora_fetch: info: setting end_of_data
ora_fetch: info: fetched 1 rows
ora_fetch: info: returning row 0 from cache:
ora_fetch: info: field     0 (140100000) data "Arnold"
ora_fetch: exit: returning 1 items
Arnold
ora_fetch: entry: ora_fetch(0x1400f7f00, 0)
ora_fetch: conv: string "0x1400f7f00" converted to csr 0x1400f7f00
check_csr: entry: check_csr(0x1400f7f00)
ora_findcursor: entry: ora_findcursor(0x1400f7f00)
ora_findcursor: exit: is a cursor
check_csr: exit: is a csr
ora_fetch: exit: end of data
ora_close: entry: ora_close(0x1400f7f00)
ora_close: conv: string "0x1400f7f00" converted to csr 0
etc.!
```

1. What is the function &ora_bind used for?
   a. to commit changes to the database
   b. to open the database
   c. to lock a record
   d. to substitute variables for placeholders in an SQL statement

2. At the end of the following script, what functions are necessary to cleanly exit?

```
#!/usr/local/bin/oraperl
$lda = &ora_login('p:whse','www_scripts','sinatra') || print $ora_errstr;
&ora_do($lda,"DROP TABLE employees") || print "$ora_errstr\n";
```

    a. &ora_bind, &ora_close
    b. &ora_close
    c. &ora_logoff
    d. &ora_close, &ora_logoff

3. Why can't &ora_do be used as follows: &ora_do($lda,"select * from sales");?
    a. It must be used with a cursor rather than a login identifier.
    b. You can't execute SQL with &ora_do.
    c. &ora_do is not used on SQL that returns rows.
    d. &ora_do only takes one argument.

4. All Oraperl defaults are in effect, and an insert statement from an &ora_do
function is not working. What could be one possible reason?
    a. The bind is not being performed correctly.
    b. The change was not committed.
    c. A long field was used.
    d. Insert statements should not be used from the &ora_do function.

WOW

In this session you'll go deeper into the Oracle database, so deep you'll be writing HTML from within it! WOW from Oracle provides a way to write scripts using procedures stored in the database itself. To understand how WOW does this, let's look at the big picture.

The WOW Architecture

WOW stands for Web-Oracle-Web, and consists of three major components that all reside on the Web server:

 A shell script for setting variables about the database, user, and password

 A C program called wowstub that is the middleman between the CGI and Oracle

 A PL/SQL package called WOW that executes PL/SQL procedures that you write yourself

The WOW software kit can be obtain free via http://dozer.us.oracle.com:8080/.

    WOW expects Oracle to be installed on the same server as the Web. This might seem like a limitation, but once you are connected to one Oracle server, it's quite easy to link to other Oracle databases on other platforms across the network.

    Figure 7-5 illustrates how a form calls a stored procedure in the Oracle database using WOW.

    But what exactly is a stored procedure? Time to find out a little more about PL/SQL.

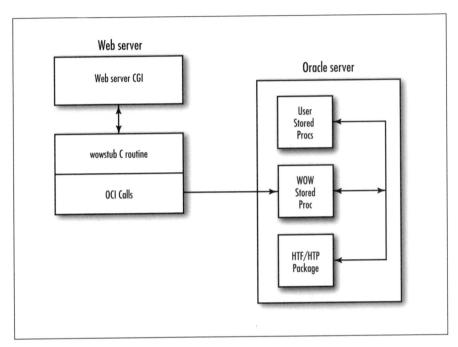

Figure 7-5
The WOW
architecture

PL/SQL

SQL is a nonprocedural language. You describe what you want, and SQL figures out how to get it. PL/SQL wraps a procedural framework around SQL. It adds structure like loops, if-then-else blocks, and other primitives to control the how and what of execution. Essentially it's a programming language, and in fact it was modeled after Ada. This makes PL/SQL a flexible tool for writing CGI scripts.

PL/SQL scripts are stored in the database server and referred to as *stored procedures*. These procedures are "compiled" by the server, and execute much more efficiently than individual SQL statements passed through client applications like Oraperl.

PL/SQL Template

A vanilla PL/SQL procedure looks something like the following:

```
procedure test (name1 IN varchar2, name2 IN varchar2)
is
nlen integer;
begin
nlen := 0;
if soundex(name1) = soundex(name2) then
    dbms_output.put_line(name1 || ' sounds like ' || name2);
else
```

continued on next page

continued from previous page

```
        nlen := length(name1);
        dbms_output.put_line('Names do not sound alike');
  end if;
  end;
```

The procedure name is "test"; it expects two variables using the same SQL datatypes you worked with in Table 7-2. A local variable *nlen* is defined as an integer; the declaration *is* indicates that what follows is the beginning of the procedure block (as opposed to the variable definitions). The length is set to zero. All assignment statements use the Ada variable := value convention. The first variable passed to the procedure is translated to soundex and tested to see if it is phonetically equivalent to the second. A message is displayed in what passes for standard output in PL/SQL, and if they don't sound alike, the length of the first variable is assigned to the variable *nlen*.

Note that the use of semicolons to terminate statements is kind of tricky. The semicolons end statements or blocks.

Oracle provides documentation on writing PL/SQL if you want to delve into the language for more sophisticated scripts. As you did with Perl, you'll just be scratching the surface of the language in this session. But while you won't be getting that deep into PL/SQL, you will learn all the mechanics of installing, testing, and accessing PL/SQL procedures from the Web.

Creating Stored Procedures

You can write PL/SQL procedures with any ASCII editor, just like any script. To install PL/SQL, however, you will need to use a client application. The most readily available one generally comes on the Oracle server; it's called SQL*Plus. It's basically a command-line interface to SQL. Here are the steps you need to follow to create and install a PL/SQL procedure, assuming you are logged in to a UNIX server that has Oracle installed.

1. Create the PL/SQL procedure with vi, emacs, or whatever editor is handy. As the first line of the procedure, instead of

```
procedure test (name IN varchar2, age IN integer)
```

use

```
create or replace procedure test (name IN varchar2,
age IN integer)
```

After you've finished entering the procedure, save the file as whatever filename you like, but make the filetype .sql.

2. Start SQL*Plus by entering

```
sqlplus
```

from the command line and log in to Oracle.

3. From the

```
SQL>
```

prompt, enter

```
SQL>@procname
```

where *procname* is whatever you called the procedure (without the .sql filetype). This will load the procedure into the SQL*Plus buffer. Now enter

```
SQL>/
```

This will compile the PL/SQL code and store it in Oracle.

4. If you get any errors, enter

```
SQL>show errors
```

Identify the line numbers in error and, if you are using vi for example, enter

```
SQL>!vi procname.sql
```

This will shell you to vi and edit the procname.sql. After you make your changes and save the file, you will be returned to the sql prompt. Reiterate step 3.

5. Enter

```
SQL>commit;
SQL>quit
```

to exit SQL*Plus and return to the UNIX command line.

Packages

A *package* is a set of related procedures. This concept was borrowed from Ada, and it wouldn't be important for your purposes except that one important piece of the WOW solution is contained in a package: the HTP/HTF procedures.

The HTP/HTF Package

This package, provided in the WOW distribution, makes it easy to send HTML back through the CGI. You can, of course, send output back without using the HTP/HTFpackage by using the dbms_output statement. Dbms_output is also a package, but it doesn't understand HTML; it's like using print in Perl. HTP/HTF is more like using CGI.pm.

Here's an example of a snippet of PL/SQL code that sends back a minimal HTML document:

```
dbms_output.putline('<TITLE>WOW Results</TITLE>')
dmbs_output.putline('Hello World!')
```

Here's code that produces the same output using the HTP/HTF package:

```
htp.htitle('WOW Results');
htp.p('Hello World');
```

In either case, you don't need to worry about the content-type header or the beginning <HTML> or closing <HTML> tags. These are taken care of by the WOW interface.

Besides these minimal functions, HTP/HTF has several more that encompass most of HTML 2.0, and parts of HTML 3.0. Here are some other useful HTP/HTF routines:

htp.header(n,'text');

where

n = header level (1—6).
'text' is the text appearing in the header.

htp.bold('text');
htp.italic('text');
htp.para;

generates a <P>

htp.preOpen;

generates <PRE>

htp.preClose;

generates </PRE>

htp.line;

generates a

htp.formOpen(*url*);

generates a <FORM ACTION="*url*">

htp.formClose;

generates the </FORM> end tag

htp.formDo(*text*);

generates a submit button with optional label

htp.formUndo(*text*);

generates the reset button with optional label

htp.p(*text*)

is a generic print. It can include text and functions (see below).

The HTP routines are procedures, and they generate output. The HTF preface works like functions, and will return, but not print, a value. This allows flexibility in building your HTML output. For example:

```
htf.formField('name',15)
```

formField is called with the HTF package, causing it to return (rather than print) the following value:

```
<INPUT TYPE='text' NAME='name' SIZE=15>
```

This can be used in a prompt for name by including this function in

```
htp.p('Enter Name: ' || htf.formField('name',15));
```

You could, of course, use

```
htp.p('Enter Name: ');
htp.formField('name',15);
```

to produce a less concise version with the same effect.

This is not the complete list of HTP routines. For a comprehensive list of all the routines in the package, consult the Oracle Web page in the installation section for this chapter.

Here is a short example of a procedure that generates an HTML form. It expects no parameters. Open a file called quiz.sql on your Web server and enter the following:

```
create or replace procedure quiz is
begin
        htp.htitle('Quiz');
        htp.formOpen('/cgi-bin/wow/quiz');
        htp.header(3, 'Enter Your Name: ' || htf.formField('name'));
        htp.p('<HR>');
        htp.p('<b>Choose: </b>' || htf.formSelectOpen('ctype'));
        htp.formSelectOption('The Prince Of Zimbago');
        htp.formSelectOption('The Prince of Chinook');
        htp.formSelectOption('The Queen of Egypt');
        htp.formSelectClose; htp.para;
        htp.formDo('Answer');
        htp.formUndo;
        htp.formClose;
end;
```

Loading the procedure into Oracle using the five steps above, and with the WOW interface installed on your system, activate this PL/SQL code from your Web browser by using the following URL:

```
http://test.com/cgi-bin/wow/quiz
```

The results are displayed in Figure 7-6.

Note that the WOW script in cgi-bin must be edited and a username and password must be supplied. Your stored procedures must be available for access from this user id. The Oracle DBA can set this up for you.

Passing Form Variables to Stored Procedures

The quiz procedure above didn't accept any input, but adding this ability to your PL/SQL scripts is not hard. The values can be passed with either an implicit GET, as in the following:

```
http://test.com/cgi-bin/wow/quiz?name=joe
```

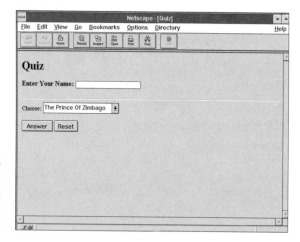

Figure 7-6
A form generated
with PL/SQL and
the HTP/HTF
package

or as POST variables within a form.

The variables passed to the script from the form must be predefined in a PL/SQL parameter list. This is the set of variables in the parentheses right after the script name. A form that passed a name and option value to the tester script would need the tester PL/SQL script to be defined as

```
procedure tester (name IN varchar2, option IN varchar2)...
```

The variables in the parameter have to have the same names as the variables in the Web form.

A Simple PL/SQL Lookup

Let's write a simple PL/SQL script to look up a text string found anywhere in a name in a database and return all the rows whose name contains the text string. The HTML for the form could look like this:

```
<HTML>
<HEAD>
<TITLE>Employee Lookup Screen</TITLE>
</HEAD>
<H2 ALIGN=center>Employee Lookup</H2>
<P>Enter any text that appears in an employee name to look up the
employee in the Corporate directory
<HR>
<FORM ACTION="http://www.test.com/cgi-bin/wow/empfind" METHOD=POST>
<TABLE>
<TD>Enter Partial Name:
<TD><INPUT TYPE="text" SIZE=25 NAME="ename" VALUE="" MAXLENGTH=60>
</TABLE>
</FORM>
</BODY>
</HTML>
```

The PL/SQL procedure this form calls would be empfind.sql and contain the following:

```
procedure empfind
        (ename in varchar2) is
        cursor c is select name from phonelist
where upper(name) like ('%' || upper(ename) || '%');
begin
htp.htitle('Search Results');
htp.header(2,'Search results for: ' || ename);
htp.para;
htp.uListOpen;
for l in c loop
        htp.item;
        htp.p(l.name);
end loop;
htp.uListClose;
wow.sig('empfind');
end;
```

Self-documentsing! Note the wow.sig in Figure 7-7. Clicking on this returns the source code for the stored procedure, shown in Figure 7-8.

The cursor, used as a variable above, is somewhat similar to the cursors you used in Oraperl. They contain the results of multirow queries. The loop extracts each row returned in a cursor. If you knew only a single row of data was coming back, say with a key field look up, you could use

```
c_name varchar2(60);
c_date date;
begin
        select name, date into c_name, c_date
        from orders where id=4444;
```

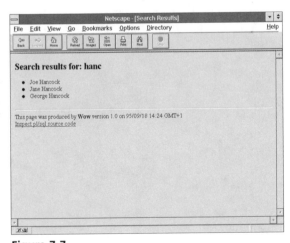

Figure 7-7
Results with wow.sig

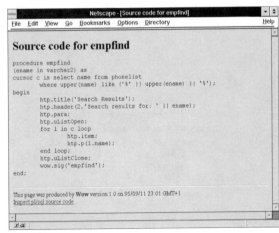

Figure 7-8
Source code

This snippet returns the values of name and date, storing them in the variables *c_name* and *c_date*.

Debugging from SQL*Plus

Before you get into the next PL/SQL example, let's look briefly at debugging PL/SQL. The five-step procedure for creating stored procedures didn't delve into how to test them. As it is for the scripts you wrote for CGI, it's generally a good idea to test and debug the execution of a script stand-alone, before introducing other variables like Web forms and gateways. This can be done for PL/SQL from SQL*Plus. You'll pick up back at the SQL> prompt, after entering *sqlplus* and logging into the database.

To test the empfind procedure above, you would enter the following two lines:

```
SQL>set serveroutput on
SQL>begin empfind('hanc'); end;
```

When you press <ENTER>, you'll get a line number prompt:

```
2
```

Enter a "/" and press <ENTER>. This executes the stored procedure empfind, passing it the variable *hanc*. You should see the HTML generated by the HTP/HTF package displayed on your screen. You can test various parameters and ensure that your procedure is working as expected before subjecting it to tests from the Web. So now, on to the project at hand.

WOW Example

With all your tools in place, let's create a sample questionnaire that will solicit data via a form and store the data entered directly into an Oracle table using WOW. Be sure to log in to Oracle with an account that the WOW login can access.

First you will need to create a table. From the SQL*Plus prompt enter the following lines:

```
SQL>create table survey
        (name  varchar2(60),
         email varchar2(60),
         itype varchar2(60),
         iother varchar2(60),
         ctype varchar2(20),
         cother varchar2(60),
         cversion varchar2(10),
         country varchar2(60));
/
SQL>commit;
SQL>quit
```

Now open a new Web page for the form and enter the following HTML:

```
<HTML>
```

```
<HEAD>
<TITLE>Web Survery</TITLE>
</HEAD>

<BODY>
<H1>Subscription Survey</H1>
<FORM METHOD="POST" ACTION="/cgi-bin/wow/survey">
Please fill out the following information for your free
subscription to <em>Motif and Metaphor:</em>.


<TABLE BORDER=5>
<TD><STRONG>Name: </STRONG><input type="text" name="name" value=""size=35 maxlength=60>
<TD><STRONG>E-Mail Address: </STRONG><input type="text" name="email" value="" size=35
maxlength=60>
<TR>
<TD><STRONG>What kind of Internet connectivity do you have:</STRONG><br>
<INPUT TYPE="radio" NAME="itype" VALUE="direct" checked>direct TCP/IP<br>
<INPUT TYPE="radio" NAME="itype" VALUE="lease">leased line SLIP/PPP to service provider<br>
<INPUT TYPE="radio" NAME="itype" VALUE="dial">dial-up SLIP/PPP to service provider<br>
<INPUT TYPE="radio" NAME="itype" VALUE="online">Online Service Provider (e.g. AOL, Prodigy,
etc.)<br>
<INPUT TYPE="radio" NAME="itype" VALUE="other">other:
<INPUT TYPE="text" NAME="itypetext" VALUE="" SIZE=20 MAXLENGTH=60><br>
<TD><STRONG>What Web client are you using:</STRONG><br>
<INPUT TYPE="radio" NAME="client" VALUE="Netscape" checked>Netscape<br>
<INPUT TYPE="radio" NAME="client" VALUE="Mosaic">Mosaic<br>
<INPUT TYPE="radio" NAME="client" VALUE="Lynx">Lynx<br>
<INPUT TYPE="radio" NAME="client" VALUE="Macweb">MacWeb<br>
<INPUT TYPE="radio" NAME="client" VALUE="Winweb">WinWeb<br>
<INPUT TYPE="radio" NAME="client" VALUE="Cello">Cello<br>
<INPUT TYPE="radio" NAME="client" VALUE="other">other:
<INPUT TYPE="text" NAME="clienttext" VALUE="" SIZE=20 MAXLENGTH=60><br>
<TR>
<TD>
<TD>
<TR>
<TD><STRONG>Country: </STRONG><input type="text" name="country" value="" size=10
maxlength=60><p>
<TD><STRONG>Web client version number:</STRONG><br>
<INPUT TYPE="text" NAME="cversion" SIZE=5 MAXLENGTH=10 VALUE=""><p>
<TR>
</TABLE>

<P><INPUT TYPE="submit" VALUE="Submit">
<INPUT TYPE="reset" VALUE="Clear"><BR>

</FORM>
</BODY>
</HTML>
```

Figure 7-9 shows what this page should look like.

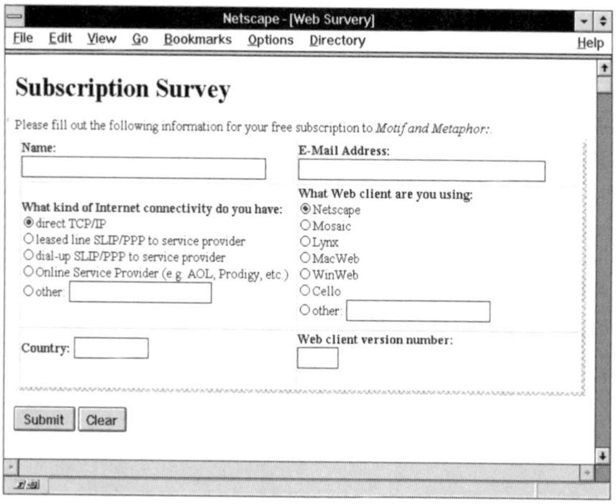

Figure 7-9
WOW
questionnaire
—the form

All that's left is the stored procedure. Use the five-step process to enter the following stored procedure into Oracle:

```
create or replace procedure survey
(name    in      varchar2,
 email   in      varchar2,
 itype   in      varchar2,
 itypetext       in      varchar2,
 client  in      varchar2,
 clienttext      in      varchar2,
 cversion        in      varchar2,
 country in      varchar2)
as
v_itext VARCHAR2(60):=NULL;
v_ctext VARCHAR2(60):=NULL;
begin
        v_itext := itypetext;
        v_ctext := clienttext;
        IF itype != 'other' THEN
                v_itext := NULL;
        END IF;
        IF client != 'other' THEN
                v_ctext := NULL;
        END IF;
        insert into surveytable values (
                name, email, itype, v_itext, client, v_ctext,
                cversion, country);
        htp.htitle(' Subscription Survey ');
        htp.header(2, 'Thank you for completing the survey');
        htp.line;
        htp.para;
```

```
htp.bold('Your first issue should be arriving shortly');
htp.para;
htp.line;
htp.italic('Copyright (1996) Motify And Metaphor, Ltd.');

end;
```

Now load the form, fill in some data, and click Submit. If all goes well, you should see results similar to those in Figure 7-10.

Advantages of Stored Procedures

WOW and its use of stored procedures offers several advantages over the interpreted SQL approach of Oraperl:

- Better performance. Procedures are compiled and stored on the server, reducing network overhead and server CPU for processing raw SQL statements.

- Reusable code. Procedures can be reused from other Web forms on other platforms since they are in the database, not embedded as functions in Perl scripts.

- Better security. Procedures are first-class Oracle objects; they can be controlled with all of the Oracle mechanisms for fine-grained protection of resources within the database.

- Skill sets. WOW allows developers conversant in PL/SQL to develop and maintain Web applications; they don't need to learn Perl.

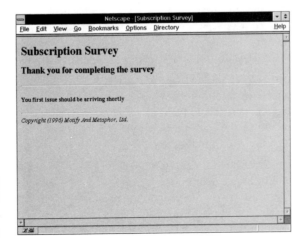

Figure 7-10
WOW
questionnaire—
the WOW update

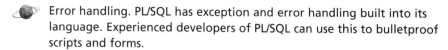 Error handling. PL/SQL has exception and error handling built into its language. Experienced developers of PL/SQL can use this to bulletproof scripts and forms.

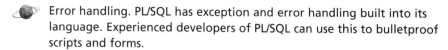 Modularization. PL/SQL's use of packages modularize large applications. Data hiding, function, and procedural overload are part of PL/SQL's inheritence, having been modeled after Ada.

That's it for Oracle. Now we'll leave for other uncharted realms of Web authoring…like Virtual Reality.

 By default WOW will display a WOW logo GIF on all your stored procedures executed from its interface. To get rid of this "feature", edit the wow.sql package. Find the line assigning the *wowgif* variable to a GIF file and replace it with the following:

```
wowgif varchar2(255) := 'NONE';
```

Reload the wow.sql package just the way you installed PL/SQL above. It will replace the old WOW with the new, GIF-less one.

An active page for WOW users and subscription to mailing list are available at http://gserver.grads.vt.edu/. This page also has extensions to the HT package for tables, etc.

1. Parameters passed from Web forms to PL/SQL procedures must
   a. have the same name as those in the PL/SQL parameter list
   b. be passed using the POST method
   c. have the same name as the fields in the database
   d be passed using the GET method

2. From the SQL*Plus prompt, what does @test followed by "/" do?
   a. executes test.sql
   b. edits test.sql
   c. executes test
   d. compiles and stores test.sql into Oracle

3. The HTP/HTF package provides a way to
   a. create HTML from PL/SQL code
   b. pass parameters to PL/SQL
   c. manipulate SQL from within PL/SQL
   d. call PL/SQL from Perl

4. A cursor variable is used in PL/SQL to
   a. control the cursor on the screen
   b. position a user at the beginning of a form text field
   c. retrieve multiple rows from a SELECT statement
   d. send output to the terminal for debugging

VIRTUAL REALITY ON THE WEB

VRML stands for Virtual Reality Modeling Language. It's the evolution of the Web into three dimensions. Like HTML, VRML has browsers, but unlike HTML, these browsers model 3D space rather than a flat mosaic of text, links, and images. This means you can actually navigate into the image on the screen, go through doors, look out windows, and circle around a landscape rift with scenes and objects. If you've played any of the classic immersive games like DOOM or Myst, you'll know exactly what this means. If not, look at Figure 7-11.

Figure 7-11 is the view from a VRML browser called WorldView, which runs on various PC Windows platforms. Note the navigational buttons at the bottom of the screen. By clicking the forward arrow on the Fly panel you move forward in the scene. Figure 7-12 shows the same scene after moving closer and entering the door seen in the distance in Figure 7-11.

Metalinks in VRML

If you move the cursor to a hyperlinked object in VRML, like a picture in the virtual saloon, it will change to a hand icon just like some Web browsers display on a hyperlink. The picture could be linked to an HTML page, so clicking on it toggles you back to your Web browser, with the results of following this URL displayed. Links in VRML can also be to other VRML worlds, or to valid MIME types.

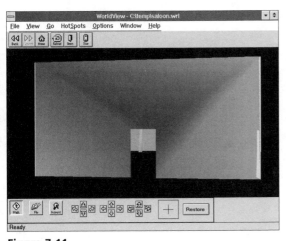

Figure 7-11
WorldView image

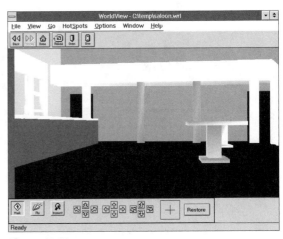

Figure 7-12
Up close and personal

At the time of this writing, VRML browsers are implemented as external helper applications to Web browsers. It won't be this way for long. Products like Netscape have announced plans to fold VRML capabilities into their HTML browsers, making a seamless transition between hypermedia and virtual worlds.

Turn Up the Bandwidth?

If JPG and GIF images that cover a screen take 300 to 500K and 60 seconds to download on a 28.8 bps link, what does an image take that can be viewed from an unlimited number of perspectives? At worst, you would need an image for each angle from which it could be viewed and a bandwidth connection the virtual size of a New York subway. Better is something like the way VRML is actually designed, a language that describes a scene and objects in plain text and lets your VRML viewer figure out how to display and manipulate the images interactively. The VRML for the image in Figure 7-12, for example, took 35K, equivalent to less than a quarter-screen's worth of a JPG image. Let's take a look at a simple VRML source file to see how this is done.

VRML Spheres

At a high level of abstraction, VRML consists of a bunch of statements, each of which defines some object (called a *node*) in 3D space. Nodes have fields that specify their orientation in the scene, their texture, color, etc. Nodes can be grouped together in *group nodes* for assigning common properties, and these group nodes act as containers for sets of related objects. A *separator* is one of these generic group nodes. For example, the following VRML:

```
#VRML V1.0 ascii
Separator {
Info {
        string "Created As An Experiment"
}
Separator {
   DirectionalLight {
        direction 0 0 -1
        }
   PerspectiveCamera {
        position -8.0 0 0
        orientation 0 0 0 1
        focalDistance 10
        }
   Separator {    # A Yellow Sphere
        Material {
                diffuseColor 1 1 0      # RGB Color
                shininess 0.8
                }
        Transform { translation 3 0 1 }
        Sphere { radius 2.3}
        }
   Separator {    # A Red Cube
```

```
Material {
        diffuseColor 1 0 0
        }
Transform { translation −5 0 1
        rotation 0 1 1 .7}
Cube {}
        }
    }
}
```

defines four objects: a light, a camera, a sphere, and a cube. The results are shown in Figure 7-13.

You can move closer or orbit around this simple scene with the navigation buttons on the VRML browser.

The entire scene required 563 bytes. It could transfer across even a slow modem link in less than a second.

To experiment with hand-coded VRML like the above, you will have to strip any <CR> (carriage return) characters from the file. VRML expects each line to be terminated with an <LF> (line feed), which is a UNIX convention, not the <CR><LF> that is used by MS-DOS.

Now let's experiment with one other feature of the language before we leave the raw VRML and look for convenient tools. Let's add a hyperlink to the sphere. When it is clicked, it should link to the Wired VRML page at: http://www.wired.com/vrml/. A link is defined with a WWWAnchor node. This is another type of group node, and it contains the node(s) that will contain a hyperlink. For example, to associate the sphere with a URL, you can enclose it with

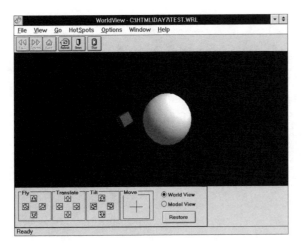

Figure 7-13
Simple VRML scene
(test.wrl)

```
Separator {      # A Yellow Sphere
      Material {
              diffuseColor 1 1 0      # RGB Color
              shininess 0.8
              }
      Transform { translation 3 0 1 }
      WWWAnchor {                # Hyperlink
              name "http://www.wired.com/vrml/"
              Sphere { radius 2.3}
              }

}
```

Now if you move the cursor over the sphere it will change to a hand, indicating you can click to follow the link. The hyperlinked sphere is shown in Figure 7-14.

The Metaverse

In 1991 Neil Stephenson wrote an underground classic called *SnowCrash*. The protagonist lived in a storage shed in real life, but with Virtual Reality goggles had a mansion on the burgeoning streets of the metaverse. VRML has caught the imagination of many, holding the promise of concepts like the metaverse tantalizingly near. Unfortunately, in its current specifications, VRML has some vexing limitations:

 No animations

 No multiuser environments

 No complex interactions

But interesting forces are at work. VRML browsers, and VRML authoring packages, are providing VRML capabilities, but also extending the specification to include the

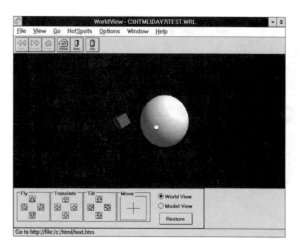

Figure 7-14
Sphere with a
hyperlink

enhancements lacking in VRML 1.0. Sound familiar? This was the tack Netscape took to provide features to enhance presentation on the Web and spur the development of the sometimes sluggish standards groups. The caveat is the same; by authoring in a specific VRML package, you may only be providing content for viewers that have incorporated these enhancements.

Extending Hyperspace

VRCreator from VREAM is a Virtual Reality creation product for Windows, Window NT, and Windows 95. It should be commercially available by the time you read this, and has extended Virtual Reality on the Web into more evolutionary areas than strict VRML.

Using VRCreator, objects have interactive properties. They can be grabbed, thrown, stretched, and carried. Not only can you navigate around objects and walls, you can bounce off them if you are so inclined. On the Windows platforms, VREAM is leveraging their product on the graphics and rendering libraries that Microsoft is layering into the operating system, making real-time, immersive Virtual Reality possible on these machines. Another interesting product, called Home Space Builder, has a more modest appeal.

Home Page or Home Space?

Figure 7-15 shows the Home Space Builder by Paragraph Internal. This product allows you to quickly create buildings, rooms, and galleries. You can use graphical images to apply textures to the walls, and you can hang pictures, provide background music, and attach various multimedia and HTML links to objects in your environment.

Home Space exports your designs as VRML. It could be used to provide a virtual office for visitors, or to provide a virtual home page for yourself. It can also be used as

Figure 7-15
Home Space
Builder

a replacement for bookmarks, allowing you to organize your Web links in rooms and buildings instead of flat menus and folders.

Build or Renovate?

Besides using a special-purpose modeler, you can also produce VRML from other 3D sources. A utility called wcv2pov, written by Keith Rule, converts a variety of 3D object formats into VRML. Figure 7-16 shows wcv2pov at work. It's loaded a clip-art 3D image of a chess piece and it's getting ready to save it as a VRML file. Menu options on wcv2pov allow you to scale, rotate, and position the object before it is exported.

Figure 7-17 shows that the export was successful. Other conversion programs exist for working with more than single objects. An intriguing one is called wadtoiv, which converts DOOM wads to VRML. A Doom wad isn't some grotty piece of gum; it's a graphics format used to design your own scenes and monsters in the popular DOOM PC game. If you want to scare people off of your home space, this is the utility you need.

Futures

VRML has incredible potential. It's easily interfaced to VR head mount displays and tracking systems, allowing the classic VR immersion experience, but it also adds more. It adds an interactive element of navigating through a number of independent systems, as opposed to the domains of a single game space. It's interesting to think about the types of scripting that might be used to create "agents" that act upon and react to objects and players in 3D space. These agents would have to run, at least in part, on the user's machine. This requirement goes beyond the scope of what you've covered with the CGI and Perl

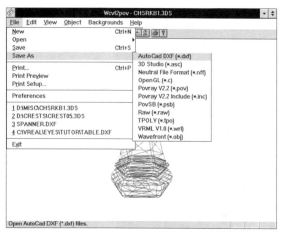

Figure 7-16
Exporting VRML from wcv2pov

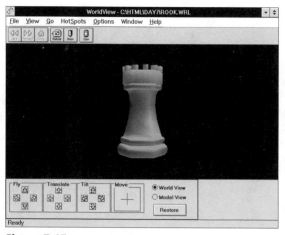

Figure 7-17
The results

scripts to date, but not beyond the scope of a powerful new scripting language designed to run on client platforms across the Web. It's called Java, and it's the topic of Session 4.

1. Why does a VRML object take up so much less size than the same object in GIF or JPEG format?
   a. VRML uses advanced compression techniques.
   b. The VRML objects have less resolution.
   c. VRML is a description language; the image is constructed by the browser.
   d. VRML sends the image down in segments.

2. How are links to URLs added to VRML objects?
   a. Through the use of HREF tags.
   b. With vendor specific hooks.
   c. With a special WWWAnchor separator section.
   d. You can't link to URLs from VRML.

3. How is VRML supported by most Web browsers?
   a. Just like HTML.
   b. As a helper application.
   c. VRML is not currently supported.
   d. By translating the VRML to HTML.

4. How could Home Space be used to organize bookmarks?
   a. by using its more extensive bookmark editor
   b. by interpreting them directly as links
   c. by providing rooms and galleries of links using visual metaphors
   d. by translating them into native VRML

JAVA AND EXECUTABLE CONTENT

Executable content, client scripts, client side includes: you don't have to author CGI scripts for very long before you begin to notice that much of what you're doing could be done better if the scripts were run by the browser instead of the server. The smart server/dumb browser model seems anachronistic as more and more power is being delivered to the desktop, in both the client hardware and the Web browser software. But before you can execute scripts on clients, you have to surmount some tough obstacles. The two most significant are the possibility of viruses and the variety of platforms and operating systems. Both of these issues have been deftly addressed by a language called *Java*, introduced by Sun Microsystems.

Java: Old or New?

Java was developed by UNIX luminary James Gosling back in early 1991. It was a language designed initially for the consumer electronics market for controlling the smarts of TV-top, video-on-demand boxes, personal digital assistants, and the like. These devices are not generally known for having abundant memory or the latest Intel processors. Java was designed to be small, portable, and extensible. It looked a lot like C++. In fact, if you've worked with C++, you'll feel right at home with Java.

In the consumer electronics market, CPUs are commodity items. It pays vendors a handsome margin to be able to go with the most inexpensive processors, and then swap brands as the market changes. To accommodate this, a language that controls these devices must not be dependent on any one architecture. It must function at a level of abstraction above the workings of any particular CPU. This is how Java was built, and this structure served it in good stead later when it hit the Internet with a base of client machines at least as diverse as their sibling programmable phones and smart toaster ovens.

Java is technically older than the Web, and it was not targeted for Web applications until Sun gave up on the set-top box market in early 1994 and discovered Java had real potential in some much bigger consumer phenomena: the Internet, online services, and desktop platforms. In doing so, Java found an ideal niche. Before uncovering what makes Java particularly suitable for Web browsers, let's take a short excursion into what executable content can do for you.

Why Executable Content?

Executable content is simply data that can be run as a program, like CGI scripts. And while CGI scripts have some advantages residing on the server, like easy access to legacy systems, indexed retrievals, and the ability to use fast RISC processors; scripts on the client have some unique advantages as well:

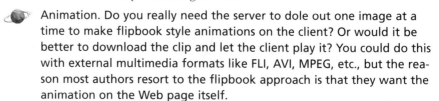 **Animation.** Do you really need the server to dole out one image at a time to make flipbook style animations on the client? Or would it be better to download the clip and let the client play it? You could do this with external multimedia formats like FLI, AVI, MPEG, etc., but the reason most authors resort to the flipbook approach is that they want the animation on the Web page itself.

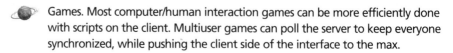 **Games.** Most computer/human interaction games can be more efficiently done with scripts on the client. Multiuser games can poll the server to keep everyone synchronized, while pushing the client side of the interface to the max.

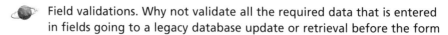 **Field validations.** Why not validate all the required data that is entered in fields going to a legacy database update or retrieval before the form

is sent, instead of trying to catch it with various iterative cycles back on the server?

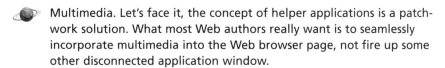 Multimedia. Let's face it, the concept of helper applications is a patchwork solution. What most Web authors really want is to seamlessly incorporate multimedia into the Web browser page, not fire up some other disconnected application window.

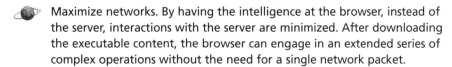 Maximize networks. By having the intelligence at the browser, instead of the server, interactions with the server are minimized. After downloading the executable content, the browser can engage in an extended series of complex operations without the need for a single network packet.

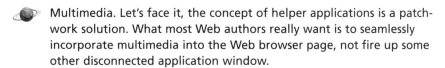 Harness client power. This is a switch. With executable content, it's possible for a server application to farm out various pieces of its work to smart browsers. Maybe you could harness the Web server contingent at your office into crunching spreadsheets during the lunch hour when their workstations are unattended!

Why Not Visual Basic?

So why do you need Java? What about putting Visual Basic binaries out on the Web, and using a Web browser that can execute them inline like <IMG> tags? Microsoft would probably agree with you. In fact, it appears Visual Basic is their de facto application language, popping up in spreadsheets and word processors in their office suite. It would be a natural step to add it to a Microsoft Web browser. But this leads to a couple of problems.

The first is security. If you were to download a page with executable content off of the Web, and this program decided that, it being April Fools' Day, it should erase your hard disk, you wouldn't be very amused. And while you would be relatively secure if you were running a Mac, you might also wonder why you weren't seeing on these pages what everyone else was raving about. Guess Visual Basic doesn't run on your machine?

The Buzz on Java

Java sidesteps both of the problems above. It has security built into the language on several levels. The first is in the language itself. It has cleaned up C's act, eliminating a lot of the areas that gave C a reputation as a good language to shoot yourself in the foot with. It protects code from itself, i.e., from making calls to places in memory that it shouldn't, from forgetting to clean up after itself, from trying to use the wrong type of data in the wrong type of operation. This level of security keeps Java programs from crashing your machine or corrupting memory used by other applications, either by accident or intent.

Another level of Java security permits application code to be digitally signed. You'll get into digital signatures more in the next sessions, but essentially this ensures that the program you are getting came from where you thought it did and hasn't been tampered with. This is a major exposure in most other types of languages, in which the executable can be modified, and the source of its origin cannot usually be verified.

The final area of security for Web authors is a cooperative level between Java and the Web browser for protecting local file systems. This interface can restrict a Java application to certain files or directories at the user's discretion. Attempts to access files or data outside of these confines result in the user being notified and prompted for permission.

Portability

Java achieves portability by not running directly on your machine. Instead, it runs in its own *virtual machine*. This virtual machine in turn is ported to the actual system environments that support Java, currently as part of the Web browser itself, but probably as part of operating systems in the future.

Various operating systems have different ways of representing data. Some represent numbers with 16 bits, some with 32. Some systems store numbers from left to right, others store them from right to left. C source code has portability problems between these systems because its data types depend on the operating system. Java's data types, by contrast, are predefined, and have the same representation across all the systems that run Java. This lets Java code be distributed as an executable, rather than source, and the executable should run on any system.

Java has cleverly addressed the two fundamental issues preventing content executables from having widespread appeal. Now that you know about Java's philosophy, let's do something with the actual language.

Components of a Java Application

A Java application consists of three pieces:

1. A Java-capable browser that executes the application.

2. The Web page that references it. This is how the application is loaded.

3. The compiled Java program on the server. This is what is downloaded by the browser to execute.

Let's look at these one by one. Figure 7-18 illustrates a Java application that has displayed the current date and time on a page. Not overly impressive, but discrete enough to get your hands around. Looking at the source HTML for this page, you discover the following:

```
<HTML>
<HEAD><TITLE>The Date Page</TITLE></HEAD>
<BODY>

The Current Date and Time Is: <applet code="DateApp.class"
                              width=300 height=75>
```

Figure 7-18
A Java application displaying the date and time

```
</BODY>
</HTML>
```

This tells the browser to load the applet named

```
DateApp.class
```

from the same directory as the HTML, and to set the initial window for the applet on the browser to 300 pixels wide by 75 pixels high. DateApp.class is the compiled version of the following Java source code:

```
import java.util.Date;
import java.awt.Graphics;
public class DateApp extends java.applet.Applet {
public void paint(Graphics g) {
  Date today = new Date();
  g.drawString(today.toString(),5,23);
  }
```

This code was created on Windows 95. When HotJava, Sun's Web browser, written entirely in Java, is downloaded from http://java.sun.com/ and unpacked on a local PC, it unpacks the Java browser, compiler, and class libraries. To compile code, you can create a file in the
```
\hotjava\classes
```

directory as a *filename*.java. If /hotjava/bin/ is not in your path, you can still compile it from the directory above using the following command at the "DOS" prompt:

```
..\bin\javac dateApp.java
```

It will compile to

```
dateApp.class
```

This file can then be transferred to your Web server, in a classes/ subdirectory.

Note that it doesn't matter which machine it is compiled on. It could be compiled on UNIX, Windows NT, or the Mac; the DateApp.class executable that results can be run on any Java-capable browser.

At the time of this writing, Java was still in its alpha release stages. Some of the syntax may have changed for the applet specification in HTML, and for the class definitions in the Java code. The final, and most recent, authority is Java's home page at http://java.sun.com/. By the time you read this, Sun should have also released their Developer's Kit for Windows 95 providing an environment for development and testing of Java applets. This will include an Applet Viewer, which allows you to run applets outside of a Web browser.

Going Further with Java

In Java, everything is a class (except numbers). A program is written by creating a new class, and creating methods in the class that can be called. If no method is specified, and the class has a main() routine, this will be executed by default. Since Java is inherently object oriented, you'll have to brush up on the principles of object-oriented programming to effectively use it. And Java is an excellent language with which to develop those concepts. If you've been holding off on learning C++ and thought Smalltalk was too esoteric, Java might be the language you've been waiting for to learn object programming.

1. What definition best fits the phrase "executable content" when referring to Java?
   a. code in a Web page that can be run by the browser
   b. content that instructs users on how to best use applications
   c. files that can be saved and executed offline
   d. parts of documents that automatically modify themselves.

2. What does Java have over Visual Basic?
   a. It can be executed on the client.
   b. It can provide local animation.
   c. It can be transmitted as executables.
   d. It can be executed by browsers as an integral part of the page.

3. Why isn't Java a risk?
   a. Very few browsers can run Java.
   b. It can only be loaded from secure networks.
   c. Access to resources on the client system are tightly controlled.
   d. It has a limited instruction set.

4. What happens if a non-Java-capable browser loads a page with a Java applet in it?
   a. It will attempt to execute it.

b. It will display it in a helper application.
c. It will ignore it.
d. It will display a message about invalid HTML.

NETSCAPE AND OLE

Netscape runs in a Microsoft Windows environment and provides interfaces for OLE and DDE links to communicate with other Windows applications. In this session you'll find out how to control Netscape from within Visual Basic. You can think of Netscape as a kind of Visual Basic control, allowing you to retrieve data from any URL and post data to CGI scripts. With just a few simple statements, your Visual Basic application can tap into the resources of the Web. To understand how this works, you'll need to understand a little about OLE automation and how Visual Basic communicates with other Windows applications.

OLE Automation

OLE stands for Object Linking and Embedding, and it's Microsoft's vision for making components in Windows reusable by other applications. OLE is a complex standard that actually encompasses in-place editing, automation, and controls. These are all ways of manipulating objects and differ in specific detail.

The OLE automation implemented by Netscape is one of these OLE flavors. In particular, OLE Automation can be thought of as a replacement for DDE, an older protocol that allows commands (usually keystrokes) to be sent and received from other applications. Instead of applications, OLE deals with objects. And if you've printed "Hello" in a Visual Basic textbox control, you've already accomplished setting and manipulating objects in Visual Basic. If you've used VBXs, you will be right at home with the following techniques.

Objects and Visual Basic

Objects, like textboxes in Visual Basic, consist of methods and properties. The following sets the textbox property in Visual Basic to accept multiple lines:

```
text1.MultiLine = True
```

Other properties that could be set include ForeColor, FontName, Text, etc. These properties can be both set and read. The familiar

```
name$ = text1.text
```

retrieves the text property from the textbox object, returning the characters the user entered in the box and assigning them to the variable *name$*.

The textbox object also has methods, which are used to make the object do things. One of these is

```
text.move left,top, width,height
```

which dynamically moves the textbox on the screen, and can also change its dimensions.

OLE and Visual Basic

OLE Automation extends the idea of controls a little further. Instead of controlling objects on your Visual Basic forms, you control objects in other applications; in this case, Netscape.

The classic technique of controlling objects through OLE animation would be something allowing the following lines:

```
Dim appAirplane
Set appAirplane = CreateObject("Airplane.Application")
appAirplane.Open
appAirplane.Throttle = "On,5"
appAirplane.Flaps = "Up, Up, Down"
appAirplane.Radio = "Is there a pilot on board?"
appAirplane.Close
```

Driving an airplane object with OLE Automation should be much like driving the textbox object. With OLE, however, you'll need to start the application in the background if it's not running (CreateObject). Activate the object (appAirplane.Open) and release it when you're finished (appAirplane.Close).

Netscape and Visual Basic

Netscape's OLE Automation won't be as cooperative as your airplane. Note the arguments passed to the OLE object properties in the appAirplane example. This assumes a Visual Basic friendly OLE object, one that understands Visual Basic parameters. Unfortunately, one of the object properties in the Netscape OLE (at the time of this writing) wanted not just a string, but a pointer to a string. Visual Basic can do this for function calls. In fact, it's common practice for interfacing with DLLs, but for OLE property assignments, it appears there is no way to pass a pointer (i.e., pass a string by reference) to an OLE object (in VB 3 that is; VB 4 can do this).

Luckily, Steve Caine wrote a DLL "wrapper" for the Netscape OLE Automation that handles the Visual Basic string conversions to and from the OLE interface. Let's use this wrapper to control Netscape from Visual Basic, with Steve's disclaimer that it is experimental (although the complete source code is included on this book's CD if you like such projects). The only difference in the wrapper from the tack taken with normal OLE objects is that you will appear to be calling functions and procedures when you are really setting object properties and calling methods. Instead of setting a variable to an object property like this:

```
content$ = Netscape.GetContentType()
```

you'll set a variable to the result from a function call:

```
content$ = NsNetGetContentEncoding()
```

A subtle difference, and one that will probably be done away with in future versions of Netscape and/or Visual Basic. The *NsNet* above is a prefix the DLL wrapper uses in front of the native OLE calls. The global definitions for the NsNet wrapper are contained in the nsnetdef.bas file and should be included in your VB project. Move the file nsnvbitf.dll to your c:\windows\system subdirectory and you're all set.

Netscape Automation, at the time of this writing, didn't register itself during installation, so you will need to run it at least once so Windows knows about it. You can then use the OLE interface in the future, or any time after this initial execution.

Netscape OLE Automation Properties

Excel spreadsheet objects have methods and properties for selecting ranges of cells and calculating formulas; Netscape's objects deal with finding and retrieving URLs. The following Visual Basic code:

```
Dim url As String
Dim buf As String
Dim n As Integer
Dim i As Integer
Dim rc As Integer
Dim msg As String
Dim wpage As String
NsNetCreate
url = Trim$(text1)
list1.Clear
rc = NsNetOpen(url, 0, "", 0, "")
wpage = ""
Do
    n = NsNetRead(buf, 512)
    If (n < 0) Then Exit Do
    wpage = wpage + buf
Loop
rc = NsNetGetStatus()
msg = NsNetGetErrorMessage()
NsNetRelease
If (rc <> 0) Then
    list1.AddItem "Error: " & Hex(rc)
    list1.AddItem "Error: " & msg
    Exit Sub
End If

n = Len(wpage)
list1.AddItem "Read " & n & " bytes"
i = InStr(1, wpage, "http:")
```

continued on next page

continued from previous page
```
Do While (i <> 0)
    list1.AddItem Mid(wpage, i, InStr(i, wpage, ">") - i)
    i = InStr(i + 1, wpage, "http:")
Loop
```

will read a URL entered in a textbox, and return all of the *http:* links in the page. Let's dissect the routine to see how it works and what can be learned for the next project.

The first OLE call is the NsNetCreate subroutine. It takes no arguments, and its purpose is to activate Netscape for OLE commands. If Netscape is not already running, you will see a minimized Netscape icon appear on your desktop. Any initialization errors will trip the Visual Basic ON ERROR exit(s), and in this case, since it is not trapped, it will just stop the program with an error message.

The NsNetOpen routine opens the URL specified in the textbox. Three things can happen here:

1. NsNetOpen finds the URL, and everything is okay. NsNetOpen returns a nonzero value (True).

2. NsNetOpen doesn't like the URL protocol type; Maybe "http" was misspelled as "httv". It returns a zero value (False). To get more information about the nature of the error, you call NsNetGetStatus, which returns a hex 0x0400, indicating an internal error, and that the server was never contacted.

3. NsNetOpen likes the URL protocol type, but the domain or page does not exist. This one is trickier. NsNetOpen will return a nonzero value (True) and continue to the next Visual Basic statement as Netscape tries to find the domain name and page in the background. By the time Netscape finds it has been duped, you're already past the NsNetOpen command with a clean bill of health. Meanwhile, Netscape sets an error code of 0x0c00 that can be retrieved via NsNetGetstatus if it's checked. (you'll catch it on the call to NsNetRead, so no worries).

The subroutine NsNetRead now retrieves the contents of the URL from Netscape, reading up to 512 bytes at a time into string "buf". NsNetRead returns the number of bytes actually read. If it returns zero, there's no data to read right now, but there may be some in a minute. If it returns -1, it's definitely finished, although it could have finished with an error, so you need to check NsNetGetStatus. While the bytes read are 0 or above, the loop keeps stuffing what's retrieved into the "wpage" string. Like any Visual Basic 3.0 string, this can only hold up to 65,500 bytes (on a good day). Luckily, unlike the browser, in OLE no inline images are downloaded with a URL, just the vanilla HTML text.

NsNetGetStatus is checked to make sure the status was zero. This is where the program would catch the bogus URL also with the status 0x0c00 and no data received in the NsNetRead loop. NsNetGetStatus can have the values shown in Table 7-3.

Error Code	Description
0x00000	Normal status.
0x0001	Username was requested.
0x0002	Password was requested.
0x0100	Netscape is currently busy, try again.
0x0200	Server reported an error; use NsNetGetServerStatus for more info.
0x0400	An internal load error, the server was never contacted.
0x0800	Netscape has suggested an error message; it can be retrieved with NsNetGetErrorMessage.

Table 7-3 *NsNetGetStatus error codes*

These values are masks, so if multiple types of errors occur, the values are meshed together. If conditions 0x0400 and 0x0800 both occurred, the error would be 0x0c00, which is the hex value of 4+8 (12 in decimal).

NsNetRelease disconnects any active connections to the OLE object. If no object is active, it doesn't do anything, so don't worry about calling it multiple times. If you don't call NsNetRelease, however, and your program exits, you could end up with a little zombie Netscape icon hanging around on your desktop that you can't close or activate or otherwise brush off.

The Sequence

That's it. In this routine:

1. NsNetCreate establishes a link to the OLE object. This only needs to be done once.

2. NsNetOpen links to a URL using Netscape and downloads the HTML.

3. NsNetRead reads what's been downloaded to the buffer from the URL.

4. NsNetClose deallocates the OLE object link.

Errors are checked with the NsNetGetStatus routine. If the message has 0x0800 in it (remember, it can be masked with other values), then NsNetGetErrorMessage() will return a string with a text error message from Netscape.

This simple routine illustrates a minimal set of OLE calls to retrieve the contents of any URL. The routine could be extended to validate URL links on a Web page, or a Web server, with just a little extra code. You could even write your own Web spider that would traverse a section of links looking for information.

More Properties

Several other OLE properties exist for the Netscape object. The complete reference is the Netscape document at http://www.netscape.com/newsref/std/oleapi.html Let's touch on a few more that are of immediate interest:

NsNetGetLastModified()

This returns a string with the date/time stamp of the last time the data retrieved by this URL was modified. Use anytime after the NsNetOpen and before NsNetRelease.

NsNetSetUsername(str)

str is a value containing the username to be used in future NsNetOpens. This is useful if you are accessing a protected page, or logging in to FTP.

NsNetSetPassword(str)

str is the password associated with the username above. You'll need this too for username/password protected URLs. Both username and password should be set before NsNetOpen is called on the URLs, or you will get the error 0x0001 and/or 0x0002 in NsNetGetStatus.

Posting Data

The example above kind of blurred through the NsNetOpen option. Here's the complete breakdown:

NsNetOpen(*url, method, postdata, postdatasize, postheaders*)

- *url* is a string with a standard URL.

- *method* is one of

0x0	GET
0x1	POST
0x2	HEAD

- *postdata* is encoded name=value pairs to be posted.

- *postdatasize* is the length of the postdata string.

- *postheaders* is one or more headers; the default for posting should be

```
Content-type: application/x-www-form-urlencoded
```

Posting Forms with Visual Basic

NsNetOpen suggests some intriguing possibilities. For example, you could use a Visual Basic data entry form for posting to the Web server, allowing local validation of

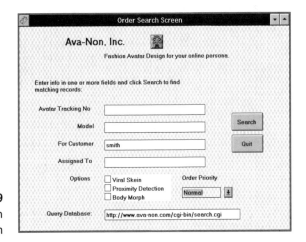

Figure 7-19
Ava-Non search
form

fields and integration with any other data sources on the PC before or after going through the CGI.

To try this out, let's take a simple input form for a fictional company illustrated in Figure 7-19.

After filling in whatever pieces of information are known, the program posts the data to a CGI script that will search for entries in a customer or order database. This example will just take it up to the point the script receives the encoded variables from the form.

On the Visual Basic form, three different types of input controls are used: Textbox, Checkbox, and Combobox. The input from each of these fields must be concatenated and encoded before it can be passed to the Web server. You'll remember from Chapter 4 that the encoded format for posted data is

```
name=value&name=value....etc.
```

with special characters like >,%,/, etc., translated to their hexadecimal equivalent and prefaced with "%", and embedded spaces replaced with "+". This is taken care of by the following Visual Basic function:

```
Function encode (ct As Control) As String
'
' Encode the text in a control for Posting to a CGI script
' Currently supports Textbox, ComboBox, and Checkbox controls
'
Dim i As Integer
Dim sWork As String
Dim sInput As String
Dim nLen As Integer
Dim sCh As String
Dim J As Integer
```

continued on next page

continued from previous page

```
sWork = ""
sInput = ""
If TypeOf ct Is TextBox Then        ' Find property that has input
    sInput = ct.Text                '    text based on control type
ElseIf TypeOf ct Is ComboBox Then
    sInput = ct.Text
ElseIf TypeOf ct Is CheckBox Then
    sInput = ct.Value
End If

nLen = Len(sInput)
For i = 1 To nLen
    sCh = Mid(sInput, i, 1)
    J = Asc(UCase(sCh))
    Select Case J
        Case 65 To 90, 48 To 57     ' Uppercase letter or number
            sWork = sWork + sCh     ' No Encoding Necessary
        Case 32                     ' Spaces encoded as +
            sWork = sWork + "+"
        Case Else                   ' Encode with %hex-value
            sWork = sWork + "%" + Hex(J)
    End Select
Next
encode = sWork
End Function
```

With the encoding function written, all that remains is to gather the input controls that will be posted and build the postdata argument to pass into NsNetOpen. This is achieved with the following:

```
Function Gather () As String
Dim sContent As String
sContent = "trackno=" + encode(trackno)
sContent = sContent + "&" + "model=" + encode(model)
sContent = sContent + "&" + "customer=" + encode(customer)
sContent = sContent + "&" + "assigned=" + encode(assigned)
sContent = sContent + "&" + "vopt= " + encode(vopt)
sContent = sContent + "&" + "popt= " + encode(popt)
sContent = sContent + "&" + "bopt= " + encode(bopt)
sContent = sContent + "&" + "priority= " + encode(priority)
Gather = sContent
End Function
```

The gather() function collects data from each of the controls on the form, encodes it, and concatenates the name=value pairs into a URL-encoded string that is returned to the caller.

Here is all that is needed now in the Search button to collect and post the data:

```
Sub Search_Click()
Dim url As String
Dim sBuf As String
Dim nLen As Integer
```

```
Dim i As Integer
Dim rc As Integer
Dim msg As String
Dim wpage As String
Dim pdata As String
Dim sHeader As String
NsNetCreate
url = Trim$(text1)

pdata = Gather()
sHeader = "Content-type: application/x-www-form-urlencoded"

rc = NsNetOpen(url, 1, pdata, Len(pdata), "sHeader")
If Not rc Then
    msg = "Open Error!"
    msg = msg + Hex(nsNetGetstatus())
    msg = msg + NsNetGetErrorMessage()
    NsNetRelease
    MsgBox msg
    Exit Sub
End If
wpage = ""
Do
    nLen = nsNetRead(sBuf, 512)
    If (nLen < 0) Then Exit Do
    wpage = wpage + sBuf
Loop
rc = nsNetGetstatus()
msg = NsNetGetErrorMessage()
NsNetRelease
If rc = 0 Then
    MsgBox wpage
Else
    MsgBox "Error: " & Hex(rc) & NsNetGetErrorMessage()
End If
End Sub
```

That's it. You collected input from a Visual Basic form, encoded what was entered, and posted it to a CGI script. To extend this example you'll probably want to do more with the results from the CGI post than just displaying it in a msgbox.

1. The Netscape browser's OLE interface allows
    a. Netscape to run on a Windows network
    b. Netscape to run in Windows
    c. Window processes to communicate with the Netscape browser as an object
    d. the Netscape browser to view OLE source

2. Which OLE method could be used in a routine to notify you of any changes to a list of URLs?
   a. NsNetOpen
   b. NsNetGetStatus
   c. NsNetGetLastModified
   d. NsNetLookup

3. To post data from the Netscape OLE interface, the data must first be
   a. retrieved
   b. checked for errors with NsNetGetStatus
   c. stored in an OLE format
   d. URL encoded

4. Why does Visual Basic 3 need to use the DLL wrapper instead of calling the Netscape OLE interface directly?
   a. because OLE is only part of the professional VB 3 product
   b. because you cannot call OLE objects from VB 3 directly
   c. because some OLE objects require pointers to strings, which VB 3 doesn't natively support
   d. for security

PGP AND SCRIPTING

Using secured servers, covered in Session 7, it is possible to encrypt all communications between Web server and browser. Secure servers have mechanisms for authenticating themselves, guaranteeing that they are who they say they are. But as important as these features are to a full-fledged commercial server, they have a couple of disadvantages for the casual corporate or organizational user.

First, at the time of this writing, secure servers are all commercial. The free servers obtainable over the Internet don't implement encryption security. Second, secure servers require "keys" that are registered with the equivalent of a key "notary." The handful of authorized notaries charge for each key, and charge again to renew them annually. You'll see why you need keys for encryption shortly, but at the same time you'll learn how to generate and use them yourself to provide protected Web documents and authenticated transactions from the server without using either a commercial server or a notarized key. Before this, let's cover some of the basics of cryptography, in order to understand its strengths and weaknesses.

What's the Secret Word?

Conventional encryption techniques use a single key to encrypt and decrypt a message. The key functions like a Cap'n Crunch decoder ring: your friend can only decrypt the message if he or she has a decoder ring, too. The problem is that anyone could get a Cap'n Crunch decoder ring, and as the cereal became popular, you could kiss your secrets good-bye. But this is the problem with single keys. Somehow you need to share the key with the people you need to have read your message, but the key must also be protected. If a key is lost, the system is compromised. You can't just send the key with the message, because if the message is intercepted, whoever did so has everything he or she needs to decrypt it. This leads to a gnarly problem with single-key encryption schemes: how to distribute the keys. If you had a secure channel to send keys over, you could just send messages over it and forget the keys.

I've Got Two Words for It

The problem remained gnarly until the public key cryptography algorithm was invented by Rivest, Shamir, and Aldeman (and called, coincidentally, the RSA algorithm). This algorithm uses two keys: a public key, and a private key. The public key you can give out to everyone. It's no secret. Probably that's why it's called public. In fact, you can post it on bulletin boards, send it in e-mail, or skywrite it, for that matter. But it has the interesting property that when it's used to encrypt a message for you, it can only be decrypted by your private key.

That's right, even the public key can't decrypt the message again. And no one else's private key will be able to decrypt it. You've given anyone a way to send you a secret message, and no one else can decrypt it. Pretty clever.

The public key and private key are mathematically related, so they work symmetrically. In fact, they are so symmetrical that you can encrypt something with your private key that will only make sense when it is decrypted with the public key! This is the technique used to "sign" your digital letters. If your signature can be decrypted with your public key, it must have been encrypted with your private one, which only you would have access to (in theory).

PGP

In 1991 Phil Zimmermann released a controversial software product called Pretty Good Privacy, PGP for short, into the public domain. It used the RSA public key encryption scheme in combination with a conventional algorithm called IDEA, making a product for the public that provided industrial strength security. This caused Phil a lot of problems with the government, and they have been investigating him since 1991 for releasing this technology to the world.

PGP and Keys

PGP runs on almost any computer platform. One of the reasons it can do this is because it's not a fancy program. In fact, it runs best at the command line, much like typical UNIX applications. There are various shells available that assist in the interface, but since you will be writing CGI scripts that use it on UNIX, let's start at the lowest common denominator.

PGP stores your public and private keys in two different files, or "keyrings." One, for public keys, is called pubring.pgp, and one, for private keys, is called secring.pgp. One of the first things you will need to do after installing PGP is to create your public/private key pair. You can do this as follows:

```
pgp -kg
```

PGP will prompt you for key size, from 256 to 1,024 bits. The larger your key size, the more secure it will be, but the longer it will take to encrypt.

Next, you will need a key identifier; this is usually your name and e-mail address, but you can put in anything you like. The convention is to enter something like

First name Last Name <username@domain>

You can have spaces, special characters, smileys, whatever.

Now you'll be prompted for a pass phrase. This is a password that is used to protect access to your private keyring. Enter a long pass phrase; at least 128 characters is recommended.

The last step will be a little strange. PGP asks you to start typing some text on your keyboard. It doesn't matter what you type; PGP uses the rhythm and intervals between your keystrokes to generate a random number used to produce your pair of keys.

Distributing Your Public Key

You're done. You now have a public and private key stored in their respective keyrings. To communicate with anyone, though, you need to distribute your public key. To extract your public key from its keyring in a form that you can send via e-mail, enter the following:

```
pgp -kxa identifier file
```

In this line, *identifier* is the first few characters of what you used for your key identifier above, and *file* is the filename to put the extracted key into. The filetype will default to .asc.

For example, to extract a public key created with an identifier:

```
Fred Noble <noble@noble.net>
```

use the following command:

```
pgp -kxa Fred test
```

A file called test.asc will be created, and it will look similar to this:

```
-----BEGIN PGP PUBLIC KEY BLOCK-----
Version: 2.6.1

mQCNAy6dYcYAAAEEAM7FPVjyZY6y+kXgFaoSk9OeKJsorWiKnxr1LTGGUw9jAdEM
3DHwzfYo7xhHJENGuRLTlN5ZuYZrOrwbXpfJbxgBe3PkprRge5yIjHnpzV32K3/U
```

```
sl7gukb2ab9OoNS+HVXyIfT3hoDfim9rVxcLeBfbntbbmmdA6a35bFXTyua5AAUR
tCxLZW5OIENlYXJsZXkgPGNlYXJsZXlfaOB3aXphcmQuY29sb3JhZG8uZWR1ZWR1Pg==
=Ybbv
-----END PGP PUBLIC KEY BLOCK-----
```

You can now send this as an attachment, paste it into an e-mail message, or put it on a Web page. Anyone with your public key can use it to encrypt a message to you.

Adding a Public Key to Your Keyring

To encrypt a message for someone, you need their public key. If they send it to you in a mail message, or you find it on a Web page, you just need to extract it to a file. Don't worry about any extraneous text before or after the key; that text will be ignored. After you have the key extracted to a file, enter the following PGP command:

`pgp -ka file`

Here, *file* is the name of the file the extracted key is in. This adds any public keys found in the file to your public keyring. Now list the keys in your public keyring with the following command:

`pgp -kv`

This lists all the users you have added to your public keyring. These are all the people you can send encrypted messages to. To encrypt a message to a user in your keyring with an identifier of Joe Blank, use the following command:

`pgp -e file Joe Blank`

In this line, *file* is the message you are encrypting, and *identifier* is the name in the User ID column in your public keyring listed above.

To decrypt a message that is encrypted with your public key, enter the following:

`pgp file`

where *file* is the filename of the encrypted file.

Signatures

Signatures can ensure that the message received was not tampered with on its way to the recipient. The message can be left unencrypted and sent via e-mail, but it will have a small block at the bottom of the message that is the encrypted signature. This signature not only tells the recipient that the message is from you, but has taken a "fingerprint" of the message, and will warn the recipient if the text has been altered in any way. To sign a message, use the following PGP command:

`pgp +clearsig=on -sat textfile -u my-identifier`

You will be prompted for your pass phrase so that PGP can read your secret key. PGP will create a file with the same filename as the text file but with an .asc filetype. Here's an example of a digitally signed text file:

```
-----BEGIN PGP SIGNED MESSAGE-----

Signed, sealed and delivered!

- -Thanks

-----BEGIN PGP SIGNATURE-----
Version: 2.6.1
```

```
iQCVAwUBMCRDuK35bFXTyua5AQHV3AP+MGhYpzyZK1G8YHjClmAUP6MzAsxQ3TVB
DsKH36vKx/k8hP74COKDEsAvkMdPjtk2WfejxXSC8owBzTYON8T9lzl/gKDOTrCO
A7xIuqLF9OiVdOYLj4wFVag+BWWUWRZDDLtF8Tx/hRiJuPCtuoFlMEEXsOPmM7uH
eAz9rxqIOjU=
=dP76
```
```
-----END PGP SIGNATURE-----
```

When the file is read with

```
pgp filename
```

PGP will examine the signature and tell you who signed it, as well as if the message authenticates or not.

PGP and CGI

You've just covered the minimum of PGP necessary for use in CGI scripts. PGP itself has many more options and techniques, and a body of literature that has sprung up to document them. For the purpose of this section though, you are now equipped to begin incorporating PGP on your server.

The technique you'll implement using PGP guarantees, through a digital signature, that the information a person receives is actually from the Web server. This is useful when the Web server is just one piece in an overall business process. If, for example, your Web forms generate a request through a Web server that is forwarded on to another department, or even another organization via e-mail, how can the recipient be sure this request

1. came from the Web server,

2. has not been tampered with.

Ordinary e-mail is notoriously easy to spoof on the Internet. In fact, some sites offer fake mail services as a prank, making it appear your e-mail was actually sent from president@whitehouse.gov. To make a Web server a credible source of a business transaction, it needs a method of authenticating itself, a method that PGP provides with its signature option. So how do you fit this into your CGI script?

Building PGP Authentication into Scripts

First, you will have to generate your server's public and private keys, and identifier as described above. Do this from the account that your Web server uses (defined in httpd.conf on NCSA servers). You'll need to make the keyring files available to the Web server, but not accessible via URLs or directory search from Web browsers.

Now use the following Perl segment:

```
#!/usr/local/bin/perl
$ENV{'PGPPASSFD'} = 0;
print "Starting...\n";
open(MAILPGP,"|pgp -fsat | mail payables@company.com ");
print MAILPGP "This Was My Password Phrase\n";
print MAILPGP "bogus\n";                 # mail message...
close(MAILPGP);
```

This will need some explanation. In the line

```
$ENV{'PGPPASSFD'} = 0;
```

the environmental variable PGPPASSFD is set to 0, which tells PGP to accept the password phrase to unlock the secret keyring from the input stream. After this, a pipe is opened to PGP, using the option string "-fsat", which encrypts and signs a file. No identifier was specified, so PGP will default to the first id found in the secret keyring. Since your Web server has only one key in this ring (its own) this will work as expected. The encrypted, signed results are in turn piped to the mail command, which mails the message to e-mail address payables@company.com. The next line

```
print MAILPGP "This Was My Password Phrase\n";
```

was the (poorly) chosen password phrase for the Web server's secret keyring. The phrase must be terminated with a line feed, \n. The next line

```
print MAILPGP "Name = $name\n";              # mail message...
print MAILPGP "Advance Requested = $amount\n"
```

is the data from the Web form that will be signed and encrypted before e-mailing out.

By protecting Web forms used to generate requests using username and password or Limit options of the server, and ensuring that all transactions that leave the server to go to external systems (like e-mail to the accounting department) are encrypted and authenticated, you can build a relatively secure application with off-the-shelf components. If you're even more paranoid, er, cautious, you can use the techniques discussed in Session 7 to create a secured server.

1. What major problem do single-key encryption techniques have to surmount?
   a. They are trivial to crack with large processors.
   b. They rely on a secure way to get the secret key to the intended recipient.
   c. They cannot be automated.
   d. They are not available for private citizens.

2. If a user of a public key encryption technique wanted to send you a message, he or she would need
   a. your private key
   b. your public key
   c. both your public and private keys
   d. his or her own public key

3. The longer the key size in public key
   a. the less secure the encryption
   b. the more keys are required
   c. the more secure the encryption
   d. the faster the encryption

4. To distribute PGP public keys
   a. you must register them with a notary
   b. they must be encrypted
   c. you can distribute them any way text is distributed
   d. you must have a license

WEB SECURITY

Most of the information circulating the Internet is not encrypted or protected from eavesdropping. Most networks are susceptible to intruders or insiders "tapping the network," just as phone lines are. In fact, one of the most popular networks, Ethernet, functions like a party line, allowing anyone to intentionally listen to traffic and pick up any "conversation" occurring at the time.

This, in addition to the media fascination with hackers both in print and at the box office, has bred distrust for the way information is used and transmitted on the Internet. And although vendors are excited about the huge potential of virtual malls, they must win consumer confidence in the security of transmitting credit card numbers, writing checks, and placing orders over the Internet. This is where secure servers come in, but they raise almost as many issues as they resolve. Let's start at the beginning, though, with what they offer for Web commerce.

What Secure Servers Do

Security features offered by the combination of secure Web servers and security-smart clients are advertised as follows.

Server Authentication

When you connect to a server to order a CD, for example, how do you know this is the server for the CD company and not a front for an unscrupulous Web form that will take your credit card number and store it, then forward your order on to the real CD company so you won't get suspicious? Later your credit card number can be used illegally, and the real CD company will probably get blamed. Especially if that was your only, or most recent transaction on the Internet.

This might seem far-fetched, but it's not that inconceivable. Just think about where you get your URLs and bookmarks today. Even obtaining these from directory services like Yahoo is no guarantee, especially since Yahoo allows companies to register themselves in the indexed directories. Other sources of bogus URL dissemination could be through Usenet News postings, e-mail lists, etc. This type of spoofing will become more common as commerce picks up.

What server authentication does is provide you with a signed certificate, based on public key technology, that the server is who it says it is. But for this to work, you need a notary to prove the key is valid. Otherwise, you have the same situation; Web server A can say it is Web server B by making up its own certificate key. If you get A's before B's, then you will believe A. The notary serves as a third party that signs the certificate key of the server. The notary's own key is, at least in the case of Netscape, embedded in your browser.

Encrypted Sessions

Even knowing that you are communicating with the right Web server doesn't in itself protect sensitive information like your credit card number. Someone could still be eavesdropping on the transactions that pass between your browser and the server. But using the public key obtained from the server, your browser can encrypt transactions that can only be decrypted by the server. So even if someone is tapping the line, all they will get is garbled data.

Digital Signatures

The server authentication key can also be used to sign documents, ensuring they're from a specific server, but what about the flip side? What if the server wants to be sure that form data came from a specific user?

The username/password authentication provided on a nonsecured server doesn't reliably authenticate clients. Usernames and passwords are not encrypted, and even if they were, they are not designed to sign a block of information the way you signed a message with PGP in the last session. At best they just indicate that an authorized user got access to the form, but not that the data from the form is the same as the data the user entered. To do this requires the user to have his or her own key.

Digital signatures are performed by the browser using a private key belonging to the user. This private key works in conjunction with the user's public key, stored in or accessible to the server, to validate data from the user. The user's signature ensures that data sent from the browser has not been tampered with, either while it was being transmitted, or anytime after it was stored in the server's database.

User Authentication

Users can be authenticated through the use of their public keys, similar to the way servers are authenticated. Their transactions can be encrypted with their private keys, and decrypted on the server, which has their public keys registered in its database (the server in this case acting as the notary). A user's public key could also be sent to the server encrypted with the server's public key, eliminating the need for the server to keep a database of user keys.

If the sessions are already encrypted, this may be sufficient protection to trust the standard username/password validation provided by the .htaccess files or their equivalent. Since the issue with passwords being transmitted in clear text is taken care of, an encrypted session may provide enough authentication, avoiding the administrative overhead of having each client generate public/private key pairs for use with the server.

Two Approaches

Two separate technologies have evolved on the Web to provide secure servers. Neither of them at the time of this writing had the blessings of the Web standards committees, but it is likely that both will be supported in the majority of Web servers and clients. The first was developed and proposed by Netscape and is called the Secure Sockets Layer, or SSL.

SSL

SSL provides the server authentication and encrypted session features discussed above. At this time, however, it does not provide digital signatures or user authentication (i.e., using public keys). SSL was designed to protect the underlying Internet protocols, not just Web traffic. This means SSL can protect FTP, News, Telnet, Gopher, and other URL protocol types, instead of just HTML documents and forms. In theory, it also means that all your current and future Internet applications can be protected with SSL.

To use SSL your server requires a digitally signed certificate from someone licensed by RSA. Currently this is only one company, VeriSign, Inc., (info@verisign.com), and it will cost you $290 the first year and $75 thereafter to renew your certificate. The clients don't need certificates or keys.

SSL protects the privacy of network traffic. This means that sensitive data, like credit card numbers, can be safely sent, and certified servers ensure they get to the right places. The encryption, however, is only in effect for traffic across the Internet. Once the document is on your browser, or on the server, it can be browsed or saved and it is no longer encrypted.

S-HTTP

S-HTTP was championed by Enterprise Integration Technologies (EIT), a Palo Alto company that was a brief stopover point for Marc Anderseen in his move from NCSA to Netscape. S-HTTP takes a different tack from the one SSL takes. Instead of trying to protect all of the underlying Internet protocols, S-HTTP protects only HTTP, the protocol spoken between the Web server and Web browser. S-HTTP provides server authentication and encrypted sessions, but only for Web traffic. It also provides digital signatures, allowing Web clients to sign a check, order, or contract.

Like SSL, S-HTTP servers require a certificate signed by a notary. At the time of this writing, the notary for S-HTTP was CommerceNet. Clients likewise require registration by a notary to use digital signatures.

Opposites or Complementary?

SSL and S-HTTP overlap in server authentication and session encryption capabilities. SSL attempts to be more encompassing at the Internet protocol layer, and S-HTTP attempts to include more enhancements, including digital signatures, specifically to the Web protocol itself. Both security models have been proposed to the World Wide Web working groups for consideration as a standard. In the interim, they are both building de facto client bases, with the Netscape browser embedding support for SSL, and the NCSA Mosaic browser, as modified by EIT for CommerceNet, embedding S-HTTP.

In May of 1995, EIT formed a joint venture with RSA to form Terisa Systems. Terisa systems in turn licensed SSL from Netscape. And while Terisa does not make products, they do sell security technologies in the form of developer kits that can be used to add both SSL and S-HTTP to commercial Web clients and servers. Some commercial servers are using this kit to provide both capabilities.

Let's look now at what these technologies mean to you as a Webmaster, and to Joe user accessing your services.

Nuts and Bolts

In both SSL and S-HTTP, server authentication and encrypted sessions require no configuration on the user's browser. In S-HTTP, generating the initial key for digital signatures requires more effort than it does in SSL. Usually this is provided on a pull-down menu of the browser that takes the user through generating a key pair, and up to the point where they need to send their identifier in to have it notarized by some authentication clearinghouse like VeriSign or CommerceNet. Here are examples of secure interactions from each approach.

SSL Examples

On Netscape's Preferences menu there are settings under Images and Security, shown in Figure 7-20. These control the message boxes that pop up warning you that you are submitting a form (the one you probably marked "Stop bugging me!) to an unsecured server. They also notify you when you are entering or leaving secure servers.

You don't need to rely on the message boxes alone, which are purposefully intrusive; you also have an indicator at the bottom of the browser whenever your transactions are connected with a secure server and your transactions are being encrypted. In Figure 7-21, the key at the bottom left of the screen alerts you to this fact.

Since everything happens at a layer below HTTP, nothing special needs to be done with your scripts to ensure this protection. After setting up the server with its certificate, the rest is business as usual.

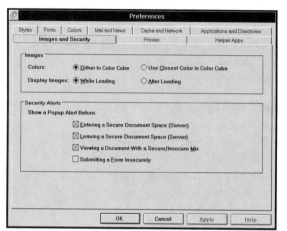

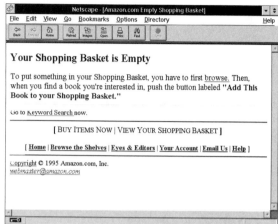

Figure 7-20
Netscape's security options

Figure 7-21
Netscape interacting with a secure server

S-HTTP Examples

S-HTTP is more complex to manage. Since it works at the HTTP level, it has actually made extensions to HTML and the CGI interface. In HTML, the hyperlink anchors to protected resources use "shttp" in the URL instead of "http". They also contain information about the server's certification. Here is a representative sample of the new anchor :

```
<a href="shttp://www.comerce.net/"
    DN="CN=Chili Peppers, Inc., OU=Persona Certificate, O=&quot;RSA Data  Security,
Inc.&quot;, C=US"
    CRYPTOPTS="SHTTP-Key-Exchange-Algorithms: recv-required=RSA;
        orig-optional=RSA, Inband
        SHTTP-Privacy-Enhancements: recv-required=encrypt;
        orig-optional=sign,encrypt">
```

The URL specifies whether the request should be signed, encrypted, and/or authenticated. Documents can come back with the embedded public key of the server, in the following HTML extension:

```
<CERTS FMT=PKCS7>
iQCVAwUBMCRDuK35bFXTyua5AQHV3AP+MGhYpzyZK1G8YHjClmAUP6MzAsxQ3TVB
DsKH36vKx/k8hP74COKDEsAvkMdPjtk2WfejxXSC8owBzTYON8T9lzl/gKDOTrCO
A7xIuqLF9OiVdOYlj4wFVag+BWWUWRZDDLtF8Tx/hRiJuPCtuoFlMEEXsOPmM7uH
eAz9rxqIOjU=
=dP76
</CERTS>
```

This key is then cached by the client and used to encrypt secure transactions to the server.

By default, transactions with S-HTTP URLs are encrypted, but don't require signatures. Signatures can be required by directives in the security configuration file on the server, or they can be requested via the HTML content header by adding the following line:

```
Content-Type: text/x-server-parsed-html
Privacy-Enhancements: sign, encrypt

<Title>Chili Peppers Order Confirmation</Title>
```

To sign the document, the user would click a Signature button on his or her browser.

A number of new CGI environment variables are also provided with information about the authorized user, their certificates, etc.

Interoperability

What happens to clients without S-HTTP support accessing your server? First, they will have a problem with the S-HTTP URL. Netscape will complain, "the URL is not recognized", and since HTTP is not protected under these encryption mechanisms, it will be served as normal, with the local access controls discussed in Chapter 5. On SSL servers, the worst that can happen is that the information that is going to the Web server will not be encrypted.

Issues

Since the Internet crosses national boundaries, there is some concern with the use of RSA, which cannot legally be exported from the U.S. For an international commerce model to be viable, it must use technology that can be freely deployed regardless of where it is rooted geographically.

Related to this are concerns about RSA holding the reins on the few commercial notaries that can certify a public key. This will be a lucrative endeavor, unless, as some analysts forecast, government agencies like the Postal Service enter the arena of public notaries. It's also unclear what leverage RSA may have with their patents, since much of their original research was government funded. A key umbrella patent for RSA technology is also up for expiration in 1997.

Microsoft is another very real contender for the position of master authenticator, and their alignment with Visa for developing a secure transaction model might introduce a third de facto standard.

Another issue being addressed on an overlapping tangent is the granularity of authorization. With the user authentication models of the S-HTTP, secure servers are still very limited with respect to protecting sets of documents, or aggregating security around groups of users. The maintenance of these sets of authorizations beyond a hundred or so users becomes an administrative nightmare.

DCE, or Distributed Computing Environment, provides a robust model for not only building hierarchical trees of authorization and management, but also for establishing domains of trust for delegating control down to the business units. This could potentially eliminate the need for the public certification at the micro (i.e., per user) level, while retaining auditability and control.

DCE has been making inroads on the DBMS and other network application levels on the Internet, and may fold into the Web with proven technology.

1. SSL provides
    a. encrypted session data and server authentication
    b. client and server authentication
    c. encrypted session data only
    d. encrypted session data and client authentication

2. S-HTTP protects
    a. all URLs
    b. only HTTP
    c. TCP/IP
    d. any network transaction

3. In Netscape, the browser checks the authenticity of a secured server by
    a. requesting authentication from a notary service on the Web
    b. using the browser's private key
    c. a server password
    d. using a notary's public key embedded in the browser to certify the server's key

4. SSL requires what changes in your Web forms?
    a. You must change protected links to "shttp" instead of "http".
    b. The forms must embed public keys.
    c. None.
    d. The forms must prompt for passwords.

DIGITAL CASH

This area of the Web is rapidly changing, and will continue to change for the foreseeable future. For those working on the Web, be it building individual pages or architecting storefronts, it's important to understand the basic payment schemes that are unfolding. This will help place the pros and cons of their variations, and assist you in understanding how to best use the available and upcoming options.

Cash, Credit, or ?

Commerce on the Internet has been compared to the U.S. banking industry in the nineteenth century. Banks had their own private currencies, and exchange was problematic, depending on how much Bank A trusted Bank B's solvency, or in some cases whether Bank A even knew of Bank B's existence. Similarly, a number of different monetary exchange schemes have been proposed, implemented, and are in limited use on the Internet today. Each offers its own vision of how commerce should be supported, and how the Internet should work as a medium of exchange. Most of these fall under two distinct categories: credit-based transactions or token-based transactions. Let's take each in turn and see what it offers.

Credit

Credit systems like Visa, MasterCard, Discovery, etc., pay vendors who can ask for their money if the vendors have two pieces of information: your account number and its expiration date. Then the credit company asks you to reimburse them for the money they paid the vendor.

Behind the scenes, the vendors who take your credit card usually use a go-between; a service that validates your card information, credits the vendor, and then collects from the charge card company. Credit systems are easily extended to the Internet.

But since the entire system depends on a 16-digit number that must be kept secret, yet is also used for every transaction, the Internet poses a new risk. Instead of requiring thieves to sift through garbage bins for carbons, where at least they have to be in the vicinity of a shop you might frequent, the Internet offers remote pilfering opportunities. Early Internet storefronts still tried to solicit credit card numbers, and tried to convince customers that it was no different from ordering over the phone. Others set up order forms, but asked you to call in with your credit card number for security purposes. Neither approach was very attractive to the Internet shopper.

A third approach, by early pioneer First Virtual Holdings, played middleman for credit transactions. A customer only needed to give their credit card number once, to First Virtual, then they could point-click-buy from any store in the First Virtual Mall. The customer used their First Virtual account number, and First Virtual sent them an e-mail confirmation of their purchase. No credit card information was transacted after the initial setup. This avoided some of the issues in the first two approaches, but introduced some limitations of its own (you had to shop at a First Virtual store). A more direct approach was imminent.

With the advent of secure servers and browsers, it becomes possible to safely transmit your credit card information across the Net. CommerceNet at http://www.commerce.net/ was one of the first to take advantage of this. In fact, with technical assistance from EIT, CommerceNet took the NCSA Web server and NCSA's Mosaic client, and built S-HTTP into both, distributing them to participants in CommerceNet. Netscape Communications markets their own Commerce Server, which provides the same transmission security using SSL. Now the emphasis seems to be shifting to online validation of credit purchases, which is part of the deal behind the Microsoft/Visa venture, and is also being pursued vigorously by Netscape.

Advantages of Credit Schemes

- They work with existing payment models.

- They're easier for customers to use and understand (at least for now).

Disadvantages of Credit Schemes

- Dependence on banks.

- Users must have a credit card.

- Detailed transaction history about consumers available and marketable.

- Cannot have transactions between individuals.

- Security? How secure (and how attractive) are the servers that contain tens of thousands of credit card numbers on the Internet? (In February 1995, a hacker, Kevin Mitnick, was arrested for stealing 20,000 credit card numbers stored on the Internet.)

E-Cash: The Dark Horse

Tokens, or e-cash, are real or virtual objects with inherent value. They can be exchanged like money. Let's examine a less extreme example first, because this is new territory, more native to the structure of the Net than the tried and true practices of plastic credit.

NetBank is a concept created by a company called Software Agents (http://www.net-bank.com/). You can send a check to Netbank and once it clears, they will send you an e-mail message with a NetCash note. This note may look something like this:

```
NetCash US $20.00 F235246-H329852WER
```

The merchant e-mails this to Netbank with the following:

```
NetCash US $20.00 F235246-H329852WER /Accept
```

At which point the note is cashed (so it can't be used again) and a new note is generated for $20 and sent to the merchant. The merchant can use this note in the future, or he or she can deposit it into an account with Netbank via

```
NetCash US $20.00 E122226-K0002352THX /Deposit 12345
```

12345 is the merchant's account number. This effectively cashes the note, and the remittance is mailed to the merchant (less a 2 percent processing fee at the time of this writing).

Merchants or customers can make change from their notes by e-mailing the note to the bank as follows:

```
NetCash US$ 10.00 E123456H789012W /Change 2 fives
would return two new coupons, each worth five dollars.
```

Other examples:

```
NetCash US$ 10.00 E123456H789012W /Change 10 ones
NetCash US$ 10.00 E123456H789012W /Change 1 five 4 ones 4 quarters
```

Netcash also has an option for you to send them a check from your (real?) bank account via e-mail. By entering the info that appears on your regular checks, they will automatically initiate the transaction with your bank (although it takes up to 10 days to clear; until then your certificates have a "pending" status).

Essentially, the whole operation is run via e-mail. If a note is intercepted, since it must be cashed from a registered account at Netbank, it's relatively easy to trace.

DigiCash

A company based in the Netherlands called DigiCash has a more radical solution (http://www.digicash.com). They hold several key patents that resolve a number of technical problems with e-cash. One in particular, which has given DigiCash a cult following, is a technique called a "blind signature." This allows the creation of unique serial numbers for currency that can be authenticated by a bank without revealing the identity of the money holder.

With DigiCash, the process unfolds as follows:

1. The consumer creates a note with a software package and submits it to the bank for signature.

2. The bank signs the note, deducting the funds from the consumer's account, and returns the signed note.

3. The consumer modifies the identifier on the note, making it anonymous, but still valid with the bank's signature.

4. The merchant can cash the signed and authenticated bank note received from the consumer.

If the e-cash is lost or stolen, the customer can reveal how the identifier was modified on the note, allowing the bank to trace that particular note.

Token Advantages

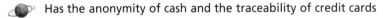 Has the anonymity of cash and the traceability of credit cards

Can be exchanged between individuals

Could save an enormous amount of overhead in record keeping for retail and financial institutions

Combats fraud

Token Disadvantages

 How is it taxed? Cyberspace is not a nation.

 Would totally reassemble the foreign-exchange system

Buying and Selling with E-Cash

Let's set up some products to sell using e-cash. These products will require cyberbucks, which is a trial currency used at DigiCash. The same techniques and principles can be employed when real cyber-dollars are used.

To purchase products with e-cash, you need an e-cash client running on your system at the same time your Web browser is running. This client is like a helper application, but it's not tied to the content of a document. Instead it is listening on a special network port for transactions with an e-cash server. When you click on an item you would like to purchase, the server contacts the e-cash client and verifies the purchase with you, then relinquishes the e-cash from your hard disk to the server you purchased from. Setting up your own server to accept e-cash is probably easier than you think.

Let's go through the four-step procedure of configuring your Web server to sell goods and accept e-cash. Here you go:

1. You'll need to set up a protected directory that holds all the files you want to sell. Restrict access to this directory to the domain digicash.com in access.conf, e.g.,

```
<Directory /usr/local/sales-stuff/>
<Limit GET POST>
order deny, allow
deny from all
allow from digicash.com
</LIMIT>
</Directory>
```

2. Create a file called price.cnf in the directory you protected with one line containing your e-cash account id (obtain from www.digicash.com) and one line containing your e-mail address. The remaining lines contain the filename, price, and description of your goods. For example:

```
Frankenburgers@myserver
fred@myserver
catalog.ps          5.50    Nice color catalog of Frankenburger products
frankendog.gif      1.50    Picture of our mascot
*.gif                .99    All other pictures 99 cents
```

3. Make a file called failed.html in the same directory as the price file. This html file will be displayed in case of payment failure.

4. Now put in links to your goods on any page as follows:

```
<A HREF="http://www.digicash.com
     /cgi-bin/shopgate2?http://www.myserver/full-path/catalog.ps>
     Download my catalog for $5.50!</A>
```

Note the pathnames in both failed.html and in the hyperlink anchor pointing to DigiCash must be full paths, not relative links.

This is the easiest technique to use e-cash. It uses DigiCash as a remote shop server to process e-cash transactions. As people buy stuff from your links, your account automatically grows. You can use your DigiCash client software to check the balance of your account as you watch the cyberbucks pour in.

Only a little more difficult is setting up your own shop server with software you can download from DigiCash.

Summary

Electronic cash is not new; it moves in bulk between financial institutions daily. What is new is that e-cash brings digital money down to the petty cash level. Like our salaries. The models discussed above will most likely coexist. Credit cards did not replace checks and cash, and e-cash will not replace established practices. But it will offer some intriguing choices.

If you are constructing a Web server to participate in electronic commerce, you will have several options. The models discussed above will still be alive and well when you are reading this. Secure transactions will be more widespread, and you will most likely be able to choose between large value added networks that will provide merchant accounts, credit validation, and secure transactions for your server, scripts, or catalogs. You can also explore other options less grounded in tradition but perhaps with more affinity for the online services and products of tomorrow. Money is, among other things, information, and the Internet has, in its short history, an established tradition of nuturing the evolution of the ways we manipulate information.

1. In a token-based system
   a. tokens represent value owed
   b. tokens represent debits to objects with inherent value
   c. tokens are objects with inherent value
   d. tokens represent cash

2. A disadvantage of using credit cards on the Internet is
   a. It doesn't work with existing payment models.
   b. It is not easily understood by customers.
   c. You cannot have transactions between individuals.
   d. Banks do not support credit cards on the Internet due to security risks.

3. How is money obtained from a user with DigiCash?
   a. Client software on the user's machine e-mails e-cash to the server.
   b. A DigiCash capable browser like Netscape must be used.
   c. Client software on the user's machine is accessed by the server when a purchase is made.
   d. It is transferred from an Internet bank account.

4. Since DigiCash is anonymous, what happens if currency is stolen?
   a. That is the risk of any token-based system; the value goes with the object.
   b. DigiCash can use their central repository to trace any e-cash issued to an individual.
   c. The individual can reveal the code used to make a particular e-cash token anonymous; with the token decoded it can be traced.
   d. The client software maintains records of all transactions, so the e-cash can be traced.

ADVANCED
SECURITY

CHAPTER 8

ADVANCED SECURITY

Small companies connecting to the Internet for the first time need to understand, if not practice, firewall technology. Luckily, this has nothing to do with slabs of asbestos, nor will you have to wear any special clothing resembling aluminum foil (unless you really want to).

Firewall is a term applied to a variety of techniques used to protect an internal network from those outside its virtual walls. Up to now, most of your Web design and application has been one-way. Even though you have created interactive forms and CGI scripts, games, and database updates and retrievals, the activity has been pretty much confined specifically to the information you wanted to offer. Unfortunately, when you hook your systems up to the Internet, you may be offering more than access to HTML.

469

If you don't want to give carte blanche to your internal data and resources, you'll need to understand how a firewall works, and decide whether you want to implement one on your own, buy protection from a provider or security consultant, or live with acceptable risk. In any case, this chapter will go over, in depth, what firewalls offer in the way of security and how they protect your network assets. For the technically inclined, there will be enough information and pointers to roll your own using equipment you probably already have at your site and software you can obtain from the Web.

WHAT FIREWALLS CAN DO

In this session, you'll learn how firewalls work. To do this, you'll dive into network protocols, and more specifically, the nuts and bolts of TCP/IP. Services, ports, and network layers form the fabric of your network perimeter, and the material a firewall is built to insulate.

How Firewalls Work

Firewalls work at the lower levels of your network. Ultimately, everything that enters and leaves your network is carried in the traffic of protocols. Network protocols come in many flavors: Windows NT runs a protocol called NetBEUI, Novell file servers use NetWare's SPX/IPX, IBM mainframes use SNA, and thickets of LANtastic, Banyan Vines, and other workgroup communications protocols abound in small offices and departments. The good news is you won't be addressing these, and you don't need to. The firewalls covered here are designed primarily to protect your environment when you connect to the Internet. And on the Internet, TCP/IP rules. So you can focus on a single protocol. The principles covered apply to most of the others, though, so you'll be learning them by proxy.

Understanding Network Protocols

Unless a Webmaster also administers a UNIX platform, or is implementing a firewall, his or her exposure to TCP/IP will probably be minimal. This session will change all that. To successfully implement or understand a firewall, you'll need to understand how TCP/IP works across the wire. You won't have to get into all the gory details, but you'll need a pretty good handle on the basics.

One of the first concepts to master in order to understand a protocol is the concept of network layers. The OSI model is most commonly used to illustrate this, and is shown in Figure 8-1.

Network Layers

Almost any network protocol can be mapped in some fashion to this model. The model helps illustrate that a network protocol performs several independent but related

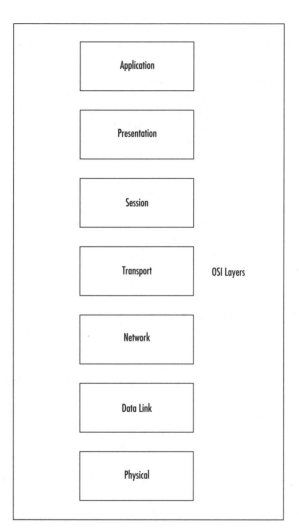

Figure 8-1
The OSI model

functions. Each function is dependent on the layer or layers beneath it. At the bottom rung, a protocol needs to have some physical medium to transport across. This could be copper wire, fiber, radio waves, or smoke signals, for that matter. Whatever physical medium is used, there needs to be some convention of using it that both sender and receiver understand. With smoke signals, blankets and hilltops would probably be part of the layer 1 standard.

Having established the physical stuff to send messages through, in, or across, you next must define how signals are bundled together to create a message. Where a message begins and ends defines the "packets" you hear about that zing around on Ethernet (a physical medium) and T1 lines (another physical medium).

The third layer is the network layer. Its job is to route the packets in the data layer to their appropriate destinations. So in this layer, you need things like network addresses.

The fourth one up is the transport layer. This layer is responsible for a little more of the big picture. It checks to make sure the packets arrived in the proper order, and asks the sender to resend any that appear damaged or missing.

The remaining three layers deal with the actual programs, like e-mail, that are running on top of the other layers. In the OSI model these three are laid out neatly with individual functions, but in TCP/IP they are basically squashed into one layer that can be referred to as the application. In Session 2 you'll see how in the OSI model TCP/IP packets are inspected by certain classes of firewalls.

TCP/IP

The TCP of TCP/IP stands for Transmission Control Protocol, and it is the transport layer (layer 4) discussed above. IP is simply Internet Protocol, and it's the network layer (layer 3). That's why people talk about IP addresses. These two layers are of major importance in building firewalls. They define where a packet is coming from, where it is trying to go, and what function it is trying to reach when it gets there. A packet's ultimate destination is usually some application, and in TCP/IP, applications are advertised as services and ports that sit on top of the transport layer.

Services and Ports

You may not realize it, but you're already familiar with services and ports. Even though it wasn't presented in precisely these terms, this is essentially what a URL is. When a Web browser tries to connect to a Web server using a URL such as http://www.easyaccess.com/, it is connecting to an IP address derived from the name www.easyaccess.com. When it reaches this IP address, it is then connecting to port 80. Ports in TCP/IP are similar in a way to ports in a harbor; they are points of entry into the system. A port in TCP/IP is associated with an application. E-mail has its own port (25), as do FTP (21) and Telnet (23). In fact, you can even connect to a TCP/IP port on a system to get the time of day (13) or a random quote (17). Table 8-1 lists some common ports and their service names on typical UNIX systems.

Service	Port
echo	7
discard	9
daytime	13
netstat	15
quote	17
chargen	19
ftp	21
telnet	23
smtp	25
time	37

Service	Port
whois	43
domain	53
tftp	69
gopher	70
finger	79
www-http	80
pop2	109
pop3	110
nntp	119

Table 8-1 *Services and ports*

Just as domain names can be used in place of an IP address for a host, service names can often be used in place of having to remember the actual port number for an application. So when someone wants to connect to your system, they specify your address, and either the port number or name of an application they want to access.

Let's take an FTP session as a representative sample of how your system services are accessed from the Internet. A remote user connects with your IP address and port 21. Your system passes the connection through to its FTP application (commonly referred to as a daemon). The FTP daemon prompts the remote user for a username and password, checks the system password file to make sure the user is okay, and then sends and receives files at the user's request until the connection is closed. Each packet going back and forth from the remote user to your system will have both the user's IP address and your own. Seems pretty secure. If users are required to log in and provide a password, what's the big deal? Who needs a firewall anyway? Let's see.

The Door Is Open

By default, a UNIX system that has services and ports for Telnet, FTP, Web, and e-mail is open to the world. When hooked to the Internet, anyone can walk up to the front door and try the lock. Most of the doors will be locked. That's the good news. UNIX protects accounts and privileged access to the system through passwords. But at such close range, a potential intruder will be able to inspect the lock. Maybe it's one they are familiar with. It may even have some well-known flaws, or a secret master key. This has been the case with several well-known system intrusions, like the Morris worm, which exploited a flaw in e-mail daemons.

Sometimes these flaws enable a user to get onto the system without an id or password. Other times, they may permit an anonymous user to access data, like the system password file. If a hacker can snag a password file, it can be run through a cracker program that identifies any passwords that are words in the dictionary, common abbreviations, etc. With a newly discovered username and a valid password, the hacker may be back at your door with a key.

Firewalls don't let a passerby off the street, much less up your driveway or sidewalk. They work like the entry to a posh estate, where you pull up to the gate and try to convince the watchman that you have an appointment with Mr. Beeg. He says your name's not on the list, and then gives you one of those looks as you peel off in your Pacer. With a firewall, Internet users can't get to the front door, or in this case, the port of a service, without first establishing the proper credentials. What these credentials are define the type of firewall being implemented. You'll learn about the two major types in the next two sessions. Before leaving this discussion of what firewalls do, though, let's cover briefly what they don't.

What Firewalls Can't Do

Firewalls are the big drawbridge across the castle moat. In other words, they don't help much if the intruder is within the grounds. If the gardener has a separate entrance to your castle, you may have a problem. When you employ firewalls, you need to be sure of your perimeter. Know what's inside and what's outside. Watch out for modem pools, software like Carbon Copy on desktops, and single users with modems that go to online providers. These are like leaving a plank across the moat in back of the castle.

Firewalls also cannot prevent attacks by "social engineering." If someone calls up one of your users and talks them into giving their password (not as difficult as you might think), or can find a way to gain access to workstations inside the firewall (were you the one having trouble with your monitor?), then technology won't be of much help. The next session begins the details of firewall construction. You will learn how a Cisco router can be configured to protect the network layers of your Intranet.

1. What's the difference between a service and a port?
    a. A service is a layer 3 protocol and a port is layer 4.
    b. A service is a layer 4 protocol and a port is layer 3.
    c. A service is an "alias" for a port.
    d. A service is a port protected by a firewall.

2. What purpose does the network layer have?
    a. It defines the medium used for communications.
    b. It advertises ports and services.
    c. It defines the way packets are addressed to nodes on a network.
    d. It makes sure packets arrive in the correct order.

3. Why is the application layer above all the other layers?
    a. Because it doesn't really exist; it's just an abstraction.
    b. Because it is independent of all other layers.
    c. Because it has higher priority in the network.
    d. Because it depends on the lower layers to handle communications.

4. How does a URL specify a port?
   a. By the IP address.
   b. By the type of URL.
   c. By user input on a form.
   d. All URLs are assigned port 80.

SESSION 2

THE NETWORK LAYER

The last session discussed how firewalls work at a conceptual level. This session shows how they work by constructing a packet filtering firewall. Packet filters are one of the two basic types of firewalls, the other being the application proxy (discussed in Session 3). The two are often used together to provide a comprehensive firewall. Packet filter firewalls are frequently very inexpensive to construct. Internet routers, for instance, can be configured to provide basic screening capabilities, and are usually already part of a site's network topology.

Packet Filters

Packet filters, sometimes referred to as packet screens, work on layers 3 and 4 of the OSI model. They look at where a packet is going and where it is coming from (the IP address in layer 3), and the service or port destination and specific flags (in layer 4). This packet information is matched against a set of rules that determine whether to let the packet through.

Figure 8-2 illustrates how a router is used to screen access from the Internet. It does this by controlling who and what gets in and out. Let's look at a packet in a little more detail to see what this means.

Controlling Who

Figure 8-3 shows the fields of a TCP/IP packet.

Note that each IP packet contains information about both source and destination IP addresses. Since TCP/IP traffic is two-way, packets are usually sent to some remote address with a local return address and a local port number. While applications on servers like Telnet and FTP have fixed port numbers, clients connecting to these services can invent a random local port number to receive information coming back. It's kind of like a phone: the addresses are the phone numbers, and the ports are the mouthpiece (the port to the server) and the earpiece (the local port, or client port). Client port numbers are higher than 1024, so they won't be confused with any of the well-known services in Table 8-1.

For example, you might Telnet to a host at address 198.4.3.10 and connect on port 23 as the destination address and port. Your Telnet client puts your own return address, say 128.140.3.4, in an address field, and generates a unique port number, say 1600, for this connection. These are the client, or "source" address and port. Your client listens

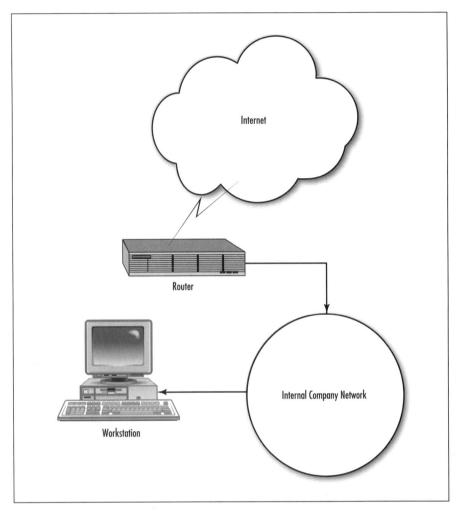

Figure 8-2
A router as a
packet filter

on port 1600 for replies from the Telnet server. This is illustrated in Figure 8-4. The servers always have the same port number. (See Table 8-1.) This way, the clients always know where to connect.

Now, say you need a firewall that would allow any of your users to get out onto the Internet, but not allow anyone from the Internet in. You might consider rules like the following:

ACTION	SOURCE	DESTINATION
allow	192.3.4.0	all
deny	all	192.3.4.0

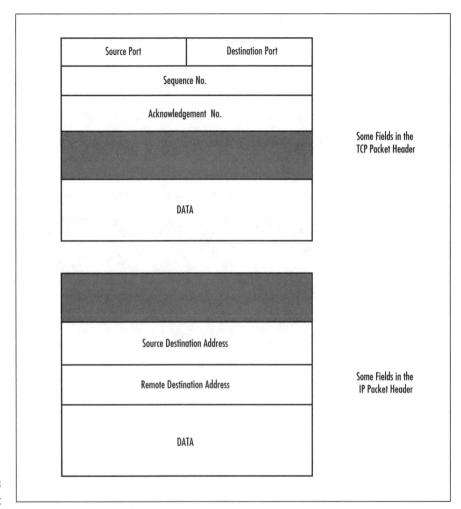

Figure 8-3
A TCP/IP packet

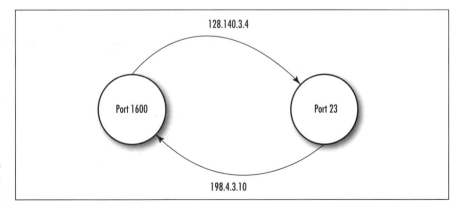

Figure 8-4
A Telnet
connection

This apparently allows any TCP packets from your network (192.3.4.0) to go anywhere they like, but doesn't allow any packets to come in. What's wrong with this? Well, it does prevent anyone from accessing your system from the Internet, but it also prevents your own people from connecting out. Why? Since traffic is blocked coming in, TCP can't establish a two-way interaction. The Internet servers your users connect to will not be able to communicate back to the clients' ports. You can fix the rules by adding some information about ports in the table.

Controlling What

Since most well-known services like the Web (HTTP), Telnet, FTP, and e-mail (SMTP) have port numbers less than 1024, and these services communicate back to your clients on ports higher than 1024, why not revise your packet filter as follows:

ACTION	SOURCE	SOURCE-PORT	DESTINATION	DESTINATION-PORT
allow	192.3.4.0	all	all	all
allow	all	all	192.3.4.0	>1024

Here the deny rule has also been dropped. Assume that anything not permitted in your table will be denied by the packet filter. This is a subtle but important point. Some routers are configured to deny everything that is not explicitly permitted, and others permit everything that is not denied. Be sure you understand the nuances of your router when configuring your firewall. Now, back to the rules at hand.

Outgoing looks the same. You can send to any destination and to any port from your local network. Incoming packets, however, are checked for which of your ports they're heading for. If their port destination is greater than 1024, you can assume they are connecting back to a session originated by one of your clients, so give it the okay. If less than 1024, they may be trying to initiate Telnet or FTP, or connect to some other application on your server, and you reject the packet.

This is better, but still not adequate. What if someone wants to send you mail? To do this they need to connect to your e-mail server on port 25. And if they want to look up your host name, they'll need to access your domain name server (DNS) on port 53. So you'll need rules to let these requests in:

ACTION	SOURCE	SOURCE-PORT	DESTINATION	DESTINATION-PORT
allow	192.3.4.0	all	all	all
allow	all	all	192.3.4.0	>1024
allow	all	all	192.3.4.12	25
allow	all	all	192.3.4.10	53
allow	all	all	192.3.4.15	53

The rules now allow connections from anyone to port 25 on host 192.3.4.12, which is the mail server. They also allow DNS requests into your DNS hosts: 192.3.4.10 and

192.3.4.15. You can continue authorizing services to specific hosts in your network, such as your Web server (port 80). This model extends to most of the other applications except FTP and services based on a transport layer known as UDP. These exceptions are covered next, so you won't run into any surprises when you sit down to actually configure your firewall. Let's start with FTP.

FTP

Why is FTP a special case? Its service port is 21, so why not just allow access to or from this port? FTP is kind of squirrelly. It actually consists of two connections. One is a two-way connection initiated by the client when it connects to the FTP server. The second is a two-way connection established by the server back to the client. Note that this is a little different from the server communicating back to the local port offered by the client. In the case of FTP, the server tries to establish a completely separate connection back to the client. It uses this as a data path for the actual sending and receiving of data. It uses the first connection as a control path to send commands that affect the data transfer. For example, you may want to cancel a transfer in midsession. Your client sends an abort command across the control connection. The second connection from the server to the client comes from the server's port 20 and requests any random high port on the client. You may be beginning to see why this requires some special handling in your filter configuration. Figure 8-5 illustrates an FTP session.

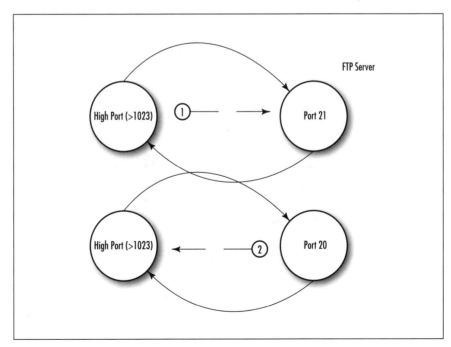

Figure 8-5
An FTP session

To allow your users to initiate FTP sessions to the Internet, you'll need to

 Allow outbound connections to ports 21 and 20

 Allow inbound connections from port 20 from the Internet to high ports on your network

Note that the last rule set permitted FTP to work because you allowed any incoming packets that had destination ports above 1024. The packets coming in from outside hosts on port 20 to a client's port on your network above 1024 would pass. The problem with such a broad rule is that it allows anyone to probe high ports on your system. In some cases you will be able to restrict access to high ports to specific host platforms, like e-mail hosts. In others, however, as in a network of PCs or Macs all capable of establishing their own FTP sessions, you may have to open the high ports to the network as a whole, or implement application proxies (covered in Session 3).

Because very few actual services reside in ports above 1024, what you are mainly screening for are unsafe applications that could allow egress through a back door. These will not, in general, be the typical application suite. They'll be custom or proprietary applications written specifically not to conflict with TCP/IP's normal range of services, such as remote SQL connections to an Oracle database. The next special case for firewall configurations is UDP.

UDP

UDP is a layer 4 transport protocol used in place of TCP for certain applications. They can be written as UDP/IP...doesn't have the same ring to it does it? UDP provides a more efficient but less reliable way of sending packets. Some of the same services offered by TCP are also available using UDP, but some UDP services are unique. In the packet filter configuration, you may also have to allow specific UDP ports and destinations through. RealAudio from Progressive Networks, for example, relies on UDP packets to efficiently "stream" audio across the Internet. If you are using these feeds in your Web browsers, you'll have to open specific UDP ports to allow them through.

Cisco Configuration

Figure 8-2 diagrammed a common topology for a business site connecting to the Internet. A router connects the business LAN to the Internet provider across a T1 line. Most of today's sophisticated routers are capable of being configured to act as packet filters, screening incoming and outgoing packets through the use of rules or access lists. In the next example, you'll see how to configure a Cisco router to act as a simple firewall and implement the following policies:

 Allow any outgoing TCP connections from your network to the Internet

 Allow incoming e-mail and domain name lookups to a specific host

 Allow FTP data connections (discussed in the example) to host 192.12.33.10

Allow connections to your Web server on host 192.12.33.10

 Protect miscellaneous exposures in the high port ranges

Due to variations in syntax with different versions of Cisco software, it is strongly recommended that you use this example only as a rough guide. Consult the specifics in your Cisco documentation when you decide to actually implement access rules at your site.

In the hypothetical Cisco router in Figure 8-2, assume the internal network is 192.12.33.0 on Ethernet interface 0, and your connection to your Internet provider is through serial interface 0. These examples also assume you are running at least Cisco IOS version 10.3. Here is the sample configuration to implement the firewall objectives described above, followed by a line-by-line commentary:

```
no ip source-route
interface ethernet 0
ip address 192.12.33.1
interface serial 0
ip address 192.12.34.1
ip access-group 101 in

router igrp
network 192.12.33.0

access-list 101 deny ip 192.12.33.0 0.0.0.255
access-list 101 permit tcp any any established
access-list 101 permit tcp any host 192.12.33.10 eq 80
access-list 101 permit tcp any host 192.12.33.10 eq ftp
access-list 101 permit tcp any host 192.12.33.10 eq smtp
access-list 101 permit tcp any host 192.12.33.20 eq dns
access-list 101 permit udp any host 192.12.33.20 eq dns
access-list 101 permit tcp any host 192.12.33.25 eq dns
access-list 101 permit udp any host 192.12.33.25 eq dns
access-list 101 deny tcp any any range 6000 6003
access-list 101 deny tcp any any range 2000 2003
access-list 101 deny tcp any any eq 2049
access-list 101 deny udp any any eq 204
access-list 101 permit tcp any 20 any gt 1023
access-list 101 permit tcp any host 192.12.33.10 gt 1023
access-list 101 permit icmp any any
```

Implicit in a Cisco access list is a statement at the end that denies everything else. So if it was not explicitly permitted in the list, it won't be allowed. The configuration begins with

```
no ip source-route
```

Source routing is a technique than can be used to circumvent firewalls by tampering with the return path. If this is not disabled, a packet can spoof its origin and the router will believe it. The next section of parameters just configure the interface. They are shown for completeness. The serial 0 interface, which is the link to the Internet, specifies access group 101 as a prefix to identify the rules that govern how incoming packets will be screened.

Next are the rules themselves:

```
access-list 101 deny ip 192.12.33.0 0.0.0.255
```

This rejects any incoming packets that are trying to masquerade as packets from your internal network.

```
access-list 101 permit tcp any any established
```

This won't be explained in great detail. Refer to the references in Session 4 if you would like to understand more specifics on how and why it works. Essentially, this rule tells the router to allow TCP sessions that are initiated and established from within your firewall. This allows you to open all outgoing connections without having to open all high-numbered ports for the connection back. It relies on a flag being set on the TCP packet after a connection has been initiated. By keying off of this flag in the packet, the filter lets the outside service finish the two-way connection back to your clients.

```
access-list 101 permit tcp any host 192.12.33.10 eq 80
```

This rule permits any outside source address or source port to connect to your Web server on host 192.12.33.10. The rest of the rules follow this same format and implement

- Incoming accessing to FTP and SMTP (e-mail) restricted to a specific host

- Domain name lookups allowed to your primary and secondary DNS, using either TCP or UDP packets

- X-window port (6000+) and OpenWindows (2000+) connection attempts denied

- NFS that uses optional TCP port 2049 denied

- Access back to any high port of one of your clients if coming from FTP's port 20 allowed

- High port connections to a single selected host allowed

- ICMP for network management messages allowed

- Everything else denied

What Wasn't Discussed

Packet filters work at very low levels of network protocol. The many filtering options and issues around potential exposures haven't even been touched on, much less exhausted. This session was meant to give you a working feel for what it entails to set up this type of firewall using equipment that you probably have onsite. Before you actually implement this, please consult some of the excellent books on the market that are dedicated specifically to firewall construction. There are dimensions of detail that would take you far afield in a session like this, but would be fascinating for those inclined to probe deeper into this challenging arena. From Webmaster to firewall consultant is both a viable and lucrative career path!

1. TCP fields include
    a. IP source and destination address
    b. username and passwords
    c. source and port destinations
    d. none of the above

2. The header fields on an IP packet include
    a. IP source and destination address
    b. fields for acknowledgment
    c. source and port destination
    d. sequence numbers

3. When you use access lists on a Cisco router, what is not explicitly permitted is
    a. allowed
    b. denied
    c. not valid
    d. not checked

4. FTP sessions contain how many two-way connections?
    a. one
    b. two
    c. none
    d. three

SESSION 3

APPLICATION PROXIES

Application proxies, also called application gateways, take security to the next level. In Session 2 you saw how packet filters and screening routers restrict what is accessible in your network, but they have a few shortcomings. Packet filters generally don't offer much in the way of auditing. It may be useful, and in some cases essential, to know who is trying to gain access to restricted services. Packet filters also don't allow much in the way of additional layers of security. They typically either accept or reject a connection based on a network address. Once allowed through, the connections are left to whatever native security is implemented on the hosts they access. Let's look at the first advantage provided by application proxies: auditing.

Auditing

Tracking connection attempts, whether successful or not, is one useful feature of this next class of firewalls. While this facility is provided with full-blown proxies, it is also implemented in a simple tool in the proxy toolkits known as a "wrapper" or "relay" function. These small applications act as a front end to your communication services. They pass packets through to the intended service, but first record information about the connection. Wrappers can also be used in conjunction with, or as replacements for, a packet filter by applying permit/deny rules before allowing the connections through to the application. They are only active during the initial connection, so they impose little overhead and are invisible to authorized users.

Wrappers are the simplest form of an application proxy. They have the advantages of being easy to implement and being transparent to users. As you will discover shortly, transparency is not a common hallmark of proxies in general.

To understand how a wrapper works, and provide a foundation for the more sophisticated proxies to be covered shortly, let's look at a public domain utility called TCP Wrapper.

TCP Wrapper

TCP Wrapper can be obtained by anonymous FTP from

```
cert.sei.cmu.edu/pub/network_tools/ tcp_wrappers_7.2.tar
```

Uncompress and unarchive the files on a UNIX system using

```
$ tar -xvf tcp_wrappers_7.2.tar
```

Then, build the modules. First, edit the REAL_DAEMON_DIR in the Makefile to point to where your network applications reside. This varies by operating system, but a common spot is /usr/sbin. The Makefile comments will guide you through this. Then compile with

```
$ make <os>
```

Where *<os>* is your flavor of UNIX operating system, (for example, aix, hp-ux, linux, and so on). You'll end up with five executables. The following of which is a key player:

```
tcpd
```

You should move tcpd into an application directory such as /usr/local/bin using the following command:

```
mv tcpd /usr/local/bin
```

Now, for any service that you would like to audit, you'll need to modify an entry in /etc/inetd.conf. For example, to monitor FTP access, change the /etc/inetd.conf entry from

```
ftp stream tcp nowait root /usr/sbin/ftpd        ftpd
```

to

```
ftp stream tcp nowait root /usr/local/bin/tcpd /usr/sbin/ftpd
```

The actual format of the entries in your /etc/inetd.conf may vary from those above, but what you accomplish is to intercept calls to the FTPD daemon with tcpd. You can continue with other services such as telnetd, tftpd, rexecd, and others with the same technique.

After making these changes, restart the inetd daemon. On most UNIX systems this is done by sending a signal to inetd's process id. To find its process id, enter the following command:

```
# ps agx | grep inetd
```

If a PID of, say, 1069 is displayed, execute

```
# kill -HUP 1069
```

to force inetd to reinitialize itself and re-read its /etc/inetd.conf file.

All accesses to Telnet will now be logged by the system log daemon syslog. By default, tcpd entries are put in the same log as sendmail. All FTP sessions to your system are now recorded. Here's an example of a single log entry; the system running tcpd is called delphi, and the FTP client is coming from a CompuServe account:

```
Feb 8 00:50:28 delphi ftpd[7711]: connect from ax11.compuserve.com
```

In and of itself this may be useful, but TCP Wrapper has additional controls in the form of two files:

```
/etc/hosts.allow
/etc/hosts.deny
```

Rules in these files permit or deny access to the service similarly to the way packet filters, discussed in Session 2, do. TCP Wrapper will check the hosts.allow file first, then hosts.deny file. The syntax of the individual rules in these files is

```
service-name: host-list [:shell-cmd]
```

To deny all access to Telnet and FTP (assuming you modified their entries in /etc/inetd.conf per above) from network 192.12.33, you would enter the following in hosts.deny:

```
telnetd, ftpd: 192.12.33
```

To disallow all finger commands from anywhere except host 192.12.44.5, enter

```
/etc/hosts.allow
      fingerd: 192.12.44.5
/etc/hosts.deny
      fingerd: ALL
```

One of the other executables built with tcpd is a program called tcpdchk. This application checks your rules and tries to diagnose any problems. Another application, tcpdmatch, is used to test the rules against hypothetical connections. For example, to test your rules against a host called peewee.bogus.com you would enter

```
tcpdmatch tftpd peewee.bogus.com
```

The tcpdmatch application reports whether this host is allowed to establish an FTP session based on the rules you've configured.

If you start monitoring several applications, you'll want to keep an eye on the size of the log files that TCP Wrapper generates. They can grow large quickly. You may also want to download another program called swatch from ftp://ftp.stanford.edu/general/security-tools/swatch. This utility can be configured to scan the syslog entries in real time to search for patterns that you specify and match them to actions. You can use it to alert you, for example, if anyone tries to access your system and is denied. If you're very compulsive, er, cautious, you could have it page you on your beeper.

Tunnels

Tunnels are similar to wrappers, but instead of passing connections through to a service on the same host, they pass them through to another host. This allows outsiders to connect to a service on an exposed host that secretly passes packets for key applications back to a host on the inside. The exposed host is usually called a *bastion* host. A packet filter can funnel all access to services like e-mail to this specific host. In turn, this host can forward the packets to some internal host unknown to, and perhaps unaddressable from, the outside world.

Wrappers and tunnels are a limited model of the application proxy. Now let's look at the full-blown package.

The Real Thing

While wrappers and tunnels operate invisibly to most users (if they are authorized), this next class of application gateways is a little more disruptive to "business as usual." They are typically used in a bastion host, discussed above, and they control connections to services both outside and inside by mediating what gets through. A bastion host configuration is shown in Figure 8-6.

If packet filters are analogous to customs searching your car at the border, Bill Cheswick of AT&T Bell Labs describes proxies as not only a search, but as having to get out of your car and take another to continue your trip!

With a proxy in place, you don't directly connect to anything. You first connect to the proxy, then the proxy asks you were you want to go. If you check out as who you say you are (authenticate), and if you are authorized to go where you want, the proxy connects you to your destination and sends all packets to the outside on your behalf, returning all those that come back. To realize the implications of this, let's walk through an example.

Say you want to FTP a file from Internet host ftp.buzzwords.com, and your application proxy/bastion host/firewall is called big.brother.com. Here's what the session would look like using typical firewall products:

```
ftp>open big.brother.com
Connected to big.brother.com
220 big.brother.com InterLock FTP Gateway 2.0 ready at Tue Dec 31 10:12:40 1996
Name (big.brother.com:fred): fred
331 Password required for fred

230 - You are authorized as Interlock user fred. Specify your remote user and destination .
Ftp>user anonymous@ftp.buzzwords.com
331 - ftp.buzzwords.com FTP server ready
331 Guest login ok, send ident as password
Password:
ftp>dir
```

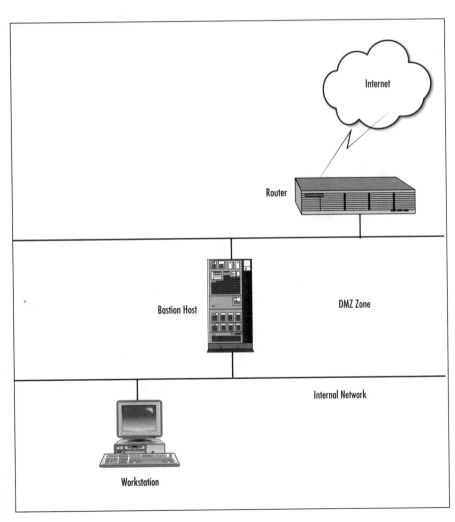

Figure 8-6
A bastion host
configuration

Everything goes through big brother. This adds an extra spin to firewalls, protecting not only who gets in, but who gets out. For pointers to commercial and public domain software that can function as this type of gateway, see Session 4.

Actually configuring an application proxy goes pretty far beyond the scope of this tutorial. Many of the commercial products have endeavored to make this a turnkey operation with mixed reviews.

Proxies are typically more secure, but less efficient, than packet filters. But there is one flavor of proxy that may even improve performance, specifically for your Web users.

Proxies and WWW

Under Netscape Options⇨Network Preferences you may have noticed a tab for Proxies. Proxies can control outbound access to Internet HTTP, and Web browsers that are "proxy aware," like Netscape, can make the experience a little less painful than the FTP example above. Once a browser is configured, it can access any Internet resource that is not forbidden to your site through a proxy host. With all of your browsers coming through a common gateway, a packet filter can be configured to restrict all outbound HTTP to just this host. This may not seem like that much of an advantage. But some proxies, like the CERN Web Server/Proxy, also cache pages that have been frequently accessed, allowing you to access sites that are popular from your network using a central cache, rather than each user caching the same information redundantly.

This can help performance when a popular application pops up on the Internet, like Sun's Java development kit, or Hubble satellite images, and you won't have megabytes of the same data competing for bandwidth with your other Internet traffic.

Adding Authentication

Another advantage of proxies is that they extend the capabilities of user authentication. The standard username/password for access to a system can become a problem if you don't trust the network a user is on, or the one a user passes through to get to your systems. A proxy can provide an extra layer, enforcing special "disposable" passwords that are good for a single login. This nullifies the exposure of eavesdropping, guessing passwords, or even hacking password files. Most application proxies allow you to hook in stronger forms of authentication for your generic services. You can do this through commercial alternatives, like SmartCards, which contain electronics to generate unique passwords every 60 seconds and vary with each card. SmartCards are effective, but somewhat expensive.

You can also adopt low-tech but useful public domain technologies like S/Key developed at Bellcore. S/Key generates a page of random numbers you can take with you to WWW and Internet conventions, allowing you to log in using one of these numbers as the password. You then cross that one off and use the next one for the next login. Anyone eavesdropping on the lines will not get any useful information, other than an expired password. S/Key can be used with the TIS firewall kit discussed in Session 4.

Well, that's it for proxies. Obviously this session didn't cover many of the details of how you would configure your topology to best use these tools, or the nuts and bolts of configuring a bastion host to protect vital services. Hopefully, though, you now have a feel for what a proxy does, and how it might be used in your environment. You've also seen proxies from the user's point of view, and how they effect access to outside services. In Session 4 you'll find out where to get these products, both commercial and home-brew, and look at some of the advantages and disadvantages of both the packet filter and proxy approaches to firewalling your data.

QUIZ 3

1. One thing proxies do that packet filters on routers generally don't is
   a. allow access based on IP addresses
   b. allow access based on ports
   c. audit access attempts
   d. protect applications from external networks

2. A TCP wrapper
   a. routes TCP packets to another host
   b. encrypts TCP packets
   c. checks and logs TCP connections
   d. shields TCP packets from eavesdroppers

3. A tunnel
   a. provides a secure path through a firewall
   b. refers to a back door in a firewall created by hackers
   c. routes TCP packets to another host
   d. makes TCP packets invisible on the Internet

4. To connect to a remote host service through an application proxy
   a. you just connect to the remote host; the proxy is transparent
   b. you have to connect to the remote host from outside the firewall
   c. is impossible, the proxy prevents this type of access
   d. you have to connect to the service on the proxy first, then the remote host

SESSION 4

STRATEGIES AND PRODUCTS

Sun Tzu is the patron saint of the security crowd, and there's an unwritten rule (up to now) that states that any discussion of firewalls or security has to include a quote from his *Art of War*. Well, here it is: "If you are ignorant of both your enemy and yourself, you are certain in every battle to be in peril."

In the last few sessions of this chapter, you've peeked into the cloak-and-dagger realms of network security. You've learned some of the exposures a host has when connecting to the Internet, and some of the ways these are exploited in the protocols that mediate transactions to host services. If the material has piqued your interest, you would do well to study firewall FAQs such as those found at

```
http://www.cis.ohio-state.edu/hypertext/faq/usenet/firewalls-faq/faq.html
http://www.greatcircle.com/firewalls/info/FAQ.html
http://www.netmanage.com/netmanage/tsupport/firewall.htm
```

Subscribe to security lists and CERT advisories at

```
http://www.sei.cmu.edu/technology/cert.cc.html
```

And you can cuddle up with some of the better texts of the trade, such as *Firewalls and Internet Security* by Cheswick and Bellovin and *Internet Firewalls and Network Security* by Karanjit Siyan and Chris Hare.

These resources will point you to the most recent developments in the firewall trade. If you would like to poke around a little more and learn with hands-on experience, one way to get started is with a firewall "toolkit," such as the one provided by Trusted Information Systems (TIS).

The TIS Toolkit

The TIS toolkit can be obtained by anonymous FTP to ftp://ftp.tis.com/pub/firewalls/toolkit/fwtk.v1-3.tar.Z. Uncompress and untar this file into a directory and you will have the source code for a variety of widgets that can be mixed and matched to implement a remarkably complete firewall solution. Let's look at some of these goodies and how they relate to concepts discussed in the last two sessions.

Netacl

This is an implementation of a TCP wrapper, like the one discussed in Session 3. Its advantage, if you are implementing more components of the TIS toolkit, is that it uses the same configuration files as the other components, allowing you to consolidate your security rules in a single location.

When implementing FTP and Telnet proxies, netacl can be used to provide internal access for the system administrator into the "regular" Telnet and FTP if they meet certain authentication and authorization criteria.

It can also be used to *chroot* anonymous FTP, locking anonymous users into a restricted directory even before the FTP daemon is contacted.

Smap

Provides a type of tunnel for e-mail. Since the sendmail application that manages e-mail is one of the most frequently exploited programs for holes in security, smap was designed to provide insulation from any bugs that might compromise security. When an outside user connects to the mail port, smap is invoked instead of sendmail. It switches to a restricted directory that contains no files or access to files other than those smap creates. Mail messages are dropped off here, and picked up next with a partner process, smapd, which has no interaction with the user, and delivers mail found in the staging area to sendmail proper.

Ftp-gw

This component implements an FTP application proxy. Like smap, and the other proxy components listed below, Ftp-gw operates in a restricted directory. Like the example in the proxy section, this gateway requires users to open an FTP session to the gateway first, and then asks the gateway to open a connection to the outside on their behalf. Outside users must authenticate themselves to this proxy before they are allowed to gain access to any FTP services offered on internal hosts behind the firewall.

Telnet-Gw, Rlogin-Gw

Telnet-Gw and Rlogin-gw work much the same as Ftp-gw, protecting Telnet and Rlogin (remote login) services with the same type of proxy intervention.

Plug-Gw

This is a generic tunnel or relay. It connects an application port on the firewall to an application port on some internal system. As part of the toolkit, it was designed primarily for Usenet News, but should work with other TCP applications as well. Tunnels allow you to "beam" into a port on an internal system, without having to establish a firewall or otherwise isolate the system as a whole, as long as the specific service on the internal system is secure.

Login-sh

When a user interactively logs in to UNIX, they usually log in to a specific "shell" or command environment. Login-sh front-ends this process with a program that requires additional authentication. A variety of new authentication protocols can be used (see Authd below) without requiring any modifications to the standard system login program. Login-sh can be enabled for selected users, and can be handy for staff that is on the road to trade shows or other locales where they will be logging in to their internal systems through "untrusted" networks or Internet providers. By adding an additional authentication requirement, like single-use passwords such as those provided by S/Key, they are protected from eavesdropping and applications running on foreign workstations that might snag a password as they access their home services.

Authd

A powerful extension in the TIS toolkit, Authd extends the authentication model for the application proxies discussed above. It offers five different types of authentication, including

 Internal plain-text password

 Bellcore's S/Key

 Security Dynamics' SecurID

 Enigma Logics' Silver Card

 Digital Pathways' SNK004 Secure Net Key

Users are matched to the type of authentication required, and Authd's security database can be managed on the bastion host, or remotely using encrypted sessions with the authsrv utility.

Administration of users in the security database can be delegated, and group administrators are able to add or delete users from their groups, allowing a single firewall to be jointly managed by a number of internal departments.

Syslogd

TIS includes a version of syslogd that works in a similar fashion to Swatch. You can specify search patterns; then when a log entry is received that matches a pattern, an alert is issued. The alert can be an arbitrary command or script.

Summary

TIS provides most of the components needed to implement a firewall on a bastion host. It is definitely oriented toward the "do-it-yourself" security crowd, and offers a very economical solution for those willing to devote the time to understanding the technical intricacies of a firewall.

Many of the serious network exposures are esoteric and highly technical. You've probably seen enough *James Bond* to know that you have to keep your knowledge of the technical tools sharp and current to keep up with the bad guys.

Come On, Do I Really Need a Firewall?

For most of you, what has been presented will probably be enough to help you understand what protection entails and to provide you with some starting points for implementing your own security measures. As dire as some of the threats appear, however, firewalls are not all that common on the Internet. Many find the basic locks and checks of a well-administered system to be sufficient. A firewall can even provide a false sense of security. If you haven't yet implemented a firewall, you can easily add capabilities like auditing or basic screening through your router to create strong deterrents for the casual hacker with a minimal investment of resources.

For others, firewalls are a basic requirement, enforced by company policy or for protection of sensitive data. For these people, it is probably necessary to hire a security manager or bring aboard a consultant for the installation of and training in one of the commercial firewall products. In both cases you will have to weigh the costs against the benefits.

The Costs

Firewalls can be very expensive, in both hardware and people costs. Packet filters, or screening routers, have the advantage using existing equipment with only additional configuration. The packet filter has a smaller impact on network performance than the application proxy, as it is working with less overhead. Nevertheless, a properly configured router that is screening services accessible from the outside can be one of the most economical and useful security measures. It requires less expertise than the application gateway or proxy approach, and limits the exposures to flaws in UNIX operating systems behind the router. If you are purchasing your connectivity through an ISP, these controls can often be implemented by your provider, and you can specify exactly what you want coming in and out of your local network.

Application proxies provide more rigorous security, but the overhead is high. Every packet is essentially duplicated as it crosses from one side of the gateway to another. These gateways can also break certain protocols, like RealAudio and other "streaming" technologies. They can make access cumbersome. Therefore, the default philosophy of shops with bastion hosts usually requires each new protocol or application to be justified and explicitly configured before it can pass through the gateway.

The Holes

Firewalls, as mentioned in the first session, are only one piece of a security policy. They can be easily circumvented if the rest of the environment is not as stringently controlled as the front door. The large metal gate in the front drive is not very effective if the back of the property is a picket fence. Things like modems connected to individual PCs can provide back doors that are hard to identify and control. Since TCP/IP is a two-way protocol, a casual user dialing out to a service may be susceptible to probes coming back down the wire without notice. The ease of programming Winsocket applications in Visual Basic makes feasible Trojan horse programs that could accept connections on high ports while playing a game, circumventing firewall strategies that are not carefully developed.

For the really paranoid, it's interesting to note that most documented computer fraud is perpetrated from within. This puts another spin on the cost/benefit equation. If the purpose of firewalls is to protect internal data, it is statistically more probable that this data will walk off on a floppy disk or cartridge tape backup than be yanked from its platform by some denizen of the Net.

These sessions have used custom-built tools to demonstrate various features and capabilities of firewalls. An easier route when you get ready to actually implement this technology may be to find a shrinkwrapped solution from one of the many firewall vendors. The marketplace is constantly changing, so the best resource would be to use a Web search engine on keywords like "Firewall and Vendor". At the time of this writing, a fairly comprehensive list was being maintained at http://access.digex.net/~bdboyle/firewall.vendor.html.

With what you've covered in these sessions, you will be able to read the technical specifications for the products and understand the lingo of the security consultants. You may even shock them with a quote from Sun Tzu.

1. The TIS Toolkit is
   a. a shrinkwrapped firewall package
   b. components you mix and match to roll your own firewall

    c. a set of utilities for configuring Cisco routers

    d. a set of unrelated firewall components

2. A packet filter is more efficient than an application proxy because

    a. It runs on faster processors.

    b. It deals with the application layer.

    c. It only performs superficial checks on a packet.

    d. It is usually connected to a high-speed network.

3. Firewalls can be circumvented if the attack

    a. is repetitive

    b. is performed from another firewall

    c. comes from inside

    d. comes from a privileged user on another UNIX host

4. One of the most commonly deployed firewalls on the Internet is

    a. the TIS Toolkit

    b. the TCP Wrapper

    c. the packet filter config on a router

    d. S/Key

BEYOND THE HTML HORIZON

CHAPTER 9

BEYOND THE HTML HORIZON

I f you write about as fast a moving target as the Web, and you write your chapters in order, the last one is destined to have some of the most exciting material. In Session 1, you'll learn how to employ a wide range of Java applets to create special effects on your pages — without writing a single line of Java code. You'll use applets already developed, kind of an upscale version of clip-art. By using off-the-shelf applets, you can Java enable your pages in a fraction of the time it would take to do so from scratch. A scrolling LED banner, for example, takes you only seconds with freeware applets, compared to days of Java coding.

Continuing the maximum-impact, minimum-effort approach, Session 2 covers creating self-contained animations by exploiting advanced features of GIF. You'll build images that animate themselves (or so it seems), without the need for scripts,

497

media players, or even freeware Java. And finally, the last session brings you back to working with Perl, where you explore a powerful object library called libwww. This library has been used to write Web spiders and robots, and you'll take it for a spin to create your very own Internet agent. So let's get started with some canned Java.

JAVA IN A CAN

Java "clip-art," or canned applets, have several advantages over traditional graphical clip-art. For starters, a well-written applet can be highly customized with parameters passed from HTML. A generic animation applet, for example, takes a series of GIF images and makes them dance across a page. The parameters make the images your own, so rather than being stuck with a steaming cup, you end up with a tool furnishing a range of presentation options for your page. Before getting into all the neat gizmos that can be added with this approach, let's revisit how applets are invoked from HTML, and how parameters are passed.

An applet is invoked from a Web page with the following HTML tag:

THE <APPLET> TAG

```
<APPLET
        code="name"
        width=n
        height=n
        [codebase="relative directory"]
        [align=""]
        [vspace=n]
        [hspace=n]
>
        <param name=x1 value=y1>
        <param name=x1 value=y2>
        </APPLET>
```

code is the name of the Java applet to be run

width is the width of the applet in pixels

height is the height of the applet in pixels

codebase is the relative directory containing the Java applet

align controls the positioning of the applet on the page

vspace is the vertical space, in pixels, around the applet

hspace is the horizontal space, in pixels, around the applet

<param> is zero or more parameter statements that pass variable names and values to the applet

The applet tag is an extension to HTML syntax. The tag tells a browser where to retrieve a Java program (or applet) to execute when the Web page is loaded. The applet tag also specifies what parameters, if any, to pass to the program. Note that an applet tag only makes sense in browsers capable of running Java; other browsers will ignore it.

Code points to the name of the Java applet. The default applet resides in the same directory as the Web page and consists of a name with a .class suffix. To call a Java applet called RunMe.class, for example, the HTML tag specifies

```
<applet code="RunMe.class" width=100 height=100>
</applet>
```

To keep applets in a subdirectory beneath the directory containing your HTML, you can use the optional parameter *codebase*, which specifies the directory containing the Java code relative to the current URL. If RunMe is in a subdirectory called MyApplets, use

```
<applet
      codebase="MyApplets"
      code="RunMe.class"
      width=100
      height=100>
</applet>
```

The applets in this session have all been designed to be driven by parameters. To pass a parameter to an applet, you specify the name of the parameter and its value. To tell RunMe that the value of the image is "balloon.gif", the HTML tag would specify

```
<applet
      codebase="MyApplets"
      code="RunMe.class"
      width=100
      height=100>
<param name="image" value="balloon.gif">
</applet>
```

Multiple parameters are usually required to control the full range of behaviors in the applets covered in the examples that follow.

Regular HTML can also be entered between the beginning and ending applet tags, and the HTML will generally (depending on the browser) be displayed if a browser is not Java capable. For example:

```
<applet
      codebase="MyApplets"
      code="RunMe.class"
      width=100
      height=100>
<param name="image" value="balloon.gif">
This would look <b>really cool</b> if your browser supported Java!
</applet>
```

Sometimes you can use an image instead of text to cover space allocated on the page for the applet:

```
<applet
        codebase="MyApplets"
        code="RunMe.class"
        width=100
        height=100>
<param name="image" value="balloon.gif">
<img src="tobad.gif" width=100 height=100>
</applet>
```

An applet can be aligned on the page much like the <IMG> tag, by using the align option:

```
<applet
        codebase="MyApplets"
        code="RunMe.class"
        align=left
        width=100
        height=100>
<param name="image" value="balloon.gif">
<img src="tobad.gif" width=100 height=100>
</applet>
```

Let's spice up your pages by using these techniques to manipulate and control a Java applet. The following applets come free with the Java Developer's Kit, and can be downloaded off the Net from http://www.javasoft.com.

Animator

Animator was written by Herb Jellinek of Sun Microsystems. It's a general purpose animation engine that displays a series of images for frame animation effects. The images can be infinitely looped or displayed with a single pass. Animator can associate sound effects with the clip, or with specific frames.

Components

Animator consist of the following .class files:

 Animator.class

 ParseException.class

 ImageNotFoundException.class

The Effect

Animator looks for a series of GIF files named T1.GIF through Tn.GIF, where n is the highest numbered frame in the animation. Individual frames can be positioned anywhere in the applet area. Pauses between frames can be specified. Animator looks for a single .au sound track file if specified and can associate individual sounds with each frame. A startup image can display while the others are loading, and a background image can be used as the scene for the animation. The parameters needed to control these effects are described below.

PARAMETER	DESCRIPTION
imagesource	URL of the directory containing the images T1.GIF through T*n*.GIF.
startup	URL of an image displayed while the animation images are downloading.
background	URL of background image.
startimage	Index of the first frame (typically "1").
endimage	Index of the last frame.
pause	Interval in milliseconds to pause between each frame.
pauses	Overrides pause above, with an array of pauses specified for each frame. Each pause separated with a | character. For example: "100|50|50|1000".
repeat	Boolean True or False to loop the animation.
positions	An array of x@y positions that specify the x,y coordinates where individual frames display. Each element is separated with a | character. For example: "5@5|50@50|0@0".
images	A list of the index sequence you want images displayed in. This allows you to repeat images. For example: "1|2|3|4|2|3|4|5|6".
soundsource	URL of the directory containing the .au sound clips.
soundtrack	URL to the sound clip played in the background.
sounds	List of clips played for each frame: "1.au|2.au|2.au|3.au". Intervals of silence can be specified by nulls; for example: "1.au||2.au".

Sample Usage

```
<applet code=Animator.class width=100 height=100>
<param name=imagesource value="images">
<param name=endimage value=10>
<param name=soundsource value="sounds">
<param name=soundtrack value=muzak.au>
<param name=sounds value="1.au|2.au|3.au|4.au|5.au|6.au|7.au|8.au|9.au|0.au">
<param name=pause value=200>
</applet>
```

The images used are T1.GIF (default starting index) through T10.GIF (specified in endimage) in the images/ subdirectory of this HTML file. Sounds clips are retrieved from the sounds/ subdirectory for a background sound track (muzak.au) and individual sounds for each frame. There is a default pause of 200 milliseconds, or 2/10ths of a second, inserted between each frame.

AudioItem

This basic but useful applet is used to play a sound clip when your page is accessed. It was written by James Gosling of Sun Microsystems.

Components

AudioItem consists of a single .class file:

 AudioItem.class

The Effect

AudioItem paints a small audio icon on the page with primitive graphics; no image file is required. It plays one or more sounds passed by parameter. If the icon is clicked, AudioItem skips to the next sound in the sequence. Setting the applet's width and height to 0 makes the audio icon invisible, leaving you with just the sound effect.

PARAMETER	DESCRIPTION
snd	URLs of sound clips separated by the | character. E.g., "hello.au|goodbye.au".

Sample Usage

```
<applet code=AudioItem.class width=0 height=0>
<param name=snd value="ghost.au">
</applet>
```

The applet is invisible on the screen. The ghost.au clip is retrieved from the directory containing this HTML page.

TickerTape

Implements a popular class of applets that display a scrolling LED sign on a page. It is freeware, written by John Criswick of Internet Conveyor.

Components

TickerTape consist of the following .class files:

 TickerTape.class

 TickerFont.class

 ISO8859.class

The Effect

TickerTape displays text set by a parameter, or retrieved from a file relative to the same directory as the HTML containing the applet. It can display the entire ISO8859 character set, and even interprets entity names like À Ñ etc. The background, frame, and LED colors can all be specified with the parameters described below.

PARAMETER	DESCRIPTION
text	Actual text string to be displayed in TickerTape.
file	Relative URL to file in same directory path as HTML using TickerTape applet.
backcolor	Background color value. Value must be one of the following: black, blue, cyan, darkgray, gray, green, lightgray, magenta, orange, pink, red, white, or yellow.
framecolor	Color of the frame surrounding the ticker tape. See valid values above.
ledcolor	Color of the LED lights (dots) themselves.
ledoffcolor	Color of the unlit LED dots.
framethick	Pixel thickness of the frame. Defaults to 1.
ledsize	Size of LED dot. Defaults to 1.
ledtype	Round (1) or square (0) LEDs, defaults to 0.
ledspacing	Pixels between LED characters, defaults to 1.
speed	Scrolling interval in milliseconds. Defaults to 100.
scrollfactor	How far the text is moved with each scroll. Defaults to 2.

Sample Usage

```
<applet code="TickerTape" width=440 height=37 align=absmiddle>
<param name=ledcolor value=magenta>
<param name=backcolor value=black>
<param name=framecolor value=black>
<param name=ledoffcolor value=black>
<param name=framethick value=1>
<param name=ledsize value=1>
<param name=ledtype value=0>
<param name=file value="quotes.txt">
</applet>
```

A message is scrolled onto the screen from the file quotes.txt in the same directory as the HTML page using this applet. The lights are in magenta on an all black background. Figure 9-1 demonstrates this effect in black and white.

ImageMap

ImageMap, written by Jim Graham, is one of the most versatile applets covered so far. Not only can it create, in essence, a client side imagemap, but it can add interactive sound and animation links as the mouse enters predefined areas of the image. There are also delayed audio effects (when a mouse stays in an area past a certain interval) and the ability to highlight sections of the image as the mouse enters.

Components

ImageMap consists of the following .class files:

ImageMap.class

ButtonFilter.class

ClickArea.class

HighlightFilter.class

HrefArea.class

HrefButtonArea.class

ImageMapArea.class

NameArea.class

RoundButtonFilter.class

RoundHrefButtonArea.class

SoundArea.class

The Effect

As the mouse enters various areas of an image, animation and sound effects are triggered. Areas are defined as highlight areas, sound areas, and link areas. This last category is the familiar hyperlink to a URL from a typical imagemap.

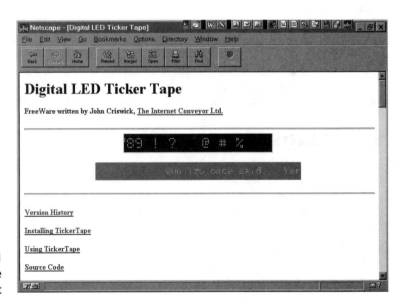

Figure 9-1
The TickerTape
applet

PARAMETER	DESCRIPTION
img	URL of the main image.
highlight	Type of highlighting for the highlight areas. Can specify brighter*n* or darker*n*, where *n* is a percentage brighter or darker; for example, brighter25 or darker10.
area*n*	Defines a rectangular area *n* of the imagemap using the following syntax: class, x, y, width, height arguments.
	Valid classes:
	SoundArea. URL of sound clip to play when mouse enters area.
	DelayedSoundArea. URL of sound clip, and millisecond interval. When mouse stays in area longer than the interval, the sound clip is played.
	LinkArea. URL to go to when mouse clicks in this area.
	NameArea. String to display on status line when mouse enters area.
	HrefButtonArea. Same as LinkArea, but also displays button border when mouse enters the area.
	RoundHrefButtonArea. Same as above; displays circular button border.
	HighLightArea. Highlights area when mouse enters. Appearance based on highlight parameter described above.
	"AniArea". Plays animation when mouse enters. Animation is a URL of a single image, with x,y coordinates defining location of individual frames within it.
	ClickArea. Display coordinates when clicked; used for debugging.

Sample Usage

```
<applet code=ImageMap.class width=320 height=200>
<param name=img value="space.gif">
<param name=highlight value="brighter20">
<param name=area1 value="SoundArea,0,0,50,50,audio/scream.au">
<param name=area2 value="NameArea,100,100,50,50,Hi!">
<param name=area3 value="HrefButtonArea,50,50,32,32,http://www.cool.com/">
<param name=area6 value="RoundHrefButtonArea,0,0,100,100,duke.wave.html">
<param name=area7 value="SoundArea,90,5,40,40,audio/beepbeep.au">
<param name=area9 value="ClickArea,0,0,320,200">
</applet>
```

A number of areas trigger various effects. Note that you can have overlapping areas, in which case the effects are applied sequentially in the order they are defined. This is a particularly useful applet for those delving into Java coding, because it dynamically loads the area "handlers." You can extend ImageMap's behavior by writing your own subclasses for new effects, and it looks for your class file if an area value specifies it. Check out the source code reference that comes with the applet for more detail.

Bar Chart

This applet, written by Sami Shaio from Sun Microsystems, displays a simple, customizable bar chart graph.

Components

BarChart consists of a single component: Chart.class.

The Effect

BarChart displays data vertically or horizontally with a variable number of bars, colors, and styles. You can set the scale, titles, and labels for the bars. You are responsible for defining the applet size large enough to contain the graph. Here are the parameters that control Bar Chart:

PARAMETER	DESCRIPTION
title	Title text for the bar chart.
columns	Number of bars on the chart.
orientation	Horizontal or vertical.
scale	Number of pixels per unit.
cn_style	When n is the column being defined, and style is the style of the bar, either solid or striped. For example, name=c1_style value="striped". Defaults to solid.
cn	Numeric quantity for the bar, the value that is being measured; for example, name=c1 value="50".
cn_label	Label on the bar.
cn_color	Color of the bar, one of the following: black, blue, cyan, darkgray, gray, green, magenta, orange, pink, red, white, or yellow. Defaults to gray.

Sample Usage

```
<applet code="Chart.class" width=250 height=150>
<param name=title value="Performance">
<param name=columns value="4">
<param name=scale value="5">
<param name=orientation value="horizontal">
<param name=c1_style value="striped">
<param name=c1 value="10">
<param name=c1_color value="blue">
<param name=c1_label value="Q1">
<param name=c2_color value="green">
<param name=c2 value="20">
<param name=c2_label value="Q2">
<param name=c2_style value="solid">
<param name=c3_style value="striped">
<param name=c3 value="5">
```

```
<param name=c3_color value="magenta">
<param name=c3_label value="Q3">
<param name=c4 value="30">
<param name=c4_color value="yellow">
<param name=c4_label value="Q4">
<param name=c4_style value="solid">
</applet>
```

This code creates a simple horizontal bar chart. Note that the parameters for the columns don't need to be specified in order. Figure 9-2 displays the results.

Nervous Text

This applet, written by Daniel Wyszynski, causes text to bounce around on the screen.

Components

NervousText consists of a single component: NervousText.class

The Effect

Nervous text is like <BLINK> with an attitude. The text oscillates inside the applet panel in random jerks and starts. Could be mistaken for a toxic overdose of caffeine.

PARAMETER	DESCRIPTION
text	Value is the string displayed.

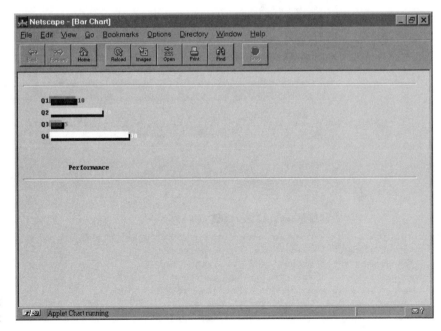

Figure 9-2
The Bar Chart
applet

Sample Usage

```
<applet code=NervousText.class width=500 height=50>
<param name=text value="Have You Had Your Coffee Today?">
</applet>
```

You'll need to adjust your applet size to fit all of your string in. A 36-point Times Roman font is used.

TourGuide Applet

This applet was written by Marc Sacoolas of SunSoft New Media Marketing, and can be found at Café de Sol at http://www.xm.com/cafe/. It automates a tour through a set of Web pages, and can optionally associate sound with each page for a rolling narrative.

Components

TourGuide consists of five class files:

 TourGuide.class

 MyCanvas.class

 MyPanel.class

 MyWindow.class

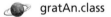 gratAn.class

The Effect

TourGuide is one of several creative applets available from Café de Sol. It can automate a presentation, or take some visitor to your page on a venture through your favorite sites or theme pages.

PARAMETER	DESCRIPTION
img	Image to display as a hot button to start the tour.
url$n$	The URLs of your destinations, url1…url$n$. The value is the actual URL string.
name$n$	The alternate names of your destinations, name1…name$n$.
sound$n$	Sound file (.au) for each destination, sound1…sound$n$.
delay$n$	Delay in seconds to spend at each destination, delay1…delay$n$.

Sample Usage

```
<applet align=middle code=TourGuide.class width=128 height=32 img=myimg.gif>
    <param name=url1 value=http://www.sun.com>
    <param name=url2 value=http://www.yahoo.com>
    <param name=url3 value=http://www.xm.com>
    <param name=url4 value=http://candlestick>
    <param name=name1 value="Sun's Home Page">
    <param name=name2 value="Yahoo's Home Page">
```

```
<param name=name3 value="XMedia's Home Page">
<param name=sound1 value=test1.au>
<param name=sound3 value=test2.au>
<param name=delay1 value=10>
<param name=delay2 value=10>
<param name=delay3 value=10>
<param name=delay4 value=10>
<applet>
```

Sources for Applets

Applets extend the function and appearance of a Web page. While they require a bit of specialization to write, they are very easy to use. A collective pool of freeware and shareware applets is rapidly developing on the Internet, providing a class of widgets that require less overhead than plug-ins, but offer more versatility than JavaScript. Please see Appendix B for a general reference to JavaScript. Some sites where you can find applets include

```
http://www.javasoft.com/applets/applets.html
http://www.gamelan.com/
http://www.xm.com/cafe/
http://www.conveyor.com/conveyor-java.html
http://www.hamline.edu/personal/matjohns/webdev/java/
```

1. Multiple parameters are passed to a Java applet by
   a. putting them in parentheses
   b. separating them with commas
   c. entering multiple parameter lines
   d. putting them in quotes

2. The codebase parameter
   a. encodes the Java applet
   b. decodes the Java applet
   c. specifies the directory in which the applet can be found
   d. notifies the browser that the applet is protected

3. An executable Java applet has a filetype of
   a. .java
   b. .html
   c. .class
   d. .exe

4. To accommodate browsers that cannot run Java applets, you should
   a. display a message within the applet tag using regular HTML
   b. check for browser type with your Java applet
   c. include Java applets only as links
   d. surround the applet tag with a comment block

Session 2

GIF ANIMATION

You may think you've done this before. If you've made it up to here, you've already used GIFs and frame animation with Perl scripts, client pulls and server pushes, and, most recently, Java applets. But what if you discovered you didn't need any of those just to display a sequence of images in a loop? What if GIF allowed you to store multiple images in a single file and had provisions for animating itself? And what if pigs could fly, eh?

Deep in the specs of GIF89a lies a curious capability, allowing for multiple images to be stored in a single file. Between these images can be inserted short headers with unusual parameters like x,y coordinates for "frames," a timer loop, flags for how an image should be removed, a pause for a keyboard event, text overlays, and comments. Strange elements for a graphics file. And stranger still that most browsers ignored these built-in GIF capabilities until Netscape 2.0 started actively interpreting them. For animations on the Web, this offers some unique opportunities.

The Alternative Animator

There seems to be no shortage of ways to animate content on the Web. Plug-ins with proprietary authoring tools, client pulls and server pushes, server side includes and Java applets all vie for your attention. Why would you need yet another method?

Each technique has its advantages, but also carries a price. Plug-in animations usually reside in large MPEG, AVI, or FLI files. A lot of application overkill for simple tasks. Client pulls and server pushes suck up network bandwidth and introduce timing variability based on network traffic. Java works pretty well, but only with Java-enabled browsers, and Java requires you to download an applet in addition to any images required. On platforms that run Netscape 2.0 but do not support Java, such as Windows 3.x, you're out of luck. And with any of the above techniques, there's a more subtle problem of meshing multiple color palettes so parts of the image that you would prefer stay put, such as the colors in the background, don't flick around like fast forward on your VCR.

How is GIF animation different? For starters, GIF contains all the animation images in a single file. Once downloaded, there's no more demand on the network. GIF doesn't require any plug-ins, other than the generic Netscape 2.0 browser, and it doesn't require Java capabilities. The multiple images in GIF frames can all share a common palette, allowing seamless animation. Best of all, with the right tool (introduced shortly), GIF animation is simple. Let's look briefly at how it works, and then jump right into some simple animations...like making a pig fly.

How It Works

A simple GIF file, with a single image, consists of two internal blocks, a header block and an image block. The header block contains information about the height and width of the frame the image should be displayed in, a background color used to fill frame space not covered by the image, and an optional global palette. The image itself has information about its own height and width and the x,y coordinates where it displays in the frame (usually 0,0). It also can have its own local palette, an interlace flag, and other miscellanea. These are the most common, but not the only, types of blocks found in a GIF89a file. As mentioned above, additional blocks can include

- Comment blocks, with text describing the image(s). Created date, author, copyright, etc. These are obviously not displayed with the image, but are visible with a utility that can look at the internal format.

- Plain text blocks. These specify text to be overlaid on the image. You can specify x,y coordinates and color of the text.

- Application blocks. These contain private data and can be used by tools and utilities that manipulate the GIF.

- Control blocks. These blocks define a color that acts transparent in the image, the delay before the next image is displayed, and how the current image is removed when the next image in the sequence is displayed.

- Loop blocks. These specify how many times multiple images are looped through when displayed.

The two most important for your purposes are the loop block and the control block. Let's see how these form the building blocks for GIF animation.

The Theory

Starting with a GIF file with a header and a single image, you can add animation by adding additional control blocks, followed by image blocks. Immediately after the header, you will also need one loop block that tells how many times to loop through the entire animation. A small two-image animation is constructed with blocks as follows:

```
<HEADER BLOCK>
<LOOP BLOCK>
<CONTROL BLOCK>
<IMAGE BLOCK>
<CONTROL BLOCK>
<IMAGE BLOCK>
```

Since the ability to insert and manipulate these GIF control blocks is missing in most graphics tools, you'll need a utility designed for the task. For Windows, this could be the GIF Construction Set by Alchemy Mindworks at http://www.north.net/alchemy/alchemy.html.

How to Build an Animated GIF

Before building the GIF animation, you'll need to have a set of images for the frames. Let's use a couple of images that come with the Java distribution kit for the Animator applet. This will give a head-to-head comparison with the same effects in Java. The image is in

`/java/demo/Animator/Images/SimpleAnimation`

It consists of two files: T1.GIF and T2.GIF, which create a simple painted candle flame on a beveled button.

Once you've located the images, you'll need to download and install the GIF Construction Set.

The GIF Construction Set (or GIFCON) is a powerful utility. It's available as book-ware, which means you have to buy a book called *The Order* by Steven Rimmer and enter a certain word from a certain page in the book to register.

Once you've installed GIFCON, load it up and open the T1.GIF image referenced above. Your opening screen should look like the screen in Figure 9-3.

Notice that GIFCON automatically created a HEADER block and an IMAGE block. If you stop here, you have a conventional GIF file. By double-clicking one of these blocks, you can edit its parameters. Figure 9-4 shows what's in the HEADER block.

The Screen width and Screen height specify the canvas area where all other images are displayed. It defaults to the size of the first image loaded, but you can change it here to make a larger canvas if you have images of varying sizes. Both T1.GIF and T2.GIF are 64x64, so this won't be a consideration.

The option for Global palette is checked, indicating that a common palette will be used for multiple images. This creates a more seamless animation. You'll see how this is used shortly. Click OK on the HEADER block and move on to the IMAGE block. Figure 9-5 shows the fields in the IMAGE block.

This screen displays the actual image, along with its size (64x64) and an option to interlace the display. The x,y coordinates position the image in the canvas defined in the HEADER. In this case the image is the same size as the canvas, so the default of 0,0 is fine.

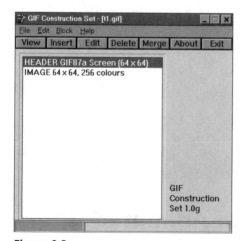

Figure 9-3
The HEADER block

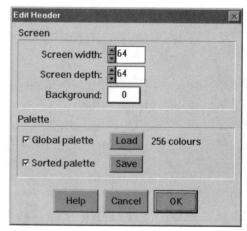

Figure 9-4
GIFCON with the first image loaded

Now let's add the next image. Choose Insert on the GIFCON menu and you'll be given a choice of control blocks. Pick IMAGE and load T2.GIF. Figure 9-6 shows what happens.

GIFCON wants to know how to map the palette. Take the default, letting GIFCON dither the current palette into the global one. You should now have the following control blocks in the GIFCON work area:

HEADER
IMAGE
IMAGE

To finish the animation, another block is very important—the CONTROL block. CONTROL blocks need to precede every IMAGE block. Highlight HEADER and choose Insert⇨Control to insert a CONTROL block between HEADER and the first IMAGE. Edit the CONTROL block by double-clicking it, and you should get a screen like Figure 9-7.

This block defines several important characteristics for animation. It defines how long the delay should be between this image and the next (in 1/100ths of a second). It defines how the image is "wiped" from the screen. The options are

- Nothing. This assumes this image will be overwritten by the next. This is the fastest "wipe," but if any part of the next image is transparent, this is not the best option.

- Leave as is. Same as nothing, as least as far as Netscape interprets it.

- Previous image. Restores with previous image.

- Background. Restores with the Netscape background color. This is used for transparent animations, where each image uses a transparent background.

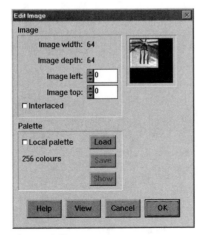

Figure 9-5
The IMAGE block

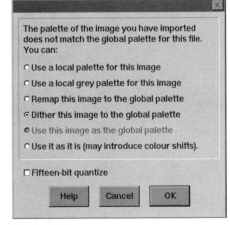

Figure 9-6
Importing another image

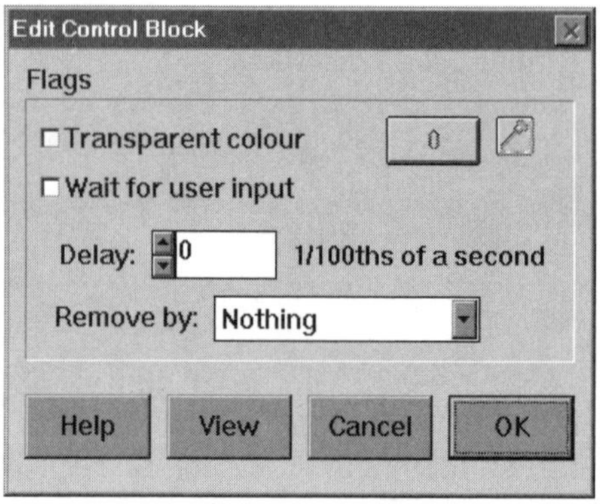

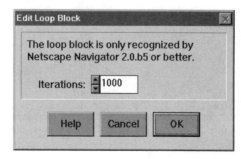

Figure 9-7
The CONTROL
block

The Transparent colour option in the CONTROL block lets you set a transparency color, either by its index number in the palette, or with the "dropper," by picking it up directly off of the image. This example won't use transparency. One image will simply flip over the other.

For this example, set the delay to 200 and let the other settings default. Repeat the procedure once more, adding a CONTROL block before the second image, with the same settings.

Now you need one more block and you're done: the LOOP block. Insert this anywhere, and double-click to edit it. Figure 9-8 shows the LOOP block dialog.

The LOOP block contains a single parameter that controls how many iterations the browser will make through the file. A value of zero means to loop indefinitely.

Save the file as something like T.GIF and you're finished! You can use this anywhere you would normally use a GIF file in Netscape (except as a background! In other browsers it will display as a single GIF, usually the first image of the animation). Wherever it displays on the page will be a small pocket of self-contained animation.

To recap what you did to create an animation, the steps were

1. Open an initial image with GIFCON. The HEADER and IMAGE blocks are created automatically.

Figure 9-8
The LOOP block

2. Edit the HEADER block and check the Global palette option.

3. Insert the remaining images. An IMAGE block is created for each; when prompted during insertion, specify "Dither this image to the global palette."

4. Insert CONTROL blocks before each IMAGE block. Set the Delay options for how the animation transitions to the next image, and set any transparent colors.

5. Insert a LOOP block to control how many times the animation is looped through.

6. Save the results as a GIF file.

Tips and Caveats

You'll discover several shortcuts and effects by experimenting with the parameters. Here are some general observations:

 The first image contains the color range used for the global palette. If possible, ensure that this image has a fairly full spectrum that the others can match. If your first image doesn't include a superset of colors for all the images, bring in the most colorful one and then insert other images before it. The first one that's loaded sets the global palette, not the first one in the sequence.

 A zero value in the loop field means infinite looping.

 You can produce "sprite" animations by starting with a background as the first image, and then using smaller images with transparent backgrounds, mapping them to different x,y coordinates in each CONTROL block to move across the background. Replace with Previous image in the CONTROL block options. You can also start sprites in the first frame and use the browser's background. Then replace with Background.

 Insert a longer delay at the start and end of the animation for the best effects. This initial delay helps Netscape to download other parts of the page without your animation hogging processor cycles.

Ideas

Try some of these ideas on a rainy day:

 Animated rulers

 Color shifts

- Little blips like a heart monitor
- Small animated sprites that traverse the ruler
- Tightwire acts
- Gradient blends
- Color cycles
- Scrolling images
- Rotating logos producing 3D-type effects
- Blinking parts of image
- Christmas lights
- Candles
- Glows

QUIZ 2

1. GIF animation works by
   a. linking to a sequence of images on the server
   b. linking to a sequence of images on a local disk
   c. embedding a sequence of images in a single file
   d. dynamically requesting images from the browser

2. The HEADER block controls
   a. the number of times the animation loops
   b. transparency colors
   c. x,y coordinates of the individual images
   d. the overall size of the frame used to display the images

3. A LOOP block with a value of 0 means
   a. Do not loop.
   b. Zero is an invalid value.
   c. Loop once and then quit.
   d. Loop indefinitely.

4. When an image is inserted and it "dithers to the global palette," this means
   a. It adds its colors to the palette.
   b. It rearranges the palette in the same order as its colors.
   c. It modifies its colors to most closely match those in the global palette.
   d. It combines the colors of all previous images with its own.

AGENTS 101

The Perl escapades that appeared earlier in this book were primarily for the purpose of creating CGI scripts. The scripts extended the functionality of the Web server, and used libraries like CGI.pm to read input from the CGI and generate HTML to return to the client. This session covers a more active facet of Perl scripts: writing agents.

Internet agents is a term used for a wide range of applications that try to automate operations on your behalf. Intelligent agents may someday be able to surf the Web for you, culling information that appeals to your unique interest, packaging it up, and dropping it off on your home page in an automated dossier. Someday may be closer than you think. Let's explore some tools similar to the CGI.pm modules that assist in writing *client* applications. As clients, these Perl scripts work on your behalf. Instead of reacting to browsers submitting forms, like CGI scripts, they appear as browsers themselves and probe servers for information.

History of Agents

The idea of agents is not really new. Several agents have been written in Perl, and have been functioning on the Internet for years. Agents appear in IRC forums in the guise of "bots." They work behind the scenes of most of the popular search engines like Excite, Yahoo, and Alta Vista in the form of Web wanderers, robots, and spiders. In fact, some of these wanderers and spiders whose job it is to traverse the Web, finding and indexing new links, were created with older versions of the modules you'll use here to build your own agent. These modules started out as Perl libraries, called libwww with Perl 4, and have since evolved into object modules with Perl 5. They are very popular as spider construction kits, but they also encapsulate powerful functionality for more general purpose agents. To start this project you'll need to download the libwww package.

Step 1. libwww: Where to Get It

The libwww package can be obtained from

```
http://www.oslonett.no/home/aas/perl/www/
```

Downloading the package and following the installation instructions adds several new modules to your Perl 5 libraries. The libraries dig pretty deeply into the elements of client/server interaction in HTTP, and although you will be working with classes higher up in the hierarchy for simplicity, you can dip into the lower levels at any time for more control and flexibility. All transmissions to and from the server are provided by objects implemented in these modules. Here's the breakdown. Indentation shows properties and methods inherited in subclasses (don't worry about what this means right now):

```
LWP::MemberMixin     Access Perl5 class variables
    LWP::UserAgent   WWW user agent class
    LWP::Protocol    Interface to various protocol schemes
        LWP::Protocol::http     http:// access
        LWP::Protocol::file     file:// access
        LWP::Protocol::ftp      ftp:// access
        LWP::Protocol::gopher   gopher:// access
        LWP::Protocol::mailto   mailto:// access

LWP::Socket          Socket creation and reading
LWP::MediaTypes      MIME types configuration (text/html etc.)
LWP::Debug           Debug logging module
LWP::Simple          Simplified functions

HTTP::Headers     MIME/RFC822 style header (used by HTTP::Message)
HTTP::Message     HTTP style message
    HTTP::Request     HTTP request
    HTTP::Response    HTTP response
HTTP::Status      HTTP status code processing
HTTP::Date        HTTP date conversion routines


URI::URL     Uniform Resource Locators
```

Other modules for controlling MIME formats, HTML, and so on are not listed. Those shown above are all that's needed to begin construction.

Step 2. Using libwww

Let's learn by building. For the first example, let's construct a simple script that, given a URL, retrieves the contents of a page off the Web. The LWP::Simple module can easily handle this. It uses several of the other LWP classes, taking care of a lot of detail to provide a simple, high-level interface. Here is all that's needed to retrieve and print a Web page:

```perl
#!/user/local/bin/perl
use LWP::Simple;
getprint("http://www.test.com/");
```

Two lines of Perl! The getprint method is obviously doing a lot behind the scenes. This simple script prints a URL to your screen. Other useful methods of the Simple module include the following:

get(url)	Gets a document. Returns the document if successful. Returns 'undef' if it fails.
getstore($url, $file)	Gets a document identified by a URL and stores it in the file. It returns the response code.
mirror($url, $file)	Gets and stores a document identified by a URL, using If-modified-since and checking of the content length. Returns response code.

IsSuccess($rc)	Checks to see if response code indicated successful request.
isError($rc)	Checks to see if response code indicated that an error occurred.
Head(url)	Gets document headers. Returns the following values if successful: ($content_type, $document_length, $modified_time, $expires, $server).

To make sure a local page always reflects the most up-to-date changes in a remote one, you can use the mirror method as follows:

```perl
#!/user/local/bin/perl
use LWP::Simple;
if (mirror("http://www.remote.com/", "mypage.html")) {
        print "Page synchronized \n";
        }
```

This is just beginning to demonstrate the power of these modules. Using two or three lines of Perl code, you've retrieved the text content of an arbitrary Web page for further manipulation, and you've checked the modification date and content size of a remote Web page and stored it locally if any updates were made.

The Simple module automates calls to an object it creates called UserAgent. UserAgent is a lower-level class module LWP and provides a few more controls than Simple. Here's how you retrieve a page using the UserAgent object. (This is essentially what Simple is doing for you in the first example.)

```perl
#!/user/local/bin/perl
use LWP::UserAgent;

$ua = new LWP::UserAgent;
$request = new HTTP::Request('GET', 'http://www.test.com/');
$response = $ua->request($request);
```

This example declares two objects: a UserAgent object and an HTTP object. The HTTP object is used to build an HTTP request. The UserAgent object is used to deliver the request and then package and return any response it receives. If you investigate the HTTP::Request object, you'll find it inherits properties and methods from the generic HTTP Method class, enabling it to set properties for building a range of legal HTTP requests including POST for submitting form data, HEAD for retrieving header data, and more esoteric options like DELETE, LINK, UNLINK, and others.

The $response variable is an object, created and returned by the UserAgent class. Its properties can be inspected for error trapping and printing the page returned by adding the following additional code:

```perl
#!/user/local/bin/perl
use LWP::UserAgent;

$ua = new LWP::UserAgent;
$request = new HTTP::Request('GET', 'http://www.test.com/');
$response = $ua->request($request);
if ($response->isSuccess) {
```

continued on next page

continued from previous page

```
        print $response->content;
} else {
        print $response->errorAsHTML;
}
```

Step 3. Fooling Forms

Sometimes an agent may have to navigate through a form to get the information it needs. If the form accepts GETs and the form data is minimal, you can often get by with packaging it all in a URL like

```
http://www.test.com/cgi-bin/form?key1=value&key2=value
```

But forms that require POSTs need more sophisticated delivery mechanisms. Fortunately, the libwww modules are up for the task. Let's extend the use of classes a little further to find out how information can be posted from a Perl agent.

A POST requires more information in the header than a GET. This information includes, among other things, the content type of the data being posted, the content length, and the MIME version. For the GET method, you used a request like the following:

```
$request = new HTTP::Request('GET', 'http://www.test.com/');
```

This sent a string to the server like

```
GET http://http.test.com/
```

For experimenting with the headers, you can inspect the request block libwww sends to the server with the following command:

```
print $request->asString(),"\n";
```

This uses the asString method of the request object to "dump" the request header to the screen. For POSTs you'll need a little more header information, but you can still use the *$request* object. Additional header fields are specified as follows:

```
$request = new HTTP::Request('POST', 'http://www.test.com/'
            ,$header,$formdata);
```

The *$header* variable is an object of the HTTP::Headers class, and the *$formdata* is the encoded field=value pairs from the form. The *$header* object is an associated array and is constructed as follows:

```
$header = new HTTP::Headers
        'Content-Type'  =>      "application/x-www-form-urlencoded",
        'Content-Length'        =>      len($formdata),
        'Accept'                =>      'text/html',
                        ;
```

The form data is the name=value pairs passed to the server and is constructed with this assignment:

```
$formdata = join('&','name=fred',"address=$addr");
```

Putting these concepts together, you can create a small script that posts data to a form and retrieves the results so they can be analyzed further:

```perl
#!/user/local/bin/perl
use LWP::UserAgent;
use HTTP::Headers;

$ua = new LWP::UserAgent;
$formdata = join('&','name=fred',"address=$addr");
$header = new HTTP::Headers
        'Content-Type'  =>      "application/x-www-form-urlencoded",
        'Content-Length'        =>      len($formdata),
        'Accept'                =>      'text/html',
        ;
$request = new HTTP::Request('POST',
                    'http://www.test.com/cgi-bin/form.exe',
                    $header,
                    $formdata
                    );
$response = $ua->request($request);
if ($response->isSuccess) {
        print $response->content;
        }
```

For the session project, let's build an agent that will wake up each morning and search through the Alta Vista Web index of Usenet for any mention of Elvis from the day before. If it finds Elvis, it e-mails a message with a link to the article. If you are using Netscape, Eudora, or any of a number of the more modern e-mail clients, you'll be able to click on this link and instantly read the article. The agent will free you up from having to trawl through the Usenet groups, alerting you only when the conditions you are tracking appear on the Internet. To kick this off, you'll want to schedule the agent to execute each day using UNIX crontab or some other batch scheduling utility on your platform of choice.

You've already been introduced to most of the tools you'll need. Now you just need to know what Alta Vista is expecting. By viewing the source of the query page, you'll discover one surprise. It uses GET rather than POST. A little unusual for complex forms. You'll also notice a number of options in the advanced query section that can be set to really home in on specific information. A few of the ones used in the agent script will be

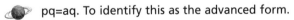 pq=aq. To identify this as the advanced form.

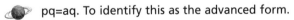 what=news. To tell Alta Vista you want to search the Usenet indexes.

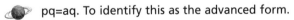 q="*string*". This is the query string. It can accept Booleans like AND, OR, NOT, and NEAR.

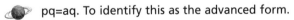 d=*dd/mmm/yy*. A from date for constraining the query.

Since this is a GET form, these values could also be discovered by doing a simple query with your Web browser and looking at the location line. It will have all the variables packed up after the URL with a ?name-value&name=value syntax.

So far so good. Let's write the first part of the script that gets everything ready.

```perl
#!/usr/local/bin/perl
use LWP::UserAgent;          # Bring in the necessary modules
use URI::Escape;             #Used to encode the GET URL String

$ua = new LWP::UserAgent;    # Create a new agent object
$query = "elvis";
#
# This next section creates a date in the format Alta Vista
# expects in the from date field. It expects a date like
# 19/Feb/96. We also want to check from yesterday
#
@month = (Jan,Feb,Mar,Apr,May,Jun,Jul,Aug,Sep,Oct,Nov,Dec);
($sec,$min,$hour,$mday,$mon,$year) = localtime(time-86400);
$yesterday = "$mday/$month[$mon]/$year";

# Build the form's expected name/value pairs
# encoding any spaces or special characters
$formdata = uri_escape(join('&',
        "q=$query",
        'fmt=.',
        "d0=$yesterday",
        'pg=aq',
        'what=news'
        ));
```

Now that everything is ready, let's add code to send the form request and read the response:

```perl
$request = new HTTP::Request('GET',
        "http://altavista.digital.com/cgi-bin/query?$formdata"
        );

$response = $ua->request($request);
$results = $response->content;
```

The content of *$results*, if successful, will be a glob of HTML that represents what would normally be returned to a browser screen. You'll need to use some of Perl's powerful parsing mechanisms to pick out the news URLs and the title of the articles:

```perl
if ($results =~ /No documents match/) {     # If nothing found
        print "No Documents Match...\n";     # nothing to do
        }
else {                                       # otherwise
        $results =~ /Documents \d/;          # Trim off the results
        $results = $';                       # a little

        # Setup output to go to e-mail address: me@test.com
        # not that the @ sign in the email address needed to be
        # "escaped" with a backslash
        #
```

```
open(MAIL,"|mail me\@test.com");
print MAIL "Subject: Agent Report\n";


# Now pick off the news URLs and the Article titles
# sending each pair found to the mail pipe
while ($results =~
        m#(news:[^"]+).*href.*href.*>(.*)</a>#gi
        ) {
                write(MAIL);
                }
        close(MAIL);
}
```

One of the trickiest parts of this will be the pattern matching to strip just the results you want from the HTML coming back. It's a good chance to learn tricks with regular expressions. The write sends the output through a format block before piping it out:

```
format MAIL_TOP=

                Alta Vista Usenet Agent Notice

    On @<<<<<<<<<<<<<<<   Your Query: @<<<<<<<<<<<<<<<<<<<<<
    $yesterday $query
    Was found in one or more Usenet Postings. Links follow...


.


format MAIL=

@<<<<<<<<<<<<<<<<<<<<<<<<<<<<<<<<<<<<<<<<<<<<<<<<<<<<<<<<<<<<<<<<<<<<<<<<<<
<<<<<<<<<<<<<<<<<<<<<<<<<<<<<<<<<<<<<<<<<<<<<<<<<<<<<<<<<<<<<<<<<<<<<<<<<<<
$2
@<<<<<<<<<<<<<<<<<<<<<<<<<<<<<<<<<<<<<<<<<<<<<<<<<<<<<<<<<<<<<<<<<<<<<<<<<<
<<<<<<<<<<<<<<<<<<<<<<<<<<<<<<<<<<<<<<<<<<<<<<<<<<<<<<<<<<<<<<<<<<<<<<<<<<<
$1
```

Extending the Design

The news agent above can be extended to search other forums for information. With a little coding you can develop your own personal newsletter with up-to-date columns on all the information you want to track in the Internet sprawl. Agents have a certain place in the future, to help us cope intelligently with information pollution. Having the ability to write and design your own mediator puts you ahead of the pack that is still waiting for the shrinkwrapped versions.

And that wraps up the session on the outer edges of HTML. While the discussion has veered a little(?) beyond your typical Web page construction, the topics should have broadened your reach and abilities and maybe even have given you a creative tug toward the far reaches of the Web, where you may soon be charting the course for others.

1. The libwww package is
   a. a set of routines for building powerful CGI scripts
   b. a set of modules for interacting with Web browsers
   c. a set of plug-ins for Netscape
   d. a set of modules to interact with Web servers

2. An agent can
   a. retrieve pages that have been modified
   b. parse information off of pages
   c. navigate through forms to retrieve information automatically
   d. all of the above

3. A Web spider or wanderer is an application that
   a. propagates itself from site to site collecting information
   b. propagates itself from client to client collecting information
   c. runs pieces of itself on several platforms
   d. usually runs from a single platform and polls other hosts for information

4. The response returned from a UserAgent request is typically
   a. a text file
   b. an object
   c. a header
   d. HTML

APPENDIX A

QUIZ ANSWERS AND CORRECTIONS

Chapter 1

Quiz 1.1

   1. b   Right!
      Else   Nope, see The Internet Phenomenon.

   2. c   Yes!
      Else   No, sorry, see Hypertext: The Way We Think.

   3. d   Correct
      Else   Nope, see Hypertext: The Way We Think.

   4. d   Right
      Else   Check under So Who Runs the Show?

Quiz 1.2

   1. c   Right
      Else   Try again after reading Types of Connections.

   2. c   Yep!
      Else   A thought question…all a provider's users are funneled onto the Internet through the provider's connection.

   3. d   Right!
      Else   See Questions to Ask.

4. b   Correct!
Else   Look under Online Services.

Quiz 1.3

1. a   Yes!
Else   Nope, see The Anatomy of HTML.

2. c   Right!
Else   Try again after checking Attributes.

3. d   Right
Else   See HTML Conventions

4. c   Exactly right!
Else   No, but try again after reading Why Not WYSIWYG.

Quiz 1.4

1. d   Right
Else   Sorry, check The Header and try again.

2. d   Yes!
Else   Nope, see the first section of the chapter.

3. c   Right!
Else   Review the HTML Tag table for the answer.

4. d   You got it!
Else   For the answer, review the opening section.

5. a   Correct
Else   The other use is found in The Title.

Quiz 1.5

1. a   Yes!
Else   No, see the section on the <BR> tag, under Quotes.

2. a   Right
Else   Nope, see Word Wrapping.

3. b   Correct
Else   Review the <PRE> Tag section, under Quotes, for the answer.

4. c   Right
Else   No, but the section Nonbreaking Space should reveal the right choice.

Quiz 1.6

1. d   Right
   Else   No, sorry, review Definition Lists.

2. c   Yes!
   Else   See Unordered Lists and give it another shot!

3. c   Correct
   Else   Er…no. See Definition Lists.

4. d   Yes
   Else   Try again after reviewing List Enhancements.

Quiz 1.7

1. d   Right
   Else   No, they can link to there! Think of someplace "unlinkable".

2. c   Yes!
   Else   Nope. Check The Anchor section.

3. a   Right
   Else   No, scan through the examples of hyperlinks for the answer.

4. c   Correct
   Else   The answer is in The Anchor section.

Chapter 2

Quiz 2.1

1. d   Right!
   Else   Nope, see The ALT Alternative.

2. d   Yes!
   Else   No, sorry, see Lynx: The Legacy of Text.

3. d   Correct
   Else   Nope, see Wrapping.

4. d   Right
   Else   Check under What Kind of Image?

Quiz 2.2

1. d   Right
   Else   Try again after reading Hyperlinks to Images.

2. d   Yep!
Else   Review Thumbnails for the answer.

3. d   Right!
Else   See the Table 2-3.

4. d   Correct!
Else   Look under Music and MIDI.

5. b   That's right
Else   Look under Configuring Helper Applications.

Quiz 2.3

1. d   Yes!
Else   Nope, see Video's Price.

2. d   Right!
Else   Sorry, check under Video Guidelines for the answer.

3. d   Correct
Else   Look under Video Guidelines for the answer to this one.

4. c   Yep!
Else   No, look under Hyperlinks To Video.

Quiz 2.4

1. c   Yes!
Else   Nope, see The COMPACT Option.

2. d   Right!
Else   Try again after checking Bullets on the Web.

3. d   Right
Else   See Converting Icons into Bullets.

4. c   Exactly right!
Else   No, but try again after reading Putting It to Use.

5. a   Yes
Else   No, but see Buttons to Navigate and try again.

Quiz 2.5

1. d   Right
Else   Sorry, check Special Characters in HTML and try again.

2. d   Yes!
Else   Nope, see Character Entities.

3. d   Right!
    Else   Review Copyright and Registered Trademark Symbols for the answer.

4. d   You got it!
    Else   For the answer, review the Comments section.

5. b   Correct
    Else   Check the Tables section again.

Quiz 2.6

1. c   Yes!
    Else   No, see Graphical Rulers.

2. d   Right
    Else   Nope, see Transparent Images.

3. d   Correct
    Else   Review Tips for Creating Rulers and Transparent Images for the answer.

4. d   Right
    Else   No, but Transparent Images should reveal the right choice.

Quiz 2.7

1. d   Right
    Else   No, sorry, review Shapes.

2. b   Yes!
    Else   See Building Imagemaps and give it another shot!

3. d   Correct
    Else   Er…no. See the File Syntax table.

4. c   Yes
    Else   Try again after reviewing Linking the Map and Image.

Quiz 2.8

1. d   Right
    Else   No, check Physical Markups and Logical Markups.

2. c   Yes!
    Else   Nope. Check Signing Your HTML.

3. d   Right
    Else   No, scan through the examples in the Physical Markups section.

4. d   Correct
    Else   The answer is in the mailto section.

Chapter 3

Quiz 3.1

1. c   Right!
   Else   Nope, see URL Syntax.

2. a   Yes!
   Else   No, sorry, see Relative versus Absolute.

3. b   Correct
   Else   Nope, see Relative versus Absolute.

4. d   Right
   Else   Check under Protected Characters.

Quiz 3.2

1. c   Right
   Else   Try again after reading the note under FTP Transfers.

2. d   Yep!
   Else   Review FTP or HTTP? for the answer.

3. b   Right!
   Else   See the Local Files section.

4. c   Correct!
   Else   Look under News URLs.

Quiz 3.3

1. b   Yes!
   Else   Nope, see Gopher.

2. c   Right!
   Else   Sorry, check under WAIS for the answer.

3. c   Correct
   Else   Look under Gopher for the answer to this one.

4. c   Yep!
   Else   No, look under Telnet and TN3270.

Quiz 3.4

1. d   Yes!
   Else   Nope, see Relative URLs.

2. d   Right!
   Else   A tricky one, check Missing Quotes.

3. d   Right
Else   See Files in the Hood.

4. d   Yes
Else   No, but review unsafe URLs and try again!

Quiz 3.5

1. b   Right
Else   Sorry, check Presentation versus Content and try again.

2. b   Yes!
Else   Nope, see Highlights.

3. d   Right!
Else   Review Don't Click Here for the answer.

4. c   You got it!
Else   For the answer, review the Page Lengths section.

Quiz 3.6

1. b   Yes!
Else   No, see the Local Home Page.

2. b   Right
Else   Nope, see Graphical Menus.

3. a   Correct
Else   Review Consistency and Content for the answer.

4. c   Right
Else   No, but Consistency and Content should reveal the right choice.

Quiz 3.7

1. a   Right
Else   No, sorry, review Label Large Files.

2. d   Yes!
Else   See Tuning Inline Images and give it another shot!

3. c   Correct
Else   Er…no. See Number of Colors.

4. c   Yes
Else   Try again after reviewing Performance.

Quiz 3.8

1. c   Right
    Else   No, check the Online Brochure section.

2. d   Yes!
    Else   Nope. Check The Combination Page.

3. c   Right
    Else   No, remember you're not confined to a single main menu.

4. b   Correct
    Else   What if they want to reuse a menu?

Chapter 4

Quiz 4.1

1. c   Right!
    Else   Nope, see What are Forms?

2. d   Yes!
    Else   No, sorry, see The <Form> Tag.

3. d   Correct
    Else   Nope, see the Submitting Forms section.

4. d   Right
    Else   Check under Submitting Forms.

Quiz 4.2

1. b   Right
    Else   Try again after reading Making Choices.

2. c   Yep!
    Else   Review Just Forget It! for the answer.

3. b   Right!
    Else   See For Spacious Fields.

4. d   Correct!
    Else   Look under Making Choices.

Quiz 4.3

1. c   Yes!
    Else   Nope, see Custom Buttons.

2. c   Right!
    Else   Sorry, check under Radio Buttons for the answer.

3. a   Correct.
   Else   Check the example in Building an Order Form.

4. d   Yep!
   Else   No, Look under Check Boxes.

Quiz 4.4

1. d   Yes!
   Else   Nope, see the note about using database tables to store form results.

2. c   Right!
   Else   You can discover this answer by experimenting with the Access import.

3. a   Right
   Else   See the discussion of check boxes in The Rough.

4. c   Yes
   Else   No, but review Tables and Forms and try again!

Quiz 4.5

1. b   Right
   Else   Sorry, check How the CGI Passes Data to Scripts and try again.

2. b   Yes!
   Else   Nope, see Sending Data Back to the User.

3. c   Right!
   Else   Review Sending Data Back to the User for the answer.

4. d   You got it!
   Else   For the answer, review the Where Do Scripts Live? section.

Quiz 4.6

1. b   Yes!
   Else   No, review the second script example.

2. c   Right
   Else   Nope, review Development and Testing examples.

3. c   Correct
   Else   Review Things That Can Go Wrong for the answer.

4. d   Right
   Else   No, but Things That Can Go Wrong should reveal the right choice.

Quiz 4.7

1. d   Right
       Else   No, sorry, review Delivering More Than HTML.

2. c   Yes!
       Else   See Other Ways Scripts Can Be Activated and give it another shot!

3. b   Correct
       Else   Er…no. See cgi.bas.

4. c   Yes
       Else   Try again after reviewing cgi.bas.

Quiz 4.8

1. c   Right
       Else   No, check the Hidden Variables section.

2. c   Yes!
       Else   Nope. Check the discussion in Real Code.

3. c   Right
       Else   No, review Hidden Variables.

4. c   Correct
       Else   See Hidden Variables.

Chapter 5

Quiz 5.1

1. c   Right!
       Else   Nope, see Your Home Page.

2. d   Yes!
       Else   No, sorry, see Connecting to Your Server.

3. c   Correct
       Else   Nope, see the Server Topologies section.

4. d   Right
       Else   Check under Server Topologies.

Quiz 5.2

1. b   Right
       Else   Try again after reviewing the entries in httpd.conf

2. c   Yep!
       Else   Review At the Starting Line for the answer.

3. c   Right!
   Else   See At the Starting Line.

4. c   Correct!
   Else   Look under UNIX for Free: The Linux Alternative.

Quiz 5.3

1. d   Yes!
   Else   Nope, see URLs and the Web Server.

2. a   Right!
   Else   Sorry, check under URLs and the Web Server for the answer.

3. c   Correct
   Else   Check the example in the SRM.CONF User Directory Directive box.

4. d   Yep!
   Else   No, Look under Fancy Directories.

Quiz 5.4

1. c   Yes!
   Else   Nope, see Limiting Access to Local Domain.

2. b   Right!
   Else   Check Creating the Password File.

3. d   Right
   Else   See Access Groups.

4. d   Yes
   Else   No, but review Other Directories and try again!

Quiz 5.5

1. a   Right
   Else   Sorry, see the discussion on the ExecCGI option under The Options
            Directive.

2. c   Yes!
   Else   Nope, see Followsymlinks under The Options Directive.

3. b   Right!
   Else   Review Server Side Includes for the answer.

4. c   You got it!
   Else   A tricky one…look closely at the statement.

Quiz 5.6

1. c   Yes!
   Else   No, review the Weaknesses section.

2. c   Right
   Else   Nope, review Tricky Protections.

3. d   Correct
   Else   Review Symbolic Links for the answer.

4. c   Right
   Else   No, but User Script Exposures should reveal the right choice.

Quiz 5.7

1. b   Right
   Else   No, sorry, review RefStats.

2. c   Yes!
   Else   See the beginning of the session and give it another shot!

3. b   Correct
   Else   Er…no. See HTML Validation.

4. c   Yes
   Else   Try again after reviewing Webcopy.

Quiz 5.8

1. c   Right
   Else   No, check the Hypermail section at the beginning of the session.

2. c   Yes!
   Else   Nope. Check the discussion in Other Options.

3. b   Right
   Else   No, review Importing Eudora.

4. b   Correct
   Else   See Using Hypermail.

Chapter 6

Quiz 6.1

1. c   Right!
   Else   Nope, see Searching with SWISH.

2. c   Yes!
   Else   No, sorry, see Searching with SWISH.

3. d   Correct
   Else Nope, see the Searching with SWISH section.

4. d   Right
   Else Check under Searching with SWISH.

Quiz 6.2

1. c   Right
   Else Try again after reviewing Glimpse and the CGI.

2. d   Yep!
   Else Review Revisiting the Indexing Options for the answer.

3. b   Right!
   Else See Using Glimpse.

4. a   Correct!
   Else Look under Using Glimpse.

Quiz 6.3

1. c   Yes!
   Else Nope, see the section All in One.

2. c   Right!
   Else Sorry, check under Hello Fred for the answer.

3. b   Correct.
   Else Check All in One.

4. a   Yep!
   Else No, look at the sample form in All in One.

Quiz 6.4

1. c   Yes!
   Else Nope, check the places in the script where the array is hardcoded.

2. d   Right!
   Else Hint: What type of image will respond to a mouse click?

3. c   Right
   Else Hint: How are sticky variables updated?

4. c   Yes
   Else Hint: The script doesn't really care what it is displaying…

Quiz 6.5

1. c   Right
     Else   Sorry, see the discussion under Manipulating Graphics.

2. a   Yes!
     Else   Nope, see Manipulating Graphics.

3. c   Right!
     Else   Review Manipulating Graphics for the answer.

4. b   You got it!
     Else   No, look at the sample script in Creating and Displaying Objects.

Quiz 6.6

1. c   Yes!
     Else   No, review the Client Pull section.

2. c   Right
     Else   Nope, review Poor Man's Web Animation.

3. c   Correct
     Else   Review Pros and Cons for the answer.

4. b   Right
     Else   No, but the section Gotchas should reveal the right choice.

Quiz 6.7

1. d   Right
     Else   Hint: How will the information be displayed after it is entered?

2. c   Yes!
     Else   See Updating the Guestbook and give it another shot!

3. b   Correct
     Else   Er...no. What optimizations does a browser make on loading HTML that might affect your script?

4. b   Yes
     Else   Hint: How could you provide a function similar to the Back arrow of a browser?

EXTRA CREDIT:

     c   Right!
     Else   Hint: What does reverse actually reverse?

Quiz 6.8

1. d   Right
    Else   No, review the GD functions in Session 5.

2. c   Yes!
    Else   Nope. Hint: How high is the odometer in your car?

3. d   Right
    Else   No, review the reason for the $| switch in Perl in Session 5.

4. d   Correct
    Else   See Perl and DBM Files and review what DBM files store.

Chapter 7

Quiz 7.1

1. d   Right!
    Else   Nope, see &ora_bind in Essential Oraperl Functions.

2. c   Yes!
    Else   No, sorry, see Shortcuts.

3. c   Correct
    Else   Nope, see the Shortcuts section.

4. b   Right
    Else   Check under Commitment.

Quiz 7.2

1. a   Right
    Else   Try again after reviewing Passing Form Variables to Stored Procedures.

2. b   Yep!
    Else   Review Creating Stored Procedures for the answer.

3. a   Right!
    Else   See The HTP/HTF Package.

4. c   Correct!
    Else   Look under A Simple PL/SQL Lookup.

Quiz 7.3

1. c   Yes!
    Else   Nope, see the section Turn Up the Bandwidth.

2. c   Right!
    Else   Sorry, check under VRML Spheres for the answer.

3. b   Correct
Else   Check Metalinks in VRML.

4. c   Yep!
Else   No, review the discussion in Home Page or Home Space.

Quiz 7.4

1. a   Yes!
Else   Nope, check Why Executable Content?

2. d   Right!
Else   No, review Why Not Visual Basic?

3. c   Right
Else   Nope, see The Buzz on Java.

4. c   Yes
Else   Hint: How do browsers typically react to HTML they do not implement?

Quiz 7.5

1. c   Right
Else   Sorry, see the discussion under Netscape and Visual Basic.

2. c   Yes!
Else   Nope, see More Properties.

3. d   Right!
Else   Review Posting Forms with Visual Basic for the answer.

4. c   You got it!
Else   No, look at Netscape and Visual Basic.

Quiz 7.6

1. b   Yes!
Else   No, review the What's the Secret Word section.

2. b   Right
Else   Nope, review the I've Got Two Words For It section.

3. c   Correct
Else   Review PGP and Keys for the answer.

4. c   Right
Else   No, but Distributing Your Public Key should reveal the right choice.

Quiz 7.7

1. a   Right
    Else   See Two Approaches under SSL.

2. b   Yes!
    Else   See Two Approaches and give it another shot!

3. d   Correct
    Else   Er…no. See Two Approaches.

4. c   Yes
    Else   No, see Two Approaches.

Quiz 7.8

1. c   Right
    Else   No, review E-cash: the Dark Horse.

2. c   Yes!
    Else   Nope. See Disadvantages under Credit.

3. c   Right
    Else   No, review Buying and Selling with E-cash.

4. c   Correct
    Else   See Digicash.

Chapter 8

Quiz 8.1

1. c   Yes!
    Else   See Services and Ports.

2. c   Right
    Else   No, see Network Layers.

3. d   Correct
    Else   See Network Layers.

4. b   Yep!
    Else   Nope, see Services and Ports.

Quiz 8.2

1. c   Correct
    Else   See Figure 8-3 A TCP/IP packet.

2. a   Yep!
    Else   No, see Packet Filter.

3. b   Right

    Else   See Cisco Configuration.

4. b   Yes!

    Else   Nope, see FTP.

Quiz 8.3

1. d   Yes!

    Else   See Auditing.

2. c   Yep!

    Else   Nope, see TCP Wrapper.

3. c   Correct

    Else   See Tunnels.

4. d   Right

    Else   No, see The Real Thing.

Quiz 8.4

1. b   Right

    Else   No, see The TIS Toolkit.

2. c   Yep!

    Else   See The Costs.

3. c   Correct

    Else   See The Holes.

4. c   Yes!

    Else   Nope, see The Costs.

Chapter 9

Quiz 9.1

1. d   Correct

    Else   No, see Java in a Can.

2. c   Yes!

    Else   See the introduction for the answer.

3. c   Yep!

    Else   Nope, the answer is in the introduction.

4. a   Right

    Else   See the introduction.

Quiz 9.2

1. c   You are correct!
   Else   Ah, no, see How It Works.

2. d   Right
   Else   See Figure 9-4 The HEADER block.

3. d   Correct!
   Else   Nope, see Tips and Caveats.

4. c   Yep!
   Else   See How to Build an Animated GIF.

Quiz 9.3

1. d   Right
   Else   No, see History of Agents.

2. d   Correct
   Else   See Extending the Design.

3. d   Yep!
   Else   Please see History of Agents.

4. d   Yes
   Else   See Using libwww.

APPENDIX B

JAVASCRIPT OBJECT REFERENCE

etscape's JavaScript consists of a subset of the Java language and a variety of objects that can be manipulated in the context of the browser. An object in JavaScript consists of methods and properties. Methods are loosely analogous to functions in traditional languages. They are routines that can be called and return results, but they are associated with specific objects. Some methods can be pointed to your own functions for handling certain conditions; these are called event handlers.

Properties are loosely analogous to variables, and an object can contain properties that influence the actions of the object, depending on which properties it is assigned. In JavaScript, properties can be other objects. An object like Window, for example, can have a property called frames, which lists all the Frame objects contained in the window.

These Frame objects in turn have their own methods and properties. By understanding the objects of JavaScript, you'll understand what can be done in the language.

Window Object

This is the top-level object in the JavaScript hierarchy. Windows contain Document, Location, and History objects.

Syntax

A window is instantiated with

Name = window.open()

Where *Name* is the name of the new window. Note that by default you are running in the current window, so any method shown in Table B-1 without the name prefix operates on the current window.

Methods

Table B-1 lists the methods associated with the Window object and describes their functions.

Method	Description
alert	Displays alert dialog box with OK button, e.g., alert("I can't find my sock!").
clearTimeout	Used to cancel an event waiting to timeout (see setTimeout below), e.g., for the example below, clearTimeout(timer1) would cancel the alert.
close	Closes specified window, or current window if none is specified.
confirm	Displays confirmation box with OK or CANCEL, e.g., confirm("Continue?"). Returns True if OK was selected, False if CANCEL.
open	Creates a new window and optionally loads a URL, e.g. myWindow = window.open ("http://www.test.com/",[WindowName], [Options]). Where myWindow is the reference used for invoking Window methods and assigning properties, URL is the URL to be loaded into the window, WindowName is the reference for TARGET properties for <FORM> and <A> tags, and Options include zero or more of the following, separated with commas: directories[=yes|no]|[=1|0] height=pixels

Method	Description
	location[=yes|no]|[=1|0]
	menubar[=yes|no]|[=1|0]
	resizable[=yes|no]|[=1|0]
	scrollbars[=yes|no]|[=1|0]
	status[=yes|no]|[=1|0]
	toolbar[=yes|no]|[=1|0]
	width=pixels
prompt	Displays a dialog box and allows user to input a value, e.g., prompt("Your Favorite Color?", [default value]), where the default value is displayed in the input field. The value in the input field is returned by this method.
setTimeout	Evaluates an instruction after specified number of milliseconds has elapsed, e.g., timer1 = setTimeout ('self.alert("Hey! It's been 5 Seconds!")',5000). Returns a TimeoutId that can be used by the next method.

Table B-1 *Window object methods*

Properties

Table B-2 describes the Window object's properties.

Property	Description
defaultStatus	The default message displayed in the window's status bar
document	The object that contains the HTML entities on the page
frames	An array of all the frames in a window
length	The number of frames in a parent window
name	The window's name
parent	A synonym for the window name of the window containing a frameset
self	A synonym for the window's name, the current window
status	A temporary message in the window's status bar

continued on next page

continued from previous page

Property	Description
top	A synonym for the window name of the topmost Navigator window
window	A synonym for the window's name, the current window

Table B-2 *Window object properties*

Event Handlers

Table B-3 describes the Window object's event handlers.

Event Handler	Description
onLoad	Routine called when window is loaded. Set by Frame and Document objects.
onUnload	Routine called when window is unloaded. Set by Frame and Document objects.

Table B-3 *Window object event handlers*

Frame Object

This object gives you control over the frames that make up your page. Frame objects are created by the <FRAMESET> HTML tags and can be manipulated through this object's methods and properties.

Syntax

The Frame object is defined with standard HTML syntax:

```
<FRAMESET>
<FRAMESET
ROWS="rowHeightList"
COLS="columnWidthList"
[onLoad="handlerText"]
[onUnload="handlerText"]>
[<FRAME SRC="locationOrURL" NAME="frameName">]
</FRAMESET>
```

Methods

Table B-4 lists the Frame object's methods and describes their functions.

Method	Description
clearTimeout	See Window's methods
setTimeout	See Window's methods

Table B-4 *Frame object methods*

Properties

The Frame object's properties are listed and described in Table B-5.

Property	Description
frames	An array referencing all the frames in a window
length	The number of child frames within a frame
name	The NAME attribute of the <FRAME> tag
parent	A synonym for the window or frame containing the current frameset
self	A synonym for the current frame
window	A synonym for the current frame

Table B-5 *Frame object properties*

To reference a frame's properties the following is used:

[*windowReference.*]*frameName.propertyName*
[*windowReference.*]frames[*index*]*.propertyName*
window.*propertyName*
self.*propertyName*
parent.*propertyName*

Document Object

This object refers to the current HTML document. You can reference entities within the document such as links, forms, and anchors. The Document object is a property of Window, so its properties and methods can be specified as

 [windowName].document.property

 [windowName].document.method

If *windowName* is not specified, the current window is assumed.

Syntax

The Document object is defined with standard HTML syntax. The onLoad and onUnload can refer to JavaScript functions or expressions.

```
<BODY
BACKGROUND="backgroundImage"
BGCOLOR="backgroundColor"
TEXT="foregroundColor"
LINK="unfollowedLinkColor"
ALINK="activatedLinkColor"
VLINK="followedLinkColor"
[onLoad="handlerText"]
```

[onUnload="*handlerText*"]>
</BODY>

Methods

The Document object's methods are listed and described in Table B-6.

Method	Description
close	Closes the output stream and forces the output to be displayed, e.g., document.close().
open	Opens an output stream so you can write to the document space, e.g., document.open("text/html"). The MIME type of the stream is specified, and can be one of the following: text/html, text/plain, image/gif, image/jpeg, image/x-bitmap or plugIn.
write	Writes HTML to the document in the current window. The format is write(expression1 [, expression 2] [, expression 3] [,…]).
writeln	Same as above but follows the write with a new line character.

Table B-6 *Document object methods*

Properties

The Document object's properties appear in Table B-7.

Property	Description
alinkColor	The ALINK attribute color
anchors	An array of all the anchors in a document
bgColor	The BGCOLOR attribute
cookie	Any associated cookies
fgColor	The TEXT attribute
forms	An array of all the forms in a document
lastModified	The date document was last modified
linkColor	The LINK attribute
links	An array of all the links in a document
location	The complete URL of a document
referrer	The URL of the calling document
title	Contents of the <TITLE> tag
vlinkColor	The VLINK attribute

Table B-7 *Document object properties*

Form Object

This object is contained within a Document object. It in turn contains objects defining check boxes, radio buttons, and selection lists in its elements property. You can use this object to post data to a server. Since a document can contain multiple forms, this object, like the frame object, can be referenced by name or by an array element, e.g.,

🪐 formName.propertyName

🪐 formName.methodName(parameters)

🪐 forms[index].propertyName

🪐 forms[index].methodName(parameters)

It can be prefaced by a document name and window name, and if these qualifiers are not specified, the current document in the current window is assumed.

Syntax

To define a form, use standard HTML syntax with the addition of the onSubmit event handler:

```
<FORM
  NAME="formName"
  TARGET="windowName"
  ACTION="serverURL"
  METHOD="GET" | "POST"
  ENCTYPE="encodingType"
  [onSubmit="handlerText"]>
</FORM>
```

Methods

The Form object has only one method, listed in Table B-8.

Method	Description
submit	

Table B-8 *Form object methods*

Properties

The properties of the Form object are listed and described in Table B-9.

Property	Description
action	String with URL to submit data to.
elements	An array of form elements.

continued on next page

continued from previous page

Property	Description
encoding	The ENCTYPE attribute.
length	The number of elements on a form, used to loop through the elements array above.
method	The METHOD attribute, e.g., "POST" or "GET".
target	The TARGET attribute. Window or frame name that responses go to after form is submitted.

Table B-9 *Form object properties*

Event Handlers

The Form object has a single event handler, described in Table B-10.

Event Handler	Description
onSubmit	A function or action to perform when the form is submitted, before it is actually transmitted to the ACTION URL. If the function returns False, the form will not be submitted, e.g., form.onSubmit="return ValidateData(this)".

Table B-10 *Form object event handlers*

Text Objects (Text, TextArea)

This is the familiar <INPUT TYPE="text"> tag, but encapsulated in an object. It can be referenced by

 textfieldName.propertyName

 textfieldName.methodName(parameters)

 formName.elements[index].propertyName

 formName.elements[index].methodName(parameters)

Its syntax is

```
<INPUT
  TYPE="text" | TYPE="textarea"
  NAME="textName"
  VALUE="textValue" | <TEXTAREA ...>value here</TEXTAREA> for Textarea
  SIZE=integer | ROWS=x COLS=y for Textarea
  [onBlur="handlerText"]
  [onChange="handlerText"]
  [onFocus="handlerText"]
  [onSelect="handlerText"]>
```

Methods

The Text object's methods are listed and described in Table B-11.

Method	Description
blur	Moves cursor off the field
focus	Positions cursor on the field
select	Selects the text in the field

Table B-11   *Text object methods*

Properties

The Text object's properties appear in Table B-12.

Method	Description
defaultValue	The default value assigned to the field
name	The name of the field
value	The current value of the field

Table B-12   *Text object properties*

Event Handlers

The Text object's event handlers are shown in Table B-13.

Event Handler	Description
onBlur	Specifies a function or operation to call when focus leaves the field. E.g., to see if the value is valid before letting the user exit this field, you can call a function <INPUT TYPE="text" VALUE="" NAME="firstname" onBlur="validate(this.value)">
onChange	A function or operation to perform when field value is changed.
onFocus	A function or operation to perform when cursor enters the field.
onSelect	A function or operation done when the contents of the field are selected.

Table B-13   *Text object event handlers*

Checkbox Object

This is the <INPUT TYPE="checkbox"> tag encapsulated in an object. It can be referenced by

  checkboxName.propertyName

checkboxName.methodName(parameters)

formName.elements[index].propertyName

formName.elements[index].methodName(parameters)

Its syntax is

```
<INPUT
  TYPE="checkbox"
  NAME="checkboxName"
  VALUE="checkboxValue"
  [CHECKED]
  [onClick="handlerText"]>
  textToDisplay
```

Methods

The Checkbox object has only one method, listed and described in Table B-14.

Method	Description
click	Sets the value to on (and kicks off the onClick event hander)

Table B-14   *Checkbox object methods*

Properties

The properties associated with the Checkbox object appear in Table B-15.

Property	Description
checked	Current checked status; lets you assign checked.
defaultChecked	Whether box is checked or not by default.
name	The name of the field.
value	The current value of the field. True indicates checked, False indicates not checked.

Table B-15   *Checkbox object properties*

Event Handlers

The sole event handler for the Checkbox object is listed in Table B-16.

Event Handler	Description
onClick	References a routine to call when the item is checked

Table B-16   *Checkbox object event handlers*

Radio Object

This is the <INPUT TYPE="radio"> tag encapsulated in an object. It can be referenced by

 radiobuttonName[index].propertyName

radiobuttonName[index].methodName(parameters)

formName.elements[index].propertyName

formName.elements[index].methodName(parameters)

Its syntax is

```
<INPUT
  TYPE="radio"
  NAME="radioName"
  VALUE="buttonValue"
  [CHECKED]
  [onClick="handlerText"]>
  textToDisplay
```

Methods

The Radio button object has only one method, shown in Table B-17.

Method	Description
click	Sets the value to on (and kicks off the onClick event hander)

Table B-17 *Radio button object methods*

Properties

The Radio button object's properties appear in Table B-18.

Property	Description
checked	Lets you assign checked.
defaultChecked	The radio button selected by default.
length	The number of radio buttons in this group.
name	The name of the field.
value	The current value of the field. True indicates checked, False indicates not checked.

Table B-18 *Radio button object properties*

Event Handlers

Radio button has only one event handler, shown in Table B-19.

Event Handler	Description
onClick	References a routine to call when the button is checked

Table B-19 *Radio button event handlers*

Select Object

This is a standard selection list, objectified and fitted with JavaScript events:

 selectname.propertyName

 selectname.methodName(parameters)

 formName.elements[index].propertyName

 formName.elements[index].methodName(parameters)

To reference items in the options array, use

 selectname.options

 selectname.options[index]

 selectname.options.length

Its syntax is

```
<SELECT
  NAME="selectName"
  [SIZE="integer"]
  [MULTIPLE]
  [onBlur="handlerText"]
  [onChange="handlerText"]
  [onFocus="handlerText"]>
  <OPTION VALUE="optionValue" [SELECTED]>
textToDisplay [ ... <OPTION> textToDisplay]
  </SELECT>
```

Methods

The Select object has two methods, which are described in Table B-20.

Method	Description
blur	Moves cursor off the object
focus	Positions cursor on the object

Table B-20 *Select object methods*

Properties

The properties of the Select object appear in Table B-21.

Property	Description
defaultSelected	The option selected by default, e.g., selectname.options[index].defaultSelected
length	The number of options in the Select.
name	The NAME of the Select object.
options	The array of <OPTION> tags
selectedIndex	Index of selected, or first selected, if multiple.
text	The text displayed by the <OPTION> tag, e.g., document.orderform.booktitle.options[i].text = "VRML Symbols";
value	Current value of item.

Table B-21   *Select object properties*

Event Handlers

The Select object event handlers are listed in Table B-22.

Event Handler	Description
onBlur	Specifies a function or operation to call when focus leaves the object
onChange	A function or operation to perform when object value is changed
onFocus	A function or operation to perform when cursor enters the object

Table B-22   *Select object event handlers*

Button Object

This is a Button object within a form. Buttons can trigger JavaScript scripts without necessarily submitting values from the form. The Button object can be referenced by

 buttonName.propertyName

 buttonName.methodName(parameters)

 formName.elements[index].propertyName

 formName.elements[index].methodName(parameters)

Its syntax is

```
<INPUT
  TYPE="button"
  NAME="buttonName"
  VALUE="buttonText"
  [onClick="handlerText"]>
```

Methods

The Button object's only method is listed in Table B-23.

Method	Description
click	Activates the onClick routine of the button

Table B-23   *Button object methods*

Properties

The two properties of the Button object appear in Table B-24.

Property	Description
name	The NAME of the button object
value	Text displayed on the face of the button

Table B-24   *Button object properties*

Event Handlers

The button object has only one event handler, which is described in Table B-25.

Event Handler	Description
onClick	Specifies a function or operation to call when the button is clicked, either with a mouse or by calling the click method from another function

Table B-25   *Button object event handlers*

History Object

The History object stores references to URLs visited during the browser session. It's not created or declared, so there is no syntax. To reference the history object, use

 history.propertyName

 history.methodName(parameters)

Methods

The History object's methods are shown in Table B-26.

Method	Description
back	Acts the same as clicking the Back button in the navigator. E.g., history.back().
forward	The same as clicking the Forward button.
go(delta | location)	Given a number relative to where you are now (e.g., 0 is this document, -1 is back, 1 is forward) or a substring of a URL in the list, this method navigates to the location.

Table B-26   *History object methods*

Properties

The History object has a single property, described in Table B-27.

Property	Description
length	The number of entries the history object contains

Table B-27   *History object properties*

Location Object

Encapsulates properties about a URL loaded in a window. It can be referenced by

[*windowReference.*]location.*propertyName*

Properties

The Location object's properties appear in Table B-28.

Property	Description
hash	The anchor name in the URL
host	The hostname:port part of the URL
hostname	The host and domain name, or IP address, of a network host
href	Entire URL
pathname	Path part of the URL
port	The protocol port of the URL
protocol	The text protocol, e.g., http:, gopher:, etc.
search	A query string if this was a GET
target	TARGET attribute, if any

Table B-28   *Location object properties*

Link Object

A hypertext link object, associated with text or images. It can be referenced by

 document.links[index].propertyName

Its syntax is

```
<A HREF=locationOrURL
   [NAME="anchorName"]
   [TARGET="windowName"]
   [onClick="handlerText"]
   [onMouseOver="handlerText"]>
   linkText
</A>
```

Properties

A Link object inherits the properties of a Location object. See that object for references.

Event Handlers

The Link object's event handlers are listed in Table B-29.

Event Handler	Description
onClick	Action to take when link is clicked. You can use this to create dynamic links, e.g., <A HREF="" onClick="this.href=dynamicURL()".
onMouseOver	Action to take when mouse enters link or image link, e.g., onMouseOver="window.status='Pick this Link!!!'; return True". Return True needs to be specified to set window.status and display the message on the status line.

Table B-29 *Link object event handlers*

Anchor Object

This is a text block that is an anchor for another link. It is accessed via

 document.anchors[index]

 document.anchors.length

Its syntax is

```
<A [HREF=locationOrURL]
   NAME="anchorName"
   [TARGET="windowName"]>
   anchorText
</A>
```

Properties

The Anchor object has only one property, shown in Table B-30.

Property	Description
length	Number of anchors in the document

Table B-30 *Anchor object properties*

An anchor object in another window can be displayed by setting its window.location.hash to the index number of the anchor desired.

String Object

String objects don't correspond to anything in the browser or HTML; instead they are built-in types carried over from the Java class libraries. They provide routines to manipulate strings of text, and come in very handy in JavaScript scripting.

A string object is a variable that has been assigned a text value, e.g.,

var test = "this is a string";

The variable name is now the string reference and can be used to set and retrieve properties and call string methods, e.g.,

 test.StringPropertyName

 test.StringPropertyMethod()

Methods

The String object's methods are listed and described in Table B-31.

Method	Description
anchor	Creates an HTML anchor with the string
big	Causes string to be displayed in <BIG> font
blink	Makes string blink <BLINK>
bold	Bolds string <B>
charAt	Finds character in string
fixed	Makes string <FIXED>
fontcolor	Sets font color for string
fontsize	Sets font size for string
indexOf	Finds substring in string
italics	Makes string italic <I>
lastIndexOf	Finds last instance of substring in string

continued on next page

continued from previous page

Method	Description
link	Makes link out of string
small	Makes string <SMALL> font
strike	Strikes out text of string <STRIKE>
sub	Makes string into subscript <SUB>
substring	Extracts a substring from string
sup	Makes string a superscript <SUP>
toLowerCase	Converts string to lowercase
toUpperCase	Converts string to uppercase

Table B-31   String object methods

Properties

The String object's sole property appears in Table B-32.

Property	Description
length	The length of the string

Table B-32   *String object properties*

Math Object

Math objects are another internal object for manipulating math variables. They are a little different from String objects in that the Math routines are used to assign values to variables, rather than act as properties and methods for variables. Usage:

var x = *MathMethod(parameters)*

Math properties are read-only and are used as constants, e.g.,

var x = *MathPropertyName*

Methods

The methods associated with the Math object are shown in Table B-33.

Method	Description
abs	Absolute value, e.g, var x = Math.abs(-5).
acos	Arc cosine in radians.
asin	Arc sine in radians.
atan	Arc tangent in radians.
ceil	The smallest integer greater than or equal to a number.
cos	Cosine.
exp	Exponent.

Method	Description
floor	The largest integer less than or equal to a number.
log	Natural logarithm.
max	The largest of a set of numbers, e.g., var biggest = Math.max(1,4,2,20).
min	The smallest of a set of numbers.
pow	Base to the exponent power of a number.
random	Pseudo-random number between 0 and 1. In 2.0 only works on UNIX Netscape.
round	Rounds a number to nearest integer.
sin	Sine.
sqrt	Square root.
tan	Tangent.

Table B-33 *Math object methods*

Properties

The properties of the Math object are listed and described in Table B-34.

Property	Description
E	Returns Euler's constant, used as x = Math.E
LN10	Natural log of 10
LN2	Natural log of 2, e.g., x = Math.LN2
LOG10E	Base 10 logarithm of e
LOG2E	Base 2 logarithm of e
PI	Value of pi
SQRT1_2	The square root of 1/2
SQRT2	The square root of 2

Table B-34 *Math object properties*

Date Object

The Date object allows you to create and work with dates (greater than or equal to 1/1/1970!). A Date object is created via

> var date = new Date(*parameters*)

where the parameters can be one of the following:

 Nothing. Creates today's date and time. For example, today = new Date().

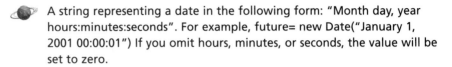 A string representing a date in the following form: "Month day, year hours:minutes:seconds". For example, future= new Date("January 1, 2001 00:00:01") If you omit hours, minutes, or seconds, the value will be set to zero.

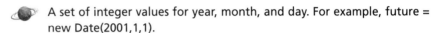 A set of integer values for year, month, and day. For example, future = new Date(2001,1,1).

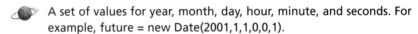 A set of values for year, month, day, hour, minute, and seconds. For example, future = new Date(2001,1,1,0,0,1).

Once a Date object is created, it can be manipulated with Date methods (it has no properties).

Methods

The methods for the Date object are given in Table B-35.

Method	Description
getDate	Returns the day of the month, an integer between 1 and 31. E.g., var x = future.getDate().
getDay	Returns the day of the week, 0=Sunday...6=Saturday.
getHours	Returns the hour.
getMinutes	Returns the minute.
getMonth	Returns the month, 0=January, 1=February, etc.
getSeconds	Returns seconds.
getTime	Returns number of milliseconds since 1 January 1970 00:00:00. Is used primarily to set the value of a Date object.
getTimeZoneoffset	Returns offset from GMT.
getYear	Returns year less 1900, e.g., 1996 returns 96.
parse	Returns milliseconds since 1 January 1970 00:00:00 from a given date.
setDate	Changes the day stored in a Date object, e.g., future.setDate(2).
setHours	Changes the hour.
setMinutes	Changes minutes.
setMonth	Changes month.
setSeconds	Changes seconds.

Method	Description
setTime	Assigns date and time to another Date object, e.g., future = new Date("Jan 1, 1999"); sameFuture = new Date(); samefuture.setTime(future.getTime()).
setYear	Changes year.
toGMTString	Returns a string of Date object converted to GMT format.
toLocaleString	Returns a string of Date object converted to local time.
UTC	Returns milliseconds from January 1, 1970 00:00:00 in Universal Coordinated Time.

Table B-35 *Date object methods*

INDEX

NOTES

NOTES

NOTES

NOTES

NOTES

NOTES

NOTES

NOTES

NOTES

NOTES

Books have a substantial influence on the destruction of the forests of the Earth. For example, it takes 17 trees to produce one ton of paper. A first printing of 30,000 copies of a typical 480-page book consumes 108,000 pounds of paper, which will require 918 trees!

Waite Group Press™ is against the clear-cutting of forests and supports reforestation of the Pacific Northwest of the United States and Canada, where most of this paper comes from. As a publisher with several hundred thousand books sold each year, we feel an obligation to give back to the planet. We will therefore support organizations that seek to preserve the forests of planet Earth.

INTERACTIVE COURSES

Waite Group Press' explosive new approach to learning programming languages offers all the flexibility of a book-based course, combined with personalized help, immediate feedback on exams, interaction with other students, and a customized Certificate of Achievement, before now available only in live, on-location classes. Each course comes with a clear, comprehensive book packed with step-by-step, hands-on lessons; a CD-ROM that contains sample code and utilities; and access to the eZone—a collection of unique Web-based features available day or night.

Learn Zone

At the end of each session, there is a quiz that can be taken online. Your personal Learn Zone charts your progress, showing you at a glance where you left off, which quizzes you've taken, and what your score is. Immediate feedback after each quiz shows you your areas of weakness, so you can go back, reread those sections, and try again. Once you've successfully completed all the exams, you may download a personalized Certificate of Achievement, suitable for framing or attaching to a resume.

This is a legal agreement between you, the end user and purchaser, and The Waite Group®, Inc., and the authors of the programs contained in the disk. By opening the sealed disk package, you are agreeing to be bound by the terms of this Agreement. If you do not agree with the terms of this Agreement, promptly return the unopened disk package and the accompanying items (including the related book and other written material) to the place you obtained them for a refund.

SOFTWARE LICENSE

1. The Waite Group, Inc. grants you the right to use one copy of the enclosed software programs (the programs) on a single computer system (whether a single CPU, part of a licensed network, or a terminal connected to a single CPU). Each concurrent user of the program must have exclusive use of the related Waite Group, Inc. written materials.

2. The program, including the copyrights in each program, is owned by the respective author and the copyright in the entire work is owned by The Waite Group, Inc. and they are therefore protected under the copyright laws of the United States and other nations, under international treaties. You may make only one copy of the disk containing the programs exclusively for backup or archival purposes, or you may transfer the programs to one hard disk drive, using the original for backup or archival purposes. You may make no other copies of the programs, and you may make no copies of all or any part of the related Waite Group, Inc. written materials.

3. You may not rent or lease the programs, but you may transfer ownership of the programs and related written materials (including any and all updates and earlier versions) if you keep no copies of either, and if you make sure the transferee agrees to the terms of this license.

4. You may not decompile, reverse engineer, disassemble, copy, create a derivative work, or otherwise use the programs except as stated in this Agreement.

GOVERNING LAW

This Agreement is governed by the laws of the State of California.

LIMITED WARRANTY

The following warranties shall be effective for 90 days from the date of purchase: (i) The Waite Group, Inc. warrants the enclosed disk to be free of defects in materials and workmanship under normal use; and (ii) The Waite Group, Inc. warrants that the programs, unless modified by the purchaser, will substantially perform the functions described in the documentation provided by The Waite Group, Inc. when operated on the designated hardware and operating system. The Waite Group, Inc. does not warrant that the programs will meet purchaser's requirements or that operation of a program will be uninterrupted or error-free. The program warranty does not cover any program that has been altered or changed in any way by anyone other than The Waite Group, Inc. The Waite Group, Inc. is not responsible for problems caused by changes in the operating characteristics of computer hardware or computer operating systems that are made after the release of the programs, nor for problems in the interaction of the programs with each other or other software.

THESE WARRANTIES ARE EXCLUSIVE AND IN LIEU OF ALL OTHER WARRANTIES OF MERCHANTABILITY OR FITNESS FOR A PARTICULAR PURPOSE OR OF ANY OTHER WARRANTY, WHETHER EXPRESS OR IMPLIED.

EXCLUSIVE REMEDY

The Waite Group, Inc. will replace any defective disk without charge if the defective disk is returned to The Waite Group, Inc. within 90 days from date of purchase.

This is Purchaser's sole and exclusive remedy for any breach of warranty or claim for contract, tort, or damages.

LIMITATION OF LIABILITY

THE WAITE GROUP, INC. AND THE AUTHORS OF THE PROGRAMS SHALL NOT IN ANY CASE BE LIABLE FOR SPECIAL, INCIDENTAL, CONSEQUENTIAL, INDIRECT, OR OTHER SIMILAR DAMAGES ARISING FROM ANY BREACH OF THESE WARRANTIES EVEN IF THE WAITE GROUP, INC. OR ITS AGENT HAS BEEN ADVISED OF THE POSSIBILITY OF SUCH DAMAGES.

THE LIABILITY FOR DAMAGES OF THE WAITE GROUP, INC. AND THE AUTHORS OF THE PROGRAMS UNDER THIS AGREEMENT SHALL IN NO EVENT EXCEED THE PURCHASE PRICE PAID.

COMPLETE AGREEMENT

This Agreement constitutes the complete agreement between The Waite Group, Inc. and the authors of the programs, and you, the purchaser.

Some states do not allow the exclusion or limitation of implied warranties or liability for incidental or consequential damages, so the above exclusions or limitations may not apply to you. This limited warranty gives you specific legal rights; you may have others, which vary from state to state.

SATISFACTION REPORT CARD

Please fill out this card if you wish to know of future updates to *HTML 3 Interactive Course*, or to receive our catalog.

First Name: _____ Last Name: _____

Street Address: _____

City: _____ State: _____ Zip: _____

E-Mail Address _____

Daytime Telephone: ( ) _____

Date product was acquired: Month _____ Day _____ Year _____ Your Occupation: _____

Overall, how would you rate *HTML 3 Interactive Course?*

☐ Excellent ☐ Very Good ☐ Good
☐ Fair ☐ Below Average ☐ Poor

What did you like MOST about this book? _____
_____
_____

What did you like LEAST about this book? _____
_____
_____

Please describe any problems you may have encountered with installing or using the disk: _____
_____

How did you use this book (problem-solver, tutorial, reference...)?
_____

What is your level of computer expertise?
☐ New ☐ Dabbler ☐ Hacker
☐ Power User ☐ Programmer ☐ Experienced Professional

What computer languages are you familiar with? _____
_____

Please describe your computer hardware:
Computer _____ Hard disk _____
5.25" disk drives _____ 3.5" disk drives _____
Video card _____ Monitor _____
Printer _____ Peripherals _____
Sound board _____ CD ROM _____

Where did you buy this book?

☐ Bookstore (name): _____
☐ Discount store (name): _____
☐ Computer store (name): _____
☐ Catalog (name): _____
☐ Direct from WGP ☐ Other _____

What price did you pay for this book? _____

What influenced your purchase of this book?
☐ Recommendation ☐ Advertisement
☐ Magazine review ☐ Store display
☐ Mailing ☐ Book's format
☐ Reputation of Waite Group Press ☐ Other

How many computer books do you buy each year? _____

How many other Waite Group books do you own? _____

What is your favorite Waite Group book? _____
_____

Is there any program or subject you would like to see Waite Group Press cover in a similar approach? _____
_____

Additional comments? _____
_____
_____

Please send to: Waite Group Press
200 Tamal Plaza
Corte Madera, CA 94925

☐ **Check here for a free Waite Group catalog.**